Considered for Withdrawal
9/92
Retention Requested by:
Dillon

CAMBRIDGE STUDIES
IN
MEDIEVAL LIFE AND THOUGHT

Edited by G. G. COULTON

FIVE CENTURIES OF RELIGION

VOLUME IV

FIVE CENTURIES OF RELIGION

BY

G. G. COULTON

VOLUME IV

THE LAST DAYS OF MEDIEVAL MONACHISM

P. H. WELSHIMER MEMORIAL LIBRARY
MILLIGAN COLLEGE
MILLIGAN COLLEGE, TENN. 37682

CAMBRIDGE
AT THE UNIVERSITY PRESS
1950

BR
252
.C6

PUBLISHED BY
THE SYNDICS OF THE CAMBRIDGE UNIVERSITY PRESS
London Office: Bentley House, N.W. 1
American Branch: New York
Agents for Canada, India, and Pakistan: Macmillan

Printed in Great Britain at the University Press, Cambridge
(Brooke Crutchley, University Printer)

BR252 .C855f v.4
$1.50
269793

PUBLISHER'S NOTE

G. G. Coulton died in March 1947. In the preceding autumn and winter he had twice worked over the proofs of this present volume, and except for a few finishing touches the book is published from his own hands.

The preface appears as he finally passed it, and without alteration. The reference there to the "fourth volume which he still hoped to get written" accordingly needs some explanation. Coulton's notes and data for a book that was to include records and extracts bearing out the argument of the present volume were put aside when, after the outbreak of war, he decided to write the concluding volume of the whole work while he still had time. Had he lived, those earlier notes would no doubt have been expanded, ordered and arranged by him, and eventually published. But when he died they were still in a fragmentary state.

After consultation with the author's literary executors, the Syndics of the Press feel that they must now regard this present volume as the completion of the whole work and have therefore closed the gap and numbered it Volume IV.

Vandy
76641
9-25-75

DEDICATION

TO MANY FRIENDS OF THE WAR-YEARS
IN CANADA AND THE UNITED STATES

AUTHOR'S PREFACE

I STILL hope against hope to get my fourth volume[1] written on the lines of volume III; that is, as one reviewer justly pointed out, rather as a collection of illustrative records than as a connected history. It will begin with food and drink and clothing, and pass on to the Choir, the Scriptorium and other daily occupations. In the late thirties, the Days of Appeasement, War loomed so inevitably on the horizon that I felt bound to hasten at all costs to my goal before cool and connected work should become impossible. Therefore, in this concluding volume, I attempt to display the full drama of successive reforms, as they were attempted by group after group in the hope of staving off the cataclysmic Reformation. I sent a carbon copy to the kind protection of Professor J. U. Nef in Chicago. When, therefore, a few months later, war broke upon us and I took my wife by doctor's orders to the generous hospitality of Toronto University, then it became possible to utilize some of my leisure in compiling a summary of *The Last Generations of Medieval Monachism* which was printed by the Medieval Academy of America in *Speculum* (vol. XVIII, no. 4, 1943). Now, at last, the Cambridge University Press is boldly facing the shortage of paper and labour, and the public is here presented with Volume V, whether IV ever materializes or not.

By this time, however, most of my books and papers are inaccessible, and I must apologize at once for shortcomings which must be practically inevitable in a work of this size, with notes of such complexity. Now and then, at Toronto, I discovered misplaced references. Here then, at home, with failing eyesight and waning energies, I cannot hope to guard against similar slips. But I must throw myself on the mercy of a public

[1] See Publisher's Note on p. v.

which has always been generous. Every one of these notes did actually represent, at one moment, an accurate reference to some source then accessible to me, and accessible, though with greater difficulty, in my library which is now permanently housed in the Library of Chicago University, in default of the List of Authorities which can make no claim to completeness in this present volume. The War deprived me of Miss Dorothy Hodder's secretarial help, to which I had owed so much in the past; and I found myself dependent upon a few fragmentary data beyond those titles which are given in my former volumes. For the Index, again, my wife has been compelled to restrict herself to proper names. Others may well correct and supplement my statements sometimes, perhaps, out of all recognition. But I end this last volume with that assurance of Montaigne which the public has not denied to its predecessors; *C'est icy un livre de bonne foy, Lecteur*.

G. G. COULTON

January 1947

CONTENTS

ABBREVIATIONS AND AUTHORITIES

ABBREVIATIONS

A.F.H. *Archivum Franciscanum Historicum.*
A.L.K.G. *Archiv für Litteratur- und Kirchengeschichte,* ed. Denifle and Ehrle.
C.A.P. *Collectanea Anglo-Premonstratensia.* Royal Historical Soc.
E.H.R. *English Historical Review.*
M.G.H. Leges. Monumenta Germaniae Historica. Leges.
M.G.H. Necrologia. Monumenta Germaniae Historica. Necrologia.
M.G.H. Scriptt. Monumenta Germaniae Historica. Scriptores.
O.E.D. Oxford English Dictionary.
P.M.L.A. *Publications of the Modern Language Association of America.*
V.C.H. *Victoria County Histories.*
AA. SS. Boll. *Acta Sanctorum* collegit J. Bollandus. Antwerp, 1643.

AUTHORITIES

Many authorities mentioned in the text and notes of the present volume have already been listed, and will be found in the sections headed Abbreviations and Authorities in volumes I, II and III of this work.

Andreas (Willy). *Deutschland vor d. Reformation.* Stuttgart, 1932.
Arbois de Jubainville (H. d'). *Études sur l'état intérieur des abbayes Cisterciennes.* Paris, 1858.
Barsch (Georg). *Das Prämonstratenser Kloster Steinfeld.* Schleiden, 1857.
Bertuch (J.). *Chronicon Portense,* ed. Schamelius. Leipzig, 1739.
Blomfield (J. C.). *The Deanery of Bicester.* Oxford, 1882.
Chambers (Sir E. K.). *Malory.* (English Assoc. Pamphlet, no. 51, 1922.)
Chmel (J.). *Zur Kritik d. Oest. Gesch.* (*Deutschriften d.k. Akad. d. Wiss. in Wien.* Phil.-hist. Cl., vol. I, 1850; II, 1851.)
Chronici Sindelfingensis, ed. C. F. Haug. Tübingen, 1836.
Dresdner, A. *Kultur- und Sittengesch. d. italienischen Geistlichkeit im* 10 *und* 11 *Jhdt.* Breslau, 1890.
Dunkin (J.). *Bullingdon and Ploughley Hundreds.* 1823.
Faucon, l'Abbé. *Essai Historique sur Le Prieuré de Saint-Vigor-Le-Grand.* Caen, 1861.
Heales (A.). *The Records of Merton Priory.* 1898.

James, M. R. *The Abbey Church of St Edmund at Bury*. (Camb. Antiq. Soc., vol. 28.)
Mirfeld (Johannes de). Ed. Hartley and Aldridge. Cambridge, 1936.
Naef (H.). *Les Origines de la Réforme à Genève*, vol. I. Geneva, 1936.
Nom[asticon] Cist[erciense], ed. Séjalon, H. Solesmes, 1892.
Pirenne (H.). *Economic and Social History of Medieval Europe*. 1937.
Richard (Abbé). *Hist. de l'abbaye de Grâce-Dieu*. Besançon, 1857.
Schlager (P., O.F.M.). *Geschichte d. Kölnischen Franziskaner Ordens-Provinz*. Cologne, 1904.
Selmer (C.). *Middle High German Translations of the Regula Sancti Benedicti*. Camb., Mass., 1933.
Swalne (E. B.). *De Kardinaal Nicolaas van Cusa, etc.* Leiden, 1838.
Vansteenberghe (E.). *Le Cardinal Nicolas de Cues*. Paris, 1920.
Wolff (G. A. B.). *Chronik des Klosters Pforta*. Leipzig, 1843–7.

INTRODUCTION

CRITICS, to whom I am grateful, have pointed out apparent contradictions in my earlier volumes which I seize this opportunity of explaining. I cannot doubt myself that the mass of generalizations collected in volume II (pp. 505ff.) may be taken as fully representative of the best medieval opinion, under the modifications which I suggest on p. 380 of that volume. How then (ask these critics) can I be right in warning readers repeatedly that "the Religious Orders have been among the main forces of European civilization; at certain times and in certain places they may have been the greatest of all civilizing forces", or, again, that "the best men of those days were as good as the best of any day: and, to the very end, a considerable proportion of these best men were in the monasteries"?* I had hoped that the facts, speaking for themselves, might give the careful reader no great trouble of adjustment on these points; but, since some of my reviewers warn me otherwise, I must begin the present volume with an attempt to reconcile this apparent contradiction. To put my explanation crudely in a single sentence: the monasteries (apart from exceptional times or places) were far from perfection, but the society which had bred them, and from which their influence was derived, was itself still further from the Christian ideal.

Everything in this world is relative, and most of us believe that, while real loyalty is one of the greatest of virtues, it must always be more or less provisional. He who, in the first Great War, was most ready to sacrifice his life for what he believed to be a cause of high civilization, might have been equally ready to admit that, a century hence, the civilization for which he was at present fighting might no longer be the highest. There is no real paradox in supposing on the one hand that monasticism was the greatest of civilizing forces for some thousand years in Europe, and that, on the other, for centuries before the Reformation, honest contemporaries confessed the lamentable gulf between monastic theory and practice, and felt this gulf to be widening instead of shrinking.

* Vol. I, p. xxiv; vol. II, pp. xi, 424.

Services which may deserve a very high reward at one moment are not necessarily of equal social value at another. These men, who had inherited the old Roman traditions of estate management on a great scale, and who had taught feudal lords and kings in this field, partly by example and partly by competition, were no longer marching in the van when once lords and kings had learned this lesson. Indeed, they often dropped to the rear; and (to take a single instance) monasticism became rather an obstacle than a stimulus to the emancipation of the serf. Those who, as missionaries, had begun by converting whole populations to Christianity, were sometimes to be found, so early as the thirteenth century, clinging to barbarous religious ideas which many men outside the cloister were outgrowing. At the very time when the best and most learned friars, such as St Thomas and St Bonaventura, had no doubt in their own minds that God would condemn the large majority of mankind to an eternity of unimaginable torment, and that the Blessed, looking down from their own heaven upon these torments, would rejoice in them as a manifestation of Divine Justice, it was to a crusading friar that the old woman at Acre told how she meant to burn Paradise and to quench hell-fire, "for I will not that any man henceforth should do well in the hopes of the guerdon of Paradise nor for fear of hell, but only for the pure love of God, who is so worthy and can do for us what is best".(1)* And, almost that same year, it was five friars who denounced Peter Garcias of Toulouse for having said: "If I could lay hold on that God who, out of a thousand men whom he had made, should save one and damn all the rest, then I would tear and rend him tooth and nail as a traitor, and would count him for a false traitor and spit in his face."(2) Dante, as a mouthpiece of Catholic common-sense, might mitigate certain horrors, and take serious liberties with ecclesiastical tradition; but the great Dominican or Franciscan philosopher could not, for it was his official task to build a coherent edifice from the separate stones of that tradition. Here and there, therefore, St Thomas illustrates the familiar truth that some disbeliefs may be more truly pious than certain cherished beliefs, and that Plutarch was right when he professed

* These small figures in parentheses refer to notes assembled at the end. The notes for each chapter are numbered separately.

far deeper sympathy with anyone who should deny the existence of Plutarch, than with another who might credit to Plutarch the deeds and passions commonly ascribed to Zeus and the rest of the Pantheon. But it is perhaps the monastic scriptorium which may most clearly illustrate my point. In many cases we can estimate the monks' services here with almost statistical accuracy. We see that their actual work was far less than has generally been claimed, even by moderate writers. Yet it remains no less true that, for whole centuries, very little writing was done in Europe except by monks. Again, the average cloisterer's ignorance of classical authors, during the five centuries with which we are mainly concerned, was very great, and his neglect of precious volumes which his house had inherited was often scandalous. Nevertheless, in the Dark Ages it was almost exclusively in monasteries that such books survived; and though, throughout the Middle Ages proper, there was no monastic school of classical learning comparable to the secular schools of Chartres and Orléans and Paris, yet, at the Renaissance, a few monks did distinguish themselves as scholars and collectors. These things, as I have said, can be measured with almost statistical accuracy; and in this field we find full evidence for the contrast which puzzles some of my critics. We know that, if we take the thousand years before the Reformation, monasticism was, on the whole, in the forefront of European civilization. But we know also that secular society had caught it up long before the Dissolution, and we shall see how the Oxford Chancellor Gascoigne could write in 1450, with no more than his usual bitter exaggeration, that the monks of his day were rather destroyers than writers of books.

Indeed, the paradox ought to be no paradox to those who take wider views in history. Why should we be surprised that an institution, most excellent for the sixth century, should more than once have dropped behind the times in later centuries, and should be justly condemned as unprogressive, or even as decadent, by the more enlightened descendants of those very populations whom at first it had educated? Ought we not rather to wonder that it could be otherwise? Again, mere *a priori* probability would strongly suggest that mankind, after many centuries of struggle and experience, is more advanced in these days of ours, both materially and intellectually, in morals and in religion, than in the distant past. To claim so much as this for our own generation is not boastful or pharisaical; it involves simply the recognition of what our forefathers have done for us. Man has hitherto shown himself a progressive animal; great teachers have not taught altogether in vain; the blood of those who have died for many different causes has been the seed of higher civilizations. That is just what we might expect, and that is just what the documents seem to show us; what, then, stands in the way of its recognition when we seem to find it in the actual records? Let us take an illustration from things too distant to awaken direct prejudices in our own day, whether political or religious. The democracy of Athens in the fifth century would be reckoned among the main factors, if not the principal factor, in the wonderful expansion of Athenian culture. Yet some features in that constitution, and especially its jury system, were impossibly equalitarian even for so small a state. The best thinkers in Athens itself, men like Thucydides and Euripides by implication and Plato explicitly, criticized the system, as it practically worked in their own day, with a freedom which shows that they recognized its actual defects more clearly than its possible remedies. If we possessed, handed down from those ancient days in Greece, anything like the mass and variety of documents which have in fact survived from the Middle Ages, then the balance of contemporary Greek criticism would probably have borne a close resemblance to that of the hundred and more witnesses whom I quote at the end of my second volume. At the same time (another close analogy), Plato apparently had no more thought of deserting the Athens which he criticized, in order to become the citizen of his admired Sparta, than those outspoken or even violent contemporary critics (with one or two possible exceptions) ever dreamed of leaving the Catholic Church. Finally, there is nobody, at this distance of time, who would wish to restore the Periclean democracy in any modern state. That institution was once living and beneficent; but at its best, it was very humanly imperfect, and now it is practically dead. Modern democracies, in all their variety, differ even more from that of Pericles than modern monasticism differs from that of the Middle Ages. Our democracies work by representative, not direct, government. Our modern monks are no longer entrenched outside and above all state laws, with vast collective wealth at their disposal, and bound, nominally, to the letter as well as the spirit of a Rule framed about A.D. 529. Is it not, therefore, of the very essence of all true historical method to bear in mind that everything is relative, and that the pioneers of one century may easily become the laggards of a later age?

I feel more and more strongly that, in our generation if in no other, the historian's most pressing task is to get at the average.* It is far easier to paint the hero or the villain; but I write neither for heroes nor for villains; I write for the kind of people whom I meet in daily life; not only for University scholars and teachers, but more for business men and artisans, who may have enough time and thoughtfulness to wonder how men lived in the distant past; and who will be helped, as well as interested, if they can realize what were their fellows' thoughts and actions under very different surroundings from ours.

* Compare Pascal, *Pensées* (ed. Brunschvicg, no. 352): "La vertu d'un homme ne doit pas se mesurer par ses efforts, mais par ce qu'il fait d'ordinaire."

CHAPTER I

COLET, MORE, AND CHARTERHOUSE

It would be difficult to find a more typical English link between the Middle Ages and the Reformation than John Colet, the great Dean of St Paul's. Colet in his later life, like St Thomas More in his earlier manhood, was strongly attracted by the idea of monastic self-surrender. More, though he defended monasticism loyally against heretical onslaughts, was quite conscious of its actual shortcomings; he occasionally tells us tales which might come from the pen of a modern scoffing Orangeman.(1) But the stricter life of the London Charterhouse attracted him; and here he was only withheld by the doubt of his own power to live exactly up to that standard. Colet was more doubtful and more exacting. Erasmus writes:

Though he yielded to none in his favour of Christian piety, yet he had very little affection for monasteries, which nowadays are often undeserving of that name. He gave them little or nothing, and did not even leave them anything at death. This was not because he disliked the Orders, but because the men themselves did not answer to their profession. For he himself wished to extricate himself altogether from the world, if he could find anywhere a community that was truly sworn to the Gospel life. Thus, when I was setting out for Italy, he commissioned me with this business, saying that among the Italians he had found certain monks of real prudence and piety. He did not judge Religion as do the common herd, since that is sometimes mere lack of intellect. He also praised a few Germans among whom there still survived vestiges of early Religion. He constantly used to affirm that he nowhere found less corrupt manners than among wedded folk, since natural affection, with the care for their children and household, forms a sort of fence which restrains them from slipping into all sorts of wickedness.

And again, later on in the same letter:

Many wondered why he built a splendid mansion within the precincts of those Carthusians who dwell hard by Richmond Palace. He said that he was preparing that dwelling for his old age, when he should be past work or broken by sickness, and thus compelled to retire from general company. There he thought to philosophize with two or three of his special friends, among whom he was wont to count me.(2)

The Carthusians boasted already then with some real truth, as they have always done ever since, that theirs is the only great Order which has never bred a Reformed Congregation: *Nunquam reformati, quia nunquam deformati*.

Such, then, was the attitude of two men than whom none had more right to fastidious choice, morally or intellectually, in that last generation of the Middle Ages. Let us compare them now with an older contemporary even more influential in his own day, Louis XI of France. In this crude contrast we shall find one thing in common: their attitude towards the monastic ideal.

In 1483 Louis was rapidly approaching his end. Comines describes him in his grim retreat of Plessis as "passing away the time in making and undoing of men"; but this was all for fear lest men should think him dead: he was "talking continually, even within a paternoster-while of his death". Yet all his right side was dead already. When the Flemish Ambassadors came to sign that treaty which outwitted and baulked our Edward IV, they found him a mere bundle of furs in a darkened chamber; he spoke with difficulty, and begged them to excuse his left hand when he swore upon the Gospels. But this man, Machiavellian before Machiavelli, had in religion the mentality of a peasant who, having outwitted his neighbour, hopes to outwit God. All this while he was studiously balancing his accounts with heaven. Every one of his innumerable pilgrimages had been a business bargain. He had heaped 12,000 crowns upon St Martin of Tours for his success in taking Perpignan; he had offered another 12,000 to the Blessed Virgin's shrine for the protection of Noyon, when Charles the Bold besieged it. His theology, like ancient barbaric law, compromised for almost any crime according to a money tariff. Therefore, in his many years of treachery and blood-guilt, he had paid the Saints at an even higher price, on the whole, than his physician, the man to whom in his last months he gave unprecedented fees. He persuaded the Pope to wring from the Archbishop of Reims that Holy Oil brought down from heaven, with which he and his ancestors had been anointed to be kings: a second similar anointing, he thought, might save him. When not only this relic had failed, but even the Pope-sent corporal which St Peter had used when he sang Mass at Rome, then it was whispered—doubtless only as a testimony to men's thoughts of him—that he drank the blood of infants. And, all these later years, he hung upon the words of a domestic hermit of his own: a friar whom he had fetched from the extremest south of Italy, who fasted and prayed more than any friar in Europe, and who founded the new Order of "Fratres Minimi", superlative in comparison with the mere "Fratres Minores" of St Francis of Assisi. Concerning this new St Francis of Pola, Comines writes:

> I never saw in my time a man of so holy life, nor by whose mouth the Holy Ghost seemed rather to speak....True it is, this Italian tongue caused somewhat the greater admiration of him....The King honoured him as if he had been the Pope himself, falling down on his knees before him and praying him to prolong his life: whereunto the hermit answered as a wise man should.

Why did this king, who had so many monks and friars at his beck, send to the farthest wilds of Italy for this Friar Minim? And why did Colet, committing himself no further with the English Carthusians than to pleasant social and intellectual intercourse, think very seriously of expatriation for the sake of the higher cloistered life? How was it that, at such moments, he looked towards Italy or Germany, and away from his own England, where religious and social life was then, and had been for many generations, more regular on an average than in any other great European country? Paradoxical as it may seem, it was just this respectable English average which did not suit the pious Colet's purpose. Continental monasticism, on the whole, had sunk lower than with us;(3) and, for that very reason, there were more violent reactions on the Continent. For instance, the English friars had always had an excellent reputation in comparison with their Continental brethren, both for regularity of life and for intellectual activity. But those three centuries between St Francis and the Reformation did not produce, from among that higher English average, one single friar canonized as a saint by the Roman Court. The whole number of English canonized saints, between the Conquest and the Reformation, was almost negligible compared with the great Continental countries. Religious contrasts were far less crude among us. We had neither such enormous abbeys nor, when monasticism had entered upon its definitely capitalistic phase, such enormous shortcomings. To the Continental abbeys, as compared with ours, we may apply something of Ovid's criticism on the Roman gods:

> Credibile est, illos pariter vitiisque locisque
> Altius humanis exseruisse caput.*

Thus Colet, a resolute and profoundly religious man, wished to venture fully if he ventured at all. He wanted some cloister where the Rule, whether of St Benedict or of St Augustine, was not only professed with average regularity and decency, but really obeyed in every important particular. This, in his day, could be found in such newly reformed Congregations as that of Sta Giustina in Italy, and Bursfelde, Melk, or Windesheim in the German Empire. The rise of these Congregations during the last four generations before the Reformation, their enthusiasms and their partial successes, form the last phase, and one of the most interesting, in medieval monastic history.

Not that there had not been many preceding periods of reform. All the weaknesses of later monasticism showed themselves very early; they became acknowledged and notorious, and periodical efforts were made to stem the tide of decay.

Sometimes these were merely sporadic and unconnected. Others were more general, and resulted in the formation of new Orders or Congregations. Here and there, again, a Church Synod or a General Council or a Pope aimed at still wider reform, and to some extent the whole waters were stirred.

* *Fasti* (I, 299): "We may believe that in their faults, as in their rank, they rose to a superhuman standard."

CHAPTER II

SPORADIC REFORMS

WHEREVER we can find a fairly complete chronicle of any house, we are pretty sure to meet with several reformers in the long series of abbots. These men's efforts can often be measured only indirectly, by the description of the disorders they found and the unpopularity they faced; but in a few cases the chronicle gives us a full-length portrait of a truly heroic figure. Abbot Samson of Bury, in Jocelin's *Chronicle* and Carlyle's *Past and Present*, is now immortal. Another such was Thomas, Abbot of Evesham, with whom I have dealt at length in chapters XXIV and XXV of my second volume, and others more briefly noticed in chapter XXXIV of my third. But here, as on many other subjects, the evidence is fullest, on the whole, from Continental abbeys. Let us take two here as described at great length in the chronicles, and as fairly typical.

The Abbey of Villers (or Villars) in Brabant was founded about 1148, with thirteen monks and five lay-brethren from St Bernard's community of Clairvaux.(1) As in the case of several other Cistercian foundations, their early hardships were such that they were often tempted to return; it was only the Saint's personal influence which kept them to their task at Villers. Presently, however, they took firm root, and prospered so rapidly that, before 1200, they had founded eight "Granges", and by 1295 they had 100 monks and 300 lay-brethren; that is, a community four or five times more numerous than the greatest of English abbeys could boast at the Dissolution. Their eighth and greatest abbot was Charles (1197–1209), brother to the Count of Sayn. Caesarius of Heisterbach (bk VIII, c. 63) tells a story illustrating the simple faith of Charles' father, whom he calls (apparently in error) a citizen of Cologne:

> He was a rich and mighty man; and, having heard that the Apostles would one day judge the world, he thought within himself: "Sin is a heavy thing, and anchor-stones* are very weighty too. So I will

* Probably the great basalt blocks which are quarried on the Rhine, and are still sometimes attached to cables for anchoring barges.

buy such stones for the future rebuilding of the Apostelkirche; then, at the Day of Judgment, when my good works are weighed against my bad, the Apostles, my judges, will cast these stones into the scale with my good works, and forthwith the other scale will kick the beam." So he bought a shipload of stones, and had them carted to a place beside the Apostelkirche.

Charles himself first studied as a clerk, and then became "a famous and doughty knight in the world". One day, riding with a fellow-knight to a tournament, he came to a meadow so beautiful that both rode through it in silence, until at last, by mutual consent, each told his thoughts to the other. Both had the same tale; the beauty of the place had reminded them how fleeting and unprofitable are all worldly things. Their first impulse now was to take the Cross; "but then", said they, "the things which we leave here will come back to our minds—our noble horses, the comely ladies, our knightly arms—and it may be that our chastity will suffer harm. Let us go, then, to these grey wolf-cowls of Himmerode, and strike a truce of five years from this haunting of tournaments." The Cistercians accepted their vows; and thus, "after a brief while, this lord Charles left his kinsfolk and his wealth; and, with many companions, he girt himself to sacred knighthood in the monastery of Himmerode. So also, by his example and exhortation, did other nobles and great men, both of holy Cologne and even of more distant places."

This, in the eyes of the chronicler, who wrote only thirty or forty years after Charles's death, was the golden time. From Himmerode Charles was promoted to the priorate of Heisterbach, where Caesarius knew and loved him; and in 1197 he was elected, most reluctantly, to the abbacy of Villers. Like many of the best men of his time, he would willingly have echoed the sentiment which one of his successors embodied in a curious jingle:

> Tu, cui donatum sine cura vivere, gratum
> Illud munus habe, nec cures culmina d'abbé.*

Dom Charles [says the chronicler] feared peril to his soul from this promotion, saying that he had not come to our Order to get liberty,

* "Thou, to whom it hath been granted to live without anxiety, take that gift gratefully, and care not for the abbot's pinnacle."

but rather to weep for having so great liberty in the World...but they compelled him to accept the burden by sentence of the General Chapter....He found at Villers only straw huts like shepherds' cotes; yet in a brief while he built two stone dormitories, for the monks and lay brethren, and certain other offices. Moreover he increased the convent both in monks and lay brethren, and endowed the granges with new buildings and lands. He knew how to fit and conform himself to all men; and thus he was enabled to draw both nobles and commoners from their vain life of this world, and by God's grace to bring them into the monastery of Villers.

Our chronicler in his preface cites fifteen nobles or knights by name, and adds: "One day, when certain great folk made a claim at law against the abbey, our abbot took with him ten of our monks of noble birth on the day fixed for treating of peace; with them he went down to the place of meeting and manfully defended the cause of the abbey with the help of these brethren." The personal influence of these men, and their studied moderation, won their adversaries completely over.

Charles, with the Grace of God to help him, kept the abbey without any great debt, and granted nearly 600 marks during his reign to other monasteries. And, by the great favour which he had with noble folk, vineyards on the Rhine and Moselle were granted to us in free gift; and that fishery in the Sambre for the profit of divine service and to solace the sick; and certain rents in Dordrecht. King Philippe-Auguste of France himself, hearing that he was in the town of Annweiler, came down from the castle of Trifels* and visited his inn and conversed with him as a friend, commanding his own marshal to take good care of the Abbot; moreover, as a pledge of love, he put a precious ring upon his finger. And it is noteworthy that, with all his incomparable favour among all men, he was most tenacious in preserving the abbey's possessions, and ever eager to increase them; nor did he ever spend them upon knights and princes, to whom his hands were ever closed; though they were freely opened to the poor and distressed, as piety and discretion demanded.

This man, who had fought so much in the world, laboured as a monk against all wars. By incredible exertions he averted one civil war when it seemed inevitable; and when, after his time, a bloody conflict broke out,

it was said on both sides that, if Charles had still been Abbot of Villers, a man so devoted to God and so gracious to men, then these

* The castle connected with the legend of Cœur-de-Lion's discovery by Blondel.

unheard-of evils would never have prevailed in our land....He had this one special virtue, that, from the time when he entered our Order, the sun never once went down upon his wrath; but, considering the monastic vow that bound him, he remitted benignly and easily all excesses committed against him, aiming singly at a pure conscience and a quiet mind....The Lord had given him this singular grace, that he enjoyed the special affection both of great and of small, both of princes and of their servants; and he was a most welcome counsellor in their assemblies, although he would never sit where men wrought against God or against the honour of holy religion.

Caesarius (who is copied word for word by the Villers chronicler) tells a story which brings the man more vividly before us than any other single episode (bk III, c. 43):

A certain noble matron, speaking with a certain Abbot of our Order under guise of secret confession, told him that she burned with great love for him. He, as a righteous and godfearing priest, set a seal upon his heart and used such words as he could find to divert this woman who had formed such wicked designs upon him. "I am an old man," he said, "unkempt and clad in rags." Yet (as he revealed unto a monk who told it to me) that lady was so exalted and so powerful that (said he) "If I were now in the world, as I once was, I should never dare to hint such a thing to her; nay, not in a single word. And now" (he said) "dost thou see how the Devil lieth in wait for us who are so dead to the world?" Now this same abbot, before his conversion, had been a knight valiant in arms, fair to see, and of great repute; and, if thou wilt know his name, he was Dom Charles, Abbot of Villers.

Thus he ruled for twelve years; and then,

after many labours and much travail which he had borne in Villers with so great success, he obtained by instant prayers to be relieved of his office by the Abbot of Clairvaux, the Mother House. For he had ever held his abbacy as a grievous thing, wherein he never spent one day without bitter fears, fearing the account which he must needs render at that last dreadful Day of Doom for the souls committed to his charge....The Abbot of Clairvaux unwillingly gave way...and Charles, freed of his burden, went back to the pleasant embraces of his Rachel at Himmerode,* hoping there to dwell unknown, and to spend the remaining days of his life in God's service and in claustral discipline. But his purpose was brought to naught, nor could he hide himself even there; for kings and princes of the earth called him to

* Medieval expositors always take Rachel as a type of the contemplative and Leah of the active life; cf. Dante, *Purg.* XXVII, 100–8.

their own business, and at last he was set over the Abbey of St Agatha, which was on the verge of ruin. Under him, this house flourished again, freed at last from debt and happily abounding in all things necessary. From this Abbey he was called by the Lord, having run his race, to receive the prize for which he had striven so well, and to join the happy company of the Saints.

It was magnificent, but some of this was not monasticism in the earliest and most real sense. St Benedict and St Bernard were men of as noble birth as Charles, but they had brought no great wealth to their abbeys. Charles lived as a poor man amid these possessions which he collected for his house; but the wealth itself tended to enervate his brethren as time went on. The Villers chronicles, unusually detailed and complete, show this plainly enough. Charles's successor rose to the cardinalate. Yearning to be at Villers again, and washing the dishes as the King of France's son had done at Clairvaux, he sent his former brethren "a golden and silver image of the Blessed Virgin, of very great price", which St Bernard would never have permitted.

Yet all the abbots down to 1250 were of exceptional merit and holiness; several also of noble birth. The abbey was a model even among the Cistercians of those parts. But we can trace definite downward steps. The eleventh abbot, William (1321–36), "sometimes betook himself to the infirmary to repair his forces, and would invite a few of the elder monks to dine there with him; but they could scarce be induced to come, since they could ill brook his sobriety and the mediocrity of his table". His charity was splendid, and the chronicler quotes from Thomas Cantimpratanus two remarkable instances:

The abbey had a grange called Scortis, wherein the lay brethren had an ox of excellent shape, bulk and strength, whose flesh a certain poor woman, great with child, conceived an unquenchable desire of eating; for she wept and was tormented as though she would die. Men gave her the fairest of ox-flesh; but this was of no avail to restrain her longing. When the abbot came to the grange and heard from a lay-brother of this woman's peril, he answered: "It is better that the ox should be slain than the woman; but do this thing secretly and fulfil the woman's desire." So the lay-brother took the ox secretly that evening, and slew and flayed him, and divided limb from limb and laid them together. Then he sent the woman that part of the ox which she had longed to eat; and she ate thereof and was restored to full health. Yet, O marvel and fearful to see! when the morrow dawned, and the lay-brother followed his servants to work, he beheld the slain ox ploughing at the plough. So, amazed beyond all belief, he hastened home, entered the chamber, and sought the flesh he had laid by; yet he found naught whatever of that ox, neither flesh nor hide nor even the blood that he had shed. Three lay-brethren who were in the grange were effective witnesses to the truth of this; nay also the butcher himself, a faithful and good man; and above all this very woman who was healed by the eating of this ox's flesh alone, and could endure no other; for, with a certain occult natural instinct, she distinguished this by the violence of her longing. The servants of the grange, however, knew naught of this; for the abbot strictly forbade lest it should be published abroad. Yet in his own mind it had such force that, whereas hitherto he had been of a parsimonious nature, he became liberal and pitiful to the poor beyond all other abbots of our Order.

Again:

A very great sum of money, perhaps 1600 pounds, was brought to this monastery at the death of a certain usurer at Namur. Many possessions were bought with this money; but then a certain man of strict conscience was elected to the abbacy; who grieved to hear what had happened. He, by selling sheep and cattle and movable goods, sent back the money to Namur, that it might be restored to all from whom it had been unjustly taken. But no man would take the responsibility of this restoration, and the money was brought again to the abbey. So this pious abbot, indignant with those who brought it back, commanded that it should be taken again and laid in the market-place before the citizens and the whole people, saying: "Let who will take it; for I renounce all claim to it, not doubting that it was unjustly won." All men, seeing this, were much edified thereby; and by common counsel they restored the money by the hands of faithful men to all who had been wronged. Moreover, within a brief space God restored it tenfold to the abbey; and, whereas hitherto it had been most slenderly endowed and almost in beggary, we have now seen it in affluence and abounding in much wealth.*

Under William's successor (1236–40) this lesson of *Date* and *Dabitur* was repeated in another form:

* Thomas, it will be noted, has to some extent exaggerated this contrast. William is the hero of yet another miracle which was more than once quoted in the Middle Ages. A spider fell into the consecrated wine at Mass; he unhesitatingly swallowed the venomous creature, and felt no harm. Only, about a year later, a pustule formed upon one of his fingers; and when it was pricked the spider crept out.

One year, when there was a dearth in the province, the brethren counted the sum of their harvest, and, as is the wont of human infirmity, were tempted (by the Devil, as was afterwards seen) to defer until harvest-time that subsidy which they had been accustomed to spend with great liberality upon the poor. That same night the fish-pond, which lay above the abbey, burst its dam and flooded the offices and grievously hurt them. The brethren, as just and godfearing men, imputed this to their sins, and especially to the counsel of avarice which they had concerted against the poor; wherefore they changed their minds and continued to succour them as before.

His successor again (1240–50) was strict enough to refuse all contributions to the new Cistercian college at the university of Paris; like many other successors of St Bernard, he distrusted this attempt to found a learned Order. But even a strict abbot cannot stem the rising tide of worldliness, as we may see from an anecdote told by the admiring chronicler:

Abbot Arnulph was so beloved by the Duke of Brabant that, when one of our lay-brethren passed by an inn, and refused to give the drinkers money for wine, and the biggest man among them ran out and took his horse from him, then the Lord Duke, hearing this, caused the man to be hanged. Moreover, when nobles or great men injured our community, the Duke would compel them to come into our chapterhouse and do us satisfaction in due form. I write not their names here, lest their posterity hear of it and avenge themselves on us.

This brings us to 1250. The next five abbots were evidently not such exceptional men as their predecessors; the nineteenth abbot, Arnulph II, was elected in 1271 and "found the house hampered with many debts and pensions; so that the monks in the monastery never tasted wine for the first year of his rule". Many, however, were no longer resident in the monastery; a custom had grown up of going and living at the granges, with the excuse of looking after the work, but in reality for enjoyment. Arnulph was obliged solemnly to warn the community that a monk's business is to pray and to keep himself unspotted from the world, "nor is it consistent with his profession to spend his attention on farming, lawsuits, sleep, tittle-tattle, wandering to and fro, or pampering his palate; especially in cases where outside business can be managed by lay-brethren or trustworthy lay folk". He had to rebuke them also for their unwillingness to receive as fellow-monks any but the upper or middle classes. He was not only a strict religious disciplinarian but a man of business, and brought the community back to such prosperity that it reached the above-mentioned total of 100 monks and 300 lay-brethren. "In the last year of his life he promised that he would give us more clothes, and would settle the whole available convent property upon the refectory; but alas! it was never done; for he had scarcely paid off our debts when he passed to the Lord."

All this time many legacies and endowments had dropped in, to add to the monks' daily comforts. One lord left money for extra wine to the reader at meals; another, for extra herrings; another for butter, and so forth. In 1300 the yearly revenue for these "pittances" or extras amounted to 400 *nigri turonenses parvi*,* a very considerable sum even if lay-brethren got their share, which is not likely.

At this point, we find growing indications of more rapid decline. In 1329 when Gerard was elected, he resigned at once in dismay at the load of debts which he had to face. There was a capital debt of some £3200 modern, and 1300 bushels of wheat were also due yearly to his creditors. His successor Henry resigned for the same cause after two months. The next, an exceptionally good man, paid off the most pressing debts by selling some of the monastic estates. Yet, even so, his successor inherited a heavy load of debt; in spite of which the chronicler praises him for having increased the conventual allowance of wine. Then follows a gap from about 1333 to 1362, during which no chronicle at all was kept; and the fifteenth-century compiler could find no materials beyond the bare abbots' epitaphs, with scattered memorials for the rest of the time. But, whenever we get a stray glimpse, it is nearly always of further decay; the debt in 1433 amounted to more than £12,000 modern.

* Apparently equivalent to the daily wage of 400 skilled masons at that time, or the price of 38 small sheep.

CHAPTER III

THE SHACKLES OF MATERIALISM

If even such a man as Charles of Villers could not shake himself and his abbey entirely free from the heavy pledges which they gave to fortune in virtue of their great wealth and worldly privileges, these hindrances were far more marked in cases where the reformer was less saintly, or the abbey more materialized already when he undertook his task. This comes out in another instance which we may take as entirely typical of its own kind: the story of St Trond as told in most welcome and unusual detail by two writers.(1)

St Trond is near Liége. Its *Chronicle* was begun not long after 1124 by Abbot Rodulf, who wrote the first seven books, and died in 1138. The next six books were written by a younger contemporary, scarcely inferior to Rodulf in his picturesqueness and wealth of detail. He was evidently an eyewitness of most that he describes; but he ends in 1136, and probably died himself during Rodulf's last illness.

In so far as space allows, I give their own words, silently omitting all that is not directly germane to the present subject:

This Rodulf was born in the village of Moustier on the Sambre, where is a convent of black nuns. His parents were plebeian, but most pious Christians, in the service of that convent. They served the poor indefatigably with hospitality and refreshment, and passed their married lives without any stain on their Christian profession.

He studied at Liége until his eighteenth year, and was ordained subdeacon; thence he accompanied to Burtscheid, near Aachen, an intimate school friend who desired to take the vows there.

Yet, all this while, he himself thought of nothing less than of becoming a monk. But by night, when the monks were wont to read from the lives of the Fathers at collation, Rodulf would hide himself in a closet hard by where he could hear and understand all that was read. Nor did he do this, as yet, so much from zeal of edification as for the sake of hearing the marvellous lives of those simple men who were there read of, and for curiosity to hear this new and simple style. When, therefore, he had often lent ear, with eager attention, not so much to this rustic style as to the marvellous sayings and deeds of those simple and most holy fathers, then he began to loathe the misery of this present life, and to be kindled into contempt for this world, and to ponder these things all night upon his bed. In brief, not many days had passed before he not only confirmed by his exhortations that companion who was somewhat hesitating on the brink of the monastic life, but he himself also took the cowl on the same day, in the 18th year of his age. When, however, he saw the Rule [of St Benedict], and noted that the brethren kept it in but few particulars, then he began to wander from monastery to monastery within the archbishopric of Cologne, sometimes staying months or even half a year there, more especially with the religious and pious Adalbero, first Abbot of Gladbach, who there had followed for a short time the monks of Siegburg,* most renowned in those days for order, religion and hospitality. The more eagerly Rodulf drank in the discipline of the place, the more heartily did he loathe the indiscipline and extreme worldliness of his own monastery.

Meanwhile Abbot Azelin died, a man whose extreme simplicity and decrepitude had led him to laxity, so that both order and worldly wealth were perishing within the monastery. He was succeeded by John, custos and dean† of the same monastery, far advanced in age and utterly unsuited for such an office; for the brethren had elected a man fit for and like unto themselves. Then Rodulf, seeing how evils were multiplied and indiscipline had grown stronger, whereby he foresaw only too plainly what would come to pass in the future, procured leave to depart. He now made his way towards Flanders, where he had heard that a strict monastic life was led. Gladbach, where he had so often dwelt, he now avoided because he felt (what indeed came to pass) that if Abbot Adalbero were to die, then that Siegburg Order so lately introduced would perish with him. Moreover, he had oftentimes, before this, suffered most grievous contumely at Burtscheid, when he was first made custos and schoolmaster, and then cellarer, and then vice-provost and provost. For, when he strove for the betterment of religion, both he and his fellow who had taken the cowl with him were reviled almost daily by the brethren who impiously resisted them; nor had they scarce any help meanwhile from the Abbot.

Wherefore, as I have said, in utter weariness and despair of amendment for that place he at length departed towards Flanders. But it

* The Abbey of Siegburg, founded in 1060, enjoyed for some years a great reputation for strictness.

† I.e. claustral prior, responsible for the discipline of the brethren.

befell that he passed by St Trond, where the Lord Abbot Dietrich gave him hospitality that night. He first enquired who and whence the stranger was, and whither he was bound, and wherefore. Then, finding him to be a young man of good purpose, comely to behold and well versed in letters, he began to strive cunningly to retain him. For he saw this young man would be profitable to him, first for the instruction of his boys in discipline and learning, and then for promotion to some inner or outer office of the monastery if such a chance should befall, as befall it did. The stranger, with many words of gratitude, showed his will to remain; whereupon the Abbot first gave the boys into his charge for their teaching in school, and then set him to write out certain most profitable compilations filled with many sentences from godly books, and the decrees of many Church Councils. Wherefore, this first year, Rodulf wrote for him that most useful volume containing much of Holy Writ, and taught the boys (who scarce knew how to decline *musa*)* not only to write prose but verse also. Yet he found it a most grievous task to teach them, since he himself could not speak the Teutonic tongue,† and some of the boys, who as yet had learnt little and whose native idiom was Teutonic, could neither understand him in Latin nor (to use the common word) in Walloon. Yet unremitting labour, which conquereth everywhere, was victorious here also; and in that year he brought them so far that they could easily understand in Latin whatsoever he could read to them. Moreover he taught them music after the doctrine of Guido‡ which he was the first to introduce into a monastery; and to the amazement of the elders he made the boys sing straight off at sight, by the help of this silent art, things which they had never learnt by ear.

In those days, as I have told in another book of this Chronicle, the aspect of this monastery was most wretched and lamentable. The brethren had no cloister or monastery but a church naked, torn, horrible and waste, and in the cloister only one rough unfinished building, in half of which they took their meals, while they slept in the other half. The brethren were as follows: first, Abbot Dietrich, (2) Bozo, the dean as he was called in the old order, which is what we now call prior, (3) Stephelin, (4) Herman called the Bald, (5) Sibert, (6) Hugo, (7) Morung, (8) Folcard, (9) Boro, (10) Reizelin. The boys in the school were Gilbert, Gerard, Thidelin, and Baldwin; but these four were only sojourners who departed afterwards.

Within about two years, Bozo the dean died, and Rodulf was chosen in his place by the voice of all the brethren. Then, girding

* *Musa*, the first declension, stands on the very threshold of Latin grammar.

† I.e. Flemish.

‡ Guido of Arezzo, Abbot of Sta Croce d'Avellino, is said to have invented the sol-fa system. His book, written about 1030, is in Migne, *P.L.* vol. 141.

himself forthwith to the amendment of the Order, he conferred daily with the elder monks in and out of Chapter, as to the Order which was kept in the old monastery while the cloister yet stood. When, therefore, they had taught him the customs of the former monastery, full of most honourable gravity and religion, he began to persuade them in kindly fashion to adopt these; and, going softly and gradually, he taught them to attempt to follow the earlier course, and thus, some day at last, to rub off the long-standing and inveterate rust of evil repute.

Wherefore Abbot Dietrich, seeing his zeal and fervour in religion, gloried and rejoiced in him above measure, and willingly suffered all claustral affairs to be disposed at his will. But Rodulf was vehemently and almost continually afflicted by certain unquiet monks from other cloisters, whom, on account of the fewness of our brethren, Abbot Dietrich suffered to lodge with us, and whom Rodulf would have compelled to live as under the Rule and discipline, which they had either never learned in their own monasteries, or had fled from with loathing. For he was wont to say that he would rather live religiously with a few, than irreligiously with many.

His first serious trouble was with their dress. When they went abroad (which, he implies, they did very freely), it was often in tunics such as "irreligious nobles" wore. An ancient brother, who claimed to have lived nearly eighty years in the abbey, and to know another preceding period of eighty by hearsay, assured him that this abuse had been imported comparatively recently by "the indiscipline and insolence of the young men". Rodulf, therefore, sent the garment of one of the recalcitrants to be standardized by the tailors; and, when the man still remained obstinate, "he was at length cast forth from the monastery, with leave to go irrevocably whithersoever he would. Meanwhile the other brethren went on daily from strength to strength in the Order, the Prior directing all his efforts to that end, and never ceasing either for this or any other contumely, nor for any man's machinations".

Moreover, he made a complete end of another evil custom which had grown up among us by the indiscipline of equally froward young monks; and not among us alone, but almost as generally among our layfolk. For on the first of the Rogation days, when our procession came to Zepperen according to ancient custom, the greater part of the brethren would beg or hire horses which they mounted forthwith, and rode to Brusthem before the procession. Thence they would gallop back to the monastery with the wanton youth of the town, at one moment giving free reins to their horses to gallop at full speed, or again suddenly reining them in, and caracoling hither and thither with poles in rest, now fleeing and now putting to flight. Thus they did all through the three Rogation days; on the second day the procession went to Falun and on the third to Mergueles. Wherefore it came to pass on those days that all those fishes or cakes which were appointed for the brethren's table were given to the men who had lent the horses, except a very few cases where monks would not get horses, or could not for love or money. The very schoolboys were devoted to this abominable custom; and those brethren who, either by choice or necessity, went on foot, while the people ran homewards after the riders, were afflicted with the most grievous weariness, not only for the length of the journey but also for that swift and unwonted pace.

Thus the Rogation days and supplicating litanies were changed among us for these mock-tournaments. Prior Rodulf, loathing this detestable abuse, refused the horse that was offered him while the rest were mounting, saying that it befitted neither layfolk nor monks, nor indeed any Christian folk whatsoever, to do their penitence and their supplications on horseback; in proof whereof he alleged their bare feet of fasting, and the fact that they covered their heads to join in these supplications to the saints and to recite their names [in these litanies]. By this and other reasons which seem pertinent, he first persuaded the lord Abbot Dietrich and then the other brethren to desist at last from this cavalcade, and from those consequent disorders which were unworthy of monks, and from that transference of their food which diminished their almsgiving. It was decided that those brethren who had strength should go on foot, while the rest stayed at home, and that the journey should so far be shortened as to afflict those who went with no excessive weariness. Thus, under his priorate, that Rogation-tide cavalcade began to cease, and it ceased during all his lifetime; and this began to please the people so much that nearly all of them were gradually brought to speak and act in like manner.

What shall I say of the solemn feast-days of St Trond, St Eucher and St Remi? Certain of our clerics, from the familiarity wherein they, as other scholars in their boyhood, had been brought up in our monastery with our own boys;* others, again, from their own religious character, had long since obtained this favour from our predecessors, that on the aforesaid feasts they should yearly come with reverence into our choir for high Mass, clad in albs like the brethren. Moreover, if it chanced that any of them sang well, then they sang the tropes which were then used among us, or the gradual or the alleluia.

* I.e. with our oblates, boys destined from the first to the monastic profession.

After this they would go with all decency on those days to the refectory, to eat with the brethren at their table; whence they would arise and sing aloud all that pertained unto the feast, and walk to the church in front of the brethren who sang their *Miserere mei Deus*. But this use, which seems to have arisen in charity and religion, began in process of time to be transformed, little by little, into superstition and vice. For whereas, at first, it was permitted only to such as we have described, and in such manner as we have described it, yet at length the evil custom had come to such a presumptuous abuse, that the priests on those days would flock thither indiscriminately from the fields, rather as to a fair than a holy-day, pressing pell-mell into our choir among the brethren and rushing without any attention to High Mass; some indecently dressed in lay garments, open in front and behind, very few in black cassocks, and even these without alb or surplice. Moreover—a thing abhorrent not only to order but also to all religious lay folk and even to all Christians—during the celebration of the secrets of the mysteries of Christ* two or three of these clerics would sit about in the choir itself around one or two of our brethren, or one cleric would sit by one monk, and thus they would go through the rest of the Mass together, with idle words and laughter and jests. When therefore, after very many unendurable disorders, they had come to the refectory, then there was such a din of divers folk at meat, such a clamour and talking even of unknown priests and clerics, that the voice of the reader from his pulpit, however loudly pitched, could scarce be heard. Moreover, the longer the meal lasted, the greater was the confusion under the influence of wine; and other guests were so many—for whosoever would might come in at random—that so many brethren were set apart for serving them as to leave scarce five or six to dine at table. How much the Provost was wont to expend on that day—or rather, how much was wrested from him—can neither be reckoned nor numbered. How utterly order and discipline were wanting among us on those days (or rather, what positive disorder and peril of souls reigned among us), I hold it more decent to bury in silence. For, when the brethren rose from table, and some of these foolish and shameless clerics snatched away all that came under their hands, forthwith an equal throng of common folk set themselves down with our servants, to wit, every man who imagined himself to have done any work on our farm at any time of the year; nor was there any limit to the din or the waste.

Rodulf put an end to this by insisting that the clergy should come reverently dressed, should not trespass among the monks in choir, "and those who would fain be at High Mass should

* I.e. the *secreta* of the Mass.

stand round the Abbot in reverent silence as befitted the feast day and the great Mystery". Further, they were to feed apart from the brethren, though "with no less abundance". "But this matter brought the Prior great and long-standing hatred and persecution, both from laity and from clergy; for the priests always met on those days at the fairs, and so stirred up that plague afresh."

Again, St Benedict's emphatic and repeated prohibition of private property was violated. At funeral Masses (which in a populous district would be fairly numerous) the celebrant monk regularly pocketed the whole offering for himself. With great difficulty, Rodulf succeeded in commuting this for "some little thing...a girdle, or a knife, or a linen napkin under his head and shoulders". But on this point he anticipates possible back-slidings: "Whatsoever be done otherwise in this matter, let our successors know that this was our decree."

Again, the cloister was so ill guarded, with a broken fence, that "there was scarce anything to prevent layfolk, and even women, from pressing through the monastery". He now made the enclosure complete: but,

seeing that this enclosure kept the brethren from pressing out of the monastery, except such as had leave, and hindered folk of both sexes from coming in (for he himself kept one key and the cellarer another) therefore he incurred the most grievous wrath and indignation of Countess Gertrude, our Advocatrix* who now lieth buried among us in the abbey, because she was no longer able to have her accustomed passage through the midst of our cloister and the congregation of the brethren. Moreover she was vehemently moved against him by many of our clergy and layfolk, especially the serfs of our manor, who complained that they were odiously shut off from their wonted passage through the cloister and from their familiarity with the brethren. But he, albeit terrible threats were launched against him, and such words flew everywhere around as might have pierced the stoutest heart, remained fearless and unshaken, dreading only lest he should fail to amend the monastery and its order. Wherefore, in order that the brethren, according to the Rule, might be more easily kept in the cloister to sit and read and sing and keep silence, by virtue of his office he caused a book-cupboard, for the first time, to be made in the

* The founder of a monastery, and his heirs after him, always possessed rights of patronage; he was called *Fundator* or *Advocatus*; hence the technical word *advowson* for a church benefice.

cloister, and stocked it with books according to the number of the brethren. Meanwhile he himself rarely ceased from writing, or noting books for music. There is extant a volume of his works with chants composed for Saints' Days, in the preface whereof thou mayest find what he wrote, what he noted, and when and wherefore. There is also another volume of the seven books which he wrote against the Simoniacs, dealing with the arguments in four books and in three with the authorities.

In other words, Rodulf warmly espoused the papal side in that Investiture struggle which then convulsed Europe, and which in many districts kindled bloody civil wars between the papal and imperial factions. Liége was in one of the most disturbed regions. For nearly every bishopric or great abbacy there were now rival papal and imperialist candidates, and the decision was often by force of arms. St Trond suffered very heavily both under Dietrich and under our Rodulf, who succeeded as abbot in 1108, and who increased his own unpopularity by introducing into the monastery, as far as he could, the reformed use of Cluny. Countess Gertrude, especially, was incensed at his firm resistance to her constant trespass upon the abbey rights.

This woman's frowardness went so far against him, that one day she swore an oath, in burning wrath, that she would not even leave to the prior his common food and clothing, unless the Abbot were deprived of his. Meanwhile the Abbot kept himself shut up in the precincts, relieving the tedium of his leisure by reading, writing of prose or verse, or singing, as a man who had no other place whither he dared to go.

It is highly significant that our pious and zealous abbot, in the full fervour of the Cluniac revival, should count confidently upon the reader's sympathy with his suffering in this temporary trial of confinement within his own precincts, according to the primitive Benedictine ideal. At length he "despaired of man's aid, and turned to the Lord". That is, he journeyed to Metz in order to worship at the shrine of Stephen the Proto-martyr, and to enlist his help. His prayers were effectual; the Countess Gertrude died shortly afterwards, and Gilbert, her heir, promised to repair the abbey's wrongs.

Yet St Trond had been "horribly wasted" in these civil wars, and the task of rebuilding was formidable indeed.

While the abbot yet feared to gird himself to so great a work, by reason of the slender substance of the Abbey, God put it into the heart of a certain matron of our town, called Ruzele, to begin the building of one pillar; which indeed she began, built, and finished at her own cost. After her example a freed serf who was bailiff of our great farm began and finished the next pillar; after whom our townsfolk, at their own cost, began four pillars, whereof they left two unfinished. Therefore Rodulf, seeing that this was the will of God and his Saints, plucked up heart and let other matters go and girded himself stoutly to this great work.

But, long before it was completed, the Devil envied this success. Civil war broke out again in 1114, and the victorious side burned the town and sacked the abbey. The workmen, who were building the roof of the apse, had barely time to escape from the flames. Yet Rodulf was undaunted.

Next year, he began to gird himself so eagerly to the task of repairing the monastery, that (so to speak) he could scarce rest even at midnight; ever would he be among the workmen to survey their labour. Before sunrise in the morning, after sunset in the evening, he would urge the masons on the one hand, and carpenters on the other, to diligence at their work. Thus in that year he completed all the walls even unto the tower, and almost roofed it with beams, still striving with all his might, from day to day, to complete the little that was left.

The whole was finished and dedicated in 1117. An interesting list of relics follows: the abbey had (among others) part of Christ's tomb, of the column at which He was scourged, of His crown of thorns, of St John Baptist's bed and cave, of the Virgin Mary's hair, of St James's clothing. Shortly afterwards, the Emperor Henry V was excommunicated by the Pope. The new Bishop of Liége, Alexander, accepted his ring and crozier from the excommunicated emperor, and so the papalists elected one Frederic as his rival. Rodulf, who took part in this election at Cologne, scarcely escaped with his life on the journey home. In the civil wars which again broke out, the townsfolk of St Trond favoured Alexander, and thus involved themselves in the general excommunication. Rodulf's position now became untenable, especially when he refused during the interdict, as a necessary point of principle, to allow Mass to be said in the abbey for the funeral of a prominent citizen's wife. To save the abbey from worse evils, he went into voluntary exile (1121). At the Synod of Cologne, he attracted the notice of the archbishop, who procured his election to the abbacy of St Pantaleon at Cologne.

And, seeing that Abbot Rodulf was a man of fine presence, and of proper sonorous voice at divine service, therefore the people of Cologne busily frequented such processions as he led, and many devout matrons also. The clergy gave him solemn reverence, unmixed with envy, as though they had the Archbishop himself before their eyes. In a brief while, and with no great labour, he fairly amended the decay of order and the broken concord among the brethren [of St Pantaleon], among whom he found an excellent virtue of pure confession, with unwearied assiduity in watchings and prayers, both secret and public. He opened to hospitality their closed (nay, locked) door. Their buildings, ruinous and unsightly, he repaired until they were worthy for the Archbishop himself, for guests, and for the Abbot; meanwhile, he suffered no diminution in the statutory food of the brethren. What with old and new, 120 cartloads of wine came that year to the monastery. He spent much on his guests, and especially on monks and canons regular, to whom his door and his table were ever free.

With the Jews he oftentimes had soft speech, neither disputing with nor reviling them, but softening the hardness of their hearts by feeling and rubbing them (to speak metaphorically) where they needed it; wherefore they so loved him, that even their womenfolk would go to see and to speak with him.

At length the Liége quarrel was settled, and Rodulf was now given a triple choice: to remain at Cologne, to go back to St Trond, or to keep both abbeys—for such pluralism was not infrequent in those days. He chose "to return to his first bride".

He had been two years and five months away, during which time Gilbert our Advocate, and his son Otto, misused the abbey revenues at their own will. Nor did they even show fit reverence for holy places; for the son lived in the abbot's lodging as in his own house, not abstaining from the embraces of his young bride even among these walls on consecrated ground.

The abbot compelled them to depart in sullen resentment.

He came back to find the Abbey possessions sorely dilapidated, and grievously oppressed with debts and usury, wherefore, from that wealth which God had given him at Cologne and which he had brought back for daily ministration, he relieved the anxiety of the whole community, especially in the matter of debts and usury. Nor was it long before he tore down to the very foundation his own lodging beside the great tower, both as loathing it for a leprous spot since the aforesaid persons had dwelt therein, and because its timbers were so rotten and broken that it could not easily be mended. In its stead he built another, hard by the new one which he himself had formerly made, with all that was needful for fit hospitality, and a chapel and orchards. He had yet another cause to hate the old building, because it was a convenient den for profane folk, who had made it (with the great tower thereunto annexed) into a strong fortress; and he feared for himself and his successors lest this should be done again.

But the new house rose slowly: and meanwhile he sat in the old.

And sometimes, sitting there alone and pondering over his cares and his past labours, and not seeing how, in his present unrest, he could find a place to weep for his sins, he began to be very heavy and sorrowful, and to consider how he might flee from his country. O!, how often did he mourn and yearn for the time when he might be able freely to obey that word of God to Abraham: *Get thee out of thy country and from thy kindred*, or to chant in all truth that verse of the Psalm: *I have gone far off flying away, and I abode in the wilderness*. Therefore he proposed to go to Rome, and, on the way, to take counsel with religious men as to the wisdom of the things which he purposed in his mind; after which, he might get the blessing of the Pope to confirm him in his purpose.

For this journey he reconciled himself with Alexander, the now expelled imperialist candidate for the bishopric of Liége, who wished to get a special personal absolution from the Pope, apart from that general absolution which he had through the Concordat of Worms. But the travellers, apart from their sufferings from robbers near Aosta, found at Rome itself "less consolation or compassion than they hoped, whether in the matter of God or man". He hints not obscurely that they found at Rome "things which they had heard at home yet had not believed", and that their escape penniless from these robbers was fatal to all hopes from the papal court.

On the other hand, concerning the purpose of his soul and of those souls committed to his charge, Rodulf had learnt from men of religion [at Rome] no more than he had learned at home from Church discipline and from books that were common both to us and to them.

Moreover, that thorn in the flesh which physicians call ciatica [*sic*] had so grown upon him that it crippled his walking; and made it impossible for him even to ride without continual torment.

Therefore

he bade farewell to the patronage of the Saints and kissed the shrines of the Apostles; then, taking the Pope's blessing with him, he determined to return with his companion aforesaid. When they were come to that above-mentioned city of Aosta, they were astonished to find that all the things taken from them by the robbers had been recovered for them by their hosts and by all the citizens! This was indeed a great and hidden judgment of God, that they should go poor to Rome, and come home rich! In brief, they came at last to the city of Basel, after many bodily sufferings and through the deadly perils of the Mount of Jove.* Rodulf took a perilous passage by boat [*naufragoso navigio*] to a spot hard by Cologne, since the aforesaid ciatica forbade him these long journeys on horseback.

Then the papalist Bishop of Liége died, and the imperialist Alexander bought the coveted prize with simoniacal bribes to the Archbishop of Cologne.

For which cause he was accused by his clergy, and summoned to the judgment seat of Pope Honorius at Rome. Then he deemed it profitable if he might take Abbot Rodulf with him. The Abbot gave him no denial; not so much for the Bishop's sake as for the yearning of that first and unfinished pilgrimage that still haunted him. The whole of his new journey was by winter, and therefore, scarce tolerable to human flesh. Yet go they did. When they reached Rome, the Abbot was robbed in his sleep by thieves—among whom, if the neighbours spake truth, was his own host—of all that he had got together for this new and old project of pilgrimage. Wherefore he again abandoned this second intention, which, so far as he could see, he felt to be contrary to God's will.

Alexander, now absolved by the Pope and full of grateful friendship for Rodulf, escorted him back. The description of their crossing of the St Bernard in the first days of January is worthy to stand side by side with John Evelyn's classic story of passing the Simplon.(2)

When once Rodulf was safely returned to St Trond, he hoped for some well-earned quiet. But "God, through his accustomed

* The Great St Bernard, still called locally *Monte Jove* or *Mont Joux*, from a Roman temple of Jupiter which stood there.

Angel of Wrath, smote our abbey, and warned the transgressors to return to their right heart. For he suffered Count Gilbert, our Advocate, and his son Otto to be filled with an evil spirit, and raised them up to persecute the household of our monastery in all that was contrary to right or justice". Yet

in all this calamity and anguish, albeit the substance of the brethren was much diminished in the matter of food and drink and raiment (for they suffered three years from these evils), yet their discipline grew not cold on that account, nor did their numbers decrease. We had now the greatest anxiety how to repair our churches that had been burnt, our mills, and our manors: we were even as men wounded in war, solicitous to cure their wounds at home. Moreover, all this while, Abbot Rodulf was afflicted not only with this grief of mind, but also with his ciatic pain, which had so eaten into his whole hip that he could scarce go either on foot or on horseback. Wherefore he built himself a convenient cell northward, well-fitted to his sickness and to his desire of a religious life. This cell was hard by the eastern apse of the minster, with a door opening into a chapel that adjoined the crypt and choir; and it was his wish to consecrate an altar in honour of St Mary, Mother of Our Lord Jesus Christ, and of the holy Bishop Basil; for the Blessed Mother of God, our Lady Mary Ever Virgin, had no special chapel in our church. But God's healing hand, which from of old was never wont to leave the body of our abbey unvexed, added now this also, that it rested mercifully upon our head, and changed his ciatic pain into a palsy.

On Friday the 17th day of March, in the 25th year of his ordination, and in Lententide, Abbot Rodulf sat at meat with his brethren in the refectory. On that day he had given the brethren a dish of fish, thus breaking their abstinence for human compassion's sake; and during the dinner there were brought unto him marsh-eels roasted on the spit, following upon which came lesser eels stewed with tender herbs; whereof when he had eaten* and had put them away from him, through a sense of greediness he laid his hand on certain apples which were in front of him, steeped in wine. Of these he tasted a little, when suddenly his left hand began to grow heavy as lead, with sudden jerks at intervals, and the corner of his mouth on that side seemed as it were to die, and his tongue to lose its wonted readiness. Though sore afraid, yet he did not put an end to the reading, but said grace with the brethren when the meal was over, and repaired to his western cell without any pain, but in great fear at this accident. Then

* *Et aviditatem sentiens abjecisset.* It is probable, however, that the real reading is *satians*: "When the edge had been taken off his hungry appetite, he put them away."

he conferred with his brethren concerning that which had befallen him in the refectory,* and rendered thanks to God, believing himself to have escaped, though indeed he had not. For, after collation, he felt his left leg benumbed little by little, so that he would not dare to go to bed without support; and awaking about midnight, he found himself bereft of all use of that leg or of his left arm. Then, fearing sore for the use of his limb and for his whole senses, he commended himself most devoutly to the prayers of the brethren, that God might still spare him a tongue for confession, and to recognize himself; which by God's mercy was granted unto him. In the autumn of that same year, the Father's correcting hand added such sickness to him that he was despaired of by the physicians, and seemed scarce the shadow of a man.

After he had escaped, though with difficulty, from that sickness, and his palsy began so far to mend that he could walk after a fashion with the help of a crutch, and could sometimes join the community in choir and cloister and chapter, he was wont to admonish the brethren most zealously to keep their Rule and turn God's indignation aside. Moreover he caused a litter to be made wherein he could conveniently be borne whithersoever he would for abbey business.

He carried out much building and was planning still more, when another calamity fell upon the abbey, this time from the side of the townsfolk. From prehistoric pagan times, peasants have propitiated the gods of fertility by drawing a plough in formal procession at the opening of the year: hence the "Plough Monday", which became a quasi-religious medieval custom, and survives in many places still.

A variant of this custom [writes Sir E. K. Chambers] may be traced in certain maritime districts, where the functions of the agricultural deities have been extended to include the oversight of seafaring. Here it is not a plough but a boat or ship that makes its rounds when the fishing season is about to begin. Ship processions are to be found in various parts of Germany; at Minehead, Plymouth and Devonport in the west of England; and probably also at Hull in the north.(3)

It is natural that it should have flourished near St Trond, in that land of rivers and canals; and, again, it was natural that a somewhat tumultuous popular festival should give opportunities for paying off old scores. Just as "serf" was a term of reproach in medieval society, so also, in a less degree, was "weaver", *textor*.

* The Rule permitted no talking in the refectory itself.

Heretics, moreover, who were rapidly growing about this time in numbers and in unpopularity, were sometimes called *textores*, either because that sedentary occupation bred them in greater numbers, or, less probably, because *textor* had become such a word of contempt in itself as to be conveniently hurled at any hated person.(4) Here, then, in the St Trond district, the Ship Procession was turned against the weavers, "a sort of craftsmen", says our chronicler, whom "the common folk hold to be wanton and proud above all other handiworkers". A certain peasant "excogitated the following device for humbling their wanton pride". "He obtained permission from the judges, and help from giddy fellows who delight in jests and novelties; whereupon he built a ship in the nearest wood and fixed wheels beneath it, so that it might be drawn along the ground; and from the powers that be he obtained a decree that the weavers should take the ropes over their shoulders and draw it by water from Korneliusmünster to Aachen." Rodulf tried vainly to persuade his townsfolk against receiving this "devilish idol", "with all its heathen passions". Meanwhile the weavers complained bitterly to each other, not without certain levelling remarks as to the value of an honest craftsman in comparison with "a noble judge in the city who oppressed orphans and robbed widows". Yet still, before this execrable idol, without intermission, "all kinds of musical instruments were braying, to the accompaniment of foul songs unworthy of the Christian religion". Moreover, between moonlight and sunrise crowds of women "leapt from their beds with hair yet dishevelled, some half-naked and others clad only in a slight robe, and burst impudently in to mingle with those who were dancing around the ship". About midnight, they dispersed with "deafening and inarticulate yells". This lasted twelve days, and the saner townsfolk began at last to weary of it: they suggested burning the ship. But the advice of the fools prevailed, and it was resolved to transfer this "sport": the ship must now be dragged farther through Duras to Léau. The Lord of Louvain, in whose territory these places lay, forbade the project; therefore at his command the men of Léau shut their gates against the ship. This led to civil war; St Trond was defeated, and all the abbey possessions were devastated—"villages, churches and mills given over to fire and ruin.... This was the fourth devastation which the Lord of Louvain wrought upon us in 26 years".

The chronicle now passes on to a story of a tenant who nearly cheated the abbey out of some property; this ends the twelfth book. The thirteenth and last book is a mere recital of arrangements made for the comforts of his monks in food, drink, and so forth. It will be noted how often these strong reforming abbots crowned their great work by increasing the statutory allowance of food and drink at the brethren's table.

CHAPTER IV

THE WIDER PROBLEM

EVIDENCE of this kind—and it meets us everywhere—proves the crying need for something more than these individual and isolated efforts. Long before the fifteenth century there had been constant calls for collective reform. It had been demanded by local Synods and great Councils, by Popes and even by the State. It would be easy to fill a volume with such evidence; but at this point it will suffice to give enough to show that the problem which confronted those two great abbeys pressed with equal force at almost every point of monasticism. The monks of Fulda, in 812, petitioned Charles the Great to the effect "that such [brethren] be chosen for Holy Orders as are learned in word and proved in holy conversation; not thieves and criminals [*scelerati*], and men totally ignorant of priestly law".(1) Already in this ninth century the question of monastic disendowment came up.(2) The historian of St-Martin-d'Autun recognizes that the real glories of his abbey were past before A.D. 1000.(3) Godfrey, Abbot of Vendôme, was one of the model prelates of St Anselm's time. "He did not tolerate any familiarities of his brethren with the inferior sex; even in others it made him impatient, saying 'How many hath it already brought to ruin! and it ceaseth not yet to destroy. To speak briefly, all who perish, and who have perished, and who will perish from now unto the end of the world, have been brought to twofold death by that sex.'"(4) The chronicler of the Bishops of Verdun, writing in 1144, deplores the fate of an excellent prelate, Rudolph, whom the wasteful and irreligious character of his subjects had compelled to resign from the abbey of St Airy at Verdun. "These monks [writes the chronicler] boast that they are condemned to this by a sort of fate; for, since the first foundation of their monastery, not one of all their abbots has died in the house, but all in exile; indeed, three of these expelled abbots are alive at the present day."(5) Concerning the monastery of Holy Trinity, founded at Strassburg in 1150, we are told that "its decay was so rapid that its restoration in 1226 was counted by some historians as its actual foundation".(6) The monasteries, especially of nuns, which were suppressed altogether or secularized, even before the middle of the thirteenth century, may be counted by the score. As early as 1210, there was only one Benedictine abbey left in the diocese of Le Puy; the two others had been secularized.(7) The Premonstratensian Order was scarcely a century old when Innocent IV and the Ecumenical Council of Lyons published statutes for the reform of its 500 monasteries (1245). These statutes show clearly the points that required serious amendment; slack visitation and want of discipline; vengeance taken by the guilty upon brethren who had spoken frankly to the visitors; fraudulent elections to abbacies; indulgence in forbidden flesh-meat; luxury in clothing; defect of hospitality and almsgiving; inconsiderate reception of choir-brethren or lay-brethren; scandal between brethren and sisters of the Order; difficulty of keeping women out of the monasteries; neglect of proper money accounts and business records; concealment of actual debts; illegal alienations by abbots; breach of the rules for silence and labour; and too great freedom outside the precincts.(8) A generation earlier Innocent III's decree *Cum ad monasterium*, incorporated in Canon Law, shows that all the worst failings of fifteenth-century Benedictinism were already notorious at the beginning of the thirteenth.(9) At Tegernsee, one of the greatest houses of the Order, the fifteenth-century chronicler records of Abbot Ulrich: "He wrote in that year 1256, in order to preserve peace in the abbey, an obituary-book which shows clearly that in those days the monks lived rather after their own will [*lege privata*] than according to the tradition of the Rule."(10) In 1274, a memorial was sent to the Pope, for his guidance at the Second Ecumenical Council of Lyons, by Humbert de Romans, Minister General of the Dominicans. In this he advises that money should be raised for financing the campaigns in the Holy Land.

> This [he says] could easily be effected by the following measures. First, to expend the superfluous treasure of the churches, their precious stones, and vessels and vestments, to buy therewith perpetual rents.*

* By putting this capital out at interest in one of the few ways permitted by medieval church law: see W. J. Ashley, *Economic History*, bk II, chap. V, § 66.

Secondly, if one or more prebends in all collegiate churches were devoted to this purpose. Thirdly, if those priories wherein sometimes a few monks dwell, not without scandal, were [dissolved and] applied to this use. Fourthly, if those utterly decayed Abbeys [*destructae*], for which there is no hope of reform, were devoted to the same purpose.(11)

In 1331, the Augustinian General Chapter in England confessed the widespread and the notorious decay of the Order.(12) These details may serve here to supplement the mass of generalizations by contemporary orthodox writers which I have already printed in my second volume, pp. 505 ff.

Hence the necessity for repeated action on the greatest scale. Such difficulties as these, pressing with more painful force from generation to generation, inevitably called for frequent intervention from the highest authorities. Society waited with increasing impatience for some collective reform. It was not so much that growing heresy and anticlericalism subjected the monks to more and more unsparing criticism. The evil began in fact at the other end: it was the chronic failure of monasticism to justify fully its enormous wealth and privileges which provided one of the main sources of heresy and anticlericalism. Monastic reform was one of the greatest and most difficult of all the tasks that faced Charles the Great. Under his son, Louis the Pious, St Benedict of Aniane compiled a body of reforming statutes which were never completely forgotten. Again, monastic reform took a conspicuous place in that earlier Renaissance of the eleventh and twelfth centuries which marks the close of the Dark and the birth of the Middle Ages. This reforming movement we may call popular in the truest sense, drawing its motive force from all classes without distinction. The Cluniacs, Cistercians, Premonstratensians, and their fellow-reformers of 1050–1150, were not only led by men of noble birth or hierarchical eminence, but they also counted many such among the ordinary rank and file of their converts. Then came the Friars, a reform which enlisted at first as many nobles as its predecessors, but which soon settled down into a predominantly democratic movement. Yet the older Orders, Benedictines and Austin Canons, still formed the most numerous portion, and by far the wealthiest and most influential, of the monastic population.

More significant still, the leaven gave way to the lump. The stimulus which should have come from the Friars was gradually less marked than the contamination which those new missionaries gradually contracted from the older, more conservative, and worldlier monastic Orders. Now it is, therefore, that Popes begin to grapple seriously with Benedictine and Augustinian reform. Gregory IX, the friend and official protector of St Francis in his struggling days, was just the man to realize most keenly both the lukewarmness of the great "possessionate" Orders, and the extent to which they acted as clogs upon the mendicants rather than as active allies. He, therefore, published a body of reforming statutes for the Benedictines which marks an epoch in monastic history (1239). Innocent IV, a few years later, republished these with slight alterations (1245). A century after Gregory, came Benedict XII, a Cistercian, who grappled even more resolutely with the problem. He saw plainly that the preceding papal statutes, with their bold proclamation of "Let there be light!" had in fact scarcely done more than to make the darkness visible. Therefore, in order to consolidate the main position, he abandoned altogether certain very important points. St Benedict, for instance, had most strictly forbidden butcher's meat; his brethren must subdue their flesh by labour and by strict abstention from the flesh of beasts. Yet Benedict XII completely ignores bodily labour, which had long since been practically abandoned, and permits flesh-eating four times a week, except in Advent and Lent. His statutes for the Benedictines run to twelve folio pages, and those for the Austin Canons are equally full.

Here, then, was a code of searching by-laws supplementary to the minutely explicit Benedictine Rule; a code specially designed to meet human frailty in these degenerate "modern" times of the late Middle Ages. This experienced and masterful Pope had designed a compromise, in face of previous failures to ensure loyalty to the Rule itself. Yet in 1338, while the ink was scarcely dry upon the document, the General Chapter of English Benedictines interpreted the Pope's permission of flesh-eating in its most liberal sense.

Within seventy-seven years of this, the papacy itself was called to account at the Council of Constance, the most learned assembly which had ever yet met in the Western Church. A main task which faced men here, as at previous Ecumenical Councils from 1215 onwards, was the Reform of the Church, "Root and Branch"—*tam in capite quam in membris*. In that field the most important question of all was this of monastic reform. Here, then, from 1415 onwards, comes the last phase. The general level of education for the population of Europe is definitely higher in 1400 than in 1300, let alone earlier generations. Printing will soon be invented; and already for nearly half a century the Brethren of the Common Life have been multiplying books with a purposeful assiduity which called for such an invention as this of the press. At Constance, men soon found that the Church must not await salvation from this or that Pope, but must learn to help herself. The final failures, both here and later at Basel, do not affect the fact that a new spirit of constitutionalism was now abroad; or, rather, a revival to some extent of ancient Christian democracy. The multitude of the fifteenth century will often be ignorant, hasty, and therefore bungling; but it will try to act for itself. Princes and nobles and great churchmen will now be far less concerned to join the monastic ranks than to force upon listless and recalcitrant cloisterers a regularity of behaviour for which all the better clergy had long clamoured in vain. It is with Constance, therefore, that the main theme of this present volume will begin.

CHAPTER V

FROM A CARTHUSIAN CELL

LET us digress, however, for one brief chapter before dealing with that most ambitious monastic reform. The historian, in his attempts to set things in orderly sequence, is always tempted to import his own thoughts, and to take what did happen as that which must have happened. At this point, therefore, let us check our calculations by referring to a contemporary of Colet; one generation older, it is true, but still sufficiently typical. Here is a witness who will tell us how Colet might have envisaged Church history if, instead of his actual English life as we know it, he had been born in Germany, had actually accomplished his "conversion" instead of merely contemplating it from afar, and had passed a long career of study and intellectual intercourse in a great Carthusian monastery there.

Werner Rolewinck, a Westphalian by birth, was a precocious student and took the monastic vows at twenty-two. He chose that Order which attracted Colet and More, and which will frequently occupy our attention in this volume. Nearly all his life was spent in the cloister at Cologne, where he died in 1502 at the age of seventy-seven. He had occupied important posts in his own Order, and earned the respectful friendship of such outside scholars as the Benedictine Abbot Trithemius. The *Allgemeine Deutsche Biographie* characterizes him as "an unusually diligent and prolific writer", who deserves more notice than he has received. His best-known work, the *Fasciculus Temporum*, is a compilation which shows no scientific advance upon its predecessors, but which for our present purpose is all the more valuable on that account. It represents the impressions of a conscientious scholar and man of business (in the monastic sense) who had set himself to summarize the current chronicles and add observations of his own. It tells us the past of the world—predominantly the ecclesiastical past—as mirrored in a mind of no great originality but of praiseworthy freedom and courage. If the book, by some miracle, had drifted to another planet, and found readers, on the one hand, completely ignorant of all that has happened in our Europe since 1500, but, on the other hand, inquisitive and clear-sighted, it could scarcely have failed to give them a sense of impending tragedy in the writer's own world. There is a Sophoclean irony in Rolewinck's frank jottings and comments. He himself may not clearly see whither he is drifting, but the reader feels more and more strongly what the orthodox Johann Geiler reports from the Emperor's lips just about the time of Rolewinck's death: "The crash must come!"—*Es muss brechen!* In its own time, the book enjoyed an almost unique popularity. First printed at Cologne in 1474, it ran to more than thirty editions in the author's lifetime; more than any other chronicle can boast.* The Spanish translation (1480) was the first book ever printed in Spain: the same year saw German and Dutch versions, and it was six times printed in French. Many of the editions were anonymous, giving the author as "a devout Carthusian at Cologne", or "a certain man most studious of history". Rolewinck himself realized the vast potentialities of that invention which was now being employed, practically for the first time as a great commercial venture, upon his own book of 72,000 words. Though the following words themselves do not appear until the edition of 1481, and are probably due to one of Rolewinck's many editors,† yet they exactly express the spirit in which he himself had recognized this new invention and pressed it into his service. They run, under the year 1457:

About this time, at the city of Mainz, was discovered that most subtle science of printing books, unheard of in all past ages. This is the art of arts, the science of sciences, by whose swift operation a desirable treasure of wisdom and knowledge, yearned after by all men through their natural instinct, hath leapt forth as from the depths of hidden darkness to enrich and enlighten this world that is seated in wickedness.‡ For, through this art, that infinite store of books which

* This was a specially favourable moment for printers to hit upon a "best seller", and flood the market with books both readable and instructive. Printing first came into the Netherlands from the Rhenish cities in 1473; by 1491 there were presses in at least nineteen different towns. (H. Pirenne, *Hist. de Belgique*, III, p. 298, cf. p. 310. Between 1525 and 1558 thirty new presses were set up in the single city of Antwerp.)

† See R. Werner, *Etude sur le Fasciculus Temporum* (1937), p. 7.

‡ I John v. 19; a text very dear to the medieval moralist: "Totus mundus in maligno positus est."

hitherto at Athens or Paris and other Universities or holy libraries were revealed to a mere handful [*paucissimis*] of students, is now published abroad in every tribe and people and nation and tongue, so that we see the literal fulfilment of that word [Proverbs i] "Wisdom preacheth abroad; she uttereth her voice in the streets; at the head of multitudes she crieth out; in the entrance of the gates of the city she uttereth her words, saying: *O children, how long will you love childishness?*" and so forth. Albeit we know that swine despise pearls, yet herein is no contrariety to the wise man's belief, to withhold him from buying the pearls.

Like practically all medieval chroniclers and moralists, Rolewinck sees in history a progressive deterioration of the human race: we read this under the years 874, 1354, 1374, and 1424. Under 1154 he tells us how a certain hermit had a revelation concerning heaven and hell. He saw 30,000 souls leave their bodies in that year; St Bernard alone went straight to heaven, and three others to purgatory, while "all the rest were plunged into hell, to be tormented for all eternity". Under 1351, another hermit saw, "in the presence of Innocent VI while he was yet a cardinal...souls going down to hell like snowflakes in a storm, and into purgatory like a few scattered flakes. Three alone did I see come into paradise; a bishop and a Roman widow, and a Carthusian prior." Thenceforward Innocent had special devotion for Religious, and above all for Cluniacs and Carthusians. Rolewinck is judicial; the partiality of John XXII for the Carthusians does not prevent our author from criticizing him freely, like other popes. In his references to Church reform, there is no clear note of optimism. The schism under Paschal II (1104) leads him to sum up the pros and cons; "The Church may be most justly compared to the moon, which waxeth and waneth and seemeth to fail altogether; yet she cometh again to the full in the light of the Everlasting Sun, which is the Lord Christ, her spouse." In 1424, half-way between the Councils of Constance and Basel, he expounds his own Theory of Development. The Church (he writes) was rich at first in her good conscience. Gradually the *con* faded out, leaving *scientia*, the knowledge which puffeth up, to gain a strong hold over the Church.

But alas! in these unspeakable days of ours, even the *sci* also hath been deleted from her, and we see only *entia* (i.e. bare existences)

governing the spouse of Christ; namely, persons who have neither conscience nor knowledge, but are as it were insensible beings. These, fearing neither God nor His saints, claim benefice upon benefice for themselves. Moreover, worse still, we see the vilest of layfolk accumulate parishes and monasteries and (horrible to relate) altar-offerings. Hence the patrimony of Christ, deputed for his ministers alone, and for distribution to the poor, cometh into the hands of tyrants and prostitutes; churches and holy monasteries are reduced to waste places. Hence we see nowadays deadly wars, destructions of cities and realms, the lamentable death of innocent folk, and innumerable evils; and we know that all these detestable things proceed from the pomp of the bishops and the insatiable greed of the prelates.

Under 1416 he relates the Council of Constance.

In this Holy Council the Christian Faith, which had seemed almost tottering to its fall for many years past, arose in strength. There the abominable schism of forty years' duration was ended: and the two heretics John Hus and Jerome [of Prague] were burned, and many good steps were taken. Moreover the Holy Council decreed that a Council lawfully assembled representeth the Church Universal, and hath power directly from Christ; and that all of any rank, even papal, are bound to obey in matters that concern the general reformation of the Church: that is in matters of faith and of morals, both in head and in members.

Even with the anti-papal measures taken by the still more democratic Council of Basel he had much sympathy (1456).

In this Council many good steps were taken for the reformation of the Church in head and in members. It had a glorious beginning, but a lowly ending and full of tribulation, by reason of the schism. Marvellous issue of [human] affairs! The Council of Constance prevailed against three Popes, casting them down and setting up a fourth, in the face of so many adversities, and of the fact that no man had confirmed it. Yet this [of Basel], though assembled and confirmed with such authority, was not able even to reduce one Pope to the measure of its purpose; nay, a single man impeded its progress. At Constance the beginning was weak and the end glorious, at Basel the precise opposite.

Again, speaking of that schism between Eugenius IV and the Anti-Pope Felix of Savoy which lasted eighteen years (1434):

The case was very new and unprecedented; for the Council of Basel deposed Eugenius, the one undoubted Pope, because (as was said) he would not observe the decrees of the Council of Constance, nor would he obey the Council of Basel, but rather contended that he must resist it. Hence ariseth a great dispute of writers on this matter, on the one part or the other; nor have they been able to agree even to the present day (1474). For one part saith, "The Council is above the Pope"; and the other "Nay, but the Pope is above the Council! May God, who is blessed above all, ever give peace to the Church, His holy spouse."

Under 1464 he writes: "A great reform of very many monasteries was carried out in divers parts of the world. And note that reforms of this sort are often recorded and have been made, but scarce any abideth; nay, after the wonted fashion, in process of time, men slide back into their earlier faintness after the death of venerable fathers." And, under that same year, comes an entry even more fateful for Church history. Boniface VIII had invented the Jubilee system, with its plenary indulgences for contributory pilgrims at Rome, as a centenary institution. Theologically, this was marked by a fatal step: such plenary indulgences were thenceforward called very frequently, even in official papal documents, "Pardons *a poena et a culpa*"—"from penalties and from guilt". Whatever attempts the schoolman and the theologian, both then and in modern times, might make to explain this phrase away, yet the unquestionable fact is that thousands of simple folk took those words at their face value—for the phrase was employed not only in the Church Latin but in the ordinary vernacular—and believed that their money bought pardon for their guilt. The popularity and pecuniary profit of these Jubilees became so enormous that Clement VI, in 1343, cut the period down to fifty years; Urban VI (1389) to thirty-three; and finally, in 1470, Paul II to its present measure. As Rolewinck puts it, he "changed the Jubilee to recur every twenty-fifth year in order that, where sin abounded, grace should more abound".(1)

Rolewinck's kind of history is not what one might expect *a priori* from a Carthusian; but, if we regard it judicially, can we point confidently to any single point in this book which would not have enlisted More's and Colet's sympathy? In his criticisms of Church life, Rolewinck is certainly less outspoken than his far more famous contemporary and brother-monk, Dionysius Cartusianus. It is too often forgotten that the papacy with which More refused to break, even at the cost of his life, differed enormously from that partially reformed Church which Europe has seen ever since the Council of Trent. We must get Trent out of our minds if we are to appreciate truly the work of Constance, where the last medieval monastic reforms had their source.

CHAPTER VI

THE COUNCIL OF CONSTANCE

THE two cases of Villers and St Trond give a fair idea of one of the greatest difficulties which confronted every individual reformer. It was almost impossible to work up any monastery to its primitive heat, so long as the religious thermometer was so low outside, not only in lay society but even in the cloister. In fortunate cases, the reformer found fellow-reformers in his neighbourhood or in his Order, with whom by action and reaction he soared higher and higher. But too frequently, even when he had conquered active resistance within his own precincts, worldliness constantly threatened to soak in from outside. Thus, throughout the fourteenth century, the feeling grew among churchmen and earnest lay-folk that a general reform was overdue. The Great Schism with its attendant scandals intensified this feeling. The Council of Constance (1415–18) set itself explicitly to the task of Root and Branch Reform—*tam in capite quam in membris*. The first step needed was to end the Schism: they swept away three papal claimants and elected a fourth from whom some real betterment might be hoped. But at that point, unfortunately, their zeal for reform cooled. The original intention had been to concentrate upon reform as soon as the three claimants had been eliminated, and thus to present the new Pope with a charter of ecclesiastical amelioration to which he might be compelled to swear adherence. This would have been a great step forward, and it was consistently supported by the English representative, Bishop Hallam of Salisbury. But this wise and pious man died before the final decision came; and he was succeeded by Cardinal Beaufort, an ecclesiastical politician who was probably the wealthiest subject under the English Crown: an actual millionaire in the Middle Ages. His vote turned the scale: Martin V was elected without the previous guarantee; and then the fundamental question of Root and Branch Reform was left in the clouds. The Council, before its dissolution, did indeed burn John Hus and Jerome of Prague on the one hand and, on the other, decree unanimously that the infallibility of the Church rests finally not upon any bare papal decision, but upon that of a General Council, which may if necessary correct the Pope in matters of faith or morals, or even condemn and depose him. But these cardinals and bishops and abbots were not prepared, in the face of papal reluctance, to enter upon an exhaustive and unsparing discussion of moral questions which so deeply concerned their own personal position. Constance was one of the most enlightened assemblies which had ever sat in the Christian Church; but it was faced by the inevitable difficulties which must confront any attempt to reform, from within, a body of enormous antiquity, wealth, and prestige. Basel, the next great Ecumenical Council after Constance, was even less successful in this direction; and those two failures were mainly responsible for the growing conviction reported by Geiler: *Es muss brechen!*

So far in anticipation: but let us now look more closely into what was said and done at Constance in the matter of monastic reform. As to the urgency of this matter there was never a moment's hesitation. It was prominent from the first preliminary proposals down to the final decrees of the Council. Jean Gerson, Chancellor of the University of Paris, sent to the Emperor Sigismund, in 1410, a memorial pleading for a General Council. He pressed for a reform of the monasteries, "in order that the monks may live in observance of their Rule". The cardinals holding abbacies *in commendam* (he said with a statistical exaggeration common in the Middle Ages) had sucked their abbeys so dry that there now remained only one-tenth of the original monastic population.(1)

Next, we have a "List of Agenda" drawn up for the future Council about a year before it actually sat. This had long been ascribed to the Italian cardinal, Zabarelli: but Finke, our latest and greatest authority, makes it tolerably certain that we must credit it to the even greater French cardinal, Pierre D'Ailly.(2) In any case the writer is certainly a cardinal and no extremist: we could not start with a better guide. Let the Council (he writes) begin its combat against heresy by remedying the appalling religious ignorance which meets us everywhere. Jean Gerson has already composed a simple manual of instruction in Latin and in French, for priests and people; let the Council supply a copy of this to every bishop. Let Church services be abridged, and the excessive number of holy-days diminished. Next, as to the papacy. The evils of past despotism are apparent; let a moderate constitutionalism be brought back into the Church. Let a General Council sit at least once every ten years, and let no pope "make wars and peace and like decisions" on his own bare responsibility. Let the cardinals be reduced in number, and proportional to the different states of Europe; thus "we shall avoid making the papacy hereditary in any single nation or race".* Thence let us pass on to reform in detail those other abuses which "have rendered the Church vile among the people". Existing laws are good enough, if only they were supported by sufficient sanctions, and by the will to enforce them. Under the present laxity "all is now falling into decay, and all men wander astray and we are on the verge of an abyss, and the papacy is steering to its own ruin"; therefore let us return to the primitive Christian system of elections, now destroyed by papal encroachment. Let none be admitted to clerical Orders save educated and reputable persons, after due examination. Let us put an end to the disgraceful pluralism of benefices. Let the prelates cease to wink at sin among the clergy in consideration of bribes: "for nowadays all such things are for sale, and are redeemed by money". Let no boy or girl be bound to the cloister before the age of puberty. Let effective measures be taken against clerical concubinage: otherwise let us frankly allow marriage. Let the prelates no longer neglect their statutory visitations. The multitudinous exemptions, which so often frustrate the visitation system, must be brought to order. Prelates must cease from illegal exactions, and the Roman Court must cease to set them a bad example here. The friars must no longer trespass so much upon the parish clergy, especially in the matter of women's confessions. Gaolers in the bishops' prisons steal the prisoners' food. The misuse of excommunication, for compelling payment of even the pettiest fines, is scandalous. In matrimonial cases, and even in the

* Yet, since that complaint was uttered, there have been only three non-Italian Popes down to the present day—Calixtus III (1455), Alexander VI (1492) and Adrian VI (1522). Thus the Italian quasi-monopoly, so far from relaxing, became increasingly tyrannous.

granting of licences for burial, excessive sums are exacted from the poor. When a child dies elsewhere than the place of its birth, the burial rights are sold for it, and in no other wise can it be buried, by hook or by crook. Priests are vicious, and "dissemble their concubines". In France, "a thousand parish parsons are wanderers upon the face of the earth"; churches are defrauded of service, children die unbaptized and adults unconfessed. Church endowments go to hirelings, while the poor are defrauded. It is a shame that at Rome there is no university, in accordance with Canon Law, and no endowment for teachers.

At the Council itself D'Ailly made another long speech.(3) This was on November 1, 1416, when the fathers had sat for a year and done very little for reform. He emphasized the fatal danger of delay; in default of immediate reform, there will be a collapse. Hallam of Salisbury had already urged the same, saying: "Reform, or within a few days the Church will suffer an eclipse".(4) First of all, cries D'Ailly, "we must remove that detestable abuse which is the source of this present Schism: viz. that one single nation or realm, whether Ultramontane or Cismontane, to the scandal of the rest of Christendom, hath so long held the papacy that it could say 'let us possess the sanctuary of God for an inheritance" (Ps. lxxxii, 13, *Vulg.*). Next, to the details. "Evil Superiors are seldom punished for their excesses: for sentence is not given quickly even against notoriously evil persons, but is deferred for many years: and often their punishment is totally neglected." By a monstrous abuse, certain prelates fight in the field, dropping their spiritual character, shedding blood and oppressing the poor. There are too many monks, and especially of the Mendicant Orders. The Indulgence system is abused. Monks should keep more strictly to their own precincts. Theology is comparatively neglected at the universities

because of the abuse of the Roman Court, which hath despised the theologians and preferred those who study the lucrative sciences [of law] in every rank of Churchmen. The early primitive theologians built up the Church, but certain pettifoggers have destroyed her, and seem to be leading her almost to utter ruin: so that some men now utter a horrible proverb, That the Church hath come to such a state that she is not worthy to be ruled but by men destined for hell—*per reprobos*.

The military monastic Orders are in special need of reform. So also are the nunneries, "which now, alas! are fallen from honesty [*dehonestata sunt*] farther than I dare to express in words". Let decayed nunneries, or monasteries of any kind, be dissolved and given "to the cloisters where Religion is maintained". Monks must beware of unjust acquisitions, especially in the matter of tithes: they must keep to their Rule in the matter of diet, "for experience proves that the keeping of this would facilitate other observances of Religion. The long prayers which had sometimes been introduced, beyond St Benedict's own requirements, should be moderated." The universities (he goes on to say) fail to give adequate instruction "in Greek, Latin, and Rhetoric, the ignorance of which subjects is in many ways harmful to the Church".

Correction should be applied to the morals of the clergy, who now, alas! are excessively corrupt in wrath, gluttony, lechery, pomp, prodigality, idleness and other kinds of vice, which grievously scandalize the laity. Especially should we strive against that most scandalous custom, or rather corruption, whereby many nowadays fear not to keep concubines publicly.* And, since the legal penalties of suspension, excommunication and irregularity are ineffective against them, the penalty of deposition from office and benefice should be brought to bear upon such incorrigible offenders in this or other public immoralities.

A third memorial to this Council was ascribed by the learned Trithemius, two generations later, to Nicolas de Clémanges, Archdeacon of Bayeux; but it is almost certainly by some contemporary at the University of Paris.(5) He voices the same complaints with even greater emphasis, and is even more explicit as to the fatal ignorance of the clergy. From the foul sources of prelatical simony and greed, he says,

flows forth that copious multitude of vile and most unworthy priests: for [the bishops], in order to get the greater gain from their ordinations, admit all comers, with very little or no distinction, to the titles which they seek....There is no enquiry into their former lives, no

* *Scandalosissimae consuetudini, seu potius corruptelae, qua plures hodie non verentur tenere publice concubinas.*

question as to their morals. What can be aptly said for their letters or learning, when we ourselves see that almost all the priests can scarce read [Latin] slowly, syllable by syllable, without tripping somewhere either in matter or in word?

Again,

How many are raised nowadays to the episcopal bench who have read, or attended lectures upon, or taught, Holy Scripture? [*Sacras litteras*] Nay, which of them has ever touched the Holy Book except upon the outside cover?...The sees are held either by ignorant and illiterate persons or, if they be men of letters, by such as have followed only Civil Law,—a subject forbidden to priests—and such learning as brings money.

Significant as these three indictments are, the cumulative force of all the rest is even more remarkable. No single speaker at the Council, I believe, is recorded to have protested against these devastating accusations. The nearest approach to such was when Leonardus Statius, General of the Dominicans, vehemently repudiated D'Ailly's suggestion that the Mendicants were too numerous and too intrusive. Yet he had nothing to say in contradiction of the more important accusations.(6) Indeed, the accusers constantly appealed to common notoriety: they enumerated, as uncontested and incontestable facts, the festering sores which cried for biting and unsparing plasters, or even for the knife.(7)

Special emphasis was laid on the shortcomings of the monasteries. At the very beginning (February 1415) an open letter was addressed to the Emperor Sigismund at Constance.(8) The Church and State are now plagued "with sword, famine and pestilence, with battles and seditions", for three main causes. First, all monks, friars and nuns

have now turned aside and departed from God's commandments and from their own Orders and Vows and Substantials* whereupon they were founded. Yet, celebrating God's mysteries daily, betraying Christ like Judas and the Jews, taking [His Body and Blood] unworthily, they are seen to be liars to God, monks in naught but their habit and their tonsure; except the Carthusian Order and very few [*paucissimis*] monasteries and monks who keep the commandments of God and of their own Order.

* The *Tria Substantialia* of monasticism were Obedience, Poverty and Chastity.

"The second cause is the lechery of the clergy." Under the Mosaic Law, wherein priests offered oxen and rams in sacrifice, they were forbidden to marry any but incorrupted virgins. Our own priests offer not brute beasts but

the Son of God, the Bread which is come down from Heaven.... Yet, alas! to such a pass is God's Church come that His priests take to themselves not only maidens as lawful wives, in violation of Canon Law, but even harlots and vile prostitutes and women cast off by their husbands, against the law, to satisfy their lust like beasts that have no understanding....Therefore be clean, you that carry for others the vessels of the Lord, or at least bring it about, by order of this present Council, that men may marry lawful wives.

"The third cause is in the simony of Religious, secular clergy and layfolk." It is as under Jeroboam, when the meanest of the people were made priests: "Whosoever would, he filled his hand and he was made a priest of the high places." Unless all these things be reformed, the world will be punished sevenfold more grievously.

John de Vinzellis (9) preached a sermon before the Council in 1417 (July 11). He described the effects of that *commendam* system which flourished under papal and princely encouragement. By this time, this had become the ordinary system by which cardinals drew incomes proportionate to their rank, and kings paid their ministers. The preacher quotes one case where the commendator had drawn 60,000 ducats from his abbey, yet had not spent 100 upon the repairs of the buildings. Hence the numbers of monks have fallen off: God's service is diminished: the few who remain "transmute the piety of religion into the hunter's art and the wantonness of utterly dissolute life.... They say: 'We are not the Abbot's monks, or the Prior's: we are My Lord Cardinal's!'" We frequently see ruined buildings —even steeples falling, and rain dripping through the broken vaults; filthy albs and tattered chasubles; "compare these things with the decency of albs and vestments and buildings in the friaries". The Body of Christ "is sometimes handled with negligence in a common piece of cloth". Relics are neglectfully kept, and the rich reliquaries sometimes profanely embezzled; the abbey charters perish uncared for. Thus famous abbeys and priories are first ruined and reduced to the state of cattle-sheds;

then licence is given to absorb them into some other house, where the greedy absorber treats the whole as his own foundation, and devotes the revenues to Masses for his own kin. In England (as I have shown in vol. III, chapter XXV) this plague of *commendam* had been encouraged by popes, but steadily resisted by kings until Wolsey's time, when it enabled the great cardinal to imitate exactly those disendowments and pompous foundations which had long been common on the Continent. The friaries escaped, of course, because none was rich enough to tempt a cardinal.

Others at Constance speak to the same effect more briefly, but not less emphatically. The Austrian ambassador complains to the Pope of the wars which fill this world; the frequent unworthiness of the clergy, with whom simony is rampant; and the "damnosa negligentia" of the prelates, especially in the matter of visitation.(10) The Church stinks of simony, says Hallam of Salisbury.(11) An anonymous petitioner complains that Rome sets the example here. "Let hunting-dogs be done away with; let us make an end of luxury, and cohabitation with women, of whom, as I hear, so great a multitude is congregated in this Holy Council that it is abominable to hear."(12) Another, probably a friar, emphasizes monastic decay.(13) Johannes Huguonetti pleads that good pastors are scarce to be found: "they feed not, but play": and grind the faces of the poor. "How many desolate and ruined churches we have! How many monasteries and other pious foundations abandoned by the pastors! How many folk die without the sacrament of baptism!" According to Bernhardus Baptizatus, a Benedictine monk,(14) "Prelates often took their pleasure with maidens and women, and, what is worse, with nuns, with whom many [Church] goods are spent." Jacobus de Camplo complains that the immorality of the clergy earns the scorn of the laity.(15) Peter v. Pulka, again: "Certainly the clergy of the Roman Court [*clerici curiales*] are said to(16) keep their own concubines, and to sell justice shamelessly in the sight of all men; they go about in the most indecent fashions of lay dress, with short doublets and tight hosen."(17) Dietrich v. Münster: "The Church has been made a den of thieves."(18) The Cistercian Marthaeus de Aula Regia: "There is no pastor nowadays who says to his flock as

St Paul did 'Ye received me as an angel from heaven'; but there are abundantly many who can say the contrary: 'Ye have repulsed me as a messenger of the Devil'." A cleric has sometimes ten or twenty or more benefices, incompatible according to Canon Law: and "we have now been waiting nearly two years in this Holy Council" for reform of that notorious scandal.(19) Another speaker says (December 19, 1417): "We see more fornicators and concubinaries among the clergy than adulterers among the laity."(20) An anonymous treatise complains of the dilapidation of churches and ornaments, the multiplicity of Religious Orders, and the ubiquity of concubinage, especially in Italy: let marriage be permitted, as it is in the Greek Church. There are too many nuns, again; these would often be better married. The marriage laws for the general population encourage the sale of dispensations, and concubinage among such as do not buy.(21) The famous Roman Court official, Dietrich v. Nieheim, writes of abbeys in ruins, and others subject to the "abominable custom" of limitation to inmates of noble birth. If "a saint from heaven" asked at the Roman Court for a bishopric or a fat abbey, none would listen unless he first paid the money. Religious life in Germany is starved by the absence of Provincial Councils and visitations, during the last hundred years or thereabouts. *Commendam* is eating like a cancer into monasticism. Indulgences lend themselves to abuse: services are neglected in the cathedrals and great churches. There is so little examination of priests that "we have come to this: very many are to be found, promoted even to Holy Orders, who have neither worthy life nor knowledge nor the other things required of priests by Canon Law". As to the universities, a man may reach the highest intellectual distinction and sue vainly for a living,

but if any ignorant freshman [*beanus*] were to come with his money-bag to the Roman Court, ready to buy any vacant Church benefice, then it would be granted forthwith, and none would first discuss his fitness, whether he were sufficiently literate and otherwise proper to obtain that benefice....So the ignoramus laughs at that other who has wearied his head with long study, and suffered perchance much fasting or miseries on that account.(22)

A Cistercian addressed to the Council, in 1415, a memorial

concerning the common vice of private property among monks. The Church (he says), once so fresh and fair, is now a wrinkled, old hag. The foulest of her blotches is the "extreme and immeasurable defection of the monks. Some folk remain unmarried, or desert their wives, in order to take the vow of continence in a monastery, after which they shamelessly marry nuns, prostitutes, divorced adulteresses and the like." *Proprietas* is not only a mortal sin (as a flat contradiction of the Rule to which we are vowed) but an obvious moral corruption. Men may thus take the vows when they shrink from hard work, "wishing to live quietly and comfortably and without care; or that they may have greater honours and wealth than in the world". If this abuse is so indulgently permitted by abbots or priors, this is either (1) of their own perversity, (2) in order to avoid criticism for their own evil lives, (3) for fear of unpopularity or deposition, or (4) "as evil and slothful servants; for the sake of their own comfort and quiet they presume to rebuke no man for this iniquity". It is mainly on account of this multitude of "proprietary" monks that God has "given the monasteries over to the indignation and hatred of kings and princes; nay, even to all the people also". "Through this vice of property almost all Religion in the world is perishing, as sad experience plainly shows. For whence come so many fornications and adulteries among monastic persons, so many feastings and drunkennesses, so much wandering abroad and indiscipline and sins, save through money, which all things obey?"(23) In the summer of 1417, the German nation sent proposals for reform to the Council. They complained that patrons of churches "and, what is worse, some Religious prelates and ecclesiastical persons", were wont to present unfit persons for institution by the bishop; "viz. knights, nobles, esquires, mere layfolk, incompetent, untaught, illiterate; nay sometimes unknown, expelled, undisciplined,* apostates and vagrants". The monks, especially, hire such men in the cheapest market for the churches which they have appropriated.

And if the bishop will not have such men (as indeed he is not bound), and refuses to institute them, then the presentors, of their own temerity, without canonical institution, presume to rule and

* Reading *discolos* for the impossible *distulos*.

govern such parish churches and their parishioners themselves,* or cause such presentees to be instituted by their conservators, asserting themselves to be thus privileged by the Holy See....Moreover, it must be noted that in the diocese of Constance nearly all the eminent and wealthier parish churches are appropriated by Religious and other persons and institutions...and, unless some remedy be applied here, the churches will be utterly reduced to naught.

They beseech the Council to revive the visitation system decreed long ago at the Lateran Council of 1215.(24)

Lukewarmly as the Council dealt with reform in comparison with other less vital matters, it still showed some sense of responsibility in connection with the abuses enumerated. It decreed that novices be not permitted to take the vows unless they could decently read and sing, nor be admitted to Holy Orders "unless competently instructed in grammar". Abbots, on appointment, are to swear that they will reside in their abbeys. Prelate may not declare war against prelate on his own authority.† Vagrant and apostate monks are to be dealt with severely, and monks are not to serve as parish priests. At least two must dwell together even in the smallest priories. Nuns must be restrained in their association with men, from which, "as experience shows, many indecent and unhonest things have been wont to be committed". "Nuns may not wander abroad, by reason of temptations to unchastity." Matters which had been most emphasized in the discussions are specially prominent in these decrees. "Since almost the whole multitude of Religious, of both sexes, is tainted with the vice of simony", therefore there is now a general pardon to all who shall confess and repent. Again, since the incontinence of the clergy has caused the greatest scandal to Catholic folk, therefore the laws must henceforth be actually enforced.(25) It will be seen that, as D'Ailly had said to begin with, and as Colet will repeat a century later in his famous Sermon to Convocation, what the Church needed everywhere was not new laws, but ordinary respect for the laws which had existed for many centuries.

* The rule of Canon Law that monks might not act as parish priests was, in fact, far more often broken in later medieval Germany than elsewhere, whether with or without papal licence.

† In Germany prelatical barons sometimes sent each other letters of defiance, and proceeded thence to war, like other barons.

The same impression emerges from the study of the Chapter of the Black Monks at the convent of Petershausen, near Constance, in 1417. This advertised itself—and apparently quite truly—as the first Benedictine Provincial Chapter ever held in Germany, though Innocent III had decreed in 1215 that these should be held in all countries every three years. England had kept far nearest to this ideal; Germany and Italy had neglected it most. This Petershausen Chapter, held under the impulse given by the Council, covered the whole great ecclesiastical province of Mainz, together with the dioceses of Bamberg and Constance. Its decrees, epoch-making in the sense that they represented the first systematic and concerted fight in Germany against growing laxity, are simply a repetition of long-standing statutes, with only the slightest additional details. Each monastic congregation is to provide, within a month, a decent place for the Eucharist; a provision which may be compared with the strong efforts made almost at the same time, by the episcopal visitors of the diocese of Lausanne, to ensure that every church had an aumbry for safe keeping of the Lord's Body, and a lamp burning before it. Monastic services, again, are to be said devoutly, "without skipping or syncopation"; and absence from services is to be punished. Monks are not to imitate worldly dress. They must obey St Benedict's prohibition of butcher's meat. The dormitories must not be divided into private cells. The porter must prevent unauthorized exits of brethren, and must on no account permit the entrance of women. A teacher must always be provided for the novices, and promising students maintained at the universities. Accounts must be faithfully kept, and shown to the visitors. Pocket-money must not be given, notwithstanding any custom which may have grown up. Nuns must obey Boniface VIII's command of strict claustration. Friars must not be permitted to transfer themselves to Benedictine houses, and then wander abroad. All these statutes must be read twice a year in every monastery, that none may plead ignorance. The whole code implies past neglect of the most ordinary rules: and there is one provision which strikes at a custom commoner in Germany than elsewhere.

We will and ordain that the number of monks instituted from of old be maintained, if the revenues suffice; if not, let there be as many as can conveniently be kept. Let them not be able in any way to defend themselves by the pretext of any privilege or custom (or, to speak more truly, corruption) whereby they plead that they should receive none but nobles, especially if there are no nobles to be received or who desire to enter the aforesaid monasteries. Yet if such be received, let them be preferred to the rest, other things being equal. (26)

While the Council was yet sitting, a desperate appeal came to it for help against the deformed abbey of Iburg, in which town the Bishop of Osnabrück had his palace. "We fear", it ran, "the obstinate wickedness and perilous rebellion of certain monks...also of certain powerful folk who stick to them and favour them in these parts....*And, if need be, let the help of the secular arm be invoked.*" (27) We shall see later, most abundantly, the significance of this last sentence here italicized.

At this point, as at many others, we have specially valuable evidence from Abbot Johann v. Trittenheim (Trithemius), who was among the most zealous reformers, yet sufficiently distant in time to survey the Council of Constance in its true proportions. In his *Chronicle of Hirschau* he tells us how Abbot Friedrich took the oath of obedience to the reformers at Petershausen with a right good will, partly "in consideration of the peril to his own soul, and partly in memory of the ancient reform at Hirschau" under St Wilhelm, who had led the Cluniac revival in Germany (1080). Yet, when Friedrich returned to his abbey, in spite of all his entreaties and tears, "all the brethren, with one accord, resisted him obstinately; wherefore, unable to make anything of his subjects, he reformed his own life and committed the business to God". Yet, adds Trithemius, the labours of the Council were not altogether vain; for three houses did reform themselves completely—Melk, Castell and Bursfelde—"and, in consequence, more monasteries also".(28).

CHAPTER VII

ITALY AND SPAIN

WE have seen how Dietrich v. Nieheim, whose position at the Roman Court gave him ample opportunities for judging, assigned to Italy a melancholy pre-eminence in the matter of ruined or extinct monasteries. Generations earlier, the Franciscan Salimbene had borne similar testimony against his own country: "Note that the Order of Black Monks of St Benedict is far better kept in the countries beyond the Alps than in Italy."(1) Moreover, the assertion can be tested in detail, for one of the most considerable and not least civilized districts of the Peninsula, by a careful analysis of G. B. Semeria's *Secoli Cristiani della Liguria*.(2) This author is constantly obliged to apologize for the scantiness of his materials, though in his case there is no question of Protestant vandalism, and the monasteries were undisturbed until the French Revolution. In some cases, he has found no data for anything but the barest skeleton. Altogether, he describes about forty houses, but many in such meagre detail—sometimes only two or three lines—that in those cases no judgment is possible. Twenty-seven, however, do lend themselves to some real judgment.

The Benedictine abbey of S. Stefano (founded 970) gradually earned great wealth through its piety and beneficence, and exercised all the rights of a sovereign prince. But Boniface IX (1401) reduced it to a *commenda*. In 1529 "there was scarcely one monk left in the abbey"; but it was then reformed and flourished until 1776, when it was apparently extinguished. S. Fruttuoso (Benedictine, tenth century) enjoyed at first a great reputation. St Catharine of Siena, in 1376, stayed there, and some of her letters are addressed to the monks. "In the sixteenth century, the abbey was secularized." S. Siro (994) began well and rose gradually to "vast possessions". At last, "through the negligence and injustice of the secular [i.e. commendatory] abbots, the abbey came almost to complete ruin, and was transferred to the Theatines". Pulx (Augustinians,

1065)—very meagre details, but apparently it went on until the French Revolution. Sta Maria del Zerbino (Cistercian, 1156) had long "an excellent reputation and full numbers". But at length, being put under *commendam*, "it succumbed to this abuse, and was suppressed in 1617".

These are typical of the whole long catalogue, as will be seen if we pass on now to the last ten houses. Tiglieto (Cistercian, 1131) was the most famous of all Italian abbeys in that Order. Yet Semeria could find but few details of its history. It was already in *commendam* at the beginning of the fifteenth century; by 1583 the monks had abandoned it, yet its considerable revenues were enjoyed by commendatory abbots, absentees of noble birth, apparently down to the French Revolution. S. Martino di Gallinaria (Benedictine, founded early) evidently lost its great reputation in process of time, fell into debt, and had to sell heavily. In 1473 the monks abandoned the convent; it was put under *commendam*, and in 1842 the abbey was still a sinecure in the papal gift. Varatella (Benedictine, about 1000) was a wealthy abbey. Gradually it became "diminished both in worldly revenues and in the number of its brethren", so that in 1315 the Bishop transferred it to the Carthusians of Casotto. Varigotti and Villaregia were apparently extinct before the Reformation. Sta Maria in Caneto (Benedictine) was suppressed by Leo X and granted to the Dominicans in 1516. San Remo (Benedictine, before 1136) "passed afterwards to the Franciscans, who abandoned it after a short time". Another priory here was suppressed in 1258. Ventimiglia (Benedictine, before 1041) was a cell to Lérins; it was apparently extinct before the Reformation. For Pigna Semeria writes: "after searching for the year of foundation and the founder's name, I am more in the dark than ever concerning this abbey. I know for certain that, like so many others, it ended at last *in commendam*."

For the nunneries, Semeria gives scarcely any details, but he sums up unfavourably: grave scandals were not infrequent.

We may fairly argue, also, from what is recorded of the three greatest of Italian houses, most directly connected with St Benedict himself: viz. Monte Cassino, Subiaco, and Farfa. Innocent III, in 1208 and 1215, had dealt severely with the first for the wastefulness of the abbot and breaches of the Rule on the monks' part (flesh-eating, hunting, private property, neglect of almsgiving, wandering abroad, and suspicion of immoralities). His bull of 1215 gives a lurid picture of life in some of the dependent cells. Yet when Honorius III came to the throne (1216) he published a flattering bull of protection for Monte Cassino, because God had disposed "that this abbey, wherein [St Benedict] both lived a most holy life and died a most holy death, should be dignified and privileged beyond all other monasteries in the West". A year later, however, he took a very different tone. His bull of 1217, I believe, has never been published in full. The Roman editor of the brief summaries from the Vatican register puts it very succinctly: commissioners were sent by the Pope "to reform and correct this abbey, which had fallen very low"—*maxime depravatum*. But Bishop Spondanus, in his *Annales*, summarizes it more frankly. He reports the Pope as writing that "he is sorely grieved that this abbey, wherefrom the Religion [i.e. the Benedictine Order] had taken its first origin, and which ought to be a light shining before all men, had nevertheless become as it were a sink of iniquity", *quasi sentina omnium vitiorum*. He therefore sends two commissioners to reform the monastery in head and members.(3) Again, under the year 1362, Abbot Tosti writes of this, his own abbey: "All, meanwhile, was squalor at Monte Cassino; and those masses of ruined walls reflected excellently the moral conditions of the monks....But those of Monte Cassino were not alone in these conditions; Regular and Secular clergy were all sick of the same disease."(4, 5)

When [in 1320], John XXII sent a reforming abbot to St Benedict's other monastery of Subiaco, the chronicler tells us that he found it "rather a cattle-stall than a house of monks".(6)

At Farfa, in 1219, Honorius III decreed "Let women be absolutely forbidden all entrance within the monastic precincts".

The scorn heaped by Boccaccio and other Italian novelists upon the clergy, and monasticism in particular, is notorious. Firenzuola (himself a monk) describes his brethren very much as Chaucer does; ambling comfortably on their fat and easy mules; "nor do they care to weary their brains with study of many books, since the knowledge gained therefrom would swell them up with the pride of Lucifer, and rob them of their monastic simplicity".(7) Masuccio, again, wrote: "A greater part of the houses of the Conventual [Franciscans] have more the semblance of robbers' caves than of habitations of the servants of God."(8) We may discount these novelists heavily; but St Catharine of Siena, in that *Dialogue* which so indignantly rebukes clerical immoralities in general, does not spare the cloisterers.(9) In her letters again, we find her pleading that "a good and virtuous Vicar General" should now be appointed for the Dominican Order, "since it hath run too wild"—*perocché egli è troppo insalvatichito*.(10) She speaks with burning scorn of the ubiquitous simony. Unworthy prelates sell Church offices to unworthy men: the Pope ought to "deprive the seller of his office if he amend not; and, for the buyer, it would be well if he gave him the prison in exchange".(11)* "Read all history", cried Savonarola to crowds of hearers at Florence, "and thou shalt not find that the Church was ever in a worse state than to-day....Almost all Religious make it their study to get food and money and tapers" which they sold again.(12)

Things were worst, perhaps, in Rome itself and the papal states. Machiavelli twice speaks of Italy as the most immoral of great European states. What goes farther to discredit Christianity is "to see that those people that are nearest neighbours to the Church of Rome are the most irreligious....Through the vicious examples of that [papal] Court, this country has lost all devotion and all religion....Therefore we Italians with our Church and our priests have this first necessary consequence, that we have become irreligious and evil." Elsewhere, speaking of the advantages of religion and morality to states, he writes: "And truly, where this goodness is not, little can be hoped for: as we can hope for nothing in those countries which in these days we see corrupted; as in Italy above others, so France and

* St Bernardino, according to his latest orthodox biographer, "was wont to say that the traveller on entering Italy could perceive a peculiar stench, the result of the shameful vices with which the country was infected" (P. Thureau-Dangin, *St B. de Sienne*, Engl. translation, p. 42). He gives no chapter-and-verse reference here, but the words are in harmony with those of his sermons. See *Pred. Volgari*, II, 98, 108, 140, 142, 150, and especially III, 135–6.

Spain retain a part of the same corruption."(13) A similar judgment had been passed two centuries earlier by the strongly pro-papal Alvarez Pelayo, a Spanish bishop who was Penitentiary to John XXII. He singled out Italy as the country *par excellence* of sodomy, sometimes even systematically organized. He wrote: "Alas, alas! within Holy Church many Religious and clerics in their lairs and their conventicles" bear this load of guilt.(14) A few years earlier than Machiavelli, the Zürich precentor Felix Hemmerlin passed a judgment similar to this.

We read of St Gregory [the Great] that, of his own bounty, he built six monasteries in Sicily, and a seventh in Rome wherein he took the vows himself; which monastery (to say nothing of the others) once flourished, and especially in his days, with a copious multitude of monks; and nowadays it is publicly apparent in the disposition of this monastery, and I myself in my time have seen, how that monastery hath scarce fed a single monk with his prior, and sometimes none at all; because the cardinals, as aforesaid, have thus eaten up the monastery and its monks....And not only in this monastery of St Gregory, but in almost all the churches and monasteries in Rome —and indeed in the whole world—there is a scarcity of Religious by reason of the lack of means and of devout persons.(15)

Fuller evidence on the relaxation of ordinary moralities in fifteenth-century Italy may be found in two works which have become classical: Burckhardt's *Renaissance in Italy* and P. Villari's *Life and Times of Savonarola*. For the later years of the sixteenth century, there are startling revelations printed from papers of suppressed Dominican houses of the kingdom of Naples in V. Spampanato's *Life of Giordano Bruno* (Messina, 1921, pp. 135–45).

The Italian nunneries had a specially dubious reputation. This is brought out in another work which has become classical, P. G. Molmenti's *History of Venice in her Private Life*; and also in G. Marcotti's *Donne e Monache* (Florence, 1884). The Venetian nuns, writes Molmenti, were commonly younger portionless daughters without real vocation; they naturally lived very much as worldlings; and the State legislated, without much success, against a class of convent-haunting men, the so-called *monachini* or *moneghini*.(16) From the official records of the Town Council at Bologna comes an almost incredible *dossier* concerning a nun's career culminating in 1432; a story strange not so much in her doings, which might be those of any person run wild in any age or place, as in the comparative impunity which she so long enjoyed.(17) Vasari, again, at the end of his *Life* of Lippo Lippi (d. 1469), tells us how Pope Eugenius IV was willing to release this friar-painter from his vows and allow him to marry the nun he had seduced; but Lippo declined the offer "in order to be able to do as he liked and to follow his appetite as he chose". In other words, legitimate marriage would have been a greater bar than monastic vows to his sexual freedom. Whether the story be literally true or not, it does at least show Vasari's opinion of monastic discipline in fifteenth-century Florence. So, again, a few generations later.

At Milan, in 1538, the Senator besought Pope Paul III to intervene, since the convents (he says) are plague-spots. At Sta Amelia, the nuns went out as they pleased. Those of Sta Caterina at Bologna had been expelled for misconduct and replaced by nuns of correcter life; but, after a while, they had forced their way back; and two Cardinals, backed up by the Administrator of the Church at Bologna, failed to dislodge them or compel them to keep the Rule: the Pope himself had to intervene.(18)

The *commendam* system had claimed, as its original justification, that the monks were proving themselves no longer fit for the original self-government of St Benedict's Rule. A typical case here is that of the great abbey of S. Prospero at Reggio-Emilia, as told by Dom Affarosi, a monk of that house.(19) He is speaking of the state to which it had been reduced in 1438, when there were sometimes only three monks besides the abbot, instead of the eighty who had lived there with ample revenues 300 years earlier. Of that small remnant he writes: "they had only the bare name of monks, or scarcely even the shadow. Treading in the steps of their prelates, more greedy of command than devoted to monastic discipline, they sought pretexts and implored patronage either to escape somehow from that yoke of subjection to which they had submitted in their vows, or to relieve themselves of the weight of an indiscreet dominion." A prominent citizen of Reggio, backed by Niccoló d'Este who was then sovereign in those parts, "represented to the Holy Father the abominable [*pessimo*] state of this, one of the famous and illustrious abbeys of Italy, rather by reason of the evil conduct of the abbots than through the wars and calamities of the times". This morally indignant citizen begged the abbacy for his son Filippo, who, "though only 22 years old, was rector of the parochial church of Sta Maria di Sesso, a village near the city; and, young as he was, he had already been married in earlier days to Todesca de Tacoli, as may be inferred from several documents, and which appears quite clearly in his will!" This Philip represented himself as one anxious to take the Benedictine vows. The Pope, "willing as We are to encourage him in this laudable proposal of his", sent two bulls on the same day, one empowering the bishop to bid the brethren receive his vows, and the other "providing" the young man with the abbacy. Shortly afterwards, we find him as abbot *in commendam*, and (to do him justice) distinctly more worthy of that dignity than the large majority of commendatory abbots. He finally added the bishopric of Comacchio to his other revenues, and then transferred S. Prospero (*minus* a considerable share of the revenues, retained for his own use) to the reformed Congregation of Sta Giustina at Padua. His epitaph in his own cathedral boasts of the churches which he built "from his own moneys" —*suo aere*. Affarosi points out that this boast is flatly contradicted by the facts, which show how all or nearly all these moneys had come from S. Prospero. At that abbey itself, his epitaph was more modest: "from his abbatial income he built, enlarged, or endowed many churches, monasteries and pious buildings in our city, and handed over to the Congregation of Sta Giustina the abbey itself, then on the verge of ruin, and almost destitute of regular observance, in order that they might restore it to monastic grace". Here we have an unusually favourable case of *commendam*. The more usual fate of abbeys under commendators is that which Miss Gertrude Robinson describes as typical among the Basilian monasteries of southern Italy. These abbeys, Greek in speech and in customs, but subject to the Pope, became isolated and therefore stagnant; the monks gradually forgot even the language in which they chanted their liturgy. There was no enduring result from the successive attempts to reform (Empress Constance about 1200; Pope Honorius III in 1221, Urban V in 1362, Eugenius IV about 1440; Cardinal

Bessarion about 1470). In 1477 the great abbey of Carbone, near Bari, fell under *commendam*; the title and income were given as a sinecure to a series of favourites who plundered the monastery. "They filched all that was valuable in the way of pictures or manuscripts: the monastery buildings and churches went to ruin; the offices and ceremonies could not be kept up for want of vestments and books; the monks starved and were forced to go from place to place begging for sustenance." By about 1500 there were only four monks in the abbey; the numbers afterwards once rose to nine, but had sunk again to three before the French armies occupied the country and suppressed the abbey (1509).(20)

For the early sixteenth century ample evidence is collected by E. Rodocanachi in *La Réforme en Italie*. This book is particularly valuable for its full exploitation of unprinted legal material. At Naples no honest women dared to attend the church of the Hieronymite friars.

Cardinal Ercole Gonzaga wrote in 1547, *à propos* of a monastery at Mantua, that there was no danger of Lutheranism slipping in, since the monks thought of nothing but eating, drinking and sleeping, except one who was "old, learned and good". A Bishop of Nicosia, of the great Orsini family, signed a document securing 500 crowns in pension to a lady whom the legal document described as "concubine of the Bishop of Nicosia". In a lawsuit of 1540, before the Governor of Rome, a woman deposed that one of her friends had formerly been sold by her father to Cardinal Cesarini.(21)

Machiavelli couples Spain with Italy on his black list. Of this country I know very little; its medieval clergy seem to have differed little from those of Italy. Their lives in the twelfth and thirteenth centuries provided an excuse for much the same heretical revolts as those which convulsed southern France at that time. The Spanish Bishop Alvarez Pelayo paints a lurid picture of clerical and monastic immoralities in general: "The Day of Doom is at our very doors." So far as the monasteries are concerned, he says nothing exceptional about his own land, whether for good or for evil. In the matter of simony, indeed, he is emphatic; "I believe that, especially in Spain, only one bishop in a hundred is not simoniacal in his ordinations of clergy and in his collations of benefices." They give Orders (he says) only for money; at a single Ordination a bishop will often earn 500 florins or more. Again, he points out that Spain was rich in fighting bishops, even personal combatants, under the special temptation of defence against the Moors.(22) A later witness is Rodrigo, Bishop of Zamora. Writing to Pope Paul II (1464–71), he laments that "many are Religious in name, but few in deed. ...Far more fail than those who advance,.... Who cannot see how plentiful and numerous the Religious are, yet who seeth not how few of them are holy?"(23)

For the Spain of a generation later, on the verge of Luther's appearance, we may accept the frank judgment of the learned Roman Catholic Bishop Hefele in his *Life of Cardinal Ximenez*. About the time when Columbus sailed for America, Queen Isabella chose for her confessor this Franciscan of exceptional learning, piety, and abstinence. Shortly afterwards, Ximenez was elected Provincial of his Order in the Two Castiles. Here, as a zealous Observantine, he utilized his certainty of royal support for the heavy task of reforming the Conventuals. He took away their endowments, thus bringing them to conformity with their Rule upon one essential point.

He expelled the unworthy members, and endeavoured to induce the better disposed to embrace the reform. To many he offered pensions, if they should wish to leave the Order, and make room for others who would be willing to lead an austere life. This offer was accepted by the Franciscans of Toledo, who, as if in mockery of Ximenez, solemnly sang, on leaving their monastery, the psalm, "In exitu Israel de Ægypto". A thousand calumnies would be sure to assail a reformer placed in such circumstances engaged in a contest against relaxed orders, and with men who preferred the good things of this life to the austerities of their rule. But Ximenez pursued his path unmoved, until at length his elevation to the archiepiscopal see of Toledo gave him opportunities of attaining his object.

This was in 1495; and Hefele describes the magnitude of his task. He writes:

Many causes had contributed to impair the morals of the Spanish clergy. (1) The bishops possessed great revenues and widely-extended domains; they also took an active part in political matters, and even [frequently] exposed themselves personally to the horrors of war. The consequence was that they either became very worldly, or were in a great measure incapacitated from properly fulfilling the duties of the sacred office which they had undertaken. (2) The number of ecclesiastics became so great in Spain, that many of them experienced what dangers to morality arise from idleness. (3) The benefices were numerous and richly endowed; hence, they attracted many to embrace the ecclesiastical state who had no real vocation or sufficient learning. Being thus deprived of two essential elements in the support of a sacerdotal life, they yielded to sensual pleasures, and the enjoyments of a dissipated mind. The evil at length became so great that the council of Aranda (in 1473) made a law that no one should be allowed to receive Holy Orders who was ignorant of the Latin language. Peter Martyr assures us that in his time a clergyman of noble birth who could preach, "was more scarce than a white crow". (4) This want of learning in the Spanish clergy favoured the rise and growth of errors under the name of Judaism,.... (5) As in the later period of the Middle Ages sins of the flesh prevailed to such an extent, so in Spain also they were even more common, because the evil example of the neighbouring Moors exercised a very destructive influence on the manners of the Christians. Another influence, probably no less disastrous, was the corruption of the Castilian court under Henry IV. Cast-off mistresses were made abbesses! The sovereigns themselves shamefully defiled the sanctity of the marriage state, and almost intentionally endeavoured to root out of their people all feelings of modesty and all detestation of impurity. It was no uncommon thing to behold the concubines seated by the side of the lawful wife, while ladies of the highest rank were not ashamed to countenance such a state of things. Open concubinage seems to have been almost as freely tolerated: public opinion was silent on the matter. No wonder, then, that this corruption reached even to the clergy; and what was a remarkable feature in the immorality of this period is the fact that the concubines were not so much blamed for their wickedness as for the extravagance of their dress. In a word, the laws of Castile declared [as in no other country of the world] that the bastards of ecclesiastics might, in the absence of any will, become lawful heirs. Such was the deep degradation into which the inferior clergy were plunged in Spain. But amongst the bishops, though in general they were not so corrupt, yet many were not without reproach....Fonseca, Archbishop of Santiago, bestowed the right of succession to the see on his own son, not, however, without great opposition on the part of Ximenez, as we shall have an opportunity of seeing later. (6) Another terrible evil was, that very frequently the bastards of kings and grandees were raised to episcopal sees, there to continue the incontinence of their fathers....Pope Sixtus IV had long protested against this abuse; but through political influence, and under a threat of seeing all the church property in Sicily confiscated, he was at last obliged to consent that the bastard should have the perpetual administration of the property belonging to the archbishopric [i.e. its revenues]. (7) This general corruption had also found its way into the monasteries. The vow of poverty was no longer observed by the Mendicant Orders; their cells were often changed into magnificent apartments, and ascetism exchanged for luxury. That Holy See, it is true, which had so often before stirred up new life in the Church, and so severely punished wickedness, was at this period occupied by Innocent VIII and Alexander VI, whose individual sins forbad them to punish the guilt of others. A prelate like Ximenez, therefore, was absolutely necessary for Spain, and also a queen like Isabella; both of whom exhibited in their unspotted lives the fairest pattern of every virtue.(24)

In face of this general corruption, even the most saintly archbishop could have done little without the secular arm behind him. But here Ximenez was particularly fortunate. Spain, while jealously claiming exceptional orthodoxy, was equally jealous of political interference from Rome. The State had often thus asserted itself very vigorously, even more definitely than now under Ferdinand and Isabella. Therefore, when the canons of Toledo Cathedral sent an envoy to Rome behind the back of Ximenez, with a commission to buy papal exemption from this inconvenient archbishop's reforms, Ximenez employed the royal police and a fast-sailing galley, caught the man, and kept him in prison long enough to serve as an effectual lesson to the canons. For this Hefele feels bound to apologize: "Ximenez exhibited a peculiarity in his character which I do not wish wholly to justify,—I mean the use of severe measures in order to promote what one may consider useful objects."(25) Yet, even with such force as this in the background, Ximenez could not compel his own canons to live a community life in the clergy-house which he built for them; nor was he able, under pressure of business, to enforce his valuable rule of holding a yearly clerical synod.(26) But he succeeded to a great extent, though not completely, in introducing the Observantine reform into his own Franciscan Order. Here, again, his success was immensely helped by the Queen's support in the face of opposition not only from the nobles, whose ancestors had their tombs in the conventual friaries, but also from the Court of Rome. The Minister General of the Franciscans was here his bitterest opponent;

a man who besieged the Queen with slanders against Ximenez which, in any less extraordinary case, could scarcely have failed of success. But Isabella was unshaken, and Ximenez was left free to exercise his full visitatorial powers, with the secular arm to back him up in case of resistance. The result was that "about a thousand Conventual friars, who were averse from reform, went over to Africa, and by their apostasy to Mahomedanism freed themselves from reform and gave themselves entirely up to the gratification of their base passions".(27)

Here, then, was a monastic reform not only the completest carried out in any country of Europe before Luther's time, but far completer than any similar achievement under the Counter-Reformation. The explanation would seem simple. Here is the only case in which we find the right sort of Churchman in alliance with the right sort of sovereign. The Primate was a man of consuming zeal for the Lord's House, and of undaunted courage. The Queen trusted him through good report and evil report, and lent him her sword, too formidable for popes themselves to face. The distinguished Dominican, J. B. Labat, in the early seventeenth century, writes frankly enough to show that the Spanish Church of his day would not have satisfied the more exacting moral and intellectual standards of modern religious communities; but it seems never to have sunk again to quite so low a state as at the accession of Ximenez.

CHAPTER VIII

FROM CONSTANCE TO BASEL

THIS survey of one Italian province, which Semeria's labours have made possible, has taken us necessarily beyond the Council of Constance, and to that extent has falsified the perspective. Let us therefore pass back now to a more general European survey of the extra-conciliar evidence, limited mainly to the generations immediately preceding 1415. We may, however, sometimes include witnesses writing later than that Council, wherever they describe the abuses as chronic and inveterate, existing long before the actual date at which the author writes, and therefore thoroughly familiar to the Fathers when they sat at Constance.

This evidence has already been anticipated in great part in my second volume (chaps. XXVI–XXVIII and Appendices 34–38). If, in spite of what Machiavelli says, the unfavourable evidence in those chapters comes more abundantly from France than from Italy, this is not because the actual French conditions were worse, but because society was there more sensitive to the moral disgrace of that gulf between theory and practice, not only among the monasteries but in the whole Church. In proportion with geographical distance from Rome, men were more able to believe in the possibility of some reform which should begin, as all true and durable betterment must necessarily begin, from Rome itself; some Root and Branch Reform, *tam in capite quam in membris*. Apart from occasional papal claims to proclaim dogma from Rome or Avignon with an *ipse dixit*, the theological centre of Western Christendom in the Middle Ages was the University of Paris. The universities of Italy were remarkable for the absence, or at best for the insignificance, of theological faculties. Rome itself, as we have seen, had not even a university of any kind in 1415.(1) The University of Paris, on the other hand, was one of the great powers of Europe. France, "The Eldest Daughter of the Church", never forgot that unique position which the baptism of Clovis had given her.* It was France who felt most natural jealousy of that quasi-monopoly enjoyed by Italy in papal elections, and who in fact had done most in the fourteenth century to break it down. So early as 1333 the theologians of Paris, on their own authority, had condemned John XXII for his pet theory concerning the Beatific Vision; and the King was even reported to have said that the Pope must recant or burn.(2) In the years preceding 1415, the ambassadors of that university had scoured Europe, canvassing everywhere for the summons of this Ecumenical Council, so long overdue. Such success as the Council had, was mainly due to its adoption of voting not by heads but by nations, after the Parisian constitutional method. And, lastly, the two greatest figures on the Constance stage were Parisian doctors of divinity, Pierre d'Ailly and Jean Gerson.

Gerson's views on monastic reform have been quoted, not indeed exhaustively but fairly fully, in my second volume, pp. 588ff. Evidence from other sources must be given here to complete the picture, for the greater part of this present volume will deal with brave and repeated attempts to realize the rather Platonic ideals of Constance. Therefore the work of those missionaries, whom we shall soon see struggling to stave off religious revolution, can be fully appreciated only in the full light of these difficult conditions which confronted them.

At the Council of Vienne, in 1311, a long and plain-spoken memorial was addressed to the Pope by one of the greatest French bishops, Guillaume Durand of Mende.(3) His first emphasis is laid upon the necessity of reform at Rome itself. Next to that, the monasteries occupy a prominent place. Let the monks be prevented from straying outside their precincts, possessing private property, or escaping episcopal visitation, or dwelling alone in priories or cells. "They should be strangers to all familiarities with nuns and other women." "The monastic Order is now almost fallen", and stern measures are needed to bring it back to the prescriptions of its own Rule and of Canon Law.

* Gibbon, *Decline and Fall*, chap. XXXVIII: "On the memorable day when Clovis ascended from the baptismal font, he alone, in the Christian world, deserved the name and prerogatives of a Catholic King. The Emperor Anastasius entertained some dangerous errors concerning the nature of the divine incarnation; and the barbarians of Italy, Africa, Spain and Gaul were involved in the Arian heresy."

A few years later, Pierre Dubois recommended to the King of France a considerable measure of monastic disendowment to finance the Crusades.(4) This had already been proposed at the Ecumenical Council of Lyons (1274) as a general European income, by Humbert de Romans, Minister General of the Dominicans.(5)

If we look at the separate Orders, the story of Fontevraud gives much the same perspective as that of the Ligurian province. The documents, numerous enough to offer a wide survey, have been summarized by Jubieu in his monograph on that abbey (pp. 11–12). In 1460, two out of the eleven dependent priories had disappeared altogether. At the zenith, in the thirteenth century, these priories had totalled 906 inmates. In 1460, the total had sunk to 33! The significance of those figures is startling, even when we have made full allowance for the Hundred Years' War, and for the fact that Fontevraud was one of the smaller Orders; and, again, that it was based on the principle of dual houses, with brethren and sisters on the same foundation, like our Gilbertines and many early Celtic monasteries. In 1509 (to use Jubieu's words) some of these nunneries had "fallen to the lowest degree of immorality" (p. 42).

In the case of some other Orders also we have documents enough for fairly full generalizations. From the early thirteenth century onwards, papal bulls complained of general Benedictine decay. At Cluny, the Abbot Ivo II (1271) decreed that no illegitimates must be admitted in future, since these "easily slide into imitation of their fathers' crimes, and frequently corrupt the morals of the rest". In 1428 it is reported by the papal visitors that Cluny, with its neighbouring priories, has become so full of transgressions both in spiritual and in temporal matters, and impunity has become so scandalous, that the State has had to interfere. This papal commission took elaborate precautions to shield from the vengeance of their brethren those monks who had disclosed the true facts. Its powers were extended to five years, with licence to call upon State help if necessary. Yet, as its modern editor confesses, though its decrees were reinforced by manifold precautions and anathemas they remained "a dead letter".(6) The Premonstratensians, again, had been in the twelfth century among the strictest and most prosperous. Yet Innocent IV, in 1245, complained that Satan had wrought havoc, if not of souls, at least of reputations in that Order: he therefore decreed an elaborate series of safeguards between its brethren and its sisters.(7) In 1438 Eugenius IV publicly rebuked the depraved morals of "the superiors, canons, lay-brethren and others who were attached to the Order".(8) The evidence from official visitations in the Order of Tiron will come more properly in a later chapter. The impression produced by these and similar records is reinforced by the study of separate houses during the century preceding the Conciliar period. We have many French monographs available, nearly all by sympathetic priests or monks, and some of them excellent. Almost without exception, these describe partial or successful reforms in the thirteenth and fourteenth centuries, breaking down more or less completely in the fourteenth and fifteenth.

The German monographs tell the same tale. Throughout the Empire prince-bishops were common; high-born and worldly statesmen or even warriors, who were often not in priestly Orders, but left all their spiritual duties to suffragans. These latter (as Dietrich v. Nieheim reported to the Fathers of Constance) buy themselves into their office, and many (*plerique*) recoup themselves by illegal extortion of fees. They show scant respect for their prince-bishops, refusing to swear obedience to them on the plea that they themselves are appointed directly by the Pope. They have also better reasons for claiming that "they have nothing to do with their metropolitans: viz. because those are sometimes crazy enough to fight as warriors, and have from time immemorial neglected altogether the visitation of their dioceses".(9) At as early a date as 1354, Trithemius gives to "all of our [Benedictine] Order, almost throughout Germany", so black a character as would, by itself, render all the words spoken at Constance comprehensible.(10)

England, in this field, shows the same paradox as in the case of Colet's choice. Our monasteries, on the whole, were least irregular; yet we have most direct and multiple evidence for their decay. Nearly all our episcopal visitations are now in print, however imperfectly exploited as yet. Their evidence bears mainly upon the disputed question of Henry VIII's

Suppression, which will come naturally at the end of this volume. But at this present point it is particularly apposite to note the evidence for the Conciliar period; that is, the facts which must have been familiar to all English delegates at Constance and Basel.

For more than a century, kings and parliaments had complained of the intolerable practice by which the ancient rights of election or presentation were now overridden by papal encroachments, and the richest spoils often went to foreigners who made no pretence of residence. Thus (it was complained) divine service and almsgiving and hospitality were already perishing, and threatened to perish at an increasing rate. Eleven such protests, of the most public and emphatic kind, are collected from the years 1307 to 1390 by J. Haller in his *Papsttum und Kirchenreform* (1903, pp. 544ff.). The case of the monasteries is not specially emphasized here. Englishmen complained in the name of the Church in general; but in the parallel protests from France (549ff.) stress is laid upon the effect of this system upon the spiritual decay of many abbeys and the ruin of their buildings. Thus no single delegate to Constance or Basel was old enough to remember the days of comparative quiet, before the first mutterings from the rising thunder-cloud of Reform. Already in 1415, men were sixty-seven years removed from the first incidence of the Black Death; from those days when the clergy, by confession of their own chroniclers, had showed themselves painfully unequal to the task of maintaining religion by personal example. The majority at Constance, and practically all at Basel, must have been still in their teens in those days described by the chronicler Knighton, when "every second man one met on the road was a lollard". All, therefore, had full experience and consciousness of those lollard accusations which found their way even into the solemn debates of Parliament, which the conservatives seldom ventured to attempt denying in their entirety, and which stirred even the warmly orthodox Henry V to insistence upon reform.

However we may discount "the moral Gower" as a satirist, there can be no such deduction from the complaint of Chaucer's other contemporary, the Dominican Bromyard, when he characterizes the monastic Orders as so corrupt that they have reduced the fair body of Holy Church to a mass of sores. Again, in 1414, a strongly anti-lollard petition from Oxford University to Henry V spoke as strongly as any lollard against the impoverishment of parishes and the neglect of almsgiving by the abbeys, and the frequency and impunity of unchastity among exempt Religious. The petitioners expressed a hope that these things would be set before the Council of Constance.(11) Seven years later, Henry V made a tour of the great shrines of England, and was impressed by the "negligence and indevotion of modern monks". He therefore empowered a committee of royal representatives to draw up thirteen articles and submit them to a very solemn assembly at Westminster: 60 prelates and more than 300 monks. The articles dealt with the usual abuses, and the abbots in their formal reply practically admitted their necessity, with small exceptions.(12) Thomas Gascoigne, Chancellor of Oxford and Hammer of the Lollards, constantly agreed with the heretics in his estimate of monastic decay, and pleaded for serious measures of disendowment. Most significant of all, perhaps, is the fact that even the most determined of anti-Wycliffite apologists did not dare to meet the heretics' accusations frankly and fully.(13)

Here, again, the story of separate abbeys supports these generalizations. The valuable series of *Victoria County Histories* makes it easy to work this out in any good public library. The reader who has patience enough to follow for himself the story of the six greatest—let us say, Westminster, St Albans, Canterbury (Christ Church), Bury, Durham and Glastonbury—will realize what light these details cast forward upon Henry V's action; and how that action, read backwards, illuminates them.

Generalizations, such as those which were uttered at Constance, demand control from as many detailed sources as possible; hence the value of these separate monastic monographs. But the *onus probandi* is very heavy upon those who would discount these generalizations by anything more than the ordinary allowance we make for medieval language, wherever the writer or speaker is intensely interested. Janssen, in his enormous *History of the German People*, pleads the lack of documents, but most absurdly; for (to go no further) proofs are specially abundant among the works of Trithemius, whom he constantly quotes whenever this suits his own purpose. Pastor, in his re-issue of Janssen, does indeed take some notice of the unfavourable evidence of Trithemius and Nider; but he apparently knows both only at second-hand, and certainly the impression he leaves is one of far more real reform than can be gathered either from those two authors or from other contemporary documents. In his own *History of the Popes*, he is even less just to those two witnesses; and he ignores nine-tenths of the contemporary evidence for monastic decay. It is only in the seventh volume (English translation) that he does justice, and then very briefly, to the extent of moral revolt among the faithful in general produced by monastic decay.(14)

Dom Ursmer Berlière, a far greater authority in this field, pleading very naturally for his own Order, bids us remember the constitutional independence of each Benedictine House, which was respected to a considerable extent even after Innocent III had attempted to impose a general system of visitation and General Chapters. This individualism of each monastery, he pleads, bred great individual differences between house and house; one might be good, while its neighbour was bad.(15) But this can only afford a warning against exaggerated smoothness of generalization. For it would be almost as impossible to suspend judgment until we had studied every house, as to refrain from judging any house in itself until we were familiar with each inmate at each particular time, with his individual particularities. We cannot go far wrong if we assume, in default of real evidence to the contrary, that well-informed and honest contemporaries tell us something near the truth in these matters. Moreover, at other times Dom Berlière himself was among the most candid, as he was perhaps the most learned, among all modern historians of his own Order. He did not disguise his conviction that, whatever may have been the statistical proportion between good and evil among the monks of 1400, the evil was sufficiently prominent to form one of the gravest of social and religious problems, if not the very gravest of all. He recognized that facts, however painful, must be faced; and that if we permit ourselves to do more than justice to the men who have our deepest sympathies, this involves proportionate injustice to others. It is no more legitimate in history than in business to pay Peter by robbing Paul.

The separate English monographs, then, show the nation entering—this will soon become unmistakable—upon the period at which the State finds it necessary to interfere. Miss Wood-Legh's recent study has shown clearly how constantly Edward III intervened among those abbeys in which he could claim a direct legal right, as representative of the founder, and therefore as *advocatus*. We shall see the same policy pursued far more dramatically, if not with such business regularity, abroad. Thus, after Wolsey had helped Henry VIII to make himself Pope as well as King, the English State intervened more rapidly and completely than in any other great country.

Very few words will now suffice for the other great World Council which, after Constance, attempted to deal with monastic reform: that of Basel (1431–49). Between the two, reform had not progressed much, with the brilliant exceptions to which we shall come in the next chapters. The Dominican Nider, himself a zealous and active reformer, took an almost fatalistic view. There are passages in his *Formicarius* (about 1430) which seem to show clearly that neither the individual was at fault, nor even the general constitution of medieval society, but the monastic system, using that word not in the sense of its first ideal, nor of its actual practice at certain times and places, but of what, as a whole, it had grown to be during the later Middle Ages. That is, a vast institution with enormous endowments and extraordinary privileges, upon which the Church insisted and which the State accepted more or less willingly; a corporation controlled no longer so much by law as by tradition and custom. And we have one most significant instance in practice. Otto v. Ziegenhain was by birth a great noble, and by office Prince-Elector of Trier (1418–30). Nider describes him as a man of singular personal piety and self-denial, "so that he seemed rather a monk than a German bishop. He was one of the most enthusiastic and courageous of those who went to combat the Hussite revolt in Bohemia (1419–)."

And, because the zeal of God's house ceased not to consume him, when he saw his canons and priests fallen from the rank of their institution, and the monasteries deformed all around, therefore he began to apply himself to holy reformation, such as he had already undertaken recently in his own life. Yet he was able to introduce it only into very few places, and into no college of secular priests. For so malignant a spirit instigated both monks and secular clergy, and such a host of vices struggled against him among them, that the walls of the ruined hierarchy could not be raised again; and, through men's evil deserts, the work of God was frustrated: not, as of old, by mere artisans [*mechanicis*], but by evil clergy and monks. For in this, contrary to what should have been right, men imbued with sacred letters—nay even men dedicated to God—resisted the reformation more stoutly than worldly folk. The holy man, seeing this, groaned in spirit and, like St Ambrose, smitten to the heart with pain at his hardened clergy, began to mourn, fearing no longer to die and be with Christ. One Sunday, with prophetic voice, by revelation as it is believed, he preached publicly that his own sojourn would now be brief, and that his rebellious clergy and people would then be visited with grievous vengeance from God.

He died, in fact, far short of old age; and the next few years were disastrous for that great ecclesiastical province, "For nearly all the canons elected the man who had most stoutly resisted (it is said) this man of God in his reformation, in order to court the good-will of others." Another faction, however, set up against him a still more worthless candidate, who took the see by force. Martin V then put in the Bishop of Speyer, "a man powerful through his worldly kinsfolk"; and the three candidates, first by ferocious litigation and then by actual war, "robbery, fire, and manslaughter", reduced the province to desolation.(16) When this was the experience of a reformer who had all the cards in his hand, and the recent doings at Constance behind him, we can understand the tone of that bull of Reform which the Assembled Fathers gave to the world from Basel in 1439.(17) Their preamble rehearses that the Augustinian Order "(we say it with pain), has fallen to no small degree, in many parts of the world from its original institution"; therefore commissioners are appointed with full powers of judicial enquiry throughout the Duchy of Brunswick: they are to hear witnesses, allot punishments, and call in the secular arm when necessary. The rest of this bull amounts to no more than this: we will now strive that, henceforth, monks shall keep those time-honoured laws which are now so commonly violated.

The two greatest figures at the Council of Basel, for the monastic historian, were Cardinal Cesarini and the future Cardinal Nicholas of Cues. When Eugenius attempted to dissolve the Council as an unlawful assembly, in January 1432, Cesarini sent him a lengthy and solemn protest. He wrote:

the degeneration and indiscipline of the German clergy hath brought me hither; for it hath wholly embittered the laity against the whole clerical order. It is greatly to be feared that, if the clergy do not amend, the laity will then fall upon the whole clergy, even as the Hussites have done; men talk aloud of such an enterprise. This degeneration it is which makes the [Hussite rebels] so bold, and to some extent justifies the errors of those folk who rage especially against the shamefulness of the clergy. So many Councils have been held in our days, without any consequent reform! The peoples did at last hope for some fruit from this [of Basel]. If this Council is now dissolved, it will be said that we are mocking God and man....Even now, there is small respect for the clergy; then, it will utterly disappear....If your Holiness brings upon yourself this disgrace [of dissolving us without reform], then there will be no more hope or faith in any man....As I see it, the axe is already laid at the root of the tree; it totters to its fall, and can no longer stand.(18)

It must be noted, moreover, that the Council suffered a humiliating check in the most important case in which it attempted to enforce its own decrees. The reformed Augustinian Congregation of Windesheim was by this time so strong that it seemed fit to be used as a lever for gradual reform of the whole Augustinian Order. The Council therefore, in January 1435, commissioned two heads of Windesheim houses to visit and, where necessary, to reform, all the Augustinians in the province of Saxony. Bishop Magnus of Hildesheim confirmed this for his own diocese in March; yet in less than a year six of the greatest Augustinian priors in that and in the neighbouring diocese of Halberstadt met in council and proclaimed their rejection of the whole scheme. The visitors were denied admission at the first monastery which they approached (1437), and here they seem to have made no further attempt. It was only in 1439 that one of them was able at last to gain admission to one of the others, and to carry out some real reforms. Yet these bishops of Hildesheim and Halberstadt were among the nine whom Grube singles out as the most efficient at that time in northern Germany; and they had at their back this Ecumenical Council, with its bull proclaiming excommunication upon any persons, and interdict upon any church where these two visitors might be rejected, and authorizing the secular arm to step in against all such rebels.(19).

But the mention of Windesheim brings us into another field altogether. We can now go back again for a few years, and note, as against the disappointingly small direct result from Constance and Basel, the success of a few Congregations founded by comparatively obscure individuals. That is the main story of the century before the Reformation. The monks, from age to age, had gradually dug themselves in; they were entrenched now in a labyrinth of zigzag traditions and customs. We shall see column after column of brave reformers advance to frontal attack, inspired with fiery religious zeal, and armed with direct weapons drawn from Canon Law. There will be brilliant successes on this or that front; but (as Nider foresaw) the passive weight of defence was too strong; column after column wasted away or lost its progressive energy. Then, at last, the State and the multitude fell upon the defenders' flank; and we had that Religious Revolution, which, more than anything else, differentiates the Europe of Constance and Basel from the Europe of to-day.

CHAPTER IX

WINDESHEIM

For the materials of this and the next few chapters posterity owes a deep debt to Johann Busch, himself one of the protagonists on this stage. He knew personally most of the men whom he describes, and was in an admirable position to gather authentic information and to judge the whole movement. His writings were first published in part by the great Leibniz in his *Scriptores*; there is a later and more accurate edition (now, unfortunately, out of print) by K. Grube in the *Geschichtsquellen der Provinz Sachsen* (1886).

Holland, which among its Frisians of the extreme north might show the crudest examples of monastic decay, bred also among its more civilized townsfolk one of the most remarkable of all medieval religious revivals. It shows us how, under the Church tutelage of past centuries, men were at last growing independent of the Church, in that narrower sense in which the clergy had so long used that word.(1)

Gerrit Groot—"Big Gerard"—has found a famous biographer in Thomas à Kempis, who had never met him but had gathered materials from several of his surviving disciples. Born in 1340, the son of a Burgomaster of Deventer, he signalized himself as a precocious student. He drifted to Paris, where he took the Master's degree in 1363 and dabbled in magic; thence he passed to Cologne, where he taught for a short time. Returning home at his father's desire, he was soon enriched through family influence. He became Canon of Utrecht and of Aachen, held other benefices, and lived the life of an ordinary cleric. An old Paris friend, now prior of the Carthusian monastery near Arnhem, warned him so plainly that he resolved to quit the world. He renounced the use of his emoluments, burned publicly his costly books on magic, clothed himself in plain grey, and braved the public ridicule. He refused the priesthood, but was ordained deacon and licensed to preach; his peripatetic revival sermons stirred the whole diocese of Utrecht. But, with all his respect for the clerical profession as such, he spoke too plainly about the black sheep, and especially concubinaries; the bishop withdrew his license, and Gerard was too loyal to refuse submission. This, however, only drew his activities into another channel. He formed a close friendship with John Cele, master of the school at Zwolle, and with Florence Radewin, Vicar of Deventer. With Cele he had visited the famous mystic Ruysbroeck in his monastery of Groenendael near Brussels, and had been impressed by the exemplary life of that community. In partnership with Radewin, he now turned to help the youth of Deventer, where there was a flourishing grammar-school. He entertained the boys at his own table with food and discourse, lent them books, and presently set them to help themselves by diligent transcription. His little band of friends and copyists began to multiply almost to embarrassment; and Radewin suggested the formation of a definite society. "Beloved Master, why should not I and these scribbling clerics, who are now of such good will, put our weekly earnings into one common fund from which we might live in equality?" Gerard answered: "Common, common? Those Mendicant friars will never suffer that, but will resist it tooth and nail, and will leave no stone unturned against it." "Well", urged Florence, "what harm would it do to try? Perchance God would grant that we should prosper." Then Master Gerard, after a brief reflexion, said, "Begin, then, in God's name! I will be your faithful defender and protector against all who rise up against you to hinder this your undertaking."(2) So the society was formed; a definite link between monasticism and ordinary life. It was, in fact, bitterly attacked by many of the friars, but defended at the Council of Constance. Members came from all classes; some gave their money to the foundation; all pooled their weekly earnings, whether from writing (and, later, printing) or from other handicrafts. There were men's and women's houses, each under a rector of its own. They founded no schools of their own, but boarded and gave religious teaching to the scholars in very many places, and in other ways led the educational revival. Groot himself did not see all this; he died in his forty-fourth year of the plague, caught from a sick friend whom he visited. The brethren long outlasted the Reformation; some became

Protestants, but most of the houses were taken over by the Jesuits; a few lingered on until their suppression by Napoleon. The movement was not only very remarkable in itself; it also forms a landmark in monastic history. Here was the watershed; the moment when men were losing faith in the monks as they were, and yet felt that the ideal must not be suffered to perish. The hierarchy was unwilling or unable to give the world a model of monastic life in harmony with the aspirations of an age which, with all its faults, had learned much since St Augustine's and St Benedict's day. But here were three men prepared to step into the breach; men of comparatively small importance individually, yet knowing what the people wanted, and able to enlist all classes in this crusade.

Busch tells us that Groot himself had advised Radewin to found a regular monastery, as a firm nucleus around which these houses could crystallize, and a fortress into which the most resolute could retire and from whence they could regulate and defend the whole movement. Whether or not the idea thus originated with Groot, it was certainly Radewin who carried it out. Two years after Groot's death (1386), a sufficient sum having been collected for a beginning, an Augustinian convent was founded at Windesheim near Zwolle. The original members, only six in number, included John, the elder brother of Thomas à Kempis. Contributions for the simple buildings came so fast that, in October 1387, the church was consecrated. For a long time, this new foundation stood in very close relation to the Brethren of Common Life. Florence Radewin was head of both institutions; it was only in 1400, under Johann Vos, that each went on its separate way. Yet, even then, Deventer tried sometimes to remind Windesheim of their common origin, and Windesheim took Deventer as its model. Therefore Radewin was most generous in his help to the monastery which had grown from his initiative. (3) The new monastery, at first, had to face a violent conservative opposition, especially from the friars, who regarded the Brethren of Common Life as mischievous rivals. But it held its ground, and was gradually joined by converts from all sides. After the first difficulties and privations had been overcome, progress was rapid. As early as 1402, Windesheim had already attracted to itself eight allied monasteries; here, then, was a Congregation, which now held its Chapter General. The first business was to draw up a code of statutes:

therefore they collected the ancient institutes of various monasteries of our Order from various provinces, and modern institutes also; for these, although they had been enacted in times past by prelates of the Church, yet were they far from conformity with the actual manners of the brethren then living, who kept the institutes only in their muniment-chests or in their libraries. For the true observance of the Rule, especially in the Köln and Mainz provinces of our Order, had by this time been long since abolished and obliterated.

And again,

Few Orders, except the Carthusians and some of the Cistercians, were in those days observers of their Rule; but in almost every Order they were rather open transgressors of the Rule and of the Three Substantial Vows [i.e. Obedience, Poverty and Chastity].(4)

Here, then, was a definite reaction from the ordinary course of monastic legislation since Benedict XII. That Pope, zealous as he was, tried to obtain reform by concessions to the frailty of "modern" generations. His successor, Clement VI, went still further on that path. But Windesheim, like St Francis, acted upon the principle that a monk of any age could live like the heroes of old, if only he had sufficient faith and courage. No concessions were made for the sake of attracting converts. The great monastery of Neuss, with its dependent houses, obtained entrance into the Congregation only after protracted negotiations. Neuwerk, an almost equally important house, never succeeded in spite of many attempts.(5) Busch tells us how definitely the General Chapter refused to accept the guardianship of the nuns of Beverwijk.(6) The Council of Constance brought a favouring breeze, if not much direct help. In the year after that Council (1419) Windesheim stood at the head of a reformed Congregation of twenty monasteries. Most of them were older foundations; some very old. Mount St Agnes (Agnetenberg), where Thomas à Kempis wrote his *Imitatio*, and his brother John was at one time prior, became a member of the Congregation in the year of its own foundation (1398); but Neuss, which joined only in 1430, had been founded as early as 1181. Thus, when Johann Busch took the vows, there were already more than twenty houses. Writing half a century later in his *Chronicle*, he enumerates eighty-one; but there were 102 later, with an aggregate of more than 1000 inmates. It then had houses in eighteen different dioceses; by 1553 it had spread to twenty-three, some as distant as Pomerania and Austria.(7)

Those first heroic days found in him an historian worthy of the subject. The first sentence of his *Chronicle* strikes a lofty note, from Ecclesiasticus xl, 1: "Let us now praise famous men, the first Fathers of our Order." In his third chapter, he comes to the great founders of Monastic Rules: Basil and Augustine, Benedict and Francis. But, since their days, "the rigour of disciplinary observance of the Rule grew gradually lukewarm, through the negligence of the superiors and the dissoluteness of their subjects", until it perished at length in practice. The superiors first, and then the brethren, fell together into the vices of *proprietas*, incontinence, and disobedience:

thus all monastic devotion, claustral religion, love of God, fear of hell, and all the exercises of virtue, in dissolute monasteries of this sort, both of men and women, died together and have vanished utterly from the sight of the living.... It is a shame to relate the abominable things which have followed in practice among the said dissolute monasteries. For those places, wherein the bodily remains of the holy Fathers their predecessors are laid with all reverence, have now become brothels of fornicators with harlots and women of all sorts and conditions, and dens of demons upon earth, wherein reigns not only unheard-of lasciviousness but also gluttony, drunkenness, *proprietas* and other evils innumerable.

They touch Christ's Body with polluted hands,

and these men, who should, as good intercessors appointed by the Church, obtain from God Almighty the remission of sins, increase of grace, and the acquisition of everlasting glory for all Christian people, do on the contrary shrink in no wise from provoking God, the Judge of all, to wrath by their abominable life and their horrible crimes.

Against this, the first founders of Windesheim declared war to the knife, taking for their armour the time-honoured statutes of earlier and purer monasticism. They strove to collect into their houses "the fine flour and cream of Christian folk...since it is very hard to find men of true contemplation and angelic purity and virginal chastity in this worldly exile and in this pilgrimage-time of our mortal life".

The manly call was manfully answered. Acquoy enumerates, partly from printed and partly from manuscript sources, the difficulties and dangers affronted by some of these new converts. The aristocratic Hendrik van Wilsem was compelled to slip away from his kinsfolk, and the wealthy Albert van Wijnbergen had to brave the fury of his own. Two others, Willem Vornken and Hendrik Walvis, "rich and delicate youths of Utrecht", sacrificed all their property to gain a foothold in this famous monastery.(8) Busch tells us of his own father's tears and his mother's despairing prayers. It was still more frequent for girls to come into conflict with their parents.

We know here of two who defied all kinds of adventures, merely to reach [the nunnery of Diepenreen; of another whose wedding-clothes lay ready, yet who stole away from her bridegroom, her old mother, her friends and kinsfolk. Elspeth Hasebroeks was considered to have been greatly helped by God, because death removed her children who hindered her retirement from the world. Folk saw no evil in dissimulation or half-truths for the deception of opposing parents.(9)

Most dramatic of all was Johann Ten Water's farewell to Vanity Fair. He was by birth "among the foremost and wealthiest citizens of Zwolle, master of Arts at Köln, formerly disciple to Gerard Groot, who by a letter called him away from the vain things of this world and from University study". Therefore,

having resolved to leave the world and enter the cloister of Windesheim, he summoned a crowd of his friends and went up to his vineyard at Zwolle. There they drank wine together in jollity; and when he had solemnly drunk to the health of each in turn, he begged them all not to refuse to pass with him to Windesheim for certain reasons. Forthwith they mounted, and escorted him thither with immense noise and glory. Then he said to them all: "O ye, my beloved kinsfolk and friends, return now each unto his own home; for it is my will to abide here for ever in the service of God." All were amazed at this speech, grieving and groaning for the desertion of so dear a friend. Yet a few, of sounder mind, congratulated and wished him good fortune, praying God to grant him perseverance in his good purpose.

Their prayer was heard, in spite of Brother Body: for "he was of tender body, unused to labour. Yet this he constantly compensated by his humility; for he gladly bore away the pots of the sick, carried laths for the carpenters, and collected in baskets the hay from the rere-dorter with the novices".

Busch, at an early page of his *Chronicle*, sums up the distinctive features of this reform (p. 26).

This is the glory of Windesheim that of the forty brethren who were invested by prior John [Vos] of Huesden and before his time one full half, to wit twenty, were canonically elected to the priorate or rectorate of divers monasteries in our Order. In those days I saw our elders at Windesheim, bearded men of ripe age, tall in stature, comely in their baldness and reverend in their white hairs, moving with notable gravity, adorned with immense honesty of manners; closing their eyes in choir and at chapter-meetings, or fixing them steadily forward; booming forth the Psalms of David with no childish or womanly treble, but with a manly vigour;* moreover our younger brethren keeping themselves in all holiness of life and custody of the senses and discipline of manners, even as their elders.

Nor, with their emphasis on Mary's or Rachel's part, did they neglect that of Martha or Leah. Busch devotes six early chapters of his *Chronicle* to this subject (v–x). First he generalizes. He emphasizes their willing poverty and abstinence, and the extreme simplicity of their dress. He writes: "I have often seen them, not only juniors but seniors also, wearing threadbare frocks and tunics and surplices, torn and patched and darned, wasted and almost consumed by age and use, so that the separate threads might easily be counted." He speaks of their plain food, their discipline, but, above all, of their hard work, in church and outside: "enormous and infinite labours", he not unjustly calls them. For they were too poor at first to depend entirely on the labours of their lay-brethren or hired workmen. Therefore, they did what has sometimes been represented as usual among medieval monks, but what in fact was very exceptional; they helped in the building of their own monastery and the exploitation of their own lands.

The choir-brethren [Busch writes] shirked no labour, however humble or despised—nay, sometimes even beyond their bodily strength. They vied for the first place, not only in orderliness and in dignity and in other gifts of grace, but also in labour and in fervour.

* *Davidica cantica reboantes*. That is, they did not indulge in fauxbourdon or falsetto singing, which had become popular in the fifteenth century but was criticized by disciplinarians. See A. F. Leach, *Visitations of Southwell Minster* (C.S. 1891), pp. lxxvii–lxxix.

For they thirsted so sore, in continual affection, for the progress of our monastery, that on every day except the great festivals they set themselves manfully to handiwork outside the cloister. On many days, and even nights, they stole certain hours from sleep and laboured hard with watchful diligence upon the copying of books, suffering no time to pass without some holy work for God. Indeed, they took into their own hands many kinds of handiwork, and matters of high art to which clerics are unaccustomed, for the sake of hastening the building and sparing expense. For the first prior of Windesheim, brother Heinrich v. Huxar, learned how to chisel stones for door and window mouldings, and to shape them and square them perfectly to the prescribed pattern. So also he learned to hew planks and beams and the like, most profitable for the various needs of the brethren, with adze and chisel and axe. Nay, to the very end of his life he ceased not to carpenter and chisel and chip, sometimes with such effort and labour that we saw the drops of sweat running from every part of his body. I have also seen other brethren of our house, choir-brethren, three or four or five or six of the most active and strongest, with masons' trowels in their hands, laying the stones and cement upon the walls of our monastery buildings and setting them true to the plumb-line. Other brethren we saw mixing the lime and sand with water and making all with great labour into cement; others cheerfully bearing stones or cement on their shoulders or in their hands; again, other brethren busying themselves most faithfully upon divers tasks for the hastening of the construction, while those of less bodily strength humbly vied with the rest, by laying stones upon the hand-barrows, or filling the porters' baskets here and there, or collecting laths to help the carpenters. All this we have seen, and much more of the sort, since in all this I was a fellow-worker and had almost all these experiences.

Meanwhile, the choir offices were in no way neglected, no hour of the day was wasted.

In short, in such fervour of spirit did they devote themselves to these holy labours, that every man, when his hard day's work was done, composed his weary limbs at night to rest and sleep. When morning came, he could scarce straighten his limbs from the stiffness of yesterday's work; yet then the resumption of labour warmed them, and they gradually recovered the strength they had lost. I have also very often seen other choir-brethren cheerfully and most joyfully drudging at rustic works, deputed to them by our superiors either for necessity or for the sake of exercise. Some in the kitchen, washing with all diligence the pots and plates and cauldrons and dishes; others in the wash-house busily labouring with their hands to cleanse the brethren's soiled garments; others kneading dough in the bake-house or labouring long in the brew-house over the ale. In harvest-time, all who were in any way able helped nimbly and faithfully at the work of gathering hay or corn with all speed, or binding or carrying, both in the fields and the granges and in our farm buildings. But, although our brethren were often compelled to drudge in many rustic and external works for the new building of our monastery and the completion of one edifice after another, yet they kept the night watches of their cell and the custody of their heart and senses with the utmost diligence. Further, whensoever they were able, they besought leave to steal hours for copying holy books in common, and, at the end of matins, which at first they were wont to read [instead of singing], they had a whole hour set aside for that purpose.

CHAPTER X

TRUE MONKS

BUSCH took the vows under the second prior since the foundation, Johann Vos of Huesden. Of him Busch gives a full-length portrait, as also of fourteen others among the elder monks; all admirably drawn, with clear individual characterization both of the outer and of the inner man. Here I must be content to reproduce the first as a fair specimen of the rest, though perhaps it has not its full share of the frank unexpected touches which give so much life to Busch's portraits.

Vos had been a model pupil of Deventer, the model school of the Brethren of Common Life, which was still in full bloom under Gerhard Groot. Groot chose the youth for his secretary, and said of him prophetically: "This is the man whom I have sought, and with whom I will work much good upon earth." After Groot's death he taught under Florentius Radewin; but he aspired to monasticism and entered Windesheim with the first struggling handful of devotees in 1388. Here (writes Busch),

although, since he had already conversed some time with the devout fathers in Radewin's house, he had put their manners, their life and their teaching into practice, yet now he began as if from the beginning to amend himself and gain further ground, laying within himself a foundation of fear of the Lord and humility and simplicity. He pondered even more sedulously upon all that might more efficaciously bring his mind to true compunction of heart, and to his earlier fervour of soul, and the perfect fear of God: namely, upon the Four Last Things; death and judgment, the pains of hell and the joys of the Kingdom of Heaven. Wherefore he oftentimes revolved in his fearful heart, and wrote upon a little slip among his daily exercises, that word which St Gregory puts into the mouth of the sinner Chrysaorius when hell was gaping for him: *Spare me until dawn, spare me until dawn!* (1)

He had, like many medieval saints, so lofty a conception of the priesthood that for some time he struggled against accepting it. When he was at last ordained, this deepened his mystical contemplation. As Busch writes:

he withdrew from the world and crept by himself into the inmost recesses of his heart; and there he made unto Christ a large upper chamber for supper, dwelling with Him therein....(2)...Living thus unto God and himself alone, he became so abstracted that when, at the meetings of the whole community, he was called upon to give his sentence upon external business, he commonly made answer "I know not"; wherefore many were wont to call him *Johnny Knownot*: yet by nature he had a sagacious mind, and men saw his prudence in speech, and he surpassed many in inborn wisdom....Hence it came to pass that, when our devout father Werner resigned the priorate through a scruple of conscience, Johann Vos was chosen in his room by unanimous vote.

Then he rose to the height of his duties.

He was grave but not austere, knowing well how to temporize; sociable and jocund among his friends and devout fathers, and gently considerate among the laity and great folk; kindly and disciplined among the brethren and the household servants; never absent from our meetings unless he were hindered by conventual or Chapter General meetings, or by guests. He neglected nothing, yet he winked at much for the moment. In his cell he was always quiet yet never idle. And (whereat we often marvelled) at the same moment he would show himself one man to the brethren, another to the devout fathers, another to layfolk and another to great men, meeting each according to the fitness of his rank and his personal quality. For, as he went forward daily in virtue, so also in experience, which is the mistress of all wisdom, he grew day by day; and he was wont to say of himself: "I, who was called to be prior of this monastery so and so many years ago, have yet to learn my daily task."...His intellect was keen, his speech prudent, his mind constant, his heart humble and his aspect venerable....It was a marvel to us all how, with such greatness of mind and so long a view over difficult affairs, he kept true humility of heart and modesty of manners in equal balance and without confusion....He was not stiff-necked in his own opinion: but, when anything great had to be done or built, he was wont first to confer privately with other more expert brethren, or even with lay-brethren and servants who had more experience in such matters; and, though most expert himself, yet he listened to various reasons before choosing that which he should lay before the convent. Yet, notwithstanding this, the brethren were free to express each his own opinion. Then, having given a kindly hearing to all the brethren, one by one, at last he would himself answer: "Beloved brethren, I have spoken also with other folk who understand these matters, and, after duly weighing both sides, such and such seems a good and fit manner of doing best and putting into execution the matter with which we are concerned. Is it your pleasure that we should do thus?"

He listened patiently even to the youngest brother:

for, as a prudent man himself, the hearing of the other men's prudence brought him not trouble but rather joy, since wisdom was thus not subtracted, but added. He loved all his brethren and to each he showed true signs of affection, in deed and speech and truth. He never kept hatred and bitterness in his heart against any man; yet, if there were aught reprehensible among the brethren, in his zeal for discipline he never omitted to correct it at the right time and place.... Whithersoever he went, whether within his own monastery or in others, and among congregations of either sex, he was always welcomed most devoutly as a holy angel of God....He did not roar and gnash his teeth like a lion in the monastery, but conversed as one that was small and of no repute among the brethren. He never proclaimed imperiously what should be done, but with all kindness and gentleness. Once the brethren, sitting with him in the orchard for recreation, agreed and said that a stone wall should be built in a certain part of the orchard, lest any brother or lay-brother should go thither. But he answered: "We will set a wall of obedience there", knowing well that no man would climb over that wall....He would not that his brethren, immediately after dinner or as they sat round the fire, should quickly slip into any idle words; "For" (as he said) "man's nature is at those times more inclined unto vanity." Moreover, he would that they should shroud their heads in their hoods when they went to the rere-dorter, as blushing that so noble a creature, the image of the most High God, should need to go thither. He said another time: "Brethren, we live too long! At the beginning of our conversion we are good and ready for everything; then we labour to progress and to grow in true virtues; but in the end we begin to grow lukewarm, able to bear nothing and to do little good, constantly intent upon our own comfort and bodily rest." He said again: "The holy men who came before us did far more than we. It is little indeed that we do for the Kingdom of Heaven, yet, if we persevere in that good, we shall be saved." When the prior happened to come upon the brethren assembled at their labour or elsewhere, then he would cough (being asthmatic) or by some other sound give notice of his coming, in order that nothing of vanity or want of discipline or carelessness might be found in them when he came; and thus the brethren grew accustomed always to love him and revere him in all places. It was said of him that he had besought and obtained from God this grace, that in his own days none of the brethren in Windesheim should die of the pestilence; for he was unwilling that the brethren should shrink from each other, as men commonly do in pestilence-time.

When he had been prior for thirty-three years, and was now sixty-one years old, he began visibly to break up. His infirmities drove him more and more within himself.

He studied to amend without delay whatsoever he remembered to have done against God's will, in thought or word or deed or by omission, recognizing clearly that no evil can remain unpunished, nor any good unrewarded, since God doth not pardon the sinner unless he be truly penitent. For he lived in vehement fear of God's awful judgment, now so close upon him; and he felt how intolerable it would be to feel even for a single hour the purgatorial flames, or that fire of hell that is not quenched, tormenting the sinful soul most bitterly even to the utmost farthing....I have seen him oftentimes sitting silently on a seat in front of the choir with his eyes fixed on the graves of the brethren whose dust lies there, meditating long upon their bodies turned to ashes and the happiness and glory of their souls reigning in heaven, while he firmly hoped himself soon to follow them. Sometimes, as I sat by his side, he would say unto me: "The Lord hath called our best brethren first unto himself, even as a dove is wont to choose the best grains of wheat." Therefore, under the daily vexation of his asthmatic chest and his painful breathing, he besought his subprior, Arnold Kalker, to reflect with the other brethren upon his retirement from the priorate and the choice of some other in his place. But, whereas one evening he had earnestly commissioned him to fulfil this duty, yet next morning, when the subprior came unto him, he had bethought himself otherwise, and said: "Beloved brother, there will be no need for you to release me from my office; God will soon free me; therefore trouble no more in that matter." And thus it came to pass; for within a brief while he began to draw near his end, and the subprior gave him the Holy Communion and anointed him according to the rites of the Church in the presence of the whole congregation of Windesheim and the prior of Nordhorn. But when he besought the brethren to pardon him and to forgive all wherein he might have offended, he did this so humbly and with such true self-knowledge and compunction of heart, that almost all were moved to tears. Thenceforward he sometimes lay, sometimes sat, sometimes stood by the fire leaning upon the shoulders of the brethren, but always struggling most painfully for breath; then again he was laid upon the bed and rested awhile. But he had compassion on those who watched by his side, and said to our lay-brother, the surgeon of the infirmary, that he should lie down and rest awhile. When the surgeon came back to him in the morning, he said: "Beloved brother, I am still here," as though he should say "I shall not long be with you." So, as his natural heat departed from his extremities to his vitals, his feet began to grow cold, and the brethren would have warmed them with fomentations and friction; but he said: "Know ye not, brethren, that when a man is about to die his feet first grow cold?" And then they ceased from their endeavours. Yet at his last moments he suffered no troubling imaginations nor wandering fantasies sent by evil angels; but in full command of his mind and reason, in very good peace and quiet of heart, he rendered his happy soul to God, in the presence of the brethren, on the Saturday after St Andrew's day, during the *Gloria in excelsis* of High Mass, a Mass of the Blessed Virgin, whom he had most specially loved, which was sung with all solemnity before Advent.

Thomas à Kempis, who was in those days at the sister monastery of Mount St Agnes, is quoted by Busch among those who received revelations assuring them of the good prior's passage direct to Paradise.

The other fourteen portraits are up to the same standard; and the public ought to welcome Mr F. Darwin's forthcoming translation of nearly all that Busch has written. Meanwhile, however, a little more may be given here. On a later page (315) Busch describes the lay-brethren also, so admirably and with so little of his too frequent prolixity, that the passage may come here almost in full.

Certain devout and competently learned men, daily observing the holy conversation of the brethren at Windesheim and greatly aspiring to our Order and habit, were found in time to be too weak by nature for continual endurance of the daily labours in choir and in cloister, wherefore they were not admitted. Other clerics of less education, very strong and constant men, who aspired to our Order, were also refused admission among the choir-monks, for other causes that moved our convent. But other prudent men, of no learning in the world, yet of good experience and great wealth, entered our monastery and lived a very praiseworthy life. Also other laymen of good will, but less rich in worldly substance, entered Windesheim likewise. All these being proved and circumspect men, living admirably among choir-monks and lay-brethren in most simple habit, in true poverty and obedience and charity, in humble and abject labour, did, after long trial, often beg at last most devoutly for the habit of lay-brethren. When therefore they did this in brotherly fashion, and were of approved life and conversation, and ceased not from their request, then at last the brethren granted their desire.

Thirteen such were clothed, at different times, by Johann Vos of Huesden.

The first was John of Soest, who for his probity's sake was shortly afterwards promoted to clerical habit and Orders, and soon passed to join the choir-brethren in Amsterdam; thence he became prior of our house near Haarlem; thence to the rectorate of the nuns in Amsterdam, where he ended his life. The second was brother Henry Loeder of Osnaburg, who began as a lay-brother at Windesheim, where he was cook and cellarer. At last he was promoted to the clericate and became prior of Vrendesweel near Nordhorn, which he ruled for twenty years in such discipline that, throughout Westphalia and Saxony and Frisia and Rhineland, he was called the Apostle of that country. The third was brother Arnold Biscop, of Stavoren in Friesland, who in the world had been very rich. He, with Thada his wife, gave themselves and all that they had to our monastery; and it was their wealth which built our choir at Windesheim. The fourth was brother Jacob Bolliken, a good and discreet man, who for a long while was our miller. The fifth was brother John Boet, who long served the brethren in the kitchen, and was most scrupulous even to the end; yet from these scruples he was freed before his death. For, seeing that he was joyful, and welcomed death, and had no embarrassment of conscience, our subprior said unto him: "John, dearest brother, where now is that scrupulous conscience of thine which seldom left thee at peace?" To whom he answered: "For that cause was I ever scrupulous until now, that at this moment I might more securely go hence without any scruple or remorse of conscience." The sixth was brother Nicholas Luter of Amersfoort, a most venerable man, excellent in all honesty of manners and words, sweet and edifying in speech, prudent in mind, exemplary in his life, loving Religion, zealous for discipline and the glory of our monastery; faithful to trust, prudent in counsel, and specially adorned with religious probity of morals. He, for more than thirty years, was our most welcome hostillar, giving honour to each guest according as his rank suggested, reverent, loving to all and beloved of all; never, in so far as in him lay, offending any man in word or deed. Moreover, in the absence of our procurator, he cared for our outward affairs and ordered the work of the lay-brethren with due regard for them. The seventh was brother Hubert of Deventer, once a pupil of Gerard Groot and Florence Radewin. He was a good tailor, and to the end of his life he glowed with zeal for claustral discipline; most strictly did he maintain the humble form of our garments, according to the fashion of his forefathers aforesaid. The eighth was brother Bartholomew Herbolt of Utrecht, a strenuous and mature man, and most zealous to maintain the Order in himself and in others; he was a good and ready and most intelligent writer of shorthand. Three times over he copied that dictionary called *Catholicon* in great volumes, the last whereof lieth continually on a desk in our choir, almost the greatest and most precious of all the volumes in our monastery. He wrote other books also, of no small size, for the library, in common. The ninth was brother Frederick of Herderwijk, a good and honest man and a most reverential [*reverencialis*] baker and brewer, sweet and mature in all his arts. The tenth was brother Andrew, son of Peter of Deventer, who was for many years our tailor. He was blood-brother to brother Gerlacus Petri,* but differing far in spirit, both inwardly and outwardly. For brother Gerlacus was always spiritually joyful in the Lord, and continually lifted up in contemplation of God; but this lay-brother was always embarrassed and scrupulous and perplexed in mind; yet he was very humble and charitable, obsequious to all men, embracing the vilest labours, fervent in work; yet his scruples made him always blame himself; and very often, confessing himself guilty, taking penance, he embarrassed himself still farther and departed from the colloquies of his brethren. At the end of his life he suffered from haemorrhage in the bladder, and ended in good peace.† The eleventh was brother Egbert of Groningen, a diligent and godfearing man, excellently versed in outward affairs and in trade, who was often assistant to the procurator. He was skilled in casting metal knobs for the books; well he loved all brethren and lay-brethren; and, by permission of his wife, who was very aged, he left the world and became a lay-brother at Windesheim. The twelfth was brother Hugo, well versed in the art of carpentry, a pious and strong man, who was once inspired by the devil to apostatize; but then he was found and brought back by the lay-brother Nicholas, and afterwards, when he had done penance in prison, he was sometimes sent for his carpentry to other monasteries of our Order. At length, after many years of very religious conversation among his brethren, he was absolved of all his sins in the presence of the prior and congregation of lay-brethren and choir-brethren, and slept happily in the Lord and is buried among his fellows in the lay-brethren's cemetery. The thirteenth was brother Mercilius of Oude Yssel, a man devoted to God and beloved of the brethren, and above all things servile and obsequious to the sick brethren, even unto their death, without a murmur. For more than forty years he was a most faithful infirmarer to our brethren, and barber and bloodletter and a most expert surgeon. In the waning of his age he was for many years bereft

* A theologian of some fame in his own day.

† There was probably some fault in the Windesheim water; Busch records of many brethren that they suffered either from such haemorrhage, or calculus or gall-stones.

of all sight by God, Disposer of all things; yet of His gift he accepted this blindness, and to the present day he hath not ceased to give unending thanks; for he is approved and known to be faithful.

Lo! with how great maturity and strictest discipline these lay-brethren of ours conversed among the brethren! by what true virtues and excellent merits they have distinguished themselves before God and man, whether Religious or secular! And indeed there were perfect men among them, baldheaded, white-haired, long-bearded,* measured in their walk, disciplined in their conversation, grave in manner, soft of speech, prudent in mind, venerable in aspect, adorned with true virtues and a glory to their monastery; men who dwelt continually, even to life's end, in such perfections of manners and words and virtues. In short, even as our choir-brethren were everywhere the glory and honour of our Order and Chapter by their most holy lives and their approved manners, so did our lay-brethren in their own rank, by their good conversation and maturity of manners and discipline, show that our monastery and Chapter were worthy of all honour and reverence. For lay-brethren can fully reach even to the highest pinnacle of holiness by the fervour of their devotion, their contemplation of God, their brotherly charity, their self-control and zeal for discipline, in so far as pertaineth to the measure of their rank; provided that, carefully avoiding follies and superfluous jesting, they strive to adapt themselves in mind and body to the aforesaid [religious] exercises, even though their state be specially dedicated to outward offices, manual labours and mechanical tasks, to be faithfully performed with humble heart and ready mind and bodily subjection.

Finally, Busch sets himself to resolve a doubt which he anticipates.

We think it right here to answer briefly those weaker souls whose timid conscience or whose trust in their own wisdom forbids them to esteem those fathers as holy or illustrious who have not been distinguished by miracles either in life or in death. We read of many most holy men in the Old and New Testaments whom the Church holdeth as true saints, and hath even canonized, yet in their lives they are recorded to have wrought no miracles; as, for example, Noah, Abraham, Isaac, Jacob, Joseph and other saints of that age down to Moses and Aaron. So also Samuel and David, Hezekiah and Josiah, Jeremiah and Ezekiel and the twelve prophets are not recorded to have wrought miracles. And, in the New Testament, the most blessed Virgin Mary, John Baptist, holiest of men, and many holy confessors

* The lay-brethren of all Orders commonly wore beards; they are often called *fratres barbati*. In the Windesheim congregation, the choir-brethren also seem to have been sometimes bearded.

and holy virgins were truly holy and most saintly; yet they never shone with miracles in all their lives, as may be most clearly seen in their lives and legends. For, as St Paul saith, miracles were given not for the believing but for the unbelievers. Miracles, in the primitive Church, were altogether necessary for the conversion of unbelievers; but, now that the number of believers hath grown, they are no longer needed; for those signs which are promised to believers in Mark [xvi. 14 ff.] will be fulfilled, as we understand, not literally but in a spiritual sense.(3)

CHAPTER XI

MODEL MONASTERIES

WINDESHEIM had become a focus of reform not only before the Council of Basel, but even before Constance. In 1415 these efforts first began to bear full fruit. In that year Heinrich Loeder, a pupil of Vos in Windesheim, went as prior to Nordhorn [dioc. Hildesheim], which had joined the Congregation of 1400. He made this house a centre of reforming activity. He passed the torch on to Böddeken, which in later times could boast of having brought twenty houses under the reform. One of these was Richenberg near Goslar, which we may choose from Busch's *De Reformatione* as a typical example of the new world that these men were making. Busch pitches the note high; but we may trust him for all essential facts. He tells how it

was reformed in 1414 by our brother Heinrich Loeder.... In this monastery, before the reform, seven brethren with their prior and a scanty community of servants could scarce get the barest necessities of food and raiment. Now [1470], in the reformed house, there are more than 73 brethren and lay-brethren, with all necessaries in abundance, living by the labours of their hands and from the nourishment of their flocks and herds; for they have more than 1000 sheep, with great numbers of horses and cows and swine. Moreover they have 18 fishponds, from which, over and above their own needs, they often sell fish to the amount of one or two hundred Rhenish florins.(1) Again, they have great store of bees, from whom they get no small fruit of honey and wax. They have corn-mills driven by water, and a mill for sawing beams and planks. They have also divers offices and lay officials; to wit, blacksmiths, carpenters, tailors, shoemakers, barbers, bakers and brewers. They possess great woods on the hills, and in the valleys they have tithe-rents and farms scattered here and there. Around the monastery they have their home-farm tilled by their own lay-brethren, from whence they carry the corn with their own horses and store it in their barns. Moreover, their lay-brethren make such store of butter and cheese from the milk of their cows and sheep that, over and above their own consumption of cheese, they sometimes sell barrels full of cheeses to other folk. (p. 482.)

At Böddeken, somewhere about 1465, Busch himself was one

76641

of the visitors (p. 490). "We found there present more than 26 choir-brethren and their prior, with 173 lay-brethren and layfolk or servants. And they had outside, in other monasteries of our Order, 56 brethren, some as priors in other houses, others rulers and confessors of nuns, others co-reformers. Moreover they have very many layfolk in many monasteries, most profitable for the progress thereof." He names nineteen houses which owe their reform directly to Böddeken, and he concludes:

And, since these brethren dwell not by any city or town or village, as do many monasteries of our Order, therefore they and other such houses abound in many flocks, whence they receive food and clothing for their needs, abounding richly in butter and milk and cheese. Moreover they daily receive many layfolk to do work of this sort; and that not only for the sake of outward labours but far more for God's sake and the gain of the Kingdom of Heaven, which they can undoubtedly earn there on earth through true obedience, pure poverty or absence of private property, and chaste continence.

The house possessed nearly 2000 sheep, 130 horses, and nearly 300 oxen and cows, with a fine vaulted church and conventual buildings to match, and with all the artificers and servants which have been enumerated at Richenberg.

Molenbeke, again (p. 492), "was formerly a house of the ladies called in common speech 'ladies with a vocation'; we found there one lady and four priests who lived upon the house". The Prior of Böddeken undertook its reform, "since the place pleased us well, albeit the buildings threatened ruin and their church, very long and broad and lofty, was a stall for horses and cows, full of dung and filth; yet it was such as might be cleaned and serve its purpose well". Hither, as to the others, Windesheim brought temporal as well as spiritual prosperity. The choir-brethren were numerous, lay-brethren and lay-folk numbered about 100, and the whole place was redolent of good example to the neighbourhood. Busch enumerates sawmills, watermills, and artificers as in Richenberg. "They have also fishponds whence they are wont to draw more than 100 Rhenish florins a year, beyond their own need. So also they do with their flocks, from which they keep what they need and sell the rest."

At Dalheim, again, where there had been a few nuns, with secular canons who drew most of the revenues, Busch describes not only the construction of a fine stone church, 180 ft. long, but also the present agricultural prosperity, with lay-brethren and artificers and servants.

> On St Francis's day we found there 24 tuns of curdled milk from their cows and sheep.... They have about 2000 sheep, 200 cows and 49 horses. Such houses, [he adds] by reason of the multitude of their flocks and the feeding of the beasts, are able to receive unto themselves many layfolk, desirous of saving their souls; and they can distribute to each the work whereunto he is apt; such folk are faithful to their brethren and serve the monastery zealously without pay in money—*sine mercede exteriori*.

Under these prosperous conditions, the prior was now undertaking to rebuild the whole monastery on a far greater scale at the crest of the hill. A fine church of hewn stone was already completed when Busch wrote (180 ft. by 30); and, when the domestic buildings had been completed on the same scale, it was purposed to leave the old house to the lay-brethren and servants and cattle.

These sawmills may surprise the modern reader: but thereby hangs a curious chapter in economic history.

Medieval Western civilization, on the material side, was extraordinarily weak in the matter of machinery. Men had clocks and windmills—both, probably, imported inventions from the East—but, though clockwork showed their capacity for elaborate and accurate mechanism, there was scarcely any application of such experience to industry until the fifteenth century, when the medieval synthesis was visibly breaking up. Even then mechanization was timid and sporadic until the full tide of the Renaissance was flowing, and religious revolution seemed more and more inevitable. Moreover, these exceptions, when narrowly examined, will be found to prove the rule. This has recently been brought out by Professor M. M. Postan in a lecture at Cambridge. The records suggest that this mechanical backwardness was due mainly if not entirely to the gild system. Side by side with the many good qualities of that system, was the disadvantage of premature standardization. The gild, while it ensured a certain level of production, was tempted to restrain any excess of that standard as pitilessly as it punished shortcomings. The hatter, who in eighteenth-century Paris invented the mixture of silk with his wool, was condemned as a traitor to his profession, and his hats were confiscated.

The craftsman must be righteous, but not righteous overmuch.

Moreover the gild system, besides resting on the assumption of stable technical standards, functioned also as an organization for regulating the *petite bourgeoisie* of the cities. They fought against anything that might give one master a competitive advantage, or enable him to expand his turnover at the expense of that of the rest; thus they opposed not only expansive investments, but also labour-saving devices. Thus industry and invention were comparatively free only in a few great cities, in Italy and Rhineland and the Netherlands, for instance, where trade was dominated not by the *petite bourgeoisie* but by large capitalists. Thus mechanical advance came seldom or never from the gild.

In the Middle Ages proper, the most elaborate and effective machines were military; the springald and mangonel and crossbow (these, again, imported from ancient Greece or Rome) and, finally, gunpowder. Next to these military mechanisms we may count the masons at great cathedrals or abbey churches, with their cranes and pulleys which still survive here and there between the rafters and the stone vaults, as at Chartres. Or we may count still more emphatically, perhaps, those lathes for turning marble columns which lay unused in the bowels of the worked-out Purbeck quarries until they were consumed by fire a century ago. Here, then, in war and in the churches, were two fields in which the gild had no voice. The feudal lord wanted the most deadly machinery that could be had for attack, and the greatest security for defence; therefore a fully developed suit of plate-armour is a marvel not only of beauty but of mechanical adaptation; and the feudal lord was often capable of imitating that Norman countess who set the best military architect to build her the best of possible castles, and then slew him to make sure of retaining her superiority. Neither gild nor religion trammelled invention in war. Nor, again, had they much retarding effect on the cathedral or abbey. The masons' gild (as Professor Douglas Knoop and Mr G. P. Jones have shown) was not organized in the same close and all-embracing fashion as others; indeed, it is doubtful in the case of very many medieval masons whether they belonged to any gild at all. Villard de Honnecourt's notebook shows us master-masons constantly discussing with each other as to fresh steps forward; and the proprietors of any projected edifice, whether church or castle, were glad to be shown any improvement. Printing, again, had no powerful gild to contend with: there was only a small scriveners' gild in London, another at York and one or two, perhaps, elsewhere in England. The painters, also, had only small gilds here and there, sometimes merely as a sub-division of the saddlers. Thus there was nothing here to prevent men from putting into practice what Marco Polo had described in the case of Chinese bank-notes, and what the makers of signets and encaustic tiles had done from time immemorial; therefore at last they began to stamp from blocks of wood little figures of saints for household worship. Thence the step was easy to cut a brief legend in prose or rhyme underneath the figure: thence, again, to fill a whole block with writing; and finally to cut movable types. Thus the press rapidly became a real machine. The craftsmanship of early printing is often magnificent; there was no lack of mechanical and artistic skill if only there had been a directing brain before the Renaissance began.

Another medieval machine was the mill. Here was a free field; here neither had the gild any claim, nor even any ecclesiastic as such. The mill was a monopoly of the manorial lord; he could do practically what he liked with it. Hence we find, at quite an early stage, not only corn-mills but fulling-mills for cloth. In the towns, these fulling-mills were often forbidden; but the gild was powerless on the countryside, where the lord of the manor was as free to add to his income by building a fulling-mill as a corn-mill. And now at last, in this fifteenth-century Germany, roughly contemporaneously with the immense development of the printing machine, we find the monks making sawmills "for planks and beams", as Busch says. This is not absolutely the first example on record; there was one at Augsburg as early as 1322, and still earlier examples may be found in the Netherlands. But when we consider that, in nine cases out of ten, the medieval house was built out of wood, we shall see at once how great an industrial advance would have been made if some great abbot in St Anselm's or St Bernard's day had thought of this simple device.

This gives all the greater honour to these Windesheim reformers who, apparently, first rendered the sawmill fairly common in Western Europe. We can quite believe that St Augustine or St Benedict, resuscitated to see the economic and mechanical activities which Busch records, might have said "It is magnificent, but it is not monasticism." Yet, at all times, the monks' most beneficent social activities had often been irrelevant to the strict Rule or even contrary to it. The most solid praise of Windesheim is in what Busch often claims for it, that it set a good example to society within the whole range of its influence. It shone as "a good deed in a naughty world", and no man can take that honour from it.

CHAPTER XII

JOHANN BUSCH

St Francis was impatient with those who sang the praises of ancient saints and martyrs, just as minstrels sing those of Roland and Oliver, with their lips alone. Busch was not of that sort; his own life will bear comparison with the lives of those brethren whom he describes as labouring to make a new world in a remote corner of the German Empire. To begin with, let him speak for himself.

So my parents would fain have sent me to the University of Erfurt, that I might be chief of all our friends and kinsfolk. But I began to think within myself: "If thou wert already Doctor, clad in thy many-coloured well-furred gowns, and enjoying the title of thy degree, while all men cried: 'Good morrow, Sir Doctor, good day!' and if after this life thou must needs go down to hell, there to burn for everlasting, what profit shouldst thou then have?" So I thought the more frequently on the eternity of hell-pains and the infinity of the heavenly glory, earnestly considering whether my mind could grasp and foresee any end to eternity. When therefore, after many weary rounds of thought, this was still impossible, then after good deliberation I determined firmly in mine own mind that I would desert the whole world with all its delights, and serve God alone for ever in some good reformed monastery. For these words *ewelike ende ommermeer* ["for ever and evermore"] compelled me to do thus and to leave my parents and my friends, whereof I had many, for God's sake and the life everlasting. Hearing this, my parents and kinsfolk strove to turn me aside, and my mother above all; for she said, "Dear son, when thou wert young, thou wouldst fain have eaten in thy bed. Thou canst not fast; wilt thou slay thyself? Moreover, they will not leave thee in one monastery, but will oftentimes send thee to others. Thou shouldst have been the head of us all; wilt thou now desert us?" and much more to the same purpose. I made soft answer to my mother, but in my heart I thought: "These are women's words; none will care to go to hell for me; if I will go to heaven, I must earn that for myself!" So I gave no heed to my father's and mother's tears, but purposed to enter the order of Canons Regular, whereof the reform had lately begun in our parts....*

* Compare the words of Peter the Precentor (of Notre-Dame-de-Paris), two centuries and a half before this: "Many monks, pitying their parents, lose their own souls" (Migne, *P.L.* CCV, 210).

What temptations I suffered as a novice, especially in the Catholic faith, God alone knoweth, from Whom nothing is hid. For God Himself was so great and glorious in my heart, that I could not conceive Him to have put on flesh and walked upon earth so poor and so despised. And when the Gospels were read in refectory, I thought that the Evangelists desired to praise that man, and then my heart cried within me, "Thou knowest, it is not true that this Jesus is God!" Yet I said within my heart, "I will die for it, that He is so." Then my heart cried within me, "Thou wilt die for it, yet shalt thou see that it shall be naught!" But when I found how our father St Augustine and the other Doctors, who lived in the world almost 400 years after Christ, said and wrote and preached that this Jesus was God, then I thought: "It is strange that those wise men were so foolish as to dare to call that man God, Whom they never saw." And, albeit I was thus tempted, yet was I a good and true Catholic; but God Almighty suffered me thus to be tempted, because in later years, taught by experience, I liberated many who were buffeted with the same temptation. How I was liberated from this trial, is contained in the letter which I wrote to one Brother Bernard, of the Order of St Benedict at Erfurt. I had also temptations of the flesh in my noviciate....My temptations of vainglory, pride, and impatience could easily be driven out, for then I fought one against one; but in those of the flesh two fought against one, for my flesh and the Devil were matched against my struggling soul. When during my noviciate I sang in the service a verse or responsory or versicle, then I thought within myself: "Our lay-folk in the nave, prostrate on their knees, are thinking with admiration, 'How good and pure a voice hath our Brother John!'" When another novice sang any part, then I murmured within myself: "Now the lay-folk are thinking, 'That sounds like a rasp!'" Rarely did one of our Brethren leave the choir or do anything, but that I had various suspicions of him, thinking within myself: "He cannot stay longer in the choir, he goeth forth because he would go hither, or thither." One was wont to spit frequently in choir; and I thought that he had many temptations which he drove forth by this continual voiding of his rheum. Thus too I had most frequent suspicions of many others; for a novice is as full of suspicions as an egg is full of meat.

Yet will I sing for ever the mercies of the Lord, Who not only liberated me from many temptations, but through those same temptations rooted me fast in good, giving me a practised tongue that I might sustain the fallen by word and deed. When therefore my profession had been performed, at Epiphany, on the very year-day of mine entrance, by reason of my parents' presence, who brought wine and flesh and white bread for the convent, I was not altogether freed from the temptations aforesaid, wherein I was immersed even to the roof of my cell throughout wellnigh all the time of my noviciate. But on St Agnes' day (for then again we communicated) all my past temptation departed utterly from my heart and senses, and then my Lord Jesus answered: "Now art thou Mine, and I am thine." And from that time until this present it hath ever been well with me, so far as in Him stood; and I began to converse with Him and oftentimes to hear His answering voice, as it may be heard in the heart within.... Whensoever after this I felt inclinations or movements to fault or sin, or when I was offended by others, I conceived certain remedies thereunto which I had found by experience of myself or by study from the Holy Scriptures, which I collected into a certain little book that I might have them at hand; whereby I brought myself back little by little to peace of mind, and withstood such evil inclinations. (pp. 394 ff.)

Elsewhere (p. 704) Busch describes the dowry he brought to Windesheim.

My mother's sister, Metta Bomgard, a devout and God-fearing matron, very rich and prudent...had procured for me when I wished to enter Religion 50 French crowns in gold, to the value of 75 Rhenish florins, and black cloth sufficient for my frock and cowl; also white cloth in abundance for my upper, middle and lower tunics, namely shirts and hosen and socks and slippers, from a husband of my kinswoman....After her death I interceded for her from the bottom of my heart with the Lord God. When I came back from Bödingen to Windesheim I heard from my mother that, at my first Mass, a Mass of the Holy Ghost which I sang on the Sunday after Michaelmas, she was freed from all pains of purgatory and flew up to everlasting joys.

Only four years after his own solemn profession, while he was yet but a deacon, he was sent as one of four emissaries to Bödingen near Köln, where a college of secular priests was being transformed into an Augustinian monastery. Here he dwelt another four years under conditions well suited to harden a young Knight of the Holy Ghost.

Very often we endured no small penury even of necessaries. For in winter, lacking the needful coverings, we laid a log of wood under our heads for pillow, and another over our feet to keep them warm. When we had not enough to eat, we appeased our roaring souls with coarse bread and butter, while our prior quoted

Si brevis est caliga
Sit tibi longa liga.*

* "If thy hose be short, let thy lace be long"—i.e. the "suspender" by which the hose hung from the waist.

That is, if there be no other food, then expel hunger with bread and butter. (p. 402.)

In 1428 he was recalled to Windesheim, and was sent next January upon a still more adventurous mission. Nothing but his own words could do justice to this strange story (p. 402).

The monastery of St Martin, in Ludinkerka, of our Order, in Friesland, in the diocese of Utrecht, which was previously an abbey of our Order, began to be reformed in the year 1428. Before its reformation there were but few priests there, and a great many lay brethren—more than thirty or forty—who had entered into an agreement with the lay brethren of a neighbouring monastery of the Cistercian Order, a mile off, that they would mutually help each other with a hundred armed men against all adversaries. The consequence was, that they had subdued all that part of Friesland. A certain vavasour, however, who lived in his own castle near the monastery, by advice of the lawyers, of whom there are plenty among the priests in Friesland, reported their ill and abominable life to the Archbishop of Utrecht. None of them was continent; all were proprietary, and they had nuns with them in the monastery, with whom they cohabited, and sometimes begat children. I knew the abbot there, a learned man, whose father had been a lay brother, and his mother a nun; yet he resigned his abbacy and entered into a monastery of our Order near Haarlem, and having there taken the vows, he ended his days well.

The bishop, however, Frederic van Blankinheym, a wise and learned man, sent thither ambassadors, men learned and skilful in the law, who, diligently examining the inmates, found that almost all the lay brethren had entered without Rule or profession, and that they had remained many years without the promised obedience. Being asked how they had come to take upon them the habit of lay brethren, they answered, "When first we came here, we saw many persons clothed with white tunics and scapularies, and at the same time expert in weapons of war; so we bought ourselves white cloth, and had it made into white tunics, white hoods, and scapularies, and put them on ourselves." It was asked whether they had heard anything about their Rule. They answered, "Never"; and they added "each of us took to himself a nun, a lay sister, or other woman of our household, with whom he cohabited without being married, and sometimes begat children". The Bishop of Utrecht, therefore, hearing this, by the advice of men learned in the law, in which he too was learned, adjudged and decreed that all the persons of this description were not monks, and never had been, but might go out and marry lawful wives, and remain secular persons; and that they might put off that habit which they had taken and resume their secular dress. Hearing this, they immediately did so, and also made protestation that they had no right or claim to the monastery or its possessions. A few, however, two or three, obtained leave to remain there, because they were old: and for a long time they retained also the women who had belonged to them, that they might wait on them in their infirmities, until all the women were expelled and the men incorporated also with the monastery of our Order hard by. After this a messenger came to Windesheim to request that they would take the monastery in hand for reformation.

Friesland, we must remember, was one of the wildest corners of Western Europe. The rough and hardy peasants of that province still smacked somewhat of what St Willibrord and St Boniface had found in them; when their king Ratbod was said to have declined baptism on the plea that, his ancestors being in hell, it was not for him to desert them in order to spend eternity with ragged beggars. It was only twenty years before Busch's visit that Pope Gregory XII acted upon a report sent to him that the twenty-two Benedictine nunneries in Friesland had gradually coalesced with men's houses, so that "many gave birth to children", while others "destroy some of their unborn fruit, or slay the children after birth".(1) Under this present Frederick of Utrecht, an exceptionally efficient prelate, Ludinkerka was apparently the only surviving instance of such open scandal. He commissioned Windesheim with the reform; and Busch was one of the two colonists sent from thence to give an example of regular life. His prior sent him off with a playful word: "Brother John, you did not profit much—*non multum profecistis*—at Bödingen by Köln; see now whether you can convert the Frisians." The material hardships proved even greater there.

Since there are few trees in Friesland, the winter winds blew all round us, and bitter frosts reigned there, so that after saying my hours I sat in my bed, covered with my clothes, to warm myself. And, since the water in the dikes and the flowing streams smacked of salt by reason of the sea hard by, which sometimes filtered in through broken banks or by the course of aqueducts, therefore that drink was very contrary to my nature.

He seems to have fallen ill: for in August he and his companion were sent to Beverwijk, where a struggling house, founded two years earlier, had called for help from Windesheim. They found two buildings which they were able to convert into chapel and dormitory respectively, with kitchen and refectory in an annexe. Then a neighbouring lord, widowed and pious, built a fine stone house on these grounds for his last days. Round this, gradually, the whole monastery was built; and Busch, writing forty years later, could congratulate himself on the flourishing state of this house. Meanwhile twenty-four monks and lay-brethren had come to Ludinkerka from Mount St Agnes in the very month when Busch left; and this reform also prospered. Busch then became spiritual adviser to a nunnery in Beverwijk. A few years later, we find him at Bronop in Holland, provisor and confessor to a nunnery of the Windesheim congregation. Looking back upon all this after nearly forty years, he falls into a series of reflexions too characteristic for anything but his own words.

I lived there for 3 years; and at the end of that time I suffered no little remorse of conscience, in that, while still a young priest, I must thus spend my time. For I oftentimes thought how my conventual brethren at Windesheim were frequenting by day and night their choir and dormitory and refectory, so high in heaven, while I was so low that I could scarce catch a sight of them above me. For me, at my young age, it was a duty to profit much day by day in observance of the Rule, in strictness of order, and in mortification of my own will and nature; I should be constraining my body to serve my spirit. Yet among the nuns I could not do this; for there I did scarce anything but what I would, reading my breviary and sometimes singing Mass. So I besought the prior of Windesheim, a zealous and strenuous man, to let me return to the monastery. At the prayer of the prioress and the sisters he postponed his consent, for I was master of the works there at the completion of their great church, which still needed roofing and covering with beams and stones. As he still delayed, I besought our procurator at Windesheim, a good and holy and godfearing man, to advise me in this matter. He answered: "Brother, I believe that he who would gladly be in his own monastery among his own brethren, and is compelled by obedience to dwell with the nuns, shall receive from God a good and excellent reward." So I dwelt there yet for a while. Yet, since my conscience rested not within me, as I saw my brethren following their own conventual course in heaven, and doubted for myself whether I also could come to heaven by following my own comforts, I finally received leave from the prior to return. There, not long after, I filled the office of sacrist for about three years, and procured the betterment of our church ornaments by sixty or eighty florins. When therefore, I departed from those nuns, they most liberally gave me a good black cassock, great and broad, made for me there by the tailor of Windesheim, and a new furred cloak, which I have worn more than thirty years, down to this present day. The cassock I wore not in Bronop but for a few days at Windesheim. Then our chamberlain at Windesheim, brother Ludolph, a man of long stature, came unto me and said: "Brother John, your new cassock is too long for you, and mine is too short. I have leave from our subprior (for the prior is not at home) that you should give me your new cassock and take my old one, which is too short for me, thus let us exchange." Then I began to think: "This brother is junior to me in Religion; does he do rightly, to ask this of me? If I said one word to the prior, or even to the subprior, they would be well content for me to keep my cassock." But, considering again, I thought: "Dost thou wish to become *proprietarius* for that cassock's sake, by clinging to it?" Thus, forthwith, with tranquil and deliberate mind, I doffed my good new cassock and gave it to the chamberlain, and received his, old and worn and threadbare. For I would fain carry down to the grave, for sweet and soft pillow and for quiet sleep, the Three Substantials of our Order—Poverty, Chastity and Obedience, which I had promised to God and to my superiors. I had no sooner done this, than I felt no small joy of conscience for my resignation. (p. 706.)

Here, then, he is again at Windesheim in this heaven on earth, booming forth the Psalms of David with the rest, learning with them to wear threadbare garments for conscience' sake, and satisfying his craving for the heroic in Religion. John Vos was now dead, but the almost equally remarkable Wilhelm Vornken reigned in his stead; the man under whose priorate at Mount St Agnes the *Imitatio* was probably written. It was he who boasted concerning Windesheim that the only creatures who ate delicately within those precincts were the guests and the swine.

After three years under him, Busch had completed his full apprenticeship to what was to be the work of his life; a work sufficient to tax not only his natural qualities but his acquired discipline to the utmost. In 1437 he left Windesheim for ever as an inmate, going forth as a missionary upon the work which made Windesheim's greatest glory; the reform of decayed monasteries in the spirit of Constance and Basel.

We have seen how the Council of Basel in 1435, by a special bull, commissioned Prior Rembert of Wittenberg and another to reform all the Augustinian houses in "Saxony" (i.e. north-west Germany), and how the greater houses openly resisted. But Rembert, as a zealous Windesheimer, was not to be beaten altogether. In 1430 he had already joined hands with Johann Dederoth, the future founder of the Benedictine Congregation of Bursfelde; it was with this man that the bull of 1435 commissioned him to visit and reform. In that same year 1435 the Council of Basel gave Dederoth visitatorial powers over other Benedictine houses. Bursfelde (already reformed by Dederoth in 1433) was in the diocese of Hildesheim, which thus became the cradle of a great movement parallel with that of Windesheim. Therefore in 1439 the Prior of Wittenberg, Rembert's successor, determined to attempt the reform of Sülte, a rich Austin monastery upon a hill overlooking Hildesheim. This site gushed with abundant springs, which ran round the conventual buildings and thence down into the city. These springs had originally been haunted by demons, until St Godehard exorcised them, since which day they had supplied the best ale of all the country round. The magistracy of Hildesheim, in gratitude for the water, "gave to the monastery every year 100 bushels of Michaelmas malt, whereof three bushels make as much ale as will fill a herring-cask". Busch, who was now Sub-prior of Wittenberg, was sent to press reform upon the wealthy and conservative brethren there. The house was one of those which in 1435 had protested publicly against that bull which the Prior of Wittenberg now invoked; but he and Busch, supported now by the bishop suffragan and the cathedral chancellor, interviewed them and persuaded them to abide by the decision of the bishop and his Chapter. These decided in favour of reform: Sülte was to admit one or two reformed brethren from outside and to lend two or three of its own brethren to other reformed houses in which they might learn their future part. The bishop and the Windesheim Chapter chose Busch for the role of visiting exemplar.

So the prior of Wittenberg gave me a shilling for pocket-money* and a clerk as my companion, saying: "Beloved brother, you will be with those folk: I would rather sit in some closet where I saw neither

* *Pro bibalibus*, literally, "for Trinkgeld".

sun or moon all the while, than be where you will be: so well do I know those fellows." This he said in the faintness of his heart; as for me, my heart swelled in my belly. The whole land was plague-strickent hen, especially Hildesheim. When I went to Wittenberg I caught the sickness; but when I turned towards Hildesheim it seemed to me that I had taken a breath of good fresh air; and thus I reflected that it was the Lord God's pleasure that I should go to Hildesheim. So I came to Sülte at eventide and was very kindly received by the provost,* Johann Driburg, in his kitchen. Then came a priest, Sir Albrecht Bonsdorp, saying: "the *domini* and brethren of the monastery have just come up from the city, full of strong ale, and are sitting in the galilee outside the church. If this father comes to them, they will slay him." So the provost, a man sixty years of age, said: "I have no place for him save only that he should sleep in the dormitory, with a brother of reasonably good will, Johann Engelken." "Well," thought I, "here is good news for a beginning!" So, because his bed was narrow, I slept that night in this brother's cell upon a chest that stood there. (p. 411.)

* In the monasteries of Austin canons, the head was called *prior* or *provost*, very seldom *abbot*.

CHAPTER XIII

THE TUG OF WAR

THE further story of Sülte must be told in some detail, since it is not only the first of Busch's great battles, but thoroughly typical of the rest.

Busch soon saw that "they kept no discipline, in choir or refectory, dormitory or cloister". In the midst of the church services "one was sitting, another standing, a third walking about.... Each did as he would, reverencing neither God nor man." But he contained himself for a week. Then he began to remonstrate with the provost and brethren. "I see that ye have no reform; ye have not the manners of Religious, but walk as worldly folk.... If ye will not accept reform from me, I will commit the matter to the Bishop and his Chapter.... The provost answered: 'Tell us what we must observe, and we will gladly listen.'" Then Busch's first stroke was against *proprietas*. He went with the provost from cell to cell and removed all private possessions found there or in the cupboards. Next he insisted on silence, as Canon Law requires for monasteries, in choir, dormitory and refectory. "This also they accepted, but kept it ill, especially when they were by themselves." He introduced Scripture-reading at meals, "and they obeyed me very well at all points, because I put my wishes before them not austerely as commands, but compassionately and by way of petition". Thus, gradually, he persuaded them to outward conformity with the Windesheim observances.

But he felt the insecurity of his position, and sought about for powerful allies. His first and strongest was the bishop's chancellor, already mentioned. He enlisted also four other notable persons at the bishop's court; especially "Johann Reem, the Bishop's official at his castle of Steuerwald, whom all the ancient brethren feared mightily; for he was a strong and efficient jailor of prisoners at that castle, and they dreaded to fall into the hands of one who, at my request, could take perverse and disobedient brethren at midnight from the monastery and clap them into the stocks and correct them at his castle". Further, Busch begged from his fellow-Windesheimer, the Prior of (now reformed) Richenberg, two reformed brethren to keep him company as teachers. One was an able business man and accountant; this man put an end to the old system by which the brethren had been accustomed to divide the revenues at the end of the year and put their dividends each into his own purse. He thus saved in his first year more than forty pounds for the monastery; probably equivalent to at least £800 to-day. The ancient brethren saw that there was no hope of breaking this iron phalanx of three Windesheimers; so there was no open opposition or even grumbling.

But Busch saw that these men's dead weight would always frustrate any such complete reform as he desired. So he got leave from the bishop and his allies to transport two of these "ancients" to some house where they would see what true reform meant. One, an ex-provost, was to be sent to Richenberg, and the other to Wittenberg. The two victims, in face of this proposition made to them in their chapter-house, "begged leave of absence for a time from the monastery, according to their wont. Then those eminent ecclesiastics asked my counsel in the matter. I answered: 'I dare not advise that', for I feared that on the first day of their going forth they would fall into fornication, since I found that none of them had kept chastity, as it was publicly noised abroad; nay, some of them have children living even to the present day." Their petition was therefore rejected. One, the ex-provost, scaled the convent wall that night by a ladder and fled into apostasy. His friends had sufficient influence to beg him off from the penalties of this crime, on condition of his spending one day in the convent prison without light or lantern. The other did indeed go to Wittenberg according to order, but slunk away three days later, and returned only in order to avoid imprisonment by the bishop. With these men, as with all the other ancient brethren, Busch had a serious difficulty. They had been accustomed to spend "certain years" outside the monastery, acting actually or nominally as parish priests to the priory's appropriated churches. They now besought Busch daily for such licences; "and I was very scrupulous here, since, when they were outside, they would not keep God's precepts; yet on the other hand, while they were all together in the convent it could not be duly reformed, since they feared not God and had little reverence for men". He sought counsel from three heads of reformed houses and a canon lawyer.

They all answered with one voice saying: "If all your ancient brethren stay together in the monastery, you will never perfectly reform it, since they will not change their life or keep the Rule. It is therefore best to give your brethren licence whensoever they beg for it, so long as they return not together, but one after one year, another after two, and so on at different times, after three or four or five or six or nine or ten years and so forth. Meanwhile, receive other reformed brethren, and learned secular clerics ready for reform, with whom ye may keep due regular observance; and then these others, returning one by one, must needs conform to you in all things. Thus you will be able, step by step, to reform your monastery. Moreover, let the brethren who beg for absence promise to live as priests in the world; then, if you find the contrary, you will be able to correct them. For they will bear themselves better in the world, for fear of men, than they bear themselves now in the monastery, where, when they are by themselves, they fear no man." Thenceforth I did thus; and so from that time the house began to reach full reform.

Busch was first appointed "reformator" at Sülte, and then prior, the sexagenarian provost being a mere figure-head. In 1440 he resigned in Busch's favour. He was not reformed himself, but favourable to reform, and gladly laid down his office in exchange for the appropriated parsonage of Lunne. As he now said to Busch: "I have sat on the horse, and I leave it to you; henceforth I sit upon my ass." There were difficulties then with the bishop, who demanded fifteen florins for confirming Busch in his new office. The old provost had advised the bishop to defer this claim, saying: "I know this man Busch; he will give you nothing beforehand, lest he seem to buy his office simoniacally; but after his confirmation we will so order matters that ye shall well have something." Busch, even afterwards, refused to be party to what seemed a simoniacal gift.

When the Bishop heard this he said: "I am not holier than the Pope, who took from me more than 300 ducats for my consecration as Bishop: yet this provost of Sülte thinks to get his office for nothing!" It was then reported that he would seize the two cows of our monastery, since he would by all means get some gain from this business.

I learned afterwards that a certain true friend of reform satisfied his will in that matter. (p. 421.)

In the next two years Busch received three trustworthy clerics as novices, one of whom afterwards became sub-prior under him: then candidates came more frequently, and he was able to send some as reformers to other houses. But meanwhile the ancient brethren were far from tranquil. Six were now out "in the world", under promise to live as priests. These "all became disobedient, and thus fell under the Bishop's excommunication". Meanwhile

almost all the city murmured against us because their own sons were expelled from Sülte, and we strangers had entered into their goods and their labours; though in fact they had not been expelled but had prayed with great insistence for a certain time of absence and had obtained it with difficulty. One of them, Wilhelm by name, drew his knife upon me in the cloister, threatening to thrust it into my body if I would not fulfil his wish forthwith. Another of the ancient brethren stood by me on that occasion, and said "If thou dost so, I will drive into your throat these tongs which I have in my hand". Then the first cried at the top of his voice *Joduit, joduit!* [the ancient Saxon battle-cry]. Then all the brethren leapt forth from their cells and gathered in the cloister where we were. So I led that brother to my cell and fulfilled his will, giving him money for the brass pot that belonged to him and his children, and that he had given up for our kitchen. Then one of the ancients, standing outside his cell, cried: "Wilhelm, if you need help, we will easily call three hundred men of the city to your aid." Then answered our procurator Herman Lau: "Boast not greatly; we also, if need be, will get three hundred men from the city to stand and fight for us." For his blood-brother and his friends were none of the least among the citizens. But, when I had Brother Wilhelm alone in my cell, I contented him with the price of his pot, and thus he remained in peace. Another brother, Friedrich Peynis, who was then outside the monastery, put a long ladder to the window of my sleeping-cell (having waded barefoot into the precincts by a ford that he knew), and would have slain me in my bed while his fellows outside gave him help. But, when he had climbed a few steps, by God's inspiration he said within himself: "Thou hast many grievous sins upon thee; wilt thou now add greater crimes?" Therefore in compunction he left the ladder and cast his naked knife into the river, and returned to his fellows by the way by which he had come. A third, standing outside our cemetery and I within, cried to me in wrath and impatience: "Thou wert first our teacher and reformer, then our prior, and now our provost set over us. Thou and thine are now in possession of our monastery, and here am I without, knowing not how and when I shall return. One provost of the cathedral at Hildesheim was slain in the castle of Steuerwald; if I had known that thou wouldst get full dominion over our monastery, how should I have cared if I had died also in Steuerwald castle for killing thee?" I answered: "The sooner you did that, the more I should love you; for then you would perforce worship my entrails as relics, and I should go the sooner to heaven." Hearing this, that I should have no small joy to be worthy of death for holy reform, he departed in confusion of heart. A fourth said: "I would not slay Father Busch, but I would advise how he should be slain as it were by himself. For he sleeps in an upper chamber, one story higher than any of us. If parched peas were strewn over that stair, then, by night, when he hastened to matins and trod upon the peas, he would fall headlong and break his neck; and it could not be proved that any man had done this." These and many other like evils, in word and in deed, beset me at the beginning of this reform; but it would be too tedious to repeat them.

The six brethren who were "out in the world", weary of living in their respective parishes under at least some semblance of priestly decorum, longed again for the fleshpots of Sülte. Therefore they appealed to the Metropolitan, the Archbishop of Mainz. He appointed a judge, who absolved them from the sentence of excommunication under which they had fallen by disobedience to the Bishop of Hildesheim. Busch, however, at once intervened and brought the true facts to light, so that the judge reversed his decision. "Thus they were thenceforth held as excommunicated and interdicted throughout the diocese of Hildesheim. Therefore, expelled from the city and in great shame, they promised the bishop forty florins if he would bring them back to the monastery, even by force. He accepted this promise, and fixed a day for their return." Busch, hearing of this, went straight to the Hildesheim chapter, which was sitting at that moment. He told them plainly that in that case he would resign at once, and take the reformed brethren away with him to reformed houses. They asked time to think it over. After a while they sent to him two dignitaries, who pleaded: "My lord Provost, bear with it for a while that the lord Bishop of Hildesheim should earn the money promised him by your ancient brethren; then, as soon as they have come in, he will cast them forth by help of the brethren that same night." Busch indignantly refused to receive them for a single day. The chapter consulted again, and finally promised to support him against the bishop.

Next day the Bishop sent letters under his seal demanding the readmission of the ancient brethren: these letters were backed up by the magistracy of Hildesheim and the Duke of Brunswick. "Moreover, three hundred citizens wished to come forth to us with them; but the consuls had forbidden that by counsel of the Burgomaster. Sitting in my cell, I saw them coming forth from the city; but I bade shut all the doors of the monastery." He satisfied the messengers by explaining that all his doings at Sülte had been in virtue of powers formally conferred upon him by bishop and chapter: he himself would come down next day and meet the ancient brethren in face of the assembled chapter. Meanwhile, however, the ancients and their supporters took advantage of this parley to slip in, before the door could be shut upon them. The consuls commanded the citizens to retire. The ancients "cast away the black mantles which they wore over their linen rochets (as is usual in our Order), and, strutting about without hoods, and their heads on high and their arms akimbo, rejoiced that they had thus gotten their monastery by force". Busch reported this to the chapter. They, "after long deliberation, considered that the Bishop and Magistracy were agreed upon the residence of the ancient brethren in their monastery. Therefore they answered nothing concerning the permanence of the reform: but, if I wished, I and the brethren whom I had clothed or received for profession might go whither we would. Put not your trust in princes!"

A Cistercian abbot, Busch's fellow-visitor and reformer, counselled him to hold his ground all the same. He had already taken an important step.

I had spoken with two of the ancient brethren, Wilhelm and Gottfried, saying: "The Bishop will not suffer me to be thus troubled by you; and, when he comes, you will be the first whom he will arrest, since you have sworn obedience to me and not kept it." They answered: "We beseech you to let us go; we will gladly depart." Therefore those two, with my consent, went forth from us. The people without asked them where the others were; and these two made answer: "They lie already in prison, and we ourselves have scarce escaped!" The people, believing this, sent them food to eat. At my command, an answer was given across the river: "They must not eat."

Busch then made terms with his two worst adversaries by granting them the parsonage of Hotteln, which was evidently a desirable position. So was it, again, with the third pair; with them also he could only make a covenant that they should behave themselves in their parishes.

When these compacts had been concluded, they begged for something to eat, for it was the twelfth hour; also that, since we were now agreed, I should go and get them absolved from their excommunication and interdict. I answered: "I will not leave this monastery unless you first depart." Otherwise they would have shut the door upon me: they would have stayed within and I without, to no small peril of the whole reform. So, after dinner, they went forth before me; and, as men under excommunication and interdict, they dared not enter the city. When I entered the city I was asked where "our novices" were, to wit, these ancient canons. I answered: "They have now left us." The Burgomaster said: "Wherefore have ye let them go? The Bishop would have fetched them thence this night, and would have set them in the stocks at his castle of Steuerwald." On the morrow the Bishop absolved them at my request. From that hour all attacks and reproaches against me, from them and their friends, ceased immediately. For they had been in the monastery, and had left it again of their own free will. (p. 425.)

This was not Busch's hardest fight, by far, in the course of his long years as reformer. But, as well as any other, it shows us the man himself; enthusiastic, bold, pertinacious, and yet with a fund of common-sense and diplomacy. There were canonized saints in the van of these fourteenth-century reforms—St Bernardino of Siena, St John Capistrano, St Vincent Ferrer—but none whose work was more methodical and enduring than that of Busch and his companions.

CHAPTER XIV

RECALCITRANT SISTERS (1)

THE nun, by Roman Canon Law, was the Bride of Christ. If she broke the vow of chastity, this was not mere fornication or adultery, but incest, just as it was incest between a priest and the woman whom he confessed, between Spiritual Father and Daughter.(1) In virtue of this theory and of the proverbial "frailty of the sex" in the Middle Ages, nuns were kept under restrictions unknown to the men's houses. Especially, from the very first years of the fourteenth century, Boniface VIII's bull *Periculoso* had insisted for the nuns upon a rule of claustration long since abandoned by the monks. In the sixty-sixth chapter of St Benedict's Rule, it is not contemplated that the ordinary monk, under ordinary circumstances, should ever go outside his precincts. The Saint agreed here with St Jerome, that a monk out of his monastery is a fish out of water: his natural end is spiritual death. Yet as early as about A.D. 1200, an earnest Benedictine complained that his brethren were almost as ubiquitous as the friars became later on: "everywhere in the streets and market-places".(2) The Augustinian Rule had no such stringent clause, but it prescribed that the canons should go abroad only two by two, for avoidance of sin or suspicion; and its expositors specified "frequent wanderings forth" as one of the main causes of monastic decay.(3) Boniface VIII, taking his ground explicitly on the too-frequent scandals in nunneries, bound them down in future to the strictest terms of St Benedict's chapter 66. His bull was seldom really kept. Attempts to enforce it became one of the chief causes of friction between visitors and visitees.(4) Equally great was the difficulty of *proprietas*. Nunneries were scarcely ever endowed from the first on anything like the men's scale. Business management, again, was far harder for women, especially when they were forbidden to move about freely and supervise their various possessions. Thirdly, the nunneries were used as dumping-grounds for younger children on an even greater scale than the men's houses. Therefore frequently even in England, and far more often on the Continent, the common endowment had shrunk to very little. Parents sent in their girl with a dowry far smaller than marriage would have required: and later in case of necessity they supplied her with money or dress or food. The sisters had thus become like paying guests at an alms-house; *proprietas* had taken the place of *paupertas* as the very foundation of the community.

By Busch's time these relaxations had become immemorial. Nobody could remember anything else; they were matters of ancient custom, which in the Middle Ages ranked beside law. The Council of Constance had set itself definitely, in the nineteenth to twenty-fourth chapters of its decrees, to break the evil customs down. Each nun must live from the common fund and in common, not upon her own little allowance from home. There must be regular claustration, neither nuns abroad nor men in the nunnery, since "very many nuns, too early professed, have been tempted by carnal lust and committed many offences which it is shameful to specify". Such claustration must be imposed upon them "under reminder of the Last Judgment, and threats of everlasting damnation". Zealous churchmen pointed out that all these prescriptions had been in Canon Law from time immemorial, and that this Law was paramount, so that any *consuetudo* contrary to its precepts was a mere *corruptela*. But human nature is stronger even than Canon Law; and the conflict was never more vividly painted than in Busch's visitations. On both sides a question of principle was at stake. To these poor women, of whom the majority would never have chosen the nunnery of their own accord, immemorial social custom was a far greater reality than such a document as their Rule—even if, which is not probable, more than two or three of them had ever read that Rule. The Canonist John of Ayton exactly expresses their mind in relation to Church law. In 1269, the Legate Ottobon (afterwards Pope Hadrian V) had published certain decrees, and added: "We strictly command, in virtue of holy obedience and with appeal to the Last Judgment, that they who find it expedient to visit the nunneries shall cause the statutes here decreed to be exactly obeyed." Upon this John of Ayton remarks (writing shortly before the Black Death):

Cause to be obeyed! but certainly this almost passeth the wit of mortal man; therefore we must here insert the proviso "so far as in them lieth"....For the nuns answer roundly to these statutes, as to others which have been decreed to check their wantonness: "The men who made these statutes sat well at their ease when they decreed these things against us, imposing such hard and intolerable restrictions!" Therefore we see plainly that these statutes are kept either ill or not at all. Wherefore then did the Holy Fathers thus labour to beat the air?

Let us take Busch's first full account of his own nunnery visitations. This was in 1455, when he had already passed a score of years as visitor and reformer. The nunnery which he now undertook was that of Wennigsen, near Hannover. He writes (p. 555):

We had the Bishop of Minden and the great folk of the land against us in all the towns; but we had for us Duke William the Elder of Brunswick, with the authority of the Pope and the Council of Basel. So the Duke, with his chief counsellor Ludolf von Barum, Roger the then prior of Wittenburg, and me, came into the nuns' choir. The prioress and all her nuns being assembled thither, the Lord Duke took off his cap and said in our presence: "Lady Prioress, and ye sisters all! I will that ye accept the reform and keep your Rule." They, standing with their hands folded on their breasts, answered with one voice: "We have all resolved in common and sworn together that we will not be reformed, nor keep our Rule. We pray you, compel us not to perjure ourselves." The Duke said: "Ye make an evil answer; be better advised." They left the choir, but came quickly back and falling on their knees, with their hands folded on their breasts, answered as before: "We have sworn together that we will not keep the reform: we pray you, make us not perjured!" The Duke again answered: "Your answer as yet is naught: therefore be better advised." So they went out, and came back again, and lying flat on their bellies on the choir pavement, with their hands folded on their breasts, they made the same reply for the third time....Then said the Duke: "Arise, I am not worthy that ye worship me." So they rose, and some of them exchanged angry words with the lord Ludolf von Barum, the Duke's councillor. Then I said to the Duke: "What profit is it that we stand here and bandy words with the nuns? Let us leave the choir and take counsel what to do now." So we departed from the choir round by the dormitory; and forthwith all the nuns lay down on their bellies in the choir with the arms and legs stretched out in the form of a cross, and bawled all through, at the top of their voices, the anthem *In the midst of life we are in death.*

We, hearing them chant like this, thought that it was that responsory: "*The heavens shall reveal the iniquity of Judas.*"* Wherefore the Duke was afraid, and feared lest his whole land should go to ruin. But I said to him: "If I were duke of this land, I would rather have that chant than a hundred florins; for it is no curse on your land, but rather a blessing and a dew from heaven: but to these nuns it is a sore rebuke and a sign of their reformation. But we are few here, four only; and the nuns are many. If they assailed us with their distaffs and with stones tied in their long sleeves, what could we do?(5) Let more be called to listen with us." Then the Duke went alone to their choir and said: "Ye chant this chant over your own bodies and souls." Then to his servants, who stood with the nuns in their choir, he said: "Come ye hither to us." So they leapt forth straightaway to us. The nuns therefore, having finished their anthem, followed those servants towards us, thinking that we would open their chests and cupboards by force and carry all off with us. So when they were all gathered round us the Duke said: "How were ye not afraid to sing the anthem *Media Vita* over me? I stretch my fingers to God's holy gospels, and swear that ye must reform yourselves, or I will not suffer you in my land. If the Bishop of Minden and your friends will withstand me in this matter, I will either drive them forth from my land, or I myself will take my staff and depart thence."

That startled the nuns, who now begged for a respite to take counsel with their friends and kinsfolk. This was allowed: a fresh day was fixed, and the Duke found himself face to face with a crowd of lay-folk demanding, as the nuns had demanded for themselves, that the convent should be permitted to go on in its old ways. The Duke naturally rejected this petition: and "Forthwith their friends and relations rushed away from the monastery, their esquires following them with their shields." The Duke was left standing outside the convent gate. He summoned the nuns to admit him: they announced that they had lost their keys. The Duke and his men, with the help of "certain countryfolk and bondmen", got hold of a long and heavy wooden bench with which they battered the gate open in true military style,

as the Duke himself had often done at the siege and storm of fortresses. So, when the gate was burst open, we entered the convent

* This was a misuse of Job xx. 27 (similar to that of the funeral anthem just above) for a curse on the principle of the Black Mass. A Church Council at Cologne had expressly forbidden this abusive employment of sacred formulas.

precincts and went up into their choir. There they all lay flat on their bellies, each in the shape of a cross, girt all round with a circle of little wooden or stone images of saints, each a cubit high and with burning tapers between them: for they hoped that, though their walls and bars could not defend them against the Duke and us, yet at least the saints thus invoked with tapers might vouchsafe to protect them. So, when they saw the Duke and us standing round them, they all rose up and came to us. Then the Lord Duke doffed his hood or cap and said before them all: "If ye will yet reform yourselves, then I will suffer you in my land; if not, then chariots are here ready to bear you from my territories, never perchance to return." They answered: "Cast away those monks from our necks, then we will gladly do all your bidding." To which he answered: "All that I say and do to you, is at their advice", pointing to Roger the Prior of Wittenberg and to me. So I said then to a nun who stood by me: "Sister, do as the Lord Duke would have you do." She answered me in indignation: "You are not my brother, why do you call me *sister*? My brother is clad in steel, and you in a linen frock!" She thought I had insulted her in that I called her "sister", and not "Klosterfrau" [*claustralem virginem*].*

At last the nuns agreed to accept the reform if a provost were given them. So Sir Dierck Kornacker, apparently a neighbouring incumbent, was chosen for their provost; and all the reformers together drew up an ordinance specifying "how many dishes of flesh and how many of milk food they were to have daily, night and morning; moreover how many furs, garments, shoes, vests and other necessaries, they should have yearly; so that they and their friends and kinsfolk might be fully satisfied". This was clear, and the Duke went home, leaving the other officials to stay the night in the convent. At dusk, the nuns sent to speak with their provost, who presently came back with a long face: "My ladies the Prioress and the nuns say that they will not abide by their promise, but will remain as they are and as they have been." Busch therefore sent a messenger in hot haste to the Duke,

praying him to come to us at daybreak with so many men in his train that, if perchance the Bishop of Minden or the nuns' friends from the castles wished to resist us and him and hinder the reformation, then

* Compare the mission-preacher Pépin, about 1500, on those "many nuns who have more vanity than piety", and are indignant if you call them *Sister* instead of *Madame* (A. Méray, II, 167).

he might put them to flight with a strong arm. So next morning Duke William came to us with 200 or 300 men; for he had scarcely gone a mile from us the evening before: and he said to me: "My lord and father Provost"—for so he was wont to call me—"I would have chosen that the Bishops of Hildesheim or Minden, or the Counts of Hoyen had defied me in mortal enmity than I should thus come with a band of soldiers against women and nuns.(6) But because you have so advised me and because it is for the health of my soul, therefore I have done and still do willingly what you desire of me."

The nuns now saw that resistance was useless, and all but one consented at Busch's bidding to swear obedience directly to the prioress. The one recalcitrant nun fell down soon afterwards in a fit, and was carried senseless to the infirmary: a fortunate event for Busch; for "the others then saw how the Lord was with us"; and all overt resistance was at an end. The nuns were forced to give up their private property, even to their cooking vessels; some however did this with such impatience as to break off the legs of their beloved cauldrons. Meanwhile Busch and Prior Roger were busy, one at each corner of the chapter-house, confessing and absolving the nuns from the excommunication incurred through their former disobedience. One cannot help pitying the poor creatures; portionless daughters of noble families, dumped into a convent because the medieval world had no other place for them; aimless creatures to whom the Three Essential Vows had never been a serious reality until now. It is impossible to read these visitations without feeling how human the unreformed Religious were. The greatest weakness of the Middle Ages was this perpetual ferment of thoroughly human affections and frailties under cover of a superhuman theory which was so seldom realized in practice.

The Duke went straightway to the Bishop of Minden, and frightened him so thoroughly that at last he not only consented to the reforms, but later on "even sent prelates of his diocese to help us". Busch, however, in spite of all his tact and patience, still had to face the risks which always threatened the too sincere monastic reformer. He had left the nuns surprised and relieved at the moderation with which he now used his complete victory, and was on his way to Wittenberg. But

when I was come to a defile in the forest, where there was scarce room for my chariot to pass, two fellows were waiting there for me, one on the right in a linen frock with a long javelin, and the other with a bent bow and a steel-headed arrow; for they would have pierced and slain me, and cried to my driver "Wait, wait!" So I said: "Good fellows, what would ye with me? desire ye aught?" One made reply: "Ye see well that we desire something." "What then?" said I. They answered: "Ye have shut the nuns up in Wennigsen, and they will never more come forth"; and he who bore the javelin ran straight to the chariot as if he would thrust me through, while the other raised his bow and arrow to shoot me: yet he was in fear, and his hands shook for dread. Then I saw death before my eyes, and thought within myself: "This is where thou wilt arise on the Last Day: for here thou shalt receive thy death-wound in breast or heart or head": for the wicker-work of the chariot prevented them from wounding me below the belt. And indeed I had with me in the carriage a hand-axe, wherewith I might somehow have defended myself if they had come near; for their bellies would have been as vulnerable as mine. Yet I spake fair and peaceable words to them, especially on hearing that they would attack me for the aforesaid nuns' sake. To him who was next me I said: "Good fellow! give me your hand"; and stretched out one of my hands to him. And I added: "We are all at one now—Bishop, Duke, the nuns' friends in the towns and even the nuns themselves. We are all at one now: give me your hand." Then he of the javelin stretched out his hand to me saying, "Good sir, you should leave the nuns at peace, for many folk, at least ten times, have lain in wait for you to take you or rob you of your horse and all that you have, to wound you or do you much harm; but the Lord Jesus hath preserved you hitherto. So leave them alone now."

The other ruffian presently moved off, whistling and raising his hand to prevent his band from coming out of the wood; and Busch went on his way in peace. The Prior of Wittenberg vowed that he would never go that road again: but Busch stoutly declined to be frightened from his duty, declaring that "he was not of so poor a stuff as to be unworthy of martyrdom": and the more timid prior was ashamed to desert him.

There were no more serious difficulties at Wennigsen: but other convents gave him greater trouble on the whole than this. At the next, Mariensee, "the nuns lived irregularly, dissolutely and incontinently, with money and property of their own, having the Bishop of Minden as their protector in this matter. For, in consideration of money received from them, he gave them power to remain in their former evil life." Yet the Duke of Brunswick, although this was contrary to the bishop's will, compelled them to reform themselves, and compelled the bishop to send him an ambassador for that purpose. "At the first visitation, the Abbess and her nuns climbed to the roof of the choir and ran about there like cats." The Duke proposed sending his retainers to scale the battlements with ladders; but, as Busch said, "this would be inexpedient: for the nuns would cast down stones to prostrate or slay the first who ascended". He finally brought them down by catching a stray nun and sending her up with a message to the effect that, unless they capitulated at once, they should be taken by force and carted off without mercy into banishment beyond the Duke's frontiers. When they were down,

the Duke asked the Abbess whether she would keep her Rule and stay in her convent; for, if she refused, she should go forthwith into a carriage and depart from his lands. So she replied at once: "I will willingly do all that you wish." Then I put the same question to all the other nuns, one by one, and all answered, "willingly!" save one young girl who scorned to obey. Then said I to the Lord Duke: "This sister scorns to obey—nay she even contradicts." So, as soon as he saw her perverse will, he stood and caught hold of her, striving to drag her to the chariot. But when he had caught her in his arms, she fell backwards and lay supine on the earth, and the Duke on her, and the other nuns on the Duke, one thrusting another upon him; so that the Duke could not rise up from her, especially because his arms were kept crushed beneath her shoulders. But, we, seeing him lie like this, let him alone, awaiting the end of the matter. At last he freed one arm from underneath her, with which he thrust away the nuns who lay on him, hurting them and making bloody bruises on their arms; for he was a man, and the nuns were like weak boys without strength to resist. When he had thrust these nuns away, he raised the back of the nun on whom he lay and freed his other arm and rose to his feet, saying to his vassals and servants standing round: "Wherefore did ye suffer your liege Lord to be thus trampled under foot by nuns?" One of them answered for the rest: "Gracious Lord, we have often stood by your side where men shot with bows and cross-bows; tell us only what we must do, and we will gladly do it"; so he said: "Whomsoever of the nuns I shall seize, do ye also seize her." He answered: "Willingly, gracious Lord." So the nuns, seeing that so it must be, consented with one accord to be reformed. For she who had been so crushed, after regaining her breath, consented also with us in all things.

They were duly confessed and absolved for their disobedience, and a solemn *Te Deum* was sung in the choir; but Busch noted that the nuns sang "in a doleful voice".

For indeed there was still more to come. The actual carrying out of the reforms was very sour to them at first.

> They utterly refused it, and when we departed from them, they began the anthem *Media Vita* in the choir, and sang it at us at the top of their voices. They followed us through the church with this chant, lighting also waxen tapers upon us and hurling them to the ground against us. (7) Moreover one young nun followed us outside the church into the cemetery, singing thrice the words *Holy God, holy and strong, holy and immortal*; then, kneeling down, she thrice bit the dust in sign of malediction against us, and cast stones and earth after us.

Busch, however, had too strong support to be defied: he came back to the nunnery with three reformed nuns, one of whom was made Abbess of Mariensee, and the reformation of the convent was thus carried out.

Grube is scandalized (p. 160) at this lay interference in monastic reform; he seems never to have asked himself what would have happened if Busch had had no physical force at his back, in the face of these infuriated women and the ruffians who were ready to fight for them outside. For more than 200 years repeated attempts had been made from within the Church to reform the monasteries by purely spiritual means. From the great Lateran Council onwards (A.D. 1215) these efforts only served to show how deeply the evil was rooted; and meanwhile the monasteries, by the confession even of apologists, grew not better but worse. A hundred years before Busch's time, the author of *Piers Plowman* had pointed out the only possible remedy. He hated a lollard worse than he hated a friar, yet he agreed entirely with Wycliffe in asserting that nothing short of physical lay interference would reform the monasteries (B, x, 312). Busch's narrative shows us again and again the impossibility of overcoming, by purely spiritual weapons, men and women who relied on their own theoretical spirituality and their name of Religious, even while their daily lives belied that profession. These disobedient, proprietary and incontinent nuns of Wennigsen, who had reduced their Rule to a mere farce, had yet complete confidence in the spiritual power of their images and their candles and their silly perversions of Church anthems into maledictions against this papal commissioner. We see here a natural result of that doctrine of the Mass as an *opus operatum*, which had been evolved in order to protect Church authority by drawing an absolute distinction between the character of the ministrant and the efficacy of the sacrament. The nuns' belief in their own curses, and the Duke's fear that there might be something in them, are not more absurd than when our English Austin Canon, John Myrc, bids the parish priest teach his flock that he who has simply been at Mass (with no proviso of attention to the service) is immune for the rest of that day from sudden death or blindness.(8) Nor, again, than the teaching that the words of the Mass should not be translated into the tongue of the profane vulgar, since the mere hearing of a Gospel and Epistle read in the unknown tongue has its spiritual effect, even as the charm works upon a deaf adder.

Miss Eckenstein, in her *Woman under Monasticism*, assures us that "in the records of Busch comparatively few charges of a coarse nature are brought against nunneries" (p. 420). Here, as elsewhere, she shows complete ignorance of his actual Latin, and has evidently relied entirely upon Dr Grube's friendly silence. The fact is that Busch brings the most definite and sweeping charges of immorality against seven out of the twenty-four nunneries which he had to reform; while by implication he condemns them all. Mariensee we have just seen. At both Marienwerder (p. 567) and Barsinghausen they were living "in incontinence and disobedience" (pp. 566–7). Derneborch (p. 588), Heyninghen (p. 600), Stederborch (p. 604) and Frankenberg (p. 607) moved him to similar judgments. Almost equally significant is his praise, where he does find a clear bill. At Weinhausen (p. 633) "these nuns kept their chastity well; for their lady the ancient abbess ruled them very strictly; for they held her in much fear and reverence and called her 'Gnädige Frau' because of her noble birth". At Wülfinghausen (p. 639) he complimented the nuns publicly: "I have never heard any suspicion of you in the matter of continence and chastity"; but he had just described with emphasis the unusual care with which these particular ladies were cloistered. At Fischbeck, again (p. 640), "they keep their chastity most diligently, because they are shut up and have no conversation with men". He also goes on to describe the strict precautions taken there, and how even the usual bed-curtains were not permitted in the dormitory. The very emphasis laid upon these three cases tells its own tale; but on p. 587 Busch is still more explicit.

> We see clearly [he says] that no convent of nuns, of whatever Order they may be (and of these there is no small number in Saxony, Meissen, and Thuringia) have persevered long in their good purpose, in holy life, and in proper reformation, without reformed fathers [to look after them]. For when nuns and sisters do not confess at certain seasons, do not communicate, do not keep up the confession of faults in Chapter at least every week, are not visited yearly by their fathers (as the Pope hath commanded that the Bishops either personally or by deputy should visit even the exempt houses every year, under his mandate and under penalty of mortal sin), then we have frequently seen and heard how such nuns and sisters quickly fall from the observance of the Rule and from religious life into a life of dissoluteness hateful to God and man, to the grievous peril of their soul and to their eternal damnation. First, losing the fear of God through the dissoluteness of their life, they fall into *proprietas* in small things; then in greater things; and then, descending farther to the personal possession of money and garments, they at last rush into the lusts of the flesh, and the incontinence of outward senses, and so to wickedness of act, not fearing to give themselves up to all filth and uncleanness. So they go not up to the stars but down to the abyss of hell.

Therefore, he urges, let prelates and nuns be careful to keep even the apparently insignificant provisions of the Rule. There is a similar passage on p. 524, where he remarks how a monk's possession of private property led almost certainly to incontinence. Finally, when he is recording the work of an excellent abbess, he remarks (p. 585): "For it is no small merit to preserve so many virgins—more than thirty persons of the weaker sex—in the custody of their virginity, in the rigour of the Order, in purity of conscience and due peace; a thing which I should truly esteem higher, from my own experience, than to work miracles." And, praising her elsewhere (p. 688), he writes: "She kept her convent so well that it is unheard of in the memory of man that any of her nuns have broken their vow of chastity, as we have oftentimes heard in many other nunneries of Saxony and Westphalia."

We must make allowance for Busch, though less than for the average medieval disciplinary enthusiast, in his attitude towards womankind. There is no reason why we should distrust what he twice reports, that convents which dreaded his coming, and had heard of him as an ogre, found him in practice a sympathetic confessor (p. 589). On the other hand, we cannot ignore his incidental remark on p. 597. After he had done much to reform that convent where the nun had trapped him in the cellar, and had acted for three years as confessor there, one clique plotted to get greater freedom by procuring a Cistercian abbot as visitor in Busch's place. The plot succeeded; the nunnery was transferred to the Cistercians. The philosopher in Busch recognizes that "nuns clad in [the Cistercian] grey have often as fair souls as those in white". But, through its wilful inconstancy, this particular convent "lost both St Augustine and me from its precincts". Busch then notes that, as things turned out, the confusion of the times involved them in such difficulties that "they would afterwards have gladly paid 1000 florins to have me back as their father, and St Augustine, in whose name they had first been founded, as patron and defender". But they had forgotten all former benefits, according to that common proverb:

> Gratia nulla perit nisi gratia sola sororum;
> Sic fuit, est et erit: *ondanc* in fine laborum.*

It is a thousand pities that the sisters had not enough Latin to immortalize in a distich their own view of some of these transactions.

* "Gratitude perisheth not, save only that of the Sisters; so was it, is, and shall be: *unthank* at the end of your labours."

CHAPTER XV

RECALCITRANT SISTERS (2)

OTHER fifteenth-century evidence shows that few reformers of nunneries came even so near to success as Busch. Cardinal Nicolas Cusanus enjoyed official and personal advantages which were given to few reformers in all recorded history. Yet, even in his own diocese and the neighbouring districts, he could do little against evil customs which by this time were immemorial. As his latest orthodox biographer writes, "One condition of reform should have been a normal system of recruitment for the nunneries." These younger daughters of the nobility were almost essentially undisciplined. In 1441, "to prevent the Benedictine nuns [of Augsburg] from receiving friends in their convent and from going out as freely as though they had not been cloistered, the iron railings had to be replaced by walls, and then the walls had to be built higher and guarded by town soldiers".(1) One of Cusanus's first acts as bishop had been to decree the complete claustration of all nunneries, in obedience to the famous bull *Periculoso* of Boniface VIII. A year later, it was found that six of the most conspicuous had paid no attention to this decree.(2) Under his own nose, at Brixen, the Franciscan nuns defied him, defied a papal brief, and after more than two years of struggle it needed another envoy directly from the Pope, and a revolution effected by him in the constitution of this nunnery, to arrive at a reform.(3) The greatest nunnery in his whole diocese was that of Sonnenburg in the Pusterthal, "where the young daughters of the Tyrolese nobility led the freest and most luxurious life under cover of the veil". These women held out against him for nearly five years; for here he was unable to use his papal instructions in their fulness, by invoking the help of the secular arm. The duke wavered between the noble culprits and this inconveniently officious bishop, whose "reforms" interfered with the time-honoured disposal of portionless daughters. After four years the abbess was brought to promise obedience and reform at a public assembly in Brixen.

But scarcely had [the Visitors] begun their reform this second time; scarcely had they again forbidden the uninterrupted journeys to [public] baths, to pilgrimage-churches and to wedding-feasts (for which the Abbess paid from the abbey funds, under the strange pretext of protecting her convent from the Cardinal's harsh treatment); scarcely had they forbidden this and, apparently, limited the full free use of the conventual income, when the demon of contradiction arose again.

Cusanus was finally provoked to measures which led to the one serious blot upon his long visitatorial work. The impenitent party among the nuns stirred up the tenantry against this "oppressive ecclesiastic"; a numerous band of armed serfs flocked to the half-reformed convent, and the cardinal's men, whether mistakenly or, as they maintained, in pure defence, fell upon these rioters and drove them off with the loss of fifty dead. The story is told only by one chronicler, and is probably much exaggerated: but certainly force bred force: and the quarrel thus raised between Cusanus and the Count of Tyrol led finally to a war which involved both Pope and Emperor, and was ended only by an imperial judicial sentence given after Cusanus's death.

Almost at the same time John, Bishop of Eichstaedt (1445–64), describes at considerable length his difficulties, and his lack of complete success, in reforming the nunnery of St Walpurga. The nuns' noble kinsfolk were sometimes ready to support them in arms. The reform involved the dismissal of some sisters, who "wandered abroad with much disgrace". Of the rest, "some simulated obedience, in order that by feigned faith they might the more cautiously deceive". At one point, the reformers had to cast down part of the wall and enter the convent by storm. The reforming nuns whom the bishop introduced were subjected to insult. In his consolatory letter, he warned them how "you will find it a far heavier burden to remove abuses and to renew good manners, than if you were instituting from the first something good or orderly".(4)

The Dominican Nider, a few years earlier than this, alludes to a notorious case in which a nunnery had successfully resisted the concentrated reforming efforts of the Cardinal of Basel: but he gives no details. On the other hand, we have very full details of the Breslau case, accessible in Fr. F. Doelle's *Martinianische Reformbewegung*.(5) Here, as in several other difficult instances, the convent was of Clarisses, the Second Order of St Francis, nominally vowed to the extremes of poverty and the strictest claustration. Their earlier self-denial brought to them, as to the friars, extreme popularity. The men's churches were soon crowded with tombs of the neighbouring nobles and richer citizens, and the nunneries became favourite almshouses for their portionless daughters. The arrangement by which the nuns' confessors were chosen from among the friars, natural enough in itself, became fatal under any serious relaxation of discipline. At Breslau, in 1506, official documents show us the friars not only singing Masses for money in the Convent of the Clarisses, but also "bearing great responsibility" for the fact that the nuns "permitted and caused frivolous songs to be sung in their church, which tended rather to pastime and to indiscipline than to devotion". The Provincial Minister, Weygnant, stepped in and reformed this with the help of another Provincial, Henning. These two restricted considerably the intercourse between the two convents, even in Spiritual and Sacramental matters. Weygnant, at the same time, tried to reform the Clarisses; but they appealed to the Minister General against this trespass upon their "privileges"; and this General granted them his protection against all measures to be taken either by the Provincial or by the Custos of Breslau: "thus wrecking the work of reform."

Yet, when Weygnant had succeeded in reforming the males, the friars, he turned again to the nuns. But here again he failed, for this abbess at Breslau was a duchess, and the nuns were noble ladies who could count upon support from their kinsfolk or fellow-nobles. Abbess Elizabeth appealed to Duke Johann of Oppeln, who sent word to the magistrates of Breslau that the nuns must not be molested. Under this purely secular protection, the ladies long refused to recognize (what Church law prescribed most definitely) that they were immediately subject to their own ministers in all questions of ecclesiastical discipline. Next, they appealed to the Cardinal Protector of the Franciscan Order at Rome. From him they procured a decree that their "privileges" should be respected, and they should be permitted "to perform divine service in quiet". The next Provincial Minister, Henning, raised the question of reform again in 1507. Abbess Elizabeth was dead, and he proposed to come and exercise his official right of attending the coming election. "His commissary was despitefully handled by the nuns, and had to return without accomplishing anything." The rest of these almost interminable quarrels and lawsuits must be cut down here to a few sentences. The ducal family were partly in complete league with the nuns, and at least inclined, like the Bishop, to insist upon a compromise. Henning in fact waived many of his visitatorial rights, and fought now mainly for a legal election, since the nuns had met secretly and illegally and chosen for abbess another duchess, niece to the reigning princess. The Princess herself at one meeting cried "sit there, you devilish friars; may all the devils of hell fetch you!" The nuns were "permitted to sit almost all day in the parlour and talk with certain worthless clerics". Their resistance to reform was supported even by some Church dignitaries, accessible to bribes. Henning, "for the sake of the Lord Duke and other lords here", was driven backwards from compromise to compromise, yielding finally to the Duke's ultimatum that the false election must be confirmed, or he would drive the Franciscans from his land. Claustration was neglected, and some of the nuns ran away, "to the great scandal of the laity". Henning attempted in vain to put down the public singing, and to stop the abbess from encouraging a few favourite nuns in feasting and "disorderly life". For, all this time, the Cardinal Protector of the Order, in Rome, was supporting the rebels. He decided in favour of their "customs and privileges", and opposed the introduction of "novelties"—i.e. of strict observance of the Rule. It was in vain that the minister decreed, among other reforming statutes: "no sister, not even the Abbess, must in future hold communion, intimate companionship or special friendship with any priest whatsoever, whether regular or secular, nor with any layman: any sister who nourishes such a friendship must now give it up, under pain of excommunication, from which no ordinary confessor can absolve." The Pope left the whole Breslau affair, practically, to the Cardinal Protector. The nuns quarrelled even among themselves; there was a sort of civil war. After eight years of manful struggle for reform, Henning, whose legal rights were transparently sound, found himself condemned by the Cardinal Protector, who fined him forty-five ducats and five gulden for his pertinacity in holding out so long!

Henning then resigned an authority which his own immediate superiors, the Minister General and the Cardinal Protector, had reduced to mockery by tying his hands behind his back. Father Doelle writes:

> Subsequent events in the Convent of Clarisses brilliantly justified Henning's struggles for reform. For Christina Victorin, the Duchess's favourite nun, permitted herself forbidden intercourse outside the convent and, after the birth of a daughter, had to be expelled from the Order. Conditions thenceforward became so hopeless that, scarcely two years after Henning's condemnation [by the Cardinal Protector], the Breslau Magistracy found itself compelled to interfere directly in the reform of the nuns.

They complained to the Pope concerning "the dissolute life of the Clarisses...to the dishonour of the Apostolic See and the scandal of many folk: let them now be properly claustrated and compelled to observe their Rule". The bishop supported this complaint, and pleaded with the Cardinal Protector. Nothing, it seems, was done. Father Doelle's concluding words are: "Margarete von Tost remained Abbess until her death in 1531. In her closing years she had the experience that, as a consequence of neglected reform, it was precisely members of her convent who were the first to marry monks."

It would seem difficult to outdo this story: yet perhaps the slightly earlier affair of Klingenthal was even more scandalous. That case is all the more significant because it concerns Pius II, who talked much of reform when he had reached the papal throne, and who is celebrated by apologetic historians as having done all that could fairly be expected of a Pope in those days. Klingenthal was the richest abbey in Basel; it had been a centre of religious mysticism in the fourteenth century, but had rapidly decayed. Nicholas V vainly attempted to reform the house. Pius II, in 1456, committed the task to the Bishop of Basel and three abbots: to these he presently added the Bishop of Constance. They failed completely, and the Senate of Basel began to protest strongly against this scandal at their doors.

Backed up by many of the nobility, they appealed to Pius II in 1462, begging for a fresh papal commission and for the support of the great reforming legate, Cardinal Cusanus. Pius, in spite of the opposition of the Bishop of Constance, sent a bull of reform; but (writes Abbé Dacheux, who gives the facts in the fullest available form for ordinary readers) "this time again, we know not why, nothing was done".(6) In 1466 the convent caught fire, and rebellious nuns were suspected of incendiarism. The nuns went on selling wine, in spite of all prohibitions, and the Bishop of Constance still hindered the reform. The Senate now called in the Dominicans, to whom Klingenthal was nominally subject; but the bishop's intrigues obtained from Sixtus IV a bull confirming the nuns' privileges of exemption (1476). Better informed, he revoked this and committed the reform to the Dominicans, the Senate, the Bishop of Basel and the Governor of Upper Alsace. The Bishop of Constance was thus eliminated, and it might be thought that victory was assured, especially as the Minister Provincial of the Dominicans, Stubach, was a man of exceptional energy, courage and prudence.

But custom and privilege formed an almost inexpugnable fortress for offenders of sufficient desperation and obstinacy. The struggle was resumed in 1480. Stubach came to Klingenthal with a considerable committee of senators and distinguished clerics, headed by an ex-bürgermeister. Here let Abbé Dacheux speak.

At his prayer, Roth addressed the nuns. He begged them over and over again, in the most conciliatory terms, to collect in the chapter house and hear the communications which it was the Provincial Minister's duty to make. Here comes a scene which we blush to relate, remembering the habit which these wretched women wore. The sisters, forgetting all dignity, though they were mostly of noble family, answered these overtures only with cries and insults. When the Provincial caused the papal bulls to be read, they interrupted the reading and ran about in the refectory, singing and reciting the responsory "Mendacious men have surrounded me". In face of such a scandal, the Provincial asked the senators present to have the recalcitrant nuns shut up, and to sequestrate their goods and those of the convent until they submitted. The senators did not dare to go so far as this; they only posted sentinels at the gates to prevent all attempts at escape. On the 10th, at the Provincial's demand, the senate caused these perverse women to be imprisoned and kept under ward; and, since they obstinately refused to obey any one but the Bishop of Constance, the convent keys were forcibly taken from them. Such is the notarial report. The Provincial, in his own report to the Pope, adds that the nuns did not confine themselves to cries and insults while the bull was read; one had armed herself with a spit, another with a cudgel, a third with a sword; they had threatened to set fire to the house, and had demanded that the friars should be delivered up to them for strangling. The nuns, for their part, related and caused to be reported in Rome that they had been shamefully maltreated, and left half-dead.

The Provincial then brought thirteen nuns from the lately reformed convent of Engelporten; he solemnly installed them at Klingenthal and offered the other nuns the choice of accepting reform or leaving the house. They flatly refused. Stubach could only beg the Pope to give him help, without which he could not hope to succeed. He appealed to the Senate of Basel for evidence of his own moderation in this affair, and the nuns' scandalous behaviour. All but two nuns remained obdurate, relying upon help from their noble kinsfolk and the Bishop of Constance, who interfered now in contempt of the Pope's bull. Stubach, therefore, most reluctantly accepted a compromise negotiated by the great lay-folk of the district.

The original nuns were bound to render their accounts and to restore the objects belonging to the convent. In return for this, their own contributions were restored, and they were at liberty to withdraw into their own families or to other convents; moreover, for a whole year they were at liberty to change their minds and return to Klingenthal for submission to the new Rule. The past was to be forgotten and forgiven; and they bound themselves not to renew discussion on the recent happenings [January 28, 1480]. On the Monday before Candlemas they promised and signed all that was asked of them, 37 in all; but, from the first day onwards, they got rid of title-deeds, money, and the lesser seal of the convent.

Pope and Emperor now took this new community formally under their protection.

It seemed that all was over; for never had a reform been carried out under conditions more favourable for duration. But here came out the worst evils of that time: the weakness of the central power, the violence and greed of the feudal aristocracy, the selfishness of the citizens, and the actual impotence of the Papacy, disarmed and abandoned by all. Nothing will serve better to exonerate the Heads of the Church from the reproach of inability to reform the Church, than the new scene which will come before my readers.

A few of the old nuns returned to Klingenthal, and a few drifted to other convents; but "the majority led a very unmonastic life, raking in the dues and rents of their former convent, and giving receipts with the lesser seal which they had stolen". The reformers were supported, nominally at least, by four powerful cardinals in Rome, the Emperor, the Governor of Alsace, another of the greatest local nobles, and the Senate of Basel. The nuns offered an enormous bribe: but Rome stood firm. The reformers bought off the unfriendly Bishop of Constance with a sop of 5 florins a year: when he died, it cost them 900 florins to buy off his successor. The rebels offered 800 florins to Sigismund of Austria, who employed a robber-knight to seize two Basel citizens on the highway and thus intimidate the Senate. It was decided to accept arbitration from Sigismund and the Swiss Cantons. The great Swiss saint, Nicholas of Flue, worked for the reformers; but the arbitrators decided against them. The Pope, "wearied by these struggles, and incapable of helping effectively the cause of the reformed nuns", attempted a compromise. The Emperor decided for the reformers, but was powerless to enforce his decree. One of the reformed nuns was sent to plead at Rome, but without avail. Even Stubach had to yield at last: the reformed nuns were sent back to their old convents and the old rebels reinstated at Klingenthal.

Such [writes Dacheux] was the issue of this laudable enterprise. The most odious role was certainly that of Sigismund, whose receipt dated August 11, 1485, still exists among the convent archives of Klingenthal, an imperishable monument of his ignominy. The Pope's role was especially melancholy; but, to explain his apparent weakness, we may plead that there was scarcely any other possible choice: he yielded to considerations of more general interest and (in modern parlance) to diplomatic pressure. The Dominican General acted similarly; for the reformed sisters, in their despair when the whole world abandoned them, had written to him, "my lord General, we are amazed that you should be willing thus to ruin us, body and soul". The General answered them that the tranquillity of Basel was the main point; the sisters must think less of their own advantage than of that of the whole Order, of the province, of the convent and of the citizens; men must not be able to accuse a few nuns of having been the cause of so many evils and dissensions. There was, unfortunately, a certain amount of truth in this. Yet it is no less true that this solution was an immense scandal, deeply afflicting to all Christians who had zeal for reform. Moreover, the coping-stone of all was that at last the Dominicans were condemned to pay to the nuns who had returned to Klingenthal the enormous sum, for that time, of 11,500 florins as damages and interest. The pious virgins had demanded even 36,000, for disturbance in their possessions *and for the harm done to their reputation*! After all, they had to reward the devotion of their protectors; and neither the lord of Klingenberg nor the Count of Thierstein nor the needy Sigismund were men to content themselves with the not very devout prayers of their clients.

The result was what might have been expected. The victorious nuns constantly complained even against the partial reforms decreed by their new confessors.

Things went so far that the Bishop of Constance tried to restore some sort of order: but the nuns appealed to the Pope and the Official of Strassburg. Later, in 1505, the Pope confided the mission to the Bishop of Basel; the nuns then appealed "to the Pope when better informed"—*ad papam melius informatum*—and gave way only when the Bishop excommunicated them. The Emperor Maximilian vainly attempted to obey the Bishop of Constance in his capacity of Papal Vicar.

Disorder grew worse and worse; between 1525 and 1555, fourteen nuns left the convent to marry lowborn men or apostate priests. Finally, the last abbess being dead, the Burgomaster of Basel took possession of the convent on condition of allowing a pension to the one remaining sister, who went back to her own family.

Meanwhile the reforming nuns struggled against a coldly indifferent world. They were driven out violently from Klingenthal by the victorious rebels, who broke open the gates and the choir doors. They wandered about the diocese of Strassburg, living on alms and vainly seeking some secure refuge. At last their confessor obtained their admission to a convent at Renting in the diocese of Metz. Here were thirty-eight Dominican Tertiaries, living by the work of their own hands and struggling to build their little convent with the alms of the faithful. These twenty-four wanderers complicated the situation very seriously:

and their confessor, through influential friends, petitioned the Pope for such an Indulgence as the neighbouring Carthusians, Franciscans and Dominicans already enjoyed. Apparently they got no answer. They appealed desperately to Louis XI of France; but just then he died. At last a beneficent canon, who in 1483 had bought up a suppressed convent at Obersteigen, gave it to the nuns on condition of a life annuity of one mark. They borrowed 400 florins for the restoration of the dilapidated buildings, and in 1485 the Pope granted an Indulgence of forty days to all who should contribute their alms. Yet they were still so poor that, three years later, they procured papal licence to break the strict rule of claustration in order to go out for harvest work with their lay-sisters, and to beg about in the villages around. At last, in 1507, they gave up the struggle, resigned their convent to the bishop, and found refuge in that of Gnadenthal. The scanty revenues of deserted Obersteigen were thenceforward added to the bishop's *mensa*—i.e. his private purse.

We must make special allowance for the nunneries, which in general (though not in this Klingenthal case) were comparatively poorly endowed from the first and increasingly impoverished as time went on. Parents very naturally said, "I can give my own daughter enough to keep her there, but not enough for other girls." Hence they shifted into the position of alms-women, each keeping tenaciously to what she had, little or much. It was quite impossible to maintain the canonical prohibition of exacting dowries. Everybody recognized that, unless each fresh nun brought a serious contribution, bankruptcy must soon follow; for the outside public had ceased to add fresh endowments except by driblets. Hence *proprietas* was often a question of life and death for the nuns.

But with monks, as a rule, it was a mere luxury. They were very seldom brought to beggary except by sheer chronic waste and mismanagement; and, even then, the possessions still left to them were so considerable that one energetic abbot could change the whole face of affairs. *Proprietas* in their case, so far from being a remedy, was generally at the root of the whole disease: it meant grabbing and squandering.

One final example must be added here, where the struggle

seemed almost equally hopeless, yet faith and persistency won a final victory. Nider is here both actor and narrator.(7) Writing in 1437 he says:

How great is the power of common and private prayer, you may learn from this which follows. Scarce nine years have passed since the convent of sisters of our [Dominican] Order, St Catharine of Nürnberg, should have been reformed by the Minister General, who at that time sojourned in our friary. All the sisters, with one voice, cried out against this reform; and thence, through their kinsfolk, they set the whole city by the ears, some saying that it was good and others saying "nay, by no means, but novelty is pernicious". Therefore we laboured many months in this matter, in order that the holy work might be performed in peace; but the business was put off from day to day by reason of the contrary opinions of the city magistrates on this matter. Meanwhile the minister sent for eleven holy reforming nuns, who came from a reformed convent, and were introduced rather furtively than openly into the convent of St Catharine, for fear of certain citizens without whose consent nothing efficient could be done. Therefore the city magistrates decided that the sisters of St Catharine should be reformed with the reform which had been already begun, if and in so far as they should not be compelled unwillingly thereunto. When we heard this—we who had borne the burden of the war against the devils' wrath—we were almost in despair of ever completing the holy reform; for all knew that not one of the sisters was willing. Therefore, in a business which was humanly so desperate, I determined to have recourse to God through public prayer. And, since at that time I preached daily in Advent, therefore on that day whereon the magistrates' emissary was to enquire in public of the nuns' will, I spoke briefly thus in my sermon. "Good children [*boni pueri*], ye know how at this time we are labouring for the reform of the Sisters of St Catharine. Hitherto I have made no mention of this in the pulpit: therefore I now pray that each person here present will pray unto the Highest that the will of Almighty God be done in this matter." Then, after dinner, the emissaries came to the convent to hear the votes of those who were invited to reform, in the presence of us who had been sent by the Minister General. Some of the magistrates' emissaries were displeased at the manner of the reform. When the nuns had been asked concerning their consent, and had withdrawn, then with scarce such delay as would suffice for saying the psalm *Miserere mei Deus* [Ps. li, A.V.] they were inspired by God's spirit, and all consented to reform. Therefore, coming to us and the emissaries, they offered themselves thereunto with tears and on their bended knees: to our joy beyond measure, and the confusion of our adversaries. And, because the City Council had put this holy business in the nuns' choice, and this was now seen to be turned to the better, therefore it committed this decision to as full execution as possible; and thus that convent is now wholly reformed.

Later on, he tells us a little more about this reform.

After the convent was closed [to outsiders], according to the Rule, and the headstrong crew of the frailer sex bowed their neck to the yoke of obedience, there came to the monastery a certain demon, who began by haunting certain nuns with unwonted noises by night. When I heard this I persuaded them not to believe that this was done by a fiend, but by cats and mice, and some craze of their heads; for I suspected here the mad fancies of women. Another day the demon came, and pressed so sore one of those who had rebelled (the sacristan, as I think) that it was thought she must be laid that day in her grave. At last, it so troubled the convent, by day and night, that it became necessary to set a watch of nuns all night long, in batches, since none dared go about alone. For this weak female sex was utterly stupefied, so that I also knew not what to do with them. At last I enjoined upon all of them to pray in private and in public, and I preached patience, and oftentimes persuaded them to trust in the Lord. But in this work, although the fiend's malice had some success (for some said: "Lo! when we walked in our old broad way these things never befel us"), yet at last, by God's grace, the devil lost more than he had gained at this game. For certain stiffnecked women whom the piety of the reformers had not availed to draw wholly with them, were so terrified by this phantom that they confessed sacramentally the misdeeds of their whole life, and laid aside their old garments, and put on a new habit according to the form of the Order, and transformed themselves into another new life. The devil, seeing this, changed his mind at last by God's grace, and I know not whither he went.

CHAPTER XVI

THE REFORMER'S DIFFICULTIES

SÜLTE, Wennigsen and Mariensee were indeed among the worst cases, but Busch's evidence is cumulative. Over and over again he shows how there was a depth of monastic degradation in so many houses that these scandalized the public more than the moderate or the few really reformed houses could edify. It is not only that in his records we find this or that sinner definitely specified, but the facts which Busch mentions only by the way, and his unstudied remarks, point to a general atmosphere of indiscipline and immorality which would not be tolerated in any civilized country of to-day.

If the civil magistrates began now to interfere more and more, this was because the monks themselves often made the most definite appeals, either to the notorious corruption of the law-courts or to physical force. Those of St Godehard at Hildesheim sent two brethren with 250 florins to buy papal exemption from Busch's visitation; but the missionaries drank the money away at Magdeburg and therefore failed at Rome (p. 533). The Abbot of St Michael in the same city, Heinrich Woltorp, "an illiterate man and reputed almost as a layman,* but astute in outward matters and cunning of speech...gained confirmation from the Holy See by paying a great sum of money for it" (p. 525). Cusanus, as papal legate, compelled this man later to resign; but he was obliged to pension him with 60 florins a year, and part of the monastery for his lodging, "because he had been confirmed by the Holy See" (p. 530). On another occasion, monks bribed three doctors of law at Leipzig to write a decision rejecting as invalid the archbishop's mandate of reform (p. 747). Once, however, things went differently under the strong and honest Nicholas V. The Landgraf of Thüringen regarded Busch's visitatorial commission from the papal legate as an

* *Pene pro laico reputatus*. The word is commonly used in the sense of "ignorant of Latin". But Busch puts it plainly on p. 526: "he could not speak Latin".

infringement of his princely rights. He moved the Emperor Frederick III, his brother-in-law, to raise the question at Rome; and his greater monasteries pawned their chalices and other ornaments to raise money for the campaign. But Nicholas, who not only had Cusanus's mission very much at heart, but who also knew something of Busch's own work, insisted that the mandate should take effect (p. 478).

The great prelates were too often lukewarm. Bishop Magnus of Hildesheim, placed by Grube among the nine who were performing their spiritual duties "in so far as their rank of Prince-Bishop permitted" (p. 11), was yet willing to sell the pass at Sülte for forty florins—roughly equivalent, perhaps, to the thirty pence of ancient Judaea.* The Bishop of Minden, Busch tells us, "took money from the [incontinent and dissolute] nuns of Mariensee and gave them power to continue in their former evil life" (p. 562). The Bishop of Verden would have accepted a similar bribe but for fear of the duke (p. 541). His visitations illustrate the complaint of his contemporary, Jacobus de Paradiso, the Carthusian, who asserted that all orthodox attempts at reform had been thwarted, hitherto, by the ill-will of the higher ecclesiastics, far more than by that of earthly princes.†

He tells us elsewhere of other threats to his life; a knife which was drawn upon him, but his companion seized a hedge-stake in his defence (pp. 591–2); and a revengeful husband whose wife had been threatened with the stake if she persisted in sorcery (p. 702). Against another monk Busch had procured a legal mandate in due form. The man cried in court: "There will be heads broken before this business is finished!" and "his blood brother, a knight of the duchy of Brunswick, sent me sealed letters of defiance, to take me and my brethren as prisoners, and slay and pillage our possessions and burn our buildings". Busch sent these to the bishop, and had reason to rejoice for once that this was the same prelate who had gone armed *cap à pie* to receive the legate. The bishop wrote to both

* When Cardinal Nicholas Cusanus came to Germany as papal legate for reform of the monasteries, this bishop astonished him by coming forth to meet him "armed from head to foot, with his military vassals and a great company" (p. 746).

† Brown's *Fasciculus*, II, 104.

knight and duke, to the effect that the defiance must be revoked or he himself would waste all the offender's lands; whereupon the duke sent word that he would not otherwise suffer the knight on his lands (p. 536). One delinquent monastery was prepared, with a garrison of nearly sixty men, to stand a siege (p. 501). The reform at Lüneburg aroused a perilous revolt in the city. The monks had given men drink to ring the alarm from the town hall. The duke and his retainers, followed by the Bishop of Verden and his, fled precipitately from the tumult in those narrow streets; and the two reforming abbots, though armed with full powers from the duke, were not permitted by the citizens to go forth into safety until they had sworn to take no action against the rioters. In process of time, it should be added, this monastery joined the reformed Congregation of Bursfelde (pp. 540ff.).

Busch vividly describes the very natural fears of his fellow-reformers in face of that raging multitude and a drawn sword at Lüneburg. The Abbot of St Michael's confessed himself hastily, as at his last hour, to the Abbot of St Godehard's, "but he received no absolution by reason of the importunity of those who pressed into the monastery". He hid in a closet, pleading, "I would gladly have received death for the cause of holy reformation, but I fear some loss of limb or spilling of brains, lest I become useless to myself and burdensome to others" (p. 542). Yet in all this affair this visitor was under the express protection of the Duke of Brunswick and the Bishop of Verden, in so far as parchment and wax seals can protect.

It was frequent for the neighbours thus to defend the dissolute monks, and especially the nuns (e.g. p. 593). Sometimes, again, the house would successfully plead papal exemption (p. 569). The frequent wars raised other difficulties. From 1444 to 1449 reigned the so-called Feud of Soest, in which "the landgraf of Thüringen hastened to the aid of the Archbishop of Cologne ...ravishing and depopulating and devastating all in his way.... So the bishops [of Hildesheim and Halberstadt] and the counts and barons and villages all round flew to arms and met him, to secure themselves lest he should plunder and waste everything. So by this occasion our reformation of the monastery of Hamersleve was broken off" (p. 486). But the worst obstacle of all was the dead weight of monks inimical to reform and inexhaustible in little tricks to thwart it. The bishop, the provost of his capital, and the famous Abbot Hagen of Bursfelde were specially concerned for the reform of St Godehard's at Hildesheim.

Yet they could not [compass this]. For my lord Helmold the abbot, a man of well composed manners, soft and prudent and quiet, thwarted indirectly by his pertinacity the whole labour of bishops and reformers. He feigned that he desired reform and that he and his brethren were reformed already; he attended the Benedictine Provincial Chapters, promised to keep the ordinances there decreed, and maintained friendships with those who were well reformed. Moreover, whenever the reformed fathers of his Order came to him or to St Michael's, he received them with all solemnity or sent them drinks,* and always posed before them as truly reformed. Again, he said that he was obeying the injunctions of the visitors deputed to him by the General Chapter. Yet neither he nor his brethren kept the Rule and the Constitutions of his Order, though they had them very plainly recorded in their books. By this his diplomacy and show of reverence and familiarity with the fathers, loving all and beloved by all, with the repute everywhere of an upright, prudent and good man, he evaded either sharing active reform with his superiors and the other heads of houses, or suffering reform in his own monastery; persisting in that partial reformation which he desired. Yet he kept his buildings in good order; nay, he even improved them well, and died in this manner of life. (p. 529.)

His successor was that illiterate Heinrich Woltorp whom Cardinal Cusanus deposed. Later, after great difficulties with the tricks and lies of the ancient brethren, this monastery was reformed under pressure from the bishop and the city council. The ancients "betook themselves to other non-reformed monasteries, wherein they have remained unto this day" (p. 538).

No wonder that the Windesheim General Chapter recorded its conviction that the safest policy was to start from the foundation, since "it is a greater labour to reform old houses than to found new, as we have learned from sure experience" (p. 368).

Yet, when in his eightieth year Busch passed to God, certainly he bore his sheaves with him. For here was a man with all the qualities for a successful reformer, short of that rare genius for victory which, whether in war or in peace, does not

* *Propinas misit*; either wine itself, as was the frequent custom, or a present of money, *Trinkgeld*.

even appear once in a century. He was devoted from boyhood to the monastic ideal; courageous, persistent, yet with a strong fund of common sense and much diplomatic skill. The resolute side of him comes out in his dealings not only with the monasteries but also with the parishes, when he was created provost of Neuwerk by Halle, and thus burdened with the onerous privilege of an archdeaconry over a wide and populous district. The lay magistrate (proconsul as Busch calls him) asked him what he intended to do in those parts; and he replied: "I intend to make a new world here" (p. 439). There was, indeed, sore need of such a man. As archdeacon, he became officially and directly responsible for the fight against concubinage among the parish clergy.

It was reported to me that a certain priest in my archdeaconry slept with his maidservant. I cited them both to appear before me. Then I said to the parson: "Sir, you are accustomed, as I hear, to sleep with your maidservant." He flatly denied this. When I insisted that it was the truth, he denied again with an oath that he had done this. Being unable to extort the truth from him in words, I said to him: "Sir, you know the Paternoster; repeat it therefore that I may hear it."* He repeated it to me wholly and exactly. When he had ended I said: "Stay here in the monastery: I wish to go forth alone." Then, finding his maidservant, I said: "I have heard that you are wont to sleep with your master." She answered, "I have so much to do with cows and calves, swine and sheep, that I have no leisure for that." Then I said: "Your master has told me as true as the Paternoster. If you say otherwise, I will expel you from the diocese of Magdeburg." She said to me in amazement: "My master the parson has told you as true as the Paternoster?" I answered, "Yes." Then she said: "The last time that he knew me was on Shrove Tuesday" (and it was about *Reminiscere* Sunday that I asked her this).† So I went to the parson, who was still within our precincts, and said: "Your maid says that you knew her on Shrove Tuesday." "How, saith she thus?" "Yes." Then said he: "Venerable father, she saith true: *mea culpa*: spare me, I beseech you: I will willingly pay a fine at your will." Then I answered in amazement and wrath: "Even now you swore that you had not done this; now you admit it. You have no conscience; you neither fear God nor reverence man. You

* Busch cites concrete instances of ignorance among the parish clergy which render this question less strange than it may seem at first sight (p. 443).

† *Reminiscere* is the second Sunday in Lent. The interval, therefore, was about eighteen days.

scarce know that you possess a soul, daring as you do to commit plain perjury." So I punished him in his purse, by wax tapers and another penance, because he had not done penance in the confessional. (p. 450.)

Another confessed his guilt: in fact, the child was there as a silent witness. Busch gave him for penance a week in the monastery, under monastic fare, and his daily breviary to read. "My official lay hard upon him that he should beg me for a different penance, and that he should give me two barrels of Nuremberg ale, which is the best in those parts. But he consented not to this, choosing rather to be put to shame before men than to spend his money." Another time, a knight came and expostulated with Busch for his strictness (p. 451).

You have decreed that the parsons must dismiss their maidservants or concubines. But there are two or three parishes on my estates in Meissen* whence the parsons have departed with their concubines, leaving their churches without pastor: therefore the parishioners have neither Mass nor sermon nor other services, but walk like pagans, almost without God. It were better that you should suffer them to retain their concubines than that the people should become as heathens.

Busch was not willing, even under those conditions, to violate the plain prescriptions of Canon Law; "so, because I did not consent, things remained as they were" (p. 451). Again, in dealing with a village witch, he was undeterred by her claim, supported by the neighbourhood, that the Archbishop of Magdeburg had frequently patronized her for his own horses (pp. 700–1). To the duke and duchess Busch spoke more than once, quite plainly, concerning their very slender chances (by his calculation) of avoiding eternal damnation. With the Duchess Helena his plain speech was so effective that she made a good end. She pleaded pathetically that, in a ducal castle, where women were so little accounted and had so hard a time, married life might be weighed before God against the monk's mortifications (pp. 776–9).

His tact and common sense, on the other hand, come out frequently in his story. One of the most interesting cases is that of his dealings with a woman of Alkmaar who had constant

* Or, possibly, "in our province of Meissen".

visions of God and His Apostles. Her husband was a fisherman; she had been wet-nurse to a rich man's child and overlain it in the night; the fear that the parents would kill her first gave her incessant hysterical tears and headaches: and then came these visions. Busch suspected here the *daemonium meridianum* of which St Bernard speaks to his brethren as one of the most dangerous spiritual enemies: the devil visiting the visionary in divine or saintly form. He began with a cross-examination suggestive of the almost contemporary trial of Joan of Arc.

"Good woman, you have seen God?" "Oftentimes have I seen him, and His Apostles to boot!" "How was God clad?" "You are a learned man, and you know wherein and how God is clad." "I know that only by hearsay; you have seen Him, and seeing is better than hearing." At last, after much pressing, she answered: "I saw God in heaven, clad in a grey coat [*grisea tunica indutum*]." Then I began to doubt the truth of the vision, and said: "In heaven there are no sheep; therefore no wool, grey or white. I fear that it is not God which appeareth to you, but the devil showeth you such figments for your deception." She answered me very resolutely that it was God indeed, who for fourteen years had shown Himself and the saints to her.

She carried in her purse a Latin charm which a sacristan had written for her, and which Busch, reading, saw to be a mere deception. He warned her that she was dealing with demoniacal delusions, to the peril of her soul. Shaken and seriously concerned, she was now willing to take his advice. It ran thus.

"In the evening, when you are wont to see these visions, before lying down to sleep, recite the *Ave Maria* thrice upon your knees. When that is done, drink forthwith a quart of hot ale, as hot as you can bear, with a little butter on the top, taking it in two or three gulps until you have finished it. Then lie down forthwith to sleep. If it be God who is wont to visit you, He will surely come again: if it be the devil, he will not return." I said this in order that she might have faith in the *Ave Maria* while I trusted to the hot ale, which in common speech is called *een warme iaute*; for I saw that her brain was troubled with her tears and fasting, and that this would restore her crazy head.

The prescription succeeded admirably. At first she was inconsolable for the loss of her visions, and told the parson of Alkmaar how the change had come. He applauded Busch's advice, and gave her money for the next night's ale. Busch, fearing a relapse, arranged with three beneficent institutions to supply her with her nightly quart for a year; and thus she gained complete freedom. He tried the same recipe, with equal success, upon another woman possessed with a devil; in this case he specifies the butter more exactly: "of the bigness of a walnut" (pp. 694, 702). In his archdeaconry a certain anchoress wished to follow a Rule which prescribed that she must never keep in her cell enough food to make a meal for a mouse. "I would not suffer her to do this, for the sake of her conscience and of mine own" (p. 655). He fought steadily against the so-called religious charms which ignorant folk bought from sacristans, probably at pilgrimage-churches (pp. 694, 702). A nun, the duke's natural daughter, ran away with the confessor of her convent, and after seven years of apostasy and promiscuity was at last condemned to be taken to a reformed nunnery for penitence. The carriage was ready, but she, with the connivance of others, feigned a sudden attack of demoniacal possession and deafness. "Then the maidens and women there present wept, saying that the Gospel of St John should be hung round her neck": a common ecclesiastical rite of exorcism. "I said to them that there was no need of this, but that they should lift her up into the chariot behind me; for, if the devil had wrought this thing, then he would not dare to mount the chariot with me" (p. 662). His combined firmness and sympathy were at last successful; and at her absolution and reconciliation in full choir "all the nuns, many in number, cried in their highest voice: 'The hosts of angels rejoice this day; for the tenth piece of silver was lost and is found'" (pp. 659ff.).

It is typical of the man's frankness that, with all his severity wherever the Church enjoined fasting, he made no profession of unnecessary abstinence: he confesses to a German appetite. In 1451, when Cusanus came as papal legate to Magdeburg, Busch was honoured with a seat at table between the cardinal and his attendant bishop.

The Archbishop provided choice and delicate food and drink; and they ate in Roman fashion. A servant, helping us with great and broad knives, put the liver of a wildfowl, or its breast or belly or some of the other flesh before him, sometimes before the Lord Cardinal, sometimes before me, sometimes before the Bishop; thus again he did with the other dishes. So, again, when any of us wished to drink, a servant, standing always before us, handed to each of us a glass of delibuto wine or of the best ale, and set down the glass again when we had drunken. Thus I ate there in great state; but when supper was done I went to my host, the Archbishop's physician, saying that I came from the Lord Cardinal's table more hungry than I had gone thither, since I had supped there not after the Saxon but after the Roman fashion. (p. 745.)

The nuns of St Mary Magdalene at Hildesheim, an excellent house, had Busch as their guest at meals while he was teaching them the full details of Windesheim observance. "They put before me a small jug of beer, yet greater than such as themselves had for each two sisters. I could have drunk it at a draught if I would. Seeing this, after I had once drunken, they forthwith brought me a greater jug." On the other hand, he was no candidate for such a drinking bout as the hospitable duke once suggested, after the fashion of great castles. Three times Busch adroitly put him off: he wanted to drink what he wanted, and not what others might want.

The fourth time the Duke (having an eye which he sought to purge and heal by rubbing with his finger), said to me: "Father, what shall I do that I may heal the itching of my eye?" I said: "If you will not be wroth, I will give you good advice." He said: "I will not." Then said I: "Never rub your eye save with your elbow-joint, and then it will heal completely." At this he said: "If you were not a man of Religion, I would become your enemy", thinking that I mocked him since he could not reach his eye with his elbow; and this was indeed my meaning, for he should not have rubbed his eye in any way. (p. 774.)

Therefore, in his last years, Busch could look back quietly upon a life of unusual success. He had thoroughly falsified the prediction of "one of our lay-brethren at Windesheim, Nicholas the guest-master", who "said to my father when I took the vows: 'Your son John will be a good cloisterer, but he will never be sent abroad, by reason of his simplicity'" (p. 789). In these years, as the fifteenth century was drawing to a close, there was still a strong tide running in favour of both Windesheim and Bursfelde, friendly rivals in the race for salvation of self and of society. Much still remained to be done, and the work would always be laborious. After relating one of the earlier attempts on his own life, he adds: "I have written this in order that those who would be good reformers should fear no adversities: if they persevere to the end, they shall have good success" (p. 592). In his forty years of hard work, whether as principal or as coadjutor, he had reformed at least forty-three monasteries of other Orders, apart from his own Austin Canons. He could truly claim that this "New Devotion", born at Deventer in semi-monastic form, taking definite claustral shape at Windesheim, and showing its finest literary fruit in the *Imitatio Christi*, had created a new world in the north-west of the Empire. In the preface to his *Liber de Reformatione*, written in his seventy-sixth year, he undertakes to record the ups and downs of the holy campaign whereby, "in this brief modern age, many great fathers, and we ourselves also, have laboured for the reform of many houses of both sexes and divers Orders, through Saxony and Meissen and Thuringia and the Mark and Westphalia and in other regions of Germany; of which houses almost all persevere to the present day in observance of their Rule" (p. 379). It is significant that this book is dedicated to two of his fellow-labourers, abbots of now reformed houses which had once given most trouble, St Michael's and St Godehard's at Hildesheim. He can reckon: "I have journeyed through and covered, since I took the vows, more than 6000 miles, with 520 miles for the reform of divers monasteries, unto almost 100 cities, besides the villages lying around or between, and to more than 30 castles."* For all this he hopes for his reward in heaven. He sees no reason to repent of having recorded evil things as well as good: the example of St Augustine and the Venerable Bede indicates this as the historian's strict duty (p. 790).

Ten years earlier, in the Epilogue to his *Chronicon Windes-*

* p. 789. *Arces*, like *castra*, may mean either castles or fortified towns or villages not great enough to be *civitates*. A year later, Busch reckons his total travels at 680 miles: in both cases the *miliare* is the German mile, equivalent probably to two and a half or three English (p. 792). Once, travelling all night at full speed, a carriage covered ten miles (p. 261). Busch describes his own journeys as having been made "sometimes on foot, sometimes on horseback, but most commonly in carriages or carts". Grube reminds us truly that, in those days, "a journey of twenty miles was an adventure; and to be further off from one's home than this was almost like being dead to it" (Introd. p. xxxviii).

hemense, he had written more at length, rather of others than of himself personally, and in a strain of triumphant exultation which is pardonable even in its exaggerations, especially where he keeps his own contributions so much in the background. He tells us first of the dire need in which Religion had found itself.

In our land, desert and barren and unfruitful, there was formerly no place of refuge, where souls could be saved and could work their own salvation, whether in the world or in Religion. For men and women, old and young, commonly trod the broad and easy way that leads to perdition. Few Orders, save the Carthusians and a few Cistercians, were then loyal to their Rule and their constitutions; but rather, in almost every Religious house, they were open transgressors thereof, and of the Three Substantial Vows [of Obedience, Poverty and Chastity]. If there had then been those who would gladly have served their Creator for the salvation of their own souls and the Kingdom of Heaven, they could scarce have found, throughout the whole province, any place apt for that purpose; for the name of Reformer of monasteries and persons, before our days, was known to very few men in remote parts. Yet now it hath filled the whole land, like sweet honey, in the mouth and in the works of all men and women, whether spiritual or secular. For in all this province there is scarce any city or town to be found, but that we may see round about it either monasteries or congregations and very many other habitations of devout folk, whether newly founded or reformed from their ancient state.

Now, however, he can appeal to the eighty reformed houses of the Windesheim Congregation, sprinkled over seventeen dioceses; houses where "by day and night, in choir and in cloister, they are busy either with God's praise or with holy work, suffering no time to pass uselessly without special exercise, either inward or outward, mental or manual; mortifying themselves and their own will in all things; manfully resisting the enemy's temptations; serving God faithfully and so taking by violence the Kingdom of Heaven, earning it thus in fact and in truth". In addition to these we must count the fifty houses of Brethren of the Common Life, descended from that foundation of Florence Radewin at Deventer, with more than a hundred houses of Tertiary women affiliated to them, "who are never idle, but, bee-like, cease not to sweat importunately for their own salvation and the winning of souls". These monasteries, or brother-houses and sister-houses, contain in some cases twenty or thirty persons, in others 200 or 300 or 400. "Who, then, can lightly count the number contained in those 80 monasteries and 150 congregations, all of whom persevere unto this day in God's grace and the hope of eternal life, in good will and in their holy purpose?" Consider, again, the countless persons who, without taking vows or joining the Brethren of Common Life, have been led by their teaching and example to a better life. In the Psalmist's words,

There is sprung up a light for the righteous in these new days. This is God's doing, who, in St Paul's words, "calleth those things which be not as though they were". For who, when these folk first began the Common Life, would ever have believed that these successes would follow? Who could have thought that such a multitude of saints would have arisen for the whole German world, from so lowly a source and so few fathers? I may call these the new miracles, wrought by Christ's disciples in the early Church, and now again renewed in these days of ours by Him who worked them then: wherefore we can give God no small thanks, that we are born in these days wherein we are able to work the salvation of our souls and to find places disposed for that purpose.... Wherein, if we remain faithful to our life's end in full obedience to our Rule and our constitutions, being perfectly purged therein, we may come to the Heavenly Realm without any future purgation; and, joining the angel-choirs in their hymns, may contemplate for ever the face of our Creator and Redeemer, Jesus Christ. May the blessed and glorious God grant this, He who is eternal life, the joy of the angels and the beatitude of all the saints, world without end. *Amen.*

CHAPTER XVII

THE WINDESHEIM INFLUENCE

THIS reform, within its own limitations—partly, perhaps by reason of those limitations—may be counted as the most successful, on the whole, between the Franciscan-Dominican revival and the Reformation. It was still living and healthy, though past its first fervour, when Luther came forward; and then the Counter-Reformation breathed fresh life into it. The very useful Appendix to Grube's monograph shows that, out of 102 houses, forty-one were still in existence when the Emperor Joseph II set himself to weed out decayed or superfluous monasteries from his dominions (1782–4). Eleven were then suppressed; the remaining thirty disappeared almost altogether at the French Revolution or in 1803. One alone survived until 1809.

Acquoy, in the second volume of his exhaustive monograph (*Het Klooster Windesheim*), devotes over 200 pages to a minute examination and estimate of the influence exercised by Windesheim "upon civilisation in general, especially moral". If his conclusions seem rather cold and cautious, we must bear in mind the spirit of Busch's time, too often ignored by modern writers.

The cloisterer's first care, and his incessant pre-occupation, was to save his own soul from hell. We have seen how frankly Busch states this, and how definitely it comes out in the character of that prior of Windesheim whom Busch revered almost to the point of worship. Even in so colossal a saint as Bernard of Clairvaux this characteristic is clearly marked.(1) Indeed, it could not be otherwise in face of medieval eschatology. We are to love our neighbour as ourself, but not before ourself: salvation is the supreme end in both cases, but our control over self is more direct than it can be over any other person, and everything we can do to fit ourselves for heaven will contribute to, not detract from, his chances of salvation. The good monk's prayers, it was felt, constituted for the whole world the most efficient safeguard against God's indignation. Cistercians, Franciscans, and Dominicans, the three most active revivalist Orders, all adopted the same legend, that the Christ of the Judgment Seat had been seen raising His hand to dash this globe to pieces, and had been withheld only by the Blessed Virgin, who pleaded for these new intercessors.(2) The cloister was a haven of salvation: but it is the essence of a haven that it should be sheltered from the great ocean. Therefore disciplinarians reminded the cloisterer that his monastery would be healthy only so long as he bore in mind the significance of that Greek word *monos*, "alone". If the Carthusians withstood the solvent forces of worldliness more successfully than any other Order, this was mainly in virtue of their fidelity to that ideal. In every Charterhouse, as at the mother-house of the Grande Chartreuse, each inmate was in effect a solitary anchorite, meeting his fellows on certain occasions but normally silent even then. St Benedict, in his Rule, contemplated very little direct communication between any monk, during his whole life, and the outside world. On the whole, it was doubtless fortunate that this sixty-sixth chapter of the Rule was not kept to the letter, and that monks often became missionaries, teachers, chroniclers, lawyers and politicians, sometimes even physicians and artists, though far less than has often been imagined. Those activities were indeed mainly beneficial; but they were secondary to the monk's profession, and even tended sometimes to contradict it. Therefore, in proportion as Windesheim succeeded in reviving the early monastic ideal, we must expect to find that it neglected those multitudinous social activities which are often credited to the medieval monastery, and which some of them did in fact sometimes exercise.

Acquoy justly describes the Windesheim ideal as a return to the Society of Jerusalem, as mirrored in Acts and elsewhere in the New Testament (pp. 333–5). This implied, on many points, an attitude of steady, and sometimes violent, opposition to "the world". Their claustral enclosure was far stricter than that of most Austin Canons (pp. 273–8). At Windesheim, the brother's love of his own cloister and cell was almost Carthusian (p. 298). Augustinians were not, like the Benedictines, forbidden normally to serve in parish cures; but Windesheim gave no encouragement to such external activities; it merely suffered them; it preferred to hire, like other Orders, secular priests for its appropriated parishes. It was only at a later stage that the General Chapter became more liberal in its permission for the canons to serve its churches (p. 314). Their dread of all associations with women, beyond the necessary business relations, was great from the first, and increased with time (pp. 279, 339). This abstraction fitted in naturally with, and even tended to foster, exaggerated ideals of introspection and mortification (pp. 291–4). In some cases this was very prejudicial to the cloisterer's health (p. 294); in many more it led to extreme mental anxiety, and, sometimes, to petty observation and censoriousness of others (pp. 295–6). "The morality of the Windesheimers is only suited for cloisterers" (p. 296).

If such were the interior conditions, how shall we judge the outside influence? They set an excellent example to the world in handiwork, fieldwork, and trade; "Yet this does not justify our speaking of their special influence upon these things" (pp. 179–85). There are but very slight traces, almost negligible, of child education in the nunneries (pp. 185–7). The congregation as a whole, though sprung originally from the Brethren of Common Life, did not concern itself especially with folk-instruction (p. 187). Among the men's houses, only one seems to have possessed a school for outsiders before the Counter-Reformation of the seventeenth century: this was St Martin's at Louvain, which had originally been a Frater-house of the Common Life. Only two more had followed this example by 1700, out of the thirty-four still existing (p. 187). The cloisterers themselves, in earlier times, were somewhat suspicious of, or even hostile to, liberal education of the university pattern (pp. 190–2). Incidentally, the *Imitatio* itself is definitely tinged with such suspicions. It was not until the seventeenth century that the Congregation, though still powerful, had a seminary of its own at Louvain University, with lecturers and professors. Acquoy emphasizes more than once the contradiction between these facts and the general impressions of modern writers. He writes (p. 185):

We are sorry to be compelled to disappoint our readers, more or less, on so important a matter; but we have no other choice.

Historical veracity and good faith demand that we should not ask after what we wish to have happened, but after what has in fact happened. Although in the monasteries which belonged to the Windesheim Chapter, especially in the Northern Dutch nunneries and in the men's houses in South Holland, various traces can be found of teaching given to non-cloisterers, yet we must consider these, in face of so conspicuous a congregation, as partly too sporadic, and partly too one-sidedly ecclesiastical in their aim, to command belief in any substantial influence upon the matter in question.

He quotes certain isolated cases, but adds: "All this gives us no right to assert that the Windesheim nunneries had any influence upon popular education." And again (p. 192) "we cannot count Windesheim as a motive force [*beweegkracht*] in the domain of instruction".

In the copying of books their activities were far greater: here they did honour to their origin from the Common Life. Yet this was almost exclusively for their own use, although they sometimes sold books, as they did fish and butter (pp. 193–5). There is no trace of their ever starting a printing-press (pp. 195–8). They collected, however, libraries admirable for that age, and thus exercised an influence, especially in later times, upon learning (pp. 198–203). They produced not many learned men (pp. 203–8). These had rather the character of painstaking and useful scholars in the hagiographical or patristic fields: they had no originality, and did not further learning as such (pp. 208–10). On the other hand, their chronicles have been of great use. Apart from Busch (one of the best in fifteenth-century Europe), they have left us many useful chronicles for northern and southern Holland and western Germany (pp. 210–22). In later times, some wrote histories of wider scope and more general content (pp. 222–6). But, after this, there was again a definite falling-off (p. 226). They published useful material as editors, but had no influence otherwise upon historiography (p. 227).

To the fine arts, this "Modern Devotion" was not favourably inclined at first. True, Windesheim supplied the best scribes and illuminators in the whole movement (pp. 229–31). Acquoy gives a long list of Windesheim illuminators from north and south Holland (pp. 232–6). Moreover, they did not disdain the new art of woodcuts (p. 236). Several of the brethren practised painting with success (pp. 237–40) and architecture (pp. 240–3,

384). They took a pride in the ornamentation of their churches (p. 243). Thus they multiplied objects of art, but gave no new direction at any point (p. 245). Church song they practised assiduously (p. 246), and had strong opinions of their own in this matter (pp. 247–9). But organ playing was long forbidden in their churches (pp. 249–51). Here again, incidentally, we have already seen Busch's admiration for the conventual plainsong. A few practised poetry with good success; but we cannot speak of any influence they exerted upon others (pp. 251–4).

Next, Acquoy passes to their conception of God and His government (pp. 255–7). They clung with the utmost loyalty to the Church tradition (p. 257). To the Pope, again, they were thoroughly loyal (p. 257). Like many other revivalists from Cîteaux onwards, they had a special love for the Virgin Mary (pp. 258–61). In saint worship, and the matter of Indulgences, they were thoroughly orthodox (pp. 261–2). Like other monastic reformers from the thirteenth century onwards, they issued "letters of fraternity" to lay-folk, granting them participation in their prayers and the merit of their good works (p. 263). They show normal medieval belief in the personality of the Devil and his spirits; in angels and ghostly apparitions (pp. 264–5). They sometimes fell into actual superstition (p. 266) and took the usual attitude towards miracles (p. 267).

To the Revolution of the sixteenth century, therefore, they were frankly hostile (pp. 268–71). Yet their conservatism led them to repudiate even so remarkable and moderate a reformer as Johann Wessel Gansfort (pp. 271–3). The new ideas did nothing to shake their conception of monastic duties (p. 273). For instance, they earnestly repudiated all personal property (p. 280), extolled obedience even to exaggeration (pp. 281–2) and clung to the traditional system of discipline and punishments (p. 283). Upon humility, again, they laid extreme stress: humility in labour (pp. 284–6), in clothing (p. 286), in diet (p. 287), in the refusal of promotion (p. 288), and, still more, in self-abasement (p. 289). The Windesheimer must "be dead to himself" (p. 291) and maintain this by continual practice (pp. 291–4).

Their pietism was strong and general (p. 297). They especially read, and sometimes produced, lives of Christ, Passionbooks, and similar writings of simple edification; not only in Latin but in the vernacular (p. 299). They copied works of the Fathers and Bibles, and paid special attention to the correctness of the text (p. 300). The individual brother often compiled little common-place-books of his own, *rapiaria*, or collections of devout exercises (p. 301). Again, some of the most distinguished have left "Testaments"; exhortations to the brethren based upon long spiritual experience, with warnings against lukewarmness or backsliding (pp. 301–2). Their piety, on the whole, took a decidedly sombre tinge (p. 303); it was, in a sense, "methodistic" (p. 304). It was strongly coloured with mysticism (p. 305) and tended at times to neurosis (p. 306). Visions and ecstasies were common (p. 307); and the aim was one of perfect abstraction (p. 308). Yet, in spite of these weak points, the piety of Windesheim was far from fruitless (p. 308).

Their claustral buildings, in their beauty and their order, must have created a great impression (p. 309). The brethren's influence upon visitors and domestics and neighbours was strongly beneficent (pp. 309–11). This was fortified also by their almsgiving and their general beneficence (pp. 311–13). Though their constitutions explicitly forbid preaching to the people in general, yet there were godly exhortations to the choir-brethren in Latin and to the lay-brethren in the vulgar tongue (pp. 315–16). Thus the Congregation did not lack good pulpit orators (pp. 317–21). Moreover, they influenced society greatly through their edifying writings (pp. 321–4). Apart from the world-famed *Imitatio*, the pious writings of Gerlacus Petrus exercised considerable influence upon his own time and beyond (pp. 322–9).

But the great and special work of Windesheim was that of conventual reformation (p. 332). Their aim here was concentrated upon the restoration of the Three Substantials, with mutual charity among the brethren (p. 338). The violent resistance of ill-disposed monks is one of the strongest testimonials to the thoroughness of these reforms (p. 340). We must not, however, blink the fact that a certain amount of egoism was mingled with this reforming energy, and that the reformers' efforts often bore little or no fruit (p. 342). The nunneries gave especial difficulty (p. 343). On the other hand, we must not forget the more indirect influence of the movement. Very many monasteries were subjected more or less definitely to the influence of Windesheim without joining the Congregation (p. 344). The Council of Basel, again, and Cardinal Nicholas Cusanus, utilized these reformed Augustinians as a lever for further influence over other Orders; the Bursfelde Congregation, especially, owed much to Windesheim (pp. 345–52). France, also, at the turn of the fifteenth century, was very directly influenced (pp. 354–68). The influence of Windesheim can be traced unmistakably in more than twenty-three dioceses of Europe (p. 369).

The relations between the Windesheim canons and the Deventer Brethren, so intimate at first, gradually loosened (pp. 369–73). This intimacy had had a double effect; while it retarded the development of the more liberal side of the Brotherhood, on the other hand it withdrew from it the ultra-monastic elements: each movement could then go forward on its own lines (pp. 373–8). The cloisterers did valuable work in protection of the Brethren against the attacks of the Mendicant Orders, moreover, they erected Frater-houses, sometimes in places where they would not otherwise have come into existence (pp. 378–9). They thus introduced the "Modern Devotion", in its early stages, to a circle to which the Brethren would have been too unofficial to gain access (p. 380).

Thus, though uncompromisingly hostile to Luther's Reformation, the Congregation did indirectly assist it. To this point Acquoy, having dealt with it briefly on p. 271, comes back more explicitly on p. 385. He sums up:

> One more final word. The question of the influence of Windesheim comes really to this: What did it do for the dissemination of Protestantism? To this we answer: The Windesheimers themselves were Protestants with heart and soul, not in the historical but yet in a high and sacred sense. They protested, especially in the region of claustral life, against all immorality. And, if we ask whether any of their influence endured also into later times, our answer must be thus. A man took a stone and cast it into the water: this formed rings, wider and wider; and continued multiplying and spreading, even though the eye could no longer distinguish the ripples.

That which may seem dry and hypercritical in this Dutch scholar's estimate will be best balanced by recalling here a few sentences from Busch's own summary of the reforms, where he has described the transformation of Böddeken from a stagnant and half-bankrupt community to a model monastery, governing a multitude of lay-brethren, servants, artisans and agricultural labourers, and concludes:

Moreover they receive many lay-folk to labour daily at work of this kind, and this not merely for the sake of material labour [*propter labores externos*], but much more for God's sake and for the gain of the Kingdom of Heaven, which undoubtedly those men can earn there on earth through true obedience, pure poverty or abandonment of private property, and chaste continence. (p. 491.)

CHAPTER XVIII

BURSFELDE IN THE ASCENDANT

We may now enter upon a far more succinct survey of the other Reformed Congregations of the fifteenth century.

Bursfelde, which alone could rival Windesheim in breadth and depth of influence, owed much in its origin to this elder sister. Its first beginnings were at that Benedictine Chapter of Petershausen which was one of the few reforming steps due directly to the Council of Constance.(1)

In this year 1417 [writes Abbot Trithemius], the Fathers of the said Council of Constance, considering that our holy Order, under the Rule of St Benedict, Legislator of Monks, (whereof Holy Church had, of old, so many Popes and Cardinals and Archbishops and Bishops and Prelates and Monks famous for their learning and sanctity) was now fallen through too great licence of life, and almost utterly and miserably desolate in both those respects, especially since for many years past there had been discontinuance of those triennial Provincial Chapters required by law, and visitations neglected and no* integrity of monastic observance according to the Rule had been maintained, therefore the Fathers, in their care for the Order, and seeking to reform that observance of the monastic rule which had long been too sadly decayed [*diu nimis collapsam*] fixed the meeting of the Chapter at the abbey of Petershausen.... When the necessary statutes had been proclaimed for the reformation of the Order, and had been confirmed by authority of the Council, then all abbots there present were compelled by authority of the Council to swear and promise by their own souls, and likewise the proctors to swear by the souls of the absent abbots whom they represented, that, within a year, they would and should admit, and thenceforth faithfully keep and practise, in their own persons and in those of their monks, this reform of religious observance which had been proposed, resolved, and put into writing in that same Council and Chapter, nor would they ever rashly recede therefrom to all time, under pain of deposition from all abbatial rights and dignities.

But, as Dom Berlière remarks, "the idea of reform always arouses susceptibilities, and often provokes resistance". There

* Reading *nulla* for the *nonnulla*, "some", of this edition, which seems excluded by the whole context.

was a comparatively obscure Benedictine monk of Nordheim near Göttingen, Johann Dederoth, whom his fellow-reformer Johann Busch describes as "a man of small stature but of great prudence, burning with zeal for God and for holy reformation". This Dederoth had been sent as representative from Nordheim to the General Chapter. At Constance, he heard Johann Vos's speech, impressive with the unstudied eloquence of deep conviction.(2) Thence, fired with enthusiasm, he "came back to his abbey and reported to his abbot and brethren all that had been done at Constance; he handed to them the chapter-decrees of Petershausen, and attempted to persuade them to practise henceforward that reform which he had sworn to accept in their name". This proposal met only with derision. "What have your oaths to do with us?" they answered: "We have promised nothing; it is for you to fulfil your own pledge." The abbey of Clus, in the same territory of Brunswick, was in lamentable spiritual decay. Not only so, but, in the words of the abbey chronicler, Clus "was not alone in its deformity, for the same reigned in almost all the houses of Saxony, Thuringia, Franconia, and Westphalia, to name only the best-known.... To tell much in few words, the whole race of cloisterers had degenerated to so great wickedness [*malitia*], that no beauty remained and no comeliness was left."(7) In 1430 Dederoth was commissioned by the Council of Basel, in company with Abbot Rembert of Wittenberg, to reform decayed monasteries in those parts. This is a remarkable testimonial to the recognition which his work had brought to him in the fifteen years since Constance. The two visitors cast their eyes upon Clus, and appealed for help, as the bull of the Council authorized, to the lord of the land. Busch tells the story on p. 518. The Abbot of Clus,

unwilling to be reformed, opposed them with hard words and deeds. Therefore Father John called upon the Duke [of Brunswick] for help, in remission of his sins. The Duke said to Prior Rembert: "Must I arrest the man, and can I do this with God's favour, since he is an anointed priest?" He answered: "If you were to arrest him without summons from the Church, you would fall under papal sentence of excommunication; but, summoned as you now are, if you arrest him you will earn remission of your sins, according to the tenor of the Council's bull. It will even be a most meritorious deed in the face of God, if through your means the monastery be thus reformed." Then the illustrious prince, Duke Otto, arrested the man and said unto him: "My Lord Abbot, if you will not be reformed, then come with me to the prison of your abbey." And he went with him to the prison. So, since no man dared to defend him by reason of the Duke's presence, Father John [Dederoth] clapped him into the prison, not to come forth unless he first resigned his abbacy. At last, making a virtue of necessity, he resigned that dignity: and then Father John became abbot and first reformer of that abbey.

The first thing he did was to insist upon a step which, though modern writers sometimes make light of it, was in fact not only one of the most emphatic precepts of the Rule but a fundamental principle with all monastic reformers: viz. the abdication of private property. On that foundation he restored the whole abbey to discipline: in the words of a chronicler who had lived through this reform of Clus, "God sent this man to save His people".

In view of this solid success, the duke persuaded Dederoth to undertake the reform of neighbouring Bursfelde, ruined not only spiritually but materially, and dismally situated. Busch, who knew it well, describes it as

built in a valley among the hills, with the river Weser which flows hard by. In winter it has but little sun, which falls upon the abbey for a few hours before and after noon; wherefore bitter cold reigned there at that season, for, thirty years ago, when I oftentimes celebrated Mass there, it thrice befell that the Blessed Cup of the Lord froze within my hands with cold; because the space between the church walls and the roof was then open, and thus the cold came in.

When Dederoth went thither, he found "the buildings in ruins and its possessions dissipated. Only one monk was left, compelled to live on the meagre produce of a single cow, the companion of his solitude." Before he died, he had turned this ruin into a focus of discipline which radiated still further under his successor Johann Hagen.

One of Dederoth's first cares had been to visit some of the houses of the Windesheim reform, to which we shall come later. He borrowed also four monks from a reformed monastery at Trier to help him at Bursfelde. Fortified thus by sound precept and example, he went on from strength to strength. The Council of Basel, like its predecessor of Constance, concerned itself seriously with the monastic question: and there Dederoth was brought into association with the contemporary reforms of Sta Giustina at Padua, of Castell, and of Melk in Austria.(3) The Abbot of Vézelay was chosen abbot-president of the Benedictines, and great efforts were made to agree upon a general body of statutes. This project, however, split partly upon the rock of nationalism, which to some extent had been responsible already for the failure at Constance.(4) The Germans strove for a strict return to the original Rule and the union of all Benedictine monasteries into a single Congregation with central authority, such as the Cluniac or Cistercian Congregations. The French and Italians, on the other side, aimed no higher than the compromise which Benedict XII had worked out between strictness and relaxation; they wished also to mitigate the rule of abstinence. Moreover, there were great obstacles in the way of that general scheme of visitation by which the Council of Basel proposed to bring all the German houses to some reasonable level of discipline. "Practical difficulties had arisen. Some abbeys, under pretext that the Chapter [General] held at Bâle would name its own visitors, neglected the authority of the special visitors and paid little attention to them; or, again, if they did admit them to a visitation, they declared that the articles of reform did not emanate directly from the Council [of Basel]." Meanwhile, however, the small group which were in sympathy with Bursfelde formed themselves into a Congregation (1446). Trithemius, writing about 1490, counted 90 abbeys in the Congregation. Later, at its height of material prosperity, it had drawn about 230 monasteries within its vortex. Cardinal Nicholas of Cusa, as papal legate, confirmed the privileges of the Congregation, and made considerable use of it in his struggle for monastic reform in Germany. Pius II again, in 1461, attempted to form one great union by uniting with Bursfelde the contemporaneous reformed Congregations of Melk and Castell, with which that of Sta Giustina might possibly have fallen in also. This project, however, failed, and all those Benedictine Congregations continued their work on separate lines, though with general harmony of purpose. Trithemius, who was himself born in that fateful year 1461, lived to see the spirit evaporating painfully from this great reform, in spite of much temporal prosperity. Addressing his fellow-abbots in a Chapter which included more than one of these reformed Congregations, he laments the brief span of every monastic reform in the past, from Charlemagne's days to the present. Even among the chosen abbeys of Bursfelde and its companions, "Behold, brother abbots, ye have in your Chapter 127 abbeys, whereof, in the three aforesaid Congregations, scarce 70 have remained under reform....We of the reformed Congregation of Bursfelde are neither very numerous nor very few; yet we fear now to fall; and indeed, within our own existence of less than eighty years, certain of our houses have in fact fallen again."(5) We must, of course, make the usual allowance here for medieval vehemence of language: indeed, in another place, Trithemius counts the successes rather than the failures. Nicholas of Cusa's legation (he writes) had truly sown good seed; some had never struck root in men's hard hearts, some had sprung up and been choked by sloth and negligence; yet a good part was still bearing fruit forty years later.(6) In fact the Bursfelde abbeys long retained some distinction above the general low monastic level. Leibniz published a fifteenth-century *Chronicle of Clus* by Heinrich Bodo, a monk of the abbey (*Scriptores*, II, 350). But this book is comparatively wooden and uninteresting: and, after all, the best testimonial to Bursfelde comes from Busch, who knew Dederoth and Hagen, and whose Windesheimers and the Bursfelders had helped each other reciprocally in the reform now of Augustinian, now of Benedictine houses. Busch writes (p. 525): "It is very marvellous that such ancient monasteries of Black Monks could be brought to so perfect reform." The force of that word *ancient* will be felt by those who remember the Windesheim maxim, that it was easier to found a new house on reformed lines than to mend the old. He continues:

For these have a very strict Rule, and many brethren who are very wandering, dissolute and lascivious and incontinent, proprietary and disobedient, perverse and rebellious; yet, in the reformed monasteries, these are now compelled to live without any property and in obedience and chastity, in the strictest due maintenance of their Rule; so that they are not permitted either to eat flesh or to go forth from their precincts or to speak at all without licence. Wherefore, unless the Lord God had set His hand to the work, and had comforted them by signs and wonders,* and had repressed the rebellious and disobedient from their folly, the hope of their reform would have utterly perished. Yet, in fact, with God's help, among many Benedictines of both sexes it has been accepted at first with pain and afterwards, when well completed, with joy; so that certain brethren and sisters who at first were bitterly opposed to holy reformation are now much rejoiced to have accepted it, and are no little delighted to pursue and fulfil it for ever in great quiet of heart and body and sweetness of mind, as I have now oftentimes heard from their own lips. Moreover, I think that their Rule gives them no small help in this matter; for it compelleth all who vow themselves thereunto to the whole discipline of the Order; since almost all things that we [Austin Canons] have in our Statutes are contained in St Benedict's Rule,† whereas that of St Augustine contains scarce anything but charity [i.e. love for God and our neighbour] and the three Substantials of Poverty, Chastity and Obedience, which it asserts in many ways.

We have a very valuable picture of life at Bursfelde in its palmy days from the pen of Martin v. Senging, a monk of Melk, who stayed there some time in 1457. He writes to a friend at Melk:

I would have you know that I came successfully hither to Bursfelde by the King's highway on the day of Saints Cosmas and Damian. God, the weather, the elect, and men and beasts have served me happily to that end; for I have come hither with my mare in good health and strong of body. But, on the way I stayed many days. At Wallsec, eight miles from Melk, I abode six days awaiting another horse; in Regensburg three, awaiting companions by reason of insecurity. In Nuremberg seven, subtly detailed by Master Conrad [afterwards monk at Melk], for in truth he showed me great charity; I believe and doubt not he would have bought me a horse with all necessaries at his own expense without any hope of repayment.

* Busch had begun this chapter with stories "of the evil fate of monks who laboured to impede the reform".

† The so-called Augustinian Rule is based upon a letter which the Saint wrote to a group of women who had vowed themselves to a religious community life. These directions were adapted to men by a change of gender and the addition of other relevant sentences from his writings; thus the tradition grew up that he, like St Benedict, had composed a formal and complete Rule. Wherever the Augustinian General Chapters had seen reason to imitate the Benedictines, they had decreed statutes based on Benedictine principles; but, to the very end, these were not quite so strict; e.g. in matters of flesh-eating and claustration.

At Bamberg I stayed one day. At Saalfeld, in a certain monastery, one day. At Erfurt St Peter, a monastery of the Bursfelde Congregation, one day. Truly I am treated here with humanity and charity. The place is solitary, surrounded on all sides with woods on the banks of a tidal river called Weser; it abounds in good fish: for instance, in great trout (which they here call salmon) and eels. There are four stewponds for fish on this same river hard-by the monastery. We have good goats' milk cheeses. I have at last learned, but with difficulty, to drink ale. They do use wine here but only on the sacrificial altar. Their conversation is praiseworthy. Quite recently the Abbot has founded another monastery in Hesse at the instance of the Landgrave, who is a patron of this monastery and a pacific prince; although Bursfelde is not in his land and lordship but in Saxony under the Duke of Brunswick. It is but a short while since three abbots offered themselves for union with Bursfelde (to wit, Ettenheimmünster, St Stephenat Würzburg and Hirschau), but they were put off to the next Bursfelde Chapter, which will be celebrated in the fourth week after Easter. The Abbey is poorly endowed and simple in its buildings. As to the simplicity of structure and endowment I know not any monastery in all Austria which doth not notably exceed it; yet none in regularity of life, for the brethren keep each other in great charity. All through summer and autumn they have manual labour with earth, and two hay harvests and the gathering of fruits from the trees and so forth, sometimes daily for two hours at a time. The Father Abbot is good and exemplary, so that we may truly say of him as the Wise Man in Ecclesiasticus: *Have they made thee ruler? be not lifted up: be among them as one of them.* Yet, in spite of our poverty, he ministers food and raiment in sufficiency to his brethren. For if he were not impeded at times by the necessity of receiving of guests and visiting monasteries, it would be his delight to continue in the regular conventual exercises with his brethren; therefore when those exercises cease he attends frequently at Matins, in Chapter and in Refectory. Nevertheless the different buildings are not so abundantly prepared for the convent as at Melk. For a few years ago, even in my time, this was a nunnery, in utter ruins, and it needed to be built almost afresh. The shaving of the brethren is done by the choir-brethren themselves, not by any secular folk, for it is remote from men and the nearest city is two good miles distant. They are shaved not in a room with a fireplace but in a cold chamber both winter and summer. Their beards are shaved every week and their tonsure every two weeks. Their cells are small and low. The partitions are of wattle plastered with clay; they have no doors but curtains. I can touch with my hand the rafter of the upper floor. The Refectory is competent, the buildings are well furnished with glass windows.

Water runs all through the rere-dorter. I have not yet seen the infirmary, but it is said to be humble. There are few vaults here. At the beginning of my arrival for four days, perhaps, I was much indisposed; thus I feared I should not survive. Impelled by this I made confession in the most pregnant sense of my whole life. Seeing that I proposed to receive the sacrament of Extreme Unction (for I feared to take the Holy Eucharist lest I should not be able to keep it down) God came and consoled me, turning my pain to good success and mitigating it. Thus for seven days I could not follow the conventual services. Then they treated me most charitably; a brother was given to me as constant companion to nurse me, my urine was sent to a physician in an imperial city three miles distant under torrents of rain. They brought me a written regimen and certain medecines, and by God's will I was restored to health. On the seventh day I joined the convent again and have remained sound to the present moment. Yet tell it not in Gath, publish it not in the streets of Ascalon: lest the daughters of the Philistines rejoice. I commend myself heartily to you. Salute the company of the lay-brethren, particularly Schleft. Commend me more intimately to the three brethren latest professed. Farewell. *Written from Bursfelde by Brother Martin on St Luke's day* 1457.

Here, for a while, we must postpone the further study of Bursfelde in especial, and look again at the whole German movement of which that reform made part; the movement which took its impulse from the Councils of Constance and Basel. This Germany of the fifteenth century claims our special attention in this volume, not only because the Great Revolt broke out in that empire, but because the Councils of Constance and Basel made it the focus of orthodox reforming activity. There are here far more original records from and about Germany than any other country. For the English sources, though unsurpassably rich in their own way, have not yet arrived at half their true value; only here and there does one of our medievalists turn aside from matters of minor interest to collect all these scattered rivulets into one channel, and filter them for general use. The social historian of our children's generation will make lavish use of our Episcopal Registers, too long neglected even by ecclesiastics.

CHAPTER XIX

THE BACKGROUND OF REFORM

FOR the actual effects of the Constance and Basel reforms we have two witnesses of the greatest value, so long as we make the usual allowance for medieval rhetoric. These are Nider and Trithemius. Between them, they exactly cover the fifteenth century. Both have already been utilized in my second volume (pp. 402–3, 487–9, 590–3, 612–16); but they need closer attention here: especially since Nider's attitude towards the need for thoroughgoing reform has been sadly misrepresented. We shall see how this good Dominican, specially noted for his reforming zeal, shows deep depression: the building is so rotten that he fears the very attempt to restore may bring it down in ruin. Pastor, by truncating the passage and introducing the words of a modern author as Nider's own, turns Nider's misgivings into fears lest those who were actually striving for reform should prove inconsiderate bunglers.* This Johann Nider (d. 1438) was a Dominican of considerable note in his day. He was a zealous and most successful mission-preacher and hammer of heretics and witches. He became prior of that great Dominican convent at Basel which was once famous for Holbein's "Dance of Death", and of which the church still stands. He was present at both World Councils, Constance and Basel: the latter commissioned him as legate to Bohemia. He did not live to see the end of the Council, for he died in 1438; but it had already sat six years (1431–7) when he wrote his *Formicarius*, a treatise on morals and theology by analogy with the habits of the ant. The book is in the form of a dialogue between a theologian and his disciple, who represents what we should call the man in the street.(1)

The theologian explains how ants build for themselves a nest which shows wonderful patience and skill; we may call it their "city".

* See my second volume, p. 592.

In this operation they have no master but God alone, by whose prompting they are ruled both in the forming and in the reforming of this edifice. Herein they show a proper type of those things which pertain to General Councils, especially those of Prelates. For these ought to reform the city of the Church Militant in its buildings, in so far as it concerneth them, wherever it suffers ruin.... For thus saw John this City coming down from heaven: thus saw he its first origin: *I saw* (he saith) *the Holy City, New Jerusalem, coming down from God out of heaven, as a bride adorned for her husband.* But alas! nowadays all is turned to the contrary. For the better portion of the ecclesiastical state is debased in great part by greed and pride, and would that it were not also by incontinence!

On this subject, and that of the chronic wars in Europe, he quotes from the Vulgate Psalms liv, lxxviii, lxxix and cvi (A.V. lv, lxxix, lxxx, cvii). Then the Disciple speaks.

In our time, when the General Council was held at Constance, in so far as I remember, there was much discussion there concerning the reformation of each rank in the City of the Church; and then I rejoiced in what men told me; for in my heart I said [with the Psalmist] *We will go gladly into the house of the Lord*; in whose gates our feet have scarce stood hitherto, for the evil of deformation. But we were baulked of our desire. Afterwards came this present Council of Basel, which prefaced nearly all its bulls with the claim of Reformation in their preambles. In that Council we have daily besought God's mercy in the words of that psalm, that He might bring it about. For that purpose a special discussion was instituted, the so-called Discussion on Reform; and now for six years men have oftentimes disputed concerning the restoration of different ranks [in the Church]; yet, even to the present day, we see no effect therefrom. Therefore I desire greatly to know whether we may have any hope of a total reformation of the Church, in head and in members, in order that we might sing joyfully with the Psalmist: *When the Lord brought back the captivity of Sion, we became like men comforted!* and so forth.

Theol. Those two Councils have not been held altogether in vain. But of that total reformation of the Church which you depict I have no hope whatsoever for the present time or for the near future; both because good will is lacking in the subjects and because the wickedness of the Church authorities [*praelatorum malitia*] impedes it, and also because it is not expedient for the sake of God's Elect, who are tested by the persecutions of wicked folk. Take an example of this in the architect's art. Suppose an architect, however skilful in his own art; if he lack suitable material, such as wood or stone, he will never build a house. Suppose, again, even excellent materials, wood or stone; if there be no builder, you will always lack a fit home and inmates. If, however, a house be not commodious for your friends, and, already built, be perchance harmful to them, why should you build it, as a prudent man? If you apply these three considerations to a total reformation of the Church, you will see in your own mind how impossible that is. But, concerning reformations in detail [*particulari*] within the City of the Church, a sort of reformation that is possible in many ranks and Religious Orders, I doubt not but we shall see these introduced day by day in certain monasteries and congregations; but God knoweth with what difficulty! For if, under this present Council of Basel, in six years not even one convent of the weaker sex, albeit with the co-operation of the secular magistrates, could be reformed, by reason of the evil lives of certain of its inmates, and the fierce support they received [*et eisdem astantem saevitiam*], what then, (I pray you) can we hope of those communities of nobles or learned men, who can defend not only with arms of steel but even, what is worse, by weapons of word and tongue, the ruins and deformities that reign in their spiritual houses?

Disc. Methinks the wickedness of the prelates is the whole cause of evil among their subjects. For, if the pastors were good, the flocks would walk after their footsteps.

Theol. You err here in part, but not wholly. For in a flock of beasts it may be as you assert; but it is not so in a society of men, who have freedom of the will. It is not thus among subjects, that they catch a facility of imitation from their prelates' virtues, as they do contrariwise and learn from them an example of vice; for the multitude find it easier to sin than to do good. [He goes on to prove this from Aristotle and Scripture.] I can teach you, by many examples of events in our time, that the people often refuse to follow the steps of a good pastor. For we have seen the Cardinal Legate of the Holy See, a man endowed with every virtue, the lord Nicholas of Santa Croce, Legate in France, a man true to the Carthusian Order both by profession and in life, a prelate who had as it were the powers of an Ordinary in common law over the realm committed officially to his Legation. Many know what progress he made in those parts. For, in the matter of reform, some resisted him to his face and appealed [to Rome]; many others avoided obedience to him by threats, and others by their own cunning devices. Again, we had in Germany, sent to us as Legate from the Pope for many years, the lord Cardinal Giuliano, whose equal methinks I have never seen among the prelates, in so far as my human frailty knoweth; yet all of us who knew that man have seen how far he was hindered in the holy work of reform, and what persecution he suffered. For many folk took no more account of his example and his precepts than if any other prelate of dubious moral reputation [*semi-infamis*] had uttered them. I know also one Mendicant Order wherein God, ten years since, raised up two good and most benevolent Heads, one of whom is Minister General of the whole Order, while the other beareth rule over a great province. Each is zealous and stout in the cause of reform as to stand in peril of death, not once only, in the face of secular folk resisting him; yet both have made but little progress among their subjects; for they have been able to reform few convents, although they had wished to reform all, but were unable to do so by reason of the intractable material.

Disc. Methinks there is much peril in the office of such prelates; and I would fain know whether they can be in a state of salvation while their subjects are so rebellious.

Theol. St Augustine, in his Rule, teacheth that not these alone, but all pastors are in peril: for there he saith unto the subjects, "Have pity upon the prelate or ruler, who, in proportion as his rank is higher than yours, goeth in the greater peril." Yet they are not in a state of perdition, if, in so far as in them lieth, they follow St Paul's teaching: *Be instant in season and out of season; reprove, rebuke, exhort with all long-suffering and doctrine.* Nevertheless, lest the rent be made worse, we must wink sometimes at the lesser faults of our subjects, where rebuke might probably lead to worse evil; even as an expert surgeon leaveth sometimes a less harmful disease in the sick man's body, lest, by curing this, he should encourage an inward and fatal wound.

Yet Nider is far from the spirit of "defeatism" in this Holy War. If he recognizes that it is the depth of the gangrene which calls for the utmost caution in surgery, it is precisely that gangrene which demands unceasing patience and vigilance. His long experience has taught him that, wherever *proprietas* reigns, "in such monasteries men scarce ever live without incontinence"; yet the overwhelming majority are in fact proprietary, and the reformer's first task must be to attack decay there, at the very root. But this first task is also his greatest difficulty; for "custom, that is, corruption", is so ancient and strong here, that the unreformed appeal to it openly as to an unwritten law superseding both Rule and Papal Statutes. Vainly, while exhorting Religious to keep the fasts and self-denial prescribed by their Rule, he tries to shame them by showing that lovers, athletes, etc., do as much or more to gain their own objects. He adds: "We see poor village-folk content with such scanty clothing in winter that, if a delicately nurtured man did the same for love of God, he would be counted a saint." The average monk was not conscious of a vocation to great asceticism, nor was he tolerant of those who thus reminded him that the Rule demanded more from him than from the ordinary decent layman. "Whenever anyone tries to renew the form of ancient religion among the perverse, by exercising good works, it can scarce be believed what opprobrium he must suffer from the evil-disposed!" Nider deeply deplores the fate of

> certain holy men in Christ's Church, especially those who dwell in monasteries where there is neither the living rule of a good superior, nor the written Rule kept by the multitude....As we have seen, alas! in many that are convents in name only, and utterly deformed monasteries, which sometimes in truth are rather holes, and dens of lost men, than tabernacles of virtues: hovels of dissoluteness more truly than porches of God's temple.(2)

Trithemius (1461–1516), abbot at Spanheim and at Würzburg, is a more authoritative witness than Nider, and far more copious. He has the surpassing value of having recorded a great mass of General Chapter proceedings and other original reforming documents on the one hand, while on the other he discusses hopes and fears most frankly and fully with his fellow-abbots, and records his own considered judgment after many years of almost unique experience. Yet he has been even more neglected by historians than Nider. I cannot explain this on any other theory than that those few apologists who have made any pretence of going fully into these matters have not dared to face his evidence. The 150 folio pages in which this contemporary judges for himself the state of German monasticism in 1500, supplying always original documentary sources for judging, give the most definite lie to Janssen's complaint that the historian has not yet sufficient evidence for making up his mind.

He delivered seven orations before the assembled abbots at Bursfelde General Chapters, between 1490 and 1500.(3) The second and third of these (1492 and 1493) deal with the "ruin" of the Benedictine Order. Both are intensely earnest. "I will not trouble to linger upon citations from Scripture or Law or worldly Philosophy, knowing that such would displease this sacred assembly, nor shall I say things doubtful or uncertain, which would need attestation from Scriptures." In fact, the whole of these orations consists of a description of Benedictinism as Trithemius beholds it under his own eyes, together with an appeal to the parallel experiences of his fellow-abbots.

"The greater part of our walls are fallen; for in many of them religion hath perished, devotion is grown cold, charity hath expired. ...A minority alone shine with reformation, while the rest, the many, still remain in desolation....Lo, how many reforms have flourished in our Order; yet men's hardened minds still shrink from that Benedictine Rule which they profess" (p. 851). Subiaco, Cluny, showed the way, and now we are assembled here as a reformed Congregation of Bursfelde. This does indeed keep the Rule in so far as we can expect from human strength, "and therefore God hath blessed it with dew from heaven and with the fatness of the earth; so that, in proportion as thou servest with greater desire in observance of the Rule, thou art more abundantly loaded by Him with bodily necessities. But beware, O venerable Mother, [Bursfelde] whom thy servants must never desert, lest fulness of bread and idleness give thee matter for sinning....Many reforms, as I have said, have flourished in the past; yet nowadays there is no vestige of them in many cases." How long, then, will this reform of ours endure? I am no prophet; [he says], but let me argue from past history. Our Congregation is sixty years old, "as strong in the many as it was fervent from the beginning in the few; although we have always weaker brethren by whom the diligence of the rest is tried. Not all men can do all things, nor has each one of us the same desire: yet public report is not corrupted by the evil of one, or of a few. There are two things which very hopefully promise perseverance for this Reform" (p. 852). Those two are, our General Chapters and our system of Visitations. "If Chapter and Visitation be dropped, Reform is annihilated." Therefore, my brethren, cling to those essentials: yet I fear that, when the present zealous generation has passed away, even those may perish. "I fear, because many pseudo-monks will arise, such as are arisen even now in our Order; men who will hate holy reformation, and detest the original name, and reduce unity to confusion." There are other Benedictines who are puffed up with pride, and scorn the lowly name of Bursfelde; but we have papal approbation. What if we have perverse members even among ourselves; "no Congregation hath ever been so holy but that it hath suffered some evil associates" (p. 853). Yet reflect upon what has been said abroad: we must take the utmost care to avoid degeneration as time goes on. Benedictinism was glorious in days past for two things, holiness and knowledge of the Scriptures: but "where those have been neglected, they have quickly brought our Order to degradation....Lofty buildings or splendid estates make not stable discipline in our Order: for riches foment vanity: if they increase, set not your heart upon them, since they despoil possessionate monks of their honesty. Lo! how many Abbots and Priors, immersed in worldly things, are utterly naked of all holiness and learning!" (p. 854). "Religion, of old, brought forth riches, until the insolent daughter hath suffocated the mother: for [as St Paul saith], they that will become rich fall into temptation and into the snare of the devil. It was the worship of God and sincere devotion which enriched our holy Order; and it is the blind ambition of monks which hath stripped it of all good things. For, when they plunged into secular business, they forthwith neglected reading the Scriptures; then the glorious colour of discipline began to fade, and all devotion expired. Then, with the neglect of spiritual things, by God's just decree even worldly things have failed....Lo, in these days all things are opportune and favourable, if only there be the will to study. Nowadays, any man may become learned at a small price. Formerly there was great scarcity of books; for they were of great price, and costly in their preparation. Now, however, through the art of printing, a huge multitude of books is brought daily to light, whereby wholesome teaching is gloriously increased. Wherefore, then, do we languish in sloth and idleness?" (p. 855).

In his next oration (1493), Trithemius is more pessimistic still. He there speaks not only of the monasteries, but of the whole body of clergy. He hints not obscurely at a coming revolution, and beseeches his brethren to do their best in preparation against this danger, before it shall prove too late. He will not quote to his assembled brethren from Plato or Aristotle or Cicero, but from a single Gospel parable: Luke x. 30.

"Not only our own body, but the whole body of Religious—nay, the body of the whole Church Militant—is going down from Jerusalem to Jericho; for it hath in most cases fallen away from its original institution. *Jericho* may be interpreted *moon*, or rather the waning thereof. Therefore whosoever falleth away from righteousness and cometh to a cesspool of vices, he goeth down from Jerusalem to Jericho." Therefore the Church is now fallen among thieves, wounded, and left half-dead. "Everywhere within the State of Christendom we see covetousness abounding with lust, pride, discord, wrath, envy, and other plagues of the soul, which, like fierce and cruel thieves, lacerate her with the most grievous wounds." She calls on the Priest, but he passes by. The Levite, "evil servant to an evil Priest, careth not for thine honour, repelleth the care of thee, hasteth not to heal thy wounds". No Good Samaritan is at hand. "Lo, those who sit to judge crimes are they who commit them, and who are glad to dissemble those of other men lest their own should be arraigned. Justice is sold for cheap bribes....Christians rage madly against each other; peace is broken between fellow-citizens, and quarrels are kindled. In former days, kings and princes were wont to build and endow monasteries and churches; but now, with few exceptions, such men are turned into thieves; they take Church goods with violence; they scorn God's priests; they contemn the commands of Christ's prelates. The love of God hath departed from men's hearts; reverence for the priesthood is gone; the honour for Church Sacraments (I say it with grief) hath expired; and we are come to [the prophet's lament]. *As with the people, so with the priest*....O priests, priests, who confound the ecclesiastical commonweal with your sins and crimes, who give yourselves to covetousness and lechery, who neglect God's worship and basely consume the alms of the faithful, how grievous is the sentence of condemnation which ye shall undergo! Ye who lead into the way of sin the people whom ye should have instructed with the word of truth and the pattern of holiness! Woe unto you, servants of voluptuousness, how near is your overthrow! There is no fear of God before your eyes, no dread of the law; ye are not afraid of the Judge within your own hearts. Your damnable conversation hath given occasion for sin unto the layfolk, since ye dare not teach well by reason of your own evil lives" (p. 856).

He goes on to characterize some of the worst offenders. He claims to have known peasants' sons who have amassed ten, twenty, thirty Church benefices, "yet they neither feed nor visit the flock committed to their charge". Therefore

I marvel not that the laity hate the clergy; for these by their morals deserve no love; since, as the Lord saith by the prophet [Malachi], the priests have been made contemptible before the people by reason of their crimes....And would that scorn fell upon evil priests alone, and injustice were not done also to the true and holy ministers of Christ! Would that the ignorant multitude did not spread the trespass of few over the whole, and that good priests were restoring that which the evil are destroying in our ecclesiastical commonweal!

Yet, presently, after this implication that the evil are in a minority, he goes on to imply the contrary with at least equal emphasis. Addressing the Church, he says:

Of old, in the days of tribulation for faith in Christ, thou wast full of bitterness; yet for thy countless multitude of holy children thou wert jocund, glad, constant and joyous; and the Lord consoled thee.

Now, however, in thy peace, by reason of the fewness of good children, thou art filled with the bitterest bitterness. Nor can we marvel; for thy pastors, with few exceptions [*paucis demptis*] are dumb dogs that cannot bark: they buy for money the leadership of thy sheep and thy children; they buy it with the blood of the innocent; they attack violently with spear and lance, not for love of Christ or for honour of thee, but for covetousness and pride and elation and insatiable lust of domination.*...Such as we see the priests nowadays in their relation to God, such also do we see them in relation to the laity. Contempt of God, nowadays, is very justly punished in the Church's priests by popular contempt; and the negligence of God's ministers is avenged by the robbery of their worldly possessions at the hands of the laity. Believe me, venerable priests, God suffereth naught without cause to be done against you. Doubtless He would defend His Church from the invasion of the plunderers, were it not that our own conversation provoketh Him to vengeance....No man in these days builds churches or founds monasteries; for, where covetousness is seen to abound among the priests, the accustomed honour and worship is denied by the layfolk. The Commonweal of the Church is come to such a pass that those who despoil her think they are doing God service. For they say: "Lo, sinful priests and monks have gotten unto themselves wealth! lo, they contemn the worship of God and spend that wealth with harlots! they have no care for honesty, no solicitude for holiness of life. Wherefore then do we delay? Why do we hesitate? Why do we not invade their worldly goods, that such criminal pride as this may be humbled?" ...Everywhere the cruelty of the Devil's satellites rages against God's priests; and those who should have been treated with honour and reverence are persecuted with hate and rapine by reason of the crimes of a few....Truly, Fathers, we must not marvel if we are left by the Lord in our necessity, since by our evil manners we strive against His commandments. Our sins alone render us contemptible before God and man....All things are full of iniquity, and not even from monasteries are crimes kept away....O Church, thou liest despoiled and well-nigh naked and half dead, while thou art inwardly despoiled of thine earlier virtues, and outwardly of worldly goods....What wilt thou answer to the Great Shepherd at the Last Judgement, when He shall begin to require His sheep from thy hands? See how the people is fallen by reason of thy sins, and the commonweal is destroyed. The Church's treasure is squandered, preaching is despised, and the profusion of Indulgences is contemned....Almost all Asia hath deserted

* In Germany, far more than elsewhere in Europe, the bishops were great princes, nearly always men of noble families, whose feuds and vendettas added fuel to the greed for a princely income.

the Christian faith; Africa hath left it; it is only in Europe that the Catholic faith surviveth, though feebly.

Thence he turns to monasticism in especial. He begins by depicting in detail its ancient glories: only thus (he says) can we rightly estimate that which we see around us to-day. Here the picture is dark (p. 861):

Devotion is not enough for the ruler of the Lord's flock, if knowledge of the Scriptures be lacking. But nowadays our monks and Abbots are neither devout nor learned; therefore they are judged unworthy to govern their monasteries. What if I said that, in these days, the Commonweal of the Church is unworthy of learned and holy teachers? for I think that no man could justly be wroth with me on that account.

Here he turns again to the monks of earlier distant ages: how busy they were in writing and in study, and how they have enriched the learned world.

"But now, where is such study among monks? Shame to relate, the man who is called great and useful in our Order is not he who cultivates and loves the knowledge of the Scriptures, but he who fouls his fingers with the grubbing of perishable riches." Worldly abbots excuse themselves on the ground that knowledge puffeth up: they say: "we would fain remain in our simplicity". "O fools and unwise, ye who hide not your slothfulness, but, to your greater confusion, show yourselves openly as enemies of holy Scriptures!...O ye ignorant Abbots, enemies to the knowledge that saveth, who spend the day in obscene gossip, who drink wine to repletion, who busy yourselves with earthly gain, who play like fools at the [gaming] table, what will ye answer to God Almighty, and St Benedict your legislator, when they shall require of you the care of your sheep?...Lo! there are more than 10,000 monasteries under the Benedictine Order; and I believe that scarce 1,000 of these have been kept in any sort of observance of the Rule—*ad aliqualem regulae observantiam*....I fear—nay, if I may say it, I know—that such [evil Abbots as I have described] can be found even among ours [of Bursfelde]: men who are reformed in name but deformed in truth" (p. 861).

He concludes with an enumeration of past and present monastic reforms, and exhorts his fellow-abbots to show themselves worthy helpers in this present movement.*

* Lord Acton's copy of this book had belonged to the "Collegium Hospitalense". A seventeenth-century hand has written on one of the blank end-pages, calling attention to these two orations as foretelling "the heresy now reigning", by reason of "the evil lives and scandals of priests".

In two other books, the *Dehortationes ad Monachos* and the *Liber Pentichus*, he speaks with even greater plainness to monastic audiences. The *Dehortationes*, published in 1486, were addressed to his brethren and dedicated to his predecessor, now Abbot of Seligenstadt; we may therefore trust them on matters of fact.(4) He condoles with his predecessor: "Now, alas, I know by experience the cause which impelled you to resign your abbacy of Spanheim, barren and fruitless, wherein you spent thirteen years from its reformation, not without continual anxiety of mind and infinite labours. I pass over the insults you received from very many brethren, all of which are daily redoubled upon mine own head." Thence, reviewing before his brethren his own three years of rule, he speaks more plainly and in greater detail. Just as the whole Bursfelde reform owed its birth at Clus rather to the State than to the Hierarchy, so was it with Spanheim. Trithemius describes how the abbey, grown wealthy, became proportionately proud and idle; so that money "gradually extinguished altogether the purity of the Order".* Thus the monks squandered their possessions, and fell for many years into so desolate a state that five brethren there, living dissolutely, could not find even the necessaries of life. Therefore the Duke of Transylvania, taking counsel in 1469 with the General Chapter, expelled the abbot and brought in four reformed brethren of the Bursfelde observance.† The new abbot raised Spanheim in about fourteen years "to the state wherein we now live". Yet even now

"we are few in number compared with the ancient inmates; and unused to field-work; nor do our sacerdotal Orders permit us to turn stones all day long with our hands and break off the service of God." Therefore "we work only in summer at the haymaking and in the autumn at the vintage. This is not only because few of you volunteer for manual work; but, I blush to say it, yet I am compelled to speak out: your labours outside the precincts and your cells bring rather destruction than health to the purity of your souls. For what work ye? and what is your zeal in work? Do ye not wander, run hither and thither, indulge in feasting and drinking, and spend the rest of the time in idle and useless words?" Therefore "I diminished your

* Elsewhere (p. 128) he reckons that it is now 200 years since "the purity of the monastic institution broke down in this abbey, as in almost all others".

† The Duke, "loathing the reprobate life of monks in his principality", forced reform upon two other houses at the same time (p. 128).

labours outside, lest ye should sin more grievously by working ill; and I have enjoined upon you such handiwork as the writing and binding of books....Would that ye should do even those works of your hands with diligence, for God's sake, lest ye should eat your bread in entire idleness. Moreover, necessity urges us to labour diligently at copying, if we would have at hand such books as might enable us to exercise each other in spiritual study. For ye see all the library we have in this abbey. A library once great and noteworthy, but so dispersed, sold, and alienated by the deformed monks our predecessors that we found no more than fourteen volumes here. True, the ingenious art of printing, lately discovered in our own day at Mainz, brings many volumes daily to birth: yet we cannot possibly buy them all, in the sore poverty wherewith we are oppressed." Therefore for God's honour, and for the avoidance of that sloth which corrupts the soul, let us write and write and write!

Later, he reviews despondently the story of all previous monastic reforms: for Trithemius is one of the very few pre-Reformation writers who were really learned in monastic history. He who falls sets himself to rise again; but monasticism, "once fallen, hath never fully risen again". Even that early Cluniac reform, which

shed the light of its honourable conduct over all the provinces of the world, left nevertheless many monasteries of divers realms in their earlier deformity. Thus, from that time onwards when our Religion first fell, there hath never been any general reformation....O, how easy is the descent to Avernus!...All (so to speak) fell; few arose again from their deformity; many are rotting in their lusts [*in suis voluptatibus computrescunt*].

Here and on a later page he recites the efforts of his own time; the reforms of Bursfelde and Melk and Castell and Sta Giustina, and the bold campaign of Cardinal Cusanus. Bursfelde is now the most living among all those; yet even this "seemeth to grow lukewarm in some of its members, and to decline again towards the earlier laxity of life".

Trithemius died a year before Luther's appearance. His contemporary Johannes Legatius was a monk of St Godehard at Hildesheim, another house which had joined the Bursfelde Congregation. He wrote his *Chronicle* about A.D. 1500. Here, in the second book, he recounts the glorious reform of Bursfelde.

But the brethren, he writes, had now gradually degenerated; "they strayed from the path of righteousness and corrupted the way of the holy Rule, becoming disobedient, unchaste and proprietary".(5)

It is in the light of these considered judgments, by men who were themselves at the centre of the reforming movement, that we must read the surviving special evidence for Bursfelde and other German reformed Congregations. It will be seen that the different points of view complement, without contradicting, each other. The Bursfelde reformer, however we may discount him as pleading *pro domo sua*, gives us in the main a true account of what he himself has seen; of brands plucked from the burning; of monasteries turned from indiscipline and scandal to order and usefulness. But he does not look beyond these successes that he records; or, when he does, he describes the unredeemed mass outside his own Congregation in lurid words. We have seen in an earlier chapter how Busch describes the general sea of monasticism outside his own comparatively quiet waters; and it is difficult or impossible to find witnesses who take a more favourable general view.

CHAPTER XX

BURSFELDE IN DECLINE

Let us now check those literary sources by formal General Chapter records. Much of what Trithemius says is corroborated, on one point after another, by the study of those records which he copied from the Benedictine Provincial Chapter archives (pp. 1003–74). What he and Bode say about Bursfelde can be even more closely checked. For here, partly in the official records of the General Chapters, and partly in the pleas and counterpleas of two bitterly opposed parties, we possess the whole story of this Congregation's gradual descent into the open violation of one of St Benedict's most important precepts, his prohibition of a flesh diet.

The long fight of the monks for flesh-food, with what was almost the final abrogation of the Rule, is planned for description in my fourth volume. Here, however, we must look again at the story, from the narrower Bursfelde point of view; for thus alone can we realise the full extent to which that great reform had cooled down by the end of the fifteenth century. St Benedict twice forbids flesh emphatically in his Rule; once in general terms as "flesh", and once as "the flesh of quadrupeds". But scarcely any clause of his Rule proved more difficult to enforce in its entirety than this. Innocent III introduced the thin end of the wedge by one important concession. Clement V, a century later, repeated his words. Then at last, in 1336, Benedict XII granted a very liberal compromise: monks might eat flesh four times a week (except at fast times) so long as this was not done in the regular refectory. In that chamber the Rule must be maintained; the irregularity must be decently cloaked.

That reforming Chapter of Petershausen in 1417, which was practically a committee of the Council of Constance, accepted tacitly the compromise of Benedict XII (1336); flesh may be eaten in moderation, *but not in the refectory*. The reformed Congregation of Melk (1418) went back to the strict Rule. So also did what may be called the sister-reform of Bursfelde. Archbishop Friedrich of Magdeburg (1445–64) used studiously to invite monks of that Congregation to his table on fast-days only, because they ate no meat.* This strict attitude was maintained for some time by both Congregations, while a heated conflict of pamphlets on either side was waged in the Benedictine Order. Some visitors tried to enforce obedience to the Rule wherever they went; others complained that the dearth of fish, and the difficulty of attracting promising novices to monasteries of such unnecessary strictness, rendered a compromise imperative.(1) Therefore we find that, in 1485, even the Bursfelde General Chapter was compelled to remind its abbots that flesh-eating was a breach of the Rule. At next year's Chapter a further prohibition was added; abbots must not set flesh before guests at their table. This addition was abrogated in 1487. In 1496, the President's speech was written for him by the celebrated Trithemius, who complained, "many monks eat flesh publicly on their journeys, and doubtless they do so in secret also": hence scandal among the faithful. Therefore the Chapter passed a strong decree against this violation of the Rule, which it renewed in 1497 and 1498. Yet these men had a loophole of the kind which makes medieval legislation so bewildering to the modern student, and which so often blunted its force in its own day. For Pius II, invoking the precedent of Benedict XII, had published a bull in 1459, which allowed flesh once or twice a week even in reformed monasteries, when the abbot thought it expedient. This was in harsh contradiction with the statute of 1451 in which Cardinal Cusanus, as papal legate and special commissioner for reform, had "most strictly forbidden" all flesh-eating "except in cases where the Rule permits". It was natural enough that Bursfelde should gradually incline more and more into the line of least resistance. As early as 1493 the abbey of Reinhardsbrunn had been allowed to join the Congregation, although its abbot explicitly refused to abandon the use of flesh. Moreover, at least ten houses possessed papal indults allowing them, under different pleas, to break the Rule; and there is no sign that they resigned these indults as members of Bursfelde. This dualism could scarcely fail to encourage further relaxation. The General Chapter of 1512 renewed the prohibitions of 1496,

* J. Busch, *Lib. Ref.* p. 745.

1497 and 1498 in far stronger language; transgressors must henceforth be punished "without mercy", as "calumniators and transgressors of their profession". It was now no longer possible to run with the hare and hunt with the hounds; the flesh-eaters broke into open revolt. The events which now follow were complicated by the fact that the Bursfelde Reform formed only one Congregation, however important, among the whole Benedictine multitude. In 1521, the Benedictine Chapter of all houses in the provinces of Mainz and Bamberg applied to Rome for an indult in favour of flesh. Out of the 129 houses in those two provinces fifty-three were Bursfeldian. A few weeks later, the General Chapter of Bursfelde met, and expressed high indignation, especially as the Mainz-Bamberg Chapter, speculating upon a favourable reply from Rome, had already presented the Congregation with a *fait accompli.* For it had given the assembled fathers permission to invite monks to their table and "comfort, restore and refresh them". Moreover, its decree had contained the words "even though they be of the Bursfelde Congregation". Under such provocation, Bursfelde expressed itself with a violence which damaged an otherwise strong case. "Let such *sensuales bestiae* as these" (so ran their decree) "read the bull of Cardinal Cusanus", with its strict prohibition. For ourselves, we will excommunicate all who dare to eat this forbidden flesh.(2) Yet, with all this violence of language, no really firm action was taken; it was a war of words, and the flesh-eaters were confident of final victory at Rome. The most eloquent advocates of the indult were the abbots of Ahusen and Vinsternau. The former rivalled his adversaries in violence: he wrote of "the pricked bubble of Bursfelde humility—these crowned asses—these two-footed beasts think to be reputed for learning and religion, while they shamelessly strive to vomit their venom upon others". The latter's lengthy treatise is printed by Volk *in extenso.*(3) Here, again, the language is violent; he makes great play with the Bursfelde blunder of "sensual beasts", and renders abuse for abuse on every page. But it is more interesting to follow his arguments. Nearly all come under the same general head: that to violate one clause of the Rule is a small thing compared with the sins of pride, pharisaism, and lack of that charity which breathes from every one of St Benedict's chapters. This argument would have had more force if the writer himself had not gone at least as far on his own side as his opponents on theirs. His other arguments are, first the old objection that fish is difficult to get—as if the monks had really been helpless in this respect, or fish had been a necessity of life for men who had abundance of eggs, butter, milk and cheese with their bread. The other, far more significant, is peculiar (so far as I know) to this time and to this controversy. "The Convents of Mendicants and other Orders abound in very learned and erudite persons whose ability and experience know how to stand excellently against the losses and inconveniences of each monastery" (in other words, men of business ability and legal training, a field in which the universities of the later Middle Ages excelled far more than in scholarship).

But we of the Benedictine Order, which aforetime shone beyond all others with fairer excellence, are now compelled to admit illiterate persons, vile and untaught, and apt to destroy monasteries with regard to both states [i.e. both spiritually and temporally], since others better fitted for our purpose never beg admittance. For this cause, alas! our holy and splendid Order must needs be miserably destituted and endangered unless a remedy be soon applied.... Hitherto, some monasteries—nay, many in number—have shrunk from the beauty of reformation, and may have been secularized by [papal] dispensation, which, if they had been more gently treated, or if severity had been sparely used, would doubtless have submitted to reform and would never have laboured for exemption from the Provincial Chapter, or from the Order altogether.

For the rest, it is no unfair specimen to quote from the next paragraph, addressed to the Bursfelde advocate.

No man will think thee more learned for that thou citest the bulls of Pope Pius and Nicholas of Cusa, confusedly scattered about the portfolio or the charters of Trithemius, in contempt of the laws of reciprocal charity, biting and rending thy superiors with the fangs of detraction, in thine insolent fury. Thou Pharisee! learn the way of truth, and first cast forth the beam from thine own eye, that thou mayest be held fit to remove the mote from thy brother's. Tell me, pray, which is the more inhuman? to eat flesh, as common law or the Pope's indult admits, or to devour in devilish fashion the raw flesh of honourable prelates, with whom thou art not held fit to consort?

This "masterly defence", as Dom Volk calls the pamphlet, was printed for circulation; one of the earliest examples of its kind.

The General Chapter of 1522 again unpacked its heart with words: it argued that these rebels were perjurers to their oath of profession; they were servants rather to the flesh than to the spirit; they were scandalizing all faithful Christians. But now the rigorists found an unexpected ally in the Prince-Bishop of Mainz, Primate of Germany. He commanded all the flesh-eating abbots to keep silence, and ordered the General Chapter of Bursfelde to take a special vote upon the issue. All present voted for maintenance of the Rule: but the rebels had continuously absented themselves from the Chapter. So did they, again, from that of 1523, which comforted itself with repeating for the third time, and thus giving constitutional fixity to, the previous prohibitions. But the flesh-eaters had now enlisted what counted far more heavily at Rome than any Chapter decrees; they employed the great banker Jakob Fugger to work for them at the papal court. This man, the richest merchant in Germany, explained to a contemporary ecclesiastic, Secretary to the Cardinal of Aragon, that his greatest revenues came from loans to bishops and abbots-elect in order to meet their bills at the Roman Court for first fruits and other similar charges. He boasted that he had thus filled every see in Germany, and some twice or thrice over.(4) With his help, a papal indult was procured permitting the Benedictines to break their Rule thrice a week; it cost only the comparatively small sum of 250 florins, at a time when three florins would buy a cask of herrings. This closed the discussion for the Provincial Chapter of Mainz and Bamberg; but it was far from deciding the whole question. On this point, we have irrefragable evidence from a most orthodox and anti-Lutheran contemporary, Heinrich Bode or Bodo, who was a monk and chronicler at that abbey of Clus which had been the mother of the Bursfelde Reform.(5) He wrote, under the date of 1523: "In this year very many Fathers of the Bursfelde Observance, burning with desire for flesh-food, caused no small perturbation of the regular constitution. I have thought right to go back some way to the source whence this crept in." At the Chapter of 1521 certain fathers complained of the backwardness of this great Congregation in higher studies, and obtained a decree that promising members should be sent to Erfurt; meanwhile, a few learned non-monastic teachers should be imported. But here came a difficulty: the chief promoter of the scheme said, "Ah! abstinence from flesh is the obstacle: that is what bars the way to monastic life for very many men of brilliant learning." On this plea, the Chapter decided to retrace its reforming steps, and go back.

Letters are sent to His Holiness and by a cunning twist of narration the use of flesh is besought for the Benedictine Order, as suffering now from long abstinence.* The Pope, melted almost completely by his condolence, wrote *Fiat quod petitur*. What shall I say? Men have followed noxious (not to say, unlawful) expedients, and fled from that which the sainted Father Benedict knew to be profitable. Now, in order to get licence for anything we will, we find a reason in the deficiencies (as we think) of our Order! Let those see to it, let those see to it, who have inflicted so deadly a wound upon our excellent Observants and our most laudable life!

He then reckons up the defaulters. From the Bursfelde prohibition of flesh there have fallen away all its monasteries in the dioceses of Magdeburg and Halberstadt. In that of Hildesheim, three have fallen, but Clus, Bursfelde, and three others have held fast.

In Thüringen they have connived with the flesh-seekers; in Franconia a few have been mindful of their fathers' rectitude; the rest were enticed by the odour of flesh. Those of the Upper Rhine held fast. But, when flesh had been permitted for a while, it began to be plain that this is no help for monastic life, but rather a cruel enemy. For soon, when flesh had been tasted, men clad themselves in soft-woven garments, wool is unfit for our dear delicate bodies; we procure linen. For the rest, I deem it best to keep silence. For flesh longeth after flesh; and, when fat is sprinkled on the fire it burneth the more fiercely. There are now constant quarrels in our Congregation between flesh-eaters and their opponents. "Lo! good reader, thou seest how nothing is enduring in human actions. The reform which began in this abbey hath not yet come to its hundredth year, and already we are drifting so easily into the old jungle" [*in antiquam reditur silvam*]. These are the Devil's nets and gins and snares and cunning arts; these are his twigs smeared with bird-lime, wherewith he hath betrayed those who were living well under life according to the Rule, even as the cunning fowler taketh his bird.... We have now come to the year 1525; that year (I would say) which hath been darkened by the shadow

* Leibniz prints "jam ob longam *caniciem* male se habenti", i.e. "from long old age". It seems a patent misreading for *carentiam*.

of death, invaded by darkness of mind, involved in bitterness; the year possessed with a whirlwind of darkness, by whose gloom the very stars were shrouded in night. For in that year the fellow Luther brought forth the iniquity which he had conceived in his inward parts; the man against whom the Church of Catholic Peace may not unjustly cry: "Let the day perish wherein I was born", and the night in which it was said, "There is a man child conceived"; a man (I say) full of quarrel and wrath and dissension and all schisms.

He goes on to describe, with natural exaggeration, the dissolution and sack of monasteries and the outcry against monks.

Once, when I was bidden to leave the abbey with another of the brethren and go to inspect the hedges of the meadows, we came suddenly upon a great multitude of men, on horse and on foot, returning from the market. When they saw us, they raised such an outcry upon us and attacked us with such jests that we blushed even before those whom we knew best; we cast down our faces and felt that both earth and heaven bellowed against us; we could scarce hold ourselves erect, for we were nigh bereft of sense by the extremity of our confusion and the foulness of these men's words. I have thought fit to write these few from among numberless ills which fell upon us monks, not without God's just judgement. Enough now of these things.(6)

Here was the fulfilment of what the General Chapter had vainly foretold: scandal and popular indignation against an Order in which even the most definitely "reformed" brethren could not always be prevailed upon to keep one of the clearest and most emphatic commands of the Rule to which they had sworn lifelong obedience.

For the final defeat of the Strict Observance was now a foregone conclusion; it was only a question of time. The Chapter of 1524 did what it could. It reminded abbots of the oath that each of them had sworn, on election, obedience to all General Chapter statutes. The concluding words of that oath ran: "I will faithfully keep them, nor will I procure absolutions from the aforesaid, all and several, nor will I use them if procured, or even if granted *motu proprio*." Upon those last words the Chapter now laid special emphasis: even a Pope's *motu proprio* could be no excuse for violation of the oath. Yet their representations were met only with the flimsiest excuses. Many abbeys (it was pleaded) were in hilly districts where fish is comparatively rare; even in the Black Forest it is difficult to find enough! Yet the Cistercians and other Reformed Orders had long since forestalled any such objection by damming up their own stream to a fishpond, or perhaps to a whole series down the valley. The pleaders ignore the fact that, even in default of hired labour, the monks of earlier ages could have done this for themselves. The Chapter of 1526 fell back into a tone of lachrymose persuasion, pleading "in the bowels of Christ" that brethren should suffer patiently a few years of abstinence, with an eternal crown of glory in prospect. In 1529 flesh-eaters are exhorted "not to lose, for the sake of a momentary delectation, that crown of all their past life in Religion which is promised, not to beginners, but to such as persevere". In 1530 they were reminded of their oath and of the excommunication decree. In 1531 the decrees of 1512, 1521, 1522, 1523 and 1530 were re-decreed. And so on from Chapter to Chapter, with a damnable iteration which speaks volumes, in itself, and which is reinforced by such impatient words as those of 1537, stigmatizing "that rancid odour of flesh, wafted again to the nostrils of our Fathers, even nauseously and indigestibly" and comparing this schism which beef and mutton are now creating in the Bursfelde Congregation with that which "the idolater Jeroboam" made in Israel with his Golden Veal. The old prohibition, with the old threats of punishment—transparently idle, by this time—are repeated at the Chapters of 1538, 1539, 1540, 1541. More and more openly and insistently, the revolt was growing. The decree of 1544 confesses: "Certain brethren are even gaping with open mouth for flesh-food"; and the few abbots who attended that Chapter dared not take any decision. In the next years, attendance was still poorer, and the demands for relaxation still more insistent. Therefore, in 1549, Paul III published a brief directed to the Congregation of Bursfelde. It insisted that all members should abstain from flesh, under the penalties already specified. Yet, at the General Chapter of that year, discussion was more heated than ever, and it was decided "to beseech the Pope, in the name of the whole Congregation, for a decision whether in future the full rule of abstinence should be kept or not". If not, then the emissaries were empowered to ask for an indult. Bursfelde had thus surrendered its main position; and the future was to show which was the stronger—the actual circumstances or the ideal. (6) At the same time, the Chapter sent to Louvain, which had then almost as high a reputation for such questions as Paris, for a formal opinion whether (*a*) it was permissible to seek a bull of dispensation or (*b*) such a bull, if obtained, could be used without wounding the conscience. Meanwhile the relaxed party sent a memorial to the new Pope, Julius III, with a repetition of the old plea.

It hath been proved by many experiences for some years past, beyond any possibility of doubt, that studious persons, apt for Religion, at this time when the early fervour is sadly languishing, shrink from entering our Order from no other cause than that its Rule (among other holy institutions of stricter discipline) lays a lifelong prohibition of flesh-eating upon those who profess it; a thing which men, as they are affected in these days of ours, regard as too strict and almost unbearable.... Unless some timely remedy for this evil be now provided, there appears no alternative than that (as aforesaid) this said Religion in these parts will gradually, but most certainly, die out through default of suitable persons.

Both Rome and Louvain, however, decided against the petitioners. They tried now to suppress these inconvenient documents: but the Chapter of 1550 decreed that, in future, no abbot should seek an indult without the consent of the whole assembled fathers. Thence arose in the Bursfelde Congregation what a chronicler records as "a grievous controversy concerning flesh-food, and consequently a division of minds"—*animorum scissura*. The formal Chapter Acts do their best to hide this, but other equally unexceptionable documents prove it; there were seventeen years of complicated litigation between the two parties, with proportional embitterment. In 1568, when the Chapter Acts mention flesh again, the rigorists had already conceded half the ground.

So far, then, had Bursfelde already gone, and in 1570 it took the last step. In consideration of the sad economic conditions caused by the continual wars, it was decreed that, by authority of the General Chapter and with the express or silent consent, of the Bishops, for the time being, flesh should be permitted for dinner on Sundays, Tuesdays and Thursdays, except during the fasts of Advent and Lent.

The account-rolls of 1612 show the following expenses for the assembled abbots in Chapter (servants included): Flesh 192 florins, poultry 60 florins and fish 25 florins. It is unnecessary to follow the further steps by which Dom Volk brings us to the modern usage among Benedictine Congregations; to the three types which allow three flesh days a week; the twelve which allow four, and the five which allow five. For Dom Volk's able plea in defence of these relaxations, and a brief discussion of them, I hope to deal some day in my fourth volume. The most definite conclusion which emerges, as I have there pointed out, is the almost negligible help which orthodox reformers actually got from Rome. Even where Paul III and Julius III pronounced definitely for obedience to the Rule, nothing was done; in fact, it was just at this point when papal decrees nominally fixed a clear theory that the practice broke down completely and finally. The reformers trod the winepress alone. They succumbed under difficulties from without and within; the pass was sold by those who should have been their most trustworthy allies. Here, four generations after William Langland, came an exact repetition of what he had described in the last few lines of *Piers Plowman*: betrayal from within the Sanctuary itself, and no resource for many honest struggling souls but to wander forth, each for himself, in search of the Christ that is to be.

CHAPTER XXI

THE GREAT LEGATION

NICHOLAS KREBS (i.e. Crayfish) was the son of a poor fisherman at Cues on the Moselle (1401). His precocious talent attracted the notice of the Count of Manderscheid, who sent the boy to the Brethren's School at Deventer. Hence he passed to Padua university, where he took his Doctorate of Laws just after he had reached the age of twenty-three. But he soon lost interest in law, took Holy Orders, and studied eagerly and deeply in Hebrew, Greek, Philosophy, Theology, Mathematics and Astronomy. His talents earned him promotion, and he was chosen as delegate to the Council of Basel, where at first he defended the conciliar constitutionalism against the papal claims. In 1433 he published what became the text-book of such claims, his *De Concordantia Catholica*. This "represented the ideal of the reforming party, a united Church reformed in soul and body, in priesthood and laity, by the action of a Council which should represent on earth the eternal unity of Heaven".(1) Soon, however, he became disillusioned, went over to the Pope, and became the right-hand man of Eugenius at the Council. In 1448 he was raised to the cardinalate, and in 1450 became Bishop of Brixen. In 1451 he was sent as legate to Germany, with extraordinary faculties and a special commission for monastic reforms, in aid of which the Pope empowered him to enlist the secular arm where necessary. This legation represents the nearest approach, during all medieval history, to a frontal attack by the papacy upon monastic abuses over so vast an area as the German Empire; therefore it deserves special attention here.

After all the discussions at Constance and Basel, matters had not gone far beyond mere words.

"Unprejudiced observers could not help seeing how few efficient bishops the German Church possessed in those days, since the majority had got their places through money or noble birth. In similar fashion, and seldom through inward vocation, the lower clergy had obtained their offices; hence many of them showed the grossest ignorance, reminiscent of the tenth and eleventh centuries, and immorality. The people, misled by blind leaders, and full of superstition, were like a flock of lost sheep," over which one might cry in the Lord's words: *I am moved with compassion toward them.*(2)

Cusanus himself said in a sermon,

The Religious Orders, with few exceptions, have now sunk into empty superficiality, as we see in many places where only the outer form of Church order is left, without the spirit of the founders. They are like pillars of gold or silver or copper; some are given up to levity, others to sophistry, others to foolish pride. True, they carry Christ upon them, but only as the statues and crosses and relics which are carried about by tricksters for filthy lucre. Yet thou knowest them by their fruits; men's spirit is shown by their works and their dealings.

His compatriot and friend and associate, Dionysius Carthusianus, echoed the same sentiments. Cusanus, in his mandate to the Archbishop of Salzburg (1451), warned the monasteries that he might have to deprive them of their privileges and emoluments if they did not reform themselves within a year. To the truly reformed, he promised in the Pope's name a Plenary Indulgence; and Scharpff rightly emphasizes the exceptional significance of this, as an Indulgence independent of any money payment from the participators. This (he notes) was apparently the usual distinction between the legate's and the ordinary practice; a distinction "which, in itself, proves that he, who otherwise was so indignant with all greed and cupidity, had not come hither in order to drive a base trade in Indulgences".(3)

For a year and a half he traversed a great part of Germany on this great reforming legation. Busch gives us a picture of his welcome at Windesheim in August 1451. He was

devoutly received by all the princes and prelates and magistrates of the land, with a great multitude of horsemen; by the whole clergy and people, Regular and Secular, hastening to meet him in crowds with their banners and crosses, and with great glory and triumph, singing all together the anthem *Advenisti desiderabilis quem expectabamus in tenebris*,* while he sat humbly on his mule with a little company from Rome, and many others from the neighbouring towns through which he had passed. (p. 337.)

* "Thou art come for whom we had longed and waited in the darkness."

He began at Salzburg, the metropolis of his own see of Brixen, in February 1451. Thence to Vienna (March 3), Regensburg, Nürnberg, Bamberg and Würzburg, where he received a solemn oath of obedience and amendment from the assembled abbots. Thence into Northern Germany, and especially the metropolitan see of Magdeburg; he was at Windesheim in August. Thence southward again to Erfurt and Halle, and back again to Magdeburg and Hildesheim. In October he was on his own Moselle, at Trier; next at Liége, where he found that the prince-bishop was living a scandalous life and committing his spiritual duties to a still more disreputable suffragan, whose very ordination was of doubtful legality. Moreover, the whole clergy denied that they were included within Cusanus's legative powers, and he shook the dust of the city from his feet.

Thence he passed into the Netherlands. Here, as in Austria and northern Germany, he had help from the secular arm. Duke Philip of Burgundy intervened on the reforming side, and besought the Pope's help. Here, also, he found active helpers in the General Chapter of Windesheim. He granted to all members of that Congregation, male and female, a Plenary Indulgence without money payment, on the sole condition of keeping certain moral precepts. Yet, even in the Netherlands, where he might seem to have all the cards in his hand, this great thinker and saintly churchman had little durable success. At his Council of Magdeburg, again, he repudiated the common deceptive form in which Indulgences were hawked about as remitting not only the penalty but the sin before God—*a poena et culpa*. Indeed, more than once he used words on this question which might well have brought a humble weaver to the stake, e.g. "Indulgence-altars, in most cases, produce only boldness to sin".(4) The cardinal addressed a brief in 1451 (September 3) to all the faithful of the diocese of Utrecht. In this he wrote: "Since we have learned, by true report from many men, both clerics and layfolk, that the nunneries of Utrecht diocese are open to all who desire to enter, and therefore, since they lack due claustration, much base and foul intercourse takes place, abominable to God, Who is then most grievously offended when those who have been dedicated to Him as brides by the solemn vow of chastity depart from their promised faith and commit adultery", a thing which even pagans punish most severely, therefore We decree effective claustration in future. All who enter such forbidden precincts shall fall under the ban of greater excommunication, whether they be clerics or lay-folk. All nuns again, who are at present absent from their convents, must now come back; and the clergy are to publish this decree of recall from every public place: here, again, upon pain of excommunication. Yet a few weeks later (November 13) we find the prioress of a great nunnery at Utrecht appealing in due legal form against this decree of the cardinal "bearing himself as Legate of the Holy See throughout Germany". Moreover, the nuns were supported here by the canons of the cathedral church, to whom Cusanus addressed a severe letter on October 27:

> We have now heard that you are scorning [Our injunctions] and have appealed against them, and that you are supporting the nuns' pretended and foolish appeal against that claustration which [Church] law prescribes....Who seeth not that ye care for naught but to live in pleasure here below, according to your own wanton desires? And where is your faith, ye who not only scorn the Lord Christ who nourisheth you [in your fat benefices], but are supporting also these jades [*mulierculis*] who would resist Him?...Certain despicable members of your Chapter, notwithstanding the legal prohibitions and the censures pronounced by Ourselves, have gone in openly to the nuns and do still go in, and hold feastings and solace with virgins dedicated to God; and yet ye suffer such fellows to associate with you in divine service, although interdict hath been laid by Us upon them, and those who thus mingle in the services are *irregulares*.

Better hold no services at all, than suffer such irreverence to grow: such abuses are intolerable; there will be revolt and disendowment in default of reform: you are steering to ruin. Amend yourselves, therefore, "lest we be compelled, with the help of the secular arm, to show you that Christ's adversaries must not live upon Christ's stipend and alms". Otherwise, "with God's help, we will show that Satan's soldiers must give way to the soldiers of Christ".(5)

This comparative failure of Cusanus in the Netherlands was not compensated by any proportionately conspicuous and lasting success elsewhere. Much was done in those eighteen months; but incomparably more remained to do.

Returning to Germany, he held a great Provincial Council at

Mainz, the metropolitan church. This, writes Scharpff, "was epoch-making in the history of Synods of Mainz; for it was the first step towards the fulfilment of those reform-decrees of Basel which had been solemnly accepted by the German nation, in that city, twelve years before". Next, he held a great Synod at Cologne, repeating the decrees of Mainz. In all three he spoke plainly concerning clerical concubinage and the abuse of Indulgences. In 1452 he attempted to end the Hussite war, but with little success. Still less success followed his endeavours to raise a crusade against the advancing Turks in 1454. In 1458 his friend Aeneas Sylvius became Pope, and Cusanus appealed to him for support in his quarrel with the Count of Tyrol concerning his bishopric of Brixen. The fight was long and complicated; there were faults on both sides, but Cusanus's fault was that of excessive zeal for the rights of the Church.(6) Pius II, on the whole, supported him, while striving for a compromise. Far more important was the cardinal's plea to his old friend for a general reform of the Church: "plea" we must call it, though it is drawn up in the form of a bull which Pius was to publish.(7) It is based upon that principle which had by this time become the classic watchword of all reformers—"Root and Branch"—*In capite et in membris*. He pleads with the Pope to proclaim himself and his Court of Rome as subject to periodical visitation. The Church is Christ's mystic Body.

The Light of the body is the eye: if the eye is evil, the body is full of darkness. But it is well known nowadays that the whole body is far from the clear light and is shrouded in gloomy shadows, especially because the eyes, which should be light, have become darkness. But since the eye, which sees the faults of others, notes not its own, therefore it cannot examine itself: it must submit to another for examination.... We, who are the eyes, should subject ourselves to such as have sound vision, lest, believing our eye to be clear, we should deceive ourselves, to our own ruin and that of the Church which we are to visit.

Let us therefore choose three Visitors, "earnest, mature men, true copies of Christ our model, who place truth before all else, and combine learning and intelligence with zeal for God: not such as strive after honour and wealth". Let them bind themselves to their duty by a solemn oath, and do their best to bring the flock back to proper respect for the sacredness of an oath: for nowadays "there is no truth and no right judgement in the people, so that men are inclined to contemn oaths and judgements". Wherever evil customs have become inveterate, men must be recalled to the prescriptions of Canon Law and the bishops' pastoral letters. Oaths, vows, and promises must be strictly kept; the man who lives otherwise is an unreality, a mere word, unworthy of the privileges which his title implies. "That man is no Religious who has apostatized, no monk, who runs about the town, no canon, if he lives contrary to Canon Law." Those who hold benefices must be made to reside and feed their flock; no man should enjoy pluralities where it is evident that he cannot perform the duties, "since no man can be in two places at the same time". Again, where the appropriation of churches by monasteries has led not to increase of God's worship among the monks, but to neglect of spiritual work in the parishes, let it be revoked: "for appropriations were not ordained in order that canons or monks should live in greater luxury and in idleness". Let serious disciplinary measures be taken "against those who, with brazen audacity, scorn the judgements either of written law or pronounced by Us and Our Legates or by their Ordinaries". "Let hospitals be so reformed that their alms go to the real poor." "Let watch be kept over Indulgence-mongers, who cease not to deceive the people when they can." "Let them also keep a watchful eye upon the enclosure and reform of the nunneries, in order to avert many scandals and God's great indignation, when those who have solemnly declared themselves the brides of God in their shameful excesses, drag many ministers of the Church and worldly folk to perdition with themselves." "Let false relics be discreetly made away; and let no false trade be driven with the miraculous Bleeding Hosts": for "gain alone is the cause why such things are oftentimes falsely fabricated by covetous men". "Let usury, adulteries, and party-quarrels be banished as far as possible from our flocks."

All the foregoing points (sums up Cusanus at this stage) are matters of such obvious common sense that "he who contradicts the Visitors contradicts his own self, and should be listened to no further, but sent away".

Thence he passes to a far more delicate matter. The whole document is drawn up as from the Pope; it is Pius himself who is supposed to be addressing the faithful throughout Christendom.

We are called *Father* [he says] because We must be the father of Fathers and Patriarchs; *Archbishop*, for it is upon Us that the care of all the Bishops falls; *Bishop*, because We are overseer of God's flock; *Priest*, "because the duties of the priestly dignity are Our principal charge". If we boast these titles, then We must plainly seek to be as We are named, and to show in deed what We declare in word. But, lest in Our own case we should deceive Ourselves by Our own Judgement, We beseech those who are chosen as Visitors in God's stead to visit Us exactly; and We assure Ourselves ready, to receive with most grateful hearts that form which in their judgement becometh Us, with regard to Our person and servants and court and all things pertaining to papal rank and office. Let them not shrink from visiting the Pope, since they recognize in him not only the Vicar of Christ but also *servus servorum Christi*.... Therefore, whosoever shall find in Us anything which edifieth not, but giveth offence to the Church, let him tell Us of it, that We may amend it. For, with God's help, We would fain escape the fearful sentence of one who giveth offence to the Church, and reap the fairest reward for Our labours in behalf of the believers upon earth, by consecrating Ourselves to the calling which by God's grace hath come unto Us, and therefore desiring willingly that the Visitors may amend any faults.

The cardinals also must submit to visitation. None needs more than from 3000 to 4000 ducats a year. Let this be straightforward income, not earned by heaping up a plurality of benefices, to the disadvantage of divine service or abbeys *in commendam*. Let no cardinal have more than forty servants at Court, or go abroad with more than twenty-four horses. Why should they not dress in white, the symbol of purity? Why covet the advertisement of crimson? "There is no fairer adornment for a Cardinal than that he should show himself like unto Christ in outward show, in rank, and in dignity, and should despise all pomp, which cometh from the Devil." In the city of Rome itself, the parish churches with their services and buildings and ornaments are in sad need of reform: so also the hospitals. Let all the hangers-on be dismissed from the Roman Court; men who are neglecting the cure of souls at home in order to pick up loaves and fishes by the basest flatteries and tricks. "Let all

Court officials be summarily dismissed who are debauched, concubinary, gamblers, quarrelsome, or such like."

This last section, running to six octavo pages, is indeed startling in its frankness. If it had ever been given to the world, under papal seal, this would indeed have been an epoch-making bull. The great scholar and reformer, speaking for the Pope's conscience, calls upon him for change of heart and life almost as decisive as that to which the anointing bishop had summoned the converted pagan Clovis: "Adore that which thou hast hitherto burned, and burn that which thou hast adored." But the converted libertine was not resolute enough for such worthy fruits of repentance; nor, if he had been, would his unconverted cardinals have suffered it. Scharpff puts the case as mildly as he can:

> Pius was too much occupied with the Eastern Question, and with the outward victory of the Church, to think of turning his attention to her inner condition, for the present, at least. Moreover, considering that Pius was so jealous for the extremest exaltation of the papal power that he seemed scarcely to remember his own earlier views, he can by no means have been inclined to condescend to reform and limitation of that power. Yet Cusanus was one of the few at the Curia—perhaps the only one—who, even amid glory and honour, did not forget what was decided at Basel for the salvation of the Church, and who now took earnestly to heart, in many free-spoken words (yet softened by the Pope's own resolutions), the amount of betterment that was still needed, and especially at the throne of the Supreme Pontiff.

He mourns that these things could not have been realized at this moment, and thus the later revolution avoided. But (he adds) Providence ruled otherwise.

Some of Cusanus's worst difficulties were with the Mendicant Orders, who had by this time usurped so many of the parish priest's privileges, yet seldom showed themselves worthy of this encroachment. He stood up boldly against the abuses which were practised at Wilsenak (Brandenburg) in the name of the Bleeding Host. For this, which had tempted Margery Kempe of Lynn to a long and difficult pilgrimage a generation earlier, and to which Eugenius IV had granted a fresh Indulgence in 1447, the philosopher and theologian in Cusanus had no sympathy whatever. He ordered the removal of the monstrance in which the so-called Bleeding Host was kept and adored. He condemned the whole belief as "a mischievous matter, plainly contradictory of our faith", which he "could not ignore without the greatest insult to God". He went in person to Wilsenak, burned the Hosts which were kept there, and substituted that which he himself had consecrated at Mass. "It is regrettable", writes Scharpff, "that such sensible and well-meaning measures lacked the desired success; but it is far more regrettable that the mercenary bishops of Havelberg, and the Wilsenak clergy who defied the Legate's commands, found support afterwards even among some of the Cardinals. The superstition held its ground far on into the sixteenth century."(8)

Even in his own diocese, we have seen in chapter XV how far Cusa's success fell short of his hopes. On the whole, therefore, this great visitor's work left a sense of disappointment among his contemporaries and successors. His support was indeed of great value for such reforms as Windesheim and Bursfelde; but the effect of his own visitations was not commensurate with the almost unique auspices under which they were undertaken. Vansteenberghe confesses this frankly: "This great reforming mission was not finished before the new building seemed to crumble everywhere: abbots break their oaths, canons return to their mistresses, priests buy their benefices; sometimes, even, the clergy appeal [to Rome] against the statutes which he wishes to impose upon them." The cardinal has to deal with "the underhand opposition of the Mendicant Orders against this envoy from Rome", and with "the open hostility, and the growing clamour behind his back, of men reformed in spite of themselves". It seems like the passage of a ship through the waves: the waters part, but join up behind, and the wake is soon indistinguishable among the waves. But "we must not suppose that his passage across Germany was useless". One chronicler records that five abbeys in North Germany were "consolidated in holy reformation"; another, Areutinus, writing about 1525, speaks of the reforms as durable, and we shall see presently what was done in the fifty-two houses visited by the reformers of Melk.(9) From all this Vansteenberghe draws an obvious moral. "Such a struggle as this [of Sonnenburg] shows how difficult it was to realize the moral reform which was desired for other houses. Such were the social conditions in the fifteenth century that, wherever there was no good will in all the parties interested, reform could be realized only by force, and force could be employed only with the aid, or at least the authorization, of the secular powers." The prince or the city magistrature, thus called in, might easily become King Stork, and scent plunder in the business. Thus, as he remarks, many of the "reforming" princes in the sixteenth century were following the example of others in the fifteenth whose own selfish interests had found their most natural expression in opposition to reforms which the Popes desired.(10)

Some modern apologists, on the other hand, have taken the facile course of inferring Cusa's success from the recital of those great auspices under which his visitations were undertaken. They arrive at this conclusion by ignoring not only the abundant side-lights which we get from dry official documents, but even the most explicit declarations of those contemporaries who knew best. Pastor, for instance, describes at length the impressive scenario of Cusanus's visitation journeys; for their durable effect, however, he has nothing to show beyond scanty references to modern and often untrustworthy Roman Catholic writers. Cusanus's greatest apparent triumph was at Würzburg, where, with four assessors, he held a Provincial Chapter attended by seventy abbots, from each of whom he exacted a solemn oath.

> Thus [writes Pastor with unction] was the good seed widely sown by the Cardinal Legate, for the seventy abbots bore back to their several houses the impulse received at Würzburg; no mere passing emotion, such as is wont to touch the heart for a moment, and then leave it unchanged, but a steadfast, earnest purpose of reform. It is possible, indeed, that, through human weakness or on account of insurmountable obstacles, some of the abbots may have failed to fulfil their promise within the appointed time, but there can be no doubt that the Würzburg Synod brought forth excellent fruit.(11)

For this particular assertion he gives no voucher but half a line of footnote: "such is Grube's opinion, J. Busch 130–131"—Grube being the modern ultramontane author of a useful but highly tendencious monograph on Busch. Yet Trithemius, who was born eleven years after this event and whose whole life was spent as a monastic reformer in those very parts, gives explicitly a very different account. He writes:

In this chapter,...All the abbots collectively and separately came in their order to the high altar of this [cathedral] church and promised, laying their hands in those of the Legate as he sat before the altar, that, within the space of a year, they would accept reform in their chapters without delay; and that they would faithfully keep it both in their own persons and those of their subjects. The proxies of those who were absent took a similar oath upon the souls of those abbots for whom they had been appointed proxies. All took the oath; but few accepted the observance within the year; thus, therefore, many became perjured.

Even for those who did their best, Trithemius quotes the parallel case of a Hirschau abbot who had taken a similar oath in 1417 at Petershausen, yet who found it impossible to persuade his monks when he got home, and therefore "committed the business to God".(12)

Again, in an address to the Abbot of Hirschau and his brethren of the Bursfelde reform, Trithemius wrote:

Where now is that reform which Cardinal Nicholas of Cusa, as Papal Legate, began with incredible zeal? Where are all those terrible oaths of all the Abbots of our province, wherewith they bound themselves, before the altar of St Stephen at Würzburg, in the hands of that Cardinal, to reform according to the Rule? Lo! brother Abbots, ye have in your Chapter 127 abbeys; yet, among these, who have joined the aforesaid Observances [of Castell, Melk and Bursfelde], scarce 70 have remained under the reform.(13)

Grube, like all the rest, ignores this unimpeachable authority, and bases his favourable inference upon nothing but the solemnity of this oath. Yet Cusanus himself, in that bull which he put into the mouth of Pius II, spoke of the necessity of bringing Christendom back to a sense of the guilt of perjury: "there is no truth and judgement in Christian folk by reason of the transgression of covenants and oaths."(14) It will be seen elsewhere that even Finke, a far greater medievalist than Pastor and a specialist upon the fifteenth century, is most unaccountably indifferent to evidence of this sort.

Indeed, Cusanus seems to have found the task too heavy in his later years; we hear little or nothing of his monastic visitations after 1452. But he preached indefatigably, and his sermons show him somewhat in the light of Tennyson's *Ulysses*:

> Among these barren crags...I mete and dole
> Unequal laws unto a savage race
> That hoard, and sleep, and feed, and know not me.

He attributes the great number of sorcerers in his diocese to deviations from faith and worship among the Tyrolese. He says: "They abound particularly in regions where Christ is worshipped, not as the Saviour of Souls, but only as dispenser and guardian of worldly goods; for this is blasphemy and idolatry. ...You know very well why saints are venerated and holy-days are kept in these mountains....Is it not mainly for the sake of getting rich harvests and cattle?" Therefore he teaches them to pray, and shows his flock how, under the word *bread* in the Lord's Prayer, we may ask for good harvest-weather, good health and all the goods that we desire.(15)

He had known in youth the intoxication of learning, and his genuine piety was touched with the breath of Renaissance. In 1440 he wrote his *De Docta Ignorantia*, a book which comes very near to pantheism, and which extorted afterwards the admiration not only of Kepler but of the avowed pantheist Giordano Bruno. In 1453 the fall of Constantinople prompted his *Dialogus de Pace*. He had always felt himself a stranger and pilgrim in that world full of wars, domestic and foreign, and now he tried to console himself and his age with the idea of a higher concord. In all religions there are some sparks of truth; let us emphasize these as much as possible and strive to minimize the differences. Something of the same spirit breathed through his criticism of the Koran. Yet, like his friend the Pope, he felt that the armed advance of the Turk must be met with a crusade; and he died, only three days before Pius II, in the midst of preparations for an expedition which never took shape (1464).

CHAPTER XXII

THE CONGREGATION OF MELK

A brief glance at those other waves of reforming energy will help to explain why Trithemius judged them to be already more spent than his own of Bursfelde.

Next to Windesheim and Bursfelde, the most effective Congregation was probably that of Melk. This abbey, on its great rock above the Danube, was one of the richest in Europe. But wealth, as usual, bred worldliness, with consequent unpopularity and contempt; so that here again, reform originated rather with the State than with the Hierarchy. Duke Albert V of Austria, who for a short time wore the imperial crown as Albert II (1438–9), was a strong and public-spirited prince. His work is briefly described by Martin, abbot of the reformed Schottenkloster of Vienna, writing about 1450.(1) Aided by excellent councillors, he set himself seriously to monastic reform: "he went to them in his own person and backed up the Visitors"—*tenuit dorsum visitatoribus*. "How else", asks Martin, "could he [and his faithful marshal] have deposed so many powerful prelates?" Busch, who attributes Albert's election as Emperor to the good impression created by his monastic reforms (p. 738), illustrates them by three anecdotes communicated to his fellow-visitor, the Provost of Hildesheim, by an Austrian correspondent. The first may suffice here (p. 736). An abbot desired reform, but the unreformed majority of his convent were too perverse and resolute in their disobedience, their private property and their incontinence. He therefore complained to the duke. Albert said: "My Lord Abbot, return to your abbey: I will come to you in person and reform them all thoroughly." He repaired thither, assembled them all in Chapter, from the cloister and from the granges, and put the question plainly in a long and reasoned speech, the purport of which was: "You are wasting in sin and idleness the endowments given for God's service. Each of you shall now promise amendment, or I will see to it that you shall have no longer power to contradict." He asked the abbot: "Do you wish for reform?" "Willingly."

Then said the Duke in the following order: "You, Dom So and So, will you also keep your Rule?" "By no means; but I wish to live as I found in this abbey when first I came hither." "But you also promised to keep the Rule of St Benedict." "Yes." "Therefore, keep that Rule which you have promised. If you will not, you shall forthwith receive the wages of your sin." The man gave evil answer: "I will not keep it, but remain as I am." The Duke ordered him out of the Chapterhouse, and put the same question to the rest in turn. Where the answer was favourable, he praised the man and bade him stand by: those who answered contumeliously were dismissed from the room. When all was done the Duke said: "My Lord Abbot, keep your Rule now with these brethren who are ready to obey. The rest, who have gone forth from us, will impede your reform no more." Then said the Abbot, "My Lord Duke, I would that it might be so; then we would reform ourselves perfectly." So, when all those affairs had been concluded for which the Duke had come, he said: "My Lord Abbot, come with me to see how your rebellious and wanton brethren are now doing." So he led him into the building chosen for that purpose, where all those disobedient brethren hung by the neck from the beams in the larder; some dead, others yet palpitating and drawing their last breath. The Abbot, sore afraid and terrified, said: "O, my Lord! What have you done?" The Duke made answer: "These men could not be reformed save by the gallows!" For he had left word with his retainers that whomsoever they saw coming from the Chapter-house, they should arrest him forthwith, put a halter round his neck, and hang him upon the appointed beams. These, in fulfilment of his commands, hanged them all in one batch.*

The second story is if anything still more grisly and cynical (p. 797). Though we must hope that neither is literally true, and that they represent rather what might have been threatened than what was actually done, we cannot altogether disregard the fact that they were handed on as *ben trovati* from one very experienced visitor to another, and by him to posterity, as significant of monastic conditions in the Austria of 1417.

In that year, Albert appealed to the new Pope, Martin V, who had just been elected at Constance for this very business of reform. The Pope sent him six monks from the newly reformed house of Subiaco, to which we must presently come. These Subiaco monks made a satisfactory reform, and one of them was

* Literally, "upon one peg", *in una cavilla*.

elected abbot, the last man having been forced to resign. It thus became a model for the province. The Schottenkloster at Vienna, with several other great houses in Austria and Bavaria, followed suit, and formed what was in name, though not in the strict legal sense, the "Congregation" of Melk. They all followed the same observance, but they had no general superior beneath the Pope. From 1460 onwards, attempts were made to effect a union between those houses and the other contemporary reformed Congregations; but these failed partly because of that particularism which St Benedict's Rule encourages between monastery and monastery, and partly for more fundamental difficulties which will presently appear. It was only in 1470 that seventeen abbots met at Erfurt and agreed to accept the Melk observance; but no general union was ever effected between Bursfelde, Melk, Sta Giustina, Castell and Monte Cassino. There is a despairing letter written in 1464 by the Abbot of Tegernsee to the Abbot of Augsburg upon this subject. He writes:

Of the very few who wish for the union, perhaps none can at this time bring it about. For at this moment, in Austria, things go ill everywhere, and worse than ever.... The clergy especially are oppressed, overtaxed, hounded away and hated by all. Monasteries are ravaged, plundered, and laid waste; nor is there any to save us or to sympathize in pity or mercy.... Some Fathers in Religion, with their brethren, are daily groaning in expectation of expulsion. How, then, can these give themselves up to holy union, now or in future, unless perchance God in His pity should mercifully vouchsafe to His servants a new year of blessing and kindness?

I have never found time to attempt an exhaustive study of any one among these minor Congregations. One thing, however, may confidently be asserted; that they produced no chronicler even remotely approaching Busch in value and interest. Yet there are many scattered documents; two of the most important emanate from the same man, Martin v. Senging, prior of the famous Schottenkloster, which for centuries had ceased to be a Scoto-Irish colony, but was one of the greatest Austrian monasteries.(2) The author had studied at Vienna University in 1424, had tried the noviciate at Subiaco but found it too hard for him, and then entered at the Schottenkloster, recently reformed but "a little less strictly" than Subiaco (1418).

Here he became abbot in 1446, and carried the reforms still further. He was associated with Cardinal Cusanus on the great reforming campaign of 1451, where he was employed to preach the visitation sermons. He resigned [in 1455], and died between 1460 and 1470. The first of these two documents, probably written about 1460, is concerned with that above-mentioned project of union between the different Benedictine reformed Congregations.(3) The papal legate, in order to bring these different reforms under one single observance, was seeking a compromise: Let all insist upon the Three Substantial Vows of Obedience, Poverty and Chastity, but leave freedom in the matter of the "accidentals". That was a specious proposition, reminiscent of the familiar distinction of substance and accidents upon which the doctrine of Transubstantiation rested; but Martin exposed its inherent absurdity. You class under "accidentals" (he writes) the command to abstain altogether from flesh, except in cases of sickness, and the strict injunction of labour. Yet our vow is one of lifelong obedience to the Rule; how then can we violate these "accidentals" without breaking our vow? "The Rule turns upon those 'accidentals'; it displays itself therein." Witness the present violent revolt in the matter of flesh-eating: a revolt which is driving some, even among the "reformers", to make such concessions as we make to a debtor, accepting 20 per cent in the hopelessness of getting any more except at the cost of yet greater loss. This, even apart from the patent logical flaw, is bad policy. If our opponents wanted real reform, they would accept the Rule; what shall we gain by whitewashing their bankruptcy, and setting imperfect Benedictines to visit and "reform" others not very much more imperfect? When once we have weakened our case like this, what chance have we against the quibbles of canon lawyers who are constantly employed to thwart us? Again, the visitand can too often retort upon the visitor, "I do as thou and thine do". Citing a concrete instance of visitatorial connivance at scandalous indiscipline, he exposes the impolicy of buying off these relaxed monasteries at such a price: "do what the Council will, these men will not long keep even the Three Substantials. Nor can we believe their promises or oaths; for, in the words of St Paul, they have cast off their first faith. I myself know one of them who, fearing visitation and reform, or perchance the loss of his abbacy, wickedly devised a way of keeping himself in office, at heavy expense for his monastery." The man simulated anxiety to join the reform of Melk, and interested the papal legate and the Duke of Austria in this project. The Abbot of Melk reluctantly consented to spare two of his model monks who should go as reformers to that abbey: one was presently recalled to the Council on business, while the other sickened suddenly under suspicion of poison and,...[here a scandalized pen has erased a whole sentence]. There remained then, on the reforming side, only two monks of the abbey itself, to whom the abbot made himself so intolerable that they obtained transference to other convents, "and the old life went on as before" (p. 516). Then came the time for a general visitation, including this house.

The abbot, seeing that he could not save his presidency, feigned a journey to the Roman court—whether he went thither we know not, or where he was lurking all that long time. To this he added useless expense of money (and even before this, he had dilapidated the convent's goods) so that it is now a good 5000 florins in debt. Yet he returned before the end of the visitation, believing perchance that it was already finished. Then, when the visitors came to his abbey and would have demanded his presence, he shut the precinct doors all round, nor would he open to any man even at the time of divine service. Hence he could no longer conceal his great fraud, but it became evident.

Moreover, it is very rare to find abbots in the two dioceses of Constance and Augsburg who can speak even a couple of sentences in Latin, or who study the Bible. They are capable of any shift; as when the legate sent them ten monks from the reform of Melk to teach them true observance, and the abbots in concert refused to receive, or pay travel money for, any monk of Melk; they insisted upon having brethren from the sister reform of Castell.

For, knowing that monks of Melk were indeed available, and that some had been deputed as reformers, whereas none had been deputed from Castell, therefore they begged for these last, that they might be credited with a will to reform. If however those of Castell had been deputed, and those of Melk absent, who can doubt that they would then have sought the reform of Melk and refused to accept that of Castell?

The Council, if it takes this disastrous decision, will shackle any really zealous abbot. He may no longer bid his monks keep St Benedict's own Rule with regard to flesh-eating, for the Council dismisses these things as "accidentals". Men founded monasteries primarily for the good of their own souls, but also in order that the monks' prayers might atone for the sins of the World. But "how shall that wrathful and exalted Judge be appeased by the prayers of such folk calling upon Him, when they praise Him with their lips and blaspheme Him with their lives?" [Matthew xv. 8; Isaiah xliii. 23]. The only remedy is a real return, both in Substantials and in "accidentals", to St Benedict's Rule—"now, alas, sadly debased" [*heu nimis collapsam!*]. Experience shows that, when one or two in a convent attempt nowadays to return to the Rule, there is intolerable friction. The statutory costume is frequently neglected; monks scandalize the public by frequenting public baths, which in the Middle Ages enjoyed an unenviable but not undeserved reputation. In short: "In the whole of Christendom scarce any Order can be found so debased [*collapsus*] as the Benedictine.... There are many runaway and wandering monks."(4)

This reference to friction between reformed and unreformed is borne out by another document among the Melk archives.(5) Ulrich v. Weilhaim, a canon regular of Diez in Westphalia, wrote a letter to the Prior of Melk in 1458 "concerning the tribulations and tempests in his monastery by reason of the introduction of more holy discipline". For nearly ten years, he says, his own tiny group has been "in such anxiety and tribulation...by reason of the holy Observance, that oftentimes we have even been weary of life". "For the present [*pro nunc*] I fear not, for I am certain that for the present we shall have progress in holy discipline." But

> I have twice been cast into prison for Observance' sake. I have sat ten days in darkness. I sang there *Te Deum Laudamus*. I was shut out from the monastery for seven weeks, but came back at once with honour. Twice have I stood before the Prince and his Councillors and answered on behalf of the Observance; and at last the Lord gave us victory, so that five brethren who were our persecutors, and enemies of regular life, have been sent and cut off from this monastery. This has happened recently.

Pez found allusions to a still more piteous letter from Ulrich, which however has been lost.

The other document is an account, very tantalizing, of the visitatorial experience of another Martin (surnamed von Zips), who had been abbot of the Schottenkloster at Vienna. It forms chapters IV and V of his dialogue called *Senatorium*.(6) He was one of the three commissioners appointed to visit the fifty-two Benedictine houses of Austria under the Great Legation of Cusanus in 1451. He lays natural stress upon the difficulties and dangers of travel; and, once, upon the perilous wrath of unreformed brethren, from which they were saved by God's mercy (p. 655). Again, he generalizes as to the exempt abbeys: in his opinion, they are more undisciplined because less often visited: in one of them "there appeared no vestige whatsoever of visitation; no written record, and no memory that it had ever been visited" (p. 638). In one abbey he records the popular tradition that it had formerly had for abbot a demon in human form, who ruled there while the true abbot was on a journey to Rome, and vanished when he returned (p. 643). Another he describes as "so poor that they very seldom drink wine, but small-beer", yet he saw no sign of their neglecting their work (p. 645). Here and there he tells us of curious relics or fairly natural miracles. He shows how, at St Georgen, where the nuns had barricaded their windows and their noble relatives were ready to defend them in arms, it was the Emperor's safe-conduct which broke down this resistance (p. 642). But, apart from that remark about exemption, the only other which brings us anywhere near to a generalization, favourable or unfavourable, concerns the question of *proprietas*. At Sankt Paul, in the valley of Lavant (Styria), the brethren did honestly give up their private hoards to the abbot, who bought fresh church plate with the money: "one 30 florins, another more, another less. . . At other monasteries, I fear that the resignation of private hoards was only in word; for we saw nought in effect, but they denied possessing anything. Yet the nuns at Görz gave up their rosaries of coral and their rings; but we saw no florins" (p. 462). Finally, Martin comes to his own famous Schottenkloster, and gives eight portraits of model monks whom he had known there.

CHAPTER XXIII

STA GIUSTINA AT PADUA

LODOVICO BARBO, of an ancient Venetian family, was born about 1382. In 1408 he was Prior of San Giorgio in Alga, that "St George of the Sea-Weed" which has inspired one of Ruskin's most remarkable drawings. We know next to nothing of his early life; but his reforming work was related by himself as an old man, in the third person.(1)

He describes the desolation of the once great abbey of Sta Giustina in the first years of the fifteenth century (p. 271). Under the despots who had long ruled Padua, the abbey of Sta Giustina

was tyrannically possessed by the Lord of that city, and its rich revenues were usurped for the most part for the sustentation of that Lord's kinsfolk. From this cause its habitable parts and the structure of its walls and all its offices were so reduced to nothing, that the Abbot and three monks could scarcely find dwellings, or rather, hovels, in this monastery, which was a receptacle of all vices and fornications and gaming; and thus this noble burial-ground was defiled with public and abominable iniquities.

Nothing but the prayers of past holy men who were buried there could have averted God's destroying wrath from this "modern Sodom" (p. 271). About 1404 a holy priest named Marco brooded and prayed over this state of things until he was assured by revelation that a dawn was at hand. Then, in 1408, it chanced that Barbo came to Padua as visitor under the reforming movement which was gradually spreading from San Giorgio. Marco hailed him at once as "he that should come". In fact, despite difficulties which at first seemed insuperable, this Barbo, a young man of twenty-six, was soon appointed Abbot of Sta Giustina, and found himself confronted with the heavy task of reform. Marco and all the rest encouraged him, except one prudent and reverend citizen. "You are young", said this man: "you have been only five years yourself in God's way: you are not so holy that your single example should provoke men to a change of soul. The Order of Black Monks is almost completely fallen throughout Italy: this abbey is infamous for the evil lives of its past inmates." And, in fact, he found a state of things which might have daunted the most experienced reformer (p. 279).

The monastery seemed so dilapidated [*diruptum*] and so utterly alien to the semblance of a Religious house, that it had rather the aspect of a cattle-stall than of a human habitation. In the outer part, where guests and such folk are now admitted, there was a chamber with an old wooden outer staircase,* and surrounded with rough deambulatories. Towards the oratory of St Martin there were, by way of sacristy,† two most squalid chambers. A great hall extended even to the wall of the church. The space of the main cloister was so open to passers-by that one could scarce determine whether it appertained to the public or to the abbey. The inner cloister, where we now see fair box-trees in winter-time, was unapproachable for the mire; and, where now stands the refectory, there were so many brambles and wild thorn-bushes that boys flocked thither oftentimes for bird-catching. Where now is the entrance to the cloister, there was a cruel prison, the receptacle of serpents and filth.... The garden was utterly bare of herbs and trees, save one: and this garden—nay, the whole abbey—was open to comers of both sexes. Men and women, when they had visited the church, went out through the choir door which leads to the dormitory stairs [*podiolum*], entering what is now the private cloister by a dilapidated gate which then stood in the corner behind the refectory door; and all passed through so boldly that even women, abominable to relate, would sometimes make use of the rere-dorter.

All this seemed so hopeless that many of Barbo's fellow-reformers refused to face it. He "left them free, rebuking them for their inconstancy and their want of fervour and hope in God". Then he set himself to do "after a fashion" without them. He found that the three monks of the abbey were willing to renounce private property. To these he was able to add two Camaldulensians from Murano and two clerics from San Giorgio in Alga. But Padua was a great city; and the immemorial commingling of these nominally cloistered monks with secular clergy and worldly folk rendered true Benedictine observance almost impossible. He sometimes thought desperately of

* *Podiolo*, not in Ducange but apparently bearing this signification: like the French *perron*.

† Reading *sacraria* for *factoria*, a word equally unknown to Ducange.

abandoning the whole project, and going out into some wilderness to save his own soul. But generally he favoured the brighter hope of finding some solitude where he and his friends might be able to serve God after the true model of St Benedict. Long and anxiously, therefore, he sought some such spot (p. 280). "But, by divine Providence, he was never able to conclude a bargain with the possessors, even though he offered great and honourable conditions. Thus, deprived of his one hope of solitude and destitute of all consolation, he returned sadly to his abbey [of Sta Giustina]." Here, in his deepest dejection, came one ray of hope. A promising young university student, Paolo di Strata, came and made his Holy Week confession to Barbo, and begged to become a monk with him. He crowned this sacrifice with steady perseverance: and "took the cowl reverently on Easter Day, 1410, on which devout and memorable day this Congregation took its birth, and the fallen Order of Black Monks in Italy rose again to observance of the Rule" (p. 282). A fellow-student came to entice Paolo back to the world, but found himself soon caught in the same net. This postulant, however, was not only very young, "but he was the only son of his father, who was a leader of the condottieri. Such a man as this would not lightly suffer to lose such a son, whom he was maintaining in costly and honourable fashion at the University: the more so, because it was known that the youth had promised marriage to a noble girl, publicly and in the present tense, though the marriage had not yet been consummated." Barbo feared here a snare of the Devil: would not this youth turn out like too many others, who promise hastily but afterwards trouble the community and "defile the worship of God"? But the youth came daily, besieging Barbo with incessant prayers, for a fortnight. Then being still refused he broke out: "Father, you should risk your own self and your life to win my soul." Barbo was shaken: "Will you hold out manfully against the snares of your kinsfolk?" "Yes, even unto death." Barbo then made this venture of faith, and braved the storm he had expected. The old condottiere tried blandishment at first; then he attacked him with threats, even of death. The final scene repeated almost exactly that which the Franciscan Salimbene tells of his own conversion nearly two centuries earlier.(2) "At last the father, raging with impatience, said, 'Truly the fellow is become crazy and mad, and if he came to me I would not take him in.' Thus, in uncontrollable fury, he left the hall, and the rest followed him, and the youth alone remained victoriously with the bishop" (p. 284).

"This marvellous victory was noised so loudly abroad in all Padua, that the abbey could not contain those who flocked thither....Within a brief space of time [Barbo] received 16 young students converted to Holy Religion." The devotion spread and grew; it was here just as it had been in the earliest Franciscan and Dominican days, when the friars' nets made their richest hauls at the Universities. "Thus the monastery was shortly so filled that the Abbot, by counsel of his brethren, was constrained to go in search of other places" (p. 285). After long search they found one that seemed exactly suitable; we shall see in a later chapter that there was no lack of decayed and derelict monasteries in fifteenth-century Italy. This was at Bassano, the priory of San Fortunato, on the banks of the Breuta, a pleasant site but "a dilapidated and poverty-stricken". In fact, it was let out to a certain Venetian cleric, who found it "a pleasant place", so much so that Barbo vainly tried to get it by offering a rent far higher than the profits he was actually receiving (p. 285). Our reformer,

feeling himself as the hammer in the [Divine] Smith's hand, besought God that He might vouchsafe to soften the heart of this cleric. O marvellous condescension of God! He Who in due season prepareth holes for the foxes and nests for the fowls, heard the Abbot's prayers and, even in that so healthy spot, no sooner had the Abbot departed than He smote this cleric's hand with a pestilent carbuncle and a fever. He, despairing of life, betook himself to the mercy of the Heavenly Physician, vowing solemnly that, if he chanced to be healed, he would freely release this monastery of San Fortunato to the monks of Sta Giustina. God heard his prayer: within a few days the fever left him and the carbuncle vanished. Thus, recovering his health, and taking only so much money as he had given to the workmen for changing this monastery [into a villa] he released it freely without any pension.

From this, Barbo went on to reform Sta Maria near Verona, and converted an almost ruined pilgrimage-church in the same neighbourhood: the new community "filled this hitherto most barren mountain with olives, almonds, and other fruit-trees".

A colony was sent to Genoa, where they raised a decayed chapel to the rank of a flourishing convent. Thence to Pavia where the university fed them with welcome recruits. One of these became a great mission-preacher.

This man, among other memorable deeds, converted the convent of Sangro, together with its Abbess, who was seized with strange compunction at one of his sermons. She rose from her seat, kindled with that spirit of compunction, and publicly proclaimed herself a miserable sinner, a condemned creature; and up to the present time, together with many nuns who serve God most devoutly, she hath given herself up to perpetual enclosure. This same monk, in the city of Genoa, made a bonfire of women's false hair and other indecent ornaments in vast quantity.... In many places he bore patiently, from those who suffered not the rebuking of their own vices and crimes, both bonds and prison and peril of death; yet, by divine protection he always came out unhurt to the glory of God. (p. 288.)

By this time the reformers felt themselves arrived at the dignity of a Congregation, with the Abbot of Sta Giustina at its head. Barbo therefore approached the new Pope set up by the Council of Constance, Martin V, who granted his approval, when he heard what great things had been done already, including the reform of the Badia, perhaps the wealthiest abbey in Florence. "But", asked Martin, "how about the Abbot?" "Holy Father, be assured that he serveth God, and is converted and weareth the habit of Holy Religion even as I do." The Pope could only reply: "I hear this in a dream!" (p. 290). For (continues Barbo), this abbot was a young Florentine noble, thrust into that great place. "He went to Constance for the Council; but there he cast away the fear of God and gave himself up to the snares of all sorts of vice; for there reigned in his house feasting and gaming and tournaments* and indecencies of all kinds." He even joined in a plot for seizing all the cardinals and drowning them; for he had a troop of reckless retainers. The plot failed: and the abbot had reason to fear for his own life; moreover, he fell into a serious illness. Now, "recognizing the abyss of his iniquities", he left the Council, returned to Florence and sent for Barbo. That interview set the seal on his con-

* Tournaments were regularly forbidden by Popes and Councils: strict disciplinarians insisted that those who were killed at that sport went straight to hell.

version; he received [some of Barbo's] reformed brethren into the Badia, and the abbot, "as a simple monk, gave himself into the Prior's hands". To free himself from further temptation, he resolved to "depart from his city and his kindred", and serve under Barbo at Sta Giustina. There, however, a sudden fever fell upon him and, after forty days, he made a most penitent and edifying end.

Another conversion almost equally striking, though in a meaner and even grotesque subject, is recorded in the same chronicle: it is recorded in my first volume (p. 85). Among this model community of Sta Giustina there was "one single reproach in Israel", one Martin, ignorant, stupid and indevout. While the rest listened to devotional reading before Compline, he would shamelessly tuck up his frock, cross his legs, look from side to side, and, "albeit the Rule forbade him to express it in words, did so blow for weariness of spirit that his puffing lungs betrayed how sick he was with weariness". He was, in short, an exact example of that "acedia", that religious boredom which disciplinarians always put among their sorest foes. The brethren vainly besought Barbo "to rid the Abbey of so foolish and undisciplined a fellow, and cast him forth". At last, Barbo had to go to Venice; and this Martin begged leave to accompany him. He refused, not wishing to let so rude a fellow be seen; but Martin's importunities overcame him at last. They had scarcely arrived in Venice when Martin caught the plague. One night they thought him dead; but he awoke suddenly and cried for the abbot. The attendant brethren feared danger for their beloved chief, and employed a pious fraud to represent him as absent from the place. He refused to believe; and to the prior, who came presently, he said, "Wherefore do you not cause our Father Abbot to be called? I will not tell you the secrets which I have to reveal to him." Yet even to the prior he spoke at large about ineffable things which astounded all who knew the man's past.

With incredible fervour he said: "I have seen the substance of all things, the order of the heavens and of all the planets.*...If Aristotle and other Philosophers and doctors of the Church came back to this life, they would surely tear all their books, for shame of the grossness

* Compare Dante, *Paradiso*, XXXIII, 106 ff.

of their own speech. If you yourselves could see Transubstantiation as it is, ye could never celebrate for marvel and sweetness of so admirable a sacrament."

He had seen St Benedict, glorious as the sun, with an infinite host of Benedictines glittering like the stars, and the Saint had assured him of salvation if only he kept patience in this fever. The brethren could no longer conceal this from Barbo: he rebuked them for their delay, came to the bedside, and asked now to hear what could not be said to any but himself. It was too late now, said Martin; he could only predict "many tribulations and contradictions to your Rule and your Congregations, not only from without but also from your sons within. But be constant and patient; for God will lead all things to His own great praise, and to the increase of the Congregation." Next Sunday he made his communion and a most edifying end (p. 296).

Barbo had indeed to suffer much from the Venetian magistrates, who were jealous of their constitutional authority over his abbey of San Giorgio in Alga, and long refused consent to its union with this Paduan Congregation. Even then, he had "even harder struggles from within", from brethren who were offended at this union. Satan stirred up an even graver scandal, that some of the abbots revolted against the central power. Barbo had to bear with a temporary secession, but at length brought them all back. And then came his crowning triumph, the reform of San Paolo Fuori le Mura. This, one of the greatest convents in Rome, had been founded round the church which claimed the very sarcophagus of St Paul. It had been enriched and adorned from century to century. The Kings of England were nominally its protectors, as those of France and Spain were of St John Lateran and of Sta Maria Maggiore respectively, "and the emblem of the Garter may still be seen amongst its decorations".(3) Crowds of modern visitors flock to see what remains there from almost the earliest Christian time: bronze gates inlaid with silver thread, mosaics, sculptures and a cloister which rivals that of the Lateran. But in Barbo's time this house was involved in the general decay at Rome; and here again we must turn to his own words, under the year 1425 (p. 300).

The church and monastery of San Paolo Fuori le Mura was so miserably forlorn that its roof was in most places destroyed and uncovered, so that it was a mere receptacle of rain and hail and snow. It befel by God's will, and when St Paul's merits demanded that the time was come for repairing so solemn religious a monastery, desolate now together with its church—it befel I say that a certain servant clad in a long beard and almost perpetual silence entered the church at San Paolo. Then, standing upright over against the wooden image of St Paul which stood by the altar of St Stephen within an iron grating and bore a naked sword of steel erect in its hand, this man gazed at it fixedly for a little while and then, raging in spirit, brake out in a loud voice: "O Paul, O foolish barbarian! What dost thou? Wherefore dost thou hold thy sword aloft? Seest thou not that thy church lieth in abominable ruin, and how negligently it is cared for? Lower that sword which thou holdest aloft and smite those who neglect thy house!" As God would have it, there stood beside the altar, listening to Mass, hard-by the same image, Lord Angiolotti, an eminent man, now Cardinal of San Marco, who was a close friend of the Pope. He, hearing the pilgrim's words (as he afterwards told Abbot Barbo), was smitten with such fear that he awaited impatiently the end of the Mass to report them forthwith to the Pope. When Mass was ended he mounted forthwith and hastened to the Pope whom he addressed briefly: "Holy Father, bad news for me and for thee." The Pope, startled and expecting some sudden attack of his enemies, replied: "What is this that thou sayst?" Then he repeated in order all that the pilgrim had cried aloud. These words so smote the Pope's heart with the fear of God that he bent himself wholly to the restoration of that monastery, and in his first secret consistory he disclosed to his cardinals the pilgrim's cry and his own resolve to restore both church and abbey.

The cardinals all agreed and chose one of themselves, the future Eugenius IV, to bear the burden of repairing not only church but monastery, both temporally and spiritually. It so happened that this same cardinal, while a young man in Minor Orders, had visited San Paolo and been appalled at its dilapidation. He had then been unable to do anything but had planned the construction of forty cells in the dormitory in provision of some future reform. He now wrote to summon Barbo with such brethren as he could bring. They came at his bidding, nineteen in all, on the Eve of St Paul's conversion.

First, Barbo beheld a church of marvellous and most excellent structure, but most miserably decayed. For, as aforesaid, the great part of its roof had fallen in and thus it appeared to the beholder as a place deserted; for the pilgrims also camping round the inner walls of the church were wont to cook divers sorts of flesh and herbs, giving themselves up commonly to gluttony and drunkenness without fear of God; moreover the herdsmen would lead their oxen and buffaloes to spend the night there as in a cattle-stall. It was right, therefore, that this pilgrim marvelled and cried aloud, seeing that the Blessed Paul wrought no rough and hard vengeance upon this great negligence of the prelates, whereby the house of the Princes of the Apostles [*principum apostolorum domus*] had become a notorious tavern (would that we might not add a brothel) and an execrable stable for stinking beasts. What shall I say of the rest of the fabric, seeing that the buildings were falling everywhere into ruin? Only the beauty of the cloister showed to beholders some token of Religion. In the refectory, dormitory, kitchen, and the chamber where nowadays the brethren are shaved, there was such abundance of cattle-litter that we could see naught but mire and stench and [the bare] roofs. Those few mean buildings which had kept their roof around the cloister had been usurped for pigsties and cattle-stalls; and brute beasts were huddled promiscuously not only in the abbey but in the church. O! the patience of God and His Apostles, who suffered so many and great unspeakable deeds to be done in their most holy house!

The cardinal now set to work and spent liberally upon the restoration (p. 303). With a monastery so solidly built as we know this to have been, and under the Italian skies, that cannot have been very difficult, for Barbo himself lays more stress upon the filth and irreverence than upon actual structural ruin. No doubt we have here the exaggerations common to nearly all medieval descriptions, whether for good or for evil: but antiquarian evidence bears out the great decay of San Paolo at this time. "On the side towards the river it was approached by a quadriporticus...in the centre of which a beautiful fountain, surmounted by a cantharus, was erected by [St] Leo I. Court and fountain perished in the fifteenth century....The fountain was seen by Cola di Rienzi in the fourteenth century; in the fifteenth it had disappeared." The vaulting of the cloister was badly restored in the sixteenth century.(4)

The cardinal's restoration was all that was needed for the practical purposes of this Sta Giustina reform. Barbo writes: "Within a short space, he purged this abbey and church perfectly, and with greatest honour to God; whereas not even the most ancient folk could remember that the church itself had been fully roofed" [*integre fuisse coopertam*]. In 1431 he was raised to the papal throne, and remained a warm protector to Barbo and San Paolo. "If I would tell of all [his benefits], I should need to write a new treatise or book." He ratified the union into a Congregation of the ten abbeys which Barbo had soon reformed.

Barbo was presently promoted himself (1437) to the Bishopric of Treviso, by express and direct choice of this Eugenius IV. His long hesitation was broken down by the representation that, from this point of vantage, he would be able to exercise decisive influence in favour of his struggling Congregation: therefore "for love of his sons he submitted to bodily separation from them".

The story is tersely summed up by one of the earliest brethren of Sta Giustina, named Arnold Wion. He writes:

> This is that Reformation which, considering God's love, leaveth self-will in the hands of others, taketh upon itself poverty and humility instead of this world's vanity and pride, loveth continence and purity instead of intemperance.... This hath wholly restored—yea, and with interest—the Divine Service that had long been neglected in monasteries; this doth enlighten the foolish, teacheth holy manners, loveth peace and concord, maintaineth charity, and, in brief, guideth every man into the way of salvation and eternal felicity according to his disposition and sensible capacity.(5)

CHAPTER XXIV

THE HOLY GROTTO AND MONTE CASSINO

We may now pass to the sister-reform of Subiaco, which was finally merged in that of Sta Giustina.

The world-famed abbey of Subiaco had grown up round the *Sacro Speco*, the Holy Grotto in which St Benedict had begun his ascetic career, before he founded Monte Cassino. In 1364, the strifes and dissensions of these monks, in a famous abbey within thirty miles of Rome, attracted papal attention.

Abbot Bartholomew, by command of the Pope, had to dismiss some of the incorrigible monks and fill their places with Religious from other monasteries. Numbers were brought in from Germany, and for many decades Subiaco was a centre of German thrift, science and art. Still, it seems, discipline was not satisfactory; for Urban VI (1378–89) abolished the Abbots for life, took away from the monks the right of election, and gave the administration and revenues to a member of the Curia.(1)

Later, in 1455, it was put permanently under the *commendam* system. The commendators, here as usual, disinterested themselves in their abbey. The first of them was Cardinal Torquemada, cousin to the Inquisitor, and the second was the future Alexander VI. Later, in 1506, Cardinal Pompeo Colonna set one of the worst examples of his time, squandering the revenues upon his own pleasures and favourites. Yet the community itself, by a rare exception, took advantage of their comparative poverty to live a regular Benedictine life for a century or more. In 1514 they joined the Congregation of Sta Giustina. Its acting abbot held thenceforth the title of Abbot General of the whole Congregation, while some cardinal or commendatory abbot still drew the greater part of the revenues. "Even after this union there were continual quarrels between Subiaco and Farfa, Subiaco and Monte Cassino, the Germans and the Italians." After this, but little is known of the abbey until the middle of the nineteenth century.

When Pius II began to interest himself in monastic reform,

and confirmed the Bursfelde Congregation (1458), he granted to it the same privileges already enjoyed by Sta Giustina. In 1514, Subiaco joined it; and before this, in 1504, Monte Cassino had come in. This, St Benedict's own abbey, was naturally recognized in popular esteem, though not in any formal sense, as the Mother House of the whole Order. It was therefore too magnificent to fall into a merely subordinate part; and the Congregation of Subiaco—Sta Giustina—Cassino was thenceforth known as *Cassinensis*. At its zenith, it included as many as 190 abbeys.

The previous story of Monte Cassino had been as chequered as that of most abbeys. There, on its great mountain, overlooking the road from Rome to Naples, it has earned the title of "the Sinai of the Middle Ages". Its greatest prosperity, spiritually and materially, was in the eleventh century. More than once, after that, it fell very low. Boccaccio described to a pupil the state in which he found its once magnificent library, somewhere about 1350—books dust-covered in a grass-grown chamber, leaves torn out or pared to the quick by monks who scraped together a little pocket-money by making little psalm-books for schoolboys, or texts for women.(2) Already before this (1321), John XXII had erected its church into a cathedral, thus creating a diocese with the bishop as abbot and the monks as Chapter. In the words of *The Catholic Encyclopaedia* (X, 527):

There is no doubt that this was done with the best of intentions, as an additional honour to the great abbey; in practice however it proved disastrous. The Bishops of Monte Cassino, nominated at Avignon, were secular prelates who never visited the diocese but who appropriated the income of the abbey to their own personal use. The number of monks thus dwindled, the observance declined, and utter ruin became a mere question of time. In view of this Urban V, who was a Benedictine monk, proclaimed himself abbot of Monte Cassino, collected monks from other houses to reinforce the community, and in 1370 appointed Andrew of Faenza, a Camaldolese, as Superior. The revival, however, was short-lived; in 1454 the system of commendatory abbots was reintroduced and lasted till 1504, when Julius II united Monte Cassino to the newly established Congregation at St Justina of Padua, which was thenceforth known as the Cassinese Congregation.

Martin v. Senging gives, incidentally, a comparison between

the strict use of wool in the monks' underwear at Subiaco, in contrast with the linen permitted in unreformed houses. Far more detailed and interesting is the letter in which an anonymous monk has left an account of his life there in 1400.(3) He was evidently from a German convent, in Bavaria, Austria or Switzerland, at a time when the German influence was strong in this reform. He arrived at Subiaco on the evening of October 17, 1399, and wrote to his friend after an experience of nearly eight months:

If thou wouldst know the life of the inmates here, I will describe it not fully but in part, beginning with the main preface that, in my simple judgement, the Rule is satisfactorily kept in accordance with the state of those who are here now, and will be more perfectly kept when the numbers are increased; for the plague hath somewhat thinned our population.

He begins with the services that are sung and those that are merely said. Thence to the important matter of rest in the intervals,

Vigils, as the Rule prescribes, take place always after Matins, both in summer and in winter; and these are so well tempered by apportionment of hours that no sleepy person can slumber securely at that time; for in summer there is always a brief interval on ordinary days between Matins and Lauds, and in winter a longer one....As aforesaid, there is always an interval; but it is never permitted to sleep in the daytime except in summer, unless under compulsion of some infirmity. At that time, the daily sleep lasts about three hours.

The fast is commonly so ordered that it lasts all winter long from Holy Cross Day (September 14) to Easter, save only for Christmas Day and Sundays; and the fast is until full moon. In Lent, however, it is until after Vespers; and then we go to table [for our single meal] at least two hours after noon, or even three. On all fast-days there is a very brief collation of drink before the reading of collation in the refectory [i.e. between Vespers and Compline]. From Easter onwards, they are refreshed twice daily until the vigil of Pentecost; but for the rest of summer they fast every Wednesday and Friday, and also on the Church fast-days. On such fast-days the daily sleep, which should come after dinner, takes place between Tierce and Sext before Mass, or sometimes after Mass, between Sext and None.

The manner of refection is so tempered that neither too much nor too little is given, but a sufficiency. Of bread and wine there is abundance; as much as a man can eat and drink. Two dishes are supplied; one is of some kind of pulse as peas or lentils or so forth, and another of cabbages or eggs cooked in a pan. To this they add vegetables; for example, an apple (or two, if they be small) or four walnuts, or figs, or chestnuts or garlic or onions. For supper the supply is moderate; it is mostly raw herbs with oil and vinegar, and, if anything be cooked, this is in small quantities; so that it is a consolation when two soft-boiled eggs are given (which however is rare) and a portion of cheese. The time for eating is so moderated as not to be long protracted; so that a gluttonous man (if such there were) cannot eat too much unless he should make undue haste. But there are few, and almost none, who do not deny themselves, at each meal, somewhat of that which is set before them and which they might lawfully consume. It was told me by one Father that a very ancient brother, when I was there, ate on the second day of the feast of Pentecost only once a day, and one course alone. The dishes in which the courses are served are of about the content of a quartale of wine, by measure of Salzburg. They have no season of consolations or of bleedings except at some principal feast; then an addition is made with a special draught of bitter wine, or the addition of some bread, or fish, or confection:* but this is very seldom in the year, as on the greatest feasts. And sometimes one or two more courses are added; and then it is done in smaller quantities.

The brethren's cells are joined together, and so open that the passer-by can see what the indweller is doing. They contain bedsteads, and the pillows are not of feathers but of sheep's wool, I think. The bed-covering is of two blankets like frocks.

Of labours, some are special and others general. The special are enjoined according to order. Some are spiritual, as that of the sacristan, who has to ring duly at all the hours, and to adorn the church with lights and so forth, and on Saturdays to ordain each man's offices for the week, as that of Lector or Acolyte or the like. Some, again, are temporal, as that of the kitchener or the table-servant. The kitcheners have to wash all the kitchen vessels for the week, each in his order, preceding and following on Saturday with the ministers or servants of the table, and at his entering and going forth to wash the feet of all the brethren at the Maunday (which is held every Saturday) and to prepare all the vessels and water for the foot-washing, and to sweep the dormitory and cloister;† and the servant entering the refectory has to clean it almost every day of the week. This same table-servant has to prepare the board and serve those who eat.

* The text seems rather faulty here: it runs "ut additio unius panis, additio piscati vel confecti".

† Here again the grammar seems faulty, but the sense fairly clear.

There are also other special labours, which are performed not weekly but in virtue of the man's office. Such are those of the Hostillar, who has to see to the guests: he is one of the priests, and all the brethren wash the guests' feet. Then, the labours of the Infirmarer, who has to see to the infirmary in all things, like a paterfamilias.... No monk ever entereth the infirmary to eat flesh there, unless some great and evident infirmity compel him, and that with a special order from the Prior. There are also other special labours committed to separate brethren. The lay-brethren are bound to bring in bread and wine and all victuals from the offices which they hold: and one is in the kitchen to cook food, and one in the bakery, and so with the other offices, such as the cobbler's and the tailor's.

The general labours are those which are performed in times of exercise: that is, after None in summer and in winter between Sext and None. They are performed by all together, both old and young, who are not occupied in any office; for instance, picking or cleaning the vegetables, beans, chick-peas or lentils, and so forth; and they are performed in a place set aside for exercises. And these labours are more common throughout the year. There are also divers other labours, as necessity may require, such as sweeping, carrying stones or wood, washing their own clothes, uprooting the weeds of the gardens in summer-time, collecting hay in the meadows and gathering grapes. Such labours are near the monastery in sequestered places far from men. Whatsoever the Prior or his Vicar command, whether in aid of the Officials or for any other cause, is done by all without any contradiction, and no man useth his own will. And for whatever thing he be corrected or rebuked, he saith *culpa mea est*, and excuseth not himself, unless perchance he be questioned, or some great necessity require it: nor, even so, without permission.

The deepest silence is kept in church, refectory, dormitory or other places. None dareth to speak unless he have first besought the blessing of his senior with whom he would fain speak. Necessities are dealt out to each man in all things, according as he may be apt and as they are to be had, as in the matter of books and so forth....

If it seem good to thee, speak to thy pupil Johann Jäger, [and tell him that] if he will make good provision for his soul and for bodily sustenance, he can safely come hither to take the cowl; for meseemeth he is well fitted. But tell him to take full sacerdotal Orders first, if that be possible, either at home or in Rome. Say the same from my part to Reinhard (who was mine own youth) but when he is of sufficient age; he could hardly bear it without discretion of years. Thou shouldst know that the beginning alone was grievous unto me, as a thing unaccustomed, and the divers temptations. Now, however, I have great consolation, for that by the mercy of the Almighty and

His Mother, though without desert and truly unworthy, have been able to come to such consolation, and all that is commanded unto me is scarce grievous in any way to my mind.

Moreover, I pray thee with all diligence, according as thy discretion can so order things, that thou wilt disclose this observance and these writings to all whom they may profit now and in future, at least in some measure of imitation, not caring if it displease some men: for, if we would please men, we are no servants of God. And specially send it in writing to Dom Andreas v. Beltenburg, for he can communicate it to that most devout parish priest in Spiez and others, to Caspar the Sacristan of Gesten and so forth. Yet guard this [letter of mine] above all things, by my most special prayers, that in this special matter, and in others, there be no special mention of me; for that is why I have long deferred writing unto thee, and have done it in fear, by reason of the perils of divers temptations and distractions.

Finally, I commit myself to thy devout prayers; and doubt not but that thou hast mine—would that I might say, devout also! Take Reinhard as a son committed unto thee, for God's sake and for mine own humble prayers; for I hope that, by the mercy of my God and by thy help, he will prosper in goodness. Farewell in Christ and in His sweetest Mother. Written in the Abbey of the Sacro Speco, in the year of Our Lord 1400 and the sixth day of June.

CHAPTER XXV

THE ITALIAN SCENE

NEXT to Busch, by far the most important and interesting visitatorial details have come down to us through Ambrogio Traversari, Minister General of the Camaldulensian Order. Moreover, those details enable us to conclude with even greater certainty what the reader must already have inferred from my preceding chapters. Whatever may have been the fitness of Benedictine or Augustinian monasticism for the needs of the Dark Ages, and however healthily, in some respects, those ideals may have adapted themselves to the changing social conditions of the Middle Ages proper, yet such adaptation had been far from perfect. In some ways the cloisterer was now behind his time, and in others far too much a man of his own age. If Busch's story goes a long way to support St Thomas More's plea that the clergy are lay-folk writ large, we may read this still more plainly in the experiences of this distinguished Italian contemporary. Busch's Germany was still mainly medieval; but Ambrose's Italy was already in the full tide of the Renaissance. Two men of his time were the first Popes who harnessed the Revival of Learning to Church uses: Nicholas V and Pius II. Though neither of those was elected in Traversari's lifetime, yet the spirit was already there. "Nicholas V saw that reform was needed; but reform was too dangerous" after the experience of Constance and Basel. "If the Papacy could not venture on reform, the next best thing was to identify itself with art and learning. To the demand of Germany for reformation Nicholas V answered by offering culture. His policy was so far wise that it enabled the Papacy to exist for sixty years before the antagonism broke out in open rebellion."(1)

One of the German reformer's worst difficulties was the too frequent indifference of the neighbouring laity to monastic decay, or even their active support of peccant cloisterers, who were their daily companions, against these meddlesome "foreigners" now imposed upon them as visitors. In Traversari's Italy the difficulty was still greater: not only did the neighbours often resent reform, but it was still more difficult to find zealous and consistent reformers in this society which was so rapidly learning to doubt or to repudiate many of the main medieval traditions. It was not only that (as Machiavelli remarked later) Italians saw the Roman Court too closely, and found serious stumbling-blocks in the petty wars between lay and ecclesiastical despots: civil wars which, despite the microscopic size of some of the belligerent territories, had all the vices of nationalism, and also the added bitterness of religious conflict, since one or other side commonly fought under Rome's anathema. Apart from and beyond these practical causes of unrest, it was in Italy that the Revival of Learning, destined to revolutionize the medieval outlook, was earliest and widest and deepest.

Chaucer's two Italian journeys were among the most important of all his life experiences, if not the most important of all. His older contemporaries, Petrarch and Boccaccio, were then studying antiquity with a fervour as yet unknown on this side of the Alps. Men were still alive who had seen the face and heard the voice of Dante, the most learned layman of his age, two centuries earlier than his first English counterpart, St Thomas More. Of the two chief Italian universities, Bologna was the foremost law school in Europe but comparatively insignificant in theology, while its morals were grievously depraved, by the reluctant confession of Benvenuto da Imola, who was himself professor there in Chaucer's day. Padua, again, was mainly a school of medicine; it was the focus of anti-Christian Averroism, and probably the birthplace of that proverb which Sir Thomas Browne has made familiar: *Ubi tres medici, duo athei*. Three of the most distinguished Italians at the turn of the fourteenth century, writing in sad earnest, describe the society of their time in words even more pessimistic than their Cisalpine contemporaries. Sacchetti, in his sermons, speaks of a widespread and deep infidelity, a denial of the immortality of the soul, which bears out Dante's boldness in filling a whole circle of his *Inferno* with such men. St Antonino, Archbishop of Florence, condemns the prevalent unbelief: and St Bernardino of Siena, complaining still more emphatically, traces to the wickedness of the clergy, cloistered and uncloistered, the fact that many men "believe in nothing higher than the roof of their own house".(2) Moreover, again and again we find the same obvious deduction: there can be no radical Church reform so long as the papal court remains such as it is.

These two currents, intellectual enlightenment and repudiation of Roman despotism, coalesce in an Italian, Marsilius, who in his native Padua had learned the advanced politics of these city-republics, and had passed on, at Paris, to a school of restless theological speculation. To find anything like a parallel in England, we must again pass on two centuries to the age of More and Colet and Erasmus. Marsilius showed a real sense of historical criticism. He applied to a spurious letter of St Clement of Rome, which had found its way to a very prominent position in Canon Law, the commonsense solvents which are admitted now by critics of every Christian denomination. Again, he proposed the most radical reforms: the State must take the Church in hand, seize her endowments, pay and control the clergy: the final decision everywhere must rest not with the Pope or his cardinals but with a Council thoroughly representative of the whole Church. Moreover, this was only one extreme example of what was going on everywhere in northern Italy. There, men had never entirely forgotten to study the Latin classics seriously. In France, the twelfth-century classical schools of Chartres and Orleans had been superseded as leaders of thought by the universities, with their fascination of scholastic philosophy for the speculative mind and of law or medicine for the practical. In Italy, scholasticism was never so strong as in France or Germany or England: but she was pre-eminent in law, and in political thought which was then a branch of jurisprudence. She was pre-eminent also in practical politics, domestic and foreign; and this concerns the present story as closely as any other factor.

We must confine ourselves to the north; for things were very different in the south, where the Emperor Frederick II, in the earlier thirteenth century, had created the most striking medieval example (next to the Roman Church) of the Totalitarian State. With the aid of Mohammedan subjects and mercenaries, he organized the country with a ruthlessness which enabled the French conquerors, Charles of Anjou and his descendants, to work the machine as easily as its creator had done. The papacy, which had called upon French invaders for help, thus gained little or nothing by the transfer. Nor did it gain, in the long run, by its other policy, however natural, of preventing any union between North and South. The Pope, with his own States forming a broad band from east to west of the peninsula, was always strong enough to prevent either North or South from absorbing the other, but never strong enough to absorb either to himself. Thus, as Machiavelli complained, the peninsula was subject to all the miseries of chronic disunion, suspicions, jealousies and wars. It was still, in his day, what Dante had called it two centuries earlier, "a hostelry of pain"—*osteria di dolore.*(3)

Yet from all this ferment something precious was distilled. Northern Italy (including Tuscany) has always had a population of remarkable natural qualities; it has perhaps produced more great names, acre for acre, than any other district of Europe. Here, the medieval emperors had played a political part very similar to that of the Popes. They were not strong enough to enforce anything like their full pretensions upon these great Italian cities, yet strong enough to prevent the Pope from fully enforcing his. Thus Milan, Genoa, Florence and the rest were able to shake off the political domination of their bishops, and to become little republics; or, strictly speaking, oligarchies, since no republic in the full modern sense was yet possible in medieval society.

In these cities, then, political experiments were tried, and political debate was carried on, with an energy and vivacity unknown elsewhere. More and more eagerly men turned to the study of the Roman historians for examples and arguments, in justification of policies which, at bottom, were always frankly realistic. The democracies, for their part, shrank from no violence or perfidy which might promise success; and the despots were, if anything, still more ruthless. For, after a few generations, the net result of all this had been the rise of the despot everywhere. Dante, from his lofty intellectual and moral pinnacle, might despise all that was petty and histrionic in those adventurers; but at last, in the fifteenth century, even his own comparatively democratic Florence succumbed; and Venice was then the only great city still free; secure in her lagoons, but hated by all others for aloofness, selfishness and greed. Elsewhere, the only variation was between a bad despot and a good —or, perhaps we should say, a less bad, in the mood of Figaro: "persuadé qu'un grand nous fait assez de bien quand il ne nous fait pas de mal".

Yet, good or bad, these despots were nearly always remarkable men, giving brilliant distinction to the later fourteenth century and the fifteenth. Courage and force of character had raised them; and those qualities were still more necessary to keep them where they stood. In many cases their sagacity was equal to their physical endowments; and often, again, they maintained artists and poets and rhetoricians to immortalize them. They ruled and taxed a population of high physical and mental average. The advantages of soil and climate, with two long sea coasts, had raised these people to a very high place in European agriculture, craftsmanship and commerce: and they were near neighbours to Greece, a mine of spiritual treasures even richer than those inherited from their own Roman forefathers. This Age of the Italian Despots, therefore, is one of the most brilliant periods of European history. Nor was its brilliancy merely superficial; for then the waning enthusiasm of medieval orthodoxy was met by a new enthusiasm of almost equal force—the Religion of Learning. We must cling advisedly to that term. This revival had its superstitions and idolatries, its bigots and its hypocrites, its pettinesses alloying almost everywhere its greatness; yet on the whole it was a true religion, raising men above their lower selves. The true monk and true scholar Ambrose of Camaldoli, to whom we must soon come in detail, in a letter to a pupil, chose with sure instinct that sentence from St Jerome: "Love the knowledge of scriptures, and thou shalt not love the faults of the flesh."(4)

This cult was fully conscious of its own novelty and its own force: its votaries felt themselves to be swimming with a great world-tide: "Bliss was it in that dawn to be alive, but to be young was very heaven." Mankind in the mass might still be miserable, but all things would finally work together for good in the case of the Elect. Political and social conditions, depressing for the many, were exhilarating, even to intoxication, for the few. Browning's *Grammarian's Funeral* can scarcely be called even a poetic exaggeration. The call of Piero de' Pazzi from the ordinary life of a wealthy young nobleman to the nobility of scholarship is comparable to that medieval summons of San Raniero from a dance to a hermitage, portrayed in the Campo Santo at Pisa.(5) The conversion of Leonardo Bruni can best be told in his own words.

At that time (at the age of nearly 30), I was studying civil law, yet not unversed in other studies; for I burned with an innate love of learning and had spent no small labour upon dialectics and rhetoric. Thus, at the coming of [the Greek refugee scholar] Chrysoloras, I was divided in mind. On the one hand, it seemed sinful to desert the study of law; on the other, I thought it a sort of crime to neglect so great an opportunity of learning Greek literature. Thus I said oftentimes to myself, as an impulsive youth: "Seeing that thou art now able to behold and converse with Homer and Plato and Demosthenes, and those other poets, philosophers, and orators of whom repute hath so great marvels to relate, and that thou canst steep thyself in this marvellous learning, wilt thou desert and abandon thine own self? Wilt thou let this occasion go, so providentially offered unto thee? Seven hundred years have now gone since any man taught Greek letters in Italy; yet we confess that all learning cometh from them; how great therefore will be the profit of learning, or the greater fame, or the increase of pleasure which will come unto thee from the knowledge of this tongue? Doctors of civil law abound everywhere; thou shalt never lack opportunity for learning that. Here, on the other hand, is that one and only Doctor of Greek letters; if once thou hast lost sight of him, thou shalt never find teacher more." Those reasons conquered me at last; I gave myself up to Chrysoloras in such a fury of study that whatsoever I had learned waking and by day was revolved by night also in my sleeping mind.(6)

Those two men are conspicuous examples of the spirit which impelled many to seek escape from the calamities of their age into a "dreamland of antiquity", noble or ignoble according to the scholar's own temperament, but often sought in the same spirit in which the monk had chosen his cloister.(7).

For in politics and social life "realism was overwhelmingly dominant". The star of despotism seemed steadily ascendant, both in Church and State. Not only were nearly all the city republics now in the hands of despots, but the papacy itself was drifting into a position of purely secular princedom, in which some great adventurer seemed certain, sooner or later, to seize supreme power and turn the papal states into a secular government like the rest. Luther's revolt, paradoxical as that may seem, was probably the main factor in Rome's salvation here.(8) For the immemorial laws were now very commonly repudiated, and through a very natural cause, since both government and police were tainted at their very source, resting upon recent violence and bloodshed. We are often told that the Middle Ages, before their break-up, had a deep and abiding respect for law; but this assertion needs qualification. Medieval law was to a very great extent customary, resting upon no statutory or strictly philosophical basis, but simply traditional; just the thing which had existed from time immemorial. Yet, as a monastic chartulary reminds us, "man is a forgetful animal"; and memory is but a shifting foundation for law. Therefore in those days it was easier than in more recent times for two adversaries, contending in diametrically opposite directions, to assert and believe, and perhaps to persuade others, that they were following the law.(9) But one of the earliest effects of the revival of learning was to depreciate custom, and to apply everywhere methods of logical criticism which were solvent of all mere tradition. Much of that which the Renaissance repudiated was not law in the strictest modern sense, but simply custom, the custom of distant and very different ages, woven into no philosophical system. Moreover, practice accorded here with a solvent force of abstract speculation. The theory of Unity in Church and in State had obviously broken down; the papacy had broken the Empire, and Europe saw by this time that Popes, the theoretical peacemakers of Christendom, had really caused as many wars as other princes. Men were becoming justly scornful of claims which their own eyes and ears flatly contradicted. They were seeking new values everywhere: and those who intended to wade through blood to success were no longer tempted to do even lip-service to obsolete or obsolescent standards. "The Italian of that time shrank, it is true, from no dissimulation in order to attain his ends, but he was wholly free from hypocrisy in matters of principle. In these he attempted to deceive neither himself nor others. Accordingly revenge was declared with perfect frankness to be a necessity of human nature."(10) It is significant that the very word *vendetta* is Italian by birth, and borrowed by many other nations. Elsewhere there may have been as many revengeful murders, or sometimes even more; yet seldom as a matter not only of ripe deliberation but even of moral duty. Dante himself tells us how the shade of Geri della Bella rebuked him as an unworthy scion who had ignored this sacred charge.(11)

Such political realism, national and international (for even the smallest state had its own national ambitions and jealousies), involved a constant struggle for survival. The completest combination of fraud and violence was what marked a man or a community for success; or, at least, for immediate success, and how small in any age is the proportion of men who habitually look farther than this! Such competition, therefore, bred an efficiency which goes far to explain the victory of the new ideas. The despot, to reach power and maintain it, must create something very different from what he had inherited from past ages. Concerning such great duchies as Milan or Urbino Burckhardt writes truly:

> Not only the state, but the Court too was a work of art and organization, and this in every sense of the word. Federigo [of Urbino] had 500 persons in his service; the arrangements of the Court were as complete as in the capitals of the greatest monarchs; but nothing was wasted; all had its object, and all was carefully watched and controlled. The Court was no scene of vice and dissipation: it served as a school of military education for the sons of other great houses, the thoroughness of whose culture and instruction was made a point of honour by the Duke. In the evening he would overlook the martial exercises of the young people of his Court on the meadows of S. Francesco, known for its magnificent view, and saw to it well that all the feats were done in the most perfect manner. (p. 25.)

Such men anticipated Napoleon's maxim of *la carrière ouverte aux talents*. This was easier in Italy than elsewhere; for there the feudal nobility had never been so close a caste, apart from the rich citizens or even the peasantry. Youth, again, had better chances here than elsewhere: Burckhardt emphasizes "the early emancipation of the young man from domestic and parental authority" (p. 228). Again: "The government, in the hands of an enlightened despot, had an incomparably more accurate acquaintance with its own country and that of its neighbours than was possessed by Northern contemporaries; and it estimated the economical and moral capacities of friend and foe down to the smallest particular. The rulers, were, notwithstanding grave errors, born masters of statistical science" (p. 52). The Renaissance created a number of schools, and an educational activity, far beyond the medieval standard; though, even in the past, Italy had been the only country possessing something resembling a real school system. The greater despots took just pride in their libraries; those of Milan, Urbino, Naples and Florence far exceeded all that the greatest monasteries or cathedrals had ever possessed. Cosimo de' Medici, about 1440 gave a blank cheque to the bookseller Vespasiano Bisticci for as many as possible of the best books. In Bistucci's own words: "I soon engaged 45 copyists, and in 22 months provided 200 volumes, following the admirable list provided by Pope Nicholas V."(12)

Thus the Italians were by far the best-read people in Europe, and this superiority was more marked even among the laity than among priests or cloisterers. The Italians came very definitely to the front in historiography. They may almost be called the inventors of systematic biography (as apart from mainly legendary stories of saints): and they were the actual inventors of blank verse in the vernacular, and of the sonnet, that poem which demands the greatest artistic precision and compression of thought. They paid more for their university professors, and were able to secure the most eminent scholars. Outside their universities, there were many minor academies or societies for discussion and mutual improvement. "Thus rearmed afresh with the culture of ancient Rome, the Italian soon felt himself in truth citizen of the most advanced nation in the world."(13) For this literary brilliancy had its political effect also: if great men in Church and State gave generously to the poet or the orator, this was almost as useful for propaganda as the vast buildings and the splendour of all their Courts. Nor was the effect here merely superficial; it is profoundly true that nothing succeeds like success, at least for as long a period as enters into most men's calculations. Rare indeed are those who can steadily resist its enchantment. Burckhardt notes how Leonardo da

Vinci, one of the greatest and most independent minds, was apparently fascinated like the rest. Ludovico "the Moor", Duke of Milan, is often cited as a typical Renaissance despot. He was knighted at thirteen; at twenty he commanded a troop of mercenaries; four years later he lost his father by murder and was himself imprisoned. Here he began to study in view of a cardinalate. Two years later he headed a rebellion; then betrayed his allies one by one; obtained the tutelage of the young duke, his nephew, and was thenceforward virtual ruler of Milan. His diplomacy was shifting and unscrupulous even for that not over-scrupulous age, and few have ever used money more freely in war or in politics. In both those fields he finally overreached himself; yet in the days of his success he attracted to his court not only a number of second-rate poets but such artists as Bramante and Leonardo. Indeed, the man seems to have had a special attraction for Leonardo, who served also as chief engineer to Caesar Borgia. Antonio Beccadelli, again, famous for his supreme elegance as a Latin stylist, was retained by Alfonso of Naples as court orator, ambassador, and historian of the reign.

This brings us to another striking characteristic of the Renaissance: its moral laxity, especially in matters of sex. Beccadelli's best-known work, *Hermaphroditus*, was a collection of elegies as licentious as anything in the pagan classics. Yet he earned a title of nobility from Alfonso, and the poet laureate's wreath from that Emperor Sigismund whose conscience had been shocked by the theological unorthodoxies of Hus and Jerome of Prague. The Universities of Bologna and Pavia honoured him; he became tutor to the Crown Prince of Naples, and died in wealth and glory. For he represented, in an extreme form, the revolt of his generation against many things which had been preached without effective contradiction, if not practised with equal consistency, for many centuries past. Among his youthful fellow-students at Siena was the future Pope Pius II, who turned to complete or comparative chastity only after long years of licence had begun to pall. The succinct summary of this brilliant man's amours and his erotic writings fill three of the liveliest pages in Creighton's *History of the Papacy*.(14) It is from his own letters, corrected and published by himself in cold blood, that we know not only the facts, but also his impenitent relish in them. Within a few days of his thirty-ninth year he wrote a letter commending to his father's care a lately born illegitimate son. There he describes in complacent detail how he seduced the mother, reminds the aged parent of his own past exploits in that field, and adds reflections which, however plausible from the strictly biological standpoint, are in crude conflict with his clerical profession.(15) For, though still lacking Sacerdotal Orders, he was probably not (as his standard biographers write) literally a layman. In his famous Bull of Retractation he describes his earlier life as "not yet initiated into Sacred Orders" (i.e. into those of sub-deacon, deacon and priest), but he is significantly silent as to Minor Orders. Clerks in Minor Orders, by ecclesiastical law, were expected to sit apart from the laity in church, to wear the tonsure in sign of their solemn consecration, and to set a moral and religious example. If they married, by that act they forfeited the clerical immunity from ordinary justice.(16) If the law decreed no such forfeiture in punishment for licentious life; if, again, as a matter of experience the lay-folk did not ordinarily expect examples of piety and regularity among the clergy in Minor Orders; and if Pius himself was able loosely to speak of himself as "inter laicos",(17) those are facts which rather increase than diminish the significance of his particular case for the student of social history. As Creighton says, his private life "was profligate, but it does not seem to have shocked men of his time, nor [to] have fallen below the common standard. His irregularities were never made a reproach to him later, nor did he take any pains to hide them from posterity. Such as he was he would have himself known—induced perhaps by literary vanity, more probably by a feeling that his character would not lose in the eyes of his contemporaries by sincerity on his part."(18) The remark had already been made by Voigt, in a sentence which Lord Acton marked with his approving pencil: "It is noteworthy that never and nowhere do we find any reproach of sexual immorality uttered by any contemporary against Aeneas Sylvius although both in earlier days and as Pope he had enemies who reviled him. The only accusers are his own letters" (I, 285). He did indeed, as Pope, write an elaborate moral apology; yet that letter might have been written not only by any layman (apart from a few words referring to his present seat on St Peter's throne) but almost by any pagan. His main excuse there is that philosophers have very commonly belied their teaching in their private lives; as though the Vicar of Christ were to be acquitted on the score that pagans have lived as ill or worse, and have seduced their readers as shamefully, or nearly so.(19) His other main excuse is the plea of youth and inexperience; yet that impenitent letter to his father was written a few days short of his thirty-ninth year. Moreover, five months after that letter, he wrote from Germany to a friend, Apostolic Scriptor at Rome: "I myself do not intend to spend all my life outside Italy: and hitherto I have taken care not to be involved in Holy Orders. For I fear continence, which, laudable though it be, is more easily proved by words than by deeds, and more suitable to philosophers than to poets." The Emperor, by this time, had crowned him poet laureate, and he was proud of the title. Let my friend (he writes) find me now some position worthy of my abilities (February 1444).(20) Eight months later again (October 31) he commissions a friend to buy him a Bible in Prague, where there are many priests who sell Bibles. He is now "an old man"; he desires "to drown himself in the depths of the Gospels".(21) Yet our next glimpse of his inner life is hardly evangelical. In 1446 (March 8) he wrote to Johann Freund at Strassburg:

Time flies; you and I are elders [*seniores*]; we ought now to think not how we may live but how we may die....Is not he a fool who loseth eternity for the sake of things temporal and momentary?... I beseech thee, flee the whole feminine gender, quit that plague; when thou seest a woman, believe her a devil....Thou mayest retort that, with my full stomach, I am an advocate for fasting. I confess, dearest brother, I am full; I am disgusted; Venus makes me sick. Moreover, it is true that my strength fails, my hair grows grey, my muscles are dried and my bones decayed; my body is seamed with wrinkles. I can no longer give pleasure to any woman, nor any woman to me. I will obey Bacchus rather than Venus: wine nourishes and rejoices me; it is a delight and a blessing: this liquor shall be sweet to me until my death....By Hercules, I have little merit in chastity; for, to tell the truth, Venus flees me more than I shudder at her: but, thank God, my appetite is no greater than my power.(22)

Yet, two days before this (March 6) he had written to his friend Campisio:

> Now I am Sub-deacon,* a step which in past time I greatly dreaded. But that levity of mind hath departed from me which made my desire to grow up among the laity. Now I love nothing more than the priesthood; if God will, I shall be deacon in a week, and shall in due course receive the priestly dignity. If you tell this to our friends Noxetanus and Jakob Calvus, I know they will marvel with you. But one must at some time choose one's way of life, and among Christians there are two, the lay and the clerical: those again, as you know, have their distinctions. My resolve is to live in St Peter's Order; wherein may God give me grace to wish and do only such things as please Him!(23)

He was certainly in priest's orders by February 1447. That same year he was made Bishop of Trieste; in 1456 he was Cardinal, and Pope in August 1458. We shall see later on how far his will and his power extended towards the great work of monastic reform. For the present, it has been necessary to dwell thus far upon his private life as typical of many even among those who sat at Basel nominally for the sake of carrying out such reforms. Among such theologians, the writings of men like Beccadelli caused no scandal: Aeneas himself, in 1444, had written to a friend, with unctuous morality, that he was now thinking more of the next world than of this; yet he had composed, almost at the same time, what Voigt characterizes as "a comedy of the brothel". A man's thoughts and actions are indeed deeply affected by his environment; but, on the other hand, we must not forget that he himself may be an important, or even decisive factor in the environment of his neighbours. If they encourage him in impenitence, so also does he encourage them. Impenitent in the long run, no doubt Aeneas Sylvius was not. Yet, even then, we see him reconciling himself with his God in an easy off-hand fashion which is almost as significant as his earlier lapses: *Dieu me pardonnera; c'est son métier*. Though an earlier contemporary, a fellow-Sienese with Aeneas, St Bernardino, denounced Beccadelli's *Hermaphroditus* publicly in his famous sermons, and though Eugenius IV proscribed the book under penalty of excommunication, yet it is St Bernardino who tells us also that the multitude is so outraged by the evil lives of the

* He could not legally have taken the Subdiaconate unless he had been already in Minor Orders.

clergy as to have lost its religious faith; and we shall presently see how far either Eugenius or Pius was able or willing to fight for effective moral reform in the face of real difficulties.

Humility, again, which the Middle Ages had preached as one of the chief Christian virtues, was now seldom extolled outside the cloister or the pulpit. For that virtue and for faith the Renaissance tended to substitute honour as the mainspring of right action: personal honour and class-honour. As Burckhardt says:

The highly gifted men of that day thought to find their strongest moral bulwark in the sentiment of honour. This is that enigmatic mixture of conscience and egoism which often survives in the modern man after he has lost, whether by his own fault or not, faith, love, and hope. This sense of honour is compatible with much selfishness and great vices, and may be the victim of astonishing illusions; yet nevertheless, all the noble elements that are left in the wreck of a character may gather round it, and from this fountain may draw new strength. It has become, in a far wider sense than is commonly believed, a decisive test of conduct in the minds of the cultivated Europeans of our own day, and many of those who yet hold faithfully by religion and morality are unconsciously guided by this feeling in the gravest decisions of their lives.(24)

We must not attempt to draw too clear a line here between the Middle Ages and the Renaissance; yet the distinction exists, if only in quantity. This, like the religion of culture, did indeed for a while satisfy the higher instincts of many men, making them good citizens and good neighbours. But the impulse here was individualistic; the word "honour" could too easily be interpreted in the sense of personal pride or personal inclinations. When Reformation and Counter-Reformation began to rehabilitate religion, many of the things dearest to the Renaissance began to lose their savour. It had done its work in stirring stagnant waters, but it was not solid enough to satisfy the whole man.

Among other serious defects, it reduced life too much to a gamble. To live healthily is, no doubt, always to live adventurously: but within reasonable limits.(25) A society in which we must swear allegiance to-day to some despot, and to-morrow to his conqueror or murderer, must necessarily exhaust itself in the end; and so did the Italian population, in spite of its fine natural qualities. The evil was increased by the incurable levity with which these political gamblers invited foreign help in their civil wars. French interference was thus the operative factor in the thirteenth century, stereotyping the division of Italy. So again in that Florentine quarrel in which Dante was exiled and condemned to the stake if ever he could be caught again in his native city. So was it again in the later fifteenth and sixteenth centuries, until Spain took up the intermeddler's role with far more cruel success. And finally, the orthodox Spaniard was willing to call in the Mohammedan as an ally in civil war. It is some consolation to the historian that, in the long run, these interventions seldom fulfilled the intervener's hopes.(26) But the mischief was there; and with it, the canker of mercenary armies marching backwards and forwards over the land, under leaders as unscrupulous as those who hired them, ready to turn at any moment and sell themselves to any who would bid high enough.

Meanwhile those who fought against all these solvent social forces were too often hampered by the opposite drawback of religious feelings so temperamental that they tended to mere superstition.

> The feeling of the upper and middle classes in Italy with regard to the Church at the time when the Renaissance culminated was compounded of deep and contemptuous aversion, of acquiescence in the outward ecclesiastical customs which entered into daily life, and of a sense of dependence on Sacraments and ceremonies. The great personal influence of religious preachers may be added as a fact characteristic of Italy.(27)

Yet such revivals were transitory, as the revivalists themselves were the first to complain. The men of whom St Bernardino tells us in his sermons, who made the priest's failings their excuse for an irreligious life, expected nevertheless the rites of religion for their deathbed and their grave. But not until then. Among the unredeemed masses of Italy, as Machiavelli knew, the one subconscious but constant religious foundation was an ancestral paganism.

All these things, when clumsily imitated by our compatriots, illustrated the proverb quoted by Ascham, that the Italianate Englishman is a devil incarnate.

CHAPTER XXVI

AMBROSE OF CAMALDOLI

ALTHOUGH this Revival of Learning was, on the whole, a solvent of orthodox beliefs, yet exceptions were fairly numerous, and sometimes striking, especially in the earlier phases of the Renaissance. Some of the most eminent Latinists were also earnest Christians; and the official Church, however lukewarm in general for the new Greek scholarship, did sometimes share the general enthusiasm, especially under Nicholas V (1447–55). This Pope gathered round him the best scholars of the day, paid them munificently, and projected great schemes for libraries and research which he unfortunately had not time to complete. But the subject of this present chapter, Ambrogio Traversari, was cut off prematurely eight years before the advent of this Pope who would have been so much to his own heart.(1)

The Order of Camaldoli, of which he was General, had had a great history in the past. The original house, far up among the mountains of the Casentino, lies under a ridge from which, when the woods have died away, the eye can travel on a clear day from the Adriatic to the Mediterranean. It was first the single hermitage of St Romualdo, and then a cluster of hermitages occupied by the few whom he persuaded to flee God's wrath by sharing his extreme austerities. His younger contemporary, St Peter Damian, bosom-friend to Gregory VII, tells how far his "pia saevitia" was prepared to go in the way of discipline. When his own father wished to take his hand from the plough, and to leave the monastery into which Romualdo had placed him, the Saint "fixed his feet fast in the stocks, and bound him with heavy chains, and chastised him with grievous stripes, taming his body so long with pious severity that, with God's healing help, he brought his mind back to a state of salvation".(2) The whole countryside was stirred to immense reverence for these Knights of the Holy Ghost; and reverence brought wealth. Their numbers increased; a document of 1072 mentions eleven monasteries. They adopted the Rule of St Benedict; and in 1102, they formed a Congregation, with statutes of its own. Their fourth General, the Blessed Rodulf, moderated the extreme severity of the ancients; but the discipline of these hermit-monks was still very strict. Each, for instance, had a pair of scales in his cell, to make sure of not consuming more than the statutory ration of bread. Yet still their wealth increased by further endowments, until, at the height of their prosperity, their possessions included the landed possessions and attendant privileges of three counts. Ambrose, in a letter defending his brethren's legal rights against encroachments by the magistracy of Florence, wrote in the plural: "We live by our own laws, and have men under our subjection; nor is our condition other than that of the Counts around us."(3) It was in Rodulf's day that the Order multiplied most rapidly. He enlarged Fontebuono, the hospice which the hermits had built at the foot of the mountain; this became henceforth a regular monastery. Then a distinction naturally grew up between these original hermit-brethren and the community-monks of the Order, the Cenobites; yet there was still but one Congregation. Thus the constitution of this Benedictine Congregation contrasted greatly with original Benedictine simplicity and common sense. From that point of view, the whole story is one of confusion and perpetual friction. The division resulted in an arrangement by which the General was elected alternately from among the Hermits and the Cenobites; until the latter grew so numerous that they broke the concordat and monopolized the office. In 1212 the confusion was increased by the formation of another centre, an off-shoot, at the abbey of S. Michele di Murano, near Venice. Meanwhile Rodulf's relaxations of the Rule had been further extended in 1174; and still further alleviations came in 1254 and 1333. Yet there was still enough of their original strictness to distinguish these men from the mass of the Benedictines. When Urban V (1369) wanted to reform the great monastery of Monte Cassino and purge it of its "vagrant and indisciplined monks", he could not find among the Benedictines any man whom he could trust with the job, and had to force it upon an unwilling Camaldulensian abbot.(4) But there remained that weakness upon which Dom Helyot comments:

I would willingly believe that the reason which compelled the majority of the Camaldulensian hermits to embrace cenobitic life was that, finding it difficult to subsist amid forests and deserts, they came and settled in towns, where they served the faithful through preaching or by confession. Yet this reason, which some authors have alleged for that change, is not very valid, since, even at a distance from towns, they would have procured the commodities of life, through the great possessions with which the faithful enriched their houses. Those which were already near towns, e.g. St Mattia and St Michele at Murano, could not have given that reason, since the former was near to Venice and Murano, and the latter in Murano itself. More probably it was rather these great possessions which made them lose the spirit of retreat and solitude, and even abandon the observance of the Rule.

The two greatest complications of Ambrose's laborious Generalate, as we shall see, were connected with the semi-independence of the original hermitage at Camaldoli, and of S. Mattia at Murano. In one of his letters, he strongly dissuades a younger abbot from making any such dual arrangement.(5)

The General Chapter of 1446 decreed that the superiors should no longer hold their office for life, but by triennial election, and should study to secure exact discipline in their monasteries. They began themselves by renouncing their offices, by way of good example....But scarcely was Eugenius IV dead, when the fervour of these Superiors cooled: the majority refused to resign at the end of their triennial term and obtained from Nicholas V permission to hold on. This lasted until 1476, when Pietro Donati, abbot of St Michele at Murano, persuaded the Venetian Senate to decree that these nine monasteries should be united in a single congregation, which began under the authority of Sixtus IV and was confirmed by Innocent VIII. This congregation, taking its name from Murano, was augmented later on by the accession of several other monasteries and was separated from the Congregation of Camaldoli or Santo Eremo. This lasted until 1513, when Leo X united the two Congregations.

There was a definite division between the stricter "Hermits" and the laxer "Conventuals".

The Abbot of Murano, who had procured this union, was the last General for life. He had been elected in 1480 and resigned in 1515, reserving for himself a pension of 300 crowns and the title of General for the rest of his life. Thenceforward the Generals were triennial; they were chosen alternately from the Hermits and the Conventuals. This lasted down to 1616, when the Congregation of Murano was finally separated from the Hermits.

To this Order Ambrose made his vows in 1401. The Traversari had been among the noblest families in Northern Italy; Boccaccio has immortalized the tragedy of one of them in his eighth *Novel* of the fifth day. Salimbene lamented the practical extinction of the main branch about the middle of the thirteenth century.(6) Ambrose's father was evidently a fairly prosperous citizen of the little town of Portico, in the folds of the Tuscan Apennines, which was defended with such walls and towers as even villages often possessed in all but the most settled districts.(7) Vespasiano Bisticci, a contemporary and generally trustworthy authority, speaks of Ambrose as "son of a poor man". His modern namesake contends for his probable descent from the lordly house; but he seems to prove no more than that Ambrose's father was one of the citizens who helped to compile the town statutes in 1384.

His first education was at Galeata, not far distant. Here was a Camaldolese monastery, but apparently no monastic school. The earliest authority speaks of his schoolmaster as "a very polished [*civile*] man of religious manners"; and Ambrose himself tells us nothing of the monastery beyond the fact that he found it in a very bad state in 1433: "We were received by the Abbot, surveyed everything and lamented its terribly ruinous state" [*ruinas ingentes miserati sumus*].(8) At the age of fourteen—against his parents' wish, a later tradition says—he went as novice to Sta Maria degli Angioli at Florence, and took the final vows in 1401. Here he doubtless studied hard from the first. By 1417 he had advanced so far in Greek as to have finished translating a treatise of St Basil and to have made some progress with St John Chrysostom's book in defence of monastic life. He acknowledged gratefully, in later years, the help which his Greek studies had received from the prior of his monastery and from Niccolò Niccoli, but not in words which enable us to assert confidently, as Dino-Traversari does, that the help from either was in teaching. Concerning the prior we have no evidence that he himself knew Greek; and even Niccoli, who was unquestionably a Greek scholar, may well in this case have earned the young monk's gratitude only by encouragement and gifts of money or books. Voigt seems to be right in concluding that Ambrose was mainly, if not entirely, self-taught in this language.

Yet certainly his monastery was unusually well situated for an enthusiastic young scholar. Florence was boiling over with intellectual life: Greek refugees were occasionally trickling into the city; and one at least of these, Demetrio Scarano, entered Sta Maria in 1416 and took the vows next year; he may well have been living in Florence as a free-lance teacher for several years before this. Be that as it may, Ambrose unquestionably became one of the best Greek, as well as Latin, scholars of his time.

The Renaissance, as a whole, owed far less to the monasteries than to "the world" outside; except of course, to the very different monks of far-off ages, when the Latin classics had found no other safe resting-place than the cloister, during the barbarian invasions and the long anarchy. It is true that Ambrose's contemporaries patronized artists: moreover Sta Maria degli Angioli was one of the very few in which we hear at this time of something like a school of scribes and miniaturists, though there seems to be no evidence that all this work was done by the monks themselves. Ambrose, writing to Leonardo Bruni, who had sent him a volume for illumination, excused the imperfections of the work on the ground that "those who were most experienced in this art are dead, and those who survive are youths who progress from day to day in that study....I grieved greatly that I myself had never applied myself to this craft [*huic opificio*]. For I would have wished to adorn with mine own hand this volume of your writing, and to put the last touches to it."(9) But work was still going on at Sta Maria; and he was more than once concerned to buy ultramarine and varnish for the painters; moreover in one letter he writes: "There have always been, and there are some even now in our monastery, who practise that art of adorning books most expertly and prettily; for such work is certainly no unworthy occupation for monastic leisure."(10) Of Jerome, his own brother in the flesh and in the Order, he writes: "he had learned from boyhood the art of embroidery, wherein he surpassed all others of our age";(11) and two of Jerome's tapestries were still shown in the sacristy of that monastery as late as 1575. One other monk of the same house, Eufrosino, was a painter.(12) In scholarship, again, though Sta Maria degli Angioli would have earned great distinction in contemporary England, yet apart from Ambrose it produced none who can be allotted even to the second rank in the European society of that day. Its library was abundant, greatly by reason of gifts from Florentine benefactors: but the colossal industry of Mehus has unearthed only three brethren whose names were known even in their own day. Dom Onufrio enjoyed the friendship of Coluccio Salutato, the famous Latinist and Chancellor of Florence. Dom Rafaello, General of the Order, was again distinguished enough to have been a correspondent of Coluccio. Thirdly, Dom Giovanni da San Damiano exchanged letters with Coluccio, who "most eagerly defended, against this monk, the study of pagan literature and especially of the poets". Giovanni's own writings seem to have been confined to translations into Italian of St Gregory's *Moralia*, Petrarch's *Remedia*, and St Bernard's *Sermons on the Song of Songs*. Even of copyists there seems to have been little activity among the brethren at Sta Maria. At the most favourable time, when their General was this Ambrose, one of the greatest book-lovers and book-seekers of that busy age, nearly all his references to scriptorial work suggest, or even more explicitly prove, the work of paid copyists. The main exception is his brother Jerome, to whom he had taught Greek, but whose accuracy as a scribe he criticizes with brotherly frankness.(13) Thus Ambrose's own bibliographical activities were mainly directed to book-hunting and the collection of hired copyists (*librarii*), and persuading patrons like the Medici or (less successfully) Eugenius IV to provide the necessary money. This was the golden age for collectors. Everywhere Greek refugees were fleeing from the Turk, sometimes bringing precious codices with them; and Italian scholars had begun to scent out the treasures long hidden, and often ignored, in Transalpine monasteries, very much as Tischendorf discovered the Codex Sinaiticus. More than one of Traversari's book-collecting friends triumphed publicly in having rescued some precious volume from its monastic "prison".(14) When his own business with the Pope took him to Rome, he wrote: "I have found far more to displease me than to give any pleasure....I have seen vast ruined dwellings and walls, and books mostly rotting and torn."(15)

Everything tends to show that Ambrose owed his learning, apart from his own inspiration and diligence, to scholars outside the walls of Sta Maria. The earliest help in that way seems to have come from a group at Santo Spirito, the Florentine convent of Austin Friars. These, who must be carefully distinguished from Busch's Austin Canons, seem to have become tinged everywhere with liberalism towards the close of the Middle Ages. In Germany that Order gave birth to Luther and several others among the most violent reformers; so also at Cambridge, as soon as Luther came forward. At Florence, this convent gradually became a sort of "free Academy, in the Platonic sense".(16) Among this group were Martino da Signa, the friend of Boccaccio, Pietro da Castelletto, who completed Boccaccio's *Life of Petrarch*, and especially Luigi de Marsigli, of noble birth, who as a young man of twenty had been introduced to Petrarch, and was now an Austin Friar. In 1382 he came back and settled at Florence, and died in 1394. He was a great adversary of the pagan Averroists; but his theology was liberal, and he encouraged free speech. This movement caused something like a split in the convent; and Voigt regards the mysticism of St Catharine of Siena, pupil to orthodox Dominicans, as a conscious reaction against this encroaching spirit of free enquiry. Santo Spirito thus formed a sort of second high school at Florence, side by side with the official university, and a bridge between the Church and the lay spirit. It was the most living theologico-philosophical academy in Italy, until Leo X reorganized the papal university of Rome, the Sapienza, and endowed it with princely munificence. There was thus in Florence no such open hostility as we often find elsewhere between Orthodoxy and the New Learning, with its dangerous tendencies and its frequent manifestations of open or even crude infidelity. Intellectual citizens met there with cloisterers and with scholars: it was "the first of those many private academies to which the free thought and scholarship of Italy were afterwards destined to owe so much".(17) There was no anti-Greek or anti-Semite movement, though one of the group, Manetti, who was also Traversari's pupil, learned Hebrew and disputed against the Jews. Again, there was no trace of that spirit, too common in the Middle Ages, which shrank from the Latin classics in their entirety and encouraged only "flores" and selections for commonplace-books. Under such influence, Ambrose of

Camaldoli became the most perfect type of orthodox humanist. Through his personality the ecclesiastico-literary centre of Florence shifted from S. Spirito to Sta Maria degli Angioli. Vespasiano writes:

It was seldom that all the worthy men whom Florence possessed at that time did not go to visit brother Ambrose; and in his time the city flourished with worthy men.... The pastime of Cosimo de' Medici and Lorenzo, and of Niccolò Niccolì and Master Paul and Ser Filippo di Ser Ugolino was to go daily to Sta Maria degli Angioli for converse with Brother Ambrose: and thither went likewise many worthy citizens and men of letters who lived at that time; and there their talk was always of worthy things; and thence it followed that this age had many singular men.(18)

To those days Ambrose owed also one of his closest and most enduring friendships, that of Niccolò Niccolì, who in later life helped younger students with a generous enthusiasm which made his house, with its rich library, a true continuation of the S. Spirito tradition, an unofficial Academy. Niccolì forms the subject of one of the most lifelike biographies in that series written by Vespasiano Bisticci, that Florentine bookseller who may almost be called co-founder of the Laurentian Library, and who was uniquely qualified to write the literary history of that time. Symonds has translated one long extract; but Voigt condenses the whole into a vivid story which I summarize briefly here for Ambrose's sake, on the principle of *noscitur a socio*.(19)

Niccolì was, on the whole, the most conspicuous figure in the group that had gathered under the patronage of Cosimo de' Medici. A plump neat man, daintily dressed, laughing and laughter-provoking, but capable of biting sarcasm at times; he had been chained to a merchant's desk until his father's death left him with a competence which enabled him to follow his own bent. Dante (whose *Commedia* he knew practically by heart) and Petrarch had shown him the way to the realms of gold in the Latin classics: he mastered their language, and even passed on to learn a little Greek. At S. Spirito he widened his purview, embracing theology and philosophy. He finally collected 800 volumes, enough in number to make a superior monastic library, and of incomparably greater literary value.

A great number of these he had copied with his own hand, and others he had annotated, collating them with other MSS. All this ran him into debt; but Cosimo allowed him to draw upon his bank, upon security of the books. These were valued after his death at 4000 sequins.* In 1430, he had drawn up a will leaving them all to Sta Maria degli Angioli, where Traversari was then prior. But in his last will, in 1437, when Traversari was Minister General and constantly absent on business, he left them to what was in effect the first public library in Italy since classical times.(20) Cosimo satisfied the creditors: he and Lorenzo were among the sixteen governors, appointed to choose the locality and the rules; and the MSS. were finally deposited at the monastery of S. Marco, one of Cosimo's recent foundations, under condition that they should be accessible to students.

Traversari was, by Niccolò's choice, the first of these governors; and this seems certainly to have been Ambrose's closest literary friendship. On his journeys he wrote to report each new find to his friend. He strove long and hard to compose the bitter quarrel between Niccolò and Leonardo Bruni. The former, for the sake of his studies, had always avoided marriage; though not on misogynistic grounds; for he and Bruni were wont to haunt the church doors on holy-days in order to ogle the pretty women. Moreover, he ended by carrying off the mistress of one of his five brothers. The whole five conspired and subjected the lady to chastisement in the public street. Bruni was the only friend who did not write in condolence to Niccolò: nay, he answered with some disdain when his friend complained of his silence. This, at any rate, was the fatal spark; but literary jealousy had probably heaped up the combustibles. Traversari was not here on the puritan side. His letters frequently end with compliments to the lady: "Salute in my name Benvenuta, that most faithful woman"; "Salute your most faithful servant Benvenuta"; and so on.† When she was ill, Niccolò turned to Ambrose and begged for his prayers.(21) By

* The sequin was practically interchangeable with the Venetian ducat and Florentine florin. As we shall see later, Ambrose estimated a first-rate copyist as worth 30 ducats a year, with board and lodging.

† Vespasiano's phrase is *una donna di tempo*—"a temporary lady", but the union seems in fact to have been permanent.

her ministrations he had what his fastidious taste always required; "clothes of the fairest crimson cloth, down to the ground"; at meals the cleanest and whitest of napkins and tablecloths; antique vases for dishes and crystal cups for his drink. "It was a dainty sight to see him at table, antique as it was in fashion", says Vespasiano.* His whole house was a museum of fine porcelain and other objects of art, less costly in those days of early collectors; and among these and his books the merry bachelor lived "like a spider in his web". But his books and his brain were at every man's service. At his death, 200 volumes were found to have been lent out. While he lived, "ten or twelve young folk might sometimes be seen sitting in his study, each with a book in hand; Niccolì spoke with each in turn, testing what he had read and how he had understood it".

Through Marsigli, then, and Niccolì, and Prior Guido of Sta Maria, and then again through his own priorate at that conspicuous monastery, within the very city of Florence, Ambrose became more or less intimate with nearly all the greatest scholars of that time, who learned to treat him as an equal. Dino has collected twenty such names, from Manetti (who had been Ambrose's pupil) to Beccadelli and Lorenzo Valla. His relations with this last, though far less intimate, were as curious as those with Niccolì. Valla, despite the fact that he rose soon afterwards to favour at the papal court under Nicholas V, was one of the most destructive critics of that day. He was probably introduced to Traversari by Beccadelli, who was often in Florence. In 1440, a year after Ambrose's death, he exploded those Pseudo-Isidorian Decretals which had been so often cited in the Middle Ages in favour of papal autocracy; thence he went on to other equally iconoclastic writings, and was commonly believed, probably with justice, to repudiate Christianity altogether. But already before this he had published a book scarcely less offensive to Church feeling. It was a dialogue entitled "Concerning Pleasure"; or "The True Good". The characters were Leonardo Bruni, pleading for the Stoic cause, Beccadelli for the Epicurean and Niccolì for Christian morality. Beccadelli, in perfect character, preaches the gospel of sheer sensu-

* "A vederlo in tavola, così antico come era, era una gentilezza."

ality. Nature had procreated us; therefore it is our duty to procreate others. Thus chastity and virginity are unnatural; and happy was that African tribe where the women, "far from being enclosed in the temple of Vesta because they had no dowry, were sheltered in that of Venus to earn one there".(22) This was not merely to attack the monks and nuns in person for their failure to maintain their ideal, as Poggio and other humanists did, but to undermine the very foundations. Valla, in this treatise, gave Niccolì a moderate and reasonable part to preach; but that was only what men heard from the pulpit in church. The real gist of the book, and that which was calculated to fascinate the public, was this Gospel of Nature; and men have been burned before and after Valla for smaller heresies than this. The Pope was Eugenius IV; and the reign of Nicholas V, who gave Valla a high position at his court for scholarship's sake, was still distant. Therefore the bold innovator sought about for shelter, and turned to some man whose scholarship and orthodoxy were above suspicion. None could serve this purpose better than Traversari. This was in 1431, when Ambrose had just received the papal commission to visit all the houses of his Order and purge them of such sexual licence and other irregularities as he might find there. His visitation, in fact, began on October 18. On September 4 we find him writing to Valla:

> Among my occupations I am reading—or rather I have run through—your *De Vero Bono*, gratefully and very willingly, if only I had been able to enjoy more leisure.... Your style is pleasant and easy, and well suited to the matter: upon your opinions I should not myself dare to pronounce a judgment, since in truth I have read it under very heavy occupations [*occupatissimus*]. But, if your opinion is even in discrepancy with the judgments of old time, who is so severe a critic as not to pardon this easily and willingly, since it is lawful for every man to discuss and feel according to his own choice?

The rest of the letter is equally guarded; and what Valla wanted was more than this. Therefore we find another letter from Ambrose (September 12). This is much longer; he has now read the book twice, not only with pleasure but with "the greatest profit". He wanders among philosophic names; he draws the ancient distinction between two kinds of love, Urania and Pandemos, the Heavenly and the Earthly; therefore, since Valla 'has placed the true and highest Good in that pleasure which proceeds from honest actions, I cannot but approve your judgment, and not only praise it but embrace it warmly....This, Lorenzo Valla, is what I dare to say in this brief moment of time, concerning your most excellent work, not only as to its character of exuberant and most polished diction, but also as to the gravity and splendour of your judgments." Six weeks after this letter, Ambrose was visiting (in the Pope's name, and with a heavy sense of responsibility in the face of great corruption) the first monastery of his series. Those two letters, unknown to his earlier editors, are now printed by Dino in his first Appendix. Almost more than anything else they enable us to measure the difficulties besetting, from the very first, this Italian effort for monastic reform.

Considering his time and place, Ambrose did perhaps almost as much as could be expected of any single man. Savonarola, soon after him, led a fierce frontal attack upon the mass of chronic abuses, and was burned for his pains. Among Ambrose's exact contemporaries the heroic Church champions were St Bernardino of Siena, St Giovanni Capistrano, and the Blessed Jacopo della Marchia; but these spent so much energy upon mission-preaching and heretic-hunting that they had little left for monastic or sacerdotal reform. Men like Busch or Dederoth, putting morals immeasurably above intellect, might well have kindled open revolt. We shall see that even our moderate Ambrose had reason to fear poison on his visitation, and his friends suspected it in his comparatively early death.(23)

Yet he had, outside his friendship with the learned, powerful friends in "the world", upon whom he could count for a good deal of support, so long as he did not attack vested interests too openly and too crudely. Eugenius IV had been Cardinal Protector of the Camaldulensian Order before his elevation to the papacy in 1431. Thus he was and remained in intimate official relations with Ambrose, first as Prior of Sta Maria, then as Superior of the Hermitage at Camaldoli and finally as Minister General and Visitor. Next we must count Lorenzo and Cosimo de' Medici, and especially the latter, to whom the first editor of Ambrose's letters writes in his dedicatory preface, perhaps with a little friendly exaggeration, "from tender years you followed his manners, his life and his teaching".(24) The Medic family were attached to him as one of the glories of their Florence; and he was faithful to them even during their temporary exile. Besides these, Ambrose's correspondence shows that his position enabled him to count upon respect, if not help, from lay magistrates everywhere, even up to the Doge of Venice; and he had powerful friends at the Roman Court.

CHAPTER XXVII

THE VISITOR'S MIND

HAVING taken stock of his friends and allies, let us now review his personal qualifications for this crusade; for crusade it was against inveterate abuses.

He was well aware of all its difficulties, and even dangers. There were not only the ordinary difficulties of travel for weeks or months at a time, considerable enough in those days. Beforehand Ambrose expressed his preference for walking: "my own choice (if my health or this rank which I unworthily occupy permit) would be to travel rather on foot than on horseback."(1) Later, when it came to practice, he wrote to Niccoli, "Farewell, sweetest friend, and pity thine Ambrogio the traveller—or rather thy runner—who was once a quiet monk: though indeed my least weariness and vexation is that of riding even to an almost intolerable heat" (p. 418). But a great deal of his work was done in the cold months, sometimes in snow or torrential rain, with peril from floods and precipices and unknown ways. His journey to Venice acquainted him with sea-sickness. He alludes more than once to his dangers in general terms. The additional commission for visiting the Order of Vallombrosa drew from him a piteous complaint of this fresh burden, "full of difficulty and peril" (p. 208). For his Venetian visitation, "we know not what awaits us, but that all agree in predicting labours and perils for us" (p. 556). To a friend who had declined a less burdensome commission, he writes sympathetically, "there might be reasons of caution for avoiding that fear and the perils of robbers" (p. 681). From the midst of his own visitations in 1433 he writes to his blood-brother in Florence: "The roaring lion lies in wait for us, nor can we find a safe foothold....Pray earnestly, I beseech, and commend me to the prayers of our brethren and of our children"—the schoolboys whose welfare he had so much at heart (p. 555). He had to fight slander and friends grown cold; he was criticized for mismanagement of difficult cases, for timidity in face of bold offenders, and even accused once of malversation. Thus to his literary correspondents he often complains bitterly of the burdens of his Generalate. He finds few trustworthy helpers, and can say with the Psalmist: "My lovers and my neighbours did stand looking upon my trouble, and my kinsmen stood afar off." Again: "O that I had the wings of a dove, for then would I flee away and be at rest!" A few weeks before his death he wrote to Lorenzo de' Medici of his longing for "rustication"; the converse of his peasants was pleasanter now than that of Pope or cardinals: he would make certain repairs at Fonte Buono, and fill some unglazed windows with those little round panes, like bottle-ends, which we see in pictures of that day (p. 346). It distresses him that he cannot come home one Christmas for the crèche at Sta Maria (p. 639). He is worried with money affairs and debts, especially since the payments to the Roman Court for ratification of his appointment as Minister General: "Lo, the year is not yet completed since my most unhappy fate, and already I have satisfied some undue claimants" (p. 528). He is thus compelled to write for money (p. 396). His sedentary life and hard work tell upon him; he suffers from indigestion, dizziness, headaches and a trembling of the hand which compels him at last to fall back upon amanuenses.

We cannot demand from a scholar that he should have the stuff of a martyr: but Ambrose was by no means lacking in courage. Much as he owed to the Pope, he could speak very plainly to him upon occasion. His first gift to him (apart from what Rome demanded from him for his Generalate) was an elegant copy of St Bernard's *De Consideratione*, in which the saint had pressed many unpleasant truths upon his old pupil Eugenius III: moreover, Ambrose explicitly drew the parallel. In the accompanying letter, he warned him against one of the greatest temptations of fifteenth-century Popes: "Transfer war from our own bowels to infidels and pagans, if need be" (p. 9). In the papal quarrel with the city of Bologna, "the matter should be treated not by force of arms but by negotiation" [*consilio*] (p. 21). Reform your priests and your monks (p. 9). Show the assembled Fathers at Basel "that evil deeds are far from meeting your approval". For men take grave exception to "that pomp of dress, that luxurious furniture, those war-chargers wherein many prelates and cardinals indulge" (pp. 63–4). In face of the crying injustice done to his brethren at Vangadicia, to which we shall presently come, he writes nominally to the papal Referendary but practically to Eugenius about his ingratitude for all his political services at the Council of Basel (p. 184; cf. p. 187). Here, indeed, he had every right to complain, since he was one of the minority of really distinguished men who had espoused the papal side from the very first, and treated the Council as an unauthorized rabble. Usually, he did in fact enjoy the Pope's favour as far as could be expected from so great a potentate who was no longer dependent upon his inferior for help. A bishop, worsted in a lawsuit against the Camaldulensians, attributed this partly to personal influence at court; and Ambrose's letters from Rome show him far less compelled to dangle hopelessly upon a few papal audiences than was the case with nearly all suitors who, like him, came comparatively empty-handed. Yet for him Rome was the modern "Babylon": "This Babylon of the West "(pp. 498, 574), a name no less disdainful because he applies it twice to Basel, with its political manœuvres which to Ambrose seemed frankly immoral. Of Rome he writes again: "I experience many things daily here, I see and hear much which moves me to immense scruples and are a stumbling-block: but of these things I had better speak tête-à-tête."

For certainly his instincts were rather for silence and compromise than for open fight. In his visitation diary he frequently puts his crudest phrases into Greek. On every page we see his tact and moderation: for this, in fact, he was more than once reproached (e.g. pp. 430, 902–3). In answer to a contrary accusation he was able to plead with truth: "No man's faults have been publicly noted [on my visitations] but such as are open, and of the slighter kind; I have taken care to chastise the more secret and graver offences by more secret admonitions" (p. 801; cf. p. 486 *caute tamen, ne quid scandali oriatur*). For this he pleads Christ's example and Virgil's famous *parcere subjectis* (pp. 429, 484). He tries long and patient persuasion with apostates, where the law prescribed their immediate arrest and imprisonment (pp. 928–9, 957). He is constantly willing to make serious concessions for the sake of peace, even when the law is plainly on his side (e.g. p. 582, the Bishop of Bologna;

p. 831, the citizens of Lucca). He listens patiently to reproof (p. 898). If in one business matter he finally acted with vigour, it was because "for a whole day I cast myself on my knees before them (I might almost say), yet to no profit" (p. 789). Distressed that his brethren at the Angioli have refused to find room for a sick monk at his recommendation, he feels sure that this is the doing of a few malcontents: since "I know that the monastery loves me: for, even though the men should lose their affection, yet the very walls will love me" (p. 531). More than once he yields, where Busch would certainly have been stricter in his obedience to the Rule. He condones *proprietas* (p. 938): he acts as godfather to a child, in face of what he knows to be the plain prohibition of Canon Law (pp. 86, 272, 763, 842). He does not object to the sale of church vestments from Sta Maria for the sake of raising the wind (p. 654), or to their receiving a rich old layman as lodger (p. 669). He writes to beg off a culprit from burning, where the context suggests sodomy as his offence (p. 265). He strongly dissuades a younger monk from unnecessary asceticism (p. 744). In two most entertaining passages of his *Itinerary*, he acts as moderator between violent disputants (*Hod.* 17, 66), and there is a similar scene in one of his letters (p. 796). A violent quarrel had broken out at Sta Maria in 1436 as to the sale of a piece of land, most advantageous pecuniarily, but bringing undesirable elements close to the cloister. The three protagonists, by an irony of history, bore the names of the three Archangels. "Raphael first broke out publicly into revilings and attacked Gabriel....Then Michael fell upon Raphael, in the presence of those citizens and of the whole convent. These must be first admonished, and rebuked with moderate vehemence" (p. 796). We have seen how Ambrose strove for peace between Niccolì and Bruni; so also he took great pains to heal the even worse quarrel, because more definitely based upon literary jealousies, between Niccolì and Filelfo (p. 302). Therefore his judgment was much sought (e.g. p. 1131). Most significant of all, in this context, is the difficult matrimonial case on which Ambrose was consulted by letter from an official in Rome, apparently a Canon Lawyer. The sordid details resemble with painful exactitude those which are quoted, almost at the same moment, by St Bernardino of Siena in one of his sermons, as a concrete instance of the unnatural vices with which he reproaches his fellow-citizens.(2) This case is of great interest, as a fresh proof that the question of the indissolubility of a valid marriage was not yet definitely closed by the Church, even after fourteen centuries of theology and Canon Law. This uncertainty is vital for the just estimate of those all-important and long-drawn negotiations between Henry VIII and Clement VII a century later.

In Church politics he was whole-heartedly papalist, not only at Basel but at the later Councils of Ferrara and Florence, where the Greek Church was persuaded to accept reunion, and Ambrose's Greek scholarship gave him a very prominent place. From the secular politics by which Italy was torn asunder he generally kept aloof; there are few allusions to them in his letters, though he warns Eugenius obliquely against the effect of his ministers' bloodthirsty doings at Bologna upon men's minds.(3) His friendship with the exiled Medici was not political but personal. Once, indeed, he breaks out impatiently against these contending despots: "What can we do, we who by the crooked condition of our times have fallen to a point where we can foresee what ought to be done, yet have power to perform nothing, since all is done at the arbitrament of a single man, who is most tenacious of his own purpose and cannot easily be turned aside from it!" (p. 447).

It remains to consider his attitude towards that matter of monastic reform in which the papal commission of 1431 called him to take so prominent a part, first for his own Order and secondly for the Vallombrosan.

One point, most strange to the modern mind, it would be fatal to ignore in this connection. The Reformation is, to us, so definitely a *fait accompli* that men of all creeds are tempted to forget that state of mind which either regarded a general revolt against the Pope as impossible, or, while fearing it subconsciously, took it into as little practical consideration as the man of forty takes the thought of his own death. Therefore this question of monastic reform, which our own historical experience shows now to have been absolutely fundamental, was treated much less seriously, even by zealous monks, than we are tempted to take for granted. All but the strongest minds are often dominated by the fatalistic thought: "It has lasted all this time, and why not for ever?" Therefore men often thought more of other considerations which, to us, are comparatively as dust in the balance. Whereas we think of it in the gross, as a question of life or death for the Church, to them it was overshadowed by the question of personal salvation for the individual. This, considered in its strictest sense, must be the decisive consideration in any Christian age. For the fifteenth century, we cannot ignore it without grave anachronism.

From the early twelfth century, at least, there had been a strong feeling in the most religious minds that a bishopric involved grave dangers to the soul. In the most unexpected quarters, we find this in the exaggerated form that few bishops can come to heaven, so great are the temptations of their office, and so impossible is it to treat worldly affairs, even from the episcopal bench, without contracting worldly stains. One of St Bernard's best pupils was convinced that, if he had accepted the see of Cambrai, he would have been damned. Pious Dominicans were scandalized when their brother Albert the Great accepted the see of Regensburg. There would have been similar scandal in Franciscan circles if St Bonaventura had accepted that of York.(4) Traversari expresses this same feeling with a vehemence which is remarkable in a man who so typically exemplifies fifteenth-century Florentine culture. His exact contemporary, St Bernardino, was offered a bishopric. To the modern mind, nothing could seem more suitable. He was a distinguished scholar, the greatest preacher of his day, a model of moral purity and courage and religious energy. Reform was the constant theme of his sermons. In his own Franciscan Order he was leader of the reformists: the new Observantine Congregation owed almost as much to him as Cistercian greatness owed to St Bernard. By Church law, every bishop was the natural Father of all non-exempt monasteries in his diocese; and, with papal help, he could do much for the exempt also. Earlier Franciscans like Pecham, Archbishop of Canterbury, and St Louis, Archbishop of Toulouse, had kept their personal poverty amidst luxurious surroundings; and Pecham had been one of the most efficient visitors of the monasteries. Cusanus, soon after this offer to St Bernardino, obtained a commission as papal legate which subjected to him, in strict law, exempt and non-exempt monasteries alike. Armed with episcopal authority, Bernardino might reasonably have said as Busch said when they gave him an archdeaconry: "I intend to make a new world here." Yet, when the Saint was designated for a bishopric, and his refusal was not yet known,* Ambrose wrote to him in no less dismay than the Dominican General had shown to Albert the Great. The whole missive must be read, or we shall miss something of the mentality of that time and place.

Most Reverend Father, with my greetings in the Lord Jesus. This brief letter I write to thy Reverence not without utmost tears and immense pain of heart, in order that thou mayest understand how grievous and terrible it is to all who have been kindled in the Lord Jesus by thy word to hear what hath been done concerning thee, and what, it seemeth, shall be done. And, albeit I know thy strength and force of mind in all great matters, yet sometimes I fear that this thing is not from heaven, that thou, Preacher of Poverty in Christ Jesus, who hast built up so many souls, panting for the Gospel life, shouldest be designated and proclaimed as Bishop. The unworthiness of this matter is so strongly asserted by all thy friends who feel with thee in the Lord Jesus, that we would not shrink from undergoing any torment in order that thou mightest free us from this fear. All thy brethren, falling at thy knees with most abundant tears, pray and beseech thee not to overthrow, not to tear up, not to uproot the devotion of the Order [of Friars Observant], and the foundation of thy religion, and that most holy edification of souls. All those who have been the fiercest and bitterest enemies to thee and to us are wishing now for this, praying for it, yearning for it with utmost desire. The Conventual Brethren of St Francis, those abortions in the Lord Jesus, are already congratulating themselves; they insult and mock at us. All who, among the people of Italy, are most devoted to the Lord Jesus fall now and are overthrown; they will neglect faith and hope and charity if thou, the admirable trumpet of Jesus Christ our Lord, thou the defender and preacher of poverty, fallest into that dignity, most unhappy for thyself! Therefore I, thy most devoted son and the meanest servant of Jesus Christ our Lord, do pray, entreat, beseech and implore thee, and supplicate with all tears from my heart and my eyes, that thou shouldst flee from this evil, and repudiate this loss of souls, and refrain from filling the mouths of those malignants who desire naught but to satisfy the rage of their own minds, asserting

* This was perhaps in 1427, when Martin V offered him the see of his native Siena; later on (1431 and 1435) he refused Ferrara and Urbino also.

how they have long since foretold among the people that this thing would come to pass, and that thou dost preach only to fish for benefices. If, as I hope, thou art wise, thou wilt sooner resolve to die for love of God than utterly to overthrow innumerable souls throughout Italy, and the foundation of all thy brethren. I believe that thou wilt be most constant even unto death, if thou neglect not those things which Christ hath wrought through thee. Farewell, my best Father in Christ Jesus our Lord.(5)

This illustrates the truth which Burckhardt emphasizes, that in the Church, as in general society, individualism was now becoming a stronger and stronger force. "Italy showed that she could give her enthusiasm only to individuals." "While architects, painters, and sculptors were working with restless activity in and for the churches, we hear at the beginning of the sixteenth century the bitterest complaints of the neglect of public worship and of these churches themselves....It is well known how Luther was scandalized by the irreverence with which the priests in Rome said Mass."(6) Yet the great mission-preachers of the earlier fifteenth century displayed already, almost as clearly as Savonarola in the latter half, the power of the living word upon the multitude. Their triumphs were as brilliant as any in the Middle Ages, and not more ephemeral.

In a few cases, they even attacked the tyrants openly, when no other man dared to speak except from some shelter. But the cloistered monk was fast losing his power in Italian society. "The North produced an *Imitation of Christ*, which worked silently at first only within the walls of the monastery, but worked for ages: the South produced men who made on their fellows a mighty but passing impression." Traversari knew, if only subconsciously, that the most living religion in Italy was represented by these preaching Observantines; and this knowledge conditioned his policy. St Bernardino as bishop would have been able to recall a minority of monasteries for a while to earlier purity; as mission-preacher, on the other hand, he was daily saving hundreds of souls. No office, except the papacy, could give him such force as he was now exercising of his own free will and impulse, as Knight of the Holy Ghost. But such feelings on the part of a great churchman like Ambrose suggest "defeatism"; an unconscious despair of the institutional Church; a sort of religious *sauve qui peut*.

For it was not as though Traversari had failed to realize the sore need of monastic reform. On March 10, 1431, just a week after the election of his old friend and Cardinal Protector to the papacy, he wrote him a long letter of advice. He trembles, of course, to preach to him now: for "Thou rulest in God's place, and must needs be God upon Earth"—*vice Dei fungeris: Deus in Terris sis necesse est*. "The world waiteth upon thy nod, and upon thy command hang not only Italy, Germany, France, Spain and the rest of the West, but Asia and Africa and all the barbarian peoples." The three most urgent matters are to end the civil wars which devastate Italy, and to reform the clergy in general, the monasteries in particular. "This you know far better than I; yet I may venture to remind you." In a similar strain he had written earlier, while Eugenius was as yet only Cardinal Protector. That letter is dated October 15, probably in 1430. The Protector has commissioned him to choose a few of his brethren as delegates to the coming General Chapter, with the object "if possible, of restoring our Order to the beauty of Regular Observance and to the image of its ancient sanctity" (p. 815). Ambrose feels not only that this mission would be a breach of their rule of claustration, but also that simple monks would be out of place "among prelates". Therefore, since the Protector's message is rather an advice than a command, he will send an open letter in lieu of personal attendance. He thanks God for this hopeful inspiration of the Cardinal Protector. We must look up to God, "*who is able of stones to raise up children unto Abraham*, and at whose command the dead arise".

Consider diligently how great was the sanctity of our Order in days of old.... Tell us, Fathers, wherefore is the face of things so changed? ...Are God's might and power less in our days than in those of our fathers, so that they, with His help, were able to do what we cannot? Who can say this, when on the contrary we see in our own age so many habitations of His servants suddenly changed from wretched lukewarmness to ardent faith and the love of God and holy Religion?* I beseech you, let our spirit be kindled to imitate them; so that this, which a few monasteries now do, ye yourselves may be willing to keep

* The allusion, of course, is to Sta Giustina, Bursfelde, Melk, Castell, and Monte Cassino.

of your own accord, each in his own house....Lo, how we see, and how we groan in silence over that enormous change and lamentable descent and perversion of manners and devastation of all Religion.*

He goes on to specify details: disuse of the monastic habit in favour of luxurious and semi-lay attire; use of body-linen and contempt of the statutes; for Camaldoli was founded upon the Benedictine Rule.

"Our chaste fasts have been succeeded by feasts, and banquets full of delicacies. Flesh-eating flourishes almost everywhere; and would that it were moderate and temperate flesh-eating! Monks of our Order wander inordinately everywhere, and are parsons of churches outside the bosom of Religion. In the same way, other things are committed which are full of disgrace, and most remote from the institutions of our Rule. Beloved Fathers, who is there that laboureth to prohibit these things? If ye, who in our Saviour's words should be the salt of the earth, do this—ye, after the model of whose lives your subjects' morals should be formed and directed—there can be no doubt that the simple monks will follow readily whither ye lead." *Facilis descensus*; but monasticism "riseth not without difficulty to the heights of virtue, especially when it hath become accustomed to vice". "Our Order hath excellent and praiseworthy constitutions; so excellent that they need no additions, if only we kept that which hath been decreed....I have suggested these things to you, beloved Fathers, not as studying to teach you (for perchance ye know these things better than I), but in zeal for Religion and with pious affection." *Lift up your eyes* (he quotes) *and look on the fields; for they are white already to harvest.*

Yet, knowing the facts as he did, he does not seem to have reflected that his friend St Bernardino might become one of the greatest of harvesters in that field. Or, if we suppose that both he and St Bernardino knew only too well how much it had cost to persuade even a few Franciscan friars to quit the multitude of Conventuals and go back to St Francis' own strict Observance, then that is only to approach by a different path the same conclusion. Neither the saint nor the scholar, in fifteenth-century Italy, was able to approach monastic reform in the spirit of Virgil's *possunt, quia posse videntur*. Neither of them possessed, in this matter, that ardent and robust hope which is an earnest of victory.

* "Religion", throughout, is used in the technical sense of "monasticism".

CHAPTER XXVIII

THE VISITOR IN ACTION

THIS attitude will become more explicable when we come to Ambrose's actual visitation records. For there, reading between the lines, we shall see that what he found in these monasteries was what, without ever having been personally at any but very few, he had already only too much reason to suspect.

His *Itinerary* (or *Hodoeporicon* as he named it in one of his little Greek pedantries) is in the form of a succinct diary, often carelessly written, and therefore obscure in detail. Moreover, even at his best, Ambrose is a man of his own time and country; he has taken great pains to break away from medieval Latin into Ciceronian, but not always with fortunate results.

The General Chapter meeting of 1431 opened on October 18 at the monastery of Urano, by the little town of Bertinoro, after which it is often named. When Ambrose wrote that anticipatory letter of October 15, 1430, he was only an intimate friend of the Cardinal Protector: but now that man has become Pope Eugenius IV. This time the new Protector, Cardinal Cervantes, summoned him personally.

> His repeated letters compelled Us,* against Our custom, to break Our rule of monastic enclosure and to repair, however unwillingly, to the Chapter: moreover We were summoned by apostolical letters also. I, Ambrose, then Sub-prior of our house, was sent with Silvester our Chamberlain, my sweetest companion, with whom I had now spent 30 years in the monastery. We left our convent on the 11th, whilst the brethren were singing their vespers, lest any trouble should arise from their tears and lamentations.

These days unfortunately happened to be plagued with torrential rain; the bridge of Forlì was swept away; and after many difficulties the two reached Bertinoro only on the very day fixed for the opening session. The cardinal, acting under a definite

* Ambrose generally uses the official *We* in this diary, but sometimes slips into the singular.

papal commission, exercised his right of choosing himself the seven "Diffinitores", i.e. the Executive Committee of the Chapter, in spite of the protests of the abbots, who would doubtless have elected a committee more tolerant of ancient customs. One of these Diffinitores was Ambrose. Their first agendum was Reform; "the Visitors' reports were read, and, with the exception of a few monasteries, no health was found in the Order."(1) On the fourth day the Diffinitores enquired into the charges against Benedetto Lanci, the Minister General of the Order; and "since very many crimes were alleged against him, the Protector asked him in moderate language to resign". He tried to brazen it out, and insulted the Protector: therefore he was quietly put into custody, and an enquiry was conducted in legal form. This brought him to his senses; after four days he fell on his knees, wept, and abdicated. Traversari was at once elected in his place. Since Lanci was suspected of having robbed the Order and amassed a considerable private hoard, he was kept in custody pending full examination. This business (to anticipate here) became long and tedious. It was desperately difficult to drag from him a real statement of accounts, or to control his behaviour in retirement. At length Traversari and his colleagues consented to whitewash this ex-general for a payment of 200 florins down; and he was allowed to live in fairly comfortable retirement, without further punishment for the *multa crimina* which had been objected against him at the Chapter. Indeed, in 1433, a few weeks after Ambrose's Encyclical Letter, he was over-persuaded to grant this man's petition for the vacant abbacy of St Zeno. He accompanied the formal letter of collation with another in which "we admonished him more secretly that he should abstain from the access of unlawful persons (*ab accessu illicito*), lest he should thereby rekindle his ancient error; for we would on no account permit this".(2)

Ambrose's first visit as General was to Bagnorea. "The prior himself was accused by the inhabitants, and grave complaints were made against him.* We appeased them all in so far as we

* It is quite evident, though formal details are seldom given, that a large number of these monasteries—perhaps the majority—had sunk to the state which Semeria shows to have been so common in the province of Liguria two or three monks—perhaps only one—inhabited the buildings and were parsons of the parish church.

could, and departed thence (October 30)". Thence to Fonte Buono, where he received the formal oath of obedience from all inmates: this is recorded of every other house. The peasants of Moggiona, subject to the monks, had certain complaints, no doubt economic, which he satisfied. Thence he went up the mountain to the Eremo (or Hermitage), i.e. the original mother-house, which had so much independence and of which he was now ex officio Superior. His next visit was at S. Giovanni, where "we exacted of the nuns that they should live in common, and that they should not demand money, in the name of dowry, from girls who entered their convent. We granted them the indulgence of receiving girls as they were wont.* We consoled them well and departed." Next day to Poplena, where "we exacted obedience from the Prior and the two monks": one of the two rare occasions on which he tells us the numbers. Here he seems to have learned something fresh; for next day he returned to S. Giovanni, where "we spoke secretly to the Abbess, concerning sister Fr. [*sic.*] concerning whom evil reports had been spread. We made diligent enquiry and learned by plain evidence that she was innocent: we consoled her and the rest and left them strengthened in God's service." Thence to Sta Margherita, and thence to St Peter "de Luco"; in many cases it is laborious to find the modern name of these places from which the monks or nuns have long since departed. Here "we found the nuns at discord, and not living in common" and admonished them to mutual charity and common life. "They consented with difficulty to this thing, which had long been unusual; we exhorted their pusillanimity gently, in so far as we could." Next day, to S. Benedetto; and on the morrow to Sta Maria degli Angioli. Here he found was trouble again with the ex-general, who was disobedient, went about as he liked, had been to the nunnery of Buldrone without valid excuse, and was conspiring against the present régime. Thence to S. Salvadore where the abbot greeted him "with five monks".

We exhorted them all, in a brief address, to live well and honestly, and religiously. Then we inspected this fair monastery and praised the Abbot's industry, desiring, if the Lord grant me success, to

* Possibly as pupils or boarders; but more probably as nuns, in view of the same phrase later in other contexts.

introduce Regular Observance there. Before Our departure, after dinner, reason compelled me to rebuke two monks, Phil. and Pet., admonishing them to keep continence henceforth; commanding them not to go henceforth alone about the streets of the city, but to behave themselves honestly in future, and as becometh servants of God.

There is no hint of actual punishment.

The next visit was at S. Felice:

We exhorted all to live well and honestly, and religiously. They seemed to admit Our exhortation gratefully and willingly, promising amendment, and that they would go on to better things. We commanded them not to leave their monastery alone and without permission, and to go honestly with cowls when there was need, and to live continently and keep the Church services more studiously by day and night. They offered themselves as ready and prompt to obey.

Next day to the nunnery of Buldrone. The abbess, examined secretly, admitted that the ex-general's inexcusable visit, as reported to Ambrose, was true. He exhorted them to common life and permitted them to receive girls. Thence to Querceto, one of the houses which gave him most trouble. Here

We rebuked them, gently reproaching them [*leniter exprobrantes*] because their convent might be suppressed by reason of their ill-famed acts; for the Chapter had decreed that they should receive no further inmates. Yet, afterwards, we blandly upraised them, and promised that, if they amended themselves and led a more honest life, We would see to it that they should have leave to receive girls.

Then back to S. Benedetto, where the ex-general was living under nominal custody of the abbot, Sebastian, who in concert with Ambrose attempted to extort from this man a straightforward financial statement. It resulted in his coming almost to blows with Sebastian, who himself had lost all control; and Ambrose had to act as peacemaker. The next serious case concerned Querceto again.

A certain Abbot* whom I had already sharply rebuked and gravely admonished, yet mingling threats with my mildness, came to me. I learned from this man's secret conversation that harlots inhabited the convent of Querceto, not nuns. Next day, fired with zeal and

* Ambrose very frequently omits names, or gives only initials, for avoidance of scandal. Thus, immediately afterwards, he writes *harlots* and *Querceto* in Greek.

with the Abbot of Volterra as my companion, I went thither. I called [all]* the women together, and began to address them, with the Abbot always at my side. As they denied the truth openly and with the brazen face of harlots, I dismissed the rest and retained the youngest. When from her also I had failed to elicit any of the truth, either by threats or by the indulgent hope of pardon, I again called in the Abbess alone, and began to attack her insolence with greater persistence. Then she, believing the younger to have revealed the whole of their doings, found herself compelled to reveal her own shame and that of her convent; though only partially, for she still refused to admit it of herself and the other elders. Then, recalling that junior and one other, I chastised both with long and most severe words, frequently exposing and reproving the singular impudence of each, and the discrepancy of their lies. Then another was brought before us, whom the Abbess had impudently excused as being absent. Then, calling all together again, and exposing that disgraceful scene in public, I commanded that henceforth they should admit no male within their walls, whether monk or friar or layman. We added threats, protesting that I would destroy and burn their convent if any rumour of ill-fame came again to Our ears. When we had departed, We castigated with sharp and reproachful words a wanton and loose young monk,† who most artfully begged to be set over that convent. He denied first, but afterwards went on to confess the truth. After this we also enjoined a penance and forbade all access. In those days We discovered many grievous disgraces in our Order, which We intend to examine in secret; for We have made her Our evidence, and reserve her.‡ Meanwhile I visited the house of Cosimo and Lorenzo [de' Medici], Our brethren and dearest friends, at his [*sic*] mother's invitation. There, having saluted them all and kissed Lorenzo's sweet little boy, I held long and protracted discourse with those my greatest friends, and besought their faithful counsel in our matter. They advised us to follow nothing so much as Our own "indifference".§ And seeing that, since Our first visitation and admonition, certain reports were brought to Us concerning the Abbot of S. F[elice] and his household, I went thither again and, assembling

* So the Lucca edition; Dino's sometimes makes small slips; here it omits *omnes*.

† *Lascivum et nepotem monachum*. Very possibly the *nepos* is here used in the invidious sense suggested by the prevailing plague of nepotism. Compare the common medieval proverb: *Saepe sacerdotes filios dixere nepotes*. "Priests have often called their sons nephews."

‡ "*Nam eam nobis indicem fecimus, atque reservamus:* apparently the Abbess, who had turned, so to speak, "King's Evidence".

§ *Nihil illi aeque ac nostram sequendam monuerunt*. The sense seems to be, in vulgar language, "grin and bear it".

them all, disclosed what I had discovered, but without naming the persons. One alone I mentioned by name, who was said to practise medicine publicly.* I warned him to turn away from the study of such a profession. Then, having strengthened the brethren with a moderate exhortation, and afterwards summoned the Abbot to our monastery, I admonished him secretly and enjoined the measures which I wished to be taken for the more cautious keeping of himself and his monastery: I commanded that the premises should be securely closed at night.

Concerning the ex-general, also, "I had discovered many nefarious things during those days".

In early December he passed through Sta Margherita, Prato Vecchio, Poppi, Fonte Buono, Soci, and the Eremo; on these he gives no comment. Then he heard of the sudden death of the Abbot of Agnano, which sent him post-haste to Arezzo to guard against irregularities in the elections. Four of the electors were absent from the house. One ambitious monk canvassed "almost the whole city, so that even the city magistrates sent Us messengers to commend him to Us". During the nine days' waiting for these absentees, all sorts of manœuvres were tried in favour of this man, whom Ambrose suspected more and more, though even canons and other Church dignitaries came and pleaded for him. At last he was able to hold an election in due form. After a Mass of the Holy Ghost he assembled them all in Chapter and told them that he was resolved to have for abbot "a man of Regular Observance". If they chose any other, he would use the powers bestowed on him by the Pope, and quash the election. "You can change your monasteries any day if you wish: but We, unless a good man be elected, will be branded with everlasting dishonour."† He suggested several names for their choice, but insisted again that they must elect some "man of the Rule"—*regularem virum*. They begged for a respite till vespers; then they made a happy choice in Giacomo, a monk of the Angioli.

* This was explicitly forbidden by statute, as tempting to *proprietas* and other irregularities.

† This shows the relaxation of the Rule at these times and places. One of the fundamental Benedictine principles is *stabilitas loci*, and in many houses this was explicitly included in the monk's lifelong profession which he signed. There are many indications in the Traversari papers of constant changes of house at the monk's petition, or even (it might almost be said) at his own will.

Meanwhile Ambrose had employed his time in further visitations. At S. Benedetto (nunnery)

We examined them all, one by one; for a sinister report of them had reached Us. We found that they differed in nothing from other convents, having nothing of Regular Observance but the enclosure; and this, in fact, they violated by the excessive licence of those who came unto them. We gravely admonished them, singly and in common. Since we had been unable to persuade them to live in common, we exacted, under heavy threats, that they should admit no man within, and should keep their enclosure unbroken.

Next day to S. Michele, where the citizens extolled the abbot, there present, with high praise, and commended the poverty of the abbey. Next day to S. Clemente, where the prior was "a very good man". Thence to Sta Flora and Sta Lucilla. Here "We summoned the nephew of the old Abbot, a restless, wanton and dissolute [*perditum*] youth, and warned him, with formal letters of excommunication and threats of privation and prison, to come at once to Us and obey Our monitions; for We had spent eight days here, and he had neglected to come to Us personally." The youth came, supported by his kinsfolk, but only so late in the evening that Ambrose could not attend to him. He fought his way through a snowstorm and floods to spend the feast of Christmas, as Head of the House, at the Eremo.

In January 1432 he took steps to bring Fonte Buono, at the foot of the mountain, to Regular Observance. He chose for this purpose a prior whom he thought he might trust, and advised him "not to forbid flesh to such as desired to eat it, in order that they might the more easily be persuaded to Observance". Then he was called to the Papal Court on business. He borrowed from Cosimo de' Medici for the expenses of his visit. He was much interested in the journey itself, especially in Lake Trasimene, but disappointed and depressed by the Eternal City, as we have already seen. In his *Hodoeporicon* he adds: "Men's manners offended me here very greatly: they are far from Our own purpose, yet custom itself compels Us to wink at them."(3) Moreover "We found at Rome certain wandering men of Our Order, running hither and thither with excessive licence. We gravely admonished them, and ordered them back to their own houses. One detestable and infamous fellow we bound in chains and sent for custody at Our monastery [the Angioli]. Another We had sent in bonds from Florence before Our departure, since he had made himself a common talk for his crimes." He could do little in Rome; Eugenius had been partly too busy, partly too unwilling to face serious difficulties.

The Pope's mind was most benign towards Us; but, in the prevailing wickedness of these times, he was unwilling to grant certain indulgences which seemed to prejudice the customs of the Court. We besought him to allow Us, after ancient fashion, to rebuke Superiors in our Order, and even to depose them if they deserved such punishment, in order that (in the Psalmist's words) We might be able to tear up the noxious [vines] and plant profitable shoots in their stead, substituting persons whom we knew to be fit. Again, We desired that monasteries should not be treated as vacant except by [the Superior's] death at the Roman Court. Again, We asked that the Superiors might get confirmation by paying the customary taxation at the Court. None of these petitions could We obtain gratis; and this last, least of all.

He did indeed get the promise of five minor concessions: but,

We were unable, for want of money, to obtain the last three bulls [of confirmation for these grants] before Our departure.

He was back in Florence by June 4. But,

while We were still at Rome, We had heard by letter of the unheard of and execrable offence of that impure fellow Mariano, Abbot of Selvamonda. On Good Friday, after Christ's passion had been read according to custom, being in love with a peasant's wife, he met with weapons this man returning from his journey, and would have smitten him; but the other, receiving the blow with a curved sword which he bore, cut off the adulterer's left thumb. When a clamour arose at this, and many folk ran together, the adulterer took refuge in the castle hard by, and then carried to Florence the wife whom he had seduced from the peasant. We summoned him; but he would not come to Us without an advocate: thus his conscience dictated. This man, being a friend, insisted that We should not detain him. We acceded to his wishes. When he came, We chastised him with the reproaches which he deserved. He began to argue his innocence, and to turn the whole business upside down. We, departing thence, would have taken him with Us that he might pay the penalty of his crime; yet, overcome by his friend's importunity, We suffered him to remain, commanding him never to appear in public places.

A few days later,

wishing to enquire closely into the matter of that abandoned fellow Mariano, We went to the spot where the crime was committed. There we examined ten witnesses separately, to extort the truth. All with one accord reported him as guilty of the greatest crime: nay, of many crimes. We wrote all the depositions and summoned the Abbot by letter to come and purge himself. He scorned to obey. Afterwards, when We came to Florence, he wearied Us with the prayers of many citizens that We should pardon him; yet he never consented to come to Us. We sought to take him; but he fled into hiding, and We found no opportunity of arrest. For the time, he escaped from Our hands. It was reported to Us concerning certain other monks of ours that some wore arms like soldiers, and others were looked upon as traitors. We grieved at Our ill-luck that, at the very outset of Our administration, so many things should arise on all sides to afflict Our soul, while scarce any glad event occurred to uplift it. We had one of these men arrested, who had fled away: upon the rest We were not yet able to lay hand.

The formal legal proceedings against Mariano detained him long from his other visitations; but about the end of August he succeeded in securing a sentence of deposition, and put the Chamberlain of Sta Maria in his place. Yet, in September,

that Mariano of whom We have spoken came back from Rome, bringing commendatory letters from Cardinal Orsini, yet he dared not come himself to Us, but enlisted Our Abbot as patron in his cause. At his instance, We at last remitted the ignominy of prison, if he would go to Venice and dwell two years in Our convent of S. Mattia to perform penance. He promised much, and, having come into Our presence and shed many tears, he obtained with difficulty to be sent to the convent of Valle Castro.

The whole story is a painful commentary on Ambrose's failure to secure, even by personal attendance upon a Pope who was his intimate friend, a restoration of those powers of summary discipline which Ministers General had wielded in the palmy days of his Order. Yet, in the case of less brazen offenders, a strong General could still succeed; for about this same time, "having caught [the Abbot of Sta Trinità] in crime, We removed him and put another worthier in his place". Meanwhile, at Florence, "We chastised with severe invectives another monk, devoted to war and arms and worldly business. He promised amendment and a return to better things: so We spared him." At Prato Vecchio "We found a grave scandal aroused in our convent by the perversity of the priest. For, either through this man's deed or his connivance, or without his prohibition, two servant-girls had fled. By reason of this matter We put him under severe compulsion and removed him thence." At Borgo San Sepolcro, "having publicly rebuked some of the monks, and exhorted all, singly and in common, to live well and honestly, We conceived good hope. We visited also the half-ruined [*semirupta*] convents of Sta Caterina and Sta Margherita, and were much cheered by the good report of the nuns. Having gently exhorted them, and persuaded them that they should live in common, We departed in gladness." The monastery of S. Giovanni was found to be badly in debt; Ambrose obtained a respite from the creditors: he forbade their letting out their cells as sleeping-rooms for clerics or lay-folk. At Anglaria, "We were displeased at the Abbot's negligence. We learned both there and at Rome and at Borgo that he was accused of very many crimes. We resolved to make diligent enquiry." At Castel Britone by Bologna, the Camaldulensian convent had long been transferred to the Frati Godenti; these were now reduced to a single brother, who farmed the place out to the Brethren of Sta Brigitta. At Bologna, "We obtained letters from the Chief Magistracy, bidding all men to favour us without delay against rebels of Our Order." Next, the brethren of the Eremo claimed exemption from his jurisdiction: "We resolved to take counsel's opinion on this point, and it was found that they were far in error." Shortly afterwards, he records in Greek the "incontinence" of an Abbot, whom it is difficult to identify (p. 40); he reserves action for the sake of "the peace of the younger monks" (p. 40). Two other houses were in low water. One he allowed to pawn fourteen pounds of altar-silver; the other, to sell possessions up to the value of 1000 florins (p. 41). At S. Damiano he found the prior accused of embezzlement as executor to a will, but looked into the case and absolved him. He permitted the ex-abbot of S. Ippolito to live in his parents' [or relatives'] house, so long as he was willing to consider himself under Obedience. But now began the long difficulty with S. Mattia at Venice. "A certain Agostino, an evil [*improbus*] youth", who had once been ejected from S. Damiano, insisted on permission to return, though Ambrose had twice assigned him to other houses, which he had rejected. One monk of S. Mattia "told Us much concerning both his own Prior and the Abbot and the state of the house and manners of the monks, which left Us overwhelmed with anxiety". Presently the Pope wrote committing to him the visitation of the Vallombrosan Order, "a most difficult province": "We groaned at this heavy and most unpleasant burden added to Us." The count welcomed him to his palace, and he began work at Poppi, hard by. Here the visitation took him "almost five whole days, and We are uncertain whether We have made any progress". Presently he returned to the visitation of his own Order in the Arezzo district.

> We found that our admonitions had been neglected; that prelates* and monks had not abstained from visiting the nuns. We were grieved; and, attacking this transgression with sharp invectives, We rebuked some of them in private, adding threats in case they should not desist. We sharply chastised the nuns of Our convent, forbidding them thenceforward to make bread for that Abbot; and We attempted to obstruct all access. One man even besought Us for permission to hear the confessions of certain nuns outside the city; We repelled his evil and untimely request with the severity which it deserved.

He wrote to Cardinal Orsini, begging to be relieved of the Vallombrosan visitations. By this time December had come, and he had to struggle through frost and snow to the neighbouring abbey of Anglaria.

> We arrived when the day declined already to evening. We found that the Abbot had left the house shortly before, in order to go to Borgo; though warned by a bell, he would not return when he found that We were there. He was riding, and took with him the boy his lover; he would not that we should see his degradation.† At the monastery We heard great complaints against the immodest and ill-famed‡ fellow. We spent the night there and conversed long on the morrow with Our deputy: We talked long of that wicked man, and thought now of deposing him.

* *Praelatus*, in medieval Latin, is sometimes used very widely, including Church dignitaries of all kinds.

† *Pergebat eques, puerum amasium suum ducens turpitudinemque suam conspici a nobis detrectavit.*

‡ Reading *infamem* for *infumare*.

He consulted his old friend, Roger, Governor of Arezzo and a distinguished lawyer, as to the measures to be taken against this "perditum hominem". Ambrose left his chamberlain to return to Anglaria and take the depositions of witnesses against the abbot, who begged vainly meanwhile for release. The Abbess of Prato Vecchio invited him to spend Christmas at her convent, but he could not go until the 26th: it impressed him favourably that one of the nuns had shut herself up as an anchoress. At S. Benedetto he found the ex-general, "broken in mind and weakened in the institute of Holy Religion: indeed the man openly protested that he could not bear this austerity of life, being old and infirm, and he pressed himself much upon Us. We strove to uplift him with good hope, promising that We would not fail him, in so far as we were honestly able. Yet We sought with many words to encourage him to perseverance in God's work." Returning to Sta Maria, he spent some time in appeasing certain discontents. There he received letters from the Captain of the Militia at Florence, and others who were strongly in favour of the Abbot of Anglaria.

We answered them all reasonably. At length, since he was said to be framing this and that contrivance, We consulted the good of his monastery. We recalled him to the cloister and substituted a worthier man who had done Us signal service, Rainerio, Prior of Bagnorea. He went thither and took peaceable possession of the monastery; but the deposed man came next day with an armed band and would have driven him out. Yet he gained nothing; for, when this was reported to Us, We sent letters to the Captain and the Magistrates, and caused private citizens to write; and wrote admonishing him [the Captain] both of the man's infamous life and of his own honour. He wrote back placidly and softly, and gave the man no further help. The man himself We also summoned by letter, commanding him under pain of excommunication to call upon Us within a certain day. He scorned to obey: nay, he would not even receive or read Our Letter. Yet We commanded this to be affixed to the doors of the Cathedral; and all learned to what penalty he was condemned, since he persevered in evil and would not come to Us.

At this point again, he turned aside to his Vallombrosan commission. He assembled a number of abbots and priors of that Order in Sta Trinità at Florence, read his papal commission, "and exhorted all to the zeal of the Lord's house and to disclose their wounds, that We might apply proper remedies to each disease". He found the abbot there to be "already a good man, and of laudable life". At S. Pancrazio also the abbot was "a man of good report". Thence to the nunnery of Sta Verdiana.

We found there, among the weaker sex, a praiseworthy order, and common life, and admirable observance, and especial honesty. We passed to another without the walls, where We found the virtue of special regular observance flourishing no less than in the first, of which it was an offshoot. We praised God that, contrary to Our anticipation and expectation, we had found so much love of God in these frailer vessels.

At Ripoli, however, "We had many reports of the Abbot's unworthy behaviour"; Ambrose made enquiry, but records no result. At S. Salvio,

We had received many and severe accusations against the Abbot, and such as seemed worthy of castigation. We were received kindly at first; then, finding Ourselves unable to extract anything by moderate means, We were indignant to be thus played with, and went another way. Then We extorted the truth, casting one into prison while the other confessed of his own accord. Then we attacked the Abbot and proceeded to rebuke his stubbornness severely, until at last he confessed and begged for mercy. We ordered him to keep within the Abbey precincts and go forth nowhere. He neglected to obey, fleeing secretly in extreme suspicion and slipping into the city; nor would he return until he had brought with him the Minister of Public Power, to protect him. We admonished him severely, and suffered him not to enter the abbey until he promised to dismiss his companion. Before this a ridiculous story had gone abroad; about the fourth hour of night I was awakened and heard that a woman was in bed with the Abbot. Roused by this foul rumour, I roused my companions, and set a guard to prevent him from fleeing by the door of his cell which gave an exit; then, lighting a taper, I knocked at the door of his cell. The Abbot awoke in astonishment, opened the door and, trembling, asked what we wanted. Then we searched every corner, admonished him in a few words, and, finding no woman, departed. That opinion had arisen and aroused suspicion because others, and I myself, had seen women [about]. Then we returned to our beds.

The ex-general Lanci now comes again upon the scene. He besought Ambrose to bestow upon him the abbacy of S. Pietro da Cerreto, dependent upon Sta Maria degli Angioli. Ambrose refused to accept that responsibility, but left the decision to others. Then there was trouble again with S. Felice; grave complaints made against the abbot and his monks: "I summoned them all one by one, rebuked their faults, and admonished them to study religious gravity." At Buldrone, again, "We admonished the nuns to admit no man to the convent, and left this same mandate with their Warden, Hilariano". Then the foul report and ancient disgrace of the convent of Querceto spread again. I had gone thither to search the truth of the matter; but, though their scandalous behaviour [*infamis earum conversatio*] compelled Us to suspect the worst, yet We could elicit nothing certain. Moreover, since there was a bad report [*turpis fama*] of the Abbot of Adelino, and We were warned by letters from grave persons, We ordered him to be taken into custody lest he should flee. At last, at his mother's prayers, We loosed him and ordered him to come speedily to Us. When he came, We rebuked him severely; but, when We found that the transgressions were not grave enough to deserve deposition, We dismissed him with admonitions to obey our precepts.

CHAPTER XXIX

UPHILL WORK

TRAVERSARI has now been visiting for seventeen months. In this time he has examined personally forty-three houses, out of a total of eighty at most; and he has received reports from others. In this brief summary I have tried to give his own words for everything of primary importance, good or bad. What impression do these bare facts, without further commentary, make upon the sympathetic reader of to-day?

Fortunately we are not left here, as in the case of nearly all other visitatorial reports, to our own unassisted judgment; for Traversari himself has summed up the whole story in an Encyclical Letter to the abbots and priors which is dated March 23, 1433. To this then we must now come.(1)

He is not only Visitor but also Minister General; in that double capacity he can and must speak freely. This Order (he says) is the Lord's vine; (yet now in the Psalmist's words) *the wild boar out of the wood doth root it up, and the wild beasts of the field devour it.* "Is not the glory of this vine almost altogether quenched, when there are scarce a remnant left in the Order (I say it weeping) who care to follow the footsteps of our holy fathers?" The divine fire is turned to lukewarmness, while each man turns his face downwards to the earth and seeks that which is his own.

There are very few [*perpauca*] remaining monasteries of our Order which are conspicuous with the beauty of holy Observance; We are justly offended that the rest should be naked of such grace. What wonder, therefore, if We groan in heart to be deputed to a task so great so laborious and so perilous,...For We, hitherto inexpert in this matter, are commanded to tend this hitherto long-neglected vine....We should be driven almost to despair, unless Our weakness should be consoled by God's grace, for Whose help We hope to all time....But Our greatest trouble lieth in this, that hitherto We seem to have advanced so little either by word or by example. All men, with the same licence, are sliding downwards by unlawful paths. There is the same [old] indiscipline in dress. Many, without cowls, go about in loose cloaks, open at every point. Even their head-gear exceeds the measure of decency, and all their garments are suited rather to the current fashions than to sober use. Many are seen to swagger about without companion.* That abstinence from flesh which the Rule prescribes is kept by scarce any. Again, among many of them there is no mention of the fasts in the Rule. How shall I speak of their under-clothing? Scarce any can be found who wear not linen shirts.† Almost all sleep naked on the softest of feather-beds,‡ so that there is no difference between worldly folk and those who call themselves soldiers of Christ. Nay, we even surpass worldlings and rich folk in our luxury and pleasures, so that that word of His prophet Hosea is fulfilled in us: *As the people, so is the priest.* For we are distinguished by no good works from worldly folk: we surpass them in no prerogative of virtue. Nay, rather (to our greater damnation and corruption), they easily surpass us in good and meritorious life. The very Abbots and Superiors of our Order often set their subjects an example of looser and daintier living: thus those men whom they should have exercised in pious endeavours, and challenged to the arduous contests of virtue, they lead down with themselves, by their evil lives, to the depths of voluptuousness. Others treat their monks not as brethren but as servants, showing themselves not as fathers but as masters, against all standards of our Order, as though the monasteries had come into their possession by plain law of inheritance; they cast out those monks which they will, and when they will, without asking leave of their Superior. What shall I say of the other ceremonies of our Rule, whereof many keep not the slightest traces? What shall I say concerning the purpose of chastity, and our sheer angelic vow? Lo! we see how some have cast it aside altogether, defiling with infamous filth the members dedicated to God. We groan and are consumed with grief at this so great dishonour of ours; we are offended at such guilt in our brethren and sons, we are tortured by that cruel wound of their damnation. Yet we cannot wonder at this; for those whose devotion is to the belly and the gorge cannot fail to fall by reason of these things. Certainly, when the belly is distended with dainty meats, then that which is beneath the belly soon demands his own. Beloved, let us now at last awaken and turn unto the Lord....For the things which We prescribe to you and propose for your obedience are not Our Own, but their first source is in our blessed father Benedict before us; next, in the constitutions handed down to us in writing, and finally ratified at the General

* *Fractus multorum ac solivagus notatur incessus.*

† This was definitely forbidden to all Benedictines.

‡ So also were feather-beds; and the monk was pledged to sleep in his day-garments. Nightshirts were practically unknown in the Middle Ages: a common phrase is "naked in bed".

Chapter of Borgo San Sepolcro and at that of Bertinoro: to wit, the decrees concerning moral decency, and garments according to the Rule, and abstention from flesh and wearing no linen shirts and other matters which pertain to decency of life and which, to Our grief, have long been neglected.

Henceforward General Chapters will be held every third year. He himself will first try persuasion and exhortation; but, when offenders are obstinate, he must take sterner measures. Meanwhile he will give further detailed instructions on his visitations. These were, in fact, resumed soon after Easter, which fell that year on April 14. The diary is pursued down to June 1434, when to our great loss it ends abruptly.

These later pages, after his General Chapter oration, are not more cheerful than the earlier. He first set himself to reform Fonte Buono "which for long had been most evilly governed". He fetched in a Superior of his own choice, and tried to turn it into a model school. "Having expelled those who had been most evilly nourished there, and who, it seemed, might corrupt the whole mass with the leaven of their own wickedness, We resolved to educate fresh boys in holiness." His correspondence frequently displays his love for these boys, and his efforts (not always conspicuously successful) to get better endowments for the school from his friend Eugenius and the wealthy Medici. At Sta Maria de Pratalia there were apparently only two monks, neither of whom was in priest's Orders. At S. Benedetto he removed a quarrelsome nun and, as she was elderly, allowed her to live in her aunt's house. The powerful family of Gambacorti compelled him unwillingly to accept their nomination of a prior at Bagnorea, instead of the man whom he himself had chosen. Next, he had difficulties with "a youthful and wanton monk, disobedient and contumacious". In May, he went to visit his farthest outposts, in Venetia. Prato Vecchio was on his way, and he again praised the nuns. But in Venetia he found one of his worst and most abiding trials.

The province contained, among others, three very important monasteries. S. Michele was now in good order: it was, in fact, destined soon afterwards to become head of the so-called Congregation of Murano, which at the turn of the fifteenth century was the most living branch of Camaldoli. Sta Maria de' Carceri also, was now a satisfactory house, under Abbot Sandelli, one of Ambrose's most trusty colleagues. S. Mattia had formerly stood high, but at this time it was, in Ambrose's words, "verging on ruin".(2) The prior

> was branded with extreme infamy at the Chapter General, and ordered to lead a hermit's life for a whole year at the Eremo; but his Abbot (who was one of the Diffinitors) obtained with difficulty, by fervent supplications, that he should be allowed to do penance in his own monastery, the infamous youth being torn from his side. He, ungrateful for this benefit, began to turn the blame upon the Abbot himself, because he had been the author of his ill report.

Ambrose, finding that the prior was not doing penance as commanded, wrote monitory letters to both abbot and prior. But in this case, as often, the culprit had powerful friends; he secured letters from Venetian nobles denying the abbot's disciplinary powers over him, the prior. Then, without completing his year of penance, this prior departed, taking the incriminated youth with him and keeping him in a dependent cell.(3) He moved on first to Faenza, then to Bologna; and there he sued his abbot in the Governor's Court. Traversari, with the plain law on his side, insisted that the man was subject to his own jurisdiction as General. The prior scorned his summons, and was excommunicated. But the fellow was obdurate; and here, as usual, Ambrose was compelled to compromise: "except that We did not permit that, on any account, that youth should dwell in his monastery, as he and his parents prayed; but We gave him letters for Murano, whither he should go on pain of excommunication." The youth suppressed these letters. Meanwhile "the Prior gave great scandal to pious minds at Bologna; for all through Lent he haunted the market square and the secular law-courts, and was said to wander about the city, even at night, alone with the boy [*cum parvulo*], not lodging in houses of Religion but in the houses of this youth". Ambrose committed his own jurisdiction to Sandelli, Abbot of the Carceri. The affair dragged on; letters were intercepted by the prior. Ambrose went himself to Venice, where he rightly chose to stay at S. Michele and to visit S. Mattia from thence. Here "We found copious matter for mourning; no less pain here than joy and edification at S. Michele".

We were overwhelmed with anxiety by the great complaint against the Prior (wherein many brethren agreed, and those the elder members), and by the foul report brought to us. All those who were of sounder mind prayed for his removal, as a man foolish, rash, wanton and unchaste, through whose negligence all was going to ruin.* We were led to believe the truth of this by the scandalous report of him which had been brought to the General Chapter, and his own previous contumacy with Us and against Our authority. This he perceived, and came to Us full of suspicion and fear; asserting that, if We instituted proceedings against him, he would seek exalted support, to wit, that of his friends and of the nobles.

Ambrose saw no way to go further at that time. His obscure style leaves us in doubt whether this, or some other, was the prior whom he found to have haunted the nunnery of Sta Cristina at Treviso and "secretly spoken there for several hours with a nun, in her bedroom, who afterwards left the convent" (p. 64). But certainly, six or seven months later, he was still in desperate difficulties with the S. Mattia case (pp. 109ff.). He was unable to go forward "because of his appeal [to the Cardinal Protector] and his noble kinsfolk, and very many other things which it would be tedious to relate". The kinsfolk were so powerful that, though Ambrose was on friendly terms with the Doge, who had promised to help him in his reforms, he found his hands tied at every point. The lawyers to whom he referred the case declared the prior's appeal frivolous and void; yet the Doge called the case before his own Council, and suspended meanwhile all action against the prior. Some even of the most respectable nobles took the prior's part; for no city was so jealous of ecclesiastical interferences as this, and here was a noble Venetian under trial. Ought a prelate (they argued) to be thus humiliated? Ambrose replied that this monastery of his Order was on the road to ruin, and that conscience bound him to do all he could for its salvation: "We

* *Utpote ineptum temerarium lascivum ac lubricum, et per cuius negligentiam perirent omnia.* While Ambrose was himself in Venice, this prior fell into such a quarrel with one of his monks "that swords were drawn on both sides, and the monks, armed with cudgels, ran hither and thither" (p. 66). When Ambrose first began to reason with him, he represented to the man that it would be unwise to drive him to extremities, since the accusations "even if they could be refuted, could not be repeated openly without immense disgrace to him; although indeed his accusers were prepared to say everything in his face" (p. 67).

cannot in decent language reveal the crimes objected to the Prior." The others promised their best efforts to bring the offender to reason and to an apology: "meanwhile, they begged Us to omit this kind of enquiry, lest We should scandalize those whom We ought to edify." On the other hand they warned the prior that refusal to apologize would cost him their support. Cosimo and Lorenzo de' Medici, then in Venice as exiles, joined in begging Traversari to compromise. There was a stirring scene, which Ambrose describes with dramatic *verve*, between him and the prior and the notary appointed to take down their words (p. 115). He tried again to get effective support from Doge and Council, but "they told me the Doge was most busy, and unable to hear me". The nobles came one by one to his monastery, begging him to accept an apology.

Wearied out, We consented, under protest that they were the ruin of the monastery, in that they did not suffer Us to take vengeance on this contumacious subject: they must impute it to themselves if things turned out ill. At length We summoned the whole congregation; he confessed his crime and begged pardon; then We absolved him from excommunication; and, appointing the principal officials of the house, We thus restored his administration to him. Almost all accepted this unwillingly and said that they would leave the monastery, even as We had foretold to those nobles.

This was about the end of January 1434. On May 15 we find him writing to his ally, Abbot Sandelli, that things were going better at S. Mattia than he had expected, and he had reported this more hopeful news to Eugenius IV (Letter no. 777). But that lame compromise is none the less humiliating in its contrast with the vigorous letter which Ambrose had written to Sandelli at the beginning of this affair. There, he specifies as one of his most cruel anxieties the fact that

the Prelates of Our Order, who should be an example to their subjects and companions...and be as the *salt of the earth*, whereby the unwisdom of the rest is salted, are now seen to *lose their savour* miserably, and to become a grievous scandal to everyone. Thou, my brother, art certainly not ignorant that, if the reparation of Our Order, now almost in ruins, can be hoped for (as indeed, by the favour of God's mercy it is to be hoped) this consisteth wholly in the right reformation of the Prelates.

This prior of S. Mattia (he continues) who will not dismiss his boy-minion and defies the Chapter's sentence, must be judged and formally condemned: if he is contumacious, "let him even be thrust into prison, and let us call in, if need be, the help of the secular arm. For it is most unworthy that we should wink at the ruin of so great and so famous a monastery".(4) The fact is, that the feeling which we call Nationalism nowadays was too strong for Ambrose. No less at the Renaissance than during the Middle Ages, these petty republics envied and jostled each other just as it is with the multiple millions of modern Japan and the multiple millions of modern China. Numerical differences do not alter the essential problem. No Venetian could easily admit the authority of a Florentine ecclesiastic over a Venetian noble; and this scoundrel was of noble birth. Something must be done to save national honour. On another occasion, when Ambrose would have wished to substitute an efficient prior for this unworthy person, his lawyer friend advised him "to appoint some Venetian, for the sake of avoiding envy".(5)

Some of the nunneries, again, gave him special distress, if only because the public scandal in those cases was greater. On May 6, 1433, he visited Sta Cristina at Treviso. Here

after a formal enquiry, We found the institution rather better than we had thought.* Therefore, having much exhorted them to live well, We made certain profitable and necessary dispositions, which We left in writing for them to keep. We consecrated one of them, a novice of lawful age and good promise, on the feast of Saint Christina, with great joy. We admitted no secular person whatever to the convent; a thing which, though it seemed somewhat severe, yet was afterwards approved by the consent and feeling of all; so that they all confessed never to have seen a more honourable and beautiful solemnity. Yet We indulged them so far as to admit pipers to Vespers, lest We should seem altogether enemies to their custom, especially on the double feast-day of the titular saint and of this consecration. One point they felt to be grievous, that We forbade their going to their parents' houses. For, whether on invitation or of their own accord, they were accustomed (and that frequently) to go thither. At their prayer, We tempered that rule so far as to allow their going in case of extreme

* "*Satis opinione meliorem*", taking *satis* in the classical sense. Sometimes, however, Ambrose seems to use it in the medieval (and modern Italian) sense of *very*.

sickness, by permission of the Abbess.* It was not possible to insist upon the good rule of their living in common, nor did We make many arrangements at that time, hoping We might be able more conveniently at another date. Having settled the convent after a fashion [*utcunque*], We passed on to visit the Prior of S. Damiano. (p. 59.)

But a few days later, when he was at Bologna,

We were much afflicted by the report of the friend of one of Our best acquaintances, who asserted that We had not been able to elicit any of the truth concerning Our convent of Sta Cristina, and that nearly all were harlots.† (p. 60.) We cannot possibly say how much sorrow this matter gave Us, when We heard what was said of them, just as We were rejoicing to have found the contrary; yet We did not put faith in his words, as unwilling to believe rather in them than in Our own experience. There were very many things which told against his words; and, first, their extreme diligence and expertness in Divine Service and the Sacred Offices, and other things which We noted in their presence, and which were utterly different from what was reported.‡

A few weeks later again, he "diligently investigated" this report on the spot. He found that there was no truth in the report of a simoniacal gift, no less than fifty florins, to his friend Sandelli for the abbess's confirmation: but, as for the rest, there was only too much truth. The abbess confessed to having borne a child (here, again, recorded in modest Greek); and there was also what we have already seen, a prior's visit to a nun's bedchamber and her departure. The abbess, again, complained that soldiers had hired a house contiguous to the nunnery, but Ambrose succeeded in getting his close friend the Chancellor to remove them, "since their propinquity was ill-famed and full of peril". He therefore "strengthened those women, prescribing to them in writing, which they received and read, that they should keep their claustration and admit no secular folk to enter, and many

* Thereby flatly disobeying the bull *Periculoso* of Boniface VIII.

† Here again Ambrose writes in the Greek. We may note, in this connexion, what he says on col. 484 of his correspondence: while committing his *Hodoeporicon* to a trusty copyist, Brother Silvestro, he insists that it must be neither transcribed nor published. Compare his words in *Hod.* 64: "Our scribe Dominico had stayed behind sick in Venice; wherefore We ourselves have written all this, as not willing to admit any other to the secret of Our visitation."

‡ Page 84: cf. Mehus 555, where he writes to his brother Jerome of the extreme delight he found in their choir-singing.

other points". He notes how, before he had visited Sta Cristina, a friendly monk of his at S. Mattia had written advising him "to turn the women out and add its possessions to S. Mattia (p. 65).* In late July "We often visited the handmaidens of Christ [at Sta Cristina], and disclosed personally to Our daughter [the Abbess] the causes of our past sorrow. She so satisfied Us that no suspicion remained" (p. 80). In mid-September, Ambrose was there again,

We rebuked two monks [of which monastery, it is difficult to make out], in the Prior's presence, at Our own convent of Sta Cristina, because they were reported to play frequently at unhonest games [*ludere assidue ludos parum honestos*]. We forbade them repeatedly to presume to enter that convent on any account, and commanded the handmaidens of Christ not to receive them. In those days they pressed upon Us with great insistence that they should be permitted, according to their custom, to visit their parents' houses. At last, reluctantly, We consented that they might go once every two years whenever it was needed, with the Abbess's permission and the other Superior's leave. (p. 86.)

Then in October, coming to Treviso wearied with travel, he went to lodge not at the men's house of S. Damiano hard by, but to Sta Cristina. "The handmaidens of Christ comforted Us with marvellous helpfulness, and were much cheered at Our sight. Very many friends flocked to Us, and brought much solace to Our sorrow." At his departure he exhorted all, singly and collectively, "to observe the holy institution, and especially to maintain inviolably the claustration of the convent" (p. 606). His last notice is in 1434, early in March.

We strove as We could to confirm them in the fear of God and the institute of their holy profession, not omitting to mention the things which We had discovered at Venice, and spurring them to the imitation of angelical purity. Our exhortation was received with the greatest congratulation, and they seemed to hang marvellously upon Our lips. We found that they had followed Our commands concerning the claustration of the convent; and We exhorted them to go forward daily in God's work. (p. 121.)

Yet, in earlier days, Ambrose's own behaviour would have been

* In January 1432 Ambrose himself was negotiating this union at the Court of Rome, with other similar unions of decayed houses in his Order (Mehus 925; cf. *Hod.* 97).

held incompatible with the strict rule of claustration; and it is not unnatural that these comfortable lodgings among the handmaidens of Christ were brought up against him by Jerome, his beloved brother in the flesh and in Religion.(6) He answered plaintively

What did I there too incautiously do? They prepared in a remoter cell the beds necessary for me and my companions. Did I even once, either by night or day, lie down to sleep there? Did I go alone to the convent, or tarry there alone? I did necessarily eat there, because the monastery of S. Damiano was too far distant for me to visit it for that cause except with great inconvenience to myself: nor did I ever eat alone. I consecrated a nun there without any noise of lay-folk, and with great quiet for the convent. Prelates of Our Order were present. We only suffered the admission of pipers in the evening; We could not cut off all their accustomed doings. I frequently admonished all the handmaidens of God together, and a few separately in the Church, not in the bedroom, since the matter called for this. I heard two Confessions, one of the girl whom I consecrated before her benediction, and one more in the Church. I gave them salutary precepts; and these were accepted with as much grace as I wrote unto thee.* I spoke of this matter with our Vicar, describing it merrily and without afterthought, as I had already written to thee. He seemed to hear most favourably, and freely confessed that I had gone thither of necessity. What other objection either he can raise, or any other, I know not, as I vehemently desire to know, that I may correct my errors. For I am weak and ignorant; I make many faults, yet in such fashion that I err not willingly, and desire to amend, in so far as it lies in me, whatsoever I have done wrong. I am the more prolix in this matter because pain wrings the words from me, so that I am weary of life; and yet the voice of mourning itself scarce suffereth me to expound what I feel.

This was written on June 16, 1433. A second letter of June 13 shows that Jerome had been only half satisfied, and had written that we must be careful to act rightly not only in God's but also in man's sight, and that a common friend had given him a less favourable account of this affair. Ambrose's reply is not very convincing: he answers: "This very admonition of yours puts me under suspicion of lying": an argument which always comes only too easily to aid our natural instinct of self-excuse.

* In a letter printed by Mehus on col. 555.

The last notice, apparently, of this convent occurs in a letter of Traversari's to Sandelli, dated June 25, but the year is unfortunately blank. Ambrose writes:

That young Canon of Treviso hath complained to Us that his sister, a girl of thirteen, has been received into Our nunnery of Sta Cristina in his absence and against his will; and, on account of its ill-fame [*infamiam*], he grieves much that she is detained there. He besought me to have her restored to him in order that she may more happily render her vows to God in some more honest place, and lest she should pass her adolescence in that nunnery with peril to her salvation and loss to her honour. We ought not to deny this just request. For you yourself know better the evil fame of this place in our estimation, and how, not without shame to us, evil is daily added to evil. For (to omit the rest) I myself, in accordance with the General Chapter decrees, forbade them to dare to receive any girl henceforth; yet they have received her after my prohibition. Moreover, I have since heard much that depresses me and vehemently afflicts my soul.

He has therefore written to the abbess to restore the girl to her kinsfolk. Since she may defy him this time as before, therefore he commits it to Sandello who is his vicar in those parts, that he should compel obedience, "lest the Lord's name be more abundantly blasphemed, if the girl be detained in a place of open dishonour against the will of her parents and brethren" (Mehus 897).

This long story is necessary to show on the one hand how much reason the Church had for her vehement efforts to create a water-tight compartment between medieval society and the nunnery, and, on the other, how often the nuns trickled out or the worldlings trickled in. This *Itinerary* is full of commands for separation, and of fulminations against the frequent intercourse in fact. It is sufficient to compare this Sta Cristina episode with what Ambrose had written two years earlier to a Tuscan prior, his trusted friend.(7)

We had resolved to send a general admonition for all the Prelates of our Order dwelling at Arezzo, and to enjoin upon them under the Obedience which they owe unto Us, that thenceforward none presume to visit Our convent of S. Benedetto, or enter it on any account, except only on the feast of its patron saint, or when they have to celebrate the solemnities of Mass there. And this duty of celebration must be fulfilled either by thee, in virtue of thy advanced age, or by some other monk of approved life....Admonish them in Our name, either separately or together, and add threats unless they amend their conduct. For We will not tolerate such disreputable [*infames*] excesses, nor leave them unpunished. Do thou altogether forbid all access, not only to this Our above-mentioned convent, but to all others where any suspicion of immorality might arise. Moreover, before We left, We appointed good and grave men as secret enquirers into this matter, lest they should think that We should be ignorant if any should transgress. We ourselves assembled the nuns of Our convent and admonished them severely for the second time, and repeated Our command that they should diligently close all access. It will be thy duty to repeat Our warnings to them.

This was written on December 29, 1431, on the morrow of that "Innocents' Day" which was the usual occasion for the Feast of Fools, Boy Bishop, or similar semi-pagan celebrations. In 1434, early in June, he visited the nunnery of Prato Vecchio on the feast of its patron saint. There

We sang Mass, Our Count and all his household being present. This immoderate throng displeased Us; though it arose from ancient custom, yet it was far from consonant with religious gravity and the honour of the institution. For the doors are opened; all men enter indiscriminately and go about as each pleases; they freely dance and drink, which We felt to be extremely improper and wicked.* And, although handmaidens of God be not present at spectacles of this sort, yet they cannot but be touched by the memory of ancient custom and a door is opened to temptations....When the festival was over, on the morrow, We assembled the whole congregation and disclosed the pain of Our heart, condemning this vicious and perilous custom. We said that We did not intend to permit such a custom to continue, since it was detestable, and utterly foreign to the institute of sanctity. We exhorted them to emulate a more honourable way of life, and to a gravity consonant with their profession, admonishing them that the convent enclosure must be opened to no man. Having strengthened them with Our admonition We departed. (p. 130.)

Thus for Ambrose, as for Busch and other visitors, it was the nunneries which created the worst difficulties. In medieval society strictness was far more necessary than in the modern, even of our post-war generation. The Sister of Charity, the nun who goes about to help the sick, secure in her white nurse's headdress, is a seventeenth-century invention. The medieval

* *Saltationibus et poculis vacant, quod summe iniquum et nefarium duximus.*

disciplinarian was haunted even to exaggeration on the one hand by "the frailty of the sex", and on the other by the solemnity of this "bridal to Christ". Therefore he demanded more than is demanded nowadays; and, human nature being what it is, he got less. The story of Sta Caterina, again (p. 127), makes one understand why at that nunnery, as earlier at Querceto, Ambrose threatened to pull the whole place down. It was even so that Abbot Samson pulled down the old cellarers' quarters at Bury St Edmunds, in loathing of what he had seen there when he was a simple monk.

CHAPTER XXX

CRIME AND PUNISHMENT

WITH erring brethren, on the other hand, both the ecclesiastical and the secular traditions of that time were far more inclined to Dogberry's indifference: "Why then, take no note of him, but let him go; and presently call the rest of the watch together, and thank God you are rid of a knave."

This has been already illustrated in the story of that Prior of S. Mattia; but even more significative, perhaps, is the career of Ambrose's predecessor as Abbot General, Benedetto Lanci. We have seen already how he had insisted on frequenting the nunnery of Buldrone "without cause", and contrary not only to ordinary discipline but to the new General's express commands (p. 16; November 24, 1431). That man's record is infamous, not only for pecuniary dishonesty, but for immorality: it must be summed up fully here even at the cost of some repetition. A few days afterwards (December 2) Ambrose "discovered many nefarious things concerning him" (p. 19). But in 1433 the man begged for mercy: would not Ambrose now appoint him as Superior to one of the small dependent monasteries? Ambrose was not firm enough to give a flat and final refusal; after much talk, he left the matter to the decision of his fellow-brethren at Sta Maria (p. 51). In the late summer of 1433 he weakened still further, and, yielding to the man's importunities, made him abbot of S. Zenone,* "admonishing him privately that he should restrain himself henceforth from illicit relations [*ab accessu illicito*] lest he should thence rekindle his ancient fault" (p. 65). In February 1434, we catch sight of him again (p. 83).

We privately rebuked the Abbot of S. Zenone, since, after We had appointed him, he had more than once been to the convent of Buldrone and spent the night there. He alleged this and that; but We admonished him severely and forbade his visiting that or any other convent henceforth. He freely promised obedience. We had

* Not the great Veronese monastery, but a smaller house at Pisa.

gone to the convent itself to enquire the truth; and, although the Abbess denied at first, We had afterwards forced the plain confession from her. We did not spare severe reproof to the Warden of the convent, who had disobeyed Our warnings.

A letter concerning this same warden, the chaplain Hilarianus, obviously referring to the same incident, has been preserved in the correspondence (No. 705; col. 808). Ambrose writes to his trusty fellow, Abbot Sebastian: "Thou knowest, brother, what foul report and what dark suspicions [*quam obscaenus rumor, quam tetra opinio*] have come to Our ears concerning that convent of Buldrone, and not to Ours alone but also to very many of Our Order." He suspects Hilarianus of connivance in the Lanci scandal, and attributes to his consciousness of guilt the fact that he is now pressing insistently for leave to retire to a chapel to which he had formerly been instituted by Lanci himself. Ambrose is indignant with the man who could deliberately "wink with his eyes and permit so disgraceful an act to be perpetrated"; he is practically convinced that Hilarianus "has lied, together with those women"; yet he cannot find sufficient evidence to convict: "it is inherent in the affair itself that proof should be difficult". Let Sebastian do what he can to wring confession from the man; otherwise there is nothing to be done.

Late in that autumn, Traversari visited the nunnery of his Order at Forlì, Lanci's native city. There, "with the greatest grief, We verified by a girl's more secret confession the disgrace of Our predecessor at this same convent, which We had learned before" (p. 97). A few months later (March 16, 1434) while Ambrose was visiting at Bologna, he was recalled post-haste to Florence: the news was

that one of Our daughters [at the Camaldulensian convent there], seduced by that impure and shameless man Benedetto, was close upon parturition. Troubled by the sinister news, and outraged by the indignity of the thing, We went thither intending, if it proved true, to drag that infamous man from his monastery and bring him in bonds, as an example for the future. When We came to the place, We certainly found her in bed; but whether after childbirth or with some other sickness, We could not verify; though certain indications seemed to attest it, which We ourselves observed in the presence of the Abbess. She arose, troubled at Our sudden arrival; yet, though We admonished her privately, We could elicit no more. And, since the matter was very suspicious, We were almost resolved to call in a physician for a medical examination. Yet we thought it better for the time to spare her modesty and Our own. Certainly all of the household denied most obstinately, and were almost indignant that such offence should be imputed to them. With tranquil mind We exhorted them in a gentle oration, yet leaving them with Our excommunication upon them, from which none but Ourselves could absolve, if they had chosen to lie unto Us. (p. 122.)

Early in June Traversari went to Pisa, summoning the abbots and priors of that district to a general visitation. It was decided to begin with S. Zenone and S. Michele.

We intended closely to scrutinize the doings of both Abbots, because We had received many complaints against them, and Our coming was expected for the purpose of examining and punishing their acts; yet no confession was elicited from them. We took care to call in privately a few lay-folk: yet not even so had We any success; whether they were indulgent through favour, or their doings had been falsely reported to Us. We intended to press more severely into this question, and to follow other methods; but news came which broke Our resolution. (p. 132.)

A rebellion had broken out in Rome against Eugenius, to the old cry of "The People and Freedom" (May 29). The Pope managed to slip away in disguise and join a boat of pirates, who consented at a great price to row him down the Tiber. From Ostia he sailed to Pisa: thence he journeyed to Florence, whither Traversari naturally hastened to welcome him. With this his *Itinerary* unfortunately ends, leaving us with only those first three years as a specimen of what an ex-general's life might be.

One more example must be given, brief but hardly less significant. It is a letter to that Abbot of S. Michele whose evil odour Ambrose brackets with Lanci's at Pisa (No. 813; col. 937; January 6, 1432).

Amidst all the thoughts and cares which waste Our flesh We are most especially disquieted by the lives of certain Prelates, who by word and example scandalize Christ's flock, and subvert and ruin by their abandoned morals those whom they ought to have edified by meritorious holy life.... Concerning thee also, brother, there hath come to Our hearing a report foul and altogether obscene and unbearable to religious ears: that thou, brother, forgetful of thy religious profession, despising the gravity and pious significance of thy sacred habit, dost spread thyself abroad in sin with too licentious liberty, and dost defile with nefarious filth those members which have been consecrated to God.

He quotes I Cor. vi. 15, II Cor. xiii. 7, and Ps. xiii. 1 (A.V. xiv); after which he proceeds:

Behold it is related on the testimony of many folks that thou hast long lived, and dost still live hitherto, in impudicity, going about the convents of nuns and prostituting to thy lust the bodies dedicated to God. Therefore, if I* leave this unnoticed, and quit you with impunity, I shall seem to favour filthiness and God will judge me not otherwise than as the author of crime. What can I do, unhappy as I am, with this hard necessity forced upon me? If I follow justice, I shall seem cruel. If I leave justice and keep to mildness, I shall be guilty of undermining the strict life. I will keep a middle course, and imitate our Lord's example, *Who desireth not the death of a sinner, but rather that he may be converted and live.* I will speak to thee as my Lord spake to the sick man that was healed: *Sin no more, lest a worse thing come unto thee.*

I will forgive thee for the past; but under this condition and threat, that I will not suffer thy further delinquency. If thou amend, thy former sins shall be forgotten by me; if thou addest fresh sin, I will strictly judge and exact the old also from thee. Therefore, brother, take care to bear thyself in future that no further foul report come to Us concerning thee. For We shall search all by strict examination, nor shall We leave unpunished whatsoever wickedness thou mayest have wrought. Many other unworthy reports, brother, have come to Our ears; of thy life and conversation rather as a worldling than as a Religious, and of other things which we omit for brevity's sake. Study to correct thy life and manners, that thou mayest wash away the guilt of thy former negligence, and earn the Lord's pardon for thy past crimes. Thou declinest already into old age: let it be enough to have lived ill hitherto. Live for God at least this remnant of life, that thou mayest be able to gain His Grace.

He goes on to commit to this man a difficult local matter depending upon strict commercial honesty; no doubt because he had nobody else at Pisa to trust. The next letter of this collection, far briefer, is very much to the same effect. It is to another abbot at Pisa named John, probably Lanci's predecessor at S. Zenone. Ambrose evidently fears that this man is embezzling money left by a dead monk; we have other indications in his writings that

* It is noticeable that Ambrose, no doubt unconsciously, slides here from the official *We* to plain *I* but resumes it again to pronounce sentence.

proprietas was common. To catch this potential thief, he can find no more honest man on the spot than the Abbot of S. Michele! But he seizes the occasion to speak plainly to this Abbot John also (col. 940; January 7, 1432):

> Know that We have learned many things concerning thy negligence and thine unchaste and very ill-famed and base life; things which deserve the severest punishment, yet which We do not rehearse for the present. Therefore We warn thee, brother, with pious affection, to desist at least in this thine extreme old age and to do adequate penance for the past. Otherwise, We will proceed against thee most severely, nor shall We lack witnesses to inform Us of thy deeds and morals.

Almost at the same moment (col. 940; January 17) he is compelled to write rebuking the Abbot of S. Felice, who is a scandal to the neighbourhood with his "unchaste" and "reprobate life and his extreme miserliness and unheard-of meanness". He is living alone in the *collapsa aedificia* of his abbey, without even a server at his disorderly Mass. Ambrose bids him keep at least one or two monks in the place, and amend his evil life; otherwise he will be compelled to punish.

Other cases might be quoted to show how this private diary of a visitor provides a better illustration, perhaps, than any other document of St Bernard, saying that impunity is the mother of habitual transgression. To approach the subject of monastic decay from one angle only, detail by detail, is to lose sight of the wood for the trees. On the one hand, it is nearly always possible to argue for the particular offender's innocence in any particular case, and for the visitor's fallibility. On the other, even our fullest records from the most earnest visitors are demonstrably far from exhaustive. For instance, this most significant S. Michele case is not even hinted at in Ambrose's diary for that year 1432; and the result of his visitation in 1434 is itself reported only in those few words in which the man is vaguely bracketed with Lanci. Thus, to approach this subject only person by person is even more hopeless than to approach it only monastery by monastery. We must indeed catch at detailed evidence for good and for bad; but we must give equal weight, or even more, to wider questions. Of those, one of the most crucial is this of impunity. It would be impossible for an historian of five centuries hence to evaluate the amount of Sunday trading in present-day London, by a study only of the legal restrictions and the records of separate prosecutions. He would find far more significance in the comparative impunity of the traders, and the indifference of the public at large.

An allied question, more fully treated in my second volume but relevant again at this point, is the great disproportion in these records of eminent offenders. Abbots and priors and important officers occur nearly always far more frequently than their numbers would warrant. We cannot attribute this entirely to their higher powers and larger freedom, connoting greater temptations. Much must certainly be attributed to the fact that their sins created greater scandal, and medieval moralists do in fact constantly measure the penalty of sin, and sometimes even its guilt, by the standard of scandal caused. Ambrose's writings show more clearly, perhaps, than any other similar records, the extent to which monastic sinners could reckon upon impunity; especially when, as was constantly the case, they had boon-companions among the neighbouring nobility or squirearchy or citizens.

We may credit Traversari with the zeal of a missionary in face of this burden which had been laid upon his unwilling shoulders, but not with that of a martyr. It speaks volumes that Eugenius, who knew the facts so well by experience, and whom Traversari had reminded of them at the most critical moment, should have been able to find no man more capable of strong and steady action within the whole of what had once been two great Orders, Camaldoli and Vallombrosa, than this kindly and sensitive scholar, whose name is scarcely known to posterity except as a humanist, and whose interest on these visitations was divided between Greek manuscripts and monastic discipline. Yet it had needed almost a revolution in that Chapter of Bertinoro to substitute him for the embezzling and disreputable Lanci, who spread contagion wherever he went. But for the firm interference of the Cardinal Protector, it is evident that the Diffinitores there elected would again have represented the old gang. Ambrose, when chosen, had to face the envy of those who seized the opportunity of representing him as a treacherous supplanter of his former chief, though a letter of his two months before the

Chapter shows him begging suspension of judgment in the Lanci case, and full freedom for the man to defend himself. When appointed, Ambrose was warned by friends of the possibility of poison: no doubt that age and that country had poison on the brain, but only too frequently in the belly also (pp. 560, 564–5, 567; compare also p. 566, *omnes mihi metuunt...pericula praedicuntur*). The Pope himself, having sent him into the den of lions, did painfully little to back him up.* So also with the hierarchy: Cardinal Orsini protected the villainous Prior of S. Mattia; the Bishop of Bologna tried to rob him of one of his smaller monasteries, and, for aught the documents show, succeeded (pp. 531, 582). He had intimate friends among high places in "the world", yet they sometimes failed him at his worst need. The Medici advised him cynically not to be righteous overmuch, and his noble Venetian friends sat upon that Sanhedrim which insisted on an immoral compromise with the Prior of S. Mattia. Even the Abbot of S. Michele di Murano, perhaps the best Superior among all Ambrose's colleagues in the Order, and the founder of that prosperity which presently raised that abbey to the head of a reformed Congregation, disappointed cruelly† his hopes of efficient help in that same matter. Pages of the correspondence are filled with Ambrose's expostulations against the excuses which his friend pleaded for lukewarmness and inactivity. Again, while some blamed him as too slack, others accused him of excessive severity. In one pathetic letter he asks how he can do justice upon those suspected sinners who find almost everywhere some fox-hole for their retreat. Can I (he asks) drag the truth from them on the rack, or roast them in the Brazen Bull of Phalaris (p. 808)? In one place, indeed, we do find the rack seriously contemplated (p. 537); but this is apparently a young criminal who probably had not taken the vows, and had committed an offence which in Italy, where clerical immunities had never been so strictly

* In addition to the cases quoted in chapter XXVIII, compare Mehus 17 with *Hod.* 46, 49. The Pope's hesitation to back him up enabled an abbot "of infamous life" to hold on for a whole year, and, even then, to hold his ground with "an armed band" until the local magistracy came to Ambrose's help.

† Col. 871–99; cf. 901, where he pleads "the difficulty of this matter, in the face of the petitions of nobles and the manœuvres [*artes*] of men of our own Order, even men of gravity".

respected as in England, would warrant the interference of the civil magistrate; such interference, indeed, Ambrose explicitly threatens. Nor does he find the way clear even when the most convincing evidence has been obtained. He writes to his dear Jerome, who has rebuked him for want of courage in the S. Mattia matter,

> Moreover, best of brothers, remember that the deprivation of a Superior must needs be delayed until the matter has long been discussed, and it is difficult to inflict any severer penalty. For the unshakable decrees of Councils [i.e. Canon Law] have prescribed that layfolk taken in the crime of adultery must be kept away from the Church Sacraments and deprived of communion and punished with greater penalties, while priests and prelates may only be deprived of their Orders, and can be smitten with no other sentence. (p. 520.)

Two years later, in fact, when he commanded a peccant monk (apparently prior) to remove the woman, his companion, "lest Our disgrace and that of Our Order be exposed to all men's eyes", he adds: "the man asserted that the Pope's Penitentiaries had absolved him up to date [*quatenus*], and that he had lived in continence for two years."

By way of commentary on Traversari's work, the reader should turn back to my second volume (pp. 596, 597), where his contemporary, St Antonino of Florence, tells briefly the Camaldulensian and Vallombrosan story of those days. This summary cannot be called more optimistic than Ambrose's own writings would, by themselves, lead us to expect.

CHAPTER XXXI

A COMMENDATORY ABBOT

But it is the abbey of Vangadicia which supplies the clearest instance of the Visitor's hands tied behind his back by his hierarchical superiors.

When Ambrose was elected to the Generalate, three cardinals held Camaldulensian abbeys—and, naturally, three of the richest—*in commendam*. Cardinal Orsini, out of respect for Ambrose and his work, resigned that of Cortona for a nominal sum of 28 ducats* by way of indemnification to Abbot Angelo, who was apparently what we may call the sub-tenant at that moment (p. 258). The two other cardinals were capable of no such generosity. Moreover, four years later, during which time he had been drudging at the wearisome and dangerous labour of reform and was now absent on fresh papal business, equally difficult and invidious, his friend Eugenius betrayed him ignominiously.

The first letter of this series is a petition from Ambrose to his "Lord and Father" Cristoforo, Papal Referendary. It is dated November 11, 1435, from Schaffhausen.(1) Ambrose has been nominated by papal decree as representative at Basel, together with Dominico de Vito, Auditor of the Sacred Palace. On his way he has learned for certain

that a very ancient and exceedingly wealthy abbacy of my Order, Sta Maria de Vangadicia, sadly neglected in spiritual matters, has fallen vacant. Our Legate, when we fell into discussion of its reformation, seemed to seek that our Pontiff should commend it to him† for a livelihood. True, he soon condemned his own suggestion, as one which would arouse suspicion in the Council. There were some of our party who advised me to beg it from the Pope for my own sustentation: but I would never agree to this (even though he should give it to me of his own accord) for very many just reasons which there is no necessity for me to rehearse here. I beseech thee,

* Ambrose estimated the value of a first-rate scribe at thirty ducats a year, "in addition to decent sustenance"—*adjecto honesto victu* (Mehus 320).

† Or, just possibly "to himself".

Father, keep my honour in mind, lest it fall into the hands of some strange man or some other Order.

In spite of this appeal to one who stood so near to the Pope, that which Ambrose feared was realized only too soon. This rich prize was given *in commendam* to the Cardinal Bishop of Bologna, no member of the Order. The transaction was a gross political job, a sop to Cerberus. It was convenient to buy off this man who had hitherto been one of the bitterest anti-papal delegates at the Council: and the trick was done behind Ambrose's back.

That was intolerable; and Ambrose wrote straight to Eugenius as former Cardinal Protector and friend, not only of the Order, but of himself, the Minister General, in person.

I cannot fail, most Blessed Father, to be sore troubled that, in mine absence, and when I was wholly busied with the affairs of your Holiness, a most noble member of our Order has been taken privily from us and commended to the Cardinal of Bologna. Nor am I so much moved by mine own discomfort (although it is shameful for me, and I blush to think that I, who seemed so dear and pleasant to your Holiness, am so neglected), as for the honour of your piety and your repute, which seemeth to be somewhat impaired, since you seemed to be acting unmercifully against your servant: and also for the imminent danger of perpetual alienation for this monastery now torn from us in your pontificate—for you yield in the grace of our love to no Pontiff, whether past or future. For who will spare Ambrose, your Holiness's little servant, a mere handful of dust and ashes, if this most blessed Eugenius, than whom (as I have said) none ever was or ever can be more beloved, hath thus crushed him? Moreover, since it was the shameless importunity of that old man which brought you, most unwillingly and against your wish and institution, to commend that abbey to him; and since you, my most holy Lord, promised me that it should be restored to us after this greybeard's death, never again to be commended to any man, therefore I am reminded to beseech your Holiness for a composition. Securing first to that old man the annual pension which he himself has fixed, let the person who has been elected Abbot [by the monks], a grave man and in my judgment most fit for this command, be set over Vangadicia, bearing the title and honour of Abbot, and receiving confirmation from your Holiness. Much profit will follow from this. In the first place, tomorrow, when this old man is dead, and the abbey is restored to our Order, with a Superior of its own, then this will be a blow to the stratagems and aims of those who now gape greedily for the prey. Again, your Blessedness will not again be wearied with this matter; for there will be the lawful excuse that monasteries cannot with any honesty be commended unless they are destitute of the comfort of a Superior.* And, though we doubt not that your Holiness will most firmly repulse these shameless and importunate men, yet there will be less business, and your ears will be less assailed, if matters are thus ordered. It might befall also, through the uncertainty of our present life, that your Holiness's successor, not equally friendly to us, might refuse to fulfil your promise; then, if the abbacy were not vacant, his attack upon it would be blunted. Add to this that, if there be an Abbot as governor, the abbey's rights and possessions will be more cautiously and better kept, nor will folk presume to usurp them promiscuously. How can we wonder if this be not the case at present, when the government is committed to a multitude of layfolk who have hired the abbey from the old man at a yearly rent of a thousand ducats?† The greybeard himself also, who is so fainthearted that, in his senile fears, he is haunted by imaginary indigence, will receive the pension as at present constituted, or one more moderate if he will, so that he will have no cause to complain of lost livelihood. Again, we shall be seen to receive a great favour from your Holiness, and shall be restored to our ancient rank. Lastly, the illustrious Marquis of Ferrara [in whose territory Vangadicia lies] and very many private citizens of that province, to whom the matter has been most distasteful, will be relieved. I pray my Lord's forgiveness if in my trouble I seem to exceed in anyway against that Cardinal. Knowing as I do how cruel and hostile his mind was towards your Holiness, and how crookedly he acted in the Council [of Basel], not only in presence but in absence, I was most indignant that he, of all men, should have asked from you a favour which tended to our disgrace and detriment. I believe that he wished thus to avenge upon your servant the fidelity and constancy wherewith I fought at the Council against his mad proceedings. Assuredly I should have been less pained and grieved if the abbey had been commended to any other Cardinal. But the thing is done, and we may grieve, yet there is no power to amend. I commend this

* The free election of abbots by their monks was laid down in the Benedictine Rule, and (by implication at least) confirmed in Canon Law. This was a heritage from the healthy traditions of early Christian days, when there was more democratic freedom in Church than in State. The Popes gradually broke this down under the pretext—often only too well founded—of interfering to secure the material and moral reform of some decayed monastery. By 1400, England was almost the only country where the richest houses were not being sucked dry by the papal "commendators". See my third volume, chapter xxv.

† An arrangement common in such cases, though in flagrant violation not only of common sense but of Canon Law, which explicitly prohibited the farming out of spiritual revenues to lay-folk.

matter to your Holiness. Nevertheless, most blessed Father, I submit myself and all my judgment under your holy feet. May Almighty God vouchsafe to keep your Holiness unharmed and prosperous in all your desires, most blessed Lord and most indulgent Father.

On the same day and in much the same terms he wrote to Placido, one of the papal chamberlains, to Cristoforo the papal referendary, and to brother Mariotto, the trusty monk whom he had put at the head of that school which lay so near to his heart. These letters alone have been preserved; but the last tells us that he was also writing to the cardinal himself, to Gregorio Corrari his nephew, "and above all to the Marquis of Ferrara" (p. 715).

A month later (May 25) we see that his plea, based not only upon Canon Law but upon the most ordinary justice, was as yet ineffectual. To the Pope he cites Christ's parable of the importunate widow. He repeats the arguments of his first letter: no money-loss to the cardinal, yet immense material and spiritual gains for the abbey. "Divine service will be incomparably better performed under a [real] Abbot than by those who perform it now, as hireling chaplains abominably treated by the lay [lessees]." He appeals to the Pope's solemn promise, and warns Eugenius that others are already gaping for this disgraceful sinecure after the cardinal's death. By confirming the abbot whom these monks have legally elected, the Pope will put a seal on his promise and stop further scandal: "it is almost more your Holiness's honour which is at stake, than our comfort." Meanwhile "I am not idle; for upon me falls the heavy restoration, in so far as my strength permits, of our almost ruined Order"—*religionis ferme collapsae*. In the same strain, he wrote to Placido, the papal chamberlain, beseeching him to use his interest with Eugenius. If his Holiness is firm here, "It will bring him much praise and honour": but if the jobbers are allowed to have their way, "it seems to detract somewhat from his Holiness's reputation, since many folk are displeased, and blame the deed". "I know indeed that he was impelled and driven by cruel necessity, and that the shameless importunity of that old man wearied him into doing that which otherwise he would on no account have done." Why should the cardinal refuse an arrangement which would guarantee to him personally all the spoils of the abbey? The real obstacle is in his nephew Gregorio at the papal court, who has given no satisfactory answer to Ambrose's letter, and is notoriously gaping after the succession to his uncle. "But I will never spare every possible effort lest this transaction, which has once been concluded to our disgrace and, not obscurely, to that of the Pontiff, should be rendered perpetual."

Here, again, nothing was done. The next four letters are all to the chamberlain (June 9, 26, 28; July 21). Ambrose has now, personally, even more reasons for complaint. His colleague at Basel, with whom he had worked in concert to uphold the Pope's cause against that majority which sought to insist upon constitutional government in the Church, has now been made a bishop; and, incidentally, has by his promotion left Ambrose to bear the whole later working expenses of their joint legation (p. 180). Now, therefore, "there are some (I groan to write it) who say that, in reward for my slavish baseness—nay, perfidy—I have been so punished by the Pontiff that my fellow-legate has promptly been raised to the episcopate, while I am robbed of a noble member [of my Congregation]. Moreover, those who bark against [our party] use that special argument; nor do they seem to build upon an absurd foundation." They quote sarcastically from St John's Gospel: "Lo, how He loved him!" Therefore Ambrose renews his most earnest supplications. "The old man" can have no real excuse but his gaping nephews (Ambrose now counts them in the plural).

If it be pleaded that [when the *commendam* was granted], there was no regular observance in the abbey, that is true, since the condition of the time hindered it; there is nothing now to hinder the restoration of that which had fled, or the establishment of that which had never been.... This old man needs help no more than I, that he should seek so earnestly to appropriate the things which are mine. No man who knows my circumstances fails to recognize how poor I am, so that my most slender revenues scarce procure a livelihood, nor can I afford to hire either a notary or a scribe—not to say scribes—to help me in very important affairs, so that I must daily write so much with mine own hand that I am ready to fail....my hand, from constant use, is already giving warnings which I must not neglect. Even now, as I write, my thumb is shaken with a tremor that is new to me.

Shortly afterwards (August 3) there is a new phase. The

cardinal, to put a colourable pretext upon his greed, has now proposed to Eugenius that, with Ambrose's help, he will reform this abbey of which he is commendator. The Pope therefore advises Ambrose to repair to Bologna and talk the matter over. Ambrose humbly, but very firmly, refuses what seems so evidently a trap. For here is the man who had been so violently hostile to Eugenius:

"I saw with mine own eyes at Basel letters full of cruelty against my Lord, written by the old man almost at the time when he was asking for the *commendam* of that abbey....I doubt not that, if convenience and occasion dictate, he is still ready to withstand my Lord....Now he seeks to put a fair colour upon his cruel deed; he would fain reform that abbey! I marvel at the man's piety! Forsooth, he coveted this abbey in sheer pity, seeing that Regular Observance was dormant there; and, in his anxiety to restore it, he procured its separation from me because he felt that I was utterly insufficient to put it upon a regular foundation!" The man now writes asking me for four model monks to work the reform of Vangadicia. This I will do only on one condition, that I am to direct the reform myself, here as elsewhere in the Order. "The fact is that he would fain reform this abbey—or rather deform it—after the fashion of the rest [that he holds *in commendam*]. I have been in that most ample monastery of S. Zenone,* which also is commended to him, and where a handful of monks were living in extreme want for everything. He has hired out our abbey [of Vangadicia]—I say *ours* in his teeth, though he may call it *his*—to layfolk, and now he bids me send thither Observant monks, to live in everlasting discord with the worldlings.† If he be attracted by the fair name of Observance, let him not reject that most just condition which I have proposed to him. Let him have his yearly wages, as much as he will, and go down therewith to hell! Let him permit the [lawfully elected] Abbot to govern the monastery, and I will not refuse to send Observant monks. My Lord, of your mercy forgive me, if I can bring no smooth words from my bleeding and aching breast. I hear that this greybeard's nephew hath already begun to possess the abbey as if by hereditary right; so that, if this be permitted to them, it will never return to us its lawful owners."

Nothing but respect for Eugenius, his friend and spiritual lord, withholds him from fighting the matter out openly with these

* Here, evidently, the great abbey whose church is one of the sights of Verona.

† *Cum secularibus*. Either the lay lessees, or those above-mentioned secular priests whom the cardinal has hired to conduct the services.

harpies. As to a friendly colloquy over this business with the cardinal, "I alive will never see him alive"—*vivum, credo, nunquam vivus videbo*. The Pope has encouraged Ambrose to go on with his literary labours, so honourable and useful to the Church. Therefore will he not now

> provide elsewhere for this old man, and supply me with the necessary assistance from my own possessions, so that I may educate boys and devote myself to translating from Greek volumes, hiring two or three copyists. For in truth I cannot write so much or so often with mine own hand, which oftentimes gives me by its tremor a plain warning not to be neglected, and (as I have said) is utterly insufficient for all [that is demanded of me].

That pathetic appeal was as vain as the others. This is the last surviving letter on this subject; and it is only too possible that the intruding cardinal outlived Traversari, the true shepherd of this sheepfold.

CHAPTER XXXII

THE POPE'S HELP

NOTHING short of that lengthy story could give a full impression of the extent to which Church reform was subordinated to Church jobbery, from the Pope in Rome down to the meanest cleric who had money or influence enough to get a hearing there. As I have had occasion to point out in my third volume, this *commendam* system, which Montalembert stigmatized as "the leprosy of monasticism", was exploited no less universally and shamelessly than that of Indulgences, since princes finally found it profitable to join in, and share the spoils with Rome. Of Eugenius we are told, by his contemporary biographer Vespasiano Bisticci, that on his deathbed he shuddered to think of the account that must be rendered to his Creator. He was heard to say "O Gabriello!" (for that was his Christian name) "How far better had it been for the salvation of thy soul that thou hadst never been Pope or Cardinal, but hadst died in thy monastery!" We have seen in St Bernardino's case how a sensitive soul might shrink from the contamination of medieval episcopacy: and the *Episcopus Episcoporum* might well fear this in an even higher degree. Was the dying Eugenius haunted by the memory of Vangadicia and the betrayal of his faithful servant? It is most improbable; there were too many other similar matters on his official papal conscience. At the Assembly of Tours (1493) the abbots of France complained to their king that, from the days of Eugenius IV onwards, "(for in earlier days there was no mention thereof), a disorderly number of commendators are in possession of abbeys, and farm them out to married folk who make their dwellings in the aforesaid abbeys, with wives and daughters, chambermaids and children".

For the canker, by this time, was at the very marrow of the body ecclesiastic. This man Eugenius, it may be pleaded, was as Creighton describes him; a ruler who aroused little personal enthusiasm even in his own party, and whose efforts for monastic reform were too narrowly centred upon his own Order, the

Franciscan. Again, one of his virtues was in itself a disadvantage to Traversari here; Eugenius bore no malice to political opponents, forgiving them easily. Though frugal in life and liberal in almsgiving, this Pope could scarcely spare to Ambrose the crumbs from under his table for two or three amanuenses, and for his cherished project of a small monastic school; yet he could afford to lavish 30,000 ducats upon a single tiara modelled by Ghiberti for state occasions. As Franciscan friar, his vows submitted him to a Rule which forbade his touching even a penny: but as Pope he found it natural to increase his worldly pomp by placing upon his own head as much money as could have sufficed to found a royal hospital, or to enrich Western theology with a whole body of translations from the Greek Fathers. However, if we seek in the records for some other Pontiff of that age, under whom this would-be reformer of two important monastic Orders would have received more efficient help, we find no encouraging result. To Bisticci, indeed, as to St Antonino of Florence (contemporaries both), Eugenius seemed a Pope specially zealous for monastic reform. The latter writes: "As one who was specially zealous for life in Religion, he suppressed [*evacuavit*] many monasteries of nuns who were living dissolutely and unhonestly, extinguishing the dignity of abbesses and sending their nuns to other monasteries." St Antonino specifies nine nunneries and five men's houses thus dealt with. Most, if not all, were apparently either in Rome or in places where he had himself been able to mark them as "most dissolute", "very dissolute and decayed", or "deformed". He adds that Eugenius brought many into the Congregation of Sta Giustina. The bad odour of the Benedictines at St Mark's in Florence impelled him to command a visitation, which resulted in its transference to reformed Dominicans, in answer to the prayers of Cosimo and Lorenzo de' Medici. St Antonino passes on to describe in detail the liberality with which those two princes built and adorned this monastery, which is still one of the artistic glories of Florence.(1) In that sense, therefore, Traversari was exceptionally fortunate, as in his personal friendship with this particular Pope. The predecessor of Eugenius, Martin V, would have been likely to give far less help. He did indeed (as we shall see in chapter XLII) publish reforming decrees for the Franciscans. But these he immediately retracted: and otherwise, throughout his reign, he strove successfully to avoid those conciliar demands on the strength of which he had been elected. His reforming bull for Cluny, in the judgment of a modern Benedictine historian, was rather political than religious in its essential motive; "he seems to have thought less of reforming Cluny than of tightening the dependence of the monastery" upon the Holy See.(2) Nor would serious reform have had more help from Eugenius's successor, who "saw that reform was needed; but reform was too dangerous".(3) The brief reign of Calixtus III (1455–8) did practically nothing for reform. Then came Pius II, of whose own early life Creighton writes truly that it "was profligate enough, but it does not seem to have shocked men of his time, nor to have fallen below the common standard....He took no other view of life than that of a selfish voluptuary, for whom the nobler side of things did not exist".(4) Though, as Pope, he seems to have lived with decency, yet he uttered no more than bare rebuke and vague threats when Cardinal Borgia, the future Alexander VI, gave a garden party at Siena to which ladies alone were admitted (fathers, husbands and brothers being explicitly excluded), and at which, for five hours, "they danced, as we have heard, with every licence, and spared no amatory enticements".(5) This was indeed a subject upon which Pius had every reason to be indulgent: it was one of his maxims that "for weighty reasons marriage was taken from the priests: for weightier [reasons] it ought to be restored".(6) And, if we go further down the list, to the Reformation and beyond, it is impossible to find any Pope under whom Traversari would have had a better chance than he had under Eugenius; scarcely, for the matter of that, half so good.

The question may be reduced, essentially, to one single sentence; the *commendam* system, confessedly, had become the canker of monasticism. It ruined the abbeys not only materially but morally, making real discipline almost impossible. It was the negation of one of the three fundamental vows from which the canon lawyers denied that even Popes could dispense: the vow of Poverty. It was equally destructive of a still older Christian principle, that of Free Election in the Church. The "abbot" of a rich house might thus—and generally did—

become a man who scarcely even pretended to live by the Rule; or indeed, who was not even a professed monk or in Holy Orders. He might be—and often was—a man of notoriously immoral life. At Constance the system was condemned in the plainest language, and no man dared to defend it. It was thus one of the things against which, by implication at least, the new Pope whom that Council elected was bound to struggle with all his might. Yet, during the century which elapsed between Constance and Luther, so far from forbidding it, Pope after Pope took advantage of the foul abuse which their predecessors had introduced. Cardinal Borgia, the future Alexander VI, and the hero of that garden party at Siena, was Commendator of one of the greatest abbeys in the world, specially hallowed by the memory of St Benedict himself. Vangadicia also might quite well have been among the houses of which this profligate sucked the revenues.

But we are told nowadays that Pius II did make reforming efforts in other directions. It is asserted that, during the six years of his pontificate, he set himself seriously to reform those evils which he had publicly preached and practised in the days before age and use had brought satiety. Pastor, in his laborious *History of the Popes*, seeks to prove the value of his reforms by references to certain documents in the Vatican Secret Archives, which however he does not lay openly upon the table.(7) The most important batch of cases thus appealed to, (but by title only), are eleven in number. When examined, they will be found testifying clearly to all the chronic relaxations or transgressions which we find in the visitatorial records; but they give very little promise of serious and radical reform.(8) They fit in with, rather than contradict, what we learn from Traversari and other sources. Only in one of these cases is it the responsible bishop or archbishop who has made the first move for reform. In one other, again, the Pope acts *proprio motu*, from facts which he had ascertained in his own native Tuscany, at Florence: here, however, he is taking notice of the scandal only towards the end of his life, when he had already reigned five years as Pope, although it was evidently of long standing. In six cases it was the lay rulers or neighbouring nobles who called the Pope's attention to facts which were scandalizing the faithful. In one case the Duchess of Milan complained that two nunneries, absorbed under papal permission by greedy outsiders, "had been reduced to be stalls and habitations for brute beasts", while the few remaining nuns wandered in beggary. Again, the two Counts Ulrich and Eberhardt of Württemberg complain of the many [*plerosque*] monks, friars, or nuns in their dominions who, "casting utterly away the discipline and observance of their Order, under transgression of their vow, lead a life somewhat worse than that of worldly folk", and "heaping up sins of their own, so far from placating God Almighty's wrath [against the world] tend rather to increase it": "They fear not to commit these detestable things, because there are none to correct such transgressions." This petition occurs twice in the papal *Register*, at six months' interval. The counts plead that reform under present conditions is hopeless: the monasteries are "rather apt to beget pupils for their incontinences". Next we find a report from "the knights and other nobles of the diocese of Regensburg (whose daughters and sisters and nieces are in the [Franciscan] nunnery at the imperial city of Eger) together with the magistrates and burghers and consuls of the said city". This nunnery, by an unusual arrangement, is doubled with a friary: there is one church for both, divided by an iron grating. But access in fact has been made possible from one building to the other, so that "certain of the said friars and nuns, loosing the reins of decency and modesty, have surrendered themselves to lubricity and wantonness, and some of the said nuns have borne children". Then, again, the Markgraf of Baden reports that his father had procured the reform of certain monasteries in his dominions; but "certain others still remain destitute of Observance according to their Rule". Lastly, even the semi-pagan Gismondo Malatesta of Rimini, who built a church dedicated to his concubine "Saint Isotta", joins with the magistrates of Cesena in protest. That city, one of the most considerable in the papal states, stood in sad need of reform in four convents, apparently all that existed there. These gave "an evil example to the whole population of the city by reason of the dissolute and evil example of life which is being led by certain nuns therein". The remedy proposed was to re-found these decayed nunneries as a single community living in the best of the four houses, "provided that the churches [of the other three] shall by no means be reduced to profane uses". Their constitution is also to be altered, upon lines which suggest the influence of the Sta Giustina reform.

This last is, perhaps, the case which casts the most favourable light on Pius II as monastic reformer. As a whole, these twelve documents from his *Register*, the best which Pastor can quote, show plainly how deep-seated the evil was, while they afford only the vaguest suggestions of real amendment. There is no hint even of a papal rebuke to the bishops (or, for exempt houses, to the Ministers General) who were responsible for letting these things go on under their eyes, without either fighting themselves or appealing for help from Rome. No hint, again, of punishment for the actual offenders. At best, a commission is appointed, with small guarantee of success where so many others had failed, for enforcing what all men admitted to be the ten-times re-enacted laws.* Far from contradicting Traversari, these papal *Registers* in the Secret Archives of the Vatican make his complaints and failures more and more intelligible.

As he was not destined to reap Busch's harvest of success, so he was not exposed so long to the heat and labour of the day. Even if we assume that, to the very last, he was visiting as busily as we see him in the fragmentary *Hodoeporicon*, this means only eight years. The exact day does not seem to have been recorded: but we can trace him to within a few days of his

* This will come out even more plainly in chapter XXXIII. Indeed, Pastor himself, in another context, confesses almost as much (III, 275). Writing of the occasion when Cusanus and Domenichi advised this Pope to appoint an energetic commission of reform, he says: "Unfortunately these extensive reforms were only partially undertaken. The fact that Pius II summoned such a man as St Antoninus to take part in his Commission, and also caused a Bull to be drafted directed against the prevailing abuses, will prove that, for a time, he seriously intended to carry out this important work. But, in the end, he did not venture to engage in a gigantic conflict with all the evils which had invaded the Church, and contented himself with opposing isolated abuses. The alarming advances of the Turks, and the struggle for the existence of Christendom, soon engrossed his attention; and, if his whole energies were not absolutely absorbed by the Turkish question, an unusual combination of troubles in Italy, France, Germany, and Bohemia, claimed a part of his care. The question of Reform was driven more and more into the background, and in the interests of the Church, this cannot be sufficiently regretted."

end. By July 1439, in the successive Councils of Ferrara and Florence, Eugenius had succeeded in recalling the Greek Church to a somewhat half-hearted reunion with Rome. That had been one of the great aims of Traversari's life, and one which brought him out at his best; for few could rival his combination of Greek and Latin scholarship. Almost at the same moment came the final rupture between Eugenius and the Council of Basel. The Council in May condemned Eugenius as a heretic, and on June 25 they decreed his deposition, and set about to elect an anti-Pope (November 5). But Eugenius, for his part, had already decreed the dissolution of the Council in September 1437: and for Traversari, as for him, it had ceased to exist from that date. Thus, in the autumn of 1439, Ambrose might reasonably look forward to a time of comparative rest. This was postponed a little by the arrival of a deputation from Armenia, seeking reunion: he wrote them a letter on September 10. Ten days later we find him writing an intimate letter to Lorenzo de' Medici. He is in retirement at Fonte Buono, that house at the foot of the great mountains of Camaldoli, which, from being at first a mere refuge on the way to the original Hermitage, was now a complete monastery. He can scarcely express his felicity to be safely in port after all these storms. For, "albeit I am not without many daily occupations, yet these are far quieter and milder than the inextricable cares of that abyss, that labyrinth; and it is far happier and more pleasant to converse with our peasants than with Cardinals and the Pope. It is delightful to rusticate, and either to restore or further to adorn our house." Therefore he begs for two chests of white Venetian glass, little round panes, such as Lorenzo knows how to procure, and such as he is now employing in his own house. For the monastery has very many windows exposed to the winter chills, and there is one of the monks who is skilful enough to set the glass. Ambrose will gladly pay the price,

for, since I have dedicated myself and my life and all my time to solitude, I think it will be worth while to strive for the betterment of our house, which (as I hope you yourself will some day come and see) is not ungracefully built in this lonely spot; and to redeem the savagery of this wilderness....I promise you that, with God's help and guidance, this desert shall bring forth sweet and plentiful and delectable fruits, when I have shaken off all my sloth and torpor, giving myself up to the most pious studies, and reposing in those delights with everlasting pleasures. Farewell, beloved Lorenzo, and fail not to accompany my leisure with your prayers and to help it with your labours.

That farewell was more solemn than either could have dreamed; for, a month later (October 20 or 21), after Ambrose had been called on business to his other monastery of S. Salvatore at Florence, death fell upon him apparently without warning. In the Middle Ages, and indeed almost down to our own grandfathers, sudden death was regarded with special horror, and often gave rise to sinister speculations. In Ambrose's case, there was the usual Italian suspicion of poison, if only remotely hinted.(9) We know through his own letters that he suffered often from indigestion, for which he liked to take ginger (p. 315); also that he had frequent headaches, and was sometimes troubled with dizziness, and had begun in 1436 to struggle against a nervous tremor in his fingers. But his health had held out well, on the whole, against the fatigue of excessive study, and, later, of those visitation journeys; thus, neither had his friends any fears nor, apparently, he himself. The least vague of our testimonies is a letter of November 8 written by Angelo Poliziano (not to be confounded with his celebrated namesake) to Michele, Traversari's fellow-monk and intimate friend.(10) He expresses his grief and amazement:

for, seeing that he was not only no old man, but fresh and almost young,* and that in his life, even to the present, he was of a good and healthy bodily composition, nor had any fresh sickness attacked him, except that he was somewhat hindered by the [*or* a?] cold, therefore at that time this death was not only unexpected but almost beyond our fear. Therefore with regard to that man [the physician] who caused Ambrose's death, giving him so inconsiderately I know not what pills, I myself, if Ambrose's life could thus be redeemed, would take him in my hands and strangle him.

Poliziano goes on to dwell upon the dead man's saintly life.

So far did this express the general feeling that some writers of his own time, and still more of the next generations, half-canonize him with the title of *Beato*.(11) "He is honoured by the

* His age in fact was fifty-three.

Church", writes his biographer in the *Catholic Encyclopaedia*, "on the 20th of November." Two years after his death, the monk Girolamo Aleotti, while expressing the hope that Leon Battista Alberti might write Ambrose's life, asserted that "his grave having been opened by chance, very many folk were able to behold flowers and snow-white lilies, a testimony to his virginity and his most innocent life". In a second letter, he asserts that this miracle was known to the Archbishop of Florence.(12) Bisticci's brief biography of Ambrose sums him up in two charming sentences: "To all these [intellectual qualities] he added holiness of life: for in that monastery [of Sta Maria degli Angioli] there were forty most holy monks, who were a model to Florence. The common opinion of Brother Angelo was that he was a virgin, for that he had entered into that monastery pure and clean and at a tender age."(13)

CHAPTER XXXIII

CUSTOM AND TRADITION

WHEN, in my second volume, I printed a catena of some 120 contemporary medieval generalizations on the monasteries, more than one critic allowed himself to hint that these had been tendentiously chosen, and that I had slipped into the unscientific method of accepting literary documents as trustworthy sources for actual historical conditions. No definite vouchers were offered by my critics in support of those injurious suspicions; therefore I could only answer that they seemed to write in ignorance, and that their own imagination was mainly responsible for this quite different evidence in the background, which they suspected me of suppressing or misinterpreting. Now, at last, this volume gives me scope for producing the official documents in far greater detail; and readers may judge for themselves whether the literary sources which I quoted are unfaithful to the actual facts. St Antonino of Florence, who was not only contemporary with Ambrogio but also his personal friend, dealt briefly with the Camaldulensians in words which I here reprint from vol. II, p. 596. After describing the brilliant beginnings of all Orders or Congregations, he describes their universal decay in his time: one by one he names them, and comes to the Camaldulensians: these "have degenerated from their founder St Romuald and are gone backwards, with the exception of very few monasteries and desert hermitages". As to the nuns, again, "a few convents have been renewed in the strict and narrow way of regular life", but the majority "went side by side with the monks in the path of relaxation"; they "walked by the broad and easy way" (*Chronicle*, part II, tit. XV, c. 23; ed. 1586, II, 561). What reader will deny that the Saint's strictures are borne out by the unquestionable facts of Traversari's life and work? In proportion as the mass of original records is more closely and widely studied, it must become more and more evident that these orthodox fifteenth-century reformers were fighting a rearguard action, and that the most brilliant of their successes could no more be final than Napoleon's after Leipzig. Traversari did his duty in this field, if not with the desperate courage of a born fighter, at least with conscientious loyalty. But on his Italian wing of the conflict the positions proved untenable; and he did not enjoy Busch's encouragement of forty years marked by a considerable preponderance of clear successes. For Italian monasticism exceeded the Continental average by as much as that average exceeded the English, in two fatal difficulties: the overruling force of custom and the unreality of vocations.

The first cannot be better illustrated than by one of the very cases to which Pastor appeals (though without quoting) in his apologia.(1) The date is 1458. Calixtus III (1455–8) had permitted the nuns of Sta Maria, outside the city of Messina, to come into a "grange" of their own within the city, leaving a few ancient nuns to keep the convent. This indult was granted "because of the wars and other sinister events which had affected the realm". The Archbishop of Messina now desired to enforce upon these city-dwelling nuns the strict claustration prescribed first in St Benedict's Rule and then, still more emphatically, upon nuns of all Orders, in the bull *Periculoso* of Boniface VIII. The abbess and sisters pleaded that "they and their predecessors in this grange had remained unenclosed from time immemorial, and had made profession of their Rule under the institutions thereof, and under this fashion of life". They were "of a too delicate complexion" to bear any stricter life than what they had found when they entered the convent as novices. "If they had been liable to compulsion for other things than those which they had experienced from the beginning, then they would certainly not have made the regular profession *in that convent*." Therefore they had represented to Calixtus that

they should not be constrained, *against the vow that they had taken* and against their will, beyond the point that law and equity required; since if they were [now] compelled to a stricter enclosure and to other unwonted things, then the people would greatly marvel, and no small prejudice and stigma might be laid upon them, who had always lived, and were still living, most honourably in the said grange; and their convent would be disappointed of many legacies and last gifts which were made on men's death-beds by reason of the *visitation of many persons*.

Calixtus had referred the question to ecclesiastical judges, on whose advice he granted the nuns the indult "that they should be allowed to remain in the state wherein they had made their profession, and should not be forced to the stricter life". The archbishop's counterplea was that,

> by reason of the aforesaid [papal] letters, and [of those given] to other nuns of divers Orders in those parts, and because of this relaxation of the reins, occasion is given in most cases [*ut plurimum*] of wandering to and fro, and of impudently transgressing the bounds of shame and honour, and of rushing forth into the field of public pleasure and contrary to Canon Law and to the opprobrium of their own Religious Orders, and at the peril of their own souls, the offence of God's majesty, a pernicious example to the faithful and a scandal to very many folk.

But Pius II, professing his special care for nunneries "to which, by reason of the frailty of the sex, in default of due enclosure, occasion is given for loosing the reins and plunging into the field of pleasure", now revokes his predecessor's indult. He therefore decrees "due enclosure" notwithstanding any customs to the contrary or any oaths that they may have taken.

The words which I have italicized need no further comment than to point out that they were not uttered in mere hasty dispute but pleaded successfully in due legal form at the Court of Rome before one Pope, and expected to weigh no less effectually with his successor also; a pontiff who, on other occasions than this, publicly advertised his special care for the purity of the nunneries.

Society, then, divided its allegiance between the Reign of Law and the Reign of Custom. It was as Gerson said: "defects long remaining uncorrected, are growing, and are found to grow from bad to worse; until at last, under the iniquitous fiction of 'custom', they are reputed lawful."* Thus we find the orthodox disciplinarian frequently protesting: "this is a *consuetudo pessima*": "*consuetudo seu potius corruptela.*" But he protested in vain; for his own position, after all, rested to an enormous extent upon the same foundation. Not only was custom everywhere the interpreter of law: *consuetudo optima legum interpres*; but, if old enough, it became actual law; true the Churchman

* See full quotation in my second volume, p. 589.

pleaded that none but good customs, favourable to religion and morality, could ever attain to this legal status, yet that plea offered temptations to selfishness so obvious as to blunt most of its force. For instance, many of the laity knew that, under this cover, their original free-will offerings had gained the compulsory powers of Statute Law, enforceable in their law-courts, under the Church's extreme spiritual penalties. Therefore, lay-folk had little sympathy with Church statutes which contradicted what their daughters or sisters had been accustomed to—except, perhaps, when it was too late, and licence had broken out into sin.

Traversari frankly confesses that custom made a General's life unbearable:

Everywhere we are oppressed with evil, and in no quarter can we be cheered with any gladder hope. The men of our Order, both Prelates and monks, weighed down with the mass of ancient custom, refuse to taste of spiritual grace, and are scarce restrained by fear from falling back into their former vices. Everywhere we suffer these distresses, so that, on the verge of shipwreck, we are compelled to cry, *Lord, save us, we perish!* (p. 864.)

This was in October, 1433, just two years after his acceptance of the Generalate, and a few weeks after his visitation of Vangadicia, where he "found nothing healthy in the abbey"; the monks, "having long lived in disorder", were utterly ignorant of real Benedictine order. Even at Monte Croce, where the site and the old buildings struck him with admiration, he lamented that there was none there who "would live according to the Rule".(2) A much later letter, written almost at the end of his life, illustrates this in detail (February 3, 1439; col. 609). He writes from Sta Maria degli Angioli to a fellow-monk:

I have seen the letter which you write to the Prior of [this] monastery concerning the coming of brother Pietro, blaming him for having dismissed him, whereas infirmities should be tolerated, in accordance with the custom of the monastery. He gave me the letter to read forthwith, and joined me in pity for the man, who would admit no remedy, and was inaccessible both to blandishments and to fear. He asserted that, unless he were let go, he would fall into madness, since he could not sleep; and other such reasons which it is a weariness even to recall. We commended him, and now we commend him again, to you, who know better all his affairs. Indeed, we would willingly have detained him if by any means it could have been done, and if he had suffered himself to be admonished; for whereas you write that he asserts me to have said publicly that I would rather men should live irregularly [*minus bene*] outside the monastery than inside, I pray you to see whether I have acted justly. I wished to abolish the inveterate custom of living too laxly, and I was anxious to reform the monastery into its ancient state; therefore I thought that we needed not soft words but severe condemnation. At the same time I thought that unprofitable members should be cut off, lest they should hinder the rest; for the whole state of the house had been overthrown by the extreme remissness and negligence of the Father Superior, and his unprofitable and mischievous tolerance. Therefore, not unreasonably, I resolved that those who would not change their manners and amend their ancient negligence should choose other monasteries for themselves; yet at the same time I exhorted all that they should settle to a religious life.

Elsewhere, he writes deprecating a friend's reproaches for his comparative tolerance of serious irregularities in a nunnery. He pleads Christ's treatment of the woman taken in adultery, and adds:

Whatsoever there is worthy of reprehension in these women, it seemed to deserve compassion rather than severity; for they are of the weaker sex, and for a long while have received no comfort of heavenly teaching, no exhortation to spiritual life; so that it is a marvel that they should not have turned out even worse. (p. 430.)

But this is "sad patience, too near neighbour to despair". To his beloved brother Jerome he writes:

Reports are daily brought to me full of discomfort; they torture me so vehemently that oftentimes I am weary of life; nothing glad comes within my view but this one hope, which I cast out as my secure anchor to keep the frail bark of my soul from shipwreck. Everywhere a lowering sky meets my eyes, and I cannot help wondering within myself that, in such desperate circumstances, and such lack of all comfort and such anxiety, the hope of some future gladder harvest does appear indeed. (June 19, 1432; col. 521.)

And, to another friend a few days earlier:

From my most quiet and tranquil shore I have been cast into a most stormy ocean, where cares sweep from side to side and toss me like waves, so that, if the Grace of God's protection were not my help, my salvation would daily be in peril. I have been set, unwilling and reluctant, as captain over an old ship almost destitute of rowers.... Think how much I must fear, inexperienced in navigation, and compelled to do a steersman's work in this almost broken ship—*navis paene dissolutae*. (p. 257.)

Popes in earlier centuries had been fully sensible of the harm done by this tyranny of custom, and had sometimes fought against it; but in the end they had capitulated ignominiously. All disciplinarians recognized St Benedict's prohibition of butcher's meat as almost a corner-stone of the Rule, especially now that the rule of manual labour had become practically obsolete. The English General Chapter repeatedly denounced flesh-eating as one of those *consuetudines* which were really *corruptelae*. Gregory IX (1227–41) quoted Christ's condemnation of those who transgress God's commandments for the sake of human traditions, in his warning to those who prefer their own customs to St Benedict's plain Rule. This, however, did not hinder the wealthy abbey of St Bavon at Ghent from procuring from Alexander IV, in 1255, dispensations from "the extreme rigour of the Rule". Nicholas IV, in 1290, repeated word for word, and with added emphasis, Gregory's warning against preferring custom to Rule. Yet this corrupt custom of flesh-eating was finally legitimated in formal terms by Benedict XII in 1336. He was a strict and courageous Pope, specially concerned for monastic reform; yet he sold the pass. Naturally, when this inch was granted from on high, the monks often took an ell. In 1332, Abbot Bourne of St Augustine's, Canterbury, decreed certain constitutions for the reform of the abbey, and caused this to be inscribed in the martyrology (from which the monks were bound to read daily) for a perpetual remembrance. But at his death, "even before his body had been laid in the tomb, they were torn out by command of the President of the Chapter and certain others, and cast into the fire, by reason of their undue restrictions".(3) Here, as in many other places, Chaucer is true to life; his Benedictine finds the Rule "old and somdel streit", and follows almost inevitably the fashion of his own day. The Dominican Nider, Ambrose's contemporary, who estimated so pessimistically the chances of reform without revolution, was constant in his complaints against the tyranny of evil custom, as one of the greatest obstacles to all serious reform.(4) So also Trithemius, our most natural and important source for Germany on the verge of the Reformation.(5) "The most scandalous sinners" (complained Cardinal Cusanus at his great Provincial Council of Mainz in 1451) "think to excuse themselves on the plea of custom, without considering that such customs are in fact corruptions and inveterate errors."(6) Bishop John of Eichstaedt (1450) complains how the unreformed Religious quote Scripture for their purpose: in defence of their now ingrained traditions and customs they say: "no man having drunk old wine straightway desireth new; for he saith: 'the old is better'"! He feels it necessary to bring a battery of other Scripture texts against them: I Cor. v. 7 and Ephes. iv. 23–4.(7) When Dederoth applied himself in earnest to the Bursfelde reform, his first plan of campaign was "to cast out the distinction between *meum* and *tuum*", and then "to awaken from their graves those brethren who were almost dead in evil custom".(8) Nider's contemporary, the Carthusian Jacobus de Paradiso, writes no less emphatically. Relaxations have become so inveterate that,

> if any man would say or do aught against them, he is looked upon as a madman: and thus the justice of God becomes injustice in human estimation, and the viciousness of the multitude is defended, and the sinner is praised in the desires of his heart, even as Scripture, in Genesis, testifieth that the men of Sodom did of old.

Complete reform may be beyond our hopes, but at least let us do our best. Let us demand the suppression of concubinage among the clergy. Among monks and friars we may demand—

> The cutting off of dissolutions and excesses; the restriction of wandering abroad, decency of dress and tonsure among both clergy and monks, adherence to the observances of their Rule, watchful observance of all monastic discipline, repression of adulteries and immodesties of all sorts.

He can scarcely believe that this will be achieved in the present age: the evils are too deep-rooted. There have been so many Church decrees, rapidly fallen into disuse: so many merely partial reforms of monasteries: each of them has been good as far as it went, but slight in comparison with our needs: on that point he corroborates Trithemius. He goes on to hint not obscurely at some great cataclysm in the near future.(9) "What can we do?" (asks an anonymous writer towards the end of the fifteenth century), "with a Prelate who sins publicly not only with married women but also with nuns and abbesses?"(10) Dionysius Cartusianus had already stated the same problem. Nuns, he writes, should be warned earnestly of the peril to their souls unless they return to something like the original observance of their Rule, and join the reforming movement. But the nun answers: "Those proceedings would be good; but our Superiors and Visitors have slid into deformation, and they live as we live."(11) Before the sixteenth century dawned, the very ideal of medieval monasticism was in most places bankrupt. One of the most conspicuous reforms was that which Marie de Bretagne, with all her prestige of royal blood, was able to work in the Order of Fontevrault. Yet that was less a victory than a compromise: some of the most important positions were abandoned; it was a "strategic retreat".(12)

The whole story is tersely summarized by Abbé Fleury, looking back upon all this from his philosophic angle of the later seventeenth century:

It is true that the Church hath sometimes borne with some abuses which had taken too deep rooting, waiting a favourable conjuncture to reform them; and hath sometimes indulged her children, for the hardness of their hearts, in the relaxation of the ancient discipline....We need only read the constitutions and canons which have authorized the several relaxations, to see that the Church never did it without regret. Many deviations came in only by common usage.(13)

This paltering with very solemn professions, and the evident effect of it upon all social morality, and the growing impatience of those lay-folk who did not take it as a mere excuse for their own irregularities, will go far to explain the immediate and immense success of the Jesuits. For here, in place of the Old Religious whom their own friends could defend only with compassionate qualifications almost more humiliating than open censure, came the New Religious who (for some generations at least) took their Rule as a sacred and inviolable bond, and who thus earned the respect even of their adversaries.

All this canker of custom had ,at bottom, one cause, the lack of real vocation: the two things helped each other by action and reaction.

Dom Ursmer Berlière, in a paper read before the Belgian Academy, has shown very plainly how hard this pressed upon the monasteries even in the twelfth century.(14) In the early thirteenth, Caesarius of Heisterbach tells us that many fled to the cloister from poverty, from debt, or from fear of prison. Unwilling vocations were complained of at the Council of Constance; and the Papal Registers give us concrete cases of children forced in by their parents or guardians.(15) The Monastère des Pénitents at Croisset, near Rouen, "received certain crazy and lunatic persons, in consideration for distinguished families who confided them secretly, to hide their shame and misfortune".(16) In this case it may conceivably have gone some way to creating something like a regular lunatic asylum; but the same cannot be said of the numerous cases where the unfit were scattered about among the good or indifferent. Guillaume Pépin, the Parisian mission-preacher of about A.D. 1500, in one of his sermons takes the sick folk gathered round the Pool of Bethesda as the type of "this multitude of folk who are literally deformed in body—lame, hunchbacked, one-eyed and the like—and who for that reason are placed by their parents into clerical Orders, especially if they are of high birth, because they would be despised in the world and useless for war". So also, says the contemporary friar, Olivier Maillard:

> You, my good citizens, if you have a defective or deformed son, you feel the need of making him into an ecclesiastic, and the same with your daughters. These unhealthy creatures enter the Church only to procure her benefices; and this they do by the intercession of harlots and concubines.

So again, at the same time, Geiler the famous cathedral preacher of Strassburg:

> We give to God the worst that we have. If among your children there happens to be a poor cripple whom you would like to see in the land where pepper grows,* then you say: "This one will make a good priest, a monk, a nun"; and you offer the child to God as one offers to St Antony a measly hog, or to St Valentine a sickly hen. Yes, that

* In modern slang, "to see them at Jericho".

is how folk do when they devote their children to the Church; they gladly give their abortion to the Lord.

So again, in another place: "Younger children are cast into Religion as we cast the worse puppies into the water."(17)

The moral effect of this was deplorable. Deformity, or merely the accident of birth, directed these boys and girls, indifferent or reluctant or even crudely rebellious, to the monastic ideal, along the steep and thorny way to heaven, while parents and first-born trod the primrose path. We see this in what Busch tells us, just by the way, as a thing too common to provoke him to any moral reflections (p. 659).

A certain nun, Sophia by name, natural daughter to Wilhelm the Elder, Duke of Brunswick, was offered by her father and her brother, Duke Friedrich, with great pomp and solemnity upon the altar at the Cistercian nunnery of Mariensee, in the diocese of Minden and the temporal dominion of her father. When she had dwelt a long time therein tolerably decently, as nuns are wont to live in unreformed houses, at length the chaplain there seduced her, for the maiden was eloquent and witty and fair.

Her subsequent career has been briefly told in chapter XIV. St Teresa wrote plainly about the moral dangers of the cloister for nuns thrust in without vocation.(18) Finally (to show how little the Counter-Reformation did to remove this difficulty) the most orthodox Père Bourdaloue almost outdid the free-thinking Diderot here. He wrote:

See how they drag the poor victim to the foot of the altar, bound hand and foot, daring not to complain, lest she should uncover her father's passion and her mother's obstinacy.... Whilst in fancy we are witnessing a sacrifice like that of Abraham, God for his part looks upon it as upon Cain's offering.... Must we see renewed, in our own days, the age in which barbarous and idolatrous parents sacrificed their children to idols?(19)

Such a system provided a veritable hothouse for perverse and ineradicable traditions.

Almost equally unfavourable to any true discipline was the system of exemptions. Here, as in the *commendam* system, there had been some original disciplinary excuse. A badly governed house deserved to be thus put under tutelage, so long as the guardian himself was a trustworthy person. So, again, many bishops were careless, perverse, or immoral; therefore to remove a great abbey from episcopal control and make it immediately dependent upon the Pope might be a great improvement, so long as the Pope could be trusted to fulfil his guardianship truly and effectively. But both systems offered such irresistible temptations for papal domination or greed that they bred abuses far greater than they had been designed to correct. Not only could a rich abbey buy exemption from the Court of Rome, but whole Orders gradually obtained the privilege. All the Mendicants were "exempt": their original piety, zeal and devotion to the papacy earned that reward. For a generation or two, this worked well; but, when the salt of the friars had lost its savour, this reward for virtue became too often a shield for vice. By the fifteenth century, more than half the Religious of Europe were "exempt". It needed a special papal commission to touch them, such as Ambrose had for his own Order and that of Vallombrosa. Moreover, even then, their charters of exemption gave them enormous powers of chicanery in the law-courts; we can see this in Ambrose's consultations with distinguished lawyers as to the legality of disciplinary measures which, at first sight, would seem to be as soundly constitutional as they were obviously needed.

Yet the abuse had long been notorious. St Bernard had emphasized it in his long monitory treatise to his pupil Eugenius III, the *De Consideratione*. There he pointed out how, though papal centralization had aimed at securing discipline, yet indiscipline had in fact been fostered by the constant appeals to the Roman Court and by the multiplicity of exemptions. At the Council of Vienne (1311) this had been one of the main points of reform insisted upon by Bishop Guillaume Durand. The *Chronicle of Bury St Edmunds*, in spite of its violent partisanship for the abbey, shows that the immoralities of some of the monks at that great house were causing public scandal in 1345, yet that the bishop was practically powerless to bring them to order.(20) Half a century later, the University of Oxford petitioned Henry V for help against the frequent monastic immoralities, especially in exempt houses.(21) Gerson, about the same time, connected the exemption system with the inefficacy of previous reforms;(22) yet the other vehement protests at the Council of Constance led to no practical amendment. About 1450, the Oxford Chancellor Gascoigne stigmatized the exempt houses as the worst.(23) A few years later, we have the judgment of a distinguished visitor and reformer, the abbot of the Schottenkloster at Vienna. A pupil asks him: "Which stand best in observance, the exempt or the non-exempt?" He answers: "Other things being equal, in our own Order of St Benedict, I think the non-exempt; for these are more often visited. In that which I have just mentioned [a great exempt house which he has not described by name], there appeared no vestige of visitation; nor had they any charter or memorial to show that their abbey had ever been visited."*(24) Yet Innocent III had insisted upon regular or frequent visitation as essential to healthy monastic life. On the verge of the Reformation, the exemption system showed no signs of real reform. It was too lucrative for Popes and the Curia, and too dangerous for any reformer seriously to touch. The Franciscans boasted that their prayers had moved God to take away Innocent IV, who had seriously curtailed their privileges granted by previous Popes. After the Reformation, the papal visitors found one of their worst obstacles in the system of exemptions.(25) Here again, the question has been summed up by Abbé Claude Fleury. He writes:

Exemptions have been the main source of the relaxation for the Regular Clergy. The Generals of the Order being distant, and the Pope still more distant, faults have often remained unpunished and abuses have taken root before they could be remedied; appeals and lawsuits have crept into regular discipline, under pretext of defending privileges.(26)

* Compare the concrete case of Egmond in chapters XXXIV and XXXV.

CHAPTER XXXIV

EGMOND: FIRST PHASE

As early as 1419, at least, John Count of Egmond and the Duke of Bavaria, as Lord of Holland, were pressing for the reform of the important Benedictine abbey of Egmond on the North Sea, near Alkmaar. Egmond was "exempt", and therefore untouchable except by the Holy See. The duke, whose ancestors had founded the abbey, was interested on the strength of his claim as "advocatus".(1) Egmond also claimed to be "advocatus"; but in any case he was interested as the nearest local magnate. The impulse had probably been given by the recent Council of Constance: we have seen how other temporal princes took heart from that Council and concerned themselves seriously with the monasteries in their dominions. The abbot, as early as 1419, had left his house and taken refuge in Utrecht, claiming reasons to dread personal violence from the Count. By mid-April, 1421, he learned that a papal visitation was impending, and on the 29th he appealed against this to the Pope, Martin V. Meanwhile, while he was still at Utrecht, the visitation was made, in accordance with a bull of January 14, by three papal commissioners. The bull rehearsed the reasons for this step. The duke had represented that the abbey

is notoriously subject to the opprobrium of desolation and deformation, that its possessions and goods are subject to waste by the detestable life and governance of its monks, who nourish not only concubines but also their offspring from them, and by sundry other crimes and excesses wherein they shrink not from damnably involving themselves, and by other disorderly means. The present Abbot and Claustral Prior have taken flight therefrom: wherefore the concourse of faithful folk to the abbey for reasons of devotion is decreasing, and devotion grows cold, and divine service is diminished there and Observance of the Rule is despised, whence arise very many scandals, to the scorn of the abbey and its Order, and the peril of the offenders' souls, and the scandal of very many folk. Therefore they must be visited forthwith, lest they go from bad to worse. (p. 32.)

The commissaries are empowered to compel witnesses to tell the truth under spiritual penalties; and they may brush aside "all papal constitutions, all statutes or customs of the abbey and of its Orders, whether reinforced by oath or papal confirmation or any corroboration whatsoever".

The visitors' confidential report to Rome is unfortunately not recorded: the only surviving documents are those which the monks themselves chose to insert in their own cartulary.

Abbot Gerard met this with a formal protest (p. 28). He claimed that the visitation of these papal commissioners in his absence was null and void: the bull had been "extorted" from the Pope. He asserted that he had ruled the house for eighteen years "laudably in spiritual and temporal matters, duly correcting such concubinacies and other excesses as had been committed by its inmates", and that the duke's predecessor, with other nobles of Holland, had been wont to pay yearly devotional visits to the house, until his adversaries [*emuli*] had forced him to flee for fear. The Count of Egmond, a member of the duke's Supreme Council, is a man who like his progenitors "has ever sought to usurp or seize upon the goods of the said house, and the Lord Abbot hath ever resisted them in so far as he was able". He himself and the prior have now fled lest Egmond's abettors should slay them.

On the morrow of the Prior's departure [April 12, 1420], many lay-folk, some of whom were abettors, servants or adherents of the said Egmond, entered at midnight through a strongly-barred window of the said abbey, breaking the iron with hammers or other instruments. Then going forthwith to the chamber over the Abbot's hall, they found there two of the Abbot's servants, whereof they slew one and smote and wounded the other, leaving him half dead; then retiring over the Abbot's chamber they wounded grievously and enormously two of the monks; and there, having violently broken with their instruments the Abbot's chests and caskets, they stole likewise from that same chamber many goods and jewels.

He values the property destroyed or taken at 1000 florins and more. "And these lay-folk, after their deed, have been constantly seen, going about unpunished in the halls of the Count of Egmond, or in their presence, and damnably boasting of this sacrilege; all of which things are a matter of public notoriety."

The abbot claims not only to have refrained from waste of the abbey goods, but also to have "recovered very many things alienated, especially by the said Egmond", who therefore procured this papal bull on false pretences, and the abbot was not legally cited to be present at the visitation. Moreover, for the last two years the duke, at the advice of Egmond and others, has ordained a certain monk of the abbey as "Economus", who receives all the rents and dues and hands them over to Egmond. Therefore, when the visitors' report is published, let it be seen whether it mentions that the monks begged them to take measures for the abbot's return in peace to his house. For "let it be known that he would always have been content to set himself to reformation provided that he might be present at the visitation; and therewith he will ever be content provided that it brings no unjust prejudice to his rank".

Here, then, is a quarrel of the kind which may be met elsewhere. The duke and count have interfered, as the English kings and continental sovereigns had long been accustomed to do, on the plea of gross mismanagement in an abbey of which they were "advocati", and therefore legally bound to see that the founders' intentions were not defrauded by neglect or cessation of Masses for their souls, constant prayers to God, and alms to the poor. There had been resistance on the monks' part, and consequent violence. Egmond may well have been far from blameless in the matter; but, in any case, that was a question for the commissioners to decide, and the abbot should have made his first protest to the Pope when the accusing bull was published, which he does not pretend not to have received, and which gave him at least three months' warning.

Sixteen out of the eighteen monks supported the abbot in written memorials. This, indeed, was to their obvious interest if there had been any truth in the charges upon which the Pope had acted. But it is significant that in this whole community not one should have been found competent to state their case in Latin; the two memorials entered in the chartulary are in Dutch, and it is in Dutch that one of the commissaries writes to argue with them. The commissaries' formal answer, on the other hand, was in Latin. After only two days' delay, they dealt with the four principal demands of the monks. These men wanted their abbot back: the commissaries reply that they should have him if he and they could arrange reasonable terms. They wanted their absent brethren; the commissaries retorted by summoning those absentees to return at once and submit to visitation, and commanded the rest, under pain of excommunication, to reveal their names and present abodes. The next complaint was that brother John, the "Rentmaster" now set over them, was dishonest: the commissaries promised to summon the man at once to bring his books and prepare his accounts. They complained that this man, with the Bailiff of Haarlem,* had come one day "with hammers and swords, and had kept the community long time against their will in the dormitory: had the commissaries permitted this?" In another memorial they had asserted that, when they tried to procure John's dismissal from his stewardship, he had replied "if you make Ian Aelwijn Rentmaster it shall cost him his life". The commissaries' reply was: "We are aware of this and other things set forth by you against brother John: and if ye know anything more that needs correction, against him or any other, we will gladly hear and do our best that all things may go their due course and be happily ordered" (p. 51). The other documents in the chartulary are simply repetitions for use in the legal proceedings which would follow upon this appeal. There our records end; and the seventeenth-century chronicler of the abbey had himself discovered no more. He writes: "Therefore the whole business was scattered to the winds"—*totum negotium fuit omnino dissipatum* (p. 25).

For the later episodes of this story we shall no longer be wholly dependent upon such documents as the monks themselves have chosen to incorporate in their chartulary.

On June 16, 1450, Nicholas V issued a bull at the request of the Duke of Burgundy, as overlord of Holland, concerning the reform of Egmond and of the nunnery of Rijnsburg, as "grievously fallen from the Rule of St Benedict, so that they have kept little or no regular observance for many years past, nor do they keep it now". He therefore commissions a trustworthy abbot at Trier to reform them, personally or by proxy, and in case of

* Who would be employed naturally enough as agent for the Duke of Egmond.

resistance to invoke the secular arm, notwithstanding any papal or other privileges they may plead in their defence (p. 75). The abbot named, as his deputy for this visitation, the Abbot of Syloe near Münster. On September 13 one Johannes Nicolai, a priest of Utrecht, protests as proctor chosen by the monks in their defence. The papal bull, he contends, was obtained on false pretences by enemies of the abbey; the Abbot of Syloe has therefore no right to touch it; he will do so at his own peril, for we appeal to Rome. The Abbot of Syloe answered this briefly: Come to the nunnery at Delft next Thursday, where you will find me and the Abbot of Trier, and we can get to business (p. 79). The next document is dated November 25; an appeal to the duke from Egmond and Rijnsburg in concert. The bull (they plead) is surreptitious; it would redound rather to ruin than to betterment, "since in visitations of this kind very many visitors bend their efforts and their labour rather to their own profit than to the common profit of the monasteries". Seeing, therefore, that these abbeys, "for the last 300 years, have lived under the defence and protection of your noble ancestors in the beauty of peace and in good government, without any such visitation and tribulation and invention of other novelties", therefore let them remain "as for the last 300 years, as aforesaid, they have been" (p. 81). After long deliberation (May 4) the duke issued a decree forbidding the Abbot of Trier "or any man not settled in our land and lordship" to vex the two abbeys with visitations, reformations, "or other novelties". He suggests as deputy visitor a Dutch or a Flemish abbot. He has written to the Prior of Sion by Delft (Congregation of Windesheim) "by whose impulse the aforesaid bull was procured", requesting him either to procure papal annulment of this bull, or to deliver it up (p. 81). This time it was the accused abbeys which had appealed with success to the secular arm. The Pope issued another bull. It is unfortunately half illegible with damp, but this much is plain, that he quashes his first bull and appoints an entirely new commission of enquiry (p. 85). We know from other sources that Cardinal Cusanus, the man who wielded far the widest and deepest powers for reform in that day, interested himself in the reform of Egmond. Yet here, again, there is no further record; and it seems plain that the effort of 1450 was as fruitless as that of 1421.

But Cusanus was a man of patient persistency. We see this from the next document, a third bull from Nicholas V (May 13, 1453). It rehearses how William, Lord of Egmond, has sent him a petition to the effect that the abbot and monks of Egmond

> notoriously [*dinoscuntur*] lead a life not monastic but dissolute, after the fashion of dissolute secular folk, and that they are sullied with incontinence. And, as the same petition added, Cardinal Nicholas of Cusa, at that time Papal Legate in those parts, sparing no labour and expense, coming for visitation to that exempt abbey was prevented by their rebellion and excesses* from bringing them back to the observance of St Benedict's Rule which they have professed, and to the effectual practice thereof according to its original institution; nay, rather, when he had left them they cared naught to keep that life which they had feigned to amend while he dwelt with them, to the peril of their own souls, the disgrace of their body and the scandal of very many folk.

William therefore, claiming to be "advocatus" of the abbey, begs the Pope to do justice there. He therefore commissions the Abbot of St Jacques at Liége with the fullest powers of visitation, reform, and punishment, notwithstanding all privileges or immunities, and to invoke the secular arm if necessary (p. 91). But here, again, the monks were able to exchange weapons; they procured from the duke a letter to William claiming that it was his own ancestors who had founded the abbey; and he would not suffer a subject's interference in his own princely business (p. 94). About the same time (in August) he wrote in the same sense to the Pope. He ignored Cusanus's visitation record, and made no attempt to defend the monks' morals except by implying that the facts still remained to be proved. But, as to William's interference, "I cannot express my amazement; nor, considering the circumstances, can I in any way be content with the sinister information which hath come from this lord William, himself a vassal of this abbey." Therefore he asks that the bull may be quashed and the cause committed to "one or two notable Prelates of the Order,

* *Et supersticiositate.* Medieval authors were commonly misled by the first two syllables of this word to apply it to any sort of excess: cf. Salimbene in M.G.H. XXXII.

of mine own or my successors' land or lordship; who, joining to themselves for the occasion some notable ecclesiastics of my Council, expert in such matters", may visit and act according to their judgment (p. 98). Here, again, the records end; and the editor writes that to this plain missive to Rome "we must undoubtedly also ascribe the fact that, this time also, the visitation of the abbey made no further progress, and even less did any reform of discipline take place" (p. 90).

The next act comes in 1471. Paul II, claiming to follow the judgment of that Abbot of Trier who had been appointed commissary in 1450, decided that the previous visitation of Egmond had proceeded "not from love and charity, but rather from hate and rancour", had appointed the Bishop of Tournai as supervisor of that abbey, with full powers of visitation except that no mention is made here of the secular arm. Paul died, however, before publishing this bull; and his successor Sixtus IV now ratifies it. Four years later he publishes a second bull, in a very different tone. It runs:

> Seeing that, as We have heard from very many trustworthy persons that in your exempt abbey of Egmond, without your default, divine service is not duly performed, and there is very grievous suspicion of dilapidation and alienation of the abbey goods, and of the incontinence of Our beloved sons the monks thereof: Seeing also that those monks have rendered no obedience whatever to Our admonitions, directed to them twice by letters in form of Brief, but (worse still), implicate themselves in worldly business and escape as far as they can from the matters of their Rule, possessing private property: Seeing also that the said abbey is in many ways deformed both spiritually and temporally: that they are ceasing from their regular observance of their Order and due celebration of divine service, so that the devotion of the faithful thereunto is continually diminishing

and ruin seems imminent. Therefore to the abbot, "of whose religion, continence, integrity and devotion we have heard sure report", he grants the commission of taking to his assistance any monks of the Order whom he can trust, and compelling the brethren "to resign with your hands" the property that they possess, and to renounce their portions which they abusively style *prebends*. They are to eat now in the common refectory, and, under pain of excommunication, no person of either sex is to enter the monastery "unless of the same Order or of some other reformed Order or by thine own express consent and licence". Secular persons are henceforward forbidden to come in. The abbot is to have full power of employing the ordinary sanctions of Canon Law against all offenders: and all this, "notwithstanding the statutes and customs of the abbey of Egmond" or papal privileges (p. 105).

Here the records fail us again for a dozen years. Then Innocent VIII, in 1487, at the request of Maximilian, Count of Holland and future Emperor, issued two bulls rehearsing how "some other monasteries of the [Benedictine] Order had, under colour of reformation, been despoiled and impoverished by their Visitors". Therefore, he accedes to the monks' supplication that they may never be visited but by their fellow-countryman, the abbot for the time being of St Peter's at Ghent. The Pope grants this in virtue of his opinion of "the sincerity of holy Religion under which, casting aside the enticements of the world, ye exhibit a devout and sedulous service to the Lord". Solicitous to secure their "tranquillity of mind, in order that they may more quietly serve the Most Highest", he issues a bill providing for them to the Day of Doom.

This day we have committed, subjected and placed [the abbey] under tutelage of the Abbot of St Peter's, and decree and command that, henceforth for perpetual time to come, they cannot and ought not to be visited by any other than the same Abbot of that house; and we have exempted them, and totally freed them, from visitation, correction, punishment and reformation by any other Visitors soever ...under excommunication for all who do contrary to this.

In his second bull he commissions the Provost of St John and the Dean of St Mary at Utrecht to watch jealously over any infringement (p. 110).

The value of the Pope's testimonial in the preamble to these bulls is sadly diminished by the next series, beginning with Innocent himself only three years later. For we now come for the first time to a full and connected story. One Theodoric Buschman, who calls himself "temporary Provost for reform", composed a chronicle of the events which he had taken part in or seen from 1490 to 1495. As the editor remarks: "If this description had not been written by a witness beyond suspicion, one would read it with the unwilling impression that we are here dealing with a *chronique scandaleuse* by one of the bitterest adversaries of monasticism and monastic life."*

He begins by reminding us that the rich endowments of this and other similar abbeys, and their numerous privileges, were always granted on the supposition that the monks would render corresponding services (p. 118). But here, "where, at first, the sluggish hearts of Christian folk were kindled to virtue by the practice of holy conversation, now, alas! an example of dissolution is given to all men, and very many occasions of scandal, and no small ruin of sin; so that this hotbed of edification is become a sink of sins". The abbot, far from restraining his monks, set them an example of vice. Sworn to poverty, he parades himself with a pomp and expense not only ultra-knightly but even ultra-baronial.† His brethren, in spite of the great wealth of the abbey, were often so extravagant that they ran into debt.

> Yet they did not receive poor wayfarers into their guest-house, Religious or other needy folk...but I have heard from very many of the monks, especially those of reformed life, that food was denied to those who begged for it after divine service. For each of the monks denied to strangers any part of what he had had prepared for himself: he gave rather to his servants or his concubines. Whomsoever they received to their hospitality, this was not done for the sake of God or of honesty, but all assembled thereunto in the utmost desire of drenching such a man in drink; nay, rather, (that I may speak more truly) to choke him. (p. 120.)

To the same subject he recurs on the next page. A nobleman told him how he went once on Maundy Thursday to confess and earn the Indulgences granted on that day. The abbot insisted on his taking malvoisie first to comfort his stomach. At last he overcame his scruples and accepted: the result was that "we filled ourselves so full of wine on that day that neither of us, for sheer drunkenness, could speak a single word". The

* P. 113. Later (p. 115) he shows in detail how far Buschman is corroborated by other sources, many of them official, and how "some exaggerations" are the most we can suspect.

† We must remember that the lord of Egmond, holding some of his estates under this great landowner, was to that extent his vassal. His remote ancestors had very likely been *ministeriales* of the abbey, and therefore unfree men.

monks imitated their abbot, and the servants their masters; the abbey became notoriously dangerous "even for strong drinkers"; men were often carried out in a fit from these drinking bouts, or even dead. It was proverbial that abbots scarcely ever died "a natural death". Buschman himself knew a priest, so notoriously concubinary that he boasted of forty children born during his priesthood, who was enticed to drink with the monks for a wager, stoup after stoup, until he fell down in apoplexy "and thus lost both his wager and his life".

I myself have seen, after this holy reformation had been effected, when a few of the old monks still abode here, as it were by necessity, having nowhere else to live, how often, or even daily, they challenged each other to mutual potations, so that they remained all night either on their benches or on the floor, unable to reach their beds for rest. You might often [*plerumque*] have seen them lying in the church, and sometimes [*quandoque*] in the dormitory, or in other places, so sunk in vomit and in such other filth that it would be foul even to speak thereof. Since St Paul saith, "Be not drunk with wine, wherein is lechery"—*luxuria*—you must think what these men's continence was in Venus when Bacchus ruled in the belly. I am ashamed to recount much of this, nor indeed is it expedient to rehearse the deeds of separate monks, lest I should seem diligent in detraction. But since their renown is so notorious that there is the plain evidence of their nourishing their children, I need no further proof.

A trustworthy witness to the old state of things "wrinkled up his face, as in abomination" and said that he marvelled God had not destroyed the abbey as He destroyed Sodom (p. 122).

Although some one might have been found among that crew who showed a certain honesty of outward life, so that he was at least less notorious for open lechery, yet I could reveal plainly enough from my own experience how things were done in secret; but I think it better to pass this over in silence. But what virtue could be found in a place where the root of all evil threw out its evergreen branches? What meritorious work can be in men who rejoice in the abominable vice of *proprietas*?

It destroys one of the Three Essentials, Obedience, and leaves the monk free to follow his own will. "How can the vice of incontinence be avoided, when men seek and obtain such shameless association with women of evil fame?"

Cardinal Cusanus, "in bulls which I myself have handled and read", commanded under the most formidable maledictions "that they should resign private property, and keep the other Substantials of the Rule". In one, by papal authority, he pronounced excommunication *ipso facto* upon all disobedient. "I have indeed seen the bull; but I confess I have found no vestige of obedience to it. From this you may clearly understand that they thus persisted to the end—under such horrible condemnation, in life and in death...what more horrible can be said or imagined, than to be excommunicate, and daily to celebrate the Mysteries of God?" Yet scarce one, even on his death-bed, showed attrition, not to say contrition; at most they were moved to care at their last moments "for their concubines and children, that they might inherit the goods they left, as I myself in their presence have seen and heard". One, when the bystanders asked him at his last gasp to repent of his sins, "answered, with such force as he still had, 'only one thing grieves me, that that dragon' [for thus he termed his abbot] 'will get my money'". Another, when death was certain, made his servant bring all his gold pieces and fondled them in his hands. His confessor, with all his pains, could extract no more than: "From the bottom of my heart I am wrung with grief that I must die!" Another, under the old state of things, had kept a tavern with a woman partner, as man and wife: "I heard him say at the beginning of the reformation, in the presence of bystanders who would have persuaded him thereunto, 'I would rather even be separated from God for ever, than submit to those cowled fellows' [for so he called the reformed monks]."

I will relate here what I had heard from a certain venerable father. He said, with sighs and groans, "I have been told by a certain person whom I believe to have received it by revelation, that for 200 years or thereabouts scarce any monk of Egmond hath come to salvation until the present time": denoting thereby the first introduction of the reform. In order that this assertion may seem more true, we must consider this proof, that all this time, and longer still, the monks were always proprietary, as may be clearly seen from the wills which they made and the judicial proceedings, wherein we find almost continual strife between the Abbot and the monks.

St Benedict (he argues in conclusion) condemned *proprietas* as the root of all evil and so it always must be; for, "whereas the monk who is sheltered by poverty remains intact, he who possesses money finds a thousand occasions for sin" (p. 126).

CHAPTER XXXV

EGMOND: FINAL SUCCESS

At last, in 1490, the tide began to turn. John III, Count of Egmond, successor to that John II who had made the abortive attempt of 1421, seems in earlier days to have been indifferent or hostile to reform. At any rate, there is no sign that he used his great influence against that scandalous bull which Maximilian had procured in 1487, commending the abbot and his monks and sheltering them against effective visitation. But now, writes Buschman, touched at heart by the Spirit of God, repenting his past misdeeds and instigated by the suggestions of some whose hearts God had touched, he obtained from Innocent VIII a bull not only reversing his own previous decision, but most explicitly exposing the falsehood of the flattering preamble of that document. It recalled the reforming attempt of Cardinal Cusanus, the monks' hypocritical conformity for so long as he was with them, the contempt with which they treated his injunctions when he was gone, and the general scandal of the faithful. All these things were notorious, and should have been known in Rome when the earlier bull had been granted. Innocent now describes the net result as

> but little reformation of the abbey and no effect [of Cusanus's visit]; nay, rather, the monks still commit divers excesses from day to day, leading a corrupt life, utterly discordant and contrary to the monastic Rule of living; for they devote themselves so publicly and shamelessly to drunkenness and gluttony and ingurgitation and dissolution that they are on the level not only of secular clerics but even of dissolute layfolk. Therefore the Count is now absolved from all pains and penalties formerly imposed on those who dared to touch this abbey:

in other words, Innocent silently reverses those two bulls of his own granted at the instance of Maximilian and, in so many words, grants the same plenary powers which had been granted to Cusanus, but, this time, to the two Presidents of Provincial Chapter of the Benedictines. They are to call in, if necessary, the secular arm; and here at last is the powerful Count of

Egmond ready to help (p. 182). The reformers were beside themselves with joy and wonder, "that this lord, so steeped in worldly business, should thus devote himself to this matter"; he who had been "a companion at the Abbot's table and a fellow-worker in his indecencies". Their only fear now was lest he should "be moved to desist by prayers or by bribes". It is like the deliverance of Israel from its Babylonian captivity by Cyrus of Persia! For Egmond sticks to his purpose; and the result will now be as we have already seen, when determined lords like the Duke of Brunswick or Albert of Austria lent themselves to monastic reform. Egmond may have had his selfish reasons also; but, in the main, he was doing the work which the Church, though she needed it for very life, had hitherto failed signally to perform.

The two reforming abbots, thus appointed, very naturally feared at first lest this fresh attempt should fail as disastrously as its predecessors, and leave the good cause with one more defeat to its account. But he of St Martin's at Cologne, though aged and infirm, was an old campaigner, in this field, and unbroken in spirit. "It is God's work", he said to his hesitant brother: and, borne in a litter to his chariot, swathed in flannels he braved the winter cold and the evil roads. The two comforted themselves in their journey by recalling Egmond's deeds of arms, and drawing hopeful conclusions from his promised help in this ecclesiastical campaign.

Meanwhile Abbot Jordan of Egmond got wind of the change, if not by sight of the actual bull. Therefore he fled, carrying with him not only great wealth in gold and silver plate, but almost all his furniture. He, for his part, consoled himself with the thought "that, of old, similar unrest of reform had been attempted; but, after a little novelty had been brought in, things slipped back again to the old way of life".

The visitors arrived in due time, and found not only closed doors at the abbey but "scarce in the township could any be found who would entertain these reverend fathers for money: for they delighted more in the fellowship of the monks, from whose purses they were nourished". The visitors vainly demanded admission in the Pope's name, pursuant to their special commission. Meanwhile the monks entered into a formal conspiracy, each pledging himself to maintain loyally this opposition to the visitors. These had no remedy but to wait until they had procured a General Chapter decree condemning and excommunicating the rebels. The monks cared nothing for this, until the Chapter, in virtue of their powers under the bull, "invoked the help of the secular arm, in order that these rebels, who cared neither for the fear of God nor for their own salvation, might be constrained by physical violence" (p. 135).

The count, bold in war, feared to lay hands upon a monk, "for he was not ignorant of that scripture, *Touch not Mine Anointed*". Even with a papal bull, he would not touch them unless the shavelings themselves would first set the example. Therefore the commissaries assembled a group of Superiors from neighbouring monasteries of both sexes, and two Professors of Divinity, and the learned Prior of the Charterhouse at Delft, "who for the most part were fellow-workers and encouragers in this business". Egmond and the commissaries now "came to the church, thinking whether by chance the counsel of salvation might find its way into their hearts. But they began to sing—nay, rather, to bellow—a solemn Mass, playing at the same time upon the organ, hoping thus, like deaf adders, not to hear the voice of the charmer. For, the more these venerable fathers and apostolical commissaries insisted upon being heard, the louder did these raise their voices and ramped and turned away their ears lest they should hear the voice of these who would charm them to their salvation. When at last all hope of quieting them was evidently dissipated, then the count, who had this cause at heart, came forward and called unto the prior, saying: "Will you rather open the doors that we may come in? otherwise at the summons of these venerable fathers, I will burst doors and hinges and enter." At last, after many shifts, he granted entrance to them, in the firm trust that his brethren would stick inviolably to the conspiracy that they had made, and thus they could frustrate the visitation; for they thought that the visitors, whatever they might say, could not dare to lay hands upon them. But "iniquity hath lied to itself". For, first, various courses were proposed to the monks: either that of their own accord they should keep with very generous mitigations the reform which was to be introduced: to wit, that they might eat flesh thrice a week, and wear linen undergarments, and sleep on feather-beds, and with only moderate fasts, etc., or else, that they should be sent, with an honourable provision, to other unreformed monasteries; or that they should be content with a provision for their livelihood and leave Egmond. To none of these would they consent nor even listen, but remained hardened in their obstinacy and conspiracy. Therefore at last the venerable fathers, having renewed all the offers which they had refused, called in the count and his vassals and laid first hands upon the men, as rebels and despisers of the Church's censures and excommunications, leading them to prison-like chambers and detaining them there for some days, in order that thus at length they might return to themselves and take to their hearts some sane thought for their own salvation. Yet lo! even when they were enclosed and restrained in such secluded places, they manifested their own madness and exorbitancy. For they pledged each other there in such wild carouse that scarce one of them could frame words for answer of a question, but they flung about like irrational beasts bereft of all discretion. The prior, though senior in years, was no saner than the rest. Meanwhile the count's retainers stood on guard lest force should be used against the visitors (p. 137).

The rebels, growing weary after some days, begged leave to hold a meeting and discuss their position. Two fled to the abbot, and, at that safe distance, conspired with him. The others were let out from their confinement, promising upon their honour that they would not flee, but stay in the count's hostel. Thus they ate and drank together, and supported each other in the hope of victory at long last. The visitors vainly cited the abbot to appear and defend himself. Losing patience at last, they summoned him peremptorily, as the bull empowered them, as an alternative to condemnation and deposition. Meanwhile the visitors called in ten reformed monks from different abbeys to come and set the example at Egmond. They took care to excite no nationalistic prejudices, bringing in no foreigners, but brethren from the duke's own dominions. The rebels gnashed their teeth at these rebels, saying to each other:

Lo! how joyfully these cowled fellows flock now to our house! How will we cast them out again when the Visitors are gone! for they firmly believed that the Count might be bent to their side.... Their cronies and boon-companions applauded them.... But at last, finding no relief or support from any, they agreed and consented that each should receive a yearly pension, with faculty for living outside.

Next day, therefore, the count and all those distinguished ecclesiastical assessors met, and formally elected Buschman himself as provost of the abbey, to carry on until the whole matter could be finally concluded. He here devotes two pages to his own sense of unworthiness, and the count's kind reassurances to him. The great man promised to lend the necessary funds, and gave 100 florins as earnest-money. He assured Buschman also of steady military support if necessary. The event proved that the electors could not have made a better choice. On the morrow, Buschman expedited the conclusion of the bargain with the monks. Their pensions were fixed, and each was left at liberty to carry off whatever he claimed as his own.

By reason of which concession they carried off almost all the furniture and utensils existing in the abbey, each replying, in answer to questions, that all this stuff was their own private property, thus proclaiming themselves as manifestly proprietary. The upshot was that, in the whole abbey there was not left, from all the pewter vessels, even as many as sufficed for the daily needs of a few men.

But the ten reformed monks were now free to live according to the Rule; and "for precaution they hired a few men-at-arms, who guarded the abbey from attack, by day and night, until something certain could be known" (p. 143). The abbot lurked meanwhile in his retreat; calculating with much probability: "I have vessels of gold and silver here, and a treasure in coin; moreover I have the abbey rents and other resources, wherewith I can easily resist these foreigners, who are poor." He therefore forbade all tenants to pay except to himself.

Meanwhile, however, many wires were pulled to detach the count. One of his councillors, having taken a heavy bribe, was continually and adroitly urgent, until another councillor opened the count's eyes to what was going on behind his back, and moved him to an explosion which frightened the other effectually (p. 143). A far more dangerous move was that which wealthy abbeys could always make: one of those appeals to Rome in which St Bernard and other saints after him had seen one of the worst dangers for Christendom. Otto of Heemskerk, who had the degree of *magister* and was secretary to Abbot Jordan, sent a cleric to Rome, "promising him in reward the sacrilegious pact that if he succeeded, his labours should be rewarded by such and such a benefice": the abbey, of course, had many at its disposal. His brief was to plead "spoliation": these foreigners had come in and robbed the abbey: from the Pope's justice they demanded restitution. The plea so far succeeded, that the cause was committed to a judge upon whose favour they could count. This man, "either for prayers or for bribes", showed favour to the old monks from the very first. Abbot Jordan's secretary came to the abbey ostentatiously and in the most hectoring and insulting mood: "the news whereof so excited the common people that, for the noise and tumult, one could scarce hear anything in the abbey, since the people were strongly of the Abbot's party." Matters seemed desperate, when Buschman saved the situation. As he forced his way through the crowd in the lower hall, he saw a paper lying on the ground, slipped it into his sleeve and brought it to the visitors and ecclesiastics in their own chamber. It turned out to be in the judge's own handwriting: he had supplied the old monks with instructions how to state their case with the greatest legal advantage. The visitors played this card with devastating effect. One of them took the judge aside as he was proceeding to the tribunal, and asked "What will you do?" "I will administer justice as the case may require." "My lord judge, do you know this handwriting?" "It is mine own hand." The other then opened it out and asked: "How do you pose as judge, when by this paper you show yourself advocate also?" The man confessed himself thus incapacitated from sitting as judge, and for the moment the reform seemed saved.

Jordan then turned to the count, and "sent him a letter full of threats and insults and plain lies, wherewith he dared to defame him to the utmost of his power". Egmond remained unmoved. Then Jordan, "sparing neither gold nor silver", appealed now to the highest civil authority. Here he succeeded. Maximilian and his son, Philip Duke of Burgundy, as sovereigns of Holland, sent the Bishop of Cambrai to remove the ten reformed monks and their provost and to restore the abbot, giving him a few brethren from Liége who would pose as "reformed" and thus manage to stultify the whole papal visitation. In pursuance of this plan, the bishop summoned Buschman to the Hague, with some of his monks, intending to delay them there with insincere negotiations, and in their absence to introduce the feigned reformers. Buschman went, but sent meanwhile post haste to Utrecht for the two papal visitors. The bishop opened the proceedings: he had come in the name of the most illustrious princes to hear the complaints of this "despoiled" Abbot Jordan, and to do justice. The visitors replied by appealing to their own papal commission, and pointing out that no merely secular prince, however great, could override this in a purely ecclesiastical matter. The bishop,

> moved to wrath, began to speak more sternly, saying, "I stand here armed with the authority of the Princes, sent hither by the unanimous counsel of the whole Court. I am no ordinary magistrate, but a Bishop; think not to contemn me, for if ye were in my territory I would clap you all into prison"; threatening especially those venerable fathers whom he called by the abject name of "beggarly friars" [*fratricellos*], a thing most indecent for a Bishop's dignity.*

The visitors, after giving themselves and him time for reflection, appealed against him as an evidently partisan judge, but declared themselves willing to hear sympathetically all that he had to say, as Henry de Berck, which might help to compose this lamentable quarrel (p. 149). The bishop left them in anger, and sent a severe warning to the count, "forbidding him in the Prince's name, under pain of loss of all his goods and of incurring their censure, from in any way presuming to interfere in any way for the monks and against their Abbot". This was serious, and the count went straight to the visitors, begging them "to consent to some sort of composition, rather than that the whole business should come to naught; 'for' (said he) 'I cannot act against the Princes' commands, by reason of my oath of fealty to them'". The reformers felt themselves lost, but betook themselves to prayer, and those who were priests said Mass for the success of the good cause. Then came breathlessly

* The bishop's formal title was Henry de Berck, by Grace of God and of the Pope Bishop and Count of Cambrai.

their ally the Divinity Professor from Haarlem, with the news that the bishop's feigned reformers were already in Haarlem, and would to-day be smuggled into Egmond. They took the news to the count and countess at their dinner. The count started up in fury: "This Bishop cometh hither as a traitor: but by God he shall not prevail! Let him go hither with his own fellows: and if he and those other fellows of his get hold of the abbey in this fashion, I will cast them out that same day, or die by the sword, so God help me!" He called his captain, bade him saddle with his company, and told the reformers: "Make all haste thither, for this night we will sup together in the abbey or I shall have been overpowered in fight and my blood will pay for it." For here, of course, he was on his own territory, and had a right to defend himself even against his liege lord in a just cause.

The bishop soon learned that his plot had been discovered; he then professed ignorance and astonishment, and promised the count to do nothing without consulting him. This rendered possible the compromise which the count now desired. He and the visitors, after long negotiations, agreed to accept as arbiter the Bishop of Cambrai, whose award speaks volumes for the bankruptcy of the strict Benedictine Rule in the fifteenth century (p. 214: October 25, 1491).*

Abbot Jordan was to retain the abbacy though this award and other legal documents assume his disgraceful misgovernment in the past. He was to have for his private use about half, apparently, of the whole ample abbey revenues. Buschman, as provost, was to govern the abbey in the spirit of the papal bull. He was to have twenty-six reformed monks of his own, but was compelled to admit also nine of the old gang—that is, just half—so long as they claimed to stay on. The others were to be pensioned off with sixty gold florins each per annum.† The nine who stay at Egmond must "expropriate themselves of all

* Another clear proof may be found on p. 190, in Jordan's formal notarial protest and appeal to the Pope. He pleads that it is illegal to compel any Religious to adopt a stricter form of life than that which is provided by modern "mitigation or innovation".

† These would probably be Rhenish florins, three of which would be equivalent to two French écus. These would be worth about £15 sterling or more, at a time when the richest English abbeys allowed their Oxford students £10.

moneys, houses, gardens, chests and keys and other things, so that they shall possess naught of these, or other goods, without the Provost's leave: they must also resign forthwith, in due legal form, whatever titles to rents or letters of revenue they may possess: so also they must assign in writing whatsoever debt they may have". They must follow divine service with the rest, and attend in the chapter-house for discipline, if not daily as the Rule prescribes, at least once a week. "Item, let all abstain from hunting, of any kind, prohibited by law; nor shall those brethren admit or keep hounds within the abbey precincts." They shall not go abroad without the provost's leave.

Considering, also, that, since the sentence recently pronounced, women are promiscuously admitted into the abbey, and are seen to enter the ambulatory,* as was revealed in the present visitation, a thing which is most incongruous for Religious, therefore let none of the brethren who are under the Provost's obedience enter the abbey without reasonable cause and licence from the Provost or, in his absence, from the Prior.

If the monks pertinaciously disobey, they may be punished even with prison. "Moreover they have promised that, if they are found sitting in potations or talking with women and, after one or two formal warnings, neither desist nor amend, then they shall lose, without further ado, the modification concerning walking abroad, and shall be obliged to remain inside the first gate, opposite the [so-called] 'Count's Building'." The other formal documents which the editor prints in illustration and corroboration of Buschman's own story show that this lame compromise had just the effect which might be anticipated. There were endless quarrels as to the partition of the property; Abbot Jordan defaulted in his payments, and the presence of the old gang in one part of the abbey, while the reformers tried to realize the Rule in another, was a constant and serious difficulty.

Matters were not mended when the abbot, fearing further steps which would endanger his present freedom, slipped off by boat into Brabant, where with his gold and silver plate and

* *Ambitum*: it may conceivably mean "precincts". The point of this otherwise obscure sentence lies in the fact that the main portion of the abbey was to be occupied by Jordan and his adherents, the reformed monks making themselves at home, as best they could, in the rest of the buildings.

coin, valued at 7000 florins, he was able to buy the support of powerful persons. One of these was an eminent prelate, the Provost of Liége, whose great influence at Court made him specially dangerous. This man sent an envoy to Rome for letters against the reformers. This envoy, a Carmelite friar and Doctor of Divinity, spent two years there, and at last procured letters "which were said to be in favour of Abbot Jordan; but their contents were so cautiously concealed that only the Abbot's partisans knew". Then comes a story in which Buschman saw the hand of God, and which he tells with special gusto and fulness of detail (p. 161). This messenger came safely from Rome to Hertogenbosch, within a few miles of Breda, where his party awaited him. He started confidently at daybreak; but a sea-fog suddenly came up, and, after many weary wanderings, he found himself hopelessly embogged as night came on. Leaving his horse up to its belly in the swamp, he struggled out and found with great difficulty a lonely farm, on the rising ground, where for a long while nobody dared to answer his desperate knockings at the door. Famished and exhausted, he asked how far he was from Breda, only to learn that he was farther now than he had been at daybreak! Next morning he paid the farm servants to fetch his horse: they reported at last that they had found it, "foul with mire", at a dry patch in a swamp belonging to Egmond abbey! The emissary wondered what this coincidence might mean: "for indeed it was a great miracle." Next day, being Christmas, Abbot Jordan rose "perchance at the hour when our Lord was born", to go to church. His servants found him lying on the floor; they asked what ailed him, and he could only stammer that all was lost: "'*t is al verloren*." He lived three days longer: "they could discover in him no sign of contrition or even of attrition." On the second day the agent from Rome arrived, but the abbot showed no sign of recognition. Buschman hopes that he may have found mercy at his last gasp: but "it is seldom that he dieth well who hath led his whole life ill".

The monks of Jordan's party kept his death profoundly secret until they had held a hugger-mugger election of their own. They chose the prior, who had been his right-hand man and the companion of his flight. The reformers held their own election in due legal form, and chose one Henry. Here was obvious matter for appeal to Rome. The old gang sent post-haste to re-engage their former proctor at the Court, Venroed. But the reformers sent a more efficient messenger, who managed to pass the other on the way and to see Venroed first: the man regretted this afterwards, but was too honourable to violate his engagement. But the magnates of the Low Countries threw their weight into the scale at Rome; and nearly all the cardinals were inclined against the reformers. "Our proctor feared that the prayers of the princes would prevail, as usual." The matter might have been risky under the best-intentioned of Popes: but here was Alexander VI, one of the most cynical and irreligious in history. It brought but a small counterpoise when they worked upon the old dowager duchess's conscience and persuaded her to procure from Duke Philip a letter revoking his own previous plea; for the adversaries stigmatized this as surreptitious. But then came another "change of the right hand of the Most High" (p. 167). Charles VIII of France, returning from his famous expedition against Naples, announced his intention of bringing his army home through Rome. Alexander protested in vain. It was at this moment that the Egmond case came before the Pope in full consistory. He began speaking of the King:

"It is this rebellious man's will to pass through Our land in spite of Us, with great force of armed men; and We know not his aim." And then he added: "Here We have before us a case of confirmation for a certain abbey in Germany, whereof one part is called reformed and the other not. Let Us give Our confirmation to the side elected by the reformers, that so God may be gracious to Us."

Thus, in the twinkling of an eye, salvation came "not by strict law, but incidentally—*non via juris sed occasionaliter*—that thanks may be given to God, Who from one evil thing can bring forth good". Even so, however, all might yet be lost. But a friendly banker met the litigants in the street, and asked the cause of their jubilation. "We are joyed at this sentence of confirmation: yet we have another perplexity." "How so?" "The Most Holy Father is on the point of leaving Rome, and we have not money enough to pay for the bull." "Well, if God helped you to the confirmation, I will help you for the money you need." "Here is a strange chance", comments Buschman; "for all bankers follow after gain." In due time, seven bulls arrived at Egmond, one sealed for the Archduke Philip. Buschman brought this to him as he sat with his councillors; among them the Counts of Egmond and Berck, who favoured the reform, and the Provost of Liége who, though the duke's most trusted ecclesiastical adviser, was its worst enemy. Philip called upon him to open and read it: "The case was almost that of Haman and Mordecai. ...O! if thou hadst seen the man's face!"—his pallor and the uncontrollable distortion of his features, especially when the two counts exchanged congratulations. The duke took it with a good grace; he would now obey His Holiness. The populace of Egmond, seeing only vaguely that everything was astir, got it into their heads that Buschman and his crew had been arrested and packed off to Liége.

For the common folk and the township hung upon the return of the old brethren, by whose feasts they were wont to be supported, and in whose companionship they had enjoyed things which it is better to hide unspoken, for indeed these banquetings were detrimental to modesty, witness the offspring which resulted from their intercourse with the unmarried, where there was no subterfuge such as covered their doings with married women. (p. 172.)

Thus, even after the seven papal bulls and the duke's consent, it was necessary to buy off the false claimant, the ex-prior, with a pension of 600 florins a year.

Abbot Henry now had a free hand; and Buschman's last four pages describe the new world he made at Egmond. He began with the House of God.

For the church was disorderly, not vaulted, the roofs not rain-proof, the whole unadorned until this reformation, the altars uncovered like unconsecrated spots. The monks' whole diligence and care had been spent first upon the adornment of their chambers with various furniture, and the little houses* in the orchard with precious glasses and stoups and goblets, to which houses women often came, shewing their feasting and drunkenness and immodesty. There, each strove to surpass the other in curiosity and expense. In these little houses we found indications of the business of their occupants: to wit, crossbows and longbows, dice, cards, bowls and vessels to serve drunkenness.

* Elsewhere he writes "domunculis; immo, quod pudet dicere, prostibulis".

These pavilions the new abbot dismantled. He raised the numbers of monks, from eighteen under Jordan, to nearly forty, restoring the church and its ornaments. Nowadays, more than thirty Masses are said daily with all devotion; whereas, under the old régime, few were in priestly Orders and those few were careless.

For, as transpired from the examination of witnesses, the monks were so given to drink that scarce one or two could be found sober next morning, who had slept off their drink and were able to say Mass. Nay, one priest of the township testified that he had oftentimes been feed to say the Conventual Mass, since all were still half-drunken....And indeed I fear that it would have been better for none to have celebrated, since their shameful life was a disgrace to the Church.

Nearly all the nine who died outside the abbey passed away without the last rites of the Church: "Nor did I ever see one of them whom the example of another's fate guided into the way of salvation": they did not even see, with Juvenal, that our neighbour's house afire is our own concern also.

His last two paragraphs deserve translation in full, as a pendant to Busch, and something of an antidote to Traversari:

Therefore God should rightly be praised, for that He hath so made this house that it can now be truly called *Egmunda*, as a place wholly cleansed [*tota mundata*]. For now the Superior no longer goeth in pompous attire, and with a company of many retainers; no longer doth he show himself, as of old, the prince of drunkards; but, attired like his brethren, he goes with humble bearing to divine service, is attentive to sobriety, gives an example of religion, and carefully fulfils St Benedict's written injunction: "Let the Abbot study to be loved rather than feared by his brethren." You may see him no longer busied with private feasts, while the servants pour out various drinks and cringe to him with vain flattery, but conforming in the refectory, as the Rule bids, to the lowly society of his brethren; and this without any exception of food and drink, so that he would not accept a single egg beyond the rest; all of which is by his own uncompelled choice. If worthy hosts come, then he receives them charitably at his own table, pouring water himself upon their hands, and showing them all courtesy according to their rank. You may see the brethren devoted to silence, quiet and cheerful, and studying virtue; so that you would rightly judge the wolves to be turned to lambs, and the wayward to holiness. For a certain Count, after

Compline, seeing all the brethren take holy water, as is their wont, from their Superior and mount together in silence to the dormitory, said in amazement and in praise: "In my time, I have seen devils dwelling here; and now I see angels!" May the Creator of all Angels vouchsafe to keep them ever in His fear and service, in His fear and reverence, through the same Christ our Lord.

It is worth noting that in 1502, when the Franciscan convent at Dordrecht "had fallen very low", the then Count of Egmond joined with the city magistrates to call upon the Papal Legate for reform. That ecclesiastical prince, writes Fr. P. Schlager, "set to with such zeal, that some thirty Conventuals went over to the Observants" (*Beiträge*, 148).

CHAPTER XXXVI

REFORM IN FRANCE

For the century from 1450 to 1550, roughly, this country offers the best field for study. It is far less complicated by political divisions and cross-currents than in Germany or Italy, where, in the absence of effective central authority, one area no larger than an English county might be pursuing a policy quite different from that of its neighbours, all equally small. France, during that century, was by far the largest area in Europe under a single strong monarchy. It was less homogeneous than England; but the royal policy was more definite. It may be summed up in a single sentence: Partnership with the Pope, yet resultant rivalry. After the Pragmatic Sanction had been made between Louis XI and Pius II, King and Pope were more or less in agreement upon one point; each was willing to let the other take as much as he could get of the Church's enormous endowments, except so far as this might prejudice his own revenues from the same source. On the other hand, such a partnership was essentially as insecure and uneasy as that of Pope and Emperor in the Middle Ages; therefore there was continual bickering. As to reform, each was willing to further it, except so far as it touched his own purse or privileges. Here, as in Germany and Italy, it was often the nobles or the princes who, in the name of a scandalized lay-folk, pressed action upon the otherwise inactive Papacy.

As I have pointed out in an earlier chapter, the need had long been severely felt. A Benedictine scholar has lately quoted a striking example. He is summarizing briefly the lengthy reforming statutes which Abbot Aymeri, in 1351, drew up for his abbey of Moutier-la-Celle. He writes:

> Far from surpassing in strictness [the papal and capitular decrees of the past], he is compelled to recall his monks not only to the obligations of every priest who has not taken the Three Vows [of Obedience, Poverty and Chastity], but also to the most elementary prescriptions of the Decalogue, binding upon all Christians. Judge

for yourselves; these Benedictines are forbidden to carry weapons, to keep "personas inhonestas" in their cells or their priories, to administer the sacraments or give the marriage-blessing without authorization, to play at dice, or commit thefts. They must thenceforth say Mass daily, attend the church services of the Rule; they may not leave the abbey or the priories without leave from the Abbot. Here we are far from the reforming bull of Benedict XII [1336], only a few years after it had been fulminated.(1)

In fact, we are already in the sphere in which even the "reforms" of Egmond, at first, could aim at no more than a very lame compromise.

The reader will find two admirable guides for this French story, better than anything I know for other countries. These are *Les Origines de la Réforme*, by the late P. Imbart de la Tour, and Professor A. Renaudet's *Pré-réforme et Humanisme*.(2) The latter, especially, treats the subject with a fulness and clarity which leave nothing to be desired. As he says in his Introduction: "Three facts dominate the evolution of religious thought in France towards the end of the Middle Ages. These are the triumph of nominalist philosophy, the re-birth of mysticism, and the appearance and development of humanism. Therefore we must begin with the last third of the fourteenth century, when the University of Paris recognized incontestably the supremacy of Ockham's doctrines." In the writings of this bold and original Englishman, Scholastic Philosophy had run its whole course. "From the point of view of the modern non-metaphysical man of science, Ockham represents the perfection of common sense."(3) His analysis of papal claims, again, was almost as unsparing as that of his contemporary Marsilius of Padua. Like him, Ockham placed the real leadership of Christendom not in Rome but in regularly-recurring Universal Councils in which (as he implies) he would grant votes to women also, since they have souls as well as men. He kept his orthodoxy, in so far as he may be said to have kept it, only by a series of water-tight compartments; separating faith from reason, he was able even to exaggerate the sacramental side of Christianity while pursuing a solvent rationalism. His doctrines, though condemned more than once at Rome, triumphed almost everywhere down to the Reformation, and Luther spoke of him as "my dear master". Hence a mystic reaction. When we read the *Imitatio* with this in mind, we see at once why Thomas à Kempis writes so often and so emphatically against the scholarship and knowledge which, so far from edifying, are inimical to the highest religion. Therefore paradoxically enough, though Ockham's doctrines tended ultimately, and in the bolder minds, to scepticism, yet their immediate effect upon the majority was rather conservative. His emphasis upon the separation between science and religion made it easier for men to trouble no further about giving reasons for the faith that was in them, so long as they had that faith, *la foi du charbonnier*. This gave a further impetus to what Erasmus and others regretted as the Judaic side of Catholicism, its emphasis on traditions and ceremonies. Thus this resolute and formidable anticlerical writer served, with the multitude, the cause of clericalism; and he who had shaken almost the very foundations of papal authority gave indirect encouragement to a fabrication so purely papal as the doctrine of Indulgences. This supplies one more cause for the comparative tardiness of the Renaissance on this side of the Alps. Italy had never been really devoted to Scholasticism; but in France and Germany and Spain and England medieval philosophy had still power to prevent men from seeing the world with new eyes, even when thought had moved so far that only the last veil remained to be torn away. At the universities, Ockhamists accepted, like the rest, that medieval eschatology which, with its emphasis on hell, tortured sensitive souls too often with paralysing scruples, yet hardened the callous sinner still further. The meticulous logic with which they argued from those unsafe premisses spared them further thought and encouraged the non-philosophical laity to lean increasingly upon what the priest did in church, even while they had increasing reasons for deploring the priest's personal life. "The Church soon realized that Ockham's teaching was more useful to her than that of St Thomas Aquinas" (p. 65). Theoretically, it should have thrown men back upon an intenser and more realistic study of the Bible. In fact, it rather encouraged than checked the time-honoured scholastic employment of the Scriptures not in full perspective, but as a mass of detached texts useful as missiles in theological disputes. What to Roger

Bacon seemed so perverse, that the study of Peter Lombard's *Sentences* was superseding that of Old and New Testament in their entirety, was even more marked and more regrettable in the last two centuries of the Middle Ages. "Thus this triumphant nominalism turned Christian dogma into a sort of holy relic which no man approached" (p. 105). "The only problem which really fascinated the Paris theologians was that of the Immaculate Conception" (p. 106); a dogma then rejected by the most learned theologians in Europe, but destined to triumph finally through the *foi du charbonnier*.

In France therefore, as in Italy, the spirit of the age was not entirely favourable to the religious, and especially the monastic, reformer. The reasons were not quite the same, but the results were very similar. In Italy, the general reaction towards paganism rendered the multitude comparatively indifferent to the higher side of Christianity, while it threw them back more upon those ceremonies, that emotional side, which it shares with most other religions. In France, the trend towards philosophic agnosticism worked in much the same direction. Ockham had shown that Catholic dogma is unprovable by logic; and can be apprehended by faith alone. Thus the intellectual field, which is open to few, is subordinated to the emotions of the many. And, on both sides of the Alps, in proportion as men believed in the Mass, they had the best reasons for believing the churchman when he taught that this was an *opus operatum*. A wafer consecrated by the worst priest in the most neglected church is as truly and wholly Christ's own Body as one consecrated by the most saintly Pope in St Peter's at Rome. It is not many steps from this to that general indifference to monastic decay which we have seen in Busch's and Traversari's story. If the worst Mass differs only in minor matters from the best, why then should not the worst abbey, like the best, be pleasing to God with its psalmody and Masses? Why should it not be doing and doing much to divert His wrath from the rest of God's creatures, the so-called "world", who find it easier to approach Him thus vicariously than directly?

Be that as it may, the fact is that we shall find the French story, though rather more favourable, not essentially different from that of Busch and of Traversari.

Next to the Carthusians, though at some distance, the Cluniacs and Cistercians had retained early strictness rather better than the large Benedictine majority. In 1458, when France was recovering from the Hundred Years' War, a certain number of reforms were effected at Cluny by a great abbot, Jean de Bourbon. In 1476, Cîteaux found its reforming abbot in Jean de Cirey. He owed his office to a revolt of good sense within the abbey itself. The monks had been misgoverned for generations by a succession of abbots "provided" to them by Popes by whom the wealthiest houses were regarded as milch-cows. They now asserted, for once, their original freedom of election, never legally abrogated and only superseded by a series of barefaced encroachments from Rome. Cirey's talents and efficiency earned him the respect of Louis XI, who knew a real man when he saw him, and whose personal failings never altogether obscured in his mind a genuine love for the well-being of his subjects. After eleven years of beneficent rule, Cirey managed to obtain from Innocent VIII a bull commissioning him as reformer of the whole Cistercian Order. But he found the task quite impossible in face of the *commendam* system, under which Pope and King conspired to rob the Church of her wealthiest, and therefore most influential, abbeys. Next year he went to Rome to plead personally for its abolition; the Pope put him off with empty promises, and sent him back to go on making bricks without straw.

At last, in 1484, came what may be called a revolt of the laity. That which in Germany and Italy had been sporadic, the interference of some prince or noble or body of magistrates to put an end to ecclesiastical scandals, was now focussed in France. It had become fairly common for papal bulls of reform to end with the clause "invoking, if need be, the help of the secular arm". We have now come to a point where the secular arm asserts its right of moving not merely in obedience to some special papal decree, but of its own accord, in the name of decency and of the public weal. At Tours, in 1484, Church reform was on the programme of Charles VIII and his Parliament, the États Généraux. Here Jean de Rély, Deputy for the clergy of Paris, came straight to the point. He said: "Among the monks of Cîteaux, of St Benedict, and of St Augustine, as among the rest, every man knows that there is no longer any Rule or devotion or religious discipline; and this is a matter most prejudicial to the King and his Kingdom." Bishops had little authority, even where the abbey had not bought "exemption" from Rome. The recent papal bull for grouping the houses into provinces, and thus securing a certain amount of system, was a dead letter. King and Pope, sometimes scrambling in rivalry, sometimes in amicable collusion, put their own nominees into the best-paid offices. Under the Pragmatic Sanction the King might gain a point here and the Pope a point there; but all was at the expense of the clergy and of religious regularity. The *commendam* system ruined all discipline; free election was practically extinct, not only in the case of abbots and priors but even of obedientiaries in the wealthier abbeys. The buildings were often in serious decay (pp. 4–7).

This initiative at Tours stirred the stagnant waters. Next year, at Sens, Archbishop Salazar held a synod which legislated for Church reform. The rampant simony must be checked; and the whole kingdom must be called to its duty of Sunday observance; for Church theory, as apart from popular practice, was strongly sabbatarian in the Middle Ages. Yet these statutes of Sens were little obeyed. The Bishop of Paris even ignored them altogether, and personal violence was offered to Archbishop Salazar in the cathedral of Notre-Dame. Yet 1488 passed without any redemption of this promise; and the reform of the clergy, above all of the cloistered clergy, which pressed more and more urgently upon serious and pious minds, was left not to cardinals or bishops or abbots, but to men who, with less hierarchical distinction, had more religious fervour and force of character. For France was now in that state where the need produces the men. As Renaudet sums up:

> In spite of the États Généraux, and negotiations with Rome, and the efforts of the Commission of Tours, the French Church was now without law or rule, as it had been on the morrow of Louis XI's death [1483] or of the Council of Basel; and here we find the perpetration of those miseries which the preamble to the Pragmatic Sanction described as long ago as 1438. (p. 8.)

How could the monasteries rise far above the general level of the clergy?

It is admitted that the rectors are non-resident; the man who does the duty and to whom, more often than not, they farm out the living, does not get a living wage; he cannot live without imposing taxes for his Sacraments and services, and struggling fiercely with the faithful whom his disorders scandalize. (p. 9.)

The most prominent of these volunteer reformers was the Breton Olivier Maillard, born about 1430. He was a Franciscan of the Strict Observance; in 1474 he became Provincial in the Order, and in 1487 Vicar General, an office to which he was re-elected in 1493. Charles VIII admired him and brought him to Court, and Innocent VIII commissioned him to persuade the King to abrogate the Pragmatic Sanction, that long-standing concordat which French kings had so often exploited to the disadvantage of the papacy. Yet this courtier and diplomat never swerved from his true character of mission-preacher. It was said, doubtless with some exaggeration, that he never passed a day without a sermon. Like his Italian contemporaries in the same field, he spoke out with the utmost frankness—not to say, roughness—on subjects where so many others found it prudent to keep silence. In 1491 he spoke plainly, under their very noses, about the shortcomings of the canons of Notre-Dame and they protested against him as a mischief-maker. Next year he preached at Paris another series of Lenten sermons, equally outspoken. He descended freely to all sorts of trivialities or vulgarities which would catch and fix the attention of the multitude. His single aim was practical, that of soul-saving; and with that aim in view he was compelled to clear the way, again and again, by dissociating himself most emphatically from what they all saw around them; the unworthiness of the clergy and the decay of the Church. He was indifferent to unpopularity: his relaxed brethren hated him, the clergy and laity had no love for the man who spared none of their vices. "He stood by himself, in a hostile Paris, as representative of the doctrines of Observantine Franciscanism" (p. 194). Equally powerful, in its way, was the voice of Raulin, heard less from the pulpit but more influential in solemn assembly. Born about 1443, he was Doctor of Theology at the Collège de Navarre in 1479, and Principal in 1481, in spite of Louis XI's disfavour.

> Like Maillard, he spoke both to simple folk and to the learned.... Like him, he was less curious of theoretical speculation than eager for moral and religious action; he saw too many vices both in the world and in the Clergy, to linger longer over abstract theses with his hearers. He saw the Church of his day full of law-suits and scandals and divisions, tormented by greed, differing profoundly from the early Church....He said: "Of old, one became Bishop by the Grace of God; nowadays the man had better call himself Bishop by the King's favour"....Ecclesiastical functions are given to children; we commit men's souls to a boy whom we would not trust with an apple....One would think that the Prelates commissioned their underlings to go about the streets and public places, collecting all the blind and lame that they could find, and bringing them into the Church. (pp. 166–7.)

He had the courage to refuse when they offered him a share of the spoils for preaching Indulgences which he suspected. He insisted that religion is far more than a mere intellectual matter; on the other hand, he repudiated much of the cheap popular devotion encouraged by monks and friars. Like St Augustine of old, and Erasmus afterwards, he was disgusted at the Judaic minutiae of piety which threatened to enslave Christ's free religion, and make us bondmen of the letter of the law. "Like Maillard, he attacked easy religion; and, with all his respect for Roman tradition, he drew from the Bible and St Paul's Epistles a deep personal faith which sustained him in his action and his propaganda" (p. 170). In May 1497, at the height of university success and of royal favour, he slipped quietly away from his Collège de Navarre and entered as a novice at Cluny. He told the whole story in a letter to the Warden of the Franciscans at Basel, that great church which still looks down upon the Barfüsserplatz.

> Invited daily to sumptuous tables, sometimes in pleasure and sometimes in constraint I lived as one of the sensual rich....But, in the midst of my errors, I witnessed terrible, awful deaths. I saw learned men ending in madness and idiocy; others dying in prodigious terror, as though they were already in the executioner's grasp....Now I have become, though tardily, a disciple of that death which teaches us how to live; I have fled from Paris and my family, and am dead in this solitude of Cluny.

And, to another friend; "In exchange for this narrow cell of mine, I hope for the immensity of Heaven" (p. 235). Henceforward another monk of Cluny, Bourgoing, was often partner of his reforming missions. Jean Quentin was Fellow of the Sorbonne as early as 1465; he became Canon of Notre-Dame in 1482, Penitentiary there in 1488, and in 1491 he was fascinated by St-François de Paule, whom Louis XI had imported in 1482. It was his house which, during their first year, sheltered the Minims when they came to Paris. Like Maillard and Raulin, he preached against easy religion; but his association with the Minims gave him, as we shall see, a certain extremism which hindered the full effect of his reforming efforts. This association, however, brought him into close contact with a far more remarkable reformer.

Jean Standonck, the son of a poor Malines cobbler, received his first schooling at Gouda. Here he imbibed very deeply the spirit of the Brethren of Common Life and of Windesheim. The semi-monastic discipline which these schools imposed upon the pupils gave a strong bent to his character. He learned there (says the *Chronicle of Windesheim*) above all "the fear of God, the horror of Hell, and the love of our Heavenly Country".(4) In 1469 he was a poor scholar at Louvain; thence he was admitted to the almonry school of Ste-Geneviève at Paris, where he suffered great privations, reading sometimes by moonlight. By 1475 he had become Licentiate in Arts, and in 1483 he was appointed Principal of the Collège de Montaigu. Here, in imitation of St-François de Paule, he renounced all personal use of money. The brother of one of his servitors was burned for heresy: thenceforward he pledged himself to a perpetual lenten fast, with such macerations of the flesh (says his subcontemporary biographer) "that one would have taken him for one of the Fathers of the Desert". Like the Brethren of Common Life and Gerson and Raulin, he saw that education must lie at the root of any durable reform. In 1490 he bought, close by the Collège de Montaigu,

a house in which he lodged scholars who, like himself in former days, had come from some distant land for study's sake, and who, like himself, were reduced to live by charity. Standonck used the fees of his rich pupils, with the alms which he collected, to supply these youths with bed, fire, and candle, and a white loaf daily. At eleven o'clock, they lined up and waited for food at the gate of the Carthusian monastery. They followed the College lectures, served their masters and their more fortunate comrades, and filled the humble offices which their own Principal had borne formerly at Ste-Geneviève. They attended religious service morning and evening. Without taking the vows, they formed a monastic community, electing one of their number as Superior. They held their Chapter at fixed dates, and there heard a sermon on the contempt of this world; then, in conventual fashion, accused themselves publicly of their faults. The Principal visited them, and preached to them of the Kingdom of God and the difficulty of reaching it. They seldom left the community except to enter some reformed monastery at his advice. (pp. 174 ff.)

In 1493, having thus collected more than eighty students, he undertook to found a new college with ecclesiastically-approved statutes. For this he obtained the consent of the Chapter of Notre-Dame, and a grant of 120 *livres tournois* per annum, from Louis de Graville, Admiral of France, who also built a hostel for the students. This effort secured support from the best members not only of the Chapter of Notre-Dame but also of the university, and seemed to promise a durable reform. But Standonck's extreme asceticism looked backward rather than forward. Even Ambrogio Traversari's educational work had suffered sadly from that disadvantage. Traversari knew Vittorino da Feltre; he admired and loved the man; yet he seems to have learned nothing from him here. His ideal school at Florence was almost as inhumanly superhuman as the monastic school of Cluny four centuries earlier.(5) Thus Standonck's refounded Collège de Montaigu became, in a few years, one of the horrors of Erasmus's youth. Even from the Brethren of Common Life he had inherited much of that Puritan tradition which, so far from owing its birth to the Reformation, was one of the most characteristic factors of medieval ethics, inherited from the early Christians.

But, if Standonck's stubborn toughness of fibre went far to frustrate his educational work, this quality was exactly what the Great Commission of Tours needed (1493). Here was a King really concerned, with all his faults, for reform; and here were all the chief figures of Church and State assembled to take counsel with him. The health of the whole realm was at stake—it may be said, of all medieval civilization—and there were many who realized the seriousness of this occasion. To this august assembly Standonck, as Canon of Beauvais, unburdened himself no less freely than in his own class-room at Paris. The salt (he said) has lost its savour; the clergy bear the heaviest responsibility for the evils of this age. Bishops enrich themselves partly by conferring Holy Orders upon "persons without virtue, unlettered, of evil reputation or unknown, without proper titles". In the monasteries, the strict rule is now a dead letter. Almsgiving is neglected; chastity is often violated. Papal exemptions cause the abbeys "to fall into great abuses and scandals". "Would it not be expedient that, without prejudice to the Holy Apostolic See, certain good persons, such as priors of convents or abbeys of neighbouring reformed monasteries, should be enabled to visit them as often as need should require?" (p. 180). Elsewhere, as a contemporary tells us, he spoke still more plainly: "the said Standonck has brought heavy charges against all cloisterers, because, as he saith, they keep not their Rule but lead a life dissolute and abominable and contrary to their vows: they are disobedient to their Superiors, and moreover there is no longer, in the Religious Orders, either chastity or poverty, but everywhere *proprietas*" (p. 52). Another deputy, Hugues de Malisset, was equally emphatic, and still more explicit as to direct papal and royal responsibility for these things.

> The first cause of disorder and dissolution comes from the fact that our Holy Father the Pope, at request from the King and certain princes, commends promiscuously monasteries and monastic churches and secular clerics, unripe both in sense and in age, inexpert in matters of [cloistered] Religion, and moreover (worse still), dissolute in their life and their dress; wherefrom the monks subject unto them take an evil example. (p. 192.)

Almost at the same moment, the pious humanist Robert of Gaguin wrote to Trithemius deploring the ruin of monastic sanctity; the lack of discipline in Western abbeys; "almost all the Orders collapsing together" (p. 204). At this same Council the abbot-general of Marmoutier pleaded for powers enabling the Prelates of the Benedictine Order to enforce the existing disciplinary statutes, "and especially the constitutions of Pope Benedict [XII], who laboured in his day to reform the said Order, which, for the above-mentioned or like reasons had fallen into great disorder".(6) The Abbot of Cîteaux emphasized that, partly through wars but still more through the *commendam* system, "priories and other commended houses are desolate and ruined, divine service diminished, and the intentions of their founders defrauded in many holy works". The numbers are reduced to a quarter of what they had been; books and charters and possessions are alientated; "women enter everywhere and the brethren go whither they will, whereby chastity and obedience are utterly destroyed, and all form of Religion is alienated". When the authorized visitors come to inspect, "scarce do they find any man to speak with; their ordinances are set at naught, and (what is most to be feared) they are often in danger of their persons".(7)

Other contemporaries sorrowfully recognized the same facts. Raulin insisted that *commendam* was ruining conventual discipline, and that monks sought out undisciplined houses where they might live at their will: therefore Church reform must begin from the Pope, as source of all commendations (p. 167). In 1498, he spoke plainly at the General Chapter of the Cluniac Order. Cloisterers, he said, ferociously resist those who seek to reform them. "Their name, formerly honourable before God, is becoming an object of scorn and mockery. We are now the reproach and the laughing-stock of all the people" (p. 132). His experience as reformer had by this time chastened all exuberant optimism: if we try to gain our ends by introducing a few reformed monks to an abbey, either the unreformed make their life a burden to them or, too often, these few righteous become leavened by the unredeemed lump: therefore the only efficacious course is to expel all and start afresh (p. 303). This, it may be remembered, was the conclusion to which experience had already brought the General Chapter of Windesheim. The great Synod of Lyons (1511) complained of the unbridled multitude of secular clergy and their ignorance; of the few Religious left in the cloister, and the decay even of those. It is a further symptom of the growing storm that it dealt also with the scandal of traffic in Indulgences. In 1515, the President of the Parlement begged the King to see that good bishops and abbots were appointed; "and good folk of Religion who are on the side of good observance and keeping of the state of

Religion and the observance of the Rule, and that the monasteries should be reformed and set upon a good footing" (p. 576). "A Chapter of Cluny affirmed, in 1504, that the ruin of monasticism grew worse from day to day. And Leo X himself wrote in 1516, 'The want of a Rule in the majority of monasteries; the immodest life of the nuns, has reached such a pitch that no man—king, prince, or faithful layfolk—retains respect for them'."(8) We can see why Michel Bureau wrote in his treatise on Reform (1496): "The word *reform* has rung so loudly in men's ears that, with whomsoever we converse, this is a most ordinary subject."(9)

Further evidence may be found in my Notes.

CHAPTER XXXVII

VISITORS' REPORTS

All this is in unison with the tone of Maillard's mission sermons, which are still among our best sources for French social and religious history of their day. In his Lententide course of 1498 he repeated the old medieval theme: those who will reach heaven are few indeed compared with the multitude who will be tortured to eternity in hell. The Church needs drastic purification: nowadays, when a child is unfit for the world, parents give him or her to the Church (p. 243). And, in 1496: "What of your priest, your Sir John, who has a fat cure of souls, yet who cannot decline in Latin his own name *Johannes*" (p. 208).

Among historians of our present generation, it has become almost as fashionable to decry such literary sources as it was in the past to overvalue them: the line of less intellectual resistance varies thus from generation to generation. But, just as the unimpeachable evidence of Traversari's diary shows us the essential truth of St Bernardino's sermons, so those of Maillard, Pépin, and other contemporaries are in general agreement with official documents. To these, therefore, we may now come.

Though the reports of orthodox monastic visitors are far rarer for France than for England, yet one very significant series has survived from the Benedictine Congregation of Tiron.(1) Imbart de la Tour drew attention to them, but found no space for details; yet those are too directly relevant to be omitted here. Tiron, like Camaldoli, was a comparatively small Congregation; but these reports supply a key to those brief generalizations which revivalists uttered from their pulpits, and indignant reformers at the solemn sessions of the États Généraux or of Ecclesiastical Synods. The first series of Tiron visits is in 1484–5; they are reported and signed not by any monk but by a professional notary, Feilletiz, whom the Abbot General employed as his secretary. Nine houses are dealt with. At B.M. de Tronchet in Brittany (November 13, 1485), they show plainly that visitations had fallen into desuetude and needed formal renewal in this year 1484. It was enjoined that a broken glass window should be repaired in the church, as also one bay of the vaulting, which threatened to fall. The other eight houses were visited in 1485. At "Castaneae" there were apparently only two monks, only one of whom was regularly resident; the Abbot General praised the building work which had been begun in the church. Next, at the priory of St-Antoine, there was again apparently only one monk in residence; it was enjoined "that he should make a missal for use in the priory, and repair the chapel windows, as soon as he conveniently could". The context suggests strongly that neither this "make" nor this "repair" mean that he was expected to do anything with his own hands. At Gué de Launois the Visitor "enjoined the Sacrist to cleanse decently, within a week, the linen cloth wherein the holy Eucharist of Christ was wrapped", and the abbot to repair the portable altar, which had been broken in two pieces. Some of the abbot's predecessors had alienated conventual possessions, and he himself had apparently lapsed into questionable business practices; the abbey's papers and muniments were in disorder, and the plate was carelessly kept. The daily reading of the Rule was neglected. At *La Palisse* the monks were not wearing the regulation habit, and the abbot was enjoined to appear personally before the Abbot General at Tiron, to answer for some matter unspecified in the record. At "Cohardinia" the priory was farmed out, to a cleric apparently, who asserted that a weekly Mass was said there. "And the visitor enjoined to the prior then absent, in the person of his farmer there present, that he should cause a missal to be made for the use of the said priory." A great part, at least, of the priory deeds were lost, and certain serious repairs were needed for the church and other buildings. At St-Michel-de-Cole, again, the priory was farmed out to the neighbouring prior of *La Roncière*, who asserted that he sang Mass there "at least twice a week". Repairs were needed; the chalice was of pewter, and needed cleaning; the chasuble needed mending. The Visitor "enjoined the prior to procure a missal for the church, and an altar-cloth". He was also bidden to repair the farm buildings thoroughly. At "*Audita*" the prior was dead, and therefore the house was at this moment in the hands of the Abbot General himself. The lands were let out on the *métayer* system to two farmers, and yielded 21 *livres* 10 *sols* in cattle alone, apart from corn; therefore the abbot decided to continue the lease as a profitable arrangement. At St-Léonard de Roncières, the abbot

enjoined upon Jean Martin, "métayer" of the priory, that, in recompense for his goods and possessions which he hath stored at the lower end* of the church or chapel of the said priory,(2) he should procure and buy at his own expense a chasuble, a stole and a maniple for the use and honour of this chapel or church, before Easter next. Also he enjoined upon the prior of the monastery, who was then absent, in the person of the said Martin, to procure a missal for use in the said chapel, and to cause to be made two glass windows, and paint therein two images, one of St Leonard, the patron saint of his Church, and the other of the Blessed Virgin or some saint of his own choice. The said Martin asserted that this prior, brother Jean Leillu, priest, celebrates Mass in the church twice every month. The Abbot enjoined also that the prior should cause the priory church or chapel to be whitewashed.

He enjoined also certain considerable repairs, which Martin was to carry out at the absent prior's expense; his rents to be sequestrated until the work had been completed. "Moreover, since (as [Martin] saith) the said chapel is polluted, seeing that the late prior, brother Jacques, used to lie in the said church with a certain woman dressed as a Franciscan nun; he ordained that it should be re-consecrated as soon as possible."

In 1486, the General Chapter of Tiron found that the abbot and monks of Joug-Dieu, instead of using the common refectory and the common dormitory "do not shrink from eating, drinking and sleeping daily in their own separate chambers, contrary to the disposition of law and of regular observance".

Next comes a series of three visitations in 1497. These are reported and signed by "Brehin, publicus apostolica auctoritate notarius et dicti Reverendi Secretarius". At Gué de Launay the Abbot General received from the convent a document acknowledging their subordination to the mother house; he records no fault. At "B.M. de Arcissis", in the diocese of

* "In inferiori parte"; it is just possible, but less probable, that the scribe means to describe a vault under the church.

Chartres, he was received by the Prior of *Resnon*, in the diocese of Séez

who was there actually resident for the time, and transacted the affairs of the lord abbot of *Arcis*, who was notoriously absent, by Antoine Garnier, sacristan of Arcis, and by the other brethren, two in number. In the Chapter-house he "held forth [*eructavit*] mellifluously concerning the Word of Truth and the teaching of the Rule, and delivered himself of wholesome warnings, rebuking and beseeching". To the sacrist of the monastery he commanded that a certain door in his quarters should be closed, or at any rate barred with a grating, as also the windows; that the latrines be furnished with a door and the church closed with a lock and key. Then, under the customary penalties, he strictly forbade the said sacrist to frequent henceforth the wife of a certain dweller hard by the said monastery, in the placed called Parvis; that he should not go to that place, but rather avoid it and the person of the said wife altogether. He likewise inhibited and strictly forbade brother Philippe Cormier to frequent from henceforth the house of one Fouquet, or to dare to talk or converse with the said Fouquet's wife, under pain etc. [*sic*], warning him that he should altogether avoid her company.

At *La Palisse* the record is obviously imperfect; it omits not only the usual notary's signature as voucher, but also the list of the community which he has promised, and all details of the "statutes and monitions or exhortations" which the Visitor is recorded to have sent, and the community to have accepted.

The next visitation among these fragmentary records is that of *Gué de Launay* in 1505 (November 6). There is now another Father Abbot, Louis; and he specifies his visitation as "primary". This document, with the next, suggests even more strongly than its predecessors that the Visitor's main preoccupation was less Church reform in the deepest sense, than to maintain the rights of the parent house over all its offspring. He preached in the chapter-house, exhorting the monks "to the observance of the Rule, and especially to obedience, the fruitful mother of all Religion and of monastic discipline". They received him dutifully, and there the record ceases. A few days later he was at Arcis (November 6). Here he paid them the bad compliment of preaching first in Latin in their chapter-house, and then translating his sermon into French. They begged for a fireplace in the dormitory, to warm themselves after matins; he directed that the abbot should reopen the old way, by which the community had been wont to pass through the calefactory, with its fireplace, as they went to and fro between dormitory and church. He prescribed also "that the abbot should glaze the unglazed windows in the church", a prescription sufficiently frequent in other visitations to remind us that medieval churches were often already in bad repair before the Reformation.(3) The secretary is now Gonessard.

Next comes an isolated report from Joug-Dieu (1510). By this time there is yet another secretary, Brehin. At *Joug-Dieu* the abbot was received by Philippe de Thère, acting as vicar to the abbot, "then notoriously absent", and seven other monks. Having assembled them in the chapter,

> he spake to them elegantly, giving many wholesome warnings from the Rule of St Benedict and from Holy Scripture. Then he spake to each in particular, rebuking them for their evil life, their evil management, saying that many abominable things [*nephanda*] had been told him concerning them; on which points they humbly submitted themselves to his constraint, forgiving them everything,* exhorting them thus to do well in future if they wished his mind to retain no recollection of such abominations.

He forbade their frequent visits to Villefranche and to the "locus" (i.e. convent) of *Chavannes*. He remained with them from December 22 to January 7, "always exhorting them to betterment, and expounding to them somewhat of Holy Scripture", and gave to some of the brethren breviaries of the use of Tiron, recently printed. The monasteries were beginning very slowly to realise the value of this new invention.

Two reports come from 1517, the second only just before Luther's appearance. First come Ferrières (July 2) where "one of the two young monks made an elegant speech in Latin words" in his honour, and the community made their due profession of obedience. At Gué de Launay (July 23) the Visitor consecrated the newly elected abbot, and his secretary has enregistered a long document rehearsing the claims made by the parent over this daughter house. It is significant that, although this document is entirely monastic, addressed from monks to monks, it is composed in French.

* *Sic*: the scribe's grammar is faulty, but the general sense is plain.

Next comes a series from the year 1528. Brehin is still secretary. At Craville la Roquefort the priory had sunk into the position of a mere "perpetual vicarage", in which two Masses weekly were celebrated for the parish. The next priory, Bacqueville, had farmed its revenues out, pretty clearly to a layman, who said that three Masses were sung there weekly, by "Dom Endes, here present and dwelling in the priory". St-Laurent-de-Ribue was also farmed out, to a lay *métayer*, who reported that one weekly Mass was celebrated.* The Visitor commanded that one bay of the church wall should be rebuilt within the year, since it threatened to fall. St-Blaise-de-Luy was farmed out, apparently to a layman: he reported two Masses weekly, one on Sundays and another "on no fixed day". St-Silvestre de Clara was immediately dependent on the parent abbey of Tiron, which had apparently absorbed both monks and revenues; one Mass was said per week in the church.

Six years later, *La Palisse* comes again into view. Because "the abbot was notoriously absent, and brother Jean Langloys, asserted to be his vicar, was lurking [*se latitabat*] at Ferté-Bernard"; the remaining twelve monks received the visitor. He ordered "that all doors of the cells [in the dormitory] shall have a window through which the prior may look into the cells whensoever it may please him". The dormitory is to be locked from Compline to Matins, and none but monks are to enter it. The church is to be locked after Vespers. The monks are no longer to wander abroad except two by two, by leave of the prior, and for some good cause: which things the Visitor laid upon the prior's conscience. They must not slip out by the side door next the bridge. They must conform their dress to the regular monastic habit. When a novice stays beyond three years without taking the vows, he must yet have his habit. As to Jean Langloys, the so-called abbot's vicar, since he had absented himself without excuse, and had told the sacrist, "I dare not face the abbot of Tiron, and therefore I am absenting myself", therefore he was now excommunicated as rebellious and disobedient, and the monks were absolved from all obedience

* We get two glimpses of this little Norman priory in the Register of Eudes Rigaud. This indefatigable Archbishop visited it twice, in 1264 and 1266; on each occasion he found that only a single monk was living there, in violation of the rule.

to him pending his repentance and satisfaction. The abbey evidently practised the often-forbidden system of clothes-money and pocket-money for the brethren, but this the Visitor tacitly allowed.

Finally, in 1559, we have a report from Tréhoudière. The Visitor

demanded of Michel le Halleur, dwelling now in the prior's house in the name of Clement Duval, the farmer of the priory...what service was performed therein. He answered that they had a Mass every Sunday, and on the five feasts of the Blessed Mary: moreover, that the prior was bound to celebrate a parochial Mass on four solemn holydays in the parish church of *Tourneur*, and in this priory yearly Masses on the two feasts of St Benedict. The visitor demanded of the said le Hasleur [*sic*] who was now prior of this priory; and he answered that the prior was the lord of Montflayne, esquire. To this prior then the visitor enjoined that he should buy another corporal and a chasuble, with a missal, for celebration of divine service. He enquired also as to the revenues of the said priory, and it was answered that the said farmer Duval, paid yearly to the said prior, as revenue of his priory, 460 *livres tournois*; upon which sum the aforesaid visitor stopped 200 *livres* for necessary repairs of the dwelling and grange and other buildings of the priory....In the presence of Sir Alexander Desportes, priest, John Desportes the elder, miller, George Leroy, husbandman, and other dwellers in the parish of *Tourneur*, witnesses.

There is no reason to suppose that Tiron was more decayed than the ordinary Benedictine standard. Before the middle of the thirteenth century, Endes Rigaud's visits in Normandy showed a number of small and decayed cells which make these records of 200 years later not only credible but natural and probable. In the light of these records, we need not wonder that the lay authorities should begin now to attack the problem in earnest. It will be noted that this first and fullest batch of Tiron visits, reviving definitely those long-neglected prescriptions of Innocent III and Benedict XII without which there was no serious hope of health in the monasteries, followed immediately upon the State action at Tours and that Synod of Sens which had caught the same inspiration of lay interference in last resort.

CHAPTER XXXVIII

INDIVIDUAL CASES

THE Tiron visitations, like so many of our parallel English records, leave us uncertain on two very important points: the personal equation of the Visitors, and their opportunities for doing their work with reasonable efficiency. When, for instance, a thing so illegal, and so manifestly prejudicial to religion, as the farming of a priory to a layman passes without comment, is this because the Visitor's moral sense was blunted, or because the evil custom was so ingrained (as we know it to have been sometimes elsewhere) that he felt it useless even to protest?

Let us now, therefore, pass in review the cases which Renaudet has collected from widely different sources, and where we know far more of the reformers' personality and the attendant circumstances. They all come so close together that strict chronological order is unnecessary: what concerns us is the essential similarity of these experiences, at Paris or fairly near, within a single generation.

Among the men's houses, the friaries were the most difficult. In Holland, a small group of reformed Dominicans had given some real promise. But in the greater field of France they failed. Standonck's friend Clérée joined them, and hoped to bring over the great Paris convent; meanwhile he tried his strength upon the important convent of Troyes, where he had the support of the municipality. The King obtained a papal bull in favour of reform here; and in 1497 Clérée attempted to bring them into conformity with the new statutes. Several of the friars ran away; the prior gave way only after nine days of imprisonment; the Minister Provincial of the Order appealed to the Parlement against these self-righteous intruders. "For the last hundred years" (retorted Clérée in public debate) "no Provincial has been known to reform a convent. It is for the Pope not to give way here, but rather to withdraw the reformed houses from obedience to their present superiors"; for it is natural that a reformed convent should be withdrawn from the jurisdiction of an unreformed Provincial. The Parlement gave judgment in his favour, and invited the Provincial to reform the rest.

The great Dominican convent of Paris—those "Jacobins", whose buildings were destined afterwards to shelter the most famous of all revolutionary clubs—yielded completely in theory. They promised to keep the Rule, gave up their keys and their private hoards from their cells: common life was re-established, and the gates were closed as the statutes demanded. The prior and subprior were deposed. But soon the younger students slid back into their former indiscipline, and the Observants, both Dominican and Franciscan, felt that further action was needed. Clérée and Maillard stepped in and secured the help of Cardinal Georges d'Amboise, whose spendid tomb is one of the greatest features in Rouen Cathedral. He was papal legate; and Alexander VI had lately acceded to his request and given him almost unlimited powers of interference and reform in all French houses whose income did not exceed 200 *livres tournois*,* notwithstanding exemptions or privileges, and with power to call in the secular arm. He now gave the Provincial six months to restore discipline by his own action. When this time of grace had expired, he agreed with Clérée that all resistance must be broken down.

About the beginning of February [1501] his Vicar, Antonio Flores, Bishop of Castellamare, visited the convent. It had been resolved that they should expel all students who were idle or ill-living, and replace them by Observantines. A few days later came Clérée with a certain number of Dominicans who belonged to the Dutch Congregation, but were all Frenchmen and taken from French convents. ...They dismissed about 120 students, under command to repair forthwith to reformed convents, and with the promise of recalling them whenever they deserved it. They protested loudly; and archers had to be called in to expel them. Next day, with a troop of armed students, they invaded the convent. "Upon one of the reformed friars, 77 years of age, they inflicted numberless injuries; they laid

* The limitation is noteworthy: it gave a precedent, consciously or not, for Henry VIII's similar limitation of his first suppressions (1536) to houses not exceeding £200 a year. Prejudiced writers, ignorant of the actual conditions, have attempted to argue from this to Henry's dishonesty or injustice. The limitation was in fact dictated by common sense; for it roughly marked off the small and impoverished houses in which discipline was commonly most decayed.

him on the floor, trod upon his belly and his stomach, and drew a knife upon him, so that he was in peril of death. Brother Jean Bernard, who held the office of Sacristan, was caught before the high altar, taken as a prisoner to the cloisters, cast to the ground and trodden under foot; his frock and his girdle were cut." The leader of the missionaries was struck with fists and staves. "There was a friar of the adverse party who had an iron mallet with which he thought to break the said Clérée's head." The reformers were driven out, and the old friars remained masters of the convent. But next day the archers appeared and laid siege to the friary; the Jacobins capitulated and admitted Clérée with his party. A few of the friars were taken to ecclesiastical prisons; the expelled students left Paris. (p. 327.)

Then came the turn of the Parisian Franciscans, the Cordeliers. In 1501, they were formally visited by Flores, the papal nuncio with Jean Rollin, Bishop of Autun. Terrified by the defeat of the Dominicans, they dared not at first to offer forcible resistance; they had recourse to comedy. As Jean d'Autun writes (in his *Chroniques de Louis XII*),

learning that the said reformers were coming, they hauled down the Body of our Lord and laid it upon the high altar; and there, all gathered together in the choir of their church and around the high altar, they set themselves to sing *Domine, non secundum peccata nostra facias nobis*. And when the said Bishops entered the choir, the said Cordeliers sang a versicle, all kneeling, wherein are the words *Adjuva nos, Deus salutaris noster*. Thus, then, they tarried a long while, chanting hymns and lauds and canticles, to the weariness of those who would have spoken to them, and who made signs to them that they should desist; but they would not; nay as soon as they had finished one they began another. Then was proclamation made, in the King's name, that they should cease and hold their peace; yet for all that they kept not silence, nor finished their chant, which endured four hours' long, so that the said Bishops returned to the Papal Legate, to whom they recounted the matters aforesaid.

Next day, the royal Procurator of the Grand Council, Pierre Bonnin, was able to obtain silence. Bishop Jean Rollin then addressed them. "He exhorted them", says Jean d'Autun, "not to touch, either themselves or by any intermediate person, either gold or silver* or house or ground.... The friars would not hear

* St Francis, in the 4th Chapter of his final Rule, had written "I strictly command all the Brethren that on no account shall they receive money or coin, whether with their own hands or through an intermediate person."

him. They asserted the need of money for their studies." Reformers were not listened to when they retorted that St Thomas Aquinas and St Bonaventura were friars who, without money, had yet studied successfully. The Cordeliers insulted Olivier Maillard, that Observantine who was at the root of this attempted reform; and the royal Procurator was not over-anxious to get into trouble for the sake of this preacher who had been accustomed to criticize men of law as frankly—not to say, fiercely—as his fellow churchmen. The semi-reforming legate, Georges d'Amboise, gave way; and Maillard retired to Languedoc, where he died within a year (p. 331).

The White Friars (Carmelites) gave much trouble also. They had a few houses of Strict Observance; and in 1502 the legate authorized a Reformed Congregation, with Albi for its centre. Those of Paris accepted a reformer, but soon wearied of him, and begged the Pope to appoint another (p. 350). They pleaded in Parlement against interference, but their plea was rejected (p. 355).

Next to the friars, the nuns gave most trouble. In France, as elsewhere, they could plead more cruel necessity than the men, and inveterate custom. Most of them had never really kept the two most emphatic papal decrees, that of strict claustration and the prohibition of dowries as savouring of simony. The story of the royal convent of Chelles is almost like that of Klingenthal. In 1483 (March 26) we find the abbess appealing to the King's Court against the bishop's intended visitation. The appeal was rejected, and the bishop's vicars visited the convent. They decreed a preliminary reform, which was not obeyed. In 1489, a new bishop visited with several of his canons. They found grave irregularities and ordered a fresh reform. The nuns appealed to the Archbishop of Sens, as Primate of the province. Then Olivier Maillard came forward, and made fresh attempts (March 1491 and April 1492). On this last occasion he came with signed letters of vicariate from the bishop, accompanied by another distinguished reformer, Jean Quentin. But (in the words of the reformers' pleas first in the Court of the Châtelet and then before the Parlement) "the said Abbess and her nuns received the said Maillard with derision and mockery, taking no account of him or of those who came with him. And the said Abbess even departed from the chapter-house when the said Maillard preached his [official] sermon [as episcopal commissioner], and made many other insolences and derisions" (p. 194). Judgment was not given until May 25, 1495: the new Bishop of Paris was determined to grapple with this scandal, and the Parlement gave him a free hand. But the nuns pleaded papal exemption; and nothing was done until 1500, when Louis XII himself issued letters for the reform of his ancestors' foundation. Then the abbess resigned. After a disputed election, a good abbess was at last elected, and the abbey became a member of the newly reformed Congregation of Fontevrault (p. 314).

So, again, with the Dominican nunnery of Poissy, another royal abbey. In 1506, Amboise, as papal legate, commissioned Clérée with full powers for reform. "He found it in the greatest disorder: there was no community of possessions; men and women came in freely; each nun had her own room, and they had even given up the dress of their Order." After violent litigation, they were bound by the judges "at least to silence and regularity" (pp. 450–2). But meanwhile difficulties were created by the long and desperate litigation between Conventuals and Observants in the Dominican Order, further embittered by nationalism, since the relaxed French resented the intrusion of reforms from Holland. Not until 1514, at the King's interference, was the quarrel appeased, at least outwardly, by Leo X, who permitted the foundation of a separate Gallican congregation. Then, at last, "an energetic intervention of [the King's] authority compelled the nuns of Poissy to obey" (pp. 570–5). But even this settlement was on a nationalistic basis: the Dutch Dominicans had reformed them, but the convent must remain subject to those of France (p. 558). At Yerres, the Bishop of Paris found that "layfolk entered freely: some lodged there. In August 1514, he warned the abbess to restore claustration, but without result; his vicars, among whom was Jean Emery, were no more successful. In December he went himself to Yerres with Etienne Gentil and Jean Raulin. The nuns refused to yield. The bishop decided to bring in forcibly a few sisters chosen from the restored convents in his diocese, and besought the King's support." Yet next year Yerres was still unruly, and another nunnery, Gerzy, needed the intervention of Queen and Parlement (pp. 566, 587).

Much trouble was given also by the sisters at the Hôtel-Dieu of Paris, that great royal hospital where, during the Black Death, the chronicler singles out these nurses and "a few Religious" as the only consecrated persons in Paris who really faced the plague and ministered to the sick.(1) Its ordinary official Visitors were the canons of Notre-Dame, at its very door. In 1482 it was found to be in a bad state (p. 220); and in 1496 there were scandalous scenes, unfortunately on both sides. The Chapter of Notre-Dame fixed a date at which the priests of their dependent parishes should dismiss from their houses all suspected women, and another at which they undertook to reform the Hôtel-Dieu. Peculation was rife there, the sick were neglected and the brethren and sisters kept ill their vows of chastity and poverty. The dishonest master, Lefèvre, was put into prison until he should render his accounts, and Jean Laisné succeeded him. Then, however,

a band of nuns and young brethren, with cudgels and kitchen knives, went up to Laisné's room, crying, "Judas, traitor, thou art dead! Thou hast sold the Master to the false Jews; but thou shalt die this hour and pay it dear." They broke in the door, and a nun armed with a hatchet would have killed him. The terrified monk was saved from their hands, but he took a malignant fever and died in a few days. The Dean [of Notre-Dame] and two other canons, who had hastened to the Hôtel-Dieu to restore peace, had to retire under fire of the insults of the nuns and brethren, the servants, and patients who had been brought from their beds: "Thieves, murderers, whoremongers! you have your fat harlots in your houses, and you come hither to destroy the Hôtel-Dieu!"

The Chapter gave way for the moment: a commission sat under appointment of the Parlement and appointed a new master; but the nuns protested that they would not obey him, and reviled as "hypocrites" the girls who made their confessions to him, in the ordinary course. All this while, real discipline was rendered almost impossible by the open quarrel between the Chapter, the bishop, and the archbishop. Months passed before it was possible to insist that sisters and brethren should conform to their monastic Rule. One sister was banished in disgrace to the hospital of Corbeil, another imprisoned, another sent home, and four were compelled to apologize publicly to the master. Yet, in less than three weeks, the fire had blazed out again, and fresh royal letters were issued without effect. To make matters worse, the newly appointed officials

showed extreme awkwardness and indiscretion; and Émery, one of the Canons, let himself go to brutal excesses. In February Sister Catharine the Blind having gone out without the Master's permission, he cast her into prison. "And this was about three in the afternoon, and she had not broken her fast; there he left her until ten of the evening, when he came with three men disguised as women, took and tied her hands, and her skirts were turned up all naked and she was enormously beaten and mutilated, cast to the ground, and two ribs broken; and they left her in such state that she spat blood and was in great danger of her person. The said Émery said that he would have done the like to the Prioress if he had found her.... Sister Jeanne la Bouchère, a nun, hath had her teeth broken by a blow from a key, by those who have been put newly into the said Hospital." On the 26th February the nuns presented a petition to the Parlement against the Chapter; the case went against them.

But they persisted, and, in April, the new master and Émery were removed, and the Chapter tried to mend matters by introducing ten or twelve brethren or sisters who were willing to keep the Rule (p. 229). In 1498 another reform was attempted, but remained incomplete. In 1504 the civil authorities stepped in. By this time, as Renaudet says, "the heroic period of reforms was past", and ecclesiastical disciplinarians relied more and more frankly upon the King's Courts and the royal officers for getting anything done. Here at the royal hospital, under the King's own eyes, was an obvious call for such interference. Raulin and three others were called in; they expelled eleven of the Augustinian sisters, and replaced them by Franciscans. But quarrels and strife still continued; so the King intervened again, and all the original staff were dismissed: for, "despite the reform of 1498, the brethren and sisters refused any obedience to [the Canons]. In the City, at Court, in the Parlement, they were held responsible for the evil administration of the hospital and the misery suffered by the sick, who, in winter, were driven by lack of room and of beds to lie pell-mell on the pavement of the wards" (p. 440). On the whole, "public opinion was more excited by the reform of nuns than of monks" (p. 449). Of the older Orders, there were five men's monasteries at Paris whose wealth and dignity put them in the first class. Ste-Geneviève alone seems to have stood in no great need of reform; the other four all gave serious trouble.

In 1486, the Benedictines at the royal abbey of St-Denis complained formally to the Parlement against their abbot, who was also Bishop of Lombez. He refuses (they said) to undertake the least repair in the buildings, which are falling into ruin. The bells "are in danger of falling, through fault of the woodwork, which is all rotten and broken." Rain comes into the church, and the cloisters, and St Clement's chapel. The stream which passes under the abbey is obstructed; the barns and stables threaten collapse. The food is insufficient; although the abbey lands produce more than 600 bushels of corn, the monks are rationed with one loaf each, and that mouldy; for the abbot sells the good wheat and reserves the damaged for his brethren. (p. 19.)

At St-Martin des Champs, the great Cluniac house of Paris, the reforming commission of 1501 found only twenty-one monks. They reported that "in course of time, through the fault, guilt and negligence of certain among their predecessors ...and of their officials, they discontinued to live in common, under obedience to the Rule....Thus they have lived for some time separately and in peculiar, as proprietaries, and at their own will, without regard for their profession and first institution and foundation, or for the great scandal which this brought to their Religion" (*ibid.*). The Abbot of Cluny at this time was Jacques d'Amboise, who had inherited something of Bourbon's reforming ideals. With the help of Raulin, he tried to bring these twenty-one monks to a strict observance of the statutes. "But the brother of the defunct Prior (who, beside the see of Barbeaux, the priory of St-Nicolas at Albi, and a canonicate at the Ste-Chapelle of Paris, 'benefices of great value'), came now to claim the *commendam* of St-Martin, which the late Prior had resigned to him by a deed sealed two days before his death, and with which, as he claimed, the Pope had 'provided' him." Raulin brought the case before the Parlement. The bishop's advocate argued, only too truly, that Amboise himself had managed to get the *commendam* of a few abbeys, in addition to his bishopric. The reformers answered "describing the ruins accumulated by this *commendam* system, denying the Bishop's assertion that he had effected repairs at Barbeaux, and accusing him of keeping 24 hounds with moneys which belonged to the poor". The Parlement dared not to decide between two such powerful litigants, and it was left to the arbitration of Cardinal Georges d'Amboise, who finally persuaded the bishop to abandon his claim (pp. 321–8). Raulin turned now to the Collège de Cluny, inhabited by Cluniac monks studying at the university. "They came, on the 2nd of February, with 13 monks from St-Martin. For fear of meeting the resistance which had almost checked Clérée at the Dominican convent, they came with an escort of archers. They forced the gates, and treated the elderly monks with the utmost rigour. Three officials were deposed and expelled. A sick brother, who was known to be hostile to reform, was left uncared-for" (p. 329). The royal abbey of St-Germain des Prés, which gives its name to the present Boulevard, was notoriously relaxed, but difficult to touch. Raulin and Bourgoing were commissioned to visit it in 1501. The monks protested afterwards to the King's Court: "the Visitors had not acted in the spirit of Apostolical correction; instead of following the seven degrees enumerated by St Benedict, they had begun with the very last, that is, expulsion. They had altered the ancient customs and ceremonies of the abbey, and reduced the offices by half. But the Court rejected their appeal" (p. 331; cf. p. 353). This it was which inspired the indignant treatise of Guy Jouenneaux, to which we shall come in chapter XXXIX. Then came the abbot's death and the election of his successor. At this time (1508) the abbey, with its immense wealth and palatial buildings, was occupied by only twenty-five monks. The prize was at once claimed by Briçonnet, Cardinal Archbishop of Reims, whom the King favoured and the monks obediently elected. This man

contented himself with drawing the conventual revenues, and seldom appeared there. But the rigorists still desired the restoration of this house; and Cardinal d'Amboise [the papal legate] approved them. Briçonnet was persuaded to resign his title, on consideration of a yearly pension, in favour of his son Guillaume, Bishop of Lodève, who befriended humanists and scholars, and sincerely favoured reform, although he himself had largely profited from the abuses which were ruining Church discipline.

The job was arranged; the Pope approved, and the new abbot entered into his father's place *in commendam*. The first effect was to compel the reformers to abandon the abbey (p. 355). But the bishop himself drew up certain articles of reform; whereupon seven of the monks revolted, and elected another. There was long and bitter legislation, with public scandal: at length, the monks were compelled to admit the Bishop of Lodève and to accept his articles of reform (p. 453). Here, then, was a commendator who had a real sense of decency; and, since the King was interested in the reform of his own abbey, the upshot was far more favourable than in many other cases. In 1513 Briçonnet called upon the reformers of Chezal-Benoît to help him and Louis XII insisted that the matter was too urgent to wait for the next sitting of the Chapter General. In January 1514, thirty reformed monks were sent to St-Germain; "the opponents fled, and were little regretted....Since men neither expected nor desired the return of the fugitives and the old monks were awaiting their first opportunity of abandoning the Rule, Briçonnet asked the [Chezal-Benoît] Chapter to establish its missionaries definitely at St-Germain, and added a few new companions" (p. 564). About the same time, another commendator, the Bishop of Auch, reformed his own abbey of Lagny by threatening the secular arm in case of resistance (p. 566).

St-Victor, the last of these five great abbeys, will come into the next chapter.

CHAPTER XXXIX

A BENEDICTINE REFORM

EVEN before the impulse given by Charles VIII at Tours, a reforming party had gathered consistency within the Benedictine Order itself. In 1479 a monk of noble birth named Pierre du Mas had been appointed to the rich abbey of Chezal-Benoît (*Casale Benedicti*), near Bourges. He at once began there a series of reforms, at great personal sacrifice to himself. He died in 1492, but his successor continued his work. Chezal-Benoît was recognized as a model abbey; and in 1494 the Pope designated its abbot, with two others, to visit and reform other Benedictine monasteries in France. Three years later, the great abbey of St-Sulpice at Bourges received for its head a monk of Chezal-Benoît, Guy Jouenneaux or Jouvenneaux (in Latin, *Guido Juvenalis*); and in 1499 St-Sulpice formally pledged itself to adopt the new reforms. A second great abbey in 1500, and in 1502 a third, threw in its lot with Chezal-Benoît. From this time forward these four monasteries virtually formed a new Congregation, and held a yearly chapter for reform and discipline; in 1505 the Congregation of Chezal-Benoît was formally and legally constituted. It was ratified in 1508 by the papal legate after consultation with the University of Paris and many eminent French ecclesiastics; and in 1516 Leo X formally approved the new Congregation, now consisting of five monasteries. The King, who had championed their cause at the papal court, now added his own formal approval. If Pope and King had been sincere in pushing Church reform even to their own pecuniary loss, the new Congregation might have had a great career before it. But it only succeeded in gaining a temporary footing in four other abbeys of monks and in a few convents of women; by the end of the sixteenth century it was practically dead. How terribly these reforms of the late fifteenth and early sixteenth century were hampered by royal and papal politics, and how little came of them in the end, may be read in Imbart de la Tour.(1)

This reform of Chezal-Benoît called forth two treatises of great importance for monastic history; the *Epistola Paraenetica* of Charles Fernand, and the *Monastice Reformationis Vindicie* of Guy Jouenneaux. Dom Ursmer Berlière, who has written the fullest account yet compiled of the Chezal-Benoît reform, has disappointingly little to say about the contents of either of these two volumes; or, indeed, about the main historical questions involved in the whole story.(2) The two men had taught at Paris University together, had joined the reformed monks about the same time, and fought with the same weapons for the same cause. Fernand's younger brother, Jean, prefixed to the treatise of Jouenneaux a long poem in which he deals even less tenderly with the unreformed monks than our author himself.

Jouenneaux was born about 1450, probably at or near Le Mans. Like the two Fernands, he acquired real distinction as a Latinist at Paris. He published a commentary upon Terence, several other classical books, and a French translation of the Benedictine Rule which has gone through ten editions.(3) He took the vows about 1492 at Chezal-Benoît, was elected Abbot of St-Sulpice at Bourges in 1497, and in 1500 was chosen by the papal commissary as his coadjutor "to visit and reform the monasteries of Benedictine monks and nuns in France".(4) He died in 1507, one of the last of that group of reformers who can be credited with real inspiration. His reforming energies provoked not only passive resistance but active and public opposition: hence his *Defence of Monastic Reform*. This was dedicated to the Parlement of Paris, and published in 1503, in answer to certain protests, and attacks upon the reformers, which had been circulated by a champion of the unreformed monks of St-Germain-des-Prés. In order to meet their main objections, Jouenneaux describes the state in which the majority of French monasteries then were; and it is this which makes his work so valuable. It portrays from within, and with convincing directness, the same state of things which can be inferred from official visitation documents, but only by a laborious process of analysis and synthesis.(5)

In the first book (chap. 5) Jouenneaux enters upon "A confutation of that feigned excuse put forth by monks, who say that they never thought of such a life [as this reformation] when they entered into the Order to which are added a few words concerning the abominable sin of private property among monks, and their false excuse in this matter." These "proprietary" monks seek to justify themselves by pleading their abbot's permission, an excuse which is at variance with plain facts. "For, when they are driven to the last resort, and commanded to restore the money to their abbot, they forthwith lay aside all shame and flatly refuse it; nay, they are ready to fight the matter at law against their own father [in God]."

As a result (chap. 7)

among those whose profession and habit would seem to proclaim them monks, many [*plerique*] I grieve to say, have nothing in common [with real monasticism], but heap up for themselves great sums of gold.... In truth they bear no mark of Religion save in their tonsure alone, and even that is so small that we see plainly how ashamed they are to be known for Religious.... You may find some of these men playing games forbidden both by church and civil law, by Pope and by Emperor; yea, and that openly, not without frequent blasphemy and execrable curses; and such men, being of honourable birth, escape all punishment even though they be public and notorious swearers (not to say, perjurers). Of such men the satirist hath well said: "the censor pardons the crow, and vexes the dove"; and all just-minded men are well aware how great a scandal is thereby generated. Some, again, frequent the clamours of the chase, galloping after wild beasts upon horses that wellnigh outrun the very greyhounds—those "hounds and slender coursing-dogs" (as the poet writes) whereof the monks fear not to nourish whole packs at the expense of the poor, feeding them on such victuals as are the poor man's right.

Here, of course, we have Chaucer's monk to the life. Then comes the vagabond of the sort which our Father Benedict expressly came to supersede. "Such monks never visit monasteries, but haunt the taverns; never in one place, but ever running up and down, hither and thither; not only with itching eyes and ears and tongues, but with itching feet also."

"We may sometimes meet such monks who lack scarce anything that knights have; whether on foot or on horseback, they bear a sword at their side as though they were ready for war. Can this sort of petty men like tyrants boast that they entered into Religion with the purpose of leading this irreligious life?"

And yet (chap. 8) they plead that "when we entered into Religion, we proposed to lead the same life which, in those days, the elder monks in our monastery were wont to lead". It is not the question, argues our pitiless reformer, what life this older generation of life *did* lead, but what they *ought to have* led. "Great numbers [*magna pars*] of them knew not even the works of the Rule, and many were frequently wandering astray from its precepts, not acknowledging it as their mistress."

Chapter 11 deals with the shame which such men bring upon their Order; "so that the name of *Monk*, once so glorious, is turned to disgrace and to derision, as is plainly proved by many men of the monastic profession. For honest monks are much concerned, if another call them by the name of their profession; as we may see from that monk who lately brought an action of slander against a secular person, upon the sole ground that this fellow had called him *Thou Monk!*" They often come in for filthy lucre's sake;

their household expenses are rather increased than diminished [by the change of profession]. They have as many servants to wait upon them, the same elaboration of meals; or rather, to confess the truth, they have incomparably more than formerly. They forget their former poverty and multiply their servants; they live the life of Bacchanals, and become far more intolerable than others who were nursed in affluence; since nothing is more intolerable than a poor man raised to wealth.

Sometimes, indeed, "a single wealthy monk may challenge the fortunes of many rich worldlings".

Chapter 13 deals with the unchristian results of *commendam* and *proprietas*.

Indeed, we may see that charity is now driven out from almost all monasteries; wherein some are hungry, and others are drunken; some are sick of surfeit and others of famine; one man's head aches for the emptiness of his belly, and another's for his fulness; some are clothed in frocks woven of fine and slender threads, and lined with outlandish furs; others die for chill and cold. Whither hath that hospitality now departed, which was so sedulously shown by the patriarchs, which our Lord commended and the Apostles prescribed, and which St Benedict so clearly commanded? It is become so utterly strange and foreign to our monasteries, that its very name hath perished in oblivion. Such Hospitality with her sister Almsgiving, hath bidden a long farewell to our convents.... You may see monks in the administration of country benefices, as they call them, (monks who, living in little separate communities of two or three persons, become, if we are to believe St Bernard, mere synagogues of Satan)—you may see such so busy and assiduous in their chase after even the smallest gains, that they far outdo secular folk. And thus, stuffed fat with gold, they go at last the way of all flesh, and their abbots inherit their savings.... Woe, woe! for we see a horrible thing in the house of God. Whom but idolaters do we see ministering, whose god is in their belly? For, in many monasteries, we may see ministers of the altar, whose duty it is to read a gospel or epistle or a lesson from the prophets, coming impudently to his ministry fulfilled with feasting and with wine, so that they do not so much sing as belch forth the sacred words; not so much recite them, as vomit them.

In Book II our author passes on from the sin of greed to that of sloth (chap. 3). The monk should exercise himself in fervent prayer, reading at certain regular hours, and manual work as a relaxation for the mind.

But (with shame I speak it), how slothful are many of our Order! ...Sometimes, sunk in sloth, they visit the men and women of the neighbourhood and fall into talk with light women [*mulierculis*], wherein they stick neither at words of shame nor biting speeches that besmirch the fair fame of others; so that, not unfrequently, all shame is lost, and they go on brazenly to detestable wickedness. For their very eyes bring ravage into [*depredantur*] their soul, and the castle of their heart is utterly overthrown, so that neither the inner wall of continence is left standing nor the outer wall of abstinence.

In chapter 9 Jouenneaux (like Maillard and Raulin and the other reformers) attacks the ideal of "easy religion".

Is not the state of Religion rather a discipline and an exercise of reaching onwards to the very perfection of Charity? A monastery's place of work is not in a vast extent of fields, nor among sunny hill-sides, nor in towns or cities, although many who profess Religion frequent such places more than their cells. They are more in the place of games than in their monastery, more in the market-place than in church, more in the busy streets than in the cloister; their hands are more accustomed to hawks or falcons than to the book of the Gospels or to manual labour. Do these things need reformation, or not?...Many who should have gone forward in Religion are become far worse than when they walked the easy ways of the world. Whence cometh this, but that, in entering Religion, their only task was to seek bodily indulgence, in process of time, in some fat "benefice" (as they call it)? Moreover, did not these men's parents pave the way for them to fill up what was wanting in their own wealth, from the patrimony of Christ, thinking more of themselves in devoting their sons to Religion, than of their children's salvation? Hence it is that no enquiry whatsoever is made into the manner of life that is fostered in such a monastery; for morals are their very last care; of morals is the latest question, or truly no question at all; nay, the many would be unwilling to suffer reformation and a regular life in his monastery, since the very hope of money, which had enticed him in, would thus be lost. This is why those who have thus taken the vows can never be brought to a regular life, since they have never tasted such a life even with the outer edge of their lips.

Chapter 10. The unreformed monks defend themselves by a casuistical distinction between "essential points" of the Rule, which it is a mortal sin to violate, and "simple warnings" contained in it, the transgression of which is only a venial fault.

Now, if the end at which we aim [that is, Poverty, Obedience and Chastity], be a matter of strict command, are not these means also, which are necessary to reach this aim, equally strictly enjoined upon us?...Do you not confess that the Three Vows are bound upon you by strict command? That, at least, you cannot deny. I ask, then; why are your papers and your parchments cumbered with these "simple warnings" which (as you suppose) no monk need touch even with the tips of his fingers?...In my opinion, these "warnings" are the prohibition of eating flesh except in case of necessity, the rules of regular fasts, of keeping silence, of using no soft beds and wearing no linen shirts, and other observances of the same kind. These, you will admit, were not added to no purpose, but are of great use, methinks, in safeguarding the three Vows. Wherefore, then, dost thou not use them as helps of the greatest utility towards the work that thou hast to do? Why then dost thou not rather command than discourage their observance?

Chapter 12:

How can these men possibly fulfil their vow of obedience while (for example) they fear not to transgress the Rule in so many things, which are called in their language simple warnings?...Nay, worse still, to patch up incongruous texts whereby they may prove to dull wits either that these frequent transgressions are no sin at all, or at least that they are scarcely sinful?...Perchance some monks could find some small palliation for their fault, when they beheld no other course of living in the whole region [where they dwelt]. But, now that the light hath appeared, what sort of excuse can they weave for themselves? For they may now see most clearly that the life is different in many [reformed] monasteries, where the monks live according to the dictates of the Rule.

Chapter 13:

Seeing that men of our profession burn with so consuming an itching to eat flesh, as if this were the human weakness of striving after all forbidden things and desiring all that hath been denied unto them, prithee let us see what St Jerome thought concerning flesh-eating. "To eat flesh" (saith Jerome) "and to drink wine, and to fill the belly to repletion, is to sow the seeds of lust: wherefore Ezekiel writeth 'This was the iniquity of thy sister Sodom; pride, fulness of bread and abundance of idleness was in her and in her daughters, neither did she strengthen the hand of the poor and needy.'"...But thou wilt say "To what purpose then were swine created?" To this we shall answer forthwith, like the give and take of boys at play, "Why then were vipers made, or scorpions?"...Swine and boars and other beasts were created for soldiers and wrestlers, shipmen and miners, and others devoted to violent labours, that such men might have food to sustain the vigour which their bodies need.

Chapter 14:

Our adversaries plead that Abraham and other Old Testament worthies ate flesh: true, but those men had not, willingly and deliberately, made a solemn profession to abstain from it. Benedict XII, it is true, did at last give way, and decree that monks might neglect their vow for three days a week. But "what impelled the Pope to issue this statute, except that the Monastic Order had become so corrupt as to eat the fat of animals, and perhaps pounded flesh also,(6) even on days when church custom forbade it? So that, (as I have heard), this hath come to pass so often at a certain great monastery, that the poor folk, coming to their wonted repast, and scenting the odour of flesh, or at least of fat, fled away in horror, choosing rather to suffer hunger than to violate the common rite of the Church.(7) Whether this be true indeed, I know not; for I have it only on hearsay. But I am compelled to believe it by a certain Council celebrated at Aix-la-Chapelle—no General Council, but a Synod of prelates—in which Synod certain assembled abbots, whose names I know not, decreed in I know not what ill-considered spirit, (for we must hope that the decree had not been considered) that monks should use [for cooking on fast days] an oil made from bacon. O noble statute, to be celebrated for many centuries! After all, no decree can make bacon into anything but bacon; out of the abundance of the heart the mouth speaketh, and their tongue hath betrayed their true manner of life. Would that they had been sleeping in their beds when they uttered such words, and when, by these vain decrees of theirs, they were not ashamed to brand their glorious Order with the mark of infamy!"...When monks unhesitatingly transgress upon the ground which layfolk avoid through reverence for the Church, they thereby heap up a grievous reproach upon the whole Order; in so much that the very name of monk, exalted once to the very stars in glorious praise, is now become a laughing stock and an abomination—[*risui pateat et horrori*].

Chapter 15. It is not as though they even restricted themselves to Benedict XII's licence.

For We know well that, wheresoever they may be, they abstain not from flesh-eating; and (which is a grave source of scandal) whithersoever they go outside the monastery, they are not ashamed to eat flesh, as if they were layfolk, publicly and indiscriminately and in the presence of all men, whether in cities and in wine-taverns or in country villages. Sometimes they eat in the houses of their gossips, although the law forbiddeth them all such relationships,(8) or again among citizens, at whose feasts they are as frequent guests, or more frequent, than even worldly-minded folk; at other times they eat in closets and in private chambers.

Chapter 16. There is equal neglect of Benedict XII's command that silence should be maintained at meals while one monk reads from some book of devotion.

See now how ye obey this mandate, ye who not only care to read nothing when ye go abroad, but even within your own walls ye defraud the law, rather affording a mere sip or foretaste of reading, at the beginning of the meal, than truly reading [throughout the repast]. For, scarce hath the briefest sound of reading reached your ears, when ye hear also "here endeth the Lesson!" and the reading is past, and busy talk settles down upon the company. Meanwhile quarrels arise, with backbiting and buffoonery and laughter and discussions, not concerning books but concerning meats. The argument is not of divine things, but of the sweetest and mellowest wine; and at length, when the mealtime hath been spent in vanities, some monk, mellow with liquor, mounteth into the pulpit, not indeed to read but to gulp forth a word or two with his sweetened breath; or, if thou wilt, to pour out wine to the company. When this man hath gulped out his strong wine for a brief space, then they arise from table, despatch the hymn as quickly as may be, and disperse each to his own fancy. Some cast off their frocks forthwith and gird themselves to a game of tennis; those who have plenty of money, are not always ashamed to lend themselves to games that the law forbids; and some will oftentimes gamble the whole night through. Others visit their neighbours, men and women, or hasten to tread the streets of the city, pretending that they are about the business of their offices. Alas! in those early days when our Order first began, who would have believed that monks would fall to such a depth of sluggardy!

These evils which we have here exposed in our Profession are no trumped-up charges, but seem to be committed everywhere in our Order....If there be any who are displeased at these words, they betray themselves, for they love not the Order if they will not condemn its corruption and its faults. Wherefore I make answer to all such men in those words of St Gregory: *Melius est quod scandalum oriatur, quam veritas relinquatur.** For this monition of ours is no detraction, but rather a loving attraction to the amending of faults.

Book III, chapter 2, deals with the monks' plea that they enjoyed papal exemptions, and nobody but a *Legatus a Latere* could legally touch them. He contends that the exemption they claim must be fictitious, since it is in contradiction to Canon Law, and he cannot believe that a Pope should "grant to vice a loose rein and give men, by his indulgence, an occasion of offending God's goodness".

Chapter 5:

Thou pleadest noisily, moreover, and croakest foolishly that divine service is diminished, and that the monastic constitutions and laudable customs are being changed. Here, as ever, thou art astray; for divine service is rather increased; nay, to speak more truly, that which hath been ruined is restored. Thinkest thou that God is truly worshipped where a man lifteth up his voice without his mind?...where there is no reverence for sacred things? where there is no silence—nay, rather contentions and quarrels. For indeed I know a monastery wherein the brethren, grown old in evil days, were so torn with mutual quarrels that, when they sang any versicle together in choir, they would cast sacks full of insults at each other, hurling threats of worldly loss backward and forward [as they sang]; and this, for the sake of Christ's tunic, which (more iniquitous than the soldiers who crucified our Lord) they tore between them,† as indeed we may see the brethren do publicly in almost all monasteries. For each monk

* "Better that scandal should arise than that truth should be abandoned"; a sentence dear to St Bernard.

† I.e. they quarrelled over their shares in the monastic endowments, the "patrimony of Christ".

claimeth his own part of Christ's patrimony; one is Almoner, and giveth no alms, but filleth his purse with the money of the poor; another is Cellarer, and should rightly be father of the monastery, next to the Abbot, caring for the food and clothing of the brethren; yet indeed his chief care is for himself. He feedeth himself, laying up money and stores for many years, and dealing meanwhile like a niggard in those things which custom biddeth him minister to the rest. Another is Hostillar, yet without hospitality; for that word is almost dead in our monasteries; since, among these deformed monks, none cares any longer to keep up hospitality. I have heard how, in one most famous monastery, there is indeed a guesten-house, but foul with dirt and squalor, containing one, or at most two beds, and those almost always neglected and rarely spread [for guests]. Yet doth St Benedict so commend hospitality to us, that he biddeth the Abbot to eat ever with the guests—not with his neighbour and acquaintance, or with the townsfolk, or with ladies and great men of this world; for in our Rule I find no mention of ladies, howsoever honourable they be, nor of intimate friends. Therefore saith St Jerome; "let women seldom or never cross the threshold of thy guesten-house; for that man cannot live with all his heart in God's presence who is open to the conversation of women."

After a quarter of a page of similar anti-feminist quotations, Jouenneaux proceeds:

Another monk is called Infirmarer, in name but not in deed, in mere sound but without true effect, for in nowise doth he affect the sick Brethren. For if, in one of these deformed monasteries, a monk be moneyless and sick, then his parents must be told of his sickness, that they may send to him if they will.* For each striveth for himself alone, and it is seldom indeed that he careth for another; and he who hath money layeth it by and storeth it up for himself, never to be brought forth until the monk shall have given up the ghost, and the Abbot shall bid men turn his whole cell upsidedown and search every corner of his furniture. Another monk is called steward—or, in their own language, Sacrist—though indeed he is far more careful of pelf than of sacred things. He is lynx-eyed for offerings and for droppings of wax tapers, oftentimes complaining that the service is too long drawn out, and that the tapers are thereby too prodigally consumed. Yet he would seem indeed to have no just matter of complaint against long-drawn services, since all hasten forth [from the church] with what speed they may, so that oftentimes it sufficeth

* The complaint that the sick are neglected appears with startling frequency in visitatorial records. In the earliest existing (Odo Rigaldi, 1248–69), it occurs almost as frequently as in later visitations; and it is dealt with in Pope Gregory IX's Statutes of 1235.

some of them to gabble the beginning and the end of their verse. What better speed than this couldst thou require, Brother Sacrist? Moreover, they are so hasty that their lips have no time to pause in the midst of the verse, nor do they keep the *dipsalma*, or interval of silence between verse and verse: in truth, they could invent no more voluble fashion of chanting, unless thou wouldst have them think the psalms, or beckon them with their fingers, instead of pronouncing the words! Thinkest thou now that these monks with their Abbot are walking in a safe way, when they have thus divided Christ's patrimony among themselves? It is for others to judge after their own conscience; but God forbid that I should walk in that way! Moreover, in some monasteries, words of contumely fall thick amidst the psalmody, and are bandied hither and thither from mouth to mouth. At matins and at other hours, the psalms must needs give place to these revilings, so that the choir of psalm-singers might rather be taken for a tavern full of drunken folk than for a choir of chanting brethren. The monks, still burdened with the flesh which they devoured at supper, and drenched with drink, sigh not with devotion but from the gorge,* and many, who know neither to temper their wine nor to use it with moderation, smell so strong of liquor that, if they had to give the kiss of peace, they would seem to be offering less a kiss than a draught of wine.

Chapter 6:

Of the extraordinary banquetings of monks, and of their more shameful belly-worship.

Moreover, this multitude of servants, which St Benedict never instituted, hath bred a certain worldly custom in some monasteries, that the monks, after Prime, betake themselves forthwith to the kitchen or to some other corner of the monastery, excepting always those who are under necessity of celebrating Mass—*necessity*, I say, for there are few in a monastery of this kind who are wont to celebrate for devotion's sake, unless this fatal money be added also†—and there, (that I may express the barbarous deed in barbarous words) they devour their "Prime-morsel" (*offam prime*), under which appellation and circumlocutory phrase is comprised hot broth with bacon or mutton floating therein. There, then, as we may well suspect, monks

* Usque adeo ut chorus psallentium judicari possit ebriorum taberna potius quam psallendi officina; pridianisque carnibus crudi adhuc monachi et ingurgitati pro suspiriis ructamina fundunt. Compare Chaucer, *Summoner's Tale*, I, 225,

"Whan they for soulës say the Psalm of Davit,
Lo, 'buf', they seye, 'cor meum eructavit'."

† Here, again, official documents of the later Middle Ages show a steadily increasing custom of paying individual monks for singing particular Masses. It was probably worse in France; but certainly it was common in England.

may be seen standing and devouring rather than eating; not so much dividing the morsels with their teeth, as swallowing them almost whole; this they do so hastily, because they are compelled to hasten straight back—I can scarce say, to the rest of their *psalmody*, but rather to the rest of the chase. Wherefore, within a brief space (so far as we may gather from conjecture) the monks may be seen, recalled by the sound of a bell, and (you will scarce restrain your laughter) either leaving their half-eaten morsels or licking their beards that drip with greasy bacon; and thus, with well-lined bellies, they return to gulp out the praises of God in most undevout haste. Whence, I ask, cometh this incubus of breakfasts and noonday meals? though this generation of monks who seek not the Lord call them "afternoon-bites"—[*pomeridianas gustationes*]. Do they spring from the Rule, or from the decrees or manners of our fathers, or from some error of heathendom?

He quotes instances from heathen philosophers to put his fellow-monks to shame. And, in the next chapter, he predicts the certainty of divine vengeance upon these prevarications of the Rule, and insists on the folly of adding fresh ceremonies, so long as these services themselves are so hastily and undevoutly performed.

Chapter 8:

It is clearly evident that unreformed monks will spend less time and labour in running through ten psalms, than reformed monks over a single psalm. Moreover, in many monasteries, and especially at the night-services, there is but one priest present, with a young boy; moreover, I have heard that one single priest has sometimes performed the night-services and taken the part of both sides of the choir, while the others, it may be guessed, are buried in wine and sleep. How then art thou bold enough to boast of the long services sung by deformed monks, when they are so oftentimes interrupted by quarrels or jests, by buffooneries or vain speech?

In chapter 10 ceremonies cloaked a growing laxity of life.

It is from such superfluities that the decay of the monastic Order hath principally come about. For, if they gabble rather than pronounce a great mass of services, then they flatter themselves that all is safe, letting fasts and handiwork go. They break the rule of silence, of poverty, and of obedience; nay, they oftentimes neglect and banish altogether both chastity and the rest of the regular observances. Would that they would sing those services which the Rule prescribeth, without additions of later invention, and would do their best to keep the other observances of the Rule; for thus would they nobly deal with their Order and with the founders of their monasteries, seeing that the pious singing of a single psalm would benefit their souls more than such a chattering of the whole psalter. For such irreverence as this doth rather provoke the Most Highest to wrath than it can appease Him; and, when a displeasing person is sent as intercessor, then the mind of the person to be appeased is rather provoked to great wrath.

And he concludes:

We have named no man by name...our disputation hath been in general terms, against the vices of men who are monks not in truth, but in name, not in effect, but in dress. Whosoever therefore takes what we have said as contumely to himself, he shall judge his own conscience, and condemn himself worse than me.

The whole treatise bears out the promises with which it started. In his Preface, Jouenneaux addresses himself to Parlement and explains that he is driven at last to frank speech by the shameless falsehoods which are now being published against those who are striving for monastic reform. He proposes as models the Carthusians, Celestines, Observantines and the Reformed Congregations of St Justina and of Germany, who owe it only to the care of their legislators and reformers that they have not "long ago come to great ruin, as our monasteries have". Charity is now grown cold in the world; heroic remedies are needed, and Jouenneaux reckons confidently upon the support of the Parlement for the reformers. "Gird up your loins, then, most reverend fathers, to fight the battles of the Lord, that after your honest efforts ye may be able to say with St Paul, 'I have fought a good fight; I have finished my course; I have kept the faith'."

CHAPTER XL

WINDESHEIM AGAIN

IN so far as these French reforms had any consistency or continuity over the whole kingdom, this was due partly to the rather fitful efforts of kings and magistrates, but mainly to Cardinal Georges d'Amboise, brother to that Jacques d'Amboise who did something towards continuing Bourbon's reforms at Cluny. From 1499 onwards, he was not only prime minister, but papal legate also; a French Wolsey, with Wolsey's hopes of the papal tiara when the time was ripe. Meanwhile, he acted as liaison-officer between Pope and King.

In 1501, he became their common representative; he was Papal Delegate and Royal Minister for reform. For nine whole years his hand, self-willed and stern, directed the breakdown of those monastic enclosures behind which abuses and vice took shelter. With a dictator's grip, he laboured to group isolated monasteries into congregations; and, after his death, the King continued to aim at pursuing this cleansing work. Yet this police work, which was but imperfectly efficacious for the inmost life of the soul, left untouched the abuses which reigned among the secular clergy, who were bound up with the royal administrative system.*

Here was a man of energy, wisdom, and some real measure of good will; reform was in the air, and he took advantage of the general feeling. In 1503, the year in which Jouennaux printed his booklet, Amboise obtained from Alexander VI special powers to overcome all resistance by force, if necessary; and it was under him that royal archers had expelled the rebellious Dominicans and Franciscans from their headquarters at Paris.

But in France, as in Germany, the widest and deepest reforms were brought about by comparatively little men: and Chezal-Benoît itself was outdone by others whose main impulse came from abroad. The Benedictines, multitudinous in their main stem and in their different branches, and unrivalled in

* Georges Goyau, in G. Hanotaux, *Hist. de la Nation Française*, vi 325.

wealth and in social prestige, did less than the far fewer Augustinians.(1)

In this latter case, the hero was a canon of Windesheim, Jean Mombaer, often called John of Brussels from his native city.(2) He was born probably a little later than 1460. His origin seems to have been modest. His schooldays were spent partly, if not wholly, at Utrecht, where he may have had as schoolfellow his later correspondent, Erasmus.(3) There he picked up something of the chief Latin classics, and learned versification. Thence he passed to that Agnetenberg (Mount St Agnes), a monastery of the Windesheim reform which was illustrious, among other things, as the home of Thomas à Kempis. Thomas, however, must have been dead, for Mombaer's entrance cannot have been earlier than 1474 and was probably between 1477 and 1480. His novice-master, Renier Koetken, was strict and even rough; here Mombaer learned patience, and devoured books. Later on, he warned his own pupils against excessive night-work, for, in the words of his contemporary biographer, he himself "at last brought on a grievous sickness by his indiscretions in study". His superiors sent him for a rest-cure as companion to the confessor of a nunnery. Yet his zeal for study persisted; he sometimes hid his books under his bed for fear lest they should be taken from him. Thence, after a while, his superiors sent him on a journey of inspection over all the libraries of the houses in the Windesheim Congregation; incidentally, he was commissioned to report on their morals also. Thus he wandered far over Holland and Western Germany, and under this his health improved. Yet he had one relapse even on these journeys; and he never became robust. After his return to Agnetenberg, not very long before 1496, he was made sub-prior of Gnadenthal. The place ill-deserved its name, "Valley of Grace"; pious contemporaries nicknamed it "Vale of Poverty" or "Vale of Tribulation". Neither he nor his fellows could bring this small decayed house to reform: Mombaer finally proposed its suppression, and confessed that he could hold out no longer against these "perils both of soul and of body". The superiors relieved him of the sub-priorate, but appointed him bursar of the house.

Then, in 1496, came a great opportunity. Koetken, prior now of Agnetenberg, had a "zeal not according to knowledge" which caused friction with his subjects. Mombaer, for his part, was uneasy at Gnadenthal; and at this moment a reformer in France besought the General Chapter of Windesheim to send volunteers for the good fight. They decided to send Mombaer, with Koetken as his second in command, for Mombaer had evidently more patience than his senior, with some real talent for friendship; moreover, he was already distinguished as a writer on spiritual subjects and on history. In this latter field he showed how a far-minded man can do good even as champion of a false tradition which he has had the misfortune to inherit from his ancestors.(4)

When Milan Cathedral was rebuilt (about 1480) the bishop and other great folk conceived what might seem the happy project of adorning it with statues of the Four Doctors of the Church. Then came, suddenly and unexpectedly, the burning question of St Augustine's dress. Two great Orders claimed him as their founder, the Austin canons (Canons Regular of St Augustine), and the Austin friars (Hermit Brethren of St Augustine). These rivals claims, smouldering for centuries, burst now into open flame. The two Orders were clad quite differently; and in every Order the habit was a sacred thing, often claimed as a peculiar passport to heaven. Is Milan now to worship St Augustine in the habit of an Austin canon or an Austin friar? The canons moved first, and the friars vehemently protested, in books which were among the early productions of the printing-press: their vicar-general in 1479 and their general himself in 1481. Thereupon two distinguished canons came into the field, one with four printed volumes in which he speaks of "that most detestable and execrable idol of St Augustine which hath lately been carved in marble at Milan Cathedral, as an image of falsehood, with a long girdle and a flowing hooded garment after the fashion of the Austin friars". So these got their way at Milan; but the canons appealed to Rome. Sixtus IV listened to all the pleas and counterpleas, and then dismissed both parties under prohibition of continuing the controversy. Soon he died, and Innocent VIII apparently removed the prohibition; for certainly the quarrel blazed out again: Debongnie quotes eleven writers of the sixteenth and seventeenth centuries who took part in it. In the eighteenth, the learned Hélyot and the Bollandists refused to judge; for by that time it was obvious to sober historians that neither party had, historically, a leg to stand upon. The main value of the incident is in the light it throws upon those rivalries which, almost more than their more serious failings, discredited nearly all the Orders on the verge of the Reformation and beyond. The quarrels between Order and Order, or between Conventuals and Observants in the same Order, resulted very naturally in suggesting to the general public that even the whole struggle for monastic reform was to a great extent a mere matter of personal rivalries or ambitions. Indeed, we find this suggested at the time.(5) Therefore it is much to Mombaer's credit that, though he naturally wrote in defence of his own Order, he did not forget that his readers had a right to expect history from him. In contrast to the negative criticism of his opponents, he tried to prove the canons' new claim by laying stress on the great men their Order had produced: he called his work *The Quest for Saints of the Order of Canons Regular*. Like nearly all medieval historians, he is at the mercy of venerable, but perfectly impossible, traditions. When he maintains that his Order dates even beyond St Augustine, to the Apostles themselves, he errs no further than Pope Gregory II did when he solemnly claimed to the Emperor Leo the Isaurian that the Apostles had been image-worshippers.(6) When he reckons that the Austin canons had had 2767 cardinals in their Order, 20,135 archbishops and bishops, and more than 100,000 mitred abbots, he does not go hopelessly beyond the Benedictine claim made in the fourteenth century for their own Order, or the blunder made to its own great disadvantage by the English Parliament of 1371, which calculated on 40,000 parishes for taxable purposes, while in fact there were only about 9000. There, Mombaer shows himself a man of his time; but he rises above it in that part of his work which forms a treatise upon the right principles of hagiographical research. There "his remarks are just; they show good sense. This little tractate, born of his own experience, is composed by a master-hand".(7) It shows that this mystic possessed a business mind and had trained himself to business habits.

In France, then, men of this kind were needed by the considerable body which was fighting for serious reform. The

Hundred Years' War had bred great disorders, worse perhaps than the civil wars of Italy and of the German Empire. A preacher before the chapter at Windesheim summed up in a sentence: "In most of the monasteries we see that both walls and manners have collapsed"—*in pluribus...et muros et mores corruisse cernimus*. The Order of Augustinian Canons "alas! lies almost utterly deformed"—*proh dolor fere totaliter deformatus jacet*.(8) In the face of these difficulties, Standonck was the natural man to call in; and Château-Landon, near Fontainebleau, was a house where the conditions cried for reform. It had been so wasted in the Hundred Years' War that, in 1468, none of the brethren was found fit to be abbot, so they elected a Franciscan friar. This man, naturally enough, proved unsuitable to a house with a Rule quite different from that of St Francis; therefore the canons repented and "proceeded to another election"—in a tavern, according to the chronicler. This new abbot, Cabrin, in course of time, signalized himself by the murder of his concubine. Meanwhile the evicted Franciscan had appealed to the abbot of the mother-house, Jacques d'Aubusson, to whom he had transferred his rights over Château-Landon. Aubusson finally vindicated those rights, partly by a formal siege of the abbey, in which soldiers fought on both sides, and partly by a compromise which bound him to buy Cabrin off with a money pension plus the priorate of St Sauveur at Melun. Then Aubusson, who had some real conscience although he was abbot only *in commendam*, looked about for means of reforming Château-Landon. He addressed himself to the greatest of the Augustinian houses, St-Victor at Paris, which still kept enough of the ancient spirit to pass for something like a model among that mass of relaxed abbeys. There, however, nothing effective was done, perhaps because Standonck had been consulted in the meantime, and was already at work in a different direction. He appealed to the Chapter of Windesheim, which, as we have seen, finally decided to send Mombaer and Koetken. It had not been easy to persuade the General Chapter to sanction this mission to a foreign country: but Standonck finally got his way. Koetken had first gone on alone as explorer; and Standonck wrote to the chapter: "If you send us six brethren of this stamp, with one lay-brother, and if half of them know French, they will see incalculable fruit."(9) But it was as a daughter rather than a sister that the Windesheim Chapter had expected to welcome Château-Landon. They wanted Aubusson to resign and to leave his abbey in the condition of a dependent priory whose prior should be revocable at will by the Windesheim Chapter. He, not unnaturally, protested: "I beseech that you will suffer my grey hairs to go to the grave in peace, with due respect to my rank." Standonck persuaded the chapter to give way; and, on receipt of a royal letter of approbation in due form, they despatched their little colony; six brethren, with a lay-brother and a servant. It was clearly understood that they were not to begin by enforcing the Windesheim régime in all its strictness. Having picked up on the way two further recruits from Standonck's Collège de Montaigu, they entered Château-Landon armed with royal and archiepiscopal letters, and an imposing escort (Michaelmas Day, 1496). The old canons resisted from the first. They even put up the notorious Cabrin again as a rival to Aubusson, and it needed a decree of the Parlement at Paris to defeat this manœuvre. Then they broke into the treasury and stole valuable charters; another night the stables went up in flames, and the abbot lost his mule with several horses. He brought in men of arms, arrested the culprits in full chapter, and committed them to prison for trial before the archbishop.(10) Yet he himself was doing injustice to the reformers with his parsimony: "the diet was measured on too sparing a scale for the robust stomachs of these 'Germans'; and it often happened that nothing was yet ready at dinner-time". They had to insist upon a regular money allowance for the kitchen; and this, again, was not always quite punctually paid. Even Mombaer began to wonder how long he could hold out. But he was encouraged by Standonck, who sent him three most promising recruits in place of the two Montaigu scholars who had dropped off.

Presently, however, unexpected difficulties came from the Archbishop of Sens, who began to scent in all this business an intrusion of foreign monks into his diocese, with privileges which might defend them against his authority. Only after long and laborious negotiations, and only through the whole-hearted support of the archbishop's penitentiary, moreover even then, only under certain definite written restrictions, was the reform finally ratified. One of these conditions was that the old unreformed canons should be permitted to live on side by side with the new. Here, as might be expected, was a fertile source of quarrel.

Meanwhile, Mombaer had other work and other vexations. The great abbey of St-Victor itself needed real reform, and Standonck moved in this matter also.(11) Some of the canons there, honourably conscientious, wanted reform for its own sake: others welcomed interference because they detested the abbot's despotism and his malversation of the revenues. Standonck appealed to Windesheim; the chapter sent explorers again, just as they had sent Koetken to Château-Landon. Mombaer, after some hesitation, fell in with Standonck and counselled an attack upon these Victorine relaxations; this would be a true work of God, a reform from whence might spread the renovation of the whole French Church. It was agreed that the Windesheim reformers should begin as gently as possible, as mere friendly counsellors. Six were sent, including one of recognized talent and learning, Cornelius Aurelius, a friend of Erasmus.(12) But those Victorines who really desired reform were too few and too timid. The abbot explained that, if reform was wanted, he himself would carry it out. Mombaer, therefore, wrote a book which, by praise of the earlier Victorines, hoped discreetly to bring back these relaxed successors to something like the purity of the past. No doubt this flattered the canons, but it did not convert them. The six missionaries again found their life hard at St-Victor. For this the evidence seems as definite as for the relaxation in other ways.(13) It looks as if the old canons maliciously starved the unwelcome intruders. A friend writes, "I found them much emaciated; they find the burden of the choir very heavy, and often they have only two courses of pottage and two herrings; no apples, and very rarely raisins; indeed one of them showed me, by his girdle, that he had lost more than half a foot in bodily compass." Mombaer was cruelly disappointed. He wrote to a friend:

This matter is a nightmare to me, and to my fellows also. I am in such anguish that my life is a burden to me. On either side I see nothing but danger, whether our dear brethren stay or go. Where is the gain, if they stay [at St-Victor] to the sacrifice of monastic regularity? and what a burden on our consciences! Yet, if they go without having obtained serious results, there will be shame for us, an outrage on our friends, and a hindrance to the whole of this work which we had begun.

Two months later, the Windesheim reformers quitted St-Victor for good, and the General Chapter felt itself cruelly humiliated.

Meanwhile, however, an opening came from Livry, where there was another of those rare commendatory abbots who had some real sense of duty. His house was in even worse case than Château-Landon; but he was willing to introduce the reformers and to raise the endowments to a level sufficient for the ideal number of twelve brethren. Livry was a dependent house of St-Victor; and this might offer some compensation for the reformers' failure at the great abbey. So Koetken went thither with one companion; and the restoration of the building was begun. But the handful of ancient brethren wanted no change; and Koetken wrote, "I see clearly that there is no hope of reform in France." Still, matters gradually improved; another reformed brother came to join Koetken, and the original brethren departed in disgust. Then came another opportunity, at the abbey of Cysoing near Lille. In the end, these three abbeys were formed into a small Congregation, under the influence of Windesheim, whose strict statutes, with slight modifications, they adopted for their own.

The first abuse which had to be destroyed for the restoration of religious regularity, was that of *proprietas*.... Mombaer's indignation blazed forth at the sight of the abuses which he found in "the noble land" of France. *Proprietas* has spread everywhere; it infects almost all the religious Orders. Worse still, this execrable custom has spread so deep that it is no longer held for a crime, and that some—even very religious and learned persons—admit it and defend it as lawful, even in public writings.

This, as we have seen, is essential for the full comprehension of reforming efforts in France, and indeed everywhere during the last two centuries of the Middle Ages.(14) Mombaer did his best at Livry, though hampered by the sudden death of his patron. Here also, after a struggle, the old unreformed members left the place; and, by 1510, Livry was a thoroughly reformed house.

Another smaller house, the Priory of Beaurepaire near Melun, was reformed amid great difficulties; and in 1499 Mombaer was able to hold a sort of Chapter-General of these four semi-Windesheim houses. Two years later he fell seriously ill, and Standonck's masterful insistence compelled him to travel in a litter to Paris for rest. There he grew worse, and died in the last days of 1501, at the age of about forty. Within the next three years, three of his Windesheim successors died, with Standonck himself. Then Livry passed again into French hands. But the work went on. In 1505 the statutes of this new Congregation were solemnly approved by the cardinal-legate, Georges d'Amboise, and, in 1515, the Bishop of Paris decreed the adhesion of St-Victor, that great Parisian house whose prestige gave it a sort of primacy over all the French Augustinians. This "inaugurated the brief Golden Age" of Mombaer's Congregation.(15). Three other houses joined presently; and there were sporadic adhesions until after 1600. But reform was dying out; in 1543 St-Victor fell again into the gulf of *commendam*, and its abbot, after becoming Bishop of Troyes, apostatized to Protestantism. Two years later, another followed; and then others again.(16) Then came the Wars of Religion. In 1625 so many houses had fallen off that no General Chapter could be held. In 1633 this Congregation of St-Victor was dissolved, and several houses, "willingly or by constraint", joined a new reform, that of Ste-Geneviève. But Mombaer's spiritual writings are still read sometimes; and it has been suggested that, on certain points, they influenced Loyola in his solitude at Manresa.

CHAPTER XLI

ROBERTUS RICHARDINUS(1)

WHEN so devoted a missionary as Mombaer was often compelled to suffer inveterate abuses, if only for a season—and this is brought out frankly in Fr. Debongnie's exhaustive monograph—we may be prepared to find still stronger evidence after his death. He found at St-Victor, in 1497, a formidable list of irregularities; yet not only was St-Victor the wealthiest and most imposing house of the Order,* but it had also a reputation for comparative regularity. The services were chanted there with greater solemnity than at Windesheim itself. But the abbot was formally accused by his brethren to the bishop for malversation: they asserted that he had engrossed most of the abbey's revenues, dressed luxuriously, commonly banqueted with friends in his lodgings instead of appearing in the refectory, neglected both divine service and the sick, and winked at grave faults while he punished peccadilloes with exaggerated severity. This complaint attracted attention to the plaintiffs themselves. A letter from Mombaer to a friend details what he found there. Common life had broken down: the brethren had each his own income and possessions; women were permitted to enter the precincts; the rules of silence and labour were broken, several brethren absented themselves from choir, and the sick were cared for not by their brethren but by their friends outside.(2) Exactly a generation later, in 1530, a little book was printed which throws almost as clear a light upon the ordinary unreformed Augustinian houses as Jouenneaux does upon the Benedictines. Alexander Mylne, Abbot of Cambuskenneth, had made that important house into something like a model for the rest of Scotland. He, and his predecessor Abbot Panter, and Abbot Reid of Kinloss, were struggling, almost alone, to redeem the Scottish abbeys from the reproach of ignorance. Among the twelve novices whom, at different times, Mylne admitted and

* The Prior of Windesheim styled it "Mother of the Order of Canons" (Debongnie, 100).

instructed, one at least went on to study at Paris and earned his Doctorate of Divinity. He calls himself Robertus Richardinus —no doubt, Richardson. Mylne had commissioned him to write an account of the Reformed Augustinians at Paris, and a brief Commentary on the Rule. Fifteen years before Richardinus's day, St-Victor had joined Mombaer's Congregation, and thirteen years after him it was destined to perish by *commendam*: 1530, therefore, is a most important date for the Augustinians. So it is also for the whole French Church. Imbart de la Tour, though the very existence of Richardinus was unknown to him, repeatedly chooses the years 1530–3. In his third volume he describes how Lutheranism, from about 1520 onwards, spread in and around Lyons, where there had always been active life with its consequent freedom of thought, and where the art of printing was fully developed (pp. 190ff.). It was among the *élite* that these ideas spread; several of the innovators were cloisterers, and from this centre Lutheranism began to radiate over France. The first burnings for heresy were in 1526 (p. 252). By 1530 the matter had come to a real crisis (pp. 201, 274, 324, 525). A new spirit was abroad: a "very wide and spiritual Christianity, resting upon the Gospel of reason, very detached from any 'theologism', but still within the framework of the Church. We shall find this conception in French Humanism after 1530." This, again, was the year in which Francis I, "under Budé's influence, made the first decisive gesture: the first Royal Lecturers were appointed". Here we have "the advent of the New Spirit". After that year we may apply to France the words of Erasmus: "At the very name of *Gospel*, we see the whole world awaking from its lethargy and casting the slough of its past." Serious attempts were now made to achieve, without rupture or bloodshed, those moderate reforms which many of the orthodox desired no less than the radicals. "One fact is certain; in the serene atmosphere of the Renaissance, the tension was relaxed. Government abandoned violent methods, and left some respite to the Lutherans." Thus we find here the moment at which reasonable men might well hope for an Erasmian rather than a Lutheran reform: it was a lull before the final storm. That, then, is the light in which we must read Richardson's book, and interpret the later Richardson of 1543, if he be (as I believe) the same man. He tells us very frankly how sick his Order is in 1530, and how little the remedies have hitherto availed. The next thirteen years showed not growth but decline in these efforts for reform from within. Nothing is more natural, therefore, than that he should have gone over to those who were fighting for reform from without.

This Richardinus of 1530 is certainly no Lutheran. He loses no opportunity of expressing his detestation for "that slimy serpent Luther, and his rotten limbs which have deservedly been cut off from the Church"; "the most damnable opinion of the Lutherans"; "Luther the herald of Antichrist" (pp. 20, 104, 106, 112; cf. p. 165). But, incidentally and unintentionally, he shows us why France, at this moment, was already honeycombed with Lutheranism.

Like nearly all writers on monastic discipline, our author finds the main source of evil in the unworthiness of abbots, priors, and other officials. Naturally enough, he sometimes aims evidently at the rival Order of St Benedict; but this is only because those points are common to both Orders: "What I [here] say of monks, must be here understood of Canons Regular, although their Rule is not quite so strict" (p. 56). But as a rule he is reporting explicitly upon his own Order, as Mylne had requested.

Some superiors, in these evil days of ours, scarce care even to know the precepts of their Rule (p. 26). They "neither keep the Rule nor enforce it, but live for the flesh and shall reap corruption" (p. 37). How many we have, heirs to Judas, who feather their own nests and those of their favourites! (p. 48). A great proportion [*bona pars*] of modern prelates care more for horses, dogs, hawks and harlots than for their brethren, even sick unto death. How many of them make a point of assisting at a brother's Extreme Unction? (p. 97). The Bishop of Paris told a friend of mine how one prelate kept no hounds but, instead, thirteen poor folk whom he fed and lodged: "These are my dogs, whose bark keeps the devil from my house." But alas! some prelates build royal palaces for themselves, or rather castles, wherein they live in luxury, with every incentive to lechery (p. 98). Meanwhile, the church and the monks' quarters are going to ruin (p. 55). The nepotism of these Abbots, and their neglect of true religious vocation, are great scandals in our day. They thrust into the monastery their little nephews, "even resisting with hands and feet, for the main reason that they may thus possess God's Sanctuary by hereditary succession; whence it cometh that those who are thus promoted for carnal love live carnally for the rest of their lives, and suffer others to live likewise (p. 157) for the sake of a fat living!"—*beneficium* (p. 46).

Like all his contemporaries, and like modern scholars as unimpeachably orthodox as Dom Berlière, Robert sees in *proprietas* the worst enemy of all. For *proprietas* is the germ of pestilent *commendam*. The common monk, amassing and nursing his little hoard, lacks only opportunity to become the abbot who lives in luxury and intemperance, sometimes far away from his ruined monastery. Among "proprietary" brethren, there is neither peace nor charity; the Benedictine Rule forbids this vice as emphatically as the Augustinian (p. 33). They sometimes even get into debt, and make their Order a laughing stock to the public (p. 34). It takes monks out into the market-place, to the scandal of lay-folk (p. 35). It "brings the Rule and Religion to naught" (p. 36). And yet "judge, my brethren, whether ye keep this precept of our Founder. Ye cannot deny that ye do most plainly violate your promised vow of poverty" (p. 37). He devotes many pages to exploding the pleas commonly adduced in favour of this vice, beginning with the strongest of all, that of "ancient custom". "This is easily met by that rule of Canon Law which ordains that, when a man possesses anything in bad faith, no length of time can give him a prescriptive right, and that [evil custom] is abuse rather than use, *corruptela* rather than *consuetudo*, aggravating rather than excusing [the offence]" (p. 175). Therefore among us Augustinians, as among strict Benedictines, let the abbot and three brethren search the cells for hidden hoards at least thrice a year (p. 39). But, nowadays, the monk and his relations even fight at law against their superiors for property* (p. 43). Robert's other points may follow now in his own order, that of the different clauses in St Augustine's so-called Rule.

God's worship is almost as neglected nowadays as the rule of poverty. Richardinus fulminates against "singers knowing not what they sing, and bellowing forth ununderstood Psalms"

* It will be noticed how exactly this answers to the facts with which Visitors had to deal, e.g. at Egmond.

(p. 28). Nor is their irreverence less than their ignorance. "If thou hadst to address the most mighty and most Christian King of France, or the most invincible and faithful King of Scotland. ...Good God! how carefully wouldst thou prepare thyself!" Yet

some do otherwise; at one moment lamenting, at another calling upon Christ, the man intermingles wordly matters. This monk, having begun Vespers, addresses those that stand by: What has been prepared in the kitchen? What sorts of fishes, and how dressed? The wine is heavily watered; the ale is frothy....Others, blown by the wind of levity, pray to God: *Have mercy upon me, O God; to thee alone have I sinned!* Yet, with their companions they intermingle jests and laughter.

To others, prayer is a load "heavier than Etna".

Either they read I know not what, or they pare their nails with their dagger. They stare all around in choir....They can scarce hear a single psalm with patience to the end. They sit as on a bed of nettles: for so doth that most watchful and busy Enemy of mankind move their inward parts and prick their posteriors that the fruit of their prayer is lost (pp. 69–70). Moreover, it is an evil custom to hold pleas at law in conventual churches, with concourse of men and women. Still worse is the paying of tithes there, with quarrels, oaths, and transgressions innumerable. Men count the money out upon the altar, with many idle words of the sort that are blameworthy everywhere, but especially in church....There are, however, occasions when need compels us to use churches for secular purposes; and it is lawful to bind maniacs to Church pillars, "for example, in that most holy and religious college founded by the Lord of Borthwick... where St Kentiern's merits often cure them....We may defend a church in war-time", but not buy or sell; "wherefore certain brethren do ill, in that they are wont to buy linen cloth from women in their church". Good prayer (like all other good customs) is out of date: "nowadays they that chant understand not even their chants" (pp. 73–4).

Richardinus, like some other monastic reformers, takes an attitude towards music which in modern popular language would be called puritanical, though in fact Milton was far from the only puritan who loved good music.(3) He was evidently irritated, as were the orthodox Visitors of Southwell Minster a little before his time, by the growing popularity of descant and faux-bourdon. He complains of the music of his day as not truly devotional but essentially undevotional; unbiblical, and unsupported by any sound Church tradition. He wonders how it could ever have grown up, especially among his own Augustinians, whose Rule seems definitely conservative here. This itching for novelty is like the itching to invent new Masses; "would that they would ruminate the New Testament, and the whole Bible, and rival the Seculars in those matters, as they do in these idle dreams!" "Good God! how much time is wasted upon vain music in England and Scotland, to the neglect of divinity and sound learning" (pp. 78–81).

The Rule saith: "Tame your flesh with fasts, and abstinence in food and drink, in so far as health permitteth." Note that last caution; he says "*tame*", not "*ruin*", your body: asceticism should be moderate. On the other hand, many are ascetics only in name. Constant eating and drinking stimulate the flesh; "this, according to Ezekiel xvi, was the iniquity of Sodom".

"Many are not content merely to take somewhat outside the dinner-hour (though even this is contrary to God and the Rule and bodily health); but they must also unmonastically practise superfluous compotations from morn to night. Therein conspiracies are often hatched, and plots against their superiors and other honest men; here are quarrels, blasphemies, contentions, murmurings, false judgements and vain suspicions. At the hour of Vespers, when they go to choir, they break silence, impede others, trouble the choir, and make themselves an evil show to all men, like drunken dogs who cannot bark. After Vespers they go to supper, and after supper to feastings, so that they sleep through prayers at Matins, or are found unfit for the service. Whether such men are servants rather of God or of their own belly, let their other brethren judge. I myself have known one who formed such a habit of drinking at the said hours, that he dared not lie down in his bed at night without a stoup at the head of his couch. It befel once that this was not there, and thus he died suddenly for thirst." Such men are epicures: it is shameful that, whereas a horse or an ass is watered only twice or thrice a day, these are always at table; like Philoxenus, who yearned for a throat as long as a crane's, and had filthy habits at table. (pp. 81–7.)

Again, St Augustine, like St Benedict, prescribed the reading aloud at table of some pious book by one of the brethren. Yet, in unreformed convents, even where this is kept up, some "shut their ears at the time of God's word, and talk of other things and impede the reader". Others, albeit they lend a hearing, yet trouble not to comprehend or retain. Chattering brethren fall into backbiting, and kindle quarrels. "In all reformed houses they keep excellently the custom of reading holy things all through dinner-time: nor is it ever broken even on Christmas Day, as I myself have seen in that most religious and famous convent of St-Victor without the walls of Paris" (p. 90). The Council of Toledo decreed that no banquet of priests should be made without Bible-reading. "But this is utterly contemned by many prelates of this age, who spend all their time with women and profane folk." Abbot Milne of Cambuskenneth is an honourable exception, yet even he does not fully satisfy the precept that the reading should last throughout the meal. But when he was present—as he usually was—he used to give a brief and profitable address in the midst of dinner, or call upon others to preach *ex tempore* "among which number was oftentimes my unworthy self....Yet many prelates consort with worldly folk, contrary to Canon Law, withdrawing from the companionship of spiritual folk and their brethren; and with such [worldlings], as they deserve, they sometimes die a sudden death" (p. 94). For this neglect of sacred things "many plead *custom*, which is often no sound defence; for our Lord said *I am the Truth*; not *I am Custom*" (p. 91).

Too often the sick are neglected.

"A good many [*bona pars*] prelates of to-day care more for, and visit more frequently, their horses and hounds and hawks and harlots, than any one of their brethren, even though he be at his last gasp. How many, pray, dost thou know, among this great crowd of prelates, who are careful to visit the brethren committed to their charge (even when, so to speak, they cling to life with the skin of their teeth,* upon the very brink of death) and to console them, or to give them the most worthy Sacrament of the Eucharist and the holy anointing oil?" Such men we may remind of Christ's words: *I was sick, and thou didst not visit me*; and we may go on to draw the moral "Because thou didst condole with the hounds, thou must now condole with devils." We must wonder, or rather grieve, at this sort of Superiors, who have so devoted themselves to earthly affections that thou shalt scarce find one in ten who is heavenly-minded and considers the future.

* *Extremis etiam (ut ita dicam) labiis animam tenentes*. Compare Job xix, 20.

They live as in baronial castles, with every incentive to lechery. In reformed houses, on the other hand, the sick are charitably cared for (p. 99).

In costume, our irregularities are sometimes so great that, at Paris, the Senate once interfered to insist upon our dressing in accordance with our profession (p. 103). Here, as on an earlier page, he quotes with approval "Father John Mombaer": "that venerable inceptor of monastic reform lately in France". The unreformed have each "a chest full of linen garments, and two or three of woollen, one or more for each day of the week, not succouring other brethren who are in need and necessity, even though they may pray pitifully and gently" (p. 103). Some are scarce content even with two featherbeds: they out-dress even their wealthy parents (p. 104). They wear linen shirts "pleasanter and far finer than silk". Their shoes and their tunics are like a layman's. "In France, the monks of one most wealthy abbey, blinded by their excessive abundance of wealth, riches and money, reached such a pitch of madness that they presumed" to beg the Pope for an indult to wear silk in their cloister and other places. He, however, "(doubtless warned by counsel of God) not only rejected their petition but prescribed the contrary as strongly as he could" (p. 106). "Alas! in these lamentable days of ours, there are such abuses among the garments of Religious that I am embarrassed to know which to specify first. Nowadays we see that men look not to warmth, but to colour [*non calor sed color*]; there is more insistence on choice clothes than on virtue....The knight cuts his mantle and the monk his cowl from the same cloth. Who would ever have thought that the Apostolic Rule [of monachism] would have come to so impious and so horrible a spectacle?" The Reformed Augustinians, on the other hand, never wear linen shirts; again, they have no costly furs, but only black sheepskins.(4)

Brethren must never walk abroad alone, but two by two. Some buzz about like flies: "now in choir, now in kitchen: here in the market-place, there in the pantry or the cloister. Meanwhile discord is sometimes sown by such among the beloved brethren in Christ: very many quarrels and disputes" (p. 110). St Augustine's Rule warns us against fixing eyes upon a woman: by which he means, with lustful intent. Therefore Religious men should go about with downcast eyes, and nuns should be veiled.

The Saint warns us to beware of woman beyond all else, because she has ever been beyond all others in harm to the human race. For woman is an animal prouder than the lion, that fiercest and proudest of brute beasts; more wanton than the ape; more venomous than the asp, more false and deceitful than those monstrous syrens. No animal, not the most ferocious, can worthily be compared with the feminine monster. The lions in their cave feared Daniel, and so did the dragon; yet mad Jezebel slew the righteous Naboth. Jonah escaped alive from the Whale's belly; yet Samson, mightiest of men, escaped not from the hands of his own wife. John Baptist lived unharmed for many years among dragons and asps; yet Herodias no sooner knew him than she slew him. Why should I say more of this matter?

Yet our Robert, who may by remote chance have been an ancestor of Robert Montgomery, fills more than two pages more with similar quotations from the Bible and the Fathers, from Plautus and from Virgil (pp. 111–15).

Yet the danger is insidious: "Monasteries should be open to no women; for if the outer doors be open, doubtless there will soon be access to the inner also. Thus, they are not barred from the church, since access to the House of Prayer is forbidden to none; but happy are those who in God's House (for God's House it is) do not works that are worthy of a devil!" The safest arrangement is that there should be a definite barrier, beyond which no women may go (p. 117). Moreover, the neglect of Augustine's prescription of manual labour brings another subtle temptation. The Rule says, "Your garments should be washed either by yourselves or by the fullers."

It would be a matter of perfection that even your inner tunics, which we call *shirts* should be washed either by yourselves or by your lay-brethren, lest our uncleannesses be seen by women, more loquacious than turtle-doves, who cannot keep silence as to their own. For in some monasteries there is a great abuse, worthy of God's punishment and man's reprehension, that every brother hath his own separate woman to wash his clothes; and with these they contract familiarities (pp. 136–7). Let no brother go alone to the public baths: he might be taken suddenly ill, and find none to help. On the other hand, if he makes a point of going with at least one or two other brethren, then "they can lead him in the right path, when he may have been overtaken with wine or ale....Again, worldly folk will have less suspicion (for commonly they put a sinister interpretation upon the doings of Religious) than if thou shouldst go too freely without a companion. (pp. 139.)

We must seek to rise above our present ignorance. As Jerome says: "Our wealth is to meditate day and night upon the Law of the Lord: ignorance of the Scriptures is ignorance of Christ." It is most important also to study upon our Rule and Statutes; in reformed convents each brother has a copy of the Statutes in his cell, and is bound to read it through in the year, in Advent and in Lent: the abbot or prior preaches upon them on Sundays and Holy Days. Ordinarily, the rules as to reading ought to be better kept than they are. An unlearned superior falls easily into contempt among his brethren; moreover, "the untaught man is seldom found gentle and charitable or humble". "In Reformed convents, there is only one Mass, that the brethren may better apply themselves to study and manual labour." Ignorance, the mother of all vices, is the principal cause of offences in monasticism. "Nor can we praise that custom of importing secular teachers to instruct the Religious, whereas the opposite should be the rule" (pp. 145–9). Instead of silent study, we now have gossip and quarrelsome words. As to gossip, "a certain most profound theologian said unto me: 'I believe that more men have been damned for want of restitution of [other men's] good name, than for any other sort of sin whatsoever'" (p. 157).

By our most evil doings, monachism hath almost come to naught; silence perisheth, holiness hath been taken away and there is no visitation nowadays or observance of the Statutes. And no wonder; for lectures are not given to the brethren, nor do the Superiors command that each should write and have [books] in his cell, in order that they may be able to fulfil [their duty] better. Certainly the Superiors are as dumb dogs that cannot bark in the cloister; they go about with kings and great folk in the cities and great halls: wherefore their voice is not heard in the cloister. In the day of wrath and vengeance, the blood of their brethren will be required at their hand. (p. 154.)

Discipline is difficult in practice, even apart from the artificial obstacles caused by papal exemptions. "Exemptions are never praiseworthy, albeit many labour to procure them. Alexander, the most worthy Abbot of Cambuskenneth, never would be exempt, even though he could; but he honestly wished to spend his life under obedience to his Bishop" (p. 159). With an offender, there should be three degrees: first warning; then correction; and lastly rebuke. But even the first is not always easy; for there are "some who not only disobey warnings, but even conceive hatred for those who blame them, and seek to slay them" (p. 119). "O! how many impieties against God and our neighbour's honour do Superiors suffer to be committed in the monastery, and wink at them!" (p. 155). Many of them neglect discipline through fear or pusillanimity or because they care more for their lordliness than for their spiritual duty (p. 160). Yet "discipline is the mistress of Religion and true piety" (p. 163). On p. 711, he sums up: Causae Totius Religionis Ruinae.

The first is the indiscreet reception of unprofitable persons. (2) The undue and negligent primary instruction of the novices we receive. (3) The reception of children, and of persons either our neighbours or in our vicinity. (4) The want of right intention in those who enter and in those who receive them. (5) The omission of study and devotion. (6) The frequent wandering of brethren and Superiors forth from the monastery. (7) The promotion of unprofitable persons and of [the Superior's] kinsfolk. (8) Excessive greed and anxiety for worldly things. (9) Omission of due correction, and winking at errors. (10) Negligent and ill-advised visitation. (11) The wickedness of these latter times, and of our evil days. (12) Too great extension of reform and of Chapters.* (13) The inexperience and greed of Superiors who have never attained to good literature.† (14) The granting of pensions and portions to each, contrary to God and the Rule, that the Superiors may free themselves from care for the necessities of the brethren, in order that they themselves may be more unrestrainedly freed for the world, as I say elsewhere. (15) The carnal love that Superiors bear to their kinsfolk. (p. 171.)

As to No. 9, winking at faults, he is far more explicit in a supplementary section.

* The evident failure of some of these reformers, by this time, leads him to fear they would have done more solid work if they had not attempted to spread their ideas so widely.

† Qui nec bonas literas attigerunt unquam.

Superiors fear where no fear is; but rather something great should be dared for the extermination of so great crime. Let their subject brethren rave and rage as they may yet they should be coerced, or at least persuaded. But, because the Superiors fear man rather than God, therefore all goes back to the old jungle—*omnis res vadit in antiquam sylvam*—Superiors fear to correct their subjects and to bring them to observance for the following reasons. (1) For their own comfort, since they wish to increase their wealth and honours. (2) In order that they may be reputed less evil if others are living evil, thus finding their glory in the evil life of others. (3) Lest they should be blamed for their own faults, or deposed from their offices, if they have not lived as they would have others live. (4) Through sloth and inertia and repose, seeing that the pastoral office cannot be exercised without many cares and labours and much watching and the Superior's own example. (p. 177.)

Here, then, was a promising pupil, sent to Paris by an exceptionally liberal and energetic abbot, and these were the fruits which he brought back from what was certainly the greatest theological seminary, and one of the best schools of Latin culture, when Erasmus was dying and the star of Loyola was rising.

Our Richardinus has sometimes been identified, and very probably, with the Robert Richardson who, in 1543, was sent as an anti-papal preacher to Scotland under the patronage of Henry VIII. That was the year in which Ignatius Loyola, having founded his association with seven other devotees in 1534, obtained solemn papal confirmation for his new Society of Jesus. If that identification be safe, then Richardson's *Commentary* gains double interest. It marks one of those crises which occur again and again in world history, when some venerable tradition has long held its ground against the innovators, until matters drift at last to the breaking point; then to most men the old equilibrium has become impossible, and each must choose one of two frankly hostile camps, accentuating the division still more sharply by his choice. It is perfectly possible that, in this Paris of 1530, Richardson and Loyola met and exchanged friendly counsel and uttered the same hopes, just as Hampden and Strafford did in England a century later. Imbart de la Tour, ignorant of Richardson's very existence and not concerned for the moment with Loyola, singles out as the crucial moment for both Reformation and Counter-Reformation the year 1530 in which the *Commentary* was written. From that year onwards (he argues), a new Spirit was abroad:

a very wide and spiritual Christianity, resting upon the gospels of reason, very detached from any "theologism", but still within the framework of the historic Church. Francis I appointed three royal lecturers in Greek, Hebrew and Mathematics: here we have "the advent of the New Spirit". After that year we may apply to France the words of Erasmus: "At the very name of *Gospel*, we see the whole world awaking from its lethargy and casting the slough of its past". Serious attempts were now made to achieve, without rupture or bloodshed, those moderate reforms which many of the orthodox desired no less than the radicals. One fact is certain; in the serene atmosphere of the Renaissance, the tension was relaxed. Government abandoned violent methods, and left some respite to the Lutherans. Thus we find here the moment at which reasonable men might reasonably hope for an Erasmian rather than a Lutheran reform: it was a lull before the final storm.

Dr Gordon Donaldson, of the General Register House at Edinburgh, has kindly given me three other references to a Robert Richardson who may well be our man:

1555. Preached a recantation sermon, but only *pro forma*. (Strype, *Memorials*, III, i, 356.)

1559, June 15. Presented to St Matthew's, Friday Street. (Kent Records, *Calendar of institutions by the chapter of Canterbury*, sede vacante (1923), p. 76.)

1571. Referred to as a Scot. (Huguenot Society, *Publications*, x, ii, 11.)

Renaudet, closing his detailed study with the appearance of Luther in 1517, shows how the fire of enthusiasm, which for one whole generation had supported the French reformers, was by that time smouldering away. The real fighters were all dead before then. Moreover, from 1504 onwards a spirit of lassitude set in (p. 437). Moreover, the movement was soon side-tracked. At the Council of Tours (1510); the Assembly of the Clergy at Lyons (1511); and that Gallican Council which shifted from Pisa to Milan, and thence back to Lyons (1513), big words had been used, yet these quarrels with the Pope about general reform of the Church were not only often futile in themselves, but they also had the disadvantage of obscuring the special need for clerical reform, both Regular and Secular. Thus "the Seculars, in 1517, are pretty well as they had been thirty years earlier" (p. 689). Standonck alone had tried to get at the root of the evil by improving religious education: but Montaigu had lost its salt under his successors. "Thus, in 1517, the reform of the Seculars was still to begin." Among the Regulars, a very small fraction were efficiently reformed. The friars were somewhat improved; but even that fire was cooling, and no attempt was made to abolish *commendam*, which "contributed with all its force to ruin a discipline which the public had now almost ceased to care about...few were interested in the restoration of the convents" (p. 692).

Intellectually, there had been a certain advance, side by side with the Renaissance outside the cloister, but not comparable to it in breadth or depth (pp. 696–7). The University, the Parlement and the cultivated middle classes are losing their respect for the Church. In the intellectual field, the real force of the reformers has been reactionary. "With rare exceptions, the Regulars, of whatever Order, will apply their strength to serve the narrowest orthodoxy. Maillard and Raulin, Bourgoing and Standonck, will have prepared beforehand the army of the Counter-Reformation" (p. 703). Chezal-Benoît was the most living centre of Benedictine study: Jouenneaux and the brothers Fernand were even noted figures in the French Renaissance; yet the General Chapter of the Congregation, in 1525, decreed: "Let none study Greek or Hebrew letters without permission of his Superior" (p. 703). This, two years after, Lefèvre d'Étaples had translated the New Testament from the Greek; and nine years after Erasmus had published his epoch-making Greek text, dedicated to Leo X! Benedictine scholarship was still, on the whole, in that backwater in which Roger Bacon found it; and even the splendid revival under the Congregation of St Maur, in the seventeenth century, never brought the Order back again to its pre-eminence of the earlier centuries.

CHAPTER XLII

GERMANY AGAIN

HAVING thus brought the Italian and the French story down to Reformation and Counter-Reformation, we may turn again to other Continental evidence before coming to the final catastrophe in England.

Much the same story meets us, whichever way we turn. But Germany, on the whole, shows worse irregularities than France: and *a fortiori*, than England. There, as in Italy, there was no one really powerful secular authority. All was nominally within the Holy Roman Empire; but in Holland on the West, and Calabria on the East, the Emperor had scarcely even the shadow of authority. Even within those far narrower boundaries to which the Empire was destined to be restricted at its revival in 1871, there was a bewildering multitude of princes and princelets and free cities, great and small, over whom the nominal sovereign was practically powerless. The prince-bishops, again, could sometimes defy the Pope as easily as a "Free-Knight" like Götz v. Berlichingen could defy the imperial ban. It would have been strange if this half-anarchy had not reflected itself in Church life.

Single cases might be quoted in bewildering detail. It is enough here to quote either frank confessions or significant stories: typical in the sense of "if they do these things in a green tree, what shall be done in the dry?"

Cardinal Cusanus, greatest among Visitors in the fifteenth century, struck in one of his sermons a note of sheer despair. "And, if we regard rightly, the whole Christian religion (with few exceptions) has degenerated into a mere outward show; even as we see in many Religious Orders, wherein the majority [of Religious] have kept only the outward habit, and nothing of the spirit of the founder of their Order."(1) Dionysius Cartusianus represents the Church as saying: "I have found great deformation and scandals, rather than edification, both in the Religious and in the Seculars of this day".(2) Again, still more explicitly: "But, alas! these for the most part have slid backwards, casting away the yoke of Christ, the institutions of the Rule, the Canons and decrees of the holy fathers, and the monastic profession; so that, where formerly all devotion abounded, and the greatest spirituality and most exemplary life, now there abounds on the contrary all aversion, foul carnality, and a scandalous life." These and similar complaints are summed up in the index: "In this author's day, the Religious Orders were sadly deformed." He speaks of few abuses more often or more bitterly than that of raising a tax by licensing clerical concubinage.(3) The Carthusian historian, Dorlandus, relates a vision of this same Dionysius. He pleaded with God, sadly confessing the comparative failure of every previous reform, and praying Him to amend His own House at last. "But, I beseech Thee, reform the deformity of Thy Church through Thine own hand and Thine own servants, and not through the fiercest enemies of Thy majesty."(4) Compare the words of his fellow-Carthusian, Jakob v. Jüterbogk: "The parents and friends of novices should take the greatest care, and guard with every effort of their mind against putting their children and friends into unreformed monasteries; for they will earn, beyond all doubt, the eternal fires of hell if they die in this state."(5) And finally, a couple of generations later, Erasmus's letter to his friend the Bishop of Basel in 1522:

What swarms of priests are nurtured in monasteries and collegiate churches! and, beyond these, we find everywhere a multitude of priests. Among these, how rare are those who live chastely? [*quanta raritas eorum qui caste vivunt?*] I speak of those who publicly keep concubines at home instead of wives; for I do not even touch upon the mysteries of more secret lusts. I speak only of things which are most notorious even to the multitude. Yet we, knowing this, are most easy in admitting men to Holy Orders, most difficult in relaxing the decree of celibacy.(6)

However heavily we discount the holy irritability of a defeated disciplinarian, or the satirical vein of Erasmus's letter to his friend, there is no excuse for ignoring this sort of evidence with the purblind laborious Janssen, or even for minimizing it as the far more candid Pastor does. Yet, here and there, he lifts the veil for a moment, and shows some general comprehension of matters which he in detail has slurred over. For instance, describing the rapid growth of heresy among the lower classes from the Great Schism onwards, he adds: "This was most natural: the smaller the chance of reform being effected by the Church, the more popular and active became the reform movement not directed by her: the higher the region that needed, but resisted reform, the more popular did this movement become."(7)

Remling, again, summing up the conditions in Rhineland and the Moselle basin, emphasizes "the disorder and indiscipline which struck such deep roots in almost all the monasteries about the middle of the fifteenth century". Most plain-spoken of all is the great Austrian archivist, J. Chmel.(8) "Whence comes this downfall of a faith which had formerly celebrated its triumphs in Austria? In pious Austria, which swarmed with churches and wherein the Catholic Church possessed more foundations and revenues than in any other German land, scarcely even excepting Bavaria!" The failures of Basel, he writes, were nowhere so fatal as in Austria. If we face history frankly, we must bring out not only the beneficent and edifying side of the Christian Church, "the most magnificent phenomenon upon earth", but also her blemishes and failures. Reform in Austria was thwarted, and the deluge came; we must lament the folly of modern apologists who refuse to learn from history.(9)

Turning from these literary sources to the evidence of concrete facts, we may take the two following cases as typical, if not of the average state of the monasteries, at least of what might go on without exciting any exceptional notice from the higher authorities. This first, in fact, we know only through a marginal note, supported by the brief confession of two chroniclers. Corvey, an abbey of the first rank in Europe, was in utter decay before 1500. One Wulfhard, a cleric of Paderborn, bought at Cologne in 1487 a copy of Rolewinck's *De Laudibus Saxoniae*. He has added in MS. to the eighth chapter of Book III, where Rolewinck has complacently enumerated the many great churches and pilgrimage-shrines in Westphalia, a note to the effect that "Corvey, once so famous, is now utterly decayed through the indiscipline of its inmates, and counts at the present day only a few vagabond monks". Another complained:

O Saxony, Saxony! if thou knowest it not in the case of other monasteries, yet behold the abbey of Corvey within thy boundaries; behold her ruins and marvel at her desolation! There the sons of dukes and princes—nay, even of kings—have shone under obedience to the Rule: there a son of the King of France hath been Abbot of those monks. Nowadays, who and how many dwellers are there? Certainly he who readeth how the abbey once was, will scarce recognize the shadow of the past in that which we now see.

And Johann Legatius cried: "That Saxon abbey of Corvey, beautiful of old, is now without beauty; golden of old, she is now of clay and almost null. She is fallen lower than Lucifer himself."(10)

The other story is much longer, but equally significant. It is from Pforta, that Cistercian abbey in Saxony which the Reformers turned into a school, of which Leopold von Ranke was the most famous scholar in modern times. A rebellion broke out there in 1516 against the new abbot. The duke appointed two commissions of enquiry in succession; the first, of Church and State dignitaries together, the second, apparently, of Churchmen alone. The details must be gathered from the abbot's own *apologia* and the notes of his private secretary who was also his kinsman. Reading between the lines we see how hopelessly destructive of discipline, and finally of morality, the system of private hoards had become. This abbot, while he was only an obedientiary in charge of a grange or cell, amassed a hoard of his own, by permission (as he now says) of his then abbot. This he gave into the hands of a serving-woman "who had served him and the monastery for 7 years". With this capital, he started her as a brewster in the neighbouring city of Naumburg: here again, as he claims, in order to supply the abbey of Pforta with ale at a cheaper rate: though it is difficult to reconcile this with the fact that all houses of any size had their brewery upon their own premises, so long as they kept any regularity of life. He bought her a house, which she occupied in her own name, since the Naumburg by-laws forbade brewing by any but householders. Apparently he put another man and his wife, named Peucker (who apparently had also served him for seven years), into the same house, for brewing and selling by retail. The original serving-woman, however, finally became distrustful of the money committed to her, and passed it on to the woman Peucker. Presently the monks of Pforta got scent of it; and here the revolt began. First, a party slipped off, in lay disguise, came to Peucker's house and demanded to see the money. Then they hastened back, broke in upon the abbot as he sat at table, and accused him of embezzling the common funds. Seven at least of the monks demanded with violence that he should dismiss his kinsman, whom he had brought into the abbey as bursar: even among the rest, only two or three seem to have shown him any sympathy. Storm-bells were rung at one time; at another, the peasants were mobilized with pitchforks and knives. The abbot was lifted bodily from his palace to his ordinary cell in the monastery, at a time when he claimed to be seriously indisposed. The first commission whitewashed him; but the duke insisted, and the second deposed him; he died soon after. It seems evident that his fate was partly decided by his sexual relations with one or both of the two serving-women. He himself claimed to have lent large sums to the duke and other great folk; and his secretary testifies as eye-witness to part of this. If, as he himself seems to have implied, the main motive of his adversaries was vulgar greed, this does not weaken the evident inference that the notorious commercialization of later monasticism was one of the chief causes for its ruin.(11)

The Egmond case gave us an insight into one remote corner of the Empire, Holland. Let us come now to another, Geneva, which for centuries had been ruled by a prince-bishop with something more, perhaps, than average regularity. Here we have an unusually valuable guide in the first volume of a remarkable monograph recently published by Dr H. Naef.(12) I give references here to his pages as we go along. He describes, one by one, all the monastic foundations within the territory of Geneva, as revealed by official documents from about 1490 onwards.

In 1534, when the priory of St-Victor was condemned to be dissolved, "it was discovered [eleven days later] that nine monks and their mistresses had already carried off the furniture and pillaged the priory". At the priory of St-Jean "there was no better order" than in those others. Outside the city was the priory of Satigny, subject to the Cathedral Chapter. Here, in January 1491, the chapter made an enquiry into "the unchaste life of the brethren". Later (November 1492) "there is no order in their service and they follow no Rule". In March 1494 these delegates were sent "to correct the brethren". In 1512 it was dissolved and annexed to the bishop's "mensa" by a bull of Julius II. The canons of the cathedral themselves appear again and again as disreputable cases; and their dependent priest-vicars were "as dissolute after women, or even more", than the rest. Naef concludes with the evidence of "Sister Jeanne, so faithful that she became Abbess of the convent". She wrote, looking back upon the first half of the sixteenth century:

> We may well call those days the time of persecution for Holy Church. It is true that the prelates and ecclesiastics of that time kept not well their vows and their estate, but revelled dissolutely in the Church's goods; keeping women in unchastity and adultery, and almost the whole people were infected with that abominable and detestable sin; whence we must recognize that worldly sin abounded in all sorts of people who provoked God's anger and His divine punishment.

And she continues on a true and significant note: "The good brethren and nuns were persecuted, and bore the secret judgement of God in share with the guilty: but we must believe that this was for their soul's health." Jeanne became abbess of the Clarisses in 1549 and was among those who refused to leave the Order when the religious revolution came (pp. 297–8).(13)

Dr Naef has given very probable reasons for his evaluation of the population of Geneva on the eve of the Reformation. He reckons from 7000 to 10,000 in 1400. In 1464 a census of houses suggests about 10,000 within the walls and 1300 in the suburbs. About 1475 he would give 11,000 or 12,000 to the city and 1700 to 2000 outside, and very few more in 1500. When, in 1484, a rich citizen arranged for a costly funeral, he provided that it should be attended by the clergy of the seven parishes, together with 400 other priests; and the context seems to show that these would come from the city and suburbs.

As to the cloistered clergy, there were twenty-four Clarisses at one time; twenty-nine Dominicans; eight Austin friars; twenty or thirty Franciscans; ten Benedictines in one house and about the same number in another. By including the crowd of clerks in lower orders or servants who depended on the cathedral and on the episcopal officers, he reckons that the clergy and their immediate dependents formed about 10 per cent. of the whole population. The bishop was also governor of the city.

CHAPTER XLIII

THE FRANCISCANS

THE friars may be dealt with far more briefly in proportion to the older Orders; for it may be said that their story is, roughly, that of the Benedictines writ large. They were more popular; they were "exempt" not only occasionally but universally; and they were more deeply decayed.

The Franciscans, in especial, were enormously numerous and influential. The Irish chronicler, John Clyn, in [1410] reckoned that his Order possessed, altogether, 1455 convents of men with 410 of women; and this was probably as little exaggerated as we can expect from a medieval calculation where great numbers are concerned.(1) But, with this numerical increase, zeal and discipline had diminished. It is fashionable here, as elsewhere, to lay exaggerated blame upon the Black Death, by emphasizing the chroniclers' swelled figures of mortality and ignoring their statements or implications as to the comparative inertia of the friars in face of that tremendous call for self-sacrifice.(2) We have multiple evidence from trustworthy witnesses long before that date. St Bonaventura, about 1260, had said that he himself would willingly be ground to powder, if only he could see the Order again as he had seen it in his boyhood. Roger Bacon, at the same time, complained not only of general monastic decay ("I exclude no Order") but added with explicit emphasis: "The new Orders [of Friars] are already horribly decayed from their first dignity."(3) Dante lamented, in bitter satire, the degeneracy both of Franciscans and of Dominicans.(4) Pierre Dubois, his slightly younger contemporary, demanded their reform as one of the most pressing social and religious necessities.(5) Nicholas de Lyra, writing his *Bible Commentary*, a few years later, expounded Ezekiel's condemnation of Aholah and Aholibah (xxiii. 4ff.) in terms of monastic decay. The elder sister betokens the older Orders, the "Possessionates"; while the younger Aholibah, even more unredeemed in her fornications, betokens the more recent "Mendicants".(6) Chaucer is definitely more critical of the friars than of the Possessionates; and the author of *Piers Plowman* is still more unfavourable. The Wycliffite writings cannot be used with anything like the same certainty: Lollard and friar, as rival popular preachers, were natural and hereditary enemies. Yet it is significant to note how far the Lollard criticisms are borne out by the details which crop up from other and widely different sources.* For one thing, the public very soon grew weary of monastic and clerical rivalries; Chaucer shows that plainly enough. At first the feud was simple between Possessionate and Mendicant; Matthew Paris shows it in his strongest partisan colours. The former regarded the latter as a pushful intruder; the latter could complain of holy violence sometimes employed to keep him out from the Lord's vineyard. Such quarrels often infecting whole cities or provinces, added much to the general unpopularity of the Religious in the later Middle Ages. The sarcasms of Erasmus do but repeat the earlier evidence which meets us on every side; and the quarrels were aggravated by economic causes. The monk could not help sympathizing mainly with the propertied classes, from which he generally sprang and who were the main protectors of his rich endowments, even when they exacted heavy toll for their protection. The friar was more democratic, yet seldom thoroughly so in the modern sense. Dom Berlière, without drawing special attention to this, has supplied factual evidence for it in his two articles on *Monastères et Sujets au Moyen Age* (*Rev. Bénéd.* October 1931, January 1932). It was not only that practically all peasants' revolts were marked by attacks upon the monasteries, and that cities often had to struggle for liberty against monastic lords; but in minor matters also there was often rivalry and bickering.

Originally, Greyfriars and Blackfriars were allies in a common cause; but not many years had passed before the friction between these two brothers became even more violent than between those cousins, as we may call them. It was not only that they were necessarily competitors for very livelihood, as Fr. Schlager quotes from a contemporary German chronicler:

* See, for instance, the notices in *The Victoria County History of Oxfordshire*, II, 120b; 135a; 142b; 147a.

Your sturdy beggar grieveth sore
to find another at your door.*

For they were rivals also for popularity and influence, in those days when interparochial were almost as important as international jealousies, and when, at the yearly cathedral processions, bloody fights might be carried on under the banners of different saints. Thus the strongest opposition to the story of St Francis's Stigmata came from Dominicans when the Saint was scarcely cold in his grave. Their scepticism, publicly proclaimed, called forth a bull from Gregory IX in 1237 and several more from Alexander IV in 1255.(7) More than two centuries later (1475) the storm broke out even more violently. St Catharine of Siena, a Dominican saint, was reputed to have received also the sacred Stigmata, the marks of Christ's wounds on hands and feet and side. The Dominicans set up her statue in their churches with those insignia, hitherto regarded as a Franciscan monopoly, which placed their founder, in the judgment of some heated minds, almost on a pedestal with Christ. The Order rose as one man in protest against this Dominican intruder, and appealed to the Pope. Sixtus IV, who was himself a Franciscan, issued two bulls in their favour. By the first, all these images of St Catharine were to have the Stigmata removed within the year, and the Dominicans are forbidden henceforth to preach this glory of their saint. By the second, this was extended to all other possible saints: St Francis must have his strict monopoly, and the church which infringed this bull must be laid under an interdict. The result may be imagined. As the Dominican historian Mortier pleads (IV, 506): "It was lawful to think and to teach that God was free to give the marks to whomsoever His pleasure might choose.... Both sides gave themselves up to regrettable invectives and acts of violence." The master-general procured from Sixtus a delay of two years before the complete enforcement of these bulls; but he could not procure their revocation. Thus, "forced by its respect for the Holy See, our Order abandoned officially and for the time, but not without hopes of *revanche*, the cause of St Catharine of Siena". The *revanche*, not complete but sufficient for practical

* It is den einen bedeler leit
Dat der ander vur der doeren steit.

purposes, came under a new Pope in 1491. For the Dominicans had never completely obeyed Sixtus IV, in spite of his fulminations. There were still statues with the forbidden marks, and Innocent VIII found reason (in his own words) to "fear that disorders may become more and more grievous". Therefore those existing were to be suffered in future; only none new must be made. (v, 6.)

But worst of all were the intestine quarrels. The civil war (for it amounted to no less) between Spirituals and Conventuals in the Franciscan Order, begun almost in the lifetime of St Francis, has been fully related in my second volume. The Spirituals (as they called themselves) were a small minority, wedded to the strictest observance of the Rule, and mostly living as St Francis himself had lived, in small scattered groups among secluded hermitages. The Conventuals (a term first used by Innocent IV in 1250) ruled in nearly all the established congregations (*conventus*). The first and most fatal of the definite steps in Franciscan downfall was when John XXII exterminated or drove into heresy almost the whole Spiritual party. When four friars were burned at Marseilles (1318) for the crime of clinging blindly and obstinately to that Rule to which they had sworn allegiance, and of thus refusing obedience to their relaxed superiors and this masterful Pope, this was in effect to decree officially that early Franciscanism had become a sin and a heresy. From a different angle, we may find equal significance in the actions of Benedict XII, who may count next to Innocent III and Gregory IX as the greatest papal reformer of monasticism. His Constitutions, which he forced upon the Franciscan General Chapter at Cahors in 1337, are rightly characterized by Fr. Holzapfel as "more suitable to the older Orders than for one of Mendicants. ... There is nothing said about tightening the rule of poverty and the prohibition of money; yet there is much about complete prohibition of flesh-food in the refectory"—a point which was absolutely foreign to the Rule.(8)

The cause which Popes practically abandoned was taken up by one earnest volunteer after another. In 1328 Philip of Majorca strove with a like-minded group to form a community in strict conformity with the Rule.(9) In 1334 Gentile da Spoleto and four companions obtained leave from the minister-general to inhabit a hermitage among the Apennines near Francis's own home; but he finally ended at the stake. The first durable success came from a lay-brother, Paolo de' Trinci, whose noble kinsfolk got the minister's permission for founding a convent of strict observance at the same remote spot. In 1373 and 1375 he even obtained letters of encouragement from Gregory XI; and when he died, aged 81, there were twenty convents in the group (1398). Paolo's work was taken up by a vicar of the general, Giovanni da Stronconio, who even procured papal exemption for three small convents which he founded. But this increased the dislike of the provincial ministers, if not for the movement itself, certainly for the creation of houses over which the Conventuals had no control. Thus the movement stumbled on until the Council of Constance (1415). All these thirty-four reformed convents were very small, either mountain hermitages or in country villages. Their total population came only to about 200, almost all lay-brethren, with only a priest here and there, as in the Saint's own days. This, of course, was numerically a negligible fraction among the many thousands of Conventuals. But the Council recognized the importance of this movement, and passed two decrees of great value: (1) Fifteen French convents were allowed to choose their own vicar-general: this was approved later by Martin V. (2) In each province, two convents were to be set aside for strict observance. The man who really made the Observantine Franciscans, as St Bernard had been the soul of the Cistercians, was St Bernardino of Siena.(10) In 1402, scarcely out of his teens, he entered the Observantine convent of Columbaio near Siena. His learning and eloquence soon marked him out for a great mission preacher; and he spent himself untiringly upon that work until his death in 1444. His sermons are among our richest sources for social and religious life in Italy. He was joined by three preachers of almost equal zeal and piety: St John Capistrano, Blessed James of the Mark, and Albert of Sarteano. These men were called the Four Pillars of the Observantine edifice. The movement spread rapidly; there were independent currents outside Italy, in France, Germany and Spain. But, in default of definite and consistent help from Rome, the friction increased in proportion as the two parties were becoming more equal in power. It was an absurdity that the living should still be chained to her dead sister: common-sense dictated the real solution for a century before it was finally taken by Leo X in 1517: that these two incompatibles should be allowed to go each on its own way. If formality had been absolutely necessary, then at least the party which upheld the Rule should have been set over those who made no pretence of strict obedience. Yet, in fact, the contrary was almost always the case. Hence came the paradox, lamented by Fr. Holzapfel even while he does his best to excuse the ministers, that (as an alternative to losing hold over a great part of his flock), "The General was thus formally driven to the side of the adversaries of Observance, and made into the stepfather of his best children" (p. 105).

In 1430 came the famous General Chapter of Assisi, where Capistrano was the leading spirit. He had consistently opposed any division in the Order, but on the one truly justifiable principle, that all should be bound to obey the Rule to which each had solemnly sworn fealty at his admission. In other words that the generals should be chosen from among the Observants. Yet he was no fanatic; and his party drew up a constitution which kept the mean between laxity and rigorism. This, having been approved by Martin V, bore from thenceforth the name of *Constitutiones Martinianae*. When Capistrano read the articles aloud in full chapter, the whole assembly gave its approval, crying: "We will stand and live and die fraternally in our Holy Order, according to these aforesaid constitutions and reforms." The general took a solemn oath to carry out these decrees, and never to obtain dispensation from the oath, but rather to refuse such if it were offered. Each brother swore solemnly to the same.

Here Fr. Holzapfel must speak again (p. 113):

> A turning-point had come in the history of the Order! Then came the unheard-of thing. It is said that, even during the Chapter, some brethren had begged for dispensation from their oath. But certain it is that on the 27th of July, some six weeks after the Chapter, the General obtained [papal] dispensation from his oath, and worked some mitigations in the Statutes. On the 25th of August, he obtained from the Pope the brief *Ad statum* which again utterly upset all the Chapter's reforms on the question of poverty.... This papal brief constitutes the *Magna Carta of the Conventuals*.

Whereas the constitutions had bound convents to sell the lands and endowments which they had so long illegally possessed, like Possessionate Orders, this illegality was now recognized by that same "reforming" Pope who had abolished it a few weeks earlier. "Hitherto, many Popes had exceptionally granted such rights to this or that convent, but expressly as an exception contradictory of the current laws of the Order: but Martin V made this exception into the rule." This (says Holzapfel) "shows clearly that there was absolutely no serious desire for a reform in the sense of the Chapter decrees....The Conventuals, with appalling injustice, did indeed wish to maintain the points of the Martinianian Constitution in so far as they restricted the rights which the Observants had hitherto enjoyed, but obtained dispensation from the prescriptions which affected themselves".

We need not further pursue the ups and downs of this struggle between 1430 and the final separation in 1517. It is true that other extraneous causes contributed to Franciscan decay and unpopularity. The Black Death had some effect here, though mainly by showing that the vast numbers of friars had quite lost, as a body, that missionary fervour which had led the first generation to work sometimes in leper hospitals. Again great schism showed within this Order, as in the Church outside, that it was impossible to distinguish the true Pope from the false; or, indeed, to be sure that either of these, or the third claimant who finally appeared, was genuine. The Hundred Years' War, and the still worse civil wars in Italy, and the general lack of national peace throughout Europe, did no doubt contribute their share. But, even though all these had been absent, we might see sufficient explanation in these constitutions, papally granted with one hand and papally annulled with the other; solemnly sworn to, but repudiated in the same breath by what was perjury in all but in name. Eugenius IV, who had himself been an Observant Franciscan, did indeed in 1431 revoke the brief *Ad statum* and recall the friars to their solemn oath. That, one may feel, was the least he could do: yet it also proved the most. Next year he revoked this revocation, under pressure from the superiors of the Order; and despite all his reputation of zeal for monastic reform Fr. Holzapfel can say no more of him than that "he remained, nevertheless, continually friendly to the Observants, and favoured their diffusion" (p. 115).

The practical result of all these "higher politics" may be read in all Franciscan records wherein the details are frankly set forth. One of the most careful of such monographs is that of Fr. F. Doelle.(11) Fr. Holzapfel's "thing unheard of" is for him the "thing unbelievable". From that time forward there were no longer two, but three families in the Order: viz. the Observantines (who held to the decrees of Constance), the Martinians (who kept also that Pope's Constitutions), and the Conventuals (who got dispensations from those Constitutions).

The result may easily be imagined. It was in vain that, here and there, Popes tried, by this or that distant interference, to put an end to the persecution of the few strict friars by that great majority for whom irregularity, continued from generation to generation, had practically superseded the Rule. Naef, in his monograph on Geneva (p. 251), emphasizes the hindrance which these constitutional quarrels put in the way of moral reforms. Father Doelle, in his painstaking and exhaustive study of the very extensive Saxon province of Germany, enables us to get a bird's-eye view from about 1470 to about 1510; that is, of the crucial years for a student of the Reformation. There are frequent gaps in the records; but, on the whole, the tale they tell is remarkably uniform; and the whole field is so wide (sixty-five convents in all) that on some most important points we may generalize with safety. Everywhere we find determined struggles, great bitterness, and partial success. The story of the nunneries has already been told above (chaps. XIV, XV). Here, as elsewhere, the men's houses caused less difficulty; for, in the first place, the friars had less frequently been consecrated to God in default of a worldly dowry; and, again, "reform" for them meant nothing so burdensome as the strict claustration of the nuns.

We find a similar story in the important province of Cologne, which has been studied by Fr. P. Schlager in an equally searching monograph.(12) He, like Fr. Doelle, bases himself to a great extent upon records hitherto unprinted; and the fuller records of Cologne enable him to bring far more detail into his story.

He sums up briefly the causes which called for this new Observance (p. 94):

As we have seen above, where I dealt with the separate settlements, there was much departure from the Rule in many convents of the Cologne province also; but, in spite of many shortcomings, the Observance was comparatively late in penetrating. Perhaps this was just because it was so sorely needed, since the friars had no longer sufficient inward strength to tear themselves away from a life that had such attractions for the sensual man; for that ancient proverb had been sadly verified among these men also: "The monk that hath a halfpenny is not worth a halfpenny." They had been welcomed with open arms; they had been loaded with benefits; possessions and revenues had been granted to them; and now that pungent word of a monk of Prüm was fulfilled: "Religion hath brought forth wealth to us; but the daughter hath devoured the mother." Therefore there seems no excessive exaggeration in what Ruysbroeck [d. 1381] said concerning the province of Cologne: "There are many brethren who beg, but few who hold to the Rule. In early days they despised possessions and honour, all the world's enjoyments and comforts: yet now they seek after these. They yearn sore for earthly goods and dignities by reason of the virtues that they sometimes practise. They desire to eat and drink well, they wear fine frocks, and nothing is too costly for them to wish for. They build great churches and most fair convents; they attract rich folk, but not that they may lead them to God. They flatter such sinners as are cheerful givers, and oppress the poor who can give nothing. They preach in word, and but little in deed. They seek the wool rather than the sheep: to wit, rather their own profit than men's salvation. In their refectory, it is but the poor brethren who take their scanty meal: the Warden, the Lector and other rich brethren, who have either revenues of their own or rich penitents in confession, enjoy themselves in rooms apart; they are proud and haughty, and know neither concord nor brotherly love." Therefore discord often reigned within the convent, and so many scandals arose that cities and citizens strove to remove them; and that is also the reason why, in the fifteenth century, settlements were no longer offered [to the friars], and why quite definite written assurances were demanded from the Observants before they were admitted. They had gambled away the confidence of the people.... Therefore the convents often fell into bitter destitution, since their endowments were insufficient for the satisfaction of all their wants.

On a later page (99), Schlager gives a concrete example. The first Observantine convent in the Cologne province was that of Gouda in Holland. The Duchess of Holland bestirred herself in 1428 for the reform of the Conventuals there, "who were leading a scandalous life". In 1436 the Duke of Burgundy "threw his influence into the scale but in vain". Then the city magistrates pressed the matter upon the Council of Basel; and at last, in 1439, the papal legate moved the bishop of the diocese to take real steps for reform. By that time, the convent seems to have become derelict. A batch of Observants were now imported from St-Omer.

The City Council exerted themselves to rebuild the convent so that it was the finest in the whole town. But their recent unfortunate experiences had made them prudent; and they required from the brethren a written promise, (1) to amass no property; (2) to beg only once a week in the same street; (3) not to receive more than 20 brethren; and (4) in case of falling away from the Rule, to quit the city of their own accord.

The citizens of Leyden demanded similar guarantees in 1445. Both in Cologne and in Strassburg, even before this date, strict measures had been taken against the multiplication of endowments for the Mendicants. The thing was most definitely contrary to the fundamental prescriptions of the Franciscan Rule, and also to the spirit of the early Dominicans; yet it had reached an intolerable height, and seriously crippled municipal finances by withdrawing much property from the taxable category. The cities met this by prescribing that, whenever real property was given or bequeathed to the Mendicants, they must sell it within a year and a day.

Thus, with the help of the secular authorities, the Observants spread in numbers and in influence, despite violent opposition from the Conventuals, lukewarmness or even opposition sometimes from the bishops, and lamentable aloofness by the Holy See. Very significant are the cases of Gottingen, Marburg and Grünberg (pp. 142 ff.). At Marburg the Observants indignantly repudiated accusations of indiscipline and immorality, made counter-accusations of violence and illegal interference, and bribed heavily enough at Rome to secure two commissions, one after another, for judgment in their case. The accusations were such as must have found plenty of evidence in the city, for or against. Both commissions decided against them, and the Conventuals, still refusing to accept reform, were expelled.

Such incidents make us understand why Traversari, writing to St Bernardino, alludes to "the Conventual brethren of St Francis, who are abortions in Jesus Christ".(13)

Even more significant is the evidence of one of the most prominent Observants, Johannes Brugman, writing about 1460. The author was perhaps the greatest mission preacher of the generation succeeding St Bernardino. He called his little treatise *Speculum Imperfectionis*, in contrast to the famous *Speculum Perfectionis* of early Franciscanism. We must discount his words by the usual allowance for a fervid pulpit orator. But, on the other hand, he does not need the still heavier discount of an Observant criticizing the Conventual abortions: for it is his own party which he is warning of its besetting weaknesses. We see, what is natural enough, that even the reformers found it hard to maintain their ideal and their discipline.(14)

He takes his brethren class by class, from the lowest upwards; and in the very first paragraph we see the gulf between this "reform" and the Franciscanism of St Francis and his companions. The Brethren Minor maintain servants for the menial duties, and fail to keep these in order: they "permit them to be idle and to see the weaknesses of the brethren". Wherever this appears, the Observance "threatens ruin". The next paragraph runs:

The second cause of the ruin of the Order is that novices are not proved, or exercised in humble obedience or comforted in devotions, nor do they see from the professed such examples as should draw them to devotion; nay, they are very often scandalized by dissolute old and young brethren. Herein also is verified that text: *Woe unto you, for ye compass sea and land to make one proselyte*; and oftentimes they think to find glistening* gold when, alas! they find clay and brass; indeed it would be safer to leave them in the world, than willingly to corrupt [*depravare*] such little ones.†

III. *Of Lay Brethren as Novices.*

...It must be noted again that we are often blamed by other cloisterers because we receive vain fellows, wandering and prodigal, the abortions of other Orders, ill-famed, outcasts, involved in debts

* Reading *nitidum* or *nitentem* for the *nitreum* of MS.

† In the treatise supplementary to this, Brugman writes "Let the Master of the young brethren exert himself above all to teach them the writings of the Order; for very few [*paucissimi*] set themselves to that study after they have taken the vows; for alas! they have forsaken the *fountain of living waters*, the things to which they are bound by law or naturally, and they *hew them out cisterns, broken cisterns*, by collecting common-place books" (*A.F.H.* IV, 316).

and so forth. Moreover, we are blamed for causing many wicked acts in the aforesaid prodigals and notorious fellows who come thus unto us: for men say in the taverns: "After I have consumed and wasted my substance in drink and dice and fornication, spending it with harlots and buffoons, I shall yet be a good Friar Minor": and thus we are become a hiding-place and a refuge for such malefactors. Moreover it cometh sometimes to pass that such folk, if they come with arms and torches and staves and crossbows, are received more reverently and quickly into our Order than Adam* clad in skins and hodden grey, however much devotion he may have and display: thus *we have multiplied the nation, but not increased the joy.*

IV. *Of the Conventuals and other Religious* [many of our converts from Conventuals to Observants are so lukewarm that they hinder more than they help]. I venture to say that, even as the Observance is maintained by good and ardent Conventuals, so by the tepid and remiss, who find it sufficient to spend this whole life in food and sleep and drink, it is utterly destroyed and frustrated and altogether dissolved. For such men are content to say the Hours with their lips, not to fornicate openly, not to possess money, not to beget sons and daughters; they think little and care still less to emulate the better graces in prayer and silence and compunction, in ceremonies and exemplary life and simplicity and deep humility. Such men are as lions, wild boars, foxes and dogs, eating and destroying the vineyard of God and of St Francis.

V. *Of the Lay Brethren.*

Although our holy Order had its origin in holy layfolk in St Francis's day, and even [is illumined] by some in our own time, yet that most holy Order threatens ruin by some who, as soon as they have taken the vows, are left to their own liberty without master or teacher, and become wanton, brazen, foolish, presumptuous [five lines more of blame]. I say nothing of those who are rendered illustrious by their humility, patience, labour, devotion, mildness, charity and other virtues; for such I reckon to be worthy of no less reverence than other clergy, except for the character of Holy Orders.....

VI. *Of the Clerics newly professed.*

[The newly-professed friars, too often, ignore all the classics of the Order, such as the *Speculum Perfectionis* and St Bonaventura's *Life of St Francis*: and Ludolph's *Life of Christ*.] Alas, and (shameful to relate!) as soon as they are weaned from the breast of the Novice-Master, either they cease altogether to study devotional books, and sink into idleness like "Brother Fly"† chattering and mocking, or else they soar up to the stars without wings, for their wings are not

* See Genesis iii, 21.

† Brugman quotes here from St Francis: see my second volume, p. 183.

yet grown, studying jurisprudence or law and all sorts of pompous or curious matters, that they may only appear and be called clerics, in mere name, as men unfounded in the rudiments. [They compile for themselves commonplace books of frivolous stuff, and treasure these with a persistent egoism which brings them under the condemnation of *proprietas*.]

VII. *Of the Priests and their Celebration and their Idleness.*

Our holy Order is in peril through the multiplication and promotion to the priesthood of unprofitable [*inutilium*] men. [The Order accepts too many *trentals*, or Mass-endowments: hence it must over-exert itself to get priests.] Moreover, among these, singers are multiplied and preferred above orators, bawlers are preferred above weepers....[Since the Brethren know] that their Superiors rejoice in the number of Masses and chants and sermons, therefore, as soon as they have come forth as chickens from the egg-shell, and have scarce reached their twenty-fifth year, though as yet unworthy of Orders, they are forthwith swelled with the spirit of ambition and aspire to the priesthood, and, if they are not promoted, they murmur and detract and backbite; moreover, when promoted, they are squeamish as to celebrating or chanting or teaching or other burdensome graces. [If required to write for the convent library, they make all sorts of difficulties; but for their own pleasure or glory, they scribble indefatigably, and show a spirit of *proprietas*]....

VIII. *Of Reformed Religions, of our own or other Orders, who come to us to take our habit and our way of life.*

"...Such Religions are either very good or very bad: either angels or devils." [Some come over with the hope of getting more liberty. Others are hypercritical of whatever is not to their own taste.]

IX. *Of the Master for Novices and Young Brethren.*

The ruin of our Order comes from default of novice-masters. [These need to be circumspect, kindly, patient.] If the master be light-minded and foolish and ill-mannered, he will ruin many souls: if, for instance, he be indevout, carnally familiar, uncontrolled, compelling the young to write books for himself...if he suffer to be occupied indiscriminately in writing commonplace-books for the brethren, he will be a cause of destruction for the Order by multiplying such [pupils].

X. *Of Confessors.*

[Good Confessors are the salvation of an Order: but with the bad,] alas! *there is death in the pot, O thou man of God!* [Some ask indiscreet questions about carnal sins;] Others seek to be carnally pleased like beasts; they receive little presents, wine, flesh, spices, perfumes and other sweet things for the care of the flesh; they are inflamed with private love for silly women [*fatuellas*]; they study to please men rather than the fear of God; they call women,* by a foolish love, their "daughters"; or absolve indiscriminately; or are accepters of persons; or enjoin foolish and indiscreet and scandalous penances; or encourage in their pride the women who wear horned headdresses or long tails; or admit to their companionship usurers and pimps and adulterers and public offenders of that kind, and commit other things worse still. Through such men doth our most holy Order threaten the greatest ruin.

XI. *Of Preachers.*

[Good preachers are a salvation to souls. But if they are bad—and here follows almost a whole page describing the sort of preacher whom Chaucer depicts in his Summoner's Tale—then the work of such men] is damnable in the preacher himself, and perilous to our most holy Order in the future.

XII. *Of the Select Brethren*† *of the Convents.*

Ruination oozes in and abounds [*manat et scaturit*] by default of the Select Brethren. [These should be the eye of the Convent, but if the man is discreet only in name, misusing his influence, and encouraging the evil brethren and discouraging the good, then] I dare say that such a man is antichrist, a fellow with sinners, a partaker with adulterers, an enemy of the Cross of Christ.

XIII. *Of the Presidents or Vicars of the Convents.*

Another "evident cause of ruin" comes from these men. These, upon whom discipline so directly depends, are too often enemies to those who expose their own defects, and "secretly relax all rigour of discipline" by working against their superior, the Warden of their Convent.

XIV. *Of the Wardens.*

Ruin may be imminent from the side of the Wardens, even as the salvation of the brethren may come from them. [Here, again, is more than a page and a half describing the bad Warden, and ending:] If they bring terrorism and persecution, by threats and revilings, against the brethren who come on visitation or who depose the Warden, then I venture to say that, where such things come to pass, there the sun goeth towards his setting, the Order towards strangling,‡ the Convent to ruin, holiness is reduced to death and observance to ashes.

This little treatise, with due reservations, renders intelligible

* *Mulierculas*, the word translated "silly women" in 2 Tim. iii, 6.

† *Discreti*, answering roughly to the *seniores* of a Benedictine abbey.

‡ In allusion to Job vii, 15, "My soul chooseth strangling, and death rather than my life."

the story of Franciscanism in the century before Luther's appearance, as told by a candid and learned historian like Holzapfel. We find the reformers themselves—quite apart from the Conventuals, who stood impenitently upon their age-long relaxations of the Rule—splitting into ten branches at different times; the force of their impulse being so personal as it was, and so dependent upon the leader's own temperament or his circumstances of time or place. It shows the Conventuals equally unable to reform themselves or to give the reformers freedom to go their own way; while Popes vacillate partly in timidity, partly in sheer muddle. Even when Leo X took the final step, and decreed this commonsense separation between two essentially irreconcilable parties, the clear and resolute words of his bull were not felt to be enough. To reinforce these, an "Instrument of Compromise and Concord" was solemnly drawn up before the Cardinal Protector; and, even a few weeks after this, Leo was compelled formally to remind the Conventuals of what he had recently decreed. "It sounds incredible that the then unreformed Conventuals should have claimed to be considered as the only true sons of St Francis; but the Pope's words permit no other interpretation."(15) Nor was this warning enough: Leo was compelled to send, four months later, a circular letter to lay and ecclesiastical princes threatening to call in the secular arm if his decision was still disputed. This appeal to lay help has already met us often before, and will soon meet us more emphatically still. So long as the friars had nothing but Canon Law and spiritual commands or penalties to fear, they were in an almost impregnable position. When Cardinal Cusanus, under express commission from Nicholas V, was making the greatest practical attempt of his age for monastic reform, one of his main difficulties lay in "the insidious opposition of the Mendicant Orders against this envoy from Rome".(16) Their exemption gave them multiple opportunities of appeal to the Pope against his own decrees or his own ministers, and of interminable litigation at the Curia. When Charles VIII held his commission for Church reform at Tours in 1483, it was emphasized that disciplinarians could often do nothing in the face of friars who could engineer favourable judgments in Rome, and cast the Visitor in the costs of the action.(17) Like the

Jesuits of later generations, they were too valuable as a papal militia, and too formidable as adversaries, to be dealt with as the Conventuals deserved. If, in Spain, the reform was far more successful than elsewhere; this was because it had the support of royalty. As Holzapfel points out, in Alexander VI's days "a papal brief could be obtained for anything"; and both parties thus trumped and overtrumped alternately (p. 146). But Ferdinand and Isabella were exceptionally powerful and resolute sovereigns. They commissioned the future Cardinal Ximenes to report on the monasteries. The result was, that a papal bull was procured (1494) giving him power of reformation over all the monasteries of Spain. The most violent resistance was offered by Ximenes's own Order, the Franciscans, who were in most need of reform. They obtained a counter-bull, prohibiting his interference: but the reform party was strong in the support of the secular arm. "The monasteries were disciplined, their 'privileges' burned, and their rents and heritages taken away and given to parishes, hospitals, etc. A large number of monks who were scandalous evil livers, and who seemed irreformable, were deported to Morocco, and the work was complete."(18)

In Geneva such reform as was obtained came from the city magistrates. The Franciscan nunnery was founded there under the strict Rule of Ste-Colette in 1477; but in 1500 it had broken that Rule by the acquisition of "important properties". Moreover, each nun had to pay entrance money, or "dowry", to the extent of 300 ducats, which was, if possible, even more un-Franciscan. On the whole, however, it seems to have commanded the respect of magistrates and people to the last. Not one of the men's houses in Genevan territory could make the same claim. Naef tells the whole story, mostly from contemporary official documents (pp. 17, 256–64). "In 1522, the Secretary Biolesii denounced an evil which contaminated the whole [Franciscan] monastery: 'Great complaints are arising concerning the friars of Rive, who are leading an unchaste and wicked life. Let the Syndics go to the Minister who is now in the city; let them offer him wine and request him to purge such unchastity from the friary and to punish the rebels'." Similarly, in the same year, the magistrates dealt with complaints that the

Dominicans at their convent of Le Palais were leading a dissolute life. Again, in 1483, the populace had threatened to tear down the new buildings of the Augustinian friars on account of forged miracles which had been exposed there, and the Duke of Savoy aided the magistrates in reforming the monastery.

For England, the Franciscan centuries are summed up by Dr A. G. Little in words which will probably be echoed by most students who have worked at the main records for themselves:(19)

What led men to take the vows of the Minorites? Excluding again the thirteenth century (when the highest motives were predominant), and confining ourselves to the later times, we must admit that, apart from those who entered the Order as boys, either from choice or at the instigation or compulsion of relatives—the leading motive was a superstitious belief in the externals of religion, in the efficacy of "the washing of cups and pots". How strong this feeling was may be seen from the fact that Latimer was at one time in danger of yielding to it. "I have thought", he wrote to Sir Edward Baynton, "that if I had been a friar in a cowl, I could not have been damned, nor afraid of death; and in my sickness I have been tempted to become a friar."

Many years later (April 16, 1901) Dr Little communicated to the British Academy a papal bull of 1498 which casts a vivid light upon Franciscan conditions in England at that period. There was only one convent—Greenwich, recently founded by Henry VII—"wherein there flourisheth Observance of the Rule". In the remaining 57 English houses "those Brethren live who are called Conventuals, and some of these lead a reprobate life". Therefore official visitors must be sent to five of these conventual houses; they must not enquire as to the morals and discipline; and those friars who will not undertake to conform to the Observance must be banished to other conventual houses. If they resist, the secular arm must be invoked. This bull, like so many others of similar importance, was never fully carried out. "Instead of five houses of bad reputation only three were handed over to the Observants, and one of those at any rate enjoyed a good repute."

CHAPTER XLIV

THE DOMINICANS (1)

THE resemblance between this powerful Order and the Franciscan, strong from their beginning, was scarcely less marked in their decay. The story may be read in Father Mortier's classical *History of the Masters-General*, a book bristling with facts and as objective in its conclusions as can fairly be expected from a distinguished and devoted member of the Order.(1)

We may begin with 1337, and Benedict XII, that Cistercian Pope who made the last general struggle for Monastic Reform throughout Western Christendom, and whose constitutions for the Possessionate Orders and the Franciscans formed a basis for all future legislation in the Middle Ages.

Just as those constitutions begin by rehearsing the pressing causes for some real change, so his dealings with the Dominicans were called forth by complaints from within. He wrote to the master-general: "It hath lately come to our Apostolic hearing, by the narrations of trustworthy members of your Order, that certain things are committed, in contravention of the honesty thereof, which greatly and grievously offend the eyes of God's Majesty." Therefore the general must come to Rome within three months, "with certain other honourable and circumspect men of your Order, to consult with us concerning opportune and wholesome remedies" (III, 116). Father Mortier writes bitterly of the "false brethren", the "serpent in the home", by whom these complaints had been made; but he makes no attempt to disprove their accusations. On the contrary, he is obliged to admit the existence of very serious abuses: and this evidence is implicitly borne out half a century earlier by Roger Bacon, together with such great Dominicans as Humbert de Romans and Hugues de St Cher. Explicitly, it is reinforced by Dante and the great mystic Ruysbroeck who were Benedict XII's contemporaries. Moreover, the contemporary Acts of the General Chapter testify plainly to the growth of *proprietas* among these Dominicans, as elsewhere, and to other "licences which ruined community life, and scandalized the faithful" (pp. 122–3). Studies, also, were sadly neglected; and there was serious indiscipline among the younger brethren (pp. 123–4).

Benedict, however, committed the tactical error of attempting to change the Dominican Constitution. The Order had begun practically to abandon one of St Dominic's main rules, the renunciation of property not only private but corporate also. Not that the Saint had either himself enforced this in practice, or even explicitly commanded it at the outset of his apostolate: but he decreed it at the General Chapter of 1220. He may have been influenced here by the Franciscan ideal; and certainly his successor Humbert de Romans, writing in 1254, takes the strict view. The Dominicans called themselves Mendicants; and Mortier can write that they were "canonically recognized as Mendicants by the Church" (p. 129). Of them, as of the Minors, it was claimed that they "followed, naked, the naked Christ".(2) Thus, though it is probable that the Saint himself, like his great disciple St Thomas Aquinas, regarded poverty only as means to an end, yet the fourteenth-century Dominicans were tempted to that pharisaical boast of poverty which sometimes made men say of the stricter Franciscans, "ye make an idol of this poverty of yours". On the other hand, it was now notorious that they were often frankly possessionate, possessing houses and endowments in common, and with pocket-money and legacies and rents in private. Therefore the misunderstanding between them and the Pope was natural enough. He, knowing that the Dominican Rule was originally modelled on that of the possessionate Austin canons, felt that it would be a real reform to bring the Rule into conformity with the apparently incorrigible practice. Let these friars drop pretensions which they seem no longer able to maintain, and fall back upon that moderate ideal which had been good enough for the greatest doctor of the Latin Church. But they, on their part, treated it as unthinkable that they should be publicly dismissed from the Mendicant ranks, especially as Benedict had made no such proposal for the Franciscans. Mendicancy might be impossible in practice, but as an idol it was far too venerable and convenient to be abandoned. The Counter-Reformation of Trent did indeed make Mendicants practically Possessionates: but the time was not yet ripe for this. Therefore, for five long years, the general fought this great Pope with a pertinacity which to Father Mortier seems heroic, and which may well command our sympathy even while we wish they had championed a better cause. The General Chapter of 1337 quietly ignored the Vicar of Christ: its acts contain no allusion to his proposal. But the general wrote to the University of Paris for counsel's opinion from one of its most famous doctors. The answer suited his purpose. Mendicity is indeed strictly commanded in the Dominican Constitutions: "but that does not mean that [possessions] are against our vow; for we do not swear to keep the Constitutions, but to obey in accordance with them". Therefore, a full General Chapter might remove the difficulty by rescinding this constitution. Nor are possessions against the Rule, "since the Canons Regular have possessions"—that is, the Austin canons upon whose Rule Dominic founded his own. The true remedy, thinks this counsellor, lies in the dispensing power of the superior. If this person judges that this or that convent cannot do its work properly on the Mendicant system, let him grant dispensations for possessions. He may grant such too easily, but that is on his own head; not on that of the brethren who take advantage of their freedom. Thus it is for the Order's visitors to punish on the one hand superiors who thus offend, but to ratify the cases in which dispensations have been reasonably granted. Finally, let the Pope relieve our indigence by revoking that bull of Boniface VIII confirmed by John XXII, to the effect that when folk desire burial in our churches and leave money for the purpose, we Mendicants are compelled to give a quarter to the parish priest.*

This casuistry was not calculated to convince a strong Pope, deeply pledged to reform. Yet it was quite enough for the general, in those days when hollow words and hollow appearances were more powerful socially than even in our own day. Just as the friar's frock had a value apart from the man inside it and a Latin sentence had occult force which no translation could possibly convey, so the very word Mendicant was

* We shall see later the deep significance of this "canonical portion" as it was technically called.

sacrosanct. The general and his brethren "repeated to each other, not without terror, that curse which St Dominic had pronounced on his deathbed against anyone who should introduce *proprietas* among his sons.... Hence his tenacity in the struggle against Benedict XII. In spite of the Pope's solicitations and disputes and threats, which lasted more than five years, he did not yield a hair's breadth. Such as he had received the Order, such he left it to his successor" (p. 136). The whole tragedy of the next two centuries is contained in that last sentence. That reform which the Council of Trent finally decreed, by way of counter-revolution, was too revolutionary for a strong Pope to carry through in 1337: the early fourteenth century knew not the days of its visitation. Mortier himself shows how impossible it was for any institution to maintain itself, in a growing and moving world, upon that slippery slope. He frankly exposes the Pope's point of view, and the solid reasons for his insistence. That "uncertainty for the morrow" which had been the breath of life to the first Mendicants, had now become hopelessly out of date. Where the friars were not endowed, each was tempted to appropriate his own collections, so that popular and plausible brethren might live in luxury while the less fortunate were in actual want: thus "the community remained poor, while the individual became a *rentier*". The general saw all these things clearly enough; Mortier rightly emphasizes his anxiety in some directions for reform, he sees clearly that the Pope had commonsense and justice on his side; yet he extols the general's heroic resistance. When he died, worn out, "it might even be said that he fell, like a brave soldier, on the battlefield" (p. 165). For in the Dominican Order, as in all other Orders or monasteries which enjoyed the fatal privilege of exemption, that selfish consideration, with its accompanying prestige of exceptional dignity, outweighed all others. The General Chapter, after the general's death, flatly rebelled against the papal decision. Benedict undertook to break down their resistance by suppressing the Chapter and forbidding a fresh election to the generalate. "But" (writes Mortier) "Popes propose, and sometimes God disposes: Benedict XII gave up the ghost on April 5, 1342" (p. 170). "The Order remained as it had been before the storm. It had stoutly resisted the hurricane, without losing root"

(p. 171). Here is what St Bernard had very plainly foretold to his pupil Eugenius III; and the whole later story of monasticism had justified his prophecy.

No trace was ever found of those constitutions which the Pope had contemplated, if not written down, for the reform of the Order. Things went on from bad to worse, and those breaches of the Rule which had begun as regrettable exceptions became gradually a rule unto themselves. But it is impossible to accept Mortier's plea that this decay was catastrophically hastened by the Black Death. This theory, of an entirely new world after the pestilence, persistently as it is repeated by Roman Catholic historians, is increasingly discredited by modern research in every field of history, economic or religious. What the pestilence did overthrow was only what was already tottering; in every thoroughly healthy direction recovery was rapid; Mortier relies mainly upon partisan evidence, uncritically employed.(3) Not only does he emphasize the recorded figures of mortality without the discount notoriously necessary for medieval writers when they deal with large numbers, but he ignores the general testimony of contemporaries upon a question far easier to decide; the extent to which friars as a body actually tended the sick. It would be difficult to find a legend more pious, and more devoid of real evidence, than that which he quotes from a dubious manuscript concerning the unselfish friars who cast out of their windows the rich offerings forced upon them by the frenzied gratitude of a population which they had tended through sickness and death. Moreover, his arguments are inconsistent with each other. He lauds the Pope as "very courageous" for remaining steadily in his vast prison-like palace at Avignon, where he shut himself up in a fumigated room from which he refused all visits or audiences! No man is recorded to have taken greater precautions for his own personal safety than this. Again, the picture of devoted friars dying like flies at their ministrations for the sick is inconsistent with the evidence of the chronicler of St-Denis, to the effect that, directly the plague was past, "certain cardinals and other prelates, with a great multitude of parish priests, rose up at the Court of Rome, against the Mendicants desiring and demanding from Pope Clement VI the suppression of their Order" (III, 265).

It fits ill with the similar fact that the popular movement of Flagellants—that "epidemic of mystical madness"—was bitterly hostile to priests and cloisterers, so that "a number of [Dominicans] lost their lives" at the hands of these zealots. Again, we have the fact which Clement VI himself could not deny in his defence of the friars, that in 1351 they were actually adding to their already sumptuous buildings. The truth is that the effects of the Black Death were mainly economic and moral. On the economic side, though some sources of supply were temporarily dried up, this was not permanently in proportion to the decrease among consumers. Those friars who were left should almost as easily as before have lived upon the alms of the faithful, if the beneficent social action of their Order had been as notorious as it was in the days of St Dominic. On the moral side again, all contemporaries looked upon the Black Death as God's call to the world for repentance. The surviving Dominicans and Franciscans should have been far more ready than their immediate predecessors to revert to the Rule of their Founders. How should the mortality of 1348–9, even though it had equalled those incredible descriptions which Father Mortier quoted as trustworthy facts—90 per cent. at Marseilles, five wretched survivors from all the great and populous city of Ursina!—have rendered the Dominicans less able to study and evangelize and live upon the alms of the faithful than in 1347.

Indeed, when Father Mortier comes to tell the later story, under Leonardo de' Mansueti (1474–80), while still maintaining his theory he gives even more incompatible evidence. He writes (IV, 494):

The disaster of the Black Death gave a finishing stroke to compulsory mendicancy. True the friars still begged—even too much—but the convents had no hesitation in accepting revenues and prebends and lands or houses. The Popes often intervened to grant the necessary permissions, or certain benevolent *sanatoria.* Yet it was felt that this was not St Dominic's Rule. So, when Blessed Raymond of Capua [1380–1399] inaugurated the Reform, he turned the ship's tiller stoutly backwards. The Observants were to resume Dominican mendicancy in all its rigour, and abandon all property. In the earlier days [of this Reform] the generous ardour of Blessed Raymond and his sons enjoyed full success, so that the man of God was able to say triumphantly to detractors of the Observants: "Though poor, we are richer than you, because the faithful, edified by our piety, give more to us than to you."

Why was it not possible to say that, even rhetorically, just after the Black Death? That question can best be answered by an intensive study of the official acts of the General Chapters. The real clue is in what Mortier mentions, but without realizing its full significance. The General Chapter of 1348 met on Whit Sunday at Lyons, more than six months after the appearance of the plague in Southern France. Yet "Garin, the Master-General, busied himself with the government of the Order as though the Plague had never happened" (III, 267). In Paris, at the height of the mortality, "the Dominican masters and students, like the Franciscans and the University professors, seemed to have continued their work without great emotion". The next Chapter was in May, 1349. "As usual, the administrative serenity [of its recorded acts] suggests no suspicion of the anguish and fears and losses of the Order. Nothing is said of plague or ruin or comfort." All this, by itself, is puzzling: but it becomes natural enough when we look more closely into the original records, as published in vol. IV of B. M. Reichert's *Monumenta Ordinis Fratrum Praedicatorum Historica*. We shall there see these plague-year Chapters in their true perspective, as compared with the acts of earlier and later years.

Let us begin with the Chapter of London in 1335, a year of rather more than usual legislative activity. I give the main decrees much more fully in my appendix: but this present very brief catalogue may easily be verified at the British Museum. The figures in brackets after each decree represent the number of times that it was repeated again before the Black Death, often with complaints of non-observance, or equally significant threats of severer punishment against offenders. The decrees are directed against neglect and sometimes "collapse" of studies (5). "The detestable abstention of brethren from community-life" (1). Confession by mutual arrangement between friar and friar. Pawning or alienation of books (1). Separate lodgings for a friar (2). Abstention from the common meals (3). Some friars sell their own Masses for a year, or more, and pocket the proceeds (1). Some shirk choir-service (4). There is much vagrancy (7). Some preach publicly against the parish clergy.

Students need better moral discipline (5). Others wander unlicensed to the Court of Rome (5).

Next year, 1336, the list contains five other decrees. Moneyless novices, if otherwise promising, must not be rejected. Persons of notoriously illegitimate birth must, as a rule, be kept out of the Order (4). The doctors (lecturers) are sometimes inadequate. Litigation is indecent for persons vowed to poverty (3). Friars go about alone, "not without grievous suspicion": let such solitary wanderers be imprisoned (3). "Grievous scandals have followed in certain parts upon the damnable temerity of certain friars who interfere in the practice of medicine"—i.e. who take fees as doctors (3).

The decrees of 1337 (apart again from repetitions) are against giving high or responsible office to friars who have ever apostasized, been convicted of unchastity, or legally committed to prison (1). Delinquents who have been "cut off from all graces of the Order" do not thereby lose their vote at elections. Many provinces are neglecting to send students to the Universities (1). Indulgences for flesh-food are sometimes given with scandalous laxity. Many friars ride on horse-back without the excuse of necessary business. Others buy themselves life-annuities, which "is contrary to our profession, and doth also notably deform our poverty".

It was in this year 1337, then, that Benedict XII planned his reform: let the pretence of holy mendicancy be given up, and let the friars entrench themselves behind the rule which other Orders were supposed to keep: viz. ample endowment for the community, but no individual ownership of anything. Let us carry our minds back to experiences which were not only in his mind, but in that of every friar worth his name: the experiences of this whole first generation of the fourteenth century. France and England had revolted against the Pope on one of the subjects which stir men's passions most deeply—the power of the purse. One of the main factors in that quarrel had been the exemption of clergy from taxation, and that exemption was most fully enjoyed by the Mendicants. John XXII had condemned, and his Inquisitors had burned, enthusiastic friars who taught the "heresy" that Christ and His Apostles had lived in absolute poverty, owning nothing either in common or individually.

Pierre Dubois had suggested, and Marsilius of Padua had reinforced, far-reaching measures of clerical disendowment. Dante, proclaiming plainly his sense of Mendicant degeneracy, had voiced the general opinion of thoughtful people, including even such distinguished friars as St Bonaventura and Cardinal Hugues de St-Cher in a previous generation.

The general, if indeed he wanted real reform above all things, was singularly unsuccessful. Between this and the Black Death, apart from repetitions of old complaints, seven more come in—extravagance in food and dress, private hoards of money, will-hunting, fisticuffs, convicted criminals employed as confessors, sometimes, at other times haunting nunneries. Moreover, the contrast is sometimes explicitly drawn between past glories and the present decay of the Order.

Then comes 1348, with only one direct reference to the Plague. "The number of our brethren has been diminished in certain districts by the general pestilence: therefore let us recruit as many novices as possible." This significant limitation of "certain districts" is further borne out by a decree licensing the fresh foundation of five houses this year, and two in the next. There are no such previous licences in our series except for two in 1335, eight in 1344 and one in 1347: nor can I trace any at all after 1352. It is true that the 1350 chapter modifies these decrees with a conditional clause: "provided that there are enough to people the existing convents". But, if the pictures of depopulation and starvation were even approximately true, it is incredible that the official records should not show more than this. Moreover, they supply not only negative but positive evidence. The three Plague years show us the chapters wrestling not only with faults which might be attributed to poverty, but sometimes to the greed for food or money or comfort. In 1348 alchemy is again forbidden. Apostasy is dealt with, and unauthorized sale of books or valuables; and forged licences or exemptions. In 1349 "the detestable excesses in the matter of eating with secular folk outside"; at University graduations, "notably excessive expenses; *proprietas*; litigation; promotions through the influence of worldly friends". In 1350 the two clauses about eating are repeated; also horse-riding, solitary vagrancy and extravagant dress, private chambers, shirking of choir-service; with other decrees repeated from before. And, after these years, though steady deterioration can indeed be traced, it is little more rapid now than that which had prompted Benedict XII's revolutionary suggestions for reform. We shall see, later, that the rich records of Cologne are far from favourable to Mortier's theory. In short, the Dominican story is practically what we see everywhere when we look closely into the results of the Black Death. That is summed up by one of the most trustworthy of medieval chroniclers, the Florentine merchant Matteo Villani.(4) The first healthy shock, he tells us, was followed by a reaction towards self-indulgence: "according to such tidings as we could hear, there was no part of the world wherein men restrained themselves to live in temperance". What was lacking in this Dominican Order after the Great Pestilence was not the power of keeping its Rule, but the will. When at last something like effective reform came, this originated here, as we have seen elsewhere, less from above than from below: not so much from Pope or Hierarchy as from a humble friar, ordinary in everything except his piety and burning zeal.

Brother Conrad, called "of Prussia", though he seems neither to have been born nor to have lived there, entered the Order with a like-minded blood-brother in 1370. He was in the Cologne convent when he attracted the notice of the general, who chose him in 1389 for the great work.

This general, Raymond of Capua (1380–1400), was the intimate friend and patron of St Catharine of Siena. Sadly impressed by what he found on his round of official visits, he set himself to the plain straightforward task of bringing his brethren back to those constitutions to which they were bound by their solemn lifelong oath, "a law very clear, and precise, and imperious".

The Generals until then [writes Mortier] for all their good intentions had completely failed. Their method had never varied. It consisted in publishing good and serious decrees in Chapter, and, always with sincere energy, recalling all the brethren to the observance of the Rule. They were invited to resume the practice of the law *en bloc*. If this somewhat easy-going method was to succeed, there should have been in the convents a compact mass of friars who were disposed to take this warning seriously. Those ordinances were like a vigorous trumpet-call which falls violently upon the nearest ears, but whose sonorous undulations spread into space and die out afar. The few friars who followed the Rule, scattered in undisciplined surroundings, without sufficient coherence or rallying-point—perhaps without hope—were content to save their own souls: they deplored the ruin of the Order, but could not transform those among whom they lived. (p. 524.)

Therefore Raymond, not content with merely sowing good seed, set himself also to prepare the ground. The visits had brought him into contact with many relaxed brethren and a few true children of the great saint. To Conrad, chief of these, he addressed a formal letter. "Unfortunately, the children of God are often hindered by the children of the world from bringing forth good fruit, either through their perverse tongues or through their ill example." Therefore he will set Conrad at the head of a chosen convent, "inhabited only by brethren resolved to serve God and to keep the Rule of the Order....I will do everything towards this object, even by having recourse to the Pope in case of need." The convent chosen was Colmar, in Alsace; and within a short time thirty brethren answered the general's appeal. Yet, even so, reform was difficult; the old brethren were supported by their friends outside, and they took away the seal. But Raymond appealed successfully to the civil magistrates. Next year, therefore, he could go a step further. He sent a circular letter to all the provinces, commanding that, in each, one convent should be set apart, with room for twelve friars at least, for those who were willing to practise observance according to the Rule. "As for the brethren whom I have collected in some convents, and the superiors whom I myself have set over them, it is my will that ye molest them in no wise, nor hinder them from following their design." Any provincial minister who has not obeyed this command within twelve months is to be deposed (p. 530). The reaction to this may be told in Father Mortier's own words (p. 531):

The decisive step was taken. It aroused a deep disturbance in the Order. It was well known that the Chapter of Vienne, in 1388, had given the General full powers for reform, and that he had appointed a few special convents wherein literal observance should be kept; but it was not expected that these Observantine convents should be imposed upon every province. This very term "Observantine convent", new to the Order, seemed an insult. That which at first had been watched with indifference, as a limited attempt destined to failure, became a menace to all, and an imminent menace. Recriminations were plentiful at the Roman Court.

Here, as among the Franciscans, the non-Observants were soon called Conventuals, as forming the great majority in the convents. Their very excuses formed the most tell-tale accusation. Their trump-card, which Raymond found it hardest to meet, was this: "Seeing that the whole Order cannot be reformed, there will in fact be two parties in the Dominican family, one observing and one not observing the Rule: in other words, two Orders instead of one." Again, "the world will notice the difference in life: they will say of the Observants: 'These are the good', and of the non-Observants: 'Those are the evil'" (p. 537). In other words, unity above all things: better keep unity in relaxation than cause separation by reform.

Yet Raymond was far from an unyielding precisian. He did all in his power to spare the relaxed either punishment or humiliation.

He showed himself generous in dispensations, even such as seem extraordinary to us nowadays, according to our present practice. At that time they were common, adapted to the manners of the day. Thus, Raymond himself granted to certain friars, for the term of their lives, rooms at their own choice, sometimes even with a garden and outhouses.... Such life-grants appear frequently in the records. (p. 536.)

Indeed, one of the most telling attacks upon Raymond was based on the fact that he himself was physically unable to keep the fasts without fainting fits, and he pleaded in defence: "I dare not claim to have been the first instigation of reform; I have only consented and yielded to the impulse given unto me." The Pope, Boniface IX, was indeed on his side: but

at the time with which our story is still concerned, papal decisions seem not to have made so deep an impression, but that men might attempt and hope to escape from them. Some at least of the provincial ministers opposed the reform. They intrigued at Rome, and even began to boast that Raymond would soon be condemned. Therefore he besought Boniface to repeat and reinforce his previous commands. The Pope consented; he wrote condemning "those who not only ignore the decree of reform, although they know it well, but will not leave others free to keep it". They even flatter themselves that they will rescind it at the coming chapter, in spite of the Apostolic See. We therefore condemn any such act in advance as null and void, and pronounce "excommunication *ipso facto* upon all who hinder, secretly or publicly, directly or indirectly, under any pretext soever, any friar from following the observance so wisely organized". (p. 543.)

Here, again, Father Mortier can best speak (p. 544).

All official struggle was now stopped. But because war was no longer legal, it must not be thought that it ceased. The decree was laid upon them, and they had to submit. Only it was always possible to shut one's convent door against reform; to vituperate it, and to hold it up to ridicule. Men did not spare this, whether covertly or violently, the hostility against reform and against the reformers lasted long years more. Not that all the adversaries were bad friars. Doubtless some among them were undisciplined; but these were also never worthy of much respect, accustomed to the life which they had always known and which they considered better adapted to the social conditions of their time.

CHAPTER XLV

THE DOMINICANS (2)

THE real facts of Mendicant "poverty" may be gathered from a famous incident in 1387. The Parisian convent, the "Jacobins", was by far the most populous and influential in the Order, and, naturally, the richest in university students and teachers. While the Franciscans had long since gone over to the doctrine of the Immaculate Conception, and their influence with the people was paramount, the more learned Dominicans still upheld St Bernard's repudiation of that doctrine as a dangerous innovation. One of their doctors, Jean de Montson, boldly preached that the doctrine was heretical, and based himself upon St Thomas Aquinas (p. 622). The Faculty of Theology and the Bishop of Paris condemned him, and it was decided that no man henceforth should take his degree at Paris without first swearing conformity with this condemnation. For the Dominicans, rightly or wrongly, "the Cause of brother Jean de Montson, reputed that of St Thomas, became that of the Order" (p. 626). Both sides now appealed to the Pope: but no Pope was destined to pronounce finally and infallibly upon this bitterly disputed question, nor would the answer be given for more than four centuries yet to come. Meanwhile, however, the chronicler of St-Denis, who is critical of these Mendicants, reports them as boasting their certain success at Rome. "Never will our doctrine be condemned! Our Order is too powerful, too world-renowned, for any man to dare touch it. True, we are Mendicants, but we have more than 40,000 crowns of gold in reserve for this purpose"—apart from the learning of our doctors, and our brother-Dominicans as ministers and confessors to Pope, Kings, and Princes.

The same spirit of fierce independence, and the same confidence in the force of custom and of worldly possessions, supported the majority of the Order in the still more important question of reform. We need not follow Mortier in detail through his two last volumes. The most he can claim is that about half the convents did at some time join the Observants, yet often under conditions which, in earlier centuries, would have been counted as notable relaxations. Here, as in all other Orders, it was a commonplace in the fifteenth century that men were too degenerate everywhere to support what their fathers had borne. Under cover of that principle, almost any irregularity could defend itself, so long as it was bold enough. The extent to which indiscipline could sometimes thrive and flourish, even close under the eyes of a so-called reforming Pope like Eugenius IV, is recorded by a Pisan annalist. In 1442, the sub-prior of the Dominicans in that city was the son of a successful condottiere. Hence he became prior, and held that office in a fashion which earned for him the essentially un-Dominican title of abbot.

He amassed great sums of money, which he left at his death; to whom, we know not. Men say that, whenever there was talk of reform, he would say: "Reform ye, if so please you; provided that I be Prior and keep such moneys as I have; neither of these will I relinquish." Meanwhile he boasted, as I have said above, that he possessed 1,400 crowns of gold; wherefore he feared neither the Minister Provincial nor other Superiors, perchance as hoping to corrupt them with money, or at least, if he were deposed from his priorate, to live in comfort outside the Order with the help of his gold. Yet he did all that he could to hinder the reform of his convent; and so long as he lived, he succeeded. The convent possesseth still some properties from this man's mother's heritage, which the father had earned by his military exploits.(1)

It was in 1422, also, that Eugenius IV tried personally, but vainly, to reform the Dominicans of Siena, so famous sixty years earlier for their support of St Catharine. After six years of struggle, in spite of support from the city magistrates, the general gave up in despair and procured papal permission to found a new convent in Siena. The brethren of San Domenico, "in spite of the papal commands, opposed reform and never gave way. This was one of the few Italian convents which never accepted the Observance at any time".(2)

Moreover, here as elsewhere the women gave more trouble than the men, and for the usual reasons: their obedience was expected to be stricter, their temptations were greater in the absence of real religious vocation, and their lapses were more conspicuous. "The worst difficulty was that of claustration. They could hardly be brought to resume that severe observance without which there is no honourable subsistence for a convent of women devoted to contemplation. Ingrained custom, and the many oppositions of parents and friends, and the diminishing fervour of the sisters, all contributed to retard the impulse of reform among them."(3) Though some real improvement came later, even Texier's energetic efforts had little effect. To realize the immense power of conservative resistance, we must grasp the extent to which irregularities had become regular. A single illustration will suffice: that question of mendicancy or private property, of plain community life or of individual privilege and comfort, which had aroused war to the knife between Benedict XII and the Order. A century later, this is the state of things as described by Mortier.(4)

> We must note it not as a novelty, but as a fact henceforth admitted by the saintliest friars and almost consecrated by custom, until it shall gain true legal force, that brethren accepted property and fixed revenues....All that was demanded from friars who had more or less revenues was to report their budget yearly to their Prior; this formality was enough to clear them from the accusation of *proprietas*. They possessed this property with permission of their Superiors, who kept the legal possession in the name of the community; this accountancy was considered as the symbolic justification.

At last, therefore, the virtue of poverty was deserted without even the time-worn tribute of hypocrisy. It was in 1475 that the General Leonardo de' Mansueti, a personal friend of Sixtus IV, obtained from him a bull which granted to all Dominican convents, without exception, the legal right of holding possessions. This, says Mortier truly, opened a new era for the Order. The *volte-face*, as he points out, was absolute. A century and a quarter earlier the general had fought to the death against a Pope who tried to compel the Order to accept frankly, what in fact they were holding more or less furtively, endowments like those of the Possessionate Orders. Now it is the General who begs as a favour what had then been rejected as treachery to St Dominic. But "Sixtus IV, who had been a Franciscan, and General Minister, knew intimately the practical situation of the Mendicant Orders. He knew by experience how difficult it was for them to find their subsistence in public charity alone" (p. 495).

The licence was granted only for property in common: but it gave a natural stimulus to *proprietas* in private. As early as 1258 the General Chapter had complained of brethren who were beginning to buy their own garments, and to choose their own stuff. Now, two centuries later, we find a preacher arraigning the shortcomings of the clergy and, with regard to the Mendicants, appealing to "those abuses which your eyes show you in their outward observance. For they wear soft clothing, after the fashion of men who are in kings' houses; they have costly feathers spread under them; scarce can you find in the cities a cloth which satisfies their moneys."(5)

Thus the fifteenth century wore to an end; and, whereas Meyer thought that about half had been "reformed" before 1470, Mortier can claim very little more for the end of the century (IV, 647). Moreover, many even of the Observants lived under conditions which, in earlier centuries, would have been blamed for notable relaxation. Löhr has summarized evidence on this point in his preface to *Teutonia* (pp. 30, 31; cf. p. 101). As for the Conventuals, all the intimate details from German sources give the same evidence of decay. Chroniclers, Visitors, Chapter Acts show the ancient troubles, all the more dangerous in proportion as they have grown older. Dangers of association with nuns or other women; "potations and commessations", wine-shops on the premises; forbidden flesh-food; vagrancy; fighting; neglect of choir or Mass; difficulties confronting the Visitors; and complaints of general decay.(6)

One very startling episode was that of the Bernese Dominicans. In 1506 they accepted as lay-brother a tailor aged 23 and named Jetzer, who was haunted then, and had been haunted at his former abode of Zurzach, by a spirit from Purgatory, swarming with worms. This spirit promised to bring other visions; and, on the eve of Lady-Day 1507, it brought St Barbara and the Virgin Mary to his cell. The more notice this ecstatic attracted, the more his visions increased. The fathers witnessed his convulsions; the whole city was soon moved. The Virgin brought him a consecrated Host which took spots of blood; on June 24 she carried him from his bed to her image in the choir, which then wept tears of blood, and was found to be bloodstained in the morning: the prior called in a magistrate to testify to this. The minister-provincial sent a commission of enquiry, which discovered no fraud. The Bishop of Lausanne came in July, somewhat sceptical: the visions slackened. But, one night in September, the Virgin appeared to the assembled brethren on the choir screen, with her golden hair and five burning tapers, and blessed the congregation. The lector took a lantern and went up: sounds of dispute were heard, and he came down, followed presently by Jetzer. Later, they found his blond wig and coronet hidden behind the organ: these they burned. It is difficult, as Mortier confesses, to doubt the complicity of some friars, and "there was one certain complicity from the first, I will call it by its true name; the complicity of folly". After this discovery of the wig,

> there remained no possible doubt; and the conscience of the faithful, deceived by these impostures, should have been enlightened. The friars did the exact opposite. Was it in ridiculous obstinacy? Was it for fear of bringing down upon the convent the mockery of their adversaries? I know not; but, instead of testifying to the truth, they aggravated the lie and made themselves its public accomplices. A few days after this pretended apparition, the delegates of the friary set out for Rome. Their mission was to submit to the Holy See the miracles wrought in their convent, with the attestations of witnesses. (v, 186.)

What, however, made all this far more serious was the theology of Jetzer's revelations. As Father Mortier puts it, from the very first this impostor spirit "spoke *Dominican*: that is, made itself the apostle of the teaching of that Order against the Immaculate Conception". It said in so many words: "The Franciscans stand up everywhere against the truth on this subject, and cheat the faithful." It was a home-thrust at these importunate rivals who had obtained from Sixtus IV a monopoly of the Stigmata, even against St Catharine of Siena (p. 187). Could this "ignorant layman", as he was described in the solemn trial, have engineered, unaided, a doctrinal dispute of that kind?

For not once, but thrice successively, it came to solemn trial. First before the Bishop of Lausanne; here Jetzer alone was condemned. Then Jetzer accused four accomplices, including the prior, sub-prior, and lector. The Dominicans answered by expelling him. But here the city magistrates intervened: they demanded that a fresh trial should put an end to this scandal. Here, the four accused confessed under torture, but retracted afterwards. Then they appealed to the Pope. After long delay, he appointed a commission. There was no torture this time; but the four dignitaries were condemned, handed over to the secular arm, and burned as "heretics, renegades and sorcerers". Jetzer was carried round the town in a paper mitre as an idiot, and expelled from the district: he finally married and died in obscurity. Much in this matter will doubtless never be cleared up. The Protestant Reuss would explain this *auto da fé* as a political job at Rome, an accord between the Order and the Pope in order to hide further scandals behind the punishment of these scapegoats. Father Mortier, on the contrary, finds it "difficult to believe that they were unjustly punished". The one thing certain is, that the affair gave a great shock to Dominican reputation in those parts. In the German province, as in Italy, the great obstacle to reform lay in the freedom with which nuns often went abroad themselves or entertained outsiders in the convent. Father Reichert sums up this evidence, with quotations, in his preface to Meyer's *Buch der Reformacio* (XVI). At the nunnery of St Agnes, "leaving the convent seems to have been certainly nothing uncommon among the unreformed sisters, 'for they had secret underground holes', 'and other ways of exit also'. Nay, when town police were set to guard the convent and 'were keeping their watch, they found some nuns who had gone out from among the unwilling sisters within, to follow after their accustomed follies'." Even stronger evidence, perhaps, is given by Fr. Löhr in his preface to *Teutonia* (p. 24, *note* 1). The opening years of the sixteenth century are far from reassuring as to the Order in general. The General Chapter of 1501, the first under Bandelli, opened on a depressing note. The general beseeches his brethren in God's name, "to abolish deformity, and repair that life according to the Rule which is almost extinct in the Order": his desire is "to reform Religion, collapsed and totally deformed".(7) The chapter decrees repeat the old, worn-out prohibitions, against "walking or vain discourse during divine service"; impunity of evil brethren and neglect of the good; vagrancy and begging on private account; abandonment of community life. "We command, under threat of eternal malediction and deprivation of every grace of the Order, that none presume to busy himself with trade or merchandize, or the art of alchemy." Wide relaxations of the original are permitted, "yet with such moderation that [the brethren] lose not the name and merit of Mendicants". Superiors may relax the rule of poverty for separate houses, "but not for the whole Order". In protection of chastity and modesty, let claustration be duly kept, "nor let [Superiors] in any way, or under any colourable pretext, allow women to enter the dormitory or other offices or the cloisters of our convents". Nuns' confessions must be heard only at the grille, parti-coloured garments and long hair are forbidden; wandering abroad without companion; "bearing weapons of attack in the convent or keeping them in their cells"; haunting of nunneries without permission; "let none be sent as confessors, especially to young nuns, but grave, mature, honest, discreet and approved brethren". "In these times of ours, we mourn to say, studies have decayed in almost every province, to the disgrace and contempt of our Order". As to the non-Observants, we must have patience, "Whensoever any convent, of scandalous life and needing reform cometh at the prayer of princes or of city councils, let the General...give orders to the provincial to reform that house in essentials, and especially in community of all goods and strict claustration and the ceremonies of the Order, in so far as human frailty shall permit, with flesh-eating thrice a week, especially where, by reason of poverty or of situation, fish cannot easily be procured."

In 1505, the general summed up in an encyclical the results of his first visitation.

I have visited many convents in Italy; I have traversed almost all France; I have gone as far as Lower Germany and even into the vast realm of Spain. I found some consolations upon the way: but greater were my reasons for sadness and mortification. I have noted—not without tears, alas!—how the beauty of our Order had faded. I have seen our holy observance corrupted, neglected, utterly forgotten; and the love of the Constitutions handed down by our fathers was extinguished in men's hearts. I shuddered with horror to see, with my own eyes, that the habit which the Queen of Angels had brought to our Order was now deformed; and to mark the immodesty of language and the relaxation of morals. I have blushed (it must be confessed) at the scandals which were common talk, and wherewith men reproached me and the Order, as though we had both been responsible for these excesses. What affliction for me to see with my own eyes the insolence of the brethren, the execrable indiscipline of the worst among them, and their lamentable weaknesses! The light of learning, that main glory of our Order, is almost extinct: I have seen this with amazement. There is no longer any zeal for salvation of souls, but begging and fierce money-getting; nothing else. What consoles me is the true and durable reform introduced into certain places; the zeal and good-will of the Observants. I rejoiced to see these new plantations which, with God's help and our support, will multiply and become the glory of our holy Order.(8)

Yet such was the ingrained laxity, that this zealous General himself was sometimes almost compelled to withdraw with one hand what he enforced with the other. His *Register*, under date of 1501, confirmed and approved the graces conferred by Chapter and Pope upon a vicar of the Order, that "he may, for his life long, inhabit the house which he hath built at his own expense in the convent, with his companions and attendants [*familia*]; and he may make a stable and a door with free exit and ingress for himself and his guests; and he may wear linen and eat flesh, and his companion may enjoy the same privileges so far as expedient. Yet none may go out or in through the said door without licence from the prior for the time being". That same year, the Prior of Heidelberg "may build from the money inherited and accruing from his parents a room or chamber in, or adjoining to, the dormitory.(9)

From Southern France, Mortier gives two examples of that against which Bandelli struggled. In 1503, at Montpellier, under the shadow of a famous university, he was welcomed by the civic authorities, and

some of the said Friars Preachers who had led the aforesaid wanton and evil life went forth from the convent, some over the walls and buildings and others how best they could, fleeing and quitting the said convent and the Dominican habit. Some of these went and set themselves in the abbey of Vallemagne, and others in that of La Merci; and the said reverend Minister General, being well and duly informed of that which hath been said, namely of the evil lives of the said Friars Preachers, reformed the said convent well and honestly, according to the Rule of the said Saint Dominic, so that, whereas there had been ten or a dozen friars, of evil condition, who had but six pence for their daily pittance, and yet could not live thereon, there are nowadays a good fifty, well conditioned, who live well and plentifully, spending daily in food-money twelve sols and a half or more. And in this convent the Father General, with the help of the town and the other inhabitants thereof, had built and repaired the dormitory chambers of the said convent, and wrought so that each sleepeth alone in his cell of the great dormitory, whereas aforetime they slept by two or three or four together in fair chambers, having each his own garden: and from five or six gardens the said General, with aid and succour of the said Consuls, bade make one single garden common and general for all the said brethren.

He opened the great gate of the convent, "to avoid the evils that were done with the little door", which he now built up, and fixed a bell which marked every entrance or issue from the convent. In the Church "he built a screen to separate the friars from the people" (v, 85). Yet this convent was not placed definitely in the list of Observants; and the General found here in Provence a Vicar-general ill suited to execute any serious project of reform. To begin with, the man was a "shameless pluralist", as Prior of St Maximin with all the revenues thereunto appertaining. It may be left to Father Mortier to characterize him here (v, 87):

Pierre Bonneti had indeed tried in 1497 to introduce a semblance of regularity into his convent. For the French Court was ill satisfied and even scandalized at the friars' conduct. His attempt came rather from fear of the King than from a desire for reform. For indeed it was very difficult for Pierre Bonneti, with his worldly ways and his personal income, to talk of penitence and poverty and life according to the Rule. For him as for his subjects, Dominican life no longer existed. His Ordinances have been preserved. He requires his brethren to keep silence during divine service; and not to walk about among the faithful in church during services and the sermons; a point which reveals the most pitiable laxity. He forbids the wearing of particoloured caps and robes open in front; but from this he exempts Masters and Graduates. He regulates the division of the *booty*: for that was the common word for the "casual" fees from private Masses. This booty should now be distributed monthly among the whole body. He tries to put a decent face upon the convent. It is forbidden to have gaming-parties at night, to keep up noise sometimes until midnight, to eat and drink in private chambers, in which it was possible to commit every disorder. But, here again, Masters and Graduates are excepted; that is, a good number of the delinquents, and not the least; men who should have been corrected first of all, as an example to lesser folk. So long as a reform touches only the small fry, it is certain to be illusory. It is almost comic, if it were not so tragic, to find Bonneti, after each ordinance, declaring gravely that he excepts Masters in Theology and Graduates of all ranks. In these conditions, nobody will be surprised to find that his reform remained a dead-letter, and had no use but to deceive the French Court for a little while. The Court desired more serious work.

Jean Clérée succeeded Bandelli in 1507. He also was an Observant; and he was one of the most learned and energetic of French churchmen. He started at once with the great convent of Paris, the Jacobins. He told them plainly: "If you have not reformed yourselves within six months, I will hand the matter over to other brethren." For, in Mortier's words, "These students of the Dominican convent allowed themselves to slide, by the common slope of that age, to life of small regularity, the excesses of which sometimes violated Christian morality" (v, 129). Clérée had the King's support, and he carried his reform through. He dealt also with the nunnery of Poissy, where the nuns were rich and powerful, and could employ all the chicaneries of the law in support of their resolution to endure no reform. Here, again, as the Chapter Acts testify with unusual emphasis, he broke down all opposition "by command of the most Christian King, and armed with powers from the Holy See" (v, 133).

Clérée's successor was the famous Cardinal Caietan, commentator of Aquinas and adversary of Luther, who aroused the antagonism of the Theological Faculty of Paris by maintaining Papal Infallibility. In other respects he was far from an extremist: indeed, his contemporaries were somewhat scandalized by his emphasis on the literal as against allegorical interpretations of the Bible. The same discretion he displayed in practical government, favouring solid rather than enthusiastic work. Mortier shows us this general "constantly at work to bring the brethren back to Observance, while leaving great latitude for indulgence. What he demands especially—and he demands it from all—is community life, the respect for claustration, and, as far as possible, the performance of penitential practices". Yet, among the Conventuals, almost any infraction of discipline was still possible here and there. At Venice, in 1526, those Dominicans who went about the city at will, and lived outside the Order, were so numerous and outrageous that the General Chapter forbade their wearing the habit, and were prepared to enforce this prohibition by appealing to the secular arm (Mortier, v, 274). Even in the official *Registers* of the Order, we sometimes find this same appeal: e.g. in that of Turriani (1494), p. 83.

An attempt was made in 1390 to introduce the Observance among English Dominicans; but it fell absolutely flat. When the sixteenth century came in, and there were already many Observantines in other lands, "England stood aloof from this Dominican revival". On the whole, "like so many others, they said to themselves that the Primitive Observance was an archaeological matter, excellent in the Middle Ages but impracticable in their times". Their relaxed usages, "after all, were ancient, and had received a sort of consecration through time".(10)

CHAPTER XLVI

CITIZENS AND CLOISTERERS

IN the concluding sentences of chapter XLV the keynote is, Monastic Reform through the City Magistracy. This is a subject so important as to need a chapter to itself. We shall see, later, its crucial value for the study of our own English Dissolution, where royal intervention was spectacular, and where economic issues were at stake to an extent which is very commonly exaggerated, but which cannot possibly be denied. For the present, it may suffice to pursue the Dominican story into a region which shows not merely one masterful person, or even one covetous class, in economic conflict with the monasteries, but the mass of a whole population. It may give food for thought to those who believe that to touch monastic endowments was to rob the poor in favour of the rich.

The convent of Friars Preachers at Cologne was founded in 1221. In 1261, when one or two of the earliest friars may conceivably have been yet alive, the General Chapter strictly commanded this convent to "correct" the new choir of its church and bring it under the law which prescribed "none but humble and mean [*mediocria*] buildings" throughout the Order (I, 4). In 1280, Albertus Magnus left considerable sums to enlarge it. Already in 1253 the friars possessed a considerable space in the best part of the city (p. 9). By 1341, or a little earlier, their possessions were so great as to arouse a revolt in the municipality (pp. 84ff.). The causes were mainly economic; but the full study of the documents does not support Löhr in his downright statement that "it would be a mistake to believe that any sort of ecclesiastico-religious opposition was at the bottom of the citizens' behaviour" (p. 84). A whole block of the city, enclosed by four streets, was coming more and more into the dead hand of these Dominicans, who had also in the outlying district six houses which served as centres of activity for their official alms-collectors (p. 15). They had also many rents elsewhere in the city. This, so contrary to the original conception, begins only just before the death of Albertus Magnus (1280), who was regarded as a champion of apostolic poverty (p. 18). But the temptation was too great, and casuists found specious excuses. Dominican nuns had been endowed from the first. Testators now left possessions to them, subject to their giving a specified proportion to the friars. Next, we find testators leaving money, sometimes considerable sums, to found an "anniversary" (the English "Year's Mind") at which Mass was said for the soul, and the brethren spent the rest on food and wine, with or without specified alms for the poor. These anniversaries became such a regular institution that friars even enforced the payments in the law courts when necessary (p. 20). From 1301 onwards, it became more and more frequent to leave money or rents to individual friars. In the first recorded case the testatrix puts it apologetically, "although he is a professed friar" (p. 22), but soon the arrangement is bold and frequent. "The members of the rich lineages and burgher-families endow their sons or kinsfolk in the Order with life-annuities" (p. 23). One, in 1336, has even 30 marks a year; in 1253 a cow or five pigs could be bought for just over a mark of Cologne.(1) One such deed of gift to a Strassburg Dominican is so strictly drawn up and attested by witnesses so numerous and so distinguished—a bishop, two priors, three future ministers-provincial, etc.—that Löhr writes: "life-rents for individual members are now allowed even in the Dominican Order, despite the contrary commands of the Constitutions" (p. 24). Thus grew up that *vita privata*, finally destructive of the community life, which became the worst hindrance to real reform. Löhr speaks of its especially rapid growth since 1348, but he gives no statistical evidence (p. 25). His actual documents (II, 160–232) seem to give thirteen cases in the eleven years before 1348, and only eight in the twenty years 1348–67, which include the severe second pestilence of 1362. In whatever other ways the Black Death may well have loosened discipline, it was not so here. It was the rapid growth of this *proprietas* which had motived Benedict XII's intervention in 1337. Popes and generals could not stem the tide, but the interference of the citizens did. In the four years between 1337 and the quarrel of 1341, the calendar of documents gives twelve clear cases of *proprietas*, and five or more anniversaries founded: the records are not always quite explicit. When at last the quarrel was ended by a composition admitting the citizens' restrictions on Mendicant acquisitiveness, the four years 1358–62 give us only two records of *proprietas*, and not a single anniversary. It was not that the practice was wholly arrested, as we shall see later; but it was obliged to seek other channels.

To that quarrel we must now come. Löhr notes the paradox that, whereas these private rents are practically unknown at Cologne until 1300, "immediately after that date, they were accepted without hesitation or contradiction by the authorities: nay, that even the best men, whose earnestness and zeal is beyond doubt, approved them" (p. 27). The only explanation he can suggest is in Boniface VIII's bull concerning the *portio canonica*, the *quarta funeralium*. That bull, as against Mendicant encroachments, compelled the friars to give up to the parish priest one quarter of whatever death-bed legacy they received. How great was this blow we may see from two documents, one from each side. The parish priest of St Columba, one of the richest parishes in Cologne, complained to the Pope in 1341 that in the last seven years, when the Franciscans had refused payment of the *quarta*, 1660 marks of money had fallen in through funerals, and two houses of stone. On the other hand, the most learned of Dominican legists at Paris, Petrus de Palude, was commissioned in 1335 to draw up a memorial in defence of the multiplication of possessions, rents, and anniversaries. The bull, he asserts, had taken away from the Dominicans "more than a quarter of their livelihood, which consisteth mainly of legacies". Unless the bull be repealed, "the brethren will commonly lack the necessaries of life, unless they receive revenues which can be kept without anxiety". We may smile at the logic of a distinguished university professor who pleads, on behalf of his Order, that the loss of one quarter of its main source of income amounts to more than a quarter of the whole. On the other hand, we may be sure that the Rector of St Columba did not understate his own case: but those two witnesses prove indisputably how fierce the economic contest over this corpse-money must have been.

Löhr, who cannot venture to deny the breach with original Dominicanism, pleads what is nowadays called Political Realism in justification of Palude's memorial. "He was reckoning with the circumstances and the movement of evolution, and he reflects the views of the widest circle" (p. 29). Analysing the origin of these endowments, he reckons that they come mainly from family inheritance of friars, but also that the numerous other gifts are "a proof of the friars' great influence on the cure of souls, and the affection which they enjoyed in Cologne". Yet, though he insists upon the absence of religious unrest in this quarrel, here again the actual documents do not bear him out.

The most enlightening of all is the first, no. 862 in his volume of documents, dated September 13, 1346. It must be noted that the Black Death is as yet undreamt-of. The Dominican Prior of Cologne complains to the Pope how

the bailiffs and rulers of the city have published abroad to the people and clergy, and have caused a certain runaway brother to preach in the convent of the said Prior and brethren, that the said Prior and brethren were not in the way and state of salvation, seeing that they persisted continually in mortal sin, and were smitten with sentence of excommunication in that, contrary to the Constitutions of the late Benedict XII and the vows of their own profession, they possessed and held, as rightful property, perpetual alms and anniversaries, or houses to pay for anniversaries, unduly bequeathed to the said Prior and brethren by Christian folk in their last wills. Moreover, the said bailiffs and rulers sought to interpret, and to distort, the statutes and vows of profession and Rule of the said brethren, compelling them to the observance thereof according to the interpretation—nay, rather the distortion—of the said bailiffs and rulers.

On this foundation, they have published tyrannical decrees against "alms and anniversaries, in common or in special" and are forbidding communication with the friars, or wills in their favour, or burials in their church. Physicians and barbers are forbidden to serve them; religious gilds must not fraternize with them. In this, the citizens are "rashly arrogating to themselves a superiority and lordship" over religious folk. However we may stress the economic issues really at stake here, it is impossible to ignore the significance of such a document for the history of lay revolt against clerical privileges. From henceforward we shall see more and more plainly, what has transpired already in other chapters of this book, the influence of the secular arm in monastic reform. Here we have the mere citizen insisting to the friar that St Dominic's Rule means what it seems to mean, and that the breach of its most important clauses is as harmful to the friar's soul as to the layman's purse.

The fight itself can be briefly told. It did not begin at Cologne. Under slightly different forms it had come earlier in four other cities of great economic importance. At Strassburg, in 1287, the Franciscans gave in to the citizens: the more steadfast Dominicans were blockaded and starved out into exile. Papal and episcopal influence, however, at last procured a decision favourable to the friars (p. 82). We must remember here what Löhr has emphasized in other places. The Mendicants held then, in Church and even in State life, a place very different from since the Reformation. They were great, world-wide corporations, bound by a thousand links to the Hierarchy. Many friars were Bishops, and had not forgotten their origin, some were even Cardinals and had the Pope's ear. Dominicans and Franciscans have had, ordinarily, at least one member each in the Sacred College. Add to these the numerous Mendicants who are busy at the Roman Court as Papal Penitentiaries or Chaplains, or in other connexions.* Again, the friars had influential and ubiquitous allies in the shape of Béguines, pious women who began rather like the modern Sisters of Charity, and whose settlements developed into a sort of hospitals or almshouses. In 1452, "when the heyday of the Béguinages was long past, out of 98 [such] convents 7 were in the neighbourhood of the Carmelite friary, 16 of the Austin Friars, 36 of the Franciscans and 39 of the Dominicans" (p. 67). Thus at Dortmund, where the citizens tried the same blockade and starvation as at Strassburg, the women frustrated this by bringing food, and a settlement was reached in 1330. At Frankfurt a/M, in 1318, the friars found it wiser to make the necessary concessions. At Neuss, the fight began in 1301, and lasted until 1334, when the city magistrates finally "bound themselves by oath, by all means in their power to hinder all sale, gift and pledge of real property to Religious folk" (p. 84).

In Cologne the first clear evidence comes from 1341. Until then, the citizens had been more patient than elsewhere. Many of the noblest families still had sons or kinsfolk among the

* For these Papal Chaplains see my chapter LI here below, "Exemptions."

Dominicans. The archbishop had a Dominican for confessor. In 1300, the then archbishop had commanded his clergy in full Synod to warn the lay-folk of their duty of remembering the cloisterers in their wills. It had become increasingly common for the dying rich to name friars as executors and beneficiaries. Thus, while the living were beginning to give less to Mendicants, these were enriched more rapidly than ever through bequests from the dead. The mass of documents from 1224 to 1340 shows forty-five Dominicans among the executors whose names are specified: only four of these were before 1300: the next twenty years give only seven; but 1320–40 gives no less than thirty-four (p. 63). In 1344, therefore, one document shows that "feeling has become too heated; it is no longer prudent to name a friar as executor" (p. 88). For, all this time, the Dominicans were adding house to house in that block of crowded streets which was already so much their own. As early as 1335, they seem to have chosen the policy of creating here an *immunitas*, a precinct which would bring the whole block under their control, and make it almost such a sanctuary as, for instance, Holy Trinity Priory was in London. Moreover,

> more and more rapidly were rents accepted for separate friars, as also for the community. Thus the citizens had only recently awoken altogether to the fact that the Preachers, and the other Mendicants also, had practically surrendered their original position as to real property and fixed incomes. Whereas, hitherto, the real property which was charitably given to them came back sooner or later to the citizens' hands, they had been accustomed to give such charities liberally, and no layman had anything to say against it. (p. 86.)

This sentence of Löhr takes too little account of the evidence from all sources, orthodox, unorthodox, or indifferent, that house-to-house begging was infinitely less profitable now in 1325 than it had been at the beginning. But the main point is indisputable, that the greatest city in Germany was threatened now, in an even extremer form, by that danger which prompted the English Statute of Mortmain. The city demanded that, as soon as the testator was dead and the legacy of real property had come by law to the friars, these must sell it as soon as possible. They must bind themselves to accept this arrangement without any appeal to whatever ecclesiastical privileges or immunities they might possess, except for the explicit judgment of the Pope himself upon the case. All Mendicants were alike included here; "a proof that the guilt of decay from their ideal height cannot be attributed to any one Order alone" (p. 92). We have already seen how the citizens exploited their moral advantage here.

The Franciscans gave way in 1345: the whole thing was too obviously in contradiction with their Founder's Rule and the earlier decisions of Saints and Popes, to be defensible against any such determined attack. The Austin friars surrendered two months later, and the Carmelites next year. But with the Dominicans it came finally to civil war on a minor scale.

One of their brethren, Heinrich Dreyse, was a well-educated man and had been chosen at least twice as executor of a death-bed will. The first time, at least, he had accepted without resistance the foundation of an anniversary for the convent and a life-rent for one of the brethren. On the second occasion, in 1336, a similar bequest was revoked later by the testatrix, quite possibly by his influence; when next we hear of him, in 1346, it is as a declared adversary of such dubious bequests; and it is significant, as Löhr points out, that Benedict XII's struggle for reform came precisely in that interval. Be that as it may, in September 1346 Heinrich Dreyse is the "runaway brother" of document no. 862, quoted earlier in this chapter. He certainly had not come forward in this role before 1344. Löhr, with pardonable loyalty to his Order, takes their side against this man who did not shrink from publishing what he held to be its treachery to the ideal; but he has nothing against the man beyond "he decidedly went too far; he took no account of the circumstances which had grown up, and which could not now be changed at once; circumstances which were accurately known to the Roman Court, and were tacitly accepted there" (p. 100). Dreyse went to the Dominican convent at Aachen, where, by order of the Cologne brethren, he was cast into prison. The Cologne citizens asserted later that this had been done with unjustifiable personal violence; and the archbishop's final decision seems in one phrase to admit the complaint. The brethren sought to transport Dreyse; the citizens of Aachen not only attacked the convoy and freed him, but also blockaded the

Aachen convent and decreed banishment against those who had abetted the violence done to him. Then the Cologne magistrates moved against their own convent. They blockaded it, as the Strassburgers had done in 1287; they decreed that none should feed the Dominicans, no physician or barber attend them, no tenant pay their rents. A watch was set with orders to forbid any hanging about their gate beyond the space of three Paternosters. But here again the women took their part. The Abbess of St Ursula's, their immediate neighbour, is definitely specified: she supplied them by night over the intervening garden wall. So they held out for eleven months at least, till about July 1347. In that year they succeeded in finding a very different set of allies: a group of those knightly adventurers whose methods come out so crudely in the *Autobiography* of Götz v. Berlichingen.

The family of Schöneburg held the castle whose ruins still look down upon Oberwesel and the Rhine, and which produced Marshal Schomberg of Dutch and Irish history. One of the family was a Cologne Dominican, Otto, who had given evidence against the celebrated mystic Meister Eckhart, when he was tried for heresy. "The Schöneburgs were a thoroughly typical medieval knightly family, loving feuds and fights; and brother Otto seems to have had the adventurous, restless spirit of his family" (p. 108). The magistrates asserted that he, with the prior's consent, called for family help in arms; and Löhr concedes:

> the Prior may possibly have threatened this feud, and Otto may by a resolute move have brought it about without express consent of his Superiors, and actually against their will: but, when the affair was started, the Cologne Dominicans, in their awkward situation, will not have been sorry to see it; nay, they may have regarded it as the aptest means of ending as soon as possible their oppression by the townsfolk. Yet, fundamentally, it was a bad mistake. (p. 109.)

The Schöneburgs sent a "Fehdebrief" (i.e. a formal declaration of private war) and, after the fashion of the times, enlisted other kindred or friendly families from castles on the Rhine and Moselle. The magistrates, on the other hand, had full sympathy and help from the secular clergy of Cologne. Though much of this might be due to the constant friction between friars and parish priests, we cannot thus rule it out altogether. After all, what the magistrates were doing was obviously healthy not only for the city but for true religion; and, when men's actions are moral, we must not quarrel with them if those same actions are convenient to themselves. It is noteworthy that, at this point, the citizens permit themselves to criticize the friars' morals. In their formal memorial to the Pope, they take their stand upon "that which we ourselves have seen by experience; namely, how very many brethren, at the time of these [religious] processions, shrink not from sporting and confabulating with their familiar béguines even in public". And, in a later sentence, "their ambition and pride and lies and detractions, and corruption and infection with many outrageous [*enormibus*] sins, by tolerance whereof we might incur God's just wrath".(2) We must not over-stress these words, written at a point where passions were at fever-heat: yet we cannot altogether ignore them. At least they were not the refuge of men who cared only for the money side, and covered this under a false and hypocritical appeal to morality. For the magistrates had at hand, and did in fact employ repeatedly in that same memorial, a moral weapon even stronger than this, in proportion to the notoriety and universality of the offence. That matter of *proprietas*, which more than one Pope in the past had treated as a mortal sin, had infected the whole Order so visibly that it could be excused only by a casuistry which was self-condemned in the eyes of thoughtful outsiders. An excuse commonly made, even in these pre-Black Death days, was that the world was decaying from generation to generation, and men could no longer be expected to live as strictly as their forefathers.

Meanwhile the Schöneburg feud dragged on. These knightly bandits laid wait for Cologne merchants on the roads; within the city they had friends who might prove traitors; the city credited them with certain destructive fires which had occurred. The friars appealed to the Papal Court at Avignon. The magistrates held to their main complaint: "the too great and excessive possession of goods in the city of Cologne". Their messenger to Avignon was attacked by the Schöneburgs, and lost a hand in the fight. The magistrates now indemnified themselves for their continued losses in war by setting up the Dominican properties for sale. Buyers were easily found. Some may well have held back, but "the great mass [of the population] could always be mustered against the clergy" (I, 119). Moreover, the magistrates were able to read out to the burghers, in full assembly, opinions from lawyers at Avignon and at some universities, to the effect that "the Friars Preachers in the city of Cologne were legally incapable of possessing houses, lands, revenues and rents, whether corporately or individually". Then the knightly robbers had their turn, and fell upon four citizens with a heavy train of wares, which they carried off to Schöneburg. The citizens now besieged the council for reprisals; and insisted that the friars, as domestic enemies who "helped the Schöneburgers with word and deed" should be expelled. If not, there was fear lest the mob should storm the convent and maltreat, or even kill, some of the friars. The council therefore decided on expulsion: and here came a dramatic scene. The prior, with some of the rest, had gone elsewhere at earlier stages of this bitter quarrel. The sub-prior refused a safe-conduct and journey money: let them use force, and so fall under the Church's curse. The council made a careful inventory of all movables in the convent, to guard against accusations of theft, and then made their men lead out the protesting sub-prior, with a gold piece for his journey money to the nearest of his country houses, and another for his companion. Of the rest some were led out, others went of their own accord (July, 1347). The matter still dragged on at law; but the friars were deeply impressed by the quiet determination with which they had been expelled: moreover, the other three Mendicant Orders had now given in. Negotiations were begun for calling off the feudal war after a truce and a parley: but these came to nothing. All seemed now to depend upon the papal decision: but litigation at Avignon was apt to be long and expensive, even in far less complicated cases than this. The pleaders for the council were a canon of St Andreas at Cologne, and the Dominican Heinrich Dreyse, whose appearance in this capacity shows that the friars had not been able to maintain their rejection of him as an apostate, and therefore excommunicate, person. But the Black Death came almost at once, and all courts went into vacation until October. This, as Löhr points out, was a stroke of ill luck for the Dominicans. There is not the least hint, in all the documents, that the citizens were in any degree softened by this visitation of God. The modern legend of a post-plague population delirious with gratitude for the priests who had manifested their divine mission at bedside and at graveside is nowhere more clearly contradicted than in this Cologne episode. To the friars, on the other hand, this long absence from their stately convent and its comforts gave continued food for reflection. Here, then, was an excellent opportunity for the Pope to intervene for direct mediation (August 27, 1349). In one letter to the King of Germany he begs him to move "Our beloved sons the nobles of Schöneburg" to renounce their feud. In another letter to the citizens of Cologne, the Pope reminds them: "Consider that these houses, possessions and revenues have been bequeathed, as it is said, with pious devotion to the said prior and brethren by your fathers and kinsfolk for the remission of their sins, and that ye, who are bound to pray for them, ought not to impede in their prayers the said prior and brethren who pray for them" (II, 337). Under cold analysis, what does this plea mean? Take a fairly recent Cologne anniversary, dated February 27, 1332 (II, 140). A rich lady, Bliza, bequeaths her corpse for burial in the Dominican church. She leaves six marks for pittances at the friars' meals, spaced over the twelve months following her death: that legacy is far behind us now. But she also leaves a yearly rent of one mark, and a horse-load of wheat, for her anniversary, that is, a special yearly Mass and prayers for her soul to perpetuity. A few months after this papal missive, Bliza's nineteenth anniversary will come. Will Mass be said for her soul on that day, and prayers offered in alleviation of her purgatorial pains? If not, why not? What is to prevent the brethren from fulfilling their statutory obligation? They have food and drink and clothing in the other convents to which they have gone, and nobody would have refused their request to carry off into exile the anniversary-book in which their solemn pledges were recorded. Does not this papal reminder lay bare the true and fundamental cause of all this quarrel? Nothing absolute, nor even any almost insuperable difficulty, hindered the full performance of Dominican duties to their benefactors, any more than of full obedience to their Rule and constitutions. Do not the Pope's words betray most clearly that the friars hoped to make the best of both worlds? Here is the problem that meets us everywhere in this later monasticism. The cloisterer enjoys privileges which assume a very lofty ideal of life: under cover of these, he is tempted to the practices of ordinary folk. It is here as so often elsewhere in the Middle Ages: while the ideal theory of Christ's Body and Blood is refined almost beyond human conception, the practice is that of the most businesslike materialism. Terms strictly cash; no credit allowed! Of true idealism, there was no more at the bottom of Dominican than of civic policy in this long quarrel. Economic considerations gradually turned the scale. A few friars made their peace separately, and trickled back. The General Chapter, during all these years, must have discussed the matter; but no decisions were taken, for their Acts are absolutely silent. At last, in 1351, we find the Dominicans treating with the city. The new archbishop was on good terms with both sides; and he was chosen as arbitrator. Very likely the Franciscans, who had long since given in, helped to bring the parties together. The archbishop practically decided for the city. Henceforward, real property is not to be collected and kept, but sold within a year: rents, again, are permissible neither to individuals nor to the community. Four friars who had already come back to the convent, and whose names are specified, must not be victimized. None of the friars who took part in the capture of Heinrich Dreyse must ever return to Cologne; and the Schöneburg coalition must indemnify the citizens as far as possible. Father Löhr, with all his natural sympathy for his own Order, cannot bring himself to agree with other of its writers who persuade themselves that the Pope must have given a verdict for the friars. He writes:

> Thus the Dominicans had to yield all that the Council demanded at first; and to this we must add the heavy expenses, the loosening of discipline which easily comes about in such difficult conditions and a grievous loss of respect and affection among the citizens. The loss was all the more sensible because there were general complaints in the Order that the beneficence of the faithful towards them had fallen off, and the convents had the greatest trouble to clothe and feed their inmates. This gave a considerable further impulse to the so-called *vita privata*, which had long since been running its course. (p. 142.)

The friars were able, in practice, to evade the strict enforcement of these terms, even while they apparently bowed to the storm. Life-rents went on without hindrance, and gradually assumed forms that really remind us of *proprietas* (I, 153). A good many transactions were apparently never registered publicly. In 1472 a lady gave the usufruct of a valuable house to brother Johann Bolant, by deed of *donatio inter vivos*. A medieval hand has noted on the back: "This is valid in the spiritual, but not in the civil court." Father Bolant was presently promoted to the office of Inquisitor (I, 152; II, 236). The convent was able to increase its possessions in the coveted block, though not at the old rate. The Anniversary Book shows far more year-minds after 1464 than before. Though the old patrician families no longer choose Dominican confessors, and the Béguines had retired into their own convents; on the other hand, the middle-class citizens and country nobility favoured them more; and, presently, the newly founded university. Thus Löhr believes those later generations to have been more economically prosperous, and to have "enjoyed the adhesion of the faithful in an increasing degree" (I, 154). The reader must judge this optimism in the light of other contemporary evidence. Even Raymond of Capua, as Löhr confesses on p. 1 of his *Teutonia*, was unable to bring the Cologne convent into the Observance in 1399.

Here, then, is the most conspicuous example of a feeling which was growing up in all the great cities. In 1438 it was strong enough everywhere to attract the attention of Eugenius IV. He addressed a severe warning to the Premonstratensian Order, stigmatizing its decay in "different countries", and calling upon the Chapter-General to act at once "in order to extinguish the unfavourable impressions which are spread abroad, and to edify those same layfolk who seemed tempted to take into their own hands the reform of the monasteries".(3)

CHAPTER XLVII

THE SECULAR ARM

THIS Cologne story, it must be repeated, serves as a correction to exaggerated accusations of tyranny and greed against layfolk in their conflicts with cloisterers. It was not only typical of the great Rhineland cities, but roughly parallel to what we find in other great urban centres of Europe. And it forms a necessary complement to that story of royal or princely intervention. To this, again, a whole chapter must be devoted: for it has been most unaccountably neglected by historians of the English Reformation. Our judgment of that revolution must depend to a great extent on this question: Was Henry VIII a clumsy innovator? or was his policy, however brutal in method, the natural and almost inevitable culmination of a long-drawn and finally irresistible lay movement? For the records seem to show, what we might expect *a priori*, that the relations between State and Monasticism followed faithfully the fluctuations of the struggle between State and Church as a whole. Charles the Great had not much more hesitation in legislating for the monasteries of his empire than Constantine would have had. Later, at the zenith of papal power and monastic prosperity—let us say, from 1150 to 1250—it was far more difficult for the laity to interfere. But at last, in the fifteenth century, popular dissatisfaction has grown so strong that the interfering prince or magistrate finds himself moving with the tide. At this present point, in dealing with Henry VIII, I speak only of his general policy of control over these great institutions, hitherto entrenched behind a network of privileges and immunities: the policy prophecied by Langland of "beating the monks for breach of their Rule". Therefore this control alone will be considered at the present point, apart from his ulterior motives and the particular methods by which he carried out this general policy.

But, to understand Henry's acts in England, we must first take note of the Continental parallels. The pre-history of the

English Reformation has too long been divorced from its Continental context. Even for England herself, there has been far too little width of view. One of our most learned scholars in this field has said truly, in connexion with an elaborate monograph on a great abbey by an exalted church dignitary: "He writes as if X—— were the only abbey that had ever existed."

Therefore I cannot help feeling a certain perversity in those critics who have accused me, all along, of promiscuous use of evidence from different dates and different countries. I have striven always to avoid promiscuity, in giving the dates, either in figures or by clear indication. Frequently I have explicitly warned against bias or exaggeration in the witnesses; even more frequently, I have specified their status clearly enough to enable the public to judge for itself. I write for readers who, from such data, are competent to draw their own inferences, or to correct the author in their own minds if they catch him misapplying his testimonies.

Therefore, except so far as I may have been unfaithful to those common-sense rules, I must remain impenitent as to the multiplication of dates and places. Indeed, it seems one of the necessities of my task: for this conviction, with which I entered upon the work forty years ago, has been strengthened by the very words of some among my severest critics. For, in those words, I have seemed to trace the utterance of minds imperfectly acquainted with this specialized field, and therefore warped (so far as judgment in this particular matter is concerned) by impressions derived from studying very different phenomena. For we cannot rightly understand medieval history if we begin with over-simplification. Generalizations learned most effectively in one distinguished lecture-room may be worse than useless when they are applied from a different angle. And, among the many truths to which our generation has attained concerning the Middle Ages, one of the most important is this: that the field is not only larger but more complex than it seemed to our ancestors. A man may have exercised a fine intellect for many years with unwearied diligence; he may even have reached a position of something like acknowledged and legitimate dictatorship in one corner, while in relation to other corners his greatest wisdom may lie in frank Socratic ignorance. Specialization in one branch will indeed give a certain flair in others: but it goes no further. Before coming to a final judgment, the critic must step forth from the mass of original documents which are at the foundation of his own life-work, in order to test a considerable proportion, at least, of that other mass which lies hard by. It may be that nothing wider than Jordan rolls between; but he must not linger on the brink if he would really know what is on the other side.

English historians have less right than others to protest against any honest attempt to survey this whole monastic field. With perhaps the most abundant sources in the world, we have made least use of them. Nobody has yet grappled seriously with the mass of material printed in my lifetime by different Record Societies. Even among those documents, while some will bear comparison with the best work of the kind abroad, others have been edited with appalling inaccuracies which seem to have completely escaped the eyes of reviewers. Moreover, even though we had done more at home, this could still be only half understood so long as it were studied in isolation from the parallel events abroad. For those events are doubly significant for us, both in their similarities and in their contrasts. The similarities were, naturally, very great. By a curious paradox, those who are least willing to admit foreign sources as analogous to English conditions are often most zealous for the exaggerated thesis that there was little or no nationalism in the Middle Ages.(1) We find in fact a great deal of nationalism when we consider that there is no essential difference between international bloodshed and inter-village bloodshed. Moreover, a good deal of evidence comes from where we should least expect: that is, from universities with their community of Latin culture, and monasteries with their still closer uniformity of Rule. We have seen in vol. III (p. 3) how there might be deadly enmity between Norman and Saxon monks; and in chapter XXXVI of this present volume that friction was inevitable between the Flemish and the French, even among reformers in the same house. The difficulty arose quite early among the Franciscans. In 1291 Edward I had to intervene with his royal authority in Ireland. He "ordered his officials in Ireland to assist Fr. Raymond, General Minister of the Order, and any other friars whom he appoints as his delegates, to restore discipline among the friars minor in Ireland. The hostility between the native Irish and the Anglo-Irish had come to a head in a free fight at a provincial chapter held at Cork on 10 June 1291." Sixteen friars were killed, and "at last the English conquered with the city's help, to the scandal of the Order". "Some years later the province was deprived of its right to elect the Provincial Minister, and the Irish and Anglo-Irish friars were separated, different houses being assigned to the rival parties."(2) Again, under Edward III,

> The feeling of nationality fostered by the long French wars was not without its influence on the friars in England and especially at the Universities. In 1369 the Chancellor caused a royal proclamation to be published at Carfax ordering all French students at Oxford, both religious and secular, to leave the kingdom. In 1388 a royal writ was issued to the Warden of the Friars Minors in Oxford at the advice of the same convent, warning him to admit no foreign friars who might reveal to the enemy "the secrets and counsel of our kingdom", and to expel any such friars for whose good behaviour he would not be responsible, or who would not pray or celebrate Masses for the King and the good estate of the realm.

Thus, in studying the details of monastic life for my earlier volumes, I have had occasion to indicate national or local differences here and there: not only in food and dress and suchlike matters, where the difference of climate rendered complete uniformity almost impossible, but in other matters wherein the cloisterer conformed, for mere comfort and convenience, to the social fashions of his environment. Thus in Germany, where central justice was comparatively weak, the carrying of daggers by monks was far more frequent and dangerous than in England, where the King's Peace was far stronger. The Italian and Spanish nuns, again, were far more accustomed than ours to play the part of society ladies, and to make their convent a resort for the idlers of the city. The French seem to have been almost as free; and in the great German cities there was distinctly more of this indiscriminate social intercourse than can be traced among us.(3)

One most important English peculiarity has been fully emphasized already in my third volume (chap. XXV); and the contrast has come out even more glaringly in chapters XXXI and XXXVI of this present volume. The fatal *Commendam* system, "the leprosy of monasticism", was only beginning to fasten upon our abbeys at the moment when Henry VIII swept both the body and the disease into one indiscriminate grave.

Another peculiarity, almost equally important, is in the matter of lay interference with the monasteries. Even among educated men, the majority seem to look upon Henry VIII as the first king to have laid his sacrilegious hand upon this holy ark. Yet it would be almost as true to reverse the medal, and claim him as among the last to follow, after his own fashion, a policy set for generations past not only by worldly princes, but by Popes themselves. We have seen repeatedly, in this present volume, how a reform was supported, and often actually initiated and pressed in spite of obstacles, by one who "bore not the sword in vain". Here, then, is the place to pause and consider this policy in its entirety, since such consideration is one of the essentials for a true standpoint in relation to the Dissolution. That revelation which we call the Reformation had been prepared on one side by Popes themselves, from the Council of Constance onwards. There, the great and burning question had been that of general church reform, in head and in members. The papacy had side-tracked this into separate and narrow channels, by arrangements with one nation after another; and this paved the way for what the Reformation finally accomplished, a system of separate National Churches acknowledging no Head but Christ. So, again, that other characteristic of the Reformation, the frank interference of State in Church affairs, had been prepared in its beginnings by the Popes. These had found themselves more and more powerless to break down the resistance of unreformed Religious in virtue of a weakness which St Bernard had denounced in the plainest terms to Eugenius III, and other great churchmen after St Bernard's example. What paralysed even the greatest reformers was the labyrinth of appeals to Rome, with interminable litigation at a court where, notoriously, money was more powerful than even in the ordinary medieval lawcourts. Popes might excommunicate, but the ghostly ban was rapidly losing its force. For here, again, one of the stock themes of all orthodox reformers was the debasement of this moral currency by its abuse against smaller folk for trivial occasions, and the impossibility of enforcing it upon those who were most notorious (if only because most powerful in arms or in money) among the sinners. Therefore it became almost common form for a papal bull to conclude with the clause "invoking, if necessary, the help of the secular arm". It would be difficult to find any later monastic reform of primary importance which had not this in the background; while, as we have seen, a startling number of cases show the secular arm not only in the last resort, but in the forefront: even princes and magistrates marching at the head of a lukewarm episcopal crusade, or, here and there, actually storming the breach over the body, so to speak, of the recalcitrant bishop or minister-general. The facts are here seen overwhelmingly significant, and yet they have been so neglected in this context, that they must be fully brought out here on the very threshold of the English conflict.

From Constantine onward, the emperor or temporal prince had been the natural protector of the Church: but protection, however logically distinguished from interference, is practically almost inseparable. The principle was unaltered even while the relations of the two parties changed. Whereas, at first, the emperor had interfered almost without question, the Popes finally reached a position in which they regarded the civil power practically as a convenient tool; as, for instance, when she handed over the heretics she had condemned to the secular arm, under the definite understanding that a magistrate who obstinately refused to burn them would be himself liable to heretication and burning. In most cases, however, there was no such definite understanding with regard to the monasteries, even in these later generations when the Pope himself invoked the secular arm. What was done, rested upon the occasionally notorious facts of intolerable abuses in some particular monastery, and the pretty certain gratitude of the best ecclesiastics for any removal of such abuses. Thus, for instance, when Innocent III strove to reform St Bénigne at Dijon, he put its revenues for a while under the joint administration of the bishop and the Duke of Burgundy.(4) Again, certain rights of interference were granted to an abbey's *advocatus* or *fundator*, the heir or representative of the original founder.

St-Maur, so famous after the Reformation for its contributions to learning, was in moral and material decay at the end of the tenth century. Its reform was initiated by no bishop, but by a pious noble and royal favourite, Count Burchard. Still more significant is the attitude of the King, Hugh Capet, towards this reform. He had promised the count that no request of his should be denied; but when he found himself asked to transfer the control of a great abbey, the statesman in him rebelled. "Since it is well known that this hath always been a royal abbey in the days of our predecessors, how should it now be separated from our royal control? For, if I grant this, it may come to pass after thy death that the house will be ruined by the wickedness of thy heirs or successors; and then shall we incur blame and harm to our souls." He therefore granted the control for a time only, in view of this particular reform. Then Burchard's prayers at last prevailed on St Maieul of Cluny to send thither a small congregation of more perfect monks. Burchard escorted these brethren, and halted at a village just across the Marne; there he sent for the monks of St Maur to meet him. He gave them, separately and collectively, a clear choice; to return to their abbey under this new and regular obedience, or to go whither they would, clad just as they were. All preferred liberty to restraint; and this reform started with a clean slate.(5) There is no century from which some such evidence could not be produced.

Charlemagne's healthy activities as *Episcopus Episcoporum* were never altogether forgotten in the Western Church. It was natural that they should be recalled in those later centuries when the lay spirit was rapidly growing: when the papacy had broken the power of the Empire, yet had so little equivalent power to put in its place. Cusanus, in his *De Concordantia Catholica*, appeals to the great emperor's example in face of what was always one of the greatest obstacles to reform.(6) With reference to Charlemagne's law against unchaste clerics he writes:

> Here we have a King summoning a Council, and ordaining with others that which is just. And would that Princes in these present days would take pains to remove public and evil faults, and especially those who create great scandals in Religion, such as the fornications of persons who have vowed chastity, among which there should be care of nuns and their custody. For St Boniface [seven centuries ago] wrote to Ethelbald, King of England, that unchastity committed with a nun is a blasphemy to God.

Through all the next chapter, Nicholas emphasizes the duty of princes to enforce Church discipline.

There was unmistakable significance in the preponderant part played by the Emperor Sigismund at Constance, his keen practical interest in Church reform until the council began to show its impotence and to stultify its own main object. Trithemius unhesitatingly puts the emperor in the forefront of one of the greatest monastic reforms of that age: "the Emperor Sigismund with his helpers, who began the reform of Melk in Austria". The verb here is in the singular: the emperor *began*, others helped.(7) Martin V himself, who had been elected at Constance in virtue of his promises for reform, was glad to find that the lay authorities were doing in France more than his own spiritual weapons could accomplish, at least in his own hesitant hand. In his bull for the reform of Cluny (1428) he expressed his pleasure at hearing that whereas hitherto "the very many disorders and excesses, committed in multiple fashion by the brethren beneficed and professed [at that great Abbey], both in spiritual and in temporal things, remain damnably unpunished, for this reason the secular arm is said to have set its hand into the aforesaid matters" and thus that the abbey will be rescued from "the opprobrium of irreparable dissolution".(8)

Among minor German princes, Wilhelm III of Thüringen played the most prominent part. In his *Church Ordinances* of 1446, without mentioning Pope or Bishops, he announced his own intention "that all Church monasteries shall be reformed and brought back to decent Church regularity, each according to the Constitutions and Rules of its Order". With regard to the parishes appropriated to monasteries, "he was anxiously set against allowing the people to be neglected by uneducated and unrespected vicars": they were to hold office for six years only, unless his council was satisfied to continue their tenure.(8*a*)

We have seen in chapter XVI how Busch credited to Sigismund's successor, Albert II, a very short way with recalcitrant monks. The Benedictine Rumpler, writing about 1504, looks back upon him as leader of the princes in monastic reform. For Melk, again, he seems to have done as much as Sigismund, or more. Brother Martin of Emmeram, in 1490, writes thus to a friend who had enquired about the origins of the Melk and

Castell reforms: "I answer briefly that Albert, Duke of Austria ...called in reformers from the Sacro Speco and Subiaco, who reformed that monastery....Rupert, Count Palatine and King of the Romans, called reformers from a certain monastery in Bohemia, and settled them in the monastery of Castell."(9) When Cusanus set about the great monastic campaign which was to be the main work of his legation in Germany, he procured a direct warning from the emperor to the Austin canons of the diocese of Salzburg: "We request and beg you with special emphasis [*Fleiss*] that you show yourself friendly and willing to such visitation, and do not resist it...in order that you and your monasteries may be brought and established in good state and order, as is right and just."(10) The evidence is strongest, perhaps, for the Mendicants. On the one hand, these mixed more among the people, and their dealings for good or for evil would be more obvious. On the other hand, they were exempt from episcopal jurisdiction, and had enormous influence at the Court of Rome, which alone was competent to judge and condemn them. Even when they were condemned there, these distant convents could often defy spiritual penalties with complete impunity: hence the necessary recourse to the secular arm. Glassberger's Franciscan *Chronicle*, under the year 1502, gives a long list of worldly potentates who favoured the Observance. In addition to the Emperor Maximilian, there are eleven kings, eight archdukes, ten dukes, five marquesses, and eleven great magistrates such as the Lords of the Swabian and Swiss Confederations.(11) There are sixteen cases in which his editors have felt the victories of Observant reformers sufficiently important to register them in the index: in eleven of these it was the secular authorities who gave the first impulse. In three cases the initiative came from bishop or archbishop, and in two from within. Fr. Löhr gives a similar list of princes who put pressure upon the Church authorities for reform among Dominicans in the province of Cologne.(12) From princes and great nobles, the impulse passed down naturally to the cities, which, as they grew in power and self-importance, insisted upon increasing interference with these hitherto untouchable corporations. This was specially marked, on the eve of the Reformation, in Germany, where the central power was so weak and the cities so strong. At Geneva, as elsewhere, it was mainly lay influence which carried the reforms.(13) Störmann shows how the citizens became more and more accustomed to regulate monastic affairs within their own territory.

It seems that the view gradually grew, that the Town Council is the secular authority over the monasteries and religious corporations within the town itself. This body gave its consent to the enlargement of a convent, admitted none but specified Orders, limited the number of convents and of their inmates, supervised and regulated their lives, reformed claustral discipline, and superintended through comptrollers the management of the monastic property. The legal justification for all such measures lay in the city's right of protectorate over the clergy and religious institutions settled, or owning property within the walls.(14)

This transference of disciplinary power from clerical to lay hands was most marked among the princes in France and Germany, and among the citizens of Germany. Heinrich Finke, the great historian of the Constance Council, pointed out the full significance of the movement forty years ago, yet it does not seem to have filtered yet into English histories. Finke, as an orthodox Roman Catholic, is naturally most struck by the disadvantages of the movement. He writes:

It is only quite recently that, from several sides at once, a phenomenon has been indicated which did more than many others to render possible the rapid spread of the Reformation. In many parts of Germany the combination of princely powers with episcopal ecclesiasticism had gradually produced a supreme and exclusive Episcopacy, or, in technical parlance, a *Summepiscopate*. This fact was already well known in the rough; but men slid dryshod over this fact without drawing the necessary conclusions. Men are now startled, as in face of some new discovery, to find what really happened. Through an adroit exploitation of the Church's weaknesses and disasters, the secular princes, in North as in South Germany, had already usurped this *Summepiscopate* before the Reformation; and this removed the necessity of any change when the new teaching broke out. We have many testimonies to the fact that this Caesaropapism showed itself not in Germany alone, but in all the more important Christian countries. At the time of the Council of Constance, serious monitors like Dietrich v. Niem drew attention to this. It was upon this phenomenon, so calamitous to the Church, that men founded the necessity for continuance of annates and the Pope's dues for confirmation and collation of benefices; for otherwise [it was argued], the Pope would be helpless*: men would reck nothing of Pope and Curia in ecclesiastical matters. [Dietrich writes] "Kings and princes...at present...interfere in Church matters to the utmost of their power: therefore the churches are in evil case almost throughout the world." Evidence of this kind has scarcely been exploited at all in recent research.(15)

It is quite true that the lay interference was not always unselfish: far from it. In this period, as in every age since the monasteries first became outstandingly wealthy corporations, feudal lords had often seized opportunities of preying upon them. Such depredations, whether under cover of law, as in less disorderly England, or by almost barefaced robbery wherever the central authority was weak, were often invited by the very circumstances of the case. It is the Benedictine Abbot Trithemius who tells us most plainly and emphatically, what others hint more briefly, that the robber's most specious excuse lay in the notorious failings of his victim. Trithemius represents them as saying: "Lo! these sinful priests and monks have gotten riches; lo! they scorn the service of God and consume their wealth with harlots!...Why therefore should we delay or hesitate? Why do we not attack their worldly goods that this wicked pride may be humbled?"† Apart from such barefaced economic greed, even in those cases where the main question was one of religious reform, the lay lord might well have mixed motives. Sometimes, again, it was the layfolk who supported Religious in their resistance to reform. There were many feudal or city magnates who had dumped a daughter into the nearest nunnery, or a son into some abbey where, even when the life was not too openly scandalous, the traditions of many generations had softened the Rule down into something closely resembling the amenities of modern club life. This must be borne in mind later, when we shall come to the reports of the English country gentry upon the monks their neighbours. But we have already seen, in chapter XV, how the thoroughly demoralized nuns of Klingenthal held their ground with strong lay support against all reform. Again, it was the Duke of Tirol

* I have pointed out elsewhere how the great banker and merchant Jakob Fugger confessed that his richest source of gain was by lending money to bishops and abbots who had to pay these enormous dues in ready money before they could get their documentary vouchers from the Roman Court.

† For full quotations see my vol. II, pp. 612ff.

who upheld, through thick and thin, the equally indefensible Abbess of Sonnenburg and her sisters against so powerful an ecclesiastic as the papal legate Cusanus.(16) It was this kind of thing which did so much to discourage Nider in the very heat of his reforming zeal. He wrote:

The whole Council of Basel was not strong enough to reform one nunnery in a town; for the townsfolk held by the nuns. How then should a council reform the whole of Christendom? If it be so difficult to reform a nunnery, how hard would it then be to reform the men's houses, especially those which are reserved for noble kin, and have great connexions....Because it is so hard to reform all Christendom, and separate estates, therefore let every man thrust his head into some corner, into some hole, and see to it that he keep God's Commandments, and do that which is right, and save his own soul.(17)

Other instances are not far to seek.(18)

But, when all is said and done, the balance of this interference would seem to be clearly on the right side. The movement did indeed give a strong impetus to the Revolution of the sixteenth century: but, on the whole, this was on the true reforming side of that Revolution. Fr. Doelle, as a good Franciscan, naturally sees the matter very much from Professor Finke's standpoint. He seems definitely apologetic in face of what the facts reveal on every page of his detailed study, that these Observantine reforms were accomplished (where they succeeded at all) often at the impulse of laymen, and practically always with worldly force in the background. He is uneasy at this constant intervention of the lay powers in what should have been purely domestic reforms within the Church. But, while the records prove the necessity of this intervention, he frankly confesses the uprightness of the laymen's motives. Speaking of the convents in Kursachsen (roughly, the modern Kingdom of Saxony), he writes: "All of these, at the end of the 15th century, accepted reform at the instigation of the secular powers—with the possible exception of Zwickau. As to the Prince Elector himself, there is no doubt that, in his zeal for reform, he followed no other aim than to uplift and to advance claustral discipline." And again, more generally:

All these reforms which were promoted or carried out by princely persons had in view (so far as our sources enable us to analyse them) only the true observance of that Rule to which men had promised obedience. We know no case in which the reformers enriched themselves from monastic property. The same may be said of those reforms which were promoted or carried out by town authorities.(19)

Yet even this lay control was, on the whole, insufficient; nor would it have wholly sufficed if it had been still more unselfish and more resolute. For Rome alone had the undisputed legal control: and Rome never set herself to monastic reform with anything like the courage and persistency with which she had undertaken, under Gregory VII, the fight for clerical celibacy. The unreformed monk could always plead "custom" for his infringements of the Rule: custom already almost immemorial, and wearing its channels deeper with every fresh generation; "Custom weighing on us with a weight heavy as frost, and deep almost as life." For in those days the motto ran in Canon Law: *Consuetudo optima legum interpres*, and tradition was often more powerful than statute. The Canon Lawyer attempted a distinction here between "pious custom" (which had the force of law) and "evil custom" (which was not truly *consuetudo* but *corruptela*) yet was too vague and academic to have much practical effect. It was like that other academic conception of a "Natural Law", which overrides in the last resort all perverse statutes of imperfect man. This was admirable as a principle, but of no more practical value in the law courts or in politics than the feeling common to all thinkers, ancient and modern, that certain commands or restrictions are incompatible with civilized society, and with civilized conceptions of justice.

Let us take one specially conspicuous case, from among scores which might be quoted. Leo X, in 1514, treated this matter of clerical discipline in that Fifth Ecumenical Council of the Lateran which set out with an ambitious programme of Church reform. In the ninth session it was thus decreed: "Concubinaries, whether they be layfolk or clerics, are to be punished according to law; nor let them have any benefit whatever from the tolerance of their superiors or from evil custom (which should rather be called corruption) by reason of the multitude of sinners, or from any other excuse whatsoever; but let them be severely punished as the law doth prescribe." Here, then, *consuetudo* and *corruptela* were wielding great practical force; here was a plain case for action. In future, the longer time this corruption could claim for its pedigree, the more inexorably ought the law to have punished offenders. Any real effort of that kind might well have frustrated Luther's rebellion. Yet, in 1524, Cardinal Campeggio found himself legate in Germany, confronted with the task of stemming "the daily increasing impiety of the heretics", Luther having now been seven years in the field. Therefore, after consultation at Regensburg with eleven princes of the Church and five secular princes, he published a series of thirty-three constitutions for Church reform, basing them explicitly upon the fact that this "most damnable" heresy "had no small occasion, partly from the abandoned [*perditis*] morals and life of the clergy, and partly from that abuse of holy sanctions and ecclesiastical decrees which can no longer be blinked." The 13th article runs "let concubinary clerics, and those who live in incontinence, be reduced to order by the penalties prescribed by the canons; let no custom protect them, nor any connivance—nay, rather any damnable negligence—of the prelates." These articles end by condemning in the strongest language all episcopal officers, archdeacons, or rural deans who wink at the violation of these decrees for the sake of money, "even though it be offered of his own accord" by the offender—a tell-tale clause: for who else but offenders should start this bargain, if it were not the so-called judges themselves? The constitutions begin with the time-honoured threat of "ecclesiastical censures and other remedies of law, invoking even, if need be, the help of the secular arm".(20)

Therefore, in spite of the explosion which shook Europe to its base in the first half of the sixteenth century, monasticism still went on halting between a State which could not interfere with full legal powers, and a Papacy which would not. It was only revolution which could cut this knot by the frank exercise of the secular arm, in orthodox as in Protestant lands. The story of the first-class abbey of Münster supplies no more than an exaggerated instance of a general tendency. In 1540 this great house was reduced to an abbot and one monk; and, as Dom Calmet writes, "the abbot governed with so little wisdom that the Bishop of Basel, being warned of the facts, wrote to him and gave him the instructions which he needed". The bishop put the abbey under the care of a neighbouring gentleman. The Emperor, the Count Palatine and the grand bailiff of Hagenau further intervened; they tied the abbot's hands to prevent further alienations, and tried to compel him to produce accounts. "It is only too certain that, since this man's rule, the abbey never recovered; and that, from thenceforward until the introduction of the Reformation, it was in the saddest state that had ever been since its foundation [in about 660]. It is true that the heresy which we shall soon see creep into the valley [about 1560] contributed no little to this."(21) For in fact, as Branche confesses, the doctrine of privilege introduced a fatal flaw into the monastic system. He writes, in his study of the Province of Auvergne: "But these reforms [of the seventeenth century] were vain. The wound was heart-deep; that fatal principle still survived among the monasteries which must needs lead them to decay....This was the feudal principle, which survived every reform in the monasteries, in all its fullness and in all its rigours."(22) Leo X had followed innumerable papal precedents when he threatened the State's interference in the last resort. But Luther's revolution inaugurated a period in which the State, impatient, swept away at one stroke the mass of custom and privilege behind which the monasteries had entrenched themselves for a thousand years.

CHAPTER XLVIII

THE ENGLISH POSITION

IN England there was no city so rich and populous as (for instance) Cologne, Bruges, Milan, or Florence. London alone would have counted as really great on the Continent; for the rest, our economy was comparatively rural. Yet with us also there are signs of that persistent economic conflict between the cloisterer and the mass of the population; signs that contradict Farmer Cobbett's well-known epigram that our Dissolution, in essence, was a robbery of the poor in favour of the rich.

It is not only that in almost every popular rising the English monasteries were attacked. We have other quite independent indications. Among those who predicted revolution if reform were too long delayed, we find some of the most exalted in rank, and the most orthodox in creed. Eugenius IV, as we have seen, sounded that note from Rome itself; and we have also specifically English warnings, quite apart from Lollards or satirists.

Bishop Grosseteste, on his deathbed (1253), rehearsed the reigning ecclesiastical abuses, and added: "Nor will the Church be freed from her Egyptian slavery but by the edge of the sword and by bloodshed."(1) The Oxford Chancellor Gascoigne, writing less than a century before the Dissolution, called repeatedly for considerable measures of disendowment: "I firmly believe that it would be a holy work for the Pope to appropriate the superfluities of monasteries and great collegiate churches and cathedrals to parish churches and the priests who actually serve them; wherein for different causes men and souls are perishing."(2) But our main interest here must be in royal action. That which led our kings to interfere in monastic affairs, and to extend that interference from age to age, was mainly a question of finance, yet it was as inextricably involved with religion and morals as mind is bound to body.

This is excellently illustrated by an incident of 1320.(3) The monks of Binham, a cell dependent upon St Albans, were adjudged by the General Chapter [*compertum est*] to be "living in disobedience, *proprietas*, and various irregularities [*insolenciis*] to the peril of their own souls, and the scandal of the whole Monastic Order". The Abbot of St Albans had excommunicated them, but they despised these spiritual thunders and were ready to resist in arms. Therefore the Benedictine General Chapter, "for the honour of the whole Order", besought Edward II "that he would deign to extend the help of the secular arm" to bring the rebels to order. Edward commanded the Sheriff of Norfolk to arrest the offenders, fourteen in number, and deliver them to the Abbot of St Albans "to be corrected according to the Rule of St Benedict". With any ordinary person, the procedure would have been simple: after forty days of excommunication these unrepentants might have been taken by the sheriff at once under the writ *significavit*. But for these sacrosanct persons the co-operation of Church and State was needed.

Here, then, we may doubt whether the offenders were punished in virtue of St Benedict's Rule or of the King's peace. But in the great majority of cases the issue was far more simple. In them, the occasion was monastic bankruptcy, or at least great financial disorder; and here the excuse for civil interference was plain enough. The abbey was under certain definite contracts with its founders or benefactors and their legal descendants. It was bound for certain Masses; often, also, for certain doles to the poor on specified anniversaries, and always to "almsgiving and hospitality", in a general undefined way. The first effects of mismanagement (or calamities) and consequent debt were, nearly always, that the number of brethren was diminished. It was very human of them to regard their own maintenance as the first charge upon the abbey revenues; and there is overwhelming evidence that the ordinary results of debt or bankruptcy were dwindling numbers and the diminution or cessation of almsgiving and of Masses for the souls of benefactors. Therefore, on a common-sense principle current both in Roman and in feudal law, such breach of contract laid the monks open to correction by the founders' representatives. Thus there could be no doubt of royal right to interfere with the embarrassed finances of royal foundations; and in a large proportion of the greater abbeys our kings could claim hereditary rights as *fundatores*, involving responsibility for the souls of their ancestors.*

Dr K. L. Wood-Legh, in her *Church Life in England under Edward III*, devotes the whole first chapter to this subject. Beginning sporadically from Edward I onwards, she notes eight cases before the beginning of her strict limitations. Then, during the reign of Edward III himself, she recounts thirty-six cases where the most serious financial difficulties, amounting sometimes to bankruptcy, called for royal interference. The usual routine was for the king to appoint a commission which took over the whole revenues, and put its officers in to maintain the monks with decency, while making such reforms and economies as should balance the budget again. The very list of abbeys thus treated during that half century tells its own tale. Among the thirty-six houses thus requiring royal interference are some of the wealthiest and most illustrious: Bury St Edmunds, Abingdon, Reading, St Frideswide, Croyland, Winchcombe, and Holy Trinity in London. When we remember that all this took place in the lifetime of the author of *Piers Plowman*, we may better understand those prophetic lines of his (B, x, 312ff.):

> Little had lords to do, to give land from their heirs
> To Religious, that have no ruth though it rain on their altars.
> In many places where those persons be, be themselves at ease,
> Of the poor they have no pity, and that is their charity.
> Yet they bear themselves as lords, their lands be so broad.
> Yet there shall come a king, and confess you Religiouses,
> And beat you, as the Bible telleth, for breaking of your Rule nuns
> And amend moniales, monkës and canons
> And putten them to their penance, to go to their first state...
> And then shall the Abbot of Abingdon, and all his issue for ever,
> Have a knock of a King, and incurable the wound.

The Lollards, naturally, were crying aloud all this time for disendowment; but the man who wrote those words shows elsewhere no sympathy with the Lollards. It is only on this point that he, the Churchman, agrees with the heretics to some considerable extent. For him, as for them, "that two-handed engine at the door stands ready to smite once, and smite no more".

* See my third volume, pp. 69ff.

Richard II and Henry IV had less freedom of action than Edward III. Both were considerably embarrassed by the political activities of the Lollards; and even Henry IV could not always feel secure on his throne. But Henry V was strong, autocratic, and a very loyal Churchman: he founded two fresh monasteries at his own expense. Such a man could not remain indifferent in the face of serious indiscipline; and in 1414 the University of Oxford appealed formally to him. Though the general tone of their petition was strongly anti-Wycliffite, yet they accused the monasteries most emphatically of scandalous quarrels, financial disorders, and unchastity; especially among the exempt Orders. Moreover, they begged for royal intervention.* Seven years later Henry did, in fact, intervene. The story is told by two Benedictine chroniclers of the time; Thomas Walsingham of St Albans and the Continuator of Croyland.(4) Henry summoned to the chapter-house at Westminster a council of 300 monastic representatives, including more than sixty abbots and priors. Walsingham writes vaguely: "For reports had been made unto the King by certain false brethren." But the Croyland story is much more explicit: these reports had been made "by the Prior, it is said, of the Charterhouse of Mountgrace, who had made his first profession in the Religion of the said Order of St Benedict". Mountgrace was Henry's own foundation; therefore this was his own protégé who now brought formal accusation against "divers abuses and excesses which seemed to reign in the said [Benedictine] Order: wherefore the King was grievously tortured in mind, and was no little moved against the Order aforesaid". As to the details of the accusation, it is Walsingham who is the more explicit. This prior asserted "that the Abbots, with their companions, had gone far astray: that the monastic Order had fallen from its primitive institutions and observances; and that it must needs be reformed by him and by none other". Walsingham proceeds:

This accusation† was the more credible because the greater part of the prelates and seniors of this Order had died out [*defecisset*], and in time its unbridled youth had succeeded. Therefore the King, with

* More fully in my second volume, p. 586. For the next incident, see *ibid.* 588.

† Or, possibly, "this reformation". The text seems to contain several scribal errors; but the general sense is plain.

only four great persons, came very humbly unto them as they were assembled in Westminster chapter-house; and, first humbly saluting them, he sat down to hear a discourse fit for that occasion by the Bishop of Exeter, Master Edmund Lacy, D.D.* When this was ended, he himself spake to them of the primitive Order of monks; and how, on that account, his ancestors and other folk had devoutly founded and endowed monasteries; then he treated of the negligences and indevotion of the modern brethren. And he delivered unto them certain articles of corrections which they must make, beseeching them suppliantly that they should return to primitive Religion, and should pray without ceasing for himself and the Church; affirming most warmly and heartily that, if they would so act, they would fear no enemy whatsoever, and he himself would put special trust in their prayers.

The result, according to Walsingham, was a thorough discussion, and "a reform (in so far as the time and the circumstances and the frailty of man seemed to permit), for the approval of the next Chapter General". Here again the Croyland monk tells a little more. The King had named three representatives of his own: his secretary, Bishop Lacy, and the Prior of Mountgrace, to meet and confer with six of the most important Benedictines: viz. the heads of Worcester, St Albans, York, Croyland, Durham, and Lenton. Their suggestions were fully discussed in various committees, with considerable modifications as they went along. Then the Abbot of St Albans was commissioned with the drafting, and "a final response was summarily concluded; to the observance whereof in future times the Fathers there present bound themselves unanimously by promise to the Lord King. Thenceforward the king's outburst of indignation was allayed, and he marvelled much: nay, he vehemently congratulated himself that he had so numerous a multitude of literates and graduates in his realm."

The text of these articles is to be found among the Chapter Acts for the year 1422. They begin: "Seeing that, among those who profess the Rule of St Benedict, there are many transgressions and irregularities [*plura exorbitancia et enormia*] which are worthy of reform, therefore, etc. etc." They treat of wandering abroad, *proprietas*, flesh-eating, and (with special emphasis and repetition) dangers to chastity. Women are not to be invited

* *Cont. Croyland* adds: "enumerating many Masses and abuses".

to eat and drink within the conventual buildings, "not even the brethren's own mothers or sisters,...except in the guestenhouse, and that by special leave and under the witness and presence of officials deputed for such receptions". Also,

> seeing that, as Augustine saith, the battles of chastity are hardest among all the conflicts of Christian men, wherein the fight is of daily occurrence and victory is rare; and since (by the same witness) he who will not avoid familiarity with women falleth quickly into ruin, nor (as the Apostle [Paul] saith) is there any remedy but in flight, ...therefore no Superior may grant leave to any monk to eat or drink in places of public entertainment outside the monastery, except with noble folk; since therefrom grievous scandals might arise, and incentives to vice.(5)

Among the same records are three other documents: viz. two separate criticisms of these articles in committee, and the final form in which they were passed by the Chapter. Others of these articles were attenuated by the monastic critics, sometimes with barefaced special pleading. In the matter of monks' pocket money (for instance) they appeal to "the ancient and wonted laudable custom [of giving such moneys]; which *consuetudo* ought not to be called *corruptela*, seeing that it hath been approved from of old by permission of holy fathers". Yet, amid these many objections, all three documents rather emphasize than minimize the prohibition of social intercourse with women. Both sets of critics point out that "the Constitutions [of the Order] run in this same sense"; and the final approved draft on this point is longer and stricter than that of the King's committee. The General Chapter appeals to the Wise Man's words, that "many have perished by looking upon women, and speech with them is as a burning fire"; and again to Jerome's warning that the consorting and speaking with women is infectious. Therefore "We adjure in the Lord all that profess our Order, and we most earnestly exhort them under precept", to respect these prohibitions, which, after all, are only repetitions from time-honoured Benedictine legislation.(6) For centuries before Colet's famous Sermon Before Convocation, orthodox reformers had anticipated him in that which he made into his main theme: what the Church needed was not new laws, but something like effective obedience to the old time-honoured legislation.

It was Henry V who dissolved wholesale the alien priories. There were many more than a hundred of these, great and small, scattered over the kingdom. Their *fundatores* were in most cases foreigners. In a large number of cases their prior was appointed by the mother-house in France, and often the brethren themselves were Frenchmen. These, in the nature of the case, were no longer men of missionary zeal. Under even greater disadvantages than these were the ordinary "cells" dependent on a great abbey. Norwich Cathedral monastery found an obvious convenience in sending difficult subjects to its cells of Yarmouth or Lynn or Aldby; and even those who were ordinarily consigned to these small outlying colonies, often of only four or five brethren, were not likely to have much of the old monastic inspiration. Nationalism came in as another difficulty; it was apt to strain relations with their English brethren or with their neighbours. Thus Henry VI complained to Eugenius IV that Pontefract Priory was sadly dilapidated because the mother-house in France "had been wont to set over it persons of foreign birth and of an utterly different tongue".(7) In many cases these priories gradually sank almost to the level of mere rent collectors for the mother-house in France; for the cell always paid a tribute, which amounted sometimes to the whole balance of its budget. For a long time past, therefore, there had been considerable grudging at the export of all this good money; and, when our French wars came, overpowering political considerations were added to the financial: for here were enemy aliens on our ground. Edward I used their revenues for his own army, and allowed none to reside nearer than twenty miles from the coast. Successive kings followed the same policy, except in times of peace. At last, in 1414, Henry V took all into his own hands. Our ambassadors at the Council of Basel pleaded successfully that Henry had obtained permission for this from Martin V; that he had devoted the revenues to other religious or educational purposes; and that he had indemnified the French houses. How far that last plea was true, we cannot tell; but, as to the confiscation in general, Gascoigne expresses satisfaction with the Pope for his share in this disendowment, and with Clement V for having "destroyed the Order of the Templars".(8)

I abridge here the further evidence which I have printed far more fully in my second volume (pp. 593, 599, 617, 633, 655ff.).

In 1441 Henry VI was compelled to address a letter to the Carmelite Order, complaining of its indiscipline: "Through the boldness of impunity all men are granted, not without very great scandal and horror, almost a free licence for transgression." The Oxford Chancellor Gascoigne, about 1450, branded the waste and luxury of the monks, and pleaded for serious royal measures of disendowment. About 1480, an Irish Cistercian abbot wrote to headquarters at Cîteaux, pleading that the Abbot-General should induce the Pope to move against "the ruin and desolation and indiscipline of our Order in Ireland". The Augustinian General Chapter, in 1518, confessed "the imminent lamentable ruin of their whole Order...both in regular observance and in temporal possessions". And, all this while, the orthodox anti-Lollard writers, violently as they retort upon many less important criticisms from the heretics, are strangely silent or modest when the context calls upon them to deal with the accusations of monastic immoralities.

We need not wonder, therefore, at the solicitude of Henry VII, a king who prized order as highly as his predecessor Henry V, or as his own contemporaries in France. Henry addressed himself very seriously to social reconstruction after the calamitous civil wars. A statute of the first year of his reign (chapter IV, November 1485) strengthened the hands of archbishops and bishops for imprisoning "priests, clerks, and Religious men" [i.e. monks and friars] for "adultery, fornication, incest,* or any other fleshly incontinency". As things now stood, bishops risked being sued for false imprisonment by culprits sufficiently powerful or shameless. Here was a long overdue intervention of the civil power in favour of ecclesiastical decency; and in 1487 (March 6) his chief minister, Cardinal Morton, sent to the clergy of his province a decree drawn up at his Provincial Synod. It rehearses the corruptions of the times: some priests and clerics neglect the tonsure and dress indistinguishably from laymen: unless this wantonness be checked without delay, "the Ecclesia Anglicana, at least in our province of Canterbury,

* By Church law, the incontinence of a parish priest with his spiritual daughter was so reckoned.

which in former times is known to have flourished in life and reputation and decency of morals, will in our days fall (which God forbid!) into the opprobrium of great desolation". Therefore these clerics who persistently flaunt in lay attire, or who wear swords or daggers, must be thrice warned to appear within a month of this "monitio", before their ecclesiastical judge. If the culprit disobeys this "monitio", or if, appearing in court, he shows himself in the incriminated dress, then he is to be suspended from his benefice or, if unbeneficed, from his office, until good behaviour.(9)

CHAPTER XLIX

THE ST ALBANS CASE (1)

THOSE were preliminary skirmishes; we come now to the first pitched battle, waged round the shrine of St Alban, whom England worshipped as her Proto-martyr, and thus gave the abbey an excuse for claiming the premier position in this country. This is a story of primary importance; it seems to have been accepted as a test case for England even in its own day. The case is complicated in itself, especially by gaps in our documentary evidence. Froude judged here, as too often elsewhere, from first impressions, and left himself open to fair criticism on technical points. But, since his time, the question has been hopelessly confused by pleadings which, under cover of moderate language, betray not only ignorance of the technicalities to which they appeal, but downright literary dishonesty. Yet such complications bring a plain challenge to succeeding historians of the period. It is one of our first duties to grapple as best we can with the actual records, and then to sum up in clear terms, so that the interested reader may trust our facts and form his own conclusions.(1)

When once Henry VII and his archbishop felt themselves firm in the saddle, they were able to deal with the monasteries as they had already dealt with the secular clergy. This had already been the task of French kings from the middle of the century; and the movement culminated in the great Assembly of Tours under Charles VIII. There he proclaimed:

> [We,] considering the great abuses, scandals and defects which are at present, and which increase daily in the estate of the Church of our Realm of France...considering further that many princes strive now with all their power in the lands under their governance, to bring order into the said abuses of the ecclesiastical state...have summoned to our presence certain notable personages of learning and good zeal, to consult upon the proper means to prevent and remedy the said abuses.(2)

The "new Monarchy" in England was naturally influenced

in its policy by its fellow monarchy in "the most compact, harmonious, united nation of the European Continent".(3) Therefore we find Henry VII moving first, at the very outset of his reign, as French kings had moved for a generation past, and then more emphatically in 1488–9. But no reform can be truly efficient which does not touch the "exempt" houses; and these, in the ordinary way, are untouchable without special powers from the Pope. Such powers, therefore, must be procured, in the teeth of all vested interests. One great abbey, at least, is sure to resist: and here it is St Albans. The case is so confused by gaps in the documentary evidence, and so hopelessly complicated in our own day by distortion and falsification of the surviving records, that it must be treated here in considerable detail.(4)

This abbey, immensely rich and powerful, had often been among the most tenacious—and this is saying much—in asserting every privilege which it could legally plead, and sometimes more. Under Whethamstede the conflicts had been long and bitter. Two bishops of Lincoln, both earnest disciplinarians, strove repeatedly but vainly to break this barrier, and submit this house to their ordinary visitations.(5) Whethamstede went personally to Rome, and secured papal protection. Again, he successfully fought off the Archbishop of Canterbury, although in ordinary law that prelate could claim right of visitation over even an exempt house, unless it could show an explicit exception for its own case. In 1433, a still more bitter fight was waged over a question unconnected with monastic discipline: was the abbot with his dependent priors to enjoy exemption from the heavy burden of collecting clerical tenths? A great trial was held at Blackfriars; the abbey was opposed by both archbishops and a majority of bishops. We have no record of the formal verdict, yet the monastic chronicler records the story in a tone of triumph which shows clearly that the bishops were beaten once again. There can be little doubt that victory came this time through a forgery almost as barefaced as that by which Cambridge University, almost at the same time, secured a judgment of exemption against the Bishop of Ely. St Albans had been founded by King Offa of Mercia. Its great chronicler, Matthew Paris, gives the text of his actual charter; the abbey possessed two other transcripts of this text with little material difference. But two centuries later, at this Blackfriars trial, Whethamstede produced a version which had been so impudently interpolated as to swell it to about double its original volume. These additions, quite apart from granting great and unusual freedom from taxes, put an entirely different face on the whole matter; for they contain limitations of the bishop's authority which are completely absent from what Offa had actually granted, and indeed which nobody but a Pope had any legal right to grant. And the forgery concludes:

But if (which God forbid!) any person, led by diabolical impulse, shall plot with deceitful mind to annul this Charter, or even to turn it to worse than Our decree, he is accursed for his audacity and cut off in this life from the community of the Faithful; and at the fearful Judgement of God, in the presence of the Legions of Heaven and the multitudes of men and the horrible minions of Hell to boot, let him be damned with the goats to suffer the unending torments of the Pit, unless he make condign satisfaction before his death.(6)

Whethamstede may or may not have forged this himself; we must transport ourselves back to an age when forgery in matters of this sort was a venial sin.(7) But, whoever forged that charter, it was effectual: St Albans thus won yet another fight for exemption.

Not, indeed, for technical exemption from the Benedictine General Chapter Visitations, theoretically triennial, which were held in England far more regularly than elsewhere. Seven visitations of St Albans are recorded in the hundred years preceding the Reformation.(8) It is quite possible that one such was, in fact, made every three years. But when we confront these General Chapter records with the independent evidence of Episcopal Visitors, we see how superficial was this domestic discipline among the Benedictines. Such a comparison bears out the complaints of orthodox reformers, that the fundamental difficulty was to find Visitors who could be trusted as less relaxed than the relaxed parties which they visited. It will be seen presently, in chapter LV, how perfunctorily was the business done, and even the attendance, at visitatorial headquarters. In chapter LIII, again, we shall find the General Chapter committing discipline at St Albans to the care of four abbeys which were themselves among the most disorderly in the diocese.

While those Chapter Records can reassure us so little on the credit side, the abbey's own muniments show us strong evidence upon the other. Walsingham's *Gesta Abbatum*, the different Registers under the names of Amundesham and Whethamstede, all published in the Rolls Series, show progressive deterioration in the abbey, checked only now and then. Abbot John de Maryns (1302–8) found himself compelled to publish a series of articles for the reform of the dependent priories, which were sheltered by the immunities of the Mother Church, and therefore protected from episcopal visitation.(9) He warns the monks against shirking divine service. Priors must not *in future* (a tell-tale phrase which Maryns uses more than once) commit irregularities in sale or lease of lands. Runaway monks must be sent, as secretly as possible, to prison at St Albans. "We forbid all monks from swearing by the wounds, or the blood, or the pains, or horribly by any member of Our Creator."* Monks are not to wander about alone, or haunt the neighbouring town or village, or "linger suspiciously outside the gates, talking with women". Again, let the touch of women be avoided, and all talk with them, except in company with a mature companion or a Superior of our Order. For their own soul's sake, let monks not transgress the prohibition of flesh-food. The "absurdity" of a monk's keeping hunting dogs must be corrected. Their drink must be regulated: on winter feast-days this recurs with dangerous frequency during the short hours of daylight. The poor must not be defrauded of the food left after meals in the refectory.

Abbot Hugh (1308–26) "was frequently wont to admit the harmful familiarity of women, beyond what his garb and his rank demanded: whereby sometimes his abbey incurred grievous expense of loss, not to say dilapidation, and he was less feared and honoured, according to the word of St Gregory: 'Moreover, if a man's life be despised, his preaching is contemned'".(10) In 1338, Abbot Michael de Mentmore issued reforming injunctions for the neighbouring and dependent nunnery of Sopwell, based upon his recent visitation there. He is here repeating earlier statutes: but these must "from henceforth" be actually kept.(11) The nunnery doors must not be opened

* The oaths which far outlived the Reformation as *Zounds*! *Sblood*! etc.

before Prime, nor left open after Curfew. No nun "may henceforward come to the parlour to speak with secular folk, but if she have her neck and face covered with a kerchief and with an orderly veil, as pertaineth to your Religion. And no person shall be suffered to enter but such as are of good fame." Workmen must not have access to the chambers, or any private place. None may "remain in the rooms at night, out of the dormitory, with guests who shall come". At the same time he "prescribed for the monk who is guardian to the nuns of Sopwell, that they permit no man, whether Secular or Regular, to enter unto the said nuns", but by licence of the Abbot or Prior of St Albans. Even with such leave, the visitor must not enter before Prime, nor stay after Collation.

In 1351 Thomas de la Mare was abbot; the greatest of all in these later generations of St Albans. He published (apart from the Constitutions which, as President of the General Chapter, he drew up for the whole Province) a set specially adapted to St Albans.(12) These show his solicitude for the same old matters with which his predecessor Maryns had dealt more briefly. Divine service needed attention: all, if possible, must attend, "abiding through the beginning and the middle and the end". The cloister must never be left unguarded; women must be kept out; monks may not speak with women except "for manifest utility and for a reasonable cause". At times when monks ought to be in the dormitory, they must not enjoy "superfluous potations or vain confabulations, as they were wont to do of old". Those practices are again forbidden whereby the real poor were so often defrauded of their due alms, especially by the sub-priors who sell what comes into their hands, "or grant it for a price". There must be no dicing or hazard in the monastery, nor chess (a game which was played for money in the Middle Ages and therefore constantly forbidden to the clergy). Tavern-haunting, and the invitation of women to eat and drink "in chambers or private places within the precincts" are strictly forbidden: so are bows, swords, and all warlike weapons. These constitutions are to be copied also into the Martiloge of each dependent priory, and read publicly at least once a year.

In 1423, when Abbot Whethamstede went to the Council of

Pavia, he decided to set his house in order first. Therefore he made a thorough visitation of the abbey and its dependent cells: for, ordinarily, these great abbots had often comparatively little intercourse with the mass of the brethren, leaving discipline to their priors. The articles of reform which Whethamstede then drew up were directly based, he tells us, upon the *detecta* and *comperta* at that visitation.(13) He repeatedly contrasts these statutes (which are now "to be inviolably observed in this monastery, in our own modern days and in future time") with what he had discovered in the past. Monks are to keep choir-service regularly, "not feigning to themselves reasons for retreating or occasions for going forth". On Sundays especially, at the service preceding Mass, "let them remain steadily in the choir, and not presume to leave it for the sake of wandering or talking elsewhere in the Church, as they were formerly wont to do". There must no longer be "noise in the choir, and too much wandering about at the time of psalmody". The standard of service has fallen so much that "in order to arouse the devotion of the lay multitude, now almost dormant",* two outside chanters must be hired. There is too often gossip instead of work in the cloister and its doors are too freely opened to passers by. The education of the juniors is neglected. The spirit of *proprietas* is growing. The visitation had showed how brethren went to their homes too frequently, and sought occasions for wandering.

Because talk with women doth oftentimes disgrace the title of wholesome reputation, and doth sometimes raise matter of scandal, ...We prohibit most strictly and command that henceforth none of the brethren (at any rate, except those upon whom it is incumbent of duty) shall have frequent talk with women, or pass, for any cause whatsoever, to the nunneries near the abbey or near Redbourn.

Redbourn itself, a cell about five miles distant, was kept as a sort of holiday resort, just as the monks of Peterborough had their cell of Oxney for "recreationes". Laxity had now crept in there:

we forbid, under pain of recalling the delinquents [to St Albans], that the brethren who take their solaces there sit up excessively or immoderately at night, by which excesses they omit those [liturgical] vigils which they are bound to keep by the statutes of their Superiors,

* Reading *pene sopitam* for *bene sopitam*.

and by custom of their religious profession. We forbid also that they ever go about with a little boy [*puerulo*], but always, wherever they go, with a companion or an adult person.

At St Albans itself, "let them not immoderately stand about or drink at the doors of the cellar or the oriel [where flesh is eaten], and specially at those times when they are bound to be with the rest in cloister or dormitory". "Let them not bring any secular folk, except guests, with them into the dormitory". In conclusion, he gilds these little pills. He grants in perpetuity the revenue of one of his manors, £30 a year, to increase their comforts in food and drink. Later on, he took advantage of his stay at the Curia to procure—let us frankly say, to purchase—a bull permitting St Albans monks to eat flesh during the fortnight from Septuagesima to Quinquagesima, while other Benedictines were fasting. His plea was their great labours, and their great distance from the sea, which made it difficult for them to procure fish. The casuistic pleas by which he glossed all this over when he came home, and proposed to avoid the "scandal to religion and refute altogether the obloquy which perchance might arise from the cause of indulgence", are too long for quotation here.(14)

All this time, on the other hand, income was diminishing: this is pointed out even by the abbey's apologists. No doubt this was in a considerable measure due to exterior economic causes, but certainly in part to the fatal policy of raising ready money by granting long leases for lump sums, with easy quit-rents. Certainly, again, the diminution of income was not balanced by serious retrenchment. The only serious diminution of expenses of which we have record is in the matter of hospitality and almsgiving, as described later in Morton's *monitio*. Abbot Wallingford's splendid altar screen, a most laudable achievement in itself, takes a different complexion when we reflect that it contributed to the semi-bankruptcy of his abbey in the next generation. One of the other graces which Whethamstede purchased at Rome was a confirmation of Boniface IX's indult permitting St Albans to farm not only their lands but their appropriated churches in this way, even to lay-folk. This irregular indult goes far to account for the disgracefully frequent changes of incumbents in the abbey benefices amounting to six in nineteen years at one parish, five in six years at another, and so on.(15)

It is evident that Henry VII, some time towards the end of 1489, made up his mind to deal with all English monasteries, without permitting the usual exceptions, and that St Albans got wind of this and determined to forestall the blow. In following the dates of the different documents, we must bear in mind that, whereas a pressing message from England might reach Rome in forty days, the usual time for a messenger was seven or eight weeks.(16) We must reckon also with the possibility of considerable delays at the Curia, to be abridged only by favour or money on one side or the other. The Evesham Chronicle gives us classic examples of these manœuvres; and the two relevant chapters of my second volume (XXIV, XXV) will help to cast striking sidelights upon this present affair.*

Our first firm date is February 6, 1490,(17) when Innocent VIII addressed a brief to Cardinal Morton. He has been informed [*accepimus*] that St Albans and its abbot are exempt from all but papal control, "yet certain detractors of them and of Religion, seeking rather their own than that which is of God, do very often strive, by various subtle means, to molest and trouble in manifold ways the aforesaid Abbot and monastery concerning this matter of exemption". If therefore this is so, Morton is to take care "that they be not unduly molested, contrary to the tenour of this their exemption; which will also be pleasing to Us".(18) It must be noted that this brief neither contains from the Pope, nor hints from the abbey, any mention whatever of the crucial matter of *visitation*. The monks thus gain one important point: the initiative is with them.

After just a month (March 6, 1490), Innocent sent Morton a bull, which shows that Henry VII himself had urged the importance of monastic reform. This bull rehearses how "it hath lately come to Our ears, not without great displeasure and bitterness

* I had hoped to finish off this St Albans case by including the two Papal bulls to Morton which are mentioned, but without detailed information of their contents, in Professor Claude Jenkins's article (*Tudor Essays*, pp. 26–74). The outbreak of war in 1939 shattered this hope; and even at the present moment I can still see no immediate prospect of getting a professional researcher from the P.R.O. or elsewhere to copy those bulls. I must therefore throw myself on the mercy of the public if it should turn out, in happier times, that their publication seriously affects my conclusions.

of mind, by the report of certain trustworthy persons", that in some of the English monasteries "the inmates have given themselves up to a reprobate sense, and put the fear of God behind their backs, and are leading a wanton and most dissolute life, to the ruin of their own souls, the offence of God's majesty, the dishonour of Religion, and the evil example and scandal of many folk".(19) The Pope proceeds to lay special emphasis on the exempt abbeys; and rehearses how he is writing "at the instance also, in this matter, of our beloved son in Christ, Henry the Seventh". Morton, therefore, is bidden to command the Ministers-General or Father-Abbots of exempt Orders to visit, within a reasonable time from this present mandate, either personally or by proxy, all their monasteries in his province, "and bring them back to the true pattern and Rule of their Order. But" (the bull continues) "where there are no such Superiors* [do thou command] the Abbots, Priors, and other prelates of the said monasteries and places that, within the specified time, they *shall reform themselves*." "If they scorn to do so (which We do not believe)", then Morton himself is to visit them, with God before his eyes, or to depute some efficient visitor. This he must do in every case, whether it be an exempt house or not. Wherever a criminal be found, whether in head or members, Morton is empowered to punish him as Canon Law requires, even unto deposition of the Head or to expelling guilty brethren as "putrid members" and bringing healthy monks into their place. Resistance is to be broken down by excommunication "without any right of appeal, and, if need be, by invoking the Secular Arm". The bull concludes with a formula of immense importance, which had grown more and more frequent as a protection against the endless appeals to Rome from monks seeking escape by the subterfuge of pleading ancient (and often forged)

* It has been asserted that this bull does not include the Benedictine houses. This is a manifest and fatal error. The Pope provides for two sorts of cases. Most of the exempt houses were exempt in virtue of their Order: in those cases, it is the Minister General of the Order who is called upon to reform the house. In other cases it is not the Order which is exempt, but only the individual house by way of rare exception; this was so at St Albans, though not to the full extent claimed by the monks. Therefore, in such cases as St Albans, it is for the Abbot to reform his house; or if (as in the case of cathedrals) the Prior is practically Abbot, or in Augustinian houses where the Superior is called Prior, the duty is laid upon them. The special significance of the words I have italicised just below will appear later on.

privileges or exemptions. No exemption whatever, granted in the past by Popes or Synods, is to hold good in this present case: those who plead any deed of exemption must be able to prove that it "makes full and express mention, word for word, of such an indult". In other words, all time-honoured privileges are swept away for this particular occasion; none can hold good unless it clearly and explicitly recites that it excepts the abbey from the operation of this present bull of March 6, 1490. The cardinal is bidden to arm himself with transcripts of this decisive bull, in order to bear down all possible opposition.

If any Roman decision could ever be counted as final, short of a decree *ex cathedra*, here is one. Here, if anywhere, we may apply the time-honoured misquotation from St Augustine, and say *Roma locuta est, causa finita.*(20) The man whom the monks stigmatize as "seeking rather his own than that which is of God" here becomes one whom Innocent VIII can trust, "having God before his eyes" to reform "those who, having put the fear of God behind their backs, are leading a most dissolute life". Moreover, this commission is reinforced by the strongest legal clause that can be invented to ward off appeal. The St Albans monks are not even to be listened to at Rome, unless they can produce a later bull explicitly quoting and annulling this of March 6.

Therefore, Morton evidently proceeded at once to obey this bull, which would have reached him about April 24. Yet the Pope's "incontestable" command was at once contested by the monks. For, on June 30, Morton is pleading for help from the only authority which could enforce discipline upon a rebellious exempt abbey. He rehearses to Innocent VIII how St Albans is resisting him on the plea of its many privileges granted by past Popes, "and perchance granted anew, since the date [of that March 6 bull"].(21) On this pretext the abbot refuses to be visited or corrected; and it is to be feared that his resistance will encourage "very many other houses of the Benedictine, Cistercian, Cluniac, Premonstratensian and other Orders" to similar rebellion. Therefore he begs for a fresh commission, expressly citing St Albans and those exempt Orders, and reinvesting him with the powers of that bull, with the same "notwithstanding" clause, reinforced this time (if indeed an absolute prohibition can in any way be logically reinforced) by a clause superseding "specially and expressly" all privileges and indults which St Albans might plead. This petition the Pope now granted in full, with the superseding clause, and letters *ad hoc* to St Albans.(22) Yet this doubly repeated "notwithstanding" clause was ignored again, a few weeks later, not only by the monastic litigants but by Rome herself. We may here bear in mind the Dominican Fr. Mortier's sentence, with its mild but double-edged irreverence: "Popes propose, but God sometimes disposes."(23) For, under date of July 3, the Vatican Archives contain a petition from St Albans. The monks plead ancient privileges of appeal to the Popes, ratified by Boniface VIII and Nicholas V: that is, between 1294 and 1455, dates which put them hopelessly out of court in the face of Innocent's later and twice-repeated *Non Obstante*. But, under cover of these *suppressiones veri* and the usual *suggestio falsi*, they manage to procure letters of protection against "certain folk who, setting the fear of God behind them, cease not to trouble the said abbey and congregation". They are therefore free now to appeal to Rome; "even though appeal be denied, in the suit which was prosecuted against them; and, after they have interposed appeal, no man shall be suffered to pronounce judgment against them or to make any innovation or with rash daring to trouble them or their possessions". Thus the Curia grants now precisely that right of appeal which it had expressly denied itself the right of ever granting, except by a formal method which it does not pretend to follow here: namely, the obvious cause of derogating from the bulls of March 6 by citing it word for word and contradicting its provisions with equal plainness. Yet the monks have now procured a document which will give them a colourable excuse for continuing the fight, perhaps *ad infinitum*. For no English court will venture to disregard outright a bull from Rome, however plainly unjust. The Pope had given Morton a bull excluding this present imbroglio as clearly as any legal phraseology could exclude it. Yet contemporaries commonly agreed that after all, he who now committed this illegality was the Pope himself, who in law can judge black to be white, if he be so inspired. The papacy, proclaimed Boniface VIII, has all Law "in the casket of its own breast": *in scrinio pectoris sui*. Even if we interpret those words in a minimizing sense (not that he can *make* all laws but that he has all right of *interpreting* them, and need not, like other men, cite law or precedent for his judgments), the effect remains practically the same. The most illegal decision (using that word in its ordinary sense) becomes legal if pronounced by St Peter's successor sitting formally in judgment. Even those who refused to admit this altogether knew that the idea was generally strong enough to ruin their case in any ecclesiastical court. Hence that scramble for bulls, that crowd of proctors and attorneys in Rome, and those floods of money spent there, which became more and more notorious as the Middle Ages wore on. Here, at St Albans, we have one of the hundreds of cases in which a "surreptitious" bull has been obtained: a bull resting upon deliberate misstatement or concealment of fact by the litigant. St Bernard had made this one of his chief complaints against the Court of Rome: that it destroyed justice by indiscriminate licence of appeal, since Popes were thus overwhelmed with the labour of deciding complicated causes between persons so remote that nothing like personal study was possible. Half a century after St Bernard, we find the fact confessed frankly by an unusually strong and legalistic Pope, Lucius III, whose decree of 1183 marks an epoch in the history of the Inquisition. A year earlier, Lucius had been appealed to in a suit between the Abbey of Ste Geneviève at Paris and the serfs of Rosuy-sous-Bois. Within a few months he delivered two decrees flatly contradictory of each other. Later, he pleaded natural ignorance: "Seeing that, by reason of the multitude of affairs which are brought before the Apostolic See, We cannot keep in Our memory the tenour of that which We have written and other things which We do, therefore We are sometimes circumvented by the wiles of certain folk, and are ignorantly led to write against that which We had before written."(24) This it was which always gave a rich abbey that advantage of protracting litigation almost indefinitely, as we have seen the Dominicans of Paris boasting for themselves. It was noted as one of Bernard's most saintly characteristics that, though his power at the Roman Court was enormous, he never took money.

Meanwhile Morton was acting upon the commands laid upon him by the bull of March 6. It seems pretty clear that he had now visited St Albans, in the practical, if not in the technical and legal, sense. The monks, behind their great walls and gates, may easily have kept him out of their precincts; we have such instances in the case of even better equipped papal visitors. But, if only half of the document here following is true, Morton would have had no difficulty in getting less formal and more trustworthy evidence from townsfolk, the parish clergy, and the neighbouring gentry. Now, therefore (July 5), he sends a formal *monitio* to St Albans, not only as archbishop and papal legate, but as one who can claim special visitatorial powers *ad hoc*. He addresses it as "a monastery dependent immediately (as it is said) upon the Church of Rome". He thus recognizes explicitly the abbey's claims, without in any way committing himself to their validity in law. Having rehearsed Innocent's bull of March 6, which constitutes him "Visitor, Inquisitor, Reformer and Judge", he announces his intention of acting now in those capacities and in obedience to that bull. Thence he proceeds:*

Whereas by the report of public notoriety and by frequent relations of *many* trustworthy persons, it hath come to our hearing that thou, the aforesaid Abbot, hast long been and art still noted *and defamed* for simony, usury, spending and dilapidation of the goods and chattels and possessions of the said abbey, and for certain other outrageous [*enormibus*] offences and excesses written here below, and art so remiss in the rule, care and administration of its goods, both spiritual and temporal, so negligent and wasteful, that in the said abbey of St Albans, where in former days regular observance *was held in great veneration*, and hospitality *was most diligently kept, yet for no small time wherein thou hast been at its head, while thou and some of thy fellow monks and brethren* (*whose blood, it is feared, shall be required of thine hand by the Strict Judge*) *have relaxed the manner and pattern of* religious living and cast off the mild yoke of contemplation, so that regular observance, hospitality, almsgiving, and other offices of piety which from of old were wont there to be exercised and administered, have decreased and do daily more and more decrease and are withdrawn by thy fault, carelessness, negligence and deed: whereby also the pious wishes of your founders are defrauded

* The words here italicized are omitted by Cardinal Gasquet in his version of this celebrated bull (pp. 42ff.) without any warning to the reader. The rest is compressed into a brief paragraph which would run to only fifteen lines of this present page, and deliberately softened down, as he softens *enormibus* to "great." See further for note (24) in Appendix.

and, the early model of life having been abandoned, not few of thy said fellow monks and brethren (which is no small cause of grief) have given themselves to a reprobate sense and, putting the fear of God behind their backs, are leading a life of wantonness, and (what is horrible to relate) they very often [*persaepe*] fear not to profane the holy places, and even the very churches of God, with the debauching of nuns and the spilling of blood and of [human] seed: and thou, among other grievous, outrageous, and heinous offences, hast first admitted as sister and nun to the cell or priory of Pray, (which thou claimest as of thy jurisdiction) a certain married woman named Elena Germyn, (who long since departed evilly from her husband) and hast afterwards promoted her as prioress there, notwithstanding that her said husband was then, and is still, living; and Dom Thomas Sudbury, thy fellow monk,* hath long since had access and hath still, unto her as adulterer to adulteress, in the said cell or priory of Pray, as it were publicly and notoriously and with impunity: even as some others of thy brethren and fellow monks have had and have still, with impunity, continual access to her and to others [*alias*, feminine plural], there and elsewhere, as unto public brothels or stews. Moreover [it is reported] that, not only in that convent of Pray, but also in the nunnery of Sapwell (which again thou claimest as of thy jurisdiction) thou dost so often change the Prioresses and Superiors at thy will and pleasure; and, whilst thou dost depose good and religious women in both places, and dost there raise to the highest dignities the evil, and sometimes fallen women [*vitiatas*], Religion is cast away, virtue is neglected, and such superfluous expenses are made that through these aforesaid and other outrageous and damnable deeds committed by some of thy fellow monks, whom thou hast made and deputed in those places to command and rule, and under the name of guardians (though they are none such, but rather thieves and notorious criminals) to dispense the goods of those priories (or rather to dissipate and consume) those places, formerly very religious, are now rendered and reputed as it were profane and infamous, and are so impoverished by thy deeds and those of thy monks, that they seem to be brought almost to naught. Thou hast also done the like in certain other cells of monks which thou claimest as subject unto thee; and even in the abbey of the glorious protomartyr Alban, of ancient fame, thou hast wasted the common possessions, its goods and jewels. Moreover thou hast cut down promiscuously and sold and alienated its woods and forests, copses and underwoods, with almost all the oaks and other great timber, to

* This man was Prior of St Andrew's at Northampton. His congregation was Cluniac; and thus, as a Black monk of St Benedict, he was fellow to the Benedictine Wallingford.

the value of 8,000 marks and more. As to thy brethren and fellow monks (certain of whom, as it is said, are given up to all the evils in the world) while some, almost utterly neglecting divine service, consort with prostitutes and harlots within and without the abbey precincts, publicly (as it were) and continually, others, ambitious for promotion and honour, for the sake of obtaining such honours and promotions, with whatever damnable simony, satisfy thy greed by stealing chalices and other church jewels, even digging out with sacrilegious audacity such as are set in St Alban's shrine; yet these men thou dost rather knowingly defend than punish or impugn. Meanwhile such of thy fellow monks who are good, living religiously and strong in virtue and counsel, those dost thou forthwith oppress, and art wont to hate. Thus, while the head is sick, the other rotten and infected members do so riot and abound in almost manifest vices that the famous reputation of this abbey is perverted with infamy, and holy Religion hath almost perished internally, while the external possessions thereof, both lands and houses and movables, are notoriously tending to desolation, to the offence of God's Majesty and the disgrace and evil example of Religion and the scandal of very many folk, whence thou art notoriously [*dignosceris*] in very great need of the office of correction and reformation, even as the said abbey needeth the same, and many of thy fellow monks and brethren dwelling therein; and for the reform of all these things We are daily importuned and made anxious. Willing, therefore, humbly to obey our most holy lord Pope, as befitteth, and to fulfil his apostolic mandate directed to Us in this matter—Abbot William aforesaid (whom already, a little before, by authority and command of the said most holy lord Pope we did personally and charitably warn that thou shouldst have reformed certain of the said outrageous deeds, yet hitherto thou hast deferred and neglected to reform them), by the same authority committed unto Us in this matter, by and according to all force, form and effect of the letters above inserted.* We do peremptorily warn, and command thee to correct and reform effectively, as to all and singular the matters above rehearsed, both thyself and thy brethren and fellow monks within the precincts of the said abbey, as also the Prioresses, Guardians and nuns of Pray and Sapwell priories within 30 days, and others thy Priors and fellow monks subjected unto thee in the remoter priories and cells within 60 days after the communication of this present letter unto thee, if it be free to reach thee, or else after the nailing thereof upon the church doors of the said abbey, or after notification otherwise law-

* That is, the papal bull of March 6, which he encloses in this monition, and which contains the all-important *non obstante* clause sweeping appeals aside.

fully made unto thee. Thou shalt also reduce them, or cause them to be reduced, to the true pattern and Rule of thine Order, according to the laudable ordinances and institutes thereof, without exception or delay: and thyself shalt henceforward desist and abstain altogether from the alienation and embezzling of the abbey's possessions and jewels, especially of woods, trees, and copses. If, however, thou hast scorned to fulfil these things, within the aforesaid term, according to Our command (or rather that of the Apostolic See), then We will proceed according to the force, tenour and effect of the aforesaid Apostolic letters, and according to the form therein prescribed unto Us; and, after the lapse of the said 30 days, We intend to come to the said abbey personally, and, by God's grace, to visit it in fact, or (if We ourselves chance to be otherwise occupied) cause it to be visited by others whom We shall choose as apt thereunto.

The rest of the document consists almost altogether of repetitions; but Morton reminds Wallingford plainly that the bull prescribes, if necessary, even the deposition of thoroughly unworthy officials.(25)

Our last Vatican document is dated July 30, 1490.(26) It is a bull addressed to Morton. The Pope expresses his solicitude for monastic reform, and continues:

For some time past, it hath been brought to our ears by report of certain trustworthy persons that, whereas the abbeys were once flourishing, yet now for some time past our beloved abbots and monks and other religious folk of the aforesaid monasteries and foundations in thy diocese and province of Canterbury have gradually relaxed their manner and rule of life and laid aside the sweet yoke of contemplation, so that regular Observance had grown cold, and not only hath the early rule of life been abandoned, but even in certain of such houses the inmates, giving themselves up to a reprobate sense and setting the fear of God behind their backs, have led a wanton and too dissolute life, to the ruin of their own souls, the offence of God's majesty, the disgrace of Religion, and the evil example and scandal of very many folk. We therefore, at the humble and instant prayer of Our beloved son in Christ, Henry VII, King of the realm aforesaid, have commanded to you, Our brother in other letters,

to warn the heads of the Exempt Orders, or, where only the single house is exempt, its abbot or prior, "as by Our authority ...that within a fixed term they must needs take heed and set themselves effectually to such a reform, and reform themselves, and do all the things aforesaid". If they disobeyed, it was for

Morton to step in, personally or by deputy, for root and branch reform.

But, as thy recent petition hath set forth, although the said Superiors, Generals and Presidents were warned and duly required —*moniti et debite requisiti*—by thee, in the power of the said letters, to perform these things within a competent term, yet they, scorning such *monitiones* and *requisitiones*, took no care to reform, correct, and restore to such regular Observance themselves and the aforesaid houses of Religion; wherefore thou wert compelled, not without grievous labours and expense, to repair to such monasteries and houses for the aforesaid purpose, sometimes directly and in person, sometimes sending fit and sufficient persons, and thou hast visited very many, correcting them and bringing them back to regular Observance, and the inmates of such houses have begun to live in peace and quiet under such Observance and do at present so live. Moreover, when thou didst set thyself, in due order, to pass on to the reform and correction, as justice did prompt, of the crimes and excesses of the monks of certain monasteries, and especially of St Alban and of St Andrew by Northampton (in the diocese of Lincoln and of the Benedictine and Cluniac Orders respectively), then Our beloved Sons the Abbot and Convent of St Alban—both for themselves and for the cells which, as they claim, [*ut praetenditur*] are subject to them—under this claim [*praetextu*] that they assert certain privileges and indults granted to the abbey and its subject cells, wherein (as it is asserted) there is the prescription that they may not be visited or corrected by any other than a Legate *de latere* from the Apostolic See; a prescription granted aforetime by the Apostolic See and (as it is asserted), confirmed and perchance freshly conceded by Ourselves since the granting to thee of such faculty [of visitation], generally or specially. So, likewise, Thomas Sudbury, Prior of the said house of St Andrew, who hath almost utterly wasted [*quasi consumpsit*] its possessions. These have refused to be visited by thee, and have appealed from such visitation and reformation to the Apostolic See; and We have committed the cases of these appeals to the hearing and final decision of our beloved sons, Masters Jerome Porcari and Francis Breiro, Our own chaplains and Auditors of the Sacred Palace; and the community* of St Andrew do desire such visitation, reformation and correction; and, seeing that it may be probably doubted lest, by such example, very many other exempt monasteries and houses of the aforesaid or any other Orders under claim [*praetextu*] likewise of similar confirmations and of other privileges perchance granted unto them, or to be granted in future,

* As apart, that is, from their incriminated prior.

may refuse to be visited, corrected and reformed, to the no small prejudice and ruin and desolation of the said monasteries and houses, therefore thou hast humbly besought that We should deign, of Our Apostolic benignity, to make fit provision for the said matters. We therefore, (who desire with utmost affection the better direction and the reform of all monasteries and religious houses, especially in these times, and considering that the state and merit of these cases have been expressed, and calling them to Ourselves in due course, and utterly quashing the aforesaid litigation), being moved by your supplications and also by the humble prayers of the aforesaid King, do by Our Apostolic letters command thee, brother, to proceed freely to such visitations, reformations and corrections in monasteries and religious houses and persons, (yet with exception of the Cistercian Order), in all matters and altogether, according to the contents and tenor of the aforesaid letters, notwithstanding any appeals hitherto made, or perchance to be made; and also to make men strictly obey whatsoever thou shalt have decreed and ordained in such matters, even to the calling upon the help of the Secular Arm, if need be, Notwithstanding....

and here follows a long series of clauses on the model of those we have seen in the first bull. Against this present one, no objection is valid from English legatine or synodical decrees, or from abbatial privileges or indults, or from anything but a papal bull mentioning this one by name and definitely derogating from it.

Beyond this point, nothing more has been discovered in the Vatican Archives, although Monsignore Mercati has assisted my search with the utmost courtesy.

CHAPTER L

THE ST ALBANS CASE (2)

THESE documents from the Papal Archives, fragmentary as they are, seem to tell a clear story so far as essentials are concerned. Morton and the King, bent on monastic reform, obtained the fullest visitatorial powers from Innocent VIII. They would naturally begin the visitation with the houses which seemed to enjoy a bad pre-eminence, St Albans and Northampton. The former resisted on the plea of very special papal exemptions; the latter, as belonging to the exempt Order of Cluny. Yet nothing that either could produce was really valid against the bull of March 6, reinforced by Innocent's answer to the supplication of June 30. Both those two documents explicitly refused to admit appeal from any party which could not quote a clause annulling *in so many words* the powers granted to Morton. But what was invalid in papal law might none the less serve its purpose in prolonging litigation at the Papal Court, so long as the litigant was wealthy enough and in sufficiently desperate straits. We have seen in previous chapters how the nuns of Klingenthal fought their Visitor against all law, and actually procured his condemnation and fine. We have seen, again, how it was complained to the King of France that this abuse was common enough to ruin all discipline; bishops dared not take upon themselves so great labour and risks.(1) Finally, we saw how Henry VII began his reign with a Statute protecting bishops against legal chicanery for having simply done their duty. Let us turn now, therefore, to the internal evidence from the records of the two incriminated houses.

From St Andrews we can learn very little directly. The house was already badly indebted in 1473. Soon after, there was a long lawsuit for the priorate, doubtless with great waste, between Thomas Sudbury and William Brekenok. Sudbury won; and in January 1489 we find the monks petitioning Henry VII in Parliament for redress.(2) There had been, for years, great trouble between one Thomas Sudbury, late pretending himself to be Prior of the said monastery, and one William Brekenok, in likewise pretending himself to be the Prior of the same; by which trouble the goods of the said place, as well ornaments of the church, as copes, vestments, corporals, chalices, basins of silver, saints* of silver, and other jewels and plate belonging to the said monastery, as their stuffs, featherbeds, coverlets, sheets, diapers, pots, pans and other such like, be clearly consumed and wasted, as notori[ous]ly is knowen; and not only that, but for either of their other support and maintenance, in their said pretended quarrels, many grants of annuities, obligations, leases and other writings of either of them hath been made, under the convent seal and otherwise, to divers persons. Please it therefore your most noble Grace, for the interest of the service of Almighty God in the said monastery, and for the reducing of the said monastery into the old ancient order,

to quash all these deeds, except such as can justify themselves at law. The King replied: "Be it done as desired." Sudbury was deposed or resigned or died in 1490: half a year at latest, after Morton's *monitio*. Henry VIII's visitor, in December 1535, reported great debts and gross financial irregularities; it is a great pity that the King's foundation should have been "thus mangled by the quondam [ruler]". The present prior is a good manager and scholar, "and pity it is that ever he came there".(3) Broken as these glimpses are, they all point the same way.

From St Albans comes far fuller evidence, but more conflicting.

One of Wallingford's predecessors, John Whethamstede, reigned twice: first from 1420 to 1440, when he resigned; then after re-election 1452–65. He has left an account of his second abbacy, published now in the Rolls Series. Equally important for his first abbacy are the *Annals* which go by the name of Amundesham, a monk of St Albans who overlapped Whethamstede. There are strong reasons in support of this attribution; and it is under that name that these are printed in the Rolls Series. These *Annals* contain many of Whethamstede's letters; moreover, his very individual and peculiar style appears also in other parts; it seems evident that he supplied much of the material for the whole book.

On pages 102–35 of the *Register* Whethamstede gives a long

* *Seyntis*. Possibly, however, *brooches*. See *sentis* in *Med. Eng. Word-List*.

and most unflattering character of Wallingford. This man, at Abbot Stoke's death (1451), was "Official General". He held five important "obediences" simultaneously: a pluralism condemned over and over again by monastic statutes, as offering too great temptations to *proprietas*. Under Whethamstede's second rule Wallingford held two, archdeacon and chamberlain. A few of the greatest abbeys, such as Westminster and St Albans, had archidiaconal rights over the appropriated parishes; and the archidiaconal system of money fines lent itself so notoriously to peculation that John of Salisbury alludes to a satirical disputation on the question whether an Archdeacon can come to heaven. Under Abbot Albon (1465–76) he was promoted to prior; and at Albon's death he was unanimously elected abbot. This, on the face of it, is obviously in his favour, as also the fact that Whethamstede apparently continued him in two offices throughout his own second reign.

Yet, writing of that reign in cold blood, "*more registrantis*", he relates circumstantially how, at the first General Audit in 1453, Wallingford presented falsified accounts. Stoke (he writes) had notoriously been a great saver; yet there was here no trace of these savings. Wallingford, therefore, the abbey's chief financial official, was an embezzler and a hoarder; and he had earned for himself that papal condemnation decreed in Canon Law, to be buried on a dung-heap as *proprietarius*. Let him go away, reflect, and produce true accounts. Wallingford

hearing this answer, departed with no small wrath of spirit; and, going to his own chamber, he broke out into such loud murmurs that not only his own accomplices heard him, but even almost all the brethren in the cloister, and spake very variously among themselves. For some, looking rather to words than to deeds, said that the Official had been prudent, wise, and politic; and that he governed all and sundry the offices under his administration very prudently and politically and also wisely. Others however, and those who judged more solidly and ripely in the matter, said that the Official had been very evil; and that, after a lapse of many years, he left his office in a most evil state at the end of last year.(4)

The brethren therefore called Whethamstede to draw up a paper as to the then state of the abbatial revenues, in order to show whether he himself or others were responsible for the disappearance of Stoke's savings. This he did, and showed statistically that there ought to be a considerable balance somewhere. Moreover, Stoke "had confessed, at the hour of death, both to his own confessor and in confession to God, that he had in hand, in coin, 1,000 marks". Therefore, Whethamstede had made enquiry concerning this sum from Wallingford, but without satisfactory answer.

Then (he continues) the Official bethought him of the Unjust Steward, and made friends with the Mammon of Unrighteousness, that is, his powerful friends among the laity: the Earl of Richmond, with Lord and Lady Sudely. It is of importance to note, what has apparently escaped both critics and apologists, that this Earl of Richmond was none other than Edmund Tudor, father to the future Henry VII. Thus Whethamstede was constantly besieged with messages from such influential outsiders, begging him "that this monk might stand as a just man in all his offices, nor be suddenly repelled or expelled, to his shame and confusion".(5) He answered in each case that he had no such present intention, "except in so far as he may have afforded us great and serious matter for deposition". At the same time he did this with almost servile civility, "recommending himself humbly in each case", to the great man or lady, as was customary at that time. He then summoned Wallingford to his presence, and began:

Brother, many great folk have interceded for thee, that by Our good will and favour thou mightest remain peaceably in all thine offices, and specially in those which are of lighter burden, yet of greater dignity among us. We are well pleased, brother, that thou shouldest so stay, provided that thou canst truly say unto Us, with that servant in the Gospel: "Lord, thou hast given unto me five talents; behold, I have gained two other talents beside them".... Go, therefore, and consider better; for, as we have already told thee, We are in no wise pleased with subtlety, or rather sterility, of rendering account.

Wallingford (so the text continues) saw now that he must render better account of his stewardship, and produced fresh balance sheets deducting nearly £200 from the alleged debts, and acknowledging 200 quarters more of grain, with £160 in coin. The abbot welcomed this sudden betterment by more than

£400: i.e. by the yearly income of more than forty well-paid parish priests. He still suspected "fraud rather than faith", but dismissed Wallingford with a compliment upon his acknowledged business ability, and the plainly expressed hope that he "would be more faithful and prudent in future...for We love not greatly to change [Our servants]".(6)

Here follows a long account of Abbot Stoke's last moments. At the Last Unction he made his sacramental confession, and took the Holy Communion with many senior brethren, including the prior, the archdeacon, the sacristan and the almoner. Then the prior pressed him to a more public confession, for he had earned a somewhat miserly reputation. He reminded him that for nearly eleven years he had been in this great office, immersed in much worldly business, and that it is hard to keep oneself quite clean from such "slime"; now at his last gasp, therefore, let him fully disburden his soul. Stoke now confessed to having amassed 1000 marks, partly at the expense of the common abbey funds. The prior pressed him:

"Father, if it please thee, where are those moneys? in thine own hand, or in another's keeping?" Then the Abbot, raising his right hand and pointing his finger to brother William Wallingford, then Official General, and to his brother Thomas Wallingford, his Senior Chaplain, said: "In thy keeping, and in thine, are all those moneys, and laid up in a certain chest within the dormitory, which ye know better."...The Prior, rejoicing in these words, returned soon afterwards to the abbey, and, assembling the brethren, openly expounded to all men the above storing of the said moneys and the Abbot's will. Then he engaged them to prayer, and exhorted them to pray without pause for his happy passing.(7)

Soon after Stoke's death, the prior called upon the two Wallingfords to bring these moneys for the general view. "They came and brought him two little chests, firmly closed and locked, affirming with solemn oaths that they had not elsewhere in their keeping anything more consigned by the Abbot." These were opened, and also the great chest in the dormitory; but these yielded only 250 marks. The prior pressed then as to the remaining 650:* they swore most solemnly, as before, that this was all. The prior was amazed, but adjourned the matter until the election of a new abbot.

* *Sic*, apparently by a slip for 750.

Whethamstede was elected, and the prior told him at once. He resolved to bide his time; and meanwhile others also revealed what they had heard at Stoke's deathbed, yet Whethamstede waited a year and a half to give the accused every chance of voluntary confession. He became more and more convinced that "Ananias and Sapphira" were in the abbey. Then at last he summoned William, who was specially suspected of holding the money, and called upon him to clear himself of this suspicion of mortal sin, *proprietas* in its grossest form. William could not deny Stoke's deathbed words; yet he was ready to swear on the Gospels that he had no such money, adding: "So help me God, and so may He stand by me in that hour when every soul shall need His help!" Whethamstede "having little credence in these words", pressed him again to confess, adding: "If thou hast aught of those moneys in thy possession, tell Us secretly or openly, and We will preserve thine honour, without blot or disgrace or little cloud of scandalization." These words are misunderstood by the editor, who interprets them as flatly inconsistent with his final compromise and "paternal" treatment of Wallingford. They simply mean that Whethamstede, after the common practice of monastic disciplinarians, was willing to forgive much so long as public scandal could be avoided. This was so usual that we sometimes find the distinction officially noted in the tariff of punishments; the same offence is more severely punished when public, than when it can be kept quiet. Even so honest a man and so strict a disciplinarian as Abbot Samson of St Edmundsbury (as his confidential biographer tells us) behaved thus to Dom Geoffrey Redhead, one of his obedientiaries who was in charge of four manors. "Hearing the *infamia* of his incontinence, he long winked at this [*dissimulavit*] perchance because this Geoffrey seemed useful to the community."(8) Having tempted William in vain with this promise, Whethamstede summoned his brother Thomas; yet from him also he got nothing but that he "swore and swore again, and bequeathed his soul to the Prince of Hell", if he had a halfpenny or a farthing of that hoard, or knew where it was. The abbot could only hint plainly that Thomas would regret this in hell; then he let the matter drop. He remembered Solomon's warning that too much wringing of the nose bringeth forth blood, and reflected that he might here "extort from the brethren hatred rather than gold". He gave up hope of discovering either the hiding place or the person of this "Second Ananias", and ended with a solemn warning to posterity. "Therefore, let all Pastors learn, who in future shall die in this abbey, to make on their deathbed a more cautious declaration of the moneys they have; for the said Abbot [Stoke] made one of such simple sort that nothing whatever came therefrom, at least to the advantage of his successor."

This *Register* was evidently written up from time to time; for, whereas the record of Whethamstede's second year ends thus, the third year resumes the story in its very first words. A call came upon the abbey to pay heavy dues to the Exchequer, and Whethamstede turned at once to Wallingford with his confessed balance of £160. To his astonishment, Wallingford disclaimed his former assertion: he had said, not that he *possessed* a balance of £160, but that he had *spent* that sum from Stoke's hoard "in repairs, and other matters pertaining to the abbey's well-being". The abbot vainly reminded him that the whole abbey had understood the Official's confession as he had. He called the prior, who testified to this general impression; the sub-prior even claimed to have heard it from Wallingford's own lips. So did Robert Beaver, adding that Wallingford had claimed to have paid £140 of that sum to the abbot. Whethamstede then challenged him to answer these witnesses here present; otherwise

> We, brother, have now found by experience what very many brethren have told me long since. For they have said of thee that, albeit thou art most prone to swear in concealment of thy transgressions, yet thou art so wont and accustomed to perjury that, even though thine oaths were made upon the Book or upon the Lord's Body, yet no faith or credence could ever be reposed thereon.

They had also reported of him in the many offices he had held, he had been "an arrant trader, studying assiduously to buy cheap and sell dear, and then applying the whole gain to thy private uses, and in no wise to the profit of thine offices".(9) Whethamstede accused him further of neglectful administration in those offices: that of chamberlain, for instance, he had left £100 in debt. Whethamstede calculated that he must have a hoard of £1000 at least, and called upon him to produce it. For (he argued) Wallingford was known to have enjoyed from his first entrance into the abbey more money than his fellows "which, as we have sufficient proof against thee, thou didst sometimes lend out at usurious interest". So again at Oxford; so when he came back to great offices at St Albans, he was notorious for selfish greed not only among the brethren, but also among the servants and the whole neighbourhood. "It is tolerable, brother, that thou shouldest have somewhat in thy purse wherewith thou shalt be able to be maintained in honest and religious fashion; but it is intolerable, and a sin for which there is no dispensation, that thou shouldest heap up gold for thyself apart." The whole speech, crammed with biblical citations and concluding with solemn appeals to the Last Judgment, fills nearly seven pages. Wallingford (according to this *Register*) "was greatly thunderstruck at these words, with even more anguish of heart than my pen can write at present: he departed in shame and tears". Whethamstede describes the man's bitter self-communings with the rhetorical prolixity of the classical historians. He went and took counsel with his brother and confederate, begging him to mediate. Thomas, then, carried his terms to the abbot: let William be restored to favour and he will not only pay this present debt to the Exchequer but also "be so cautious in future, so provident and careful, that within the space of two years he will make you possessor of £200 or £300 in your treasury".(10) Whethamstede, rejoicing in the conversion of this "son of perdition", promised that if the next two years did in fact produce such fruit, he would "admit him to the grace of his favour, and treat him thenceforth as paternally as though he had never gone astray". William, rejoiced at this answer, "thenceforward applied his sense and knowledge unto the performance in deed of that which he had promised in word, and laboured very efficaciously. Thus and under this form was that brother restored back again to himself, and brought to concede, by implication, that he had not only in his purse the aforesaid sum,* but also various moneys besides".

* That is, this considerable payment to the Exchequer, of which Whethamstede had reminded his brethren: "That Court is as it were outside the law and hath no mercy; nor is it wont to spare any man, specially when there is money still to be paid" (p. 125). By Michaelmas, William had found £300 to pay the most pressing debts (p. 135).

This story is not only dramatic but essentially consistent and natural, when we have made allowance for Whethamstede's habitual self-intoxication with rhetoric. Whethamstede, who had been in touch with the abbey even during the period of his resignation, must have known Wallingford well from the very beginning of his career; and this picture of a thoroughly capable but equally unscrupulous business man is natural enough. We shall see in chapter LVII how truly the monks themselves pleaded the extent to which they were enslaved to worldly business by their numerous estates. I have traced in my third volume (pp. 266ff. and chapters XXI–XXIV), the progressive casuistry by which *proprietas* had been whittled down from a mortal sin to a practice so regular that it could plead the quasi-legal force of custom, so long as it was not too gross and public. For centuries before this time disciplinarians had complained of the opportunities offered to these obedientiaries, especially in wealthy abbeys, and most of all when they held a multiplicity of offices, for spending liberally on their own pleasures and hoarding for the future. When Chaucer's Shipman told of the monk of St Denis, able to suborn the merchant's wife with the loan of a hundred francs (rather more than the yearly pay of a French mounted squire on active service at that time),(11) his hearers knew that the picture, if exceptional, was still possible enough. Benedictine General Chapters guard explicitly against the sin of usurious trading; so also do the Dominicans, nominally Mendicant as they were.(12)

Lingard, the most learned and candid among Roman Catholic historians of the English Reformation, makes no mention of the St Albans case; and, with regard to the monasteries in general, he agrees with Cardinal Pole that the monks of that generation were, with few exceptions, "utterly degenerate from the founders of their institution".(13) Professor G. Constant, who comes nearest to Lingard in learning and (though *longo intervallo*, in accuracy) omits it also from the brief introductory sketch to his *Reformation in England*.(14) But two apologists for Wallingford have, comparatively recently, used Riley's denial of Whethamstede's authorship as a basis for their contentions; Cardinal Gasquet and Mr Rushbrook Williams.(15) Therefore we must face the objections raised by those three writers to what, on the face of it, is a damning indictment.

Their strongest evidence, by far, is drawn from the Obituary book printed by Riley as Appendix D to the first volume of the *Register*. This book covers six abbatial reigns: Whethamstede, Stoke, Whethamstede, Albon, Wallingford, and Ramryge. The last is very brief: Riley suggests that it was finished about A.D. 1423 [*sic* for 1523], very shortly after Ramryge's death in 1519, but it says scarcely anything about him. By far the greatest part of the book is devoted to Whethamstede's work: ten pages beyond what has been printed in the Rolls volume, making thirty-two in all. Wallingford has four pages: the remaining three abbots have only four between them.

The list of Wallingford's achievements was drawn up partly in 1484, and partly 1490; and it runs partly in the very unusual form of a solemn official testimonial. There seems to be complete agreement among critics that it was drawn up in answer to some definite attack upon the abbey, whether actually launched or apprehended. The four paragraphs which concern the present question run as follows:(16)

Here, moreover, I will speak of and plainly show how he was afterwards elected as Abbot by acclamation [of the Community, *quonam pacto, per Sancti viam Spiritus*], and having taken the pastoral office, in the few years that have passed since, that is fourteen,* he paid for the debts of his predecessor, as is most clearly proved by the accounts of his Official, to the amount of £1830. In addition to this he set up that most ornamental, sumptuous and lofty screen of the high altar, which is a great glory to the church, pleasantly delights the eyes of all who see it, and to all examining it is the most wonderful work in the kingdom: the cost of this extends to £733. Then, it is no light praise for him to have finished happily our Chapter House at his great cost, for he spent on its construction £1000. Then he arranged for the making and structure of two windows in the church, one in the north part near the Sacristy, the other in the southern part near the clock; on these he expended £100. Beyond this, for the purchase of various lands (to endow) a perpetual Mass in honour of the name of Jesus every Friday for ever, and for saying a daily Mass specially for his own soul, the celebrant each day to receive 5*d.*; and this expense came to £100. Also he paid £60 for the making of a mitre

* This shows that, though Ramryge's testimonial is dated 1484, the obituary as it stands was not drawn up before 1490.

and two pastoral staves. Also for the building of his Chapel and tomb on the south near the High Altar, with most proper railings and a marble slab with his figure on it, with other ornaments of the Chapel, he expended £100 sterling. Moreover, we should not forget how many and very great costs and heavy burdens he sustained in his old age, when he strenuously defended the liberties and immunities of this Monastery against the Archbishop and High Chancellor of England [Cardinal Morton]; and how valiantly and manfully resisting his power and great might he appealed to Rome. He sent his monk John Thornton to Rome and boldly cited the Archbishop himself and his Dean of Arches to appear. In the end, this our best and most Reverend Father and most worthy Abbot obtained a most just victory, and preserved intact and inviolate all our privileges, to our great honour and immense utility. May God and St Alban, our perpetual patron here and everywhere, be praised. What is, moreover, most wonderful, praiseworthy and memorable is, that this our best of Fathers after so many and such great expenses, after such an immense number of burdens, left this Monastery free and without any the least debt: although for many years in buildings and lawsuits and many other things he had spent so great a sum of money for the honour and liberty of the Monastery.

The total sum of money mercifully expended on all the above-named burdens and benefits by the aforesaid Right Rev. Father, William Wallingford, for the benefit of this Monastery, both when he held the offices of Cellarer, Archdeacon, Prior and Kitchener, as well as in the days of his Abbacy and Pastoral dignity, is £8600. *7s.* *6d.*

And in testimony of all the foresaid, and as a most brilliant example to all to come, We, Thomas Ramridge, then Prior, and we the other fathers and brethren, conventuals of this Monastery, signify the truth to all men by our common seal, and by the unanimous consent of all of us collectively, and assent of each individually, by this private writing we testify that all these things were lovingly and benignly accomplished and done by the said most worthy Father, in the year of Our Lord 1484, the 8th day of the month of August.

From the foregoing, therefore, we can see most clearly how useful and how beloved he has been to his Monastery. Wherefore let all of us with true hearts most devoutly pray day and night to the Almighty God for him; namely, that He may deign to give him a most fitting reward in heaven for his deeds on earth. Amen.

This document (claims Cardinal Gasquet) constitutes a complete answer to the accusations recorded in Whethamstede's *Register* and Morton's *monitio*. Yet, on analysis, the "answer" appears scarcely more relevant than were those decisions which

Wallingford had procured from Rome, as opposed to those procured by Morton.

Its silence is damning on the points which not only seem most important to the modern historian, but must also have had immense significance for Wallingford's contemporaries, and for the reputation of the whole English Church. Quite apart from the weighty legal significance of Morton's words, *monitio* and *diffamatio*, he thrice stigmatizes the sins of St Albans as "notorious"; they were matters of "public fame"; he himself was "daily importuned" to come down and reform scandals which were a "disgrace and evil example of Religion". All this, the essence of Morton's *monitio*, this Ramryge testimonial ignores and spends itself in irrelevancies, just as the monks had ignored the Pope's *non obstante* clauses at Rome. It matters little to them that the archbishop and papal legate should have pilloried them publicly as fornicators, dilapidators, shirkers of almsgiving and even of their own daily services. Wallingford is extolled, not for meeting and refuting these charges, but for having "preserved all our privileges whole and untouched, to our great honour and utility". In fact, the incident exactly bears out the complaint of Chancellor Gascoigne, a generation earlier, that "Almost all corrections of souls are destroyed nowadays by appeals to, or inhibitions from, the Court of Arches in London". He instances the appeal of "a certain vicar of abominable fame and wicked life", who was so immoderate and litigious that it needed an exceptionally courageous bishop "after long vexation in the Court of Arches", to bring him to book (*Lib. Ver.* 32–4).

We must here bear constantly in mind, what I have not seen emphasized elsewhere, the triple cord of Henry VIII's preamble to his Act of Dissolution. It specifies the three main reasons which call, now at last, for decisive action by the State. These are: (1) extravagance, waste, and debt; (2) immorality; and (3) impenitence; the episcopal visitations of the last 200 years have brought little or no amendment; monastic "vicious living" is now "rooted and infected" in custom. Preambles are bad evidence in many ways; but at least they show where an accuser believes his strength to lie. These are the accusations, therefore, which we must test at every point by critical study of outside evidence. These three counts are most explicitly rehearsed in

Morton's *monitio* to St Albans. How far were they met in this excusatory document which is now claimed as a complete rebuttal?

Extravagance and waste. The Whethamstede obituary, with a long list of his expenses on (building, books, scholarship, etc.) gives a still longer list of his acquisitions. It is written of him emphatically elsewhere: "Furthermore, it is worthy of equal commemoration and admiration, that for the acquisition of all these possessions he never sold timber beyond the ordinary".(17) Stoke, again, acquired a manor for the abbey, with a little more property. Albon, in his reign of ten and a half years, "increased the revenues of his abbey...to the sum of forty marks a year". When we come to Wallingford, one of his four pages is devoted to what he had spent as archdeacon and in the other offices which he accumulated under Stoke and Whethamstede. "He erected sumptuously a Library and a Bakehouse of stone." After his election to the abbacy, "he won no little praise by happily consumating the Chapter-house with his own moneys; upon the completion of this he spent £1000". Yet the Whethamstede obituary has already told us that it was that abbot, not Wallingford, who, in his first reign, collected materials for this library and completed it during his second; the bare building, apart from glazing, desks, and battlements, cost more than £150. The chapter-house also Whethamstede "proposed to rebuild with fair hewn stone [*lapidibus politis*], and got so far as to leave an easy task for his successor; upon this he spent more than £100. As to the bake-house, Whethamstede pulled it almost all down and built one "than which, in the opinion of many, there is none much finer, at least in any abbey, within this realm. And in the building of that house he is said to have spent, through the hands of brother William of Wallingford (who was then his official) in money, apart from food and drink and other various expenses, beyond the sum of £200".(18)

Therefore, even if there were no exaggeration in the Wallingford obituary, it would come only to this, that during at least thirty years spent as business man during three abbacies, he had been responsible for the payment of £8600 as agent for abbot and community, and had fine buildings and rich ornaments to show for this. Or that later, as abbot, he had spent through his own official the sum of £2562 on buildings and ornaments. The yearly income of the abbey was, according to different computations, £2102 or £2510.(19)

But, in comparing it with the Whethamstede record, we find that Ramryge and the brethren are giving Wallingford exclusive credit for that which had in fact been done by his forerunner in library, bake-house, and chapter-house. Moreover, that sum of £1000 for the chapter-house, added to what Whethamstede had spent, seems suspiciously large. We must not omit the fact that Wallingford is credited earlier in the obituary with the "nurture and education; at his own cost and at great expense", while he was archdeacon, of ten young monks.(20) But this, again, can mean only that he diverted to that most laudable purpose a certain amount of conventual funds,* unless we are to follow Whethamstede's accusation of *proprietas*, and suppose the archdeacon to have made sufficient personal savings from his many offices to meet this "great expense". The supposition is probable enough *a priori*, but it would not help to whitewash Wallingford as a true Benedictine. The only case, I believe, in which this testimonial strays away from mere expenditure, and uses the word "acquisition", is where Wallingford enriched the abbey with a lump sum of £100. But this gift he definitely earmarked to be spent on Masses in perpetuity for his own soul.† Apart from the asserted payment of his predecessor's debts, there is nothing to disprove more than the merest fraction of the gravest among Morton's accusations in the economic field: "simony, usury, spending and dilapidation of the goods and chattels and possessions". Here, as everywhere in medieval documents, we must make allowance for the possibility of great exaggeration. It may well be that timber had not been cut down to more than a quarter of the 8000 marks which Morton specifies. Yet the "many trustworthy witnesses" to whom he appeals can scarcely have been so utterly mistaken in a matter which must have been under their very nose. The abbey might most

* The stipend paid at St Albans for its university students, of which it generally had three, was £10 a year.

† It is worth while noting this 5*d*. a day for the celebrant, as affording a measure for all these moneys with which we have to deal. It agrees with evidence from other sources: a chaplain could be hired at that date for £7. 12*s*. 1*d*. a year: that is, about eleven marks.

boldly have challenged the archbishop's judgment on this point; yet there is no such testimonial to him as there was to Whethamstede, that all his great expenses had been met without waste of timber or "pledging even of the smallest jewel of the abbey". Here again was a point verifiable with equal certainty by Morton, if the abbey had met his challenge to trial in England, instead of taking refuge at the Roman Court. In connexion with this question of Wallingford's wastefulness it must be noted that, though his successor Ramryge was himself a steady business man, yet the abbey owed 4000 marks at his death, and was almost bankrupt.(21)

Thus the testimonial, at the best, is by no means incompatible with Whethamstede's picture of Wallingford as an astute business man from youth upwards, unscrupulous in the acquisition of money and ostentatious in its use.(22) Nor will any careful student of visitatorial records or monastic chronicles find any inherent improbability where the modern apologists plead it, in the fact that such a man as this was promoted first to a priorate and then to an abbacy. Nor, again, that such an election should be officially recorded as "unanimous"; an assertion which is made not only in Ramryge's testimonial but in Wallingford's own *Register*. Yet (as the editor points out) in that *Register* "it is only the preliminaries that are given; for, somewhat singularly the account of the election itself is missing, the leaf or leaves containing it having been torn out, apparently on purpose".(23) This leaves room, obviously, for possible manipulation of the facts.

We come now to the second count, *immorality*. Nunneries were by law inaccessible to men, except a few specified ecclesiastics upon spiritual business; nuns, again, were bound by the famous bull *Periculoso* to stay within their convent precincts, with negligible exceptions.* We must not lightly assume that the scandals which Morton had heard from "frequent re-

* Though the neglect of this bull seems to have been distinctly less frequent and scandalous in England than on the Continent, yet we cannot ignore such evidence as Dionysius Cartusianus gives us from Holland about this time. In one of his dialogues, Christ, as the Spouse, exhorts the Sponsa, the nun, to keep her vows and to obey the bull of Boniface VIII. To this the nun objects "Those processes would be good; but our Superiors and our Visitors are fallen into irregularity—*ad deformationem sunt lapsi*—and live just as we do." (*Opera*, vol. XXXVIII, p. 251.)

lations of many trustworthy persons" were exactly true in all the particulars rehearsed. Yet there must at least have been very serious suspicions, or the abbey itself would have hastened to rebut them openly. Of this there is not a hint in the apologetic obituary, though the latter part of it was evidently composed in, or after, the very year which had begun with Innocent's bull of March 6, rehearsing the grievous reports brought to his ears concerning the exempt abbey. We may, in fact, go back many years earlier. One of Whethamstede's accusations against Wallingford runs: "Therefore for these causes and for divers other causes *which We disclose not at present*, *out of respect for thine honour*, all the brethren are compelled, as also We with them, to believe, conjecture and conclude that thou aboundest in money far more than is written in these aforesaid [accusations]."(24) The phrase here italicized, or its equivalents, with their natural avoidance of plain words for ugly things, are familiar to all students of visitatorial records. Moreover, all who have read in *Past and Present*, or the original *Chronicle* of Jocelin, will remember how Abbot Samson, when once he came into power,

> commanded that men should tear down, to their very foundations, the Sacristan's chambers in the cemetery, as unworthy to stand upon earth, by reason of the frequent bibations and certain things not to be mentioned—*quedam tacenda*—which he had witnessed, willy-nilly, when he was Subsacristan. And he caused all to be so levelled that within a year, where a noble building had stood, we saw beans growing and nettles rioting where the wine-casks had lain.(25)

The plea that St Albans had apparently been fairly regularly visited, every three years, by the General-Chapter delegates, will presently be dealt with.*

Henry VIII's third point, *refusal of reform*, comes out plainest of all. Cardinal Gasquet, who was sufficiently ignorant to assert that marriages were invalid in the Middle Ages if made without the consent of a parish priest,(26) ignores Canon Law no less grossly in his plea for Wallingford. He writes concerning the *monitio*: "On the face of the document it professes to be merely the statement of reports....It purports to be merely a statement

* See my second volume, chapters XVII, XVIII, and chapters LIII, LIV here below.

that grave reports were in circulation.... Charges, or rather rumours.... Their face value is, at the worst, that they remain to this day 'not proven' by any evidence whatsoever." He even ventures to suggest that this document was comparable to the "general pardons" sometimes procured for protection against accusations of all sorts of crimes, "mere legal fictions", with "no reference to actualities".(27) It is astounding that this outrageous misinterpretation of the legal significance of an archiepiscopal *monitio* should have passed current now for a whole generation, since they were first published in *The Tablet* for January 1909, without evoking correction, or even any breath of criticism, from students of Canon Law in Cardinal Gasquet's own Church.

This *monitio*, in fact, was part of an ordinary process, familiar in its day even to those who had no pretence to be lawyers. It was bound up with the process to which Chaucer alludes in his well-known reference to the writ *Significavit*. It was part of that Inquisitorial Law which, however repugnant to modern ideas of justice, had its own *raison d'être* in the Middle Ages, and played only too prominent a part in Tudor life. It rested upon *denunciatio*. A person who had any private complaint, and meant to sue, must first warn the accused, pleading with him as a friend; this was a *caritativa* or *evangelica monitio*. Only when this failed, might he denounce the man to the judge, subject of course to penalty for frivolous accusation. The judge, then made inquisition: he notified the charge to the accused, told him that he was *diffamatus* of such and such an offence, and called upon him to rebut the accusation. A *diffamatus* who made no attempt to purge himself was condemned *ipso facto* by his refusal, even under such a *denunciatio privata* as this.

Stronger still was the presumption against him if the warning was given *ex officio*, from one who was not only his denouncer but his judge; as the archdeacon and the bishop were in matters of faith or morals. Here, the *monitio caritativa* was an unnecessary preliminary. The judge might say to the accused: "I hear what seems substantial evidence against you. You are *diffamatus*: therefore purge yourself, or you stand condemned and I must sentence you to the appropriate punishment." Morton, as archbishop and legate, would always have wielded that power completely: not only against any non-exempt house, but even, normally, against the exempt.* In this case of St Albans, he wielded it no less completely at this present moment; for we have seen how Innocent VIII, at Henry's request, had given him powers sweeping away all such defences; we have seen this in the last chapter. All the skirmishing done by the monks at Rome had produced no decision derogatory to that bull. Thus Morton, as special delegate, had even more right than as archbishop to deal summarily. Yet he had given them every possible chance; he had condescended to begin with a *caritativa monitio*; nor had he appealed, as the bull warranted, to the secular arm. Only now at last does he give a *peremptoria monitio*, in this document which the apologist grotesquely represents, in reliance upon the candid reader's ignorance of legal technicalities, as an almost meaningless matter of "common form".

Even more grotesque is the ignorance of actual medieval conditions displayed in another apology which, to an unsuspicious reader, might seem one of the most specious of all. Cardinal Gasquet writes:

> Perhaps the most astonishing part of this astonishing document is the clause directing Wallingford to correct the supposed abuses himself. If Archbishop Morton himself believed one half of these reports, the Abbot was a man of utterly abandoned life; and to leave to him the correction of the supposed abuses was nothing short of a criminal neglect of the duty with which he was charged by the Bull of Innocent VIII....An order is conveyed to Abbot Wallingford, who, if the tales reported by Morton were only partially true, was a hopelessly bad and incompetent man, himself to correct what was amiss.(28)

Yet (incredible as it may seem) the Pope himself, in that bull of July 30 (from which Cardinal Gasquet quotes to suit his purpose on p. 53, while suppressing some of its most important points), employs this very method which we are asked to regard as "a criminal neglect of duty". Rehearsing the scandals at St Albans and St Andrew's, Northampton, he commands Morton to bid those two prelates, with their brethren, "reform themselves and

* Even when a house was immune from episcopal visitation, the Metropolitan had a right to visit, unless he, like the Bishop, had been specifically excluded. C. R. Cheney, *Episcopal Visitation*, etc. p. 47.

do all the things aforesaid" if they wished to avoid forcible reform from without. The same prescription is made, in slightly different words, in a document which Cardinal Gasquet himself had edited not long before (*Collectanea Anglo-Premonstratensian*, III, 103). For in this matter, as often elsewhere in Canon Law, the influence of biblical precedent is strong and natural. The prophets constantly admonish Israel to purge herself of sin, or Jehovah will come down to purge her: the analogy is almost as close as that of the *monitio caritativa* to Matthew xviii, 15–18. In that light, as in that of common-sense, the clause is eminently reasonable; and in fact it is frequent in visitatorial records. Finally, it is argued that we have strong proof of Wallingford's innocence in the fact that Morton did not depose him, but left him to flicker out in the summer of 1492.* Mr Rushbrooke Williams even exaggerates upon the cardinal here: "Modern opinion has therefore no choice but to acquit Wallingford and his house of the charges put forward in Morton's letter." Again, "whatever the worth of this [Ramryge testimonial] may be as evidence of Wallingford's morality, it does at any rate show that he was respected by his convent, who could have had no possible motive in maintaining, after his death, that he was an admirable ruler if in truth the contrary were the case".(29) Those are suppositions so gratuitous, and so important, in spite of their plausibility, that I must leave it to my two next chapters. For in fact the frequent impunity of the greatest transgressors, and the blind *esprit de corps* which constantly impelled monks to close their ranks and ignore every other consideration in their resistance to any outside authority, and, consequently, the ferocious energy with which they fought for the acquisition or maintenance of untouchability, are among the first lessons taught by a careful study of actual visitation documents.

* A document of about June 20, 1492, refers to him as "late Abbot" (Pantin, III, 223, 233).

CHAPTER LI

EXEMPTION WHOLESALE

"PROBABILITY", writes Bishop Butler, "is the very guide of life": and it must be our guide in history. The historian deals with a mass of evidence; from this he selects the most probable. Probability guides him, to begin with, between this and that witness, it is the touchstone by which he tests the characters of each, and is inclined to believe one man rather than another. It is Probability which gives weight to a witness's admissions to the disadvantage of his friend or in favour of his enemy: on the other hand, it compels us from the very first to discount a friend's praise or an enemy's blame. Probability, again, after thus judging the witness himself, weighs the tale that he tells. However trustworthy a man may otherwise be, the historian rightly discredits him at a point where he tells us what seems inherently incredible. On the other hand, when the story seems in itself striking and credible, probability compels us to give it careful consideration; personal distrust cannot absolve us from giving it a fair hearing and facing it as a bare possibility.(1)

The last chapter has shown us a conflict of probabilities. Not, it is true, so sharp a contrast on careful consideration as seems at first sight, but still some real conflict, even though the Roman pronouncements in favour of St Albans bear only the most distant and superficial relation to the real question of Morton's *monitio*. The cardinal's claims were amply justified at Rome; yet we cannot find that he ever pursued them to the end, even with the King at his back. The monks' testimonial to Wallingford, in which all scholars recognize either an answer to Whethamstede and Morton or an anticipation of the latter's attacks in Rome, does little more than to praise him warmly yet vaguely as a *pius et optimus pater*, and to emphasize what he spent (either independently or as Whethamstede's mere official) yet without specifying any list (of the kind almost universal in the case of truly successful abbots), of lands, houses and rents added to the abbey properties. Most significant of all, perhaps, is the emphasis laid upon the large sums spent in Rome on this exemption quarrel, and the claim of a just victory gained there. All these things challenge our judgment as to probabilities; and in fact it is upon probabilities that Wallingford's defenders mostly rely. "It would scarcely be necessary to point out the absurdity of these charges"; "there is little reason to suppose that [Morton's] main motive was other than political"; "that matters were precisely as Morton suggests is on the face of it incredible". So writes Mr Rushbrooke Williams, inspired throughout by a radically anachronistic confusion between thought and life in the fifteenth century and in the twentieth. Cardinal Gasquet is still bolder; quoting from the late Professor J. S. Brewer:

> Can the same stream send forth waters both sweet and bitter? Are the higher realizations of artistic beauty...compatible with the disordering, vulgar and noisy pursuits of an unscrupulous avarice or ambition? Will men that gather meanly scatter nobly? Will any magic convert the sum total of sordid actions into greatness of any kind?(2)

Such a plea is as false in history as in psychology. It was at the beginning of this very fifteenth century that an orthodox friar complained: "It is to be feared that the solemn making of churches and the good arranging of them...is more of pomp and pride than to the worship of God"; for (he continues) the people meanwhile "despise God day and night with their wicked qualities".(3) And, in the middle of that same century, one of the most unscrupulous of tyrants immortalized himself and his mistress by employing Leon Battista Alberti to erect in her honour a church which is one of the marvels of European architecture, but in which "everything both within and without contributes to the profane and pagan character which it was Sigismondo's purpose to impress upon the Christian church".(4) The sculptors were still at work on that church in 1465, when Wallingford was paying for some of the buildings extolled in his obituary. Anachronisms of this kind, and equally false psychological pleas, are a temptation to all of us who pursue through history any coherent thread which we think to have found. To those who pride themselves on impartiality, and who are indeed often comparatively impartial, it comes sometimes in its subtlest form: that of concluding that contradictories cancel each other out, even where the documents (if the judge could find time to study them) would suggest 90 per cent. against 10. Relying on probabilities alone, we are tempted to say: "The thing refutes itself; it is too exaggerated to be credible." Yet in history, as in physical science, things do sometimes occur which stagger imagination; and, immense as may be the force of moral revolt in the long run, it is a dangerous fallacy to assume its decisive influence in any particular case. Mankind are as tolerant of naked iniquity, now and then or here and there, as they are of scandalous oppression.

Even more dangerous, in this chapter of religious history, is the fallacy of Impunity and Innocence. It rests, to begin with, on the gross anachronism of assuming that legislation and sanction corresponded to each other in Tudor England almost as closely as they do in modern Britain. Yet (to give one clear and typical instance which I have quoted more than once elsewhere) at a great and well-governed city like Norwich, in 1289, violators of most important municipal laws nearly always enjoyed mitigation of the prescribed penalty, often obtained further mitigation or even complete indemnity out of court, and paid, in the aggregate, only a small fraction of such fines as still remained nominally to their account. Out of a nominal £72. 18*s*. 10*d*., only £17. 0*s*. 2*d*. was with difficulty collected. St Thomas More, again, had among his most saintly characteristics that, being a judge, he took no bribes. We must not be surprised, therefore, to find anomalies of this kind at many other points in Tudor society.

Keeping St Albans, then, as a test case in Reformation history—and none better could be found—let us now illustrate it by other notable cases elsewhere. How does the story of this abbey explain others, or others explain this abbey? How far, upon a wider survey, can we accept these two main pleas of Moral Revolt, or Impunity and Innocence? Let us take, in necessary brevity, a few illustrative cases. And let us choose these, deliberately, with a maximum of variety both in time and in place.

The first is in 1173, from Bury St Edmunds, one of the half-dozen greatest in the kingdom. The story is told by a monk who saw and heard it all, Jocelin of Brakelond, whose *Chronicle* forms the text of Carlyle's *Past and Present*.(5) In this year, when

Jocelin was still a novice, the abbey was of decent regularity on the whole, but the abbot's mismanagement in his old age, and his constant borrowings from the Jews, had plunged it into almost hopeless debt. One Jew alone held bonds for £1200 *plus* interest. The King heard of this, and sent his almoner to enquire officially into the state of this royal abbey. He was admitted to the chapter house, and told his errand, demanding the truth "in virtue of obedience".

So the Prior rose and spake, as one for all. He said that the abbey was in a good state, and that the Order was well and religiously kept within, and business without was well and discreetly managed; yet that we were somewhat in debt, as our other neighbours were, but that there was no debt which weighed heavily upon us. The Almoner, hearing this, expressed his great pleasure to hear this evidence of the congregation—that is, of the Prior who spake for us. At another time the Prior answered in the same words; (and so did Master Geoffrey of Coutances, speaking and excusing the Abbot), when Archbishop Richard, in his right as Papal Legate, came to our Chapter-house, before we possessed such an exemption as we now have. So I, who was then in my noviciate, spake of these things to my Master, who taught me the Orders and to whose care I was deputed, to wit, Master Samson, who was afterwards Abbot. I said: "What is this that I hear? Wherefore dost thou hold thy peace, seeing and hearing these things, thou who art a claustral monk,* and covetest not to be an obedientiary, and fearest God rather than man?" But he answered and said: "My son, the child lately burned dreadeth the fire; thus is it with me and many others. Hugh the Prior hath lately been deposed from his office and banished [to one of our cells], Denis and H. and R. of Hingham have but lately come back from exile. I likewise was cast into prison, and afterwards sent to Castleacre, because we spake up for the common good of our abbey against the will of the Abbot. This is the hour of darkness: this is the hour when flatterers reign and obtain credence; their power hath been reinforced, and we can do naught against it. These things must be dissembled for a while: may God look upon them and judge!" There came tidings unto Abbot Hugh that Richard, Archbishop of Canterbury, intended to come and make an enquiry in our abbey in virtue of his legatine office; and the Abbot took counsel and sent to Rome and procured exemption from the said Legate's power. When the messenger came home from Rome, there was naught to pay that which he had promised to the Pope and the Cardinals, except,

* I.e., of the rank and file, unofficial.

among our furniture,* the cross over the High Altar, and the images of Mary and John which Archbishop Stigand had adorned with much weight of gold and silver and given unto St Edmund. Moreover, some of our brethren, who were of the Abbot's most familiar friends, said that the very shrine of St Edmund ought to be stripped of its jewels [*excrustari*] for the sake of such exemption, not observing that great peril might spring from such liberty; for, if perchance we had some Abbot who chose to squander the abbey goods and ill treat his brethren, there will be no person to whom the brethren could complain of the Abbot's injustice; for he will fear neither Bishop nor Archbishop nor Legate, and impunity will give boldness in delinquency.

How far the event justified this, I have shown in my second volume (pp. 249–51). That incident occurred in 1345; the bishop was Bateman, a strong ruler, skilled lawyer, and founder of Trinity Hall at Cambridge. The sins of this exempt abbey (he publicly asserted) cried to heaven; the abbot defended his monks, and was himself chargeable with things "whereof we say nothing here, for reverence of his dignity". Their papal exemption defended them from his visitation, but he appointed a commission of clergy to sit at Ipswich, take evidence, and report to him, "lest the foul contagion of these monks should infect his flock, and their blood be required at his hands at the Last Day". The abbot appealed to Rome, Bateman lost his case, and died in the Holy City wailing with his last breath: "Buri, Buri! Seynt Edmond, Seynt Edmond!"

In about 1200, not twenty years after that purchase of exemption by the abbey of St Edmund, Bishop Stephen of Tournai, with another bishop and two abbots as coadjutors, set himself to reform the abbey of St Martin at Tournai. The story fills a page of my second volume (p. 306); it equals or outdoes that of St Albans, taking the latter at its worst. (6)

Let us next take the Evesham case, to which I devoted chapters XXIV and XXV of my second volume. Here, again, the whole story is told by one of the monks; and he, afterwards, was elected head. Abbot Marleberge was on the whole a fine character; yet in the history which he records for contemporaries and posterity in his beloved abbey, he records again and again, nearly always with express or implied approval, things which

* *Ex circumstantiis*, literally "from the things that stood around us".

would besmirch a modern abbot's reputation. The editor of his *Chronicle*, though far from unsympathetic to monasticism, puts this plainly enough.(7)

It is sadly suggestive to learn, in the course of these details, from the formal accusation brought by Marleberge on behalf of the monks against the Abbot, that the prosecution of the latter was caused not so much by his notorious immorality as by his injustice and harshness towards themselves; nay, that they would have thought it more conducive to the honour of their house to have concealed the character of his private life, had it been possible, than to have revealed it. Even at the last his profligacy is alleged only as filling up the measure of his unworthiness, while the stint of the monks' allowances in food and clothes, the rough behaviour exhibited towards them, and the violation of the rules of ordinary monastic routine and discipline, are pressed as the leading points in his accusation.

For here, as at St Albans, the main bone of contention was, confessedly, the question of exemption from visitation by the Bishop of Worcester. Abbot Roger's immoralities were notorious to all, within and outside the abbey. His amours were promiscuous (p. 119); Marleberge tells how he himself replied, during the trial at Rome (when Innocent III commanded "that I should now speak of his incontinence"), "Holy Father, since the aforesaid [accusations of open simony, waste, and embezzlement, with neglect of proper food and clothing for the brethren[suffice for his deposition, wherefore should I uncover the nakedness of my father?" Indeed it was only upon the Pope's insistence that he told the full story, specifying six unmarried and two married women by name (p. 244; cf. p. 143). Yet the community bargained with Roger that, if he would only mend his personal extravagance and restore their comforts, then, even though the bishop should gain his cause at Rome and assert his normal right of visitation, "which we especially feared", then "we would never, in the Bishop's presence, object to our Abbot anything which should make for his deposition, but would stand faithfully by his person against the Bishop, if he would change his ways and stand by us in the cause of the abbey" (p. 121; cf. pp. 124–8). So firm were they in this conspiracy, that, "although we had a sort of civil war [*bellum quasi intestinum*] with our Abbot, nevertheless we prosecuted and defended the case so manfully and diligently against the Bishop, as the final event proved, that the archbishop himself and other magnates marvelled, saying that they had never seen such monks" (p. 130). Marleberge, who was a consummate lawyer, exulted in his final stroke at the Roman Court. He had gained his great victory, in the matter of exemption; but Master Robert boasted of having another case entrusted to him by his employer "which I should find unanswerable". Therefore, "after the fashion of litigants", when Innocent III had liberally "granted many special indulgences to my adversary, then one day when they were read in public audience, I stood out as opponent and spake against them at all points, albeit they in no wise concerned me". This brought about a bargain: Marleberge promised to cease his opposition at the Court, if Master Robert would abandon his "unanswerable" case, which Marleberge himself specifies as follows:

The Bishop of Worcester...since the monks, as I have often told you would not agree with him that inquisition should be made into the Abbot's person through them, made this inquisition through witnesses of our neighbours [*conpatriotas nostros*] under testimony of all the Church dignitaries of his diocese and sent it to the lord Pope with their seals appended.* This was the cause which Master Robert renounced; he broke the seals and handed the written scroll to me without the knowledge of any man but me and himself, and we were made friends together, nor did we set ourselves any more to grieve each other in any matter. And so it came about that our Abbot should not be deposed by the lord Pope; for if he had seen this inquisition, wherein great enormities were contained, he would undoubtedly have deposed him. So also it had come about earlier in England that he should not be deposed by the Bishop.

For this, as Marleberge reminds us, was only one in a series of Roger's similar escapes, whether by bribery or by sheer luck. He had begun by giving Bishop John of Coutances £40 on condition that "he should not take personal notice of him" at the visitation. The next bishop, Malgere, "would consent to no simoniacal pact", but yet he postponed his coming for some other time" (p. 115). As against the archbishop, Roger boasted that he was safe, because "he had done [him] such service that he was secure in that quarter"; the archbishop indignantly

* Such a document would have constituted, in a more solemn form, such a *diffamatio* "by the witness of many credible persons" as moved Morton to enquire into St Albans.

repudiated this insinuation (p. 126). When, in 1206, the papal legate held a council at Reading, Roger "sat in his mitre with the Bishops and obtained grace of the Lord Legate, and gave to the Legate's nephew rents to the value of ten marks" (p. 202). When at last, in 1213, a papal legate decided for his deposition, yet "he departed before publishing any statute on this matter; wherefore the Abbot hath oppressed us worse than before, until the present day, saying that our complaint had cost him to spend more than £200 upon the Legate, all of which he intended to take from the goods which had been assigned to us" by the commissioners whom the legate had appointed to end this "civil war". For it must be remembered that, to Abbot Marleberge, his predecessor's wickedness in starving the brethren and letting the buildings go to ruin, and the bishop's tyranny in demanding ordinary rights of visitation over the monks, form the whole main thread of the story: moral questions come in only incidentally (p. 246). Nor was the erring abbot alone in his reliance upon the omnipotence of money at the Roman Court; the Children of Light shared his confidence to the full. Marleberge, encouraging his brethren to the fight, said no more than the truth when he insisted upon this as fundamentally an economic war. We have seen, in chapter XLV, how confident the Dominicans of Paris were of success at Rome, with their "40,000 crowns of gold" in reserve. Evesham, it is true, had at this moment no such reserve: it was half-bankrupt, through Roger's mismanagement; but "fear not your poverty or the expenses of litigation: for if we will pawn our manors, or borrow at usury either from the Jews or from Romans at the Roman Court, under the statutory penalties, we shall find men who will lend us a thousand marks, or as much more as we will, under witness of our seal; for the convent is, as it were, immortal". The bishop, on the other hand, can raise but little money; for his warranty is only personal: he may pledge a manor to-day, and at his death tomorrow the deed becomes worthless: "therefore we are stronger in the matter of expenses than the Bishop" (p. 113). Therefore in 1205, when Marleberge came and his two brethren to Rome to plead that double cause at the court of Innocent III, "we borrowed four hundred marks, and made presents to the Lord Pope to the value of £100 sterling, and the Cardinals and the

Court to the value of 100 marks yet they would not accept this until many of them ascertained that we had no case in the Court". This punctilio cannot have meant very much: for the story shows that they were come openly to urge their case as soon as occasion should come to get a hearing (p. 146). The whole story is a detailed comment upon St Bernard's complaint against the abbots of two generations earlier: "They rob their monasteries, in order to purchase exemption: they buy themselves off from obedience": they aspire to the episcopal mitre and insignia, and why do they not go to the length of aspiring to the bishop's power of conferring Holy Orders?(8) Or, again, upon the complaint of Richard Archbishop of Canterbury to Alexander III, that Malmesbury's claim to exemption "has destroyed the yoke of obedience, wherein was our one hope of salvation and remedy for former transgressions".(9)

The fourteenth century supplies us with less detailed evidence of this sort: monastic chronicles are then far rarer, while the official records of Visitors are not yet so common. But the fifteenth century shows cases which cast much light on this kind of document: cases which I have already recorded in this volume. By far the strongest evidence in favour of Wallingford would seem to lie in that formal testimonial, signed by his successor and the whole community. In chapter XIV we have seen the Wennigsen nuns binding themselves by solemn oath to reveal nothing to the Visitor, and publicly pleading that the breach of such oath would involve them in the mortal sin of perjury. We have seen, again, in chapter XXXV, how the Egmond Prior "trusted firmly that his brethren would cleave inviolably to the conspiracy they had made" against the Visitor's enquiry. This was exactly at the time of Morton's *monitio*; and, probably within a few months of this, we find Abbot Trithemius warning Visitors to make this their first question of all: Has your abbot entered into some such conspiracy with you in view of my visitation?(10) Thus we sometimes find Visitors taking the initiative, and pronouncing excommunication *ipso facto* upon all who may conceal the truth on the plea of some oath that they have taken.

Chapter XXIX of this present volume, again, gives us a very close parallel to St Albans in the Prior of St Mattia at Venice, who maintained himself so stubbornly by favour of his powerful lay friends that the Minister General, who had the law indisputably on his side, and was a personal friend of the Pope, living less than a week's journey distant, could not punish the man for haunting a neighbouring nunnery and carrying about with him a youth under suspicious circumstances, and for dissipating the house's revenues, even to ruin, but was finally driven to leave him in office and accept a humiliating compromise. The story of the ex-General of Camaldoli in the next chapter (xxx) might afford even better excuse for that off-hand modern judgment: "the thing is on the face of it incredible."

Finally, here is one more concrete case which may help us to interpret the evidence from St Albans. In 1527, on the verge of our English Reformation, the Minister General of the Dominicans was struggling to purge the monasteries of his Order in the south of France. One of the most important of these in every way, and unique as the first of all St Dominic's foundations, was the double house of La Prouille. This was mainly a women's convent, superintended by the Saint himself: then he handed on the care to a convent of brethren built hard by. The prior of this convent in 1527—and therefore, shepherd of those nuns—was one Adrien de Nullay. The General, Silvestri, had decreed in the General Chapter of 1525, deposing him from his priorate and "prohibiting him under pain of excommunication *ipso facto*, which we impose in this present letter, with preface of the triple canonical monition, from interfering or meddling in any way with the said convent or its appurtenances".(11) The same Chapter condemned him to the penalties of *gravior culpa* for disobedience and contempt of that letter.(12) Notice of these decrees was sent to him on September 26. "In case of refusal to obey, all Superiors of the province of Toulouse and of the congregation of France had orders to arrest him and cast him into prison." Silvestri, to reach his end more easily, had asked the Pope for a bull, so that de Nullay's deposition was done in the name of Pope, Chapter General, and Master of the Order. From this display of juridical force, it may be guessed that de Nullay had strong bonds in the convent of La Prouille, and that peace was far from reigning there. In fact, though dismissed by these three authorities, including the

Supreme Pontiff, the prior took no notice of this sentence. Silvestri, writing from Paris on July 28, 1527, evidently yielding to strong pressure, consented to relieve the culprit from all the censures which he had incurred by his scandalous disobedience, on condition that he would recognize his deposition and retire within his own Congregation; otherwise, by this present letter all the former censures were *ipso facto* inflicted upon him afresh. The prior persisted all the same in his rebellion. In spite of the plainest prohibitions, he went back to the nunnery of La Prouille. Silvestri, who was at Toulouse on September 18, cited him to appear before him within two days. He could act with authority in the convent of La Prouille, because, in order to avoid all conflicts of jurisdiction, he had obtained from Clement VII that the convent should be directly subject to himself, as it had been before. This bull of Clement's shows that half the nuns were following de Nullay in his revolt.(13) Here the documents leave us in the lurch. We cannot say whether the culprit obeyed this formal command to appear for judgment, "under pain of prison in case of refusal", or whether Silvestri carried out his visitation of La Prouille. Probably not, thinks Mortier, and adds: "Yet it seems very extraordinary that the Master General did not visit this famous convent; was he afraid of the trouble which awaited him there?" Decrees followed decrees against this prior; but he bade defiance to the injunctions of his superior and the sentences of excommunication. In 1528 (January 28) the General had to depose the prioress, sub-prioress, and other officials of the nunnery who supported de Nullay. In July the Regent of Toulouse received orders to arrest and imprison him, with appeal to the secular arm if necessary, together with three other friars of that convent, "by reason of certain grave offences [*quaedam enormia*] committed by them". He was still at large on August 10. Later on, La Prouille became an Observantine convent, but the battle between de Nullay and the allies—General, Chapter, and Pope—seems to have been drawn at best, and possibly a clear victory for the bold criminal.(14)

The evidence here produced is, in my belief, typical, at least in the sense that it presents only in a magnified form the difficulties of discipline which were to be found almost everywhere. All honour to the Church for what she had done to civilize the barbarian conquerors; yet there came a time at which the nurslings were fast outgrowing this tutelage. As early as the twelfth century, the immense power of the papacy, centralized in all its ramifications, was beginning to hamper real freedom of thought. The most original thinkers were discouraged, or even silenced, by the hierarchy quite as often as they were assisted. Not to mention the Vaudois (with whom modern religious thought agrees more closely than with the Inquisitors who burned them), Abailard had no equal in the Christian philosophers of his day, yet he was extinguished by the authorities. Roger Racon, after him, spent many of his best years of life in prison, and fought his way through endless difficulties, for similar reasons: and the work even of Aquinas was too original to escape without serious episcopal condemnation in France and in England. In succeeding centuries, the Church became still less fitted for this censorship which she claimed over a thinking and growing society. The task was becoming more and more impossible; knowledge was overflowing too rapidly the limits of any central executive. So, again, with discipline; the machinery which had done such good work in earlier centuries became hopelessly out of date; the needs of a whole Europe could not be met by a dictator and his committees in Rome. So it was also with monasticism: its original cloistered and fugitive virtue had lost, at the crown of the Middle Ages, the intense courage and concentration of St Benedict and his fellows. Monks broke their bounds by going out into the world and working there most wholesomely in their best days, but more selfishly as time went on. The world's spirit, again, soaked gradually but irresistibly into the cloister. Yet, to the very end, the world's discipline had little hold, in law, upon even the most ordinary monastery; while the many exempt houses were almost inexpugnably entrenched against current law. Thus, an entirely false situation has been created. It is another fatal anachronism, though not uncommon, to think of the Tudor monastery in terms of its modern successor, where the brethren, who are usually men with a sense of real vocation, live as a tiny minority in a not wholly sympathetic world, and therefore under vigilant criticism from outside.

My evidence, then, is typical of what might often happen under medieval conditions, and (as I think will appear later) of what did happen only too frequently, though perhaps in less gross and spectacular forms. And I must again draw attention to the wide diversities at time, place, and circumstance in my list. The time ranges from about 1140 to 1527. The place varies between Suffolk, Belgium, Worcestershire, western and central Germany, the frozen swamps of Holland and the Venetian lagoons, Tuscany and Provence with their vines and olives. In time, we begin with the great century of saints—Bernard, Francis and Dominic—and end when Martin Luther is in the forefront of the scene. We begin with Popes who carried Rome's fame and influence to its zenith in Eugenius III, Alexander III and Innocent III. Thence our list passes through a commonplace series of Popes (except so far as we may count Eugenius IV as exceptional by reason of his reputation as a monastic reformer) down to Innocent VIII of St Albans and Morton memory, and Alexander VI of unsavoury fame, and Clement VII who, with his eye upon the gamble of international politics, took so unconscionably long to decide whether Henry VIII was sacramentally wedded or not. The governments include almost every type of medieval constitution. The prime actors against these deformed abbeys were no less diversified. At Bury, it was a king and an archbishop; later on, an unusually energetic bishop. Thence our list will run thus:—Official Visitor; Abbot General; Count; Minister General with Pope's friendly help; Minister General backed up by Pope, General Chapter, and the Secular Arm.

Through all that diversity, then, run two clear threads. The first is that of Exemption. Wennigsen alone, in this list, did not enjoy formal exemption; for, though Egmond had no such privilege normally, the Pope took the peccant abbey for a time under his wing, and thus frustrated the efforts of the Ordinary. In every one of these cases, as at St Albans, we find not a community willing to face official enquiry and justify themselves by evidence, but men ferociously bent upon escape from any such ordeal. An abbey would sell its soul for exemption, almost in a literal sense, since medieval disciplinarians, when they deal with the question, are practically unanimous in charging it with the loss of countless souls. At Evesham, those who were most anxious for exemption did indeed, in discussion, argue that this would give them a juster judge, and one better able to correct real abuses, than the ordinary bishop. Yet, almost in the same breath, Marleberge destroys this by describing complacently how the papal legate was more bribable, in that long controversy, than one of the two bishops, and how cleverly he himself had juggled away the risk of full papal enquiry into Abbot Roger's iniquities. Again, though there was some truth in the expense caused to the monks by episcopal visits, and in their fear of oppressive exertion of rights (medieval bishops being such as they were) yet this cannot possibly have been the main motive; for monks were ready to buy this immunity, in ready money, for a price at Rome which would have covered episcopal procurations for two or three centuries to come; while, on the other hand, it was a mere commonplace that the world was unlikely to last many generations longer.(15) Such, then, was the working of that exemption system which, comparatively young and modest in St Bernard's day, attained such proportions in the fifteenth century that St Antonino could write concerning his own Italy "almost all Religious are exempt from the jurisdiction of the Ordinaries".(16) In England only five or six individual houses claimed exemption, on more or less tenable grounds; but whole Orders or Congregations were exempt in the mass—Cistercians, Cluniacs, Gilbertines, Premonstratensians, Carthusians, Brigittines and the four Orders of Friars. Excluding the nunneries, over which in many cases the bishops had gradually asserted their jurisdiction, the exempt houses numbered about 285 at the Dissolution, with a probable population of about 3150. The 113 non-exempt houses contained about 3380 inmates: thus the exempt Religious were very nearly half our monastic population.(17)

We must not, however, suppose that this obsession of immunity was mainly due to the conscious guilt of irregularity in the abbey, or even to the far more general and subtler temptation of making the best of both worlds, and living in the cloister a more comfortable life, on the whole, than outside in these troubled times. Marleberge, side by side with the minute and business-like care with which he assured to the brethren, by solemn contract, such food and drink and comforts as few men enjoyed except nobles or well-to-do citizens, was a remarkable character, capable of devotion to a high ideal. But the monastic ideal, even at the crown of the Middle Ages, had its earthly as well as its heavenly side. Patriotism was very prominent, and sometimes in its intensest forms: love and pride for the Order, and even more strongly for one's own house. As Marleberge writes: the "wretches" at Evesham who were willing to accept the ordinary episcopal jurisdiction of other abbeys, "understood not that to enslave a monastery that was born free, and to thrust it back into servitude, is profanation of a Holy Place": "this freeborn abbey would become as a bondman for ever".(18) The Benedictine Order had begun in what we may call parochialism: each abbey was to be an autonomous unit, except so far as the monk was subject in the last resort, as all others were, to the bishop of his diocese. Innocent III did indeed, in 1215, institute something like a federal system, of General Chapters and regular visitations, after the model introduced so successfully by the Cistercians. But this never worked very regularly on the Continent; and even in England, where it worked best, it never obliterated the original tendency to individualism: intense conventual patriotism; the temptation of "My Order, right or wrong!" and, still more strongly, of "My abbey, right or wrong!" This was perfectly compatible, as also in worldly politics, with fierce intestine dissensions. Marleberge himself tells this in the plainest Biblical language; there was "civil war" between Roger and his monks; yet, when the two parties were confronted with the bishop, they at once coalesced, and Marleberge does not hesitate to recall the story of Pilate and Herod in Luke xxiii, 12: "And the same day our Abbot and his Convent were made friends together; for before they were at enmity between themselves." To reckon probabilities or improbabilities without reference to this, is to fall into a fatal anachronism.

CHAPTER LII

IMPUNITY

We have now seen how the St Albans case, viewed not through modern spectacles but in the light of the previous four centuries of monastic history, definitely substantiates two out of the three accusations upon which Henry VIII based his Act of Dissolution. Waste and debt are written in unexceptionable records, often backed up by exact figures, from the thirteenth century down to the Reformation. Lack of reform, again, is equally evident, "for 200 years or more". Two centuries had elapsed, almost exactly to the month, between Henry's action and the last attempt of any Pope to enforce general statutes of reform upon all the Orders: Benedict XII in 1336–7. No historian has ever ventured to plead that those two centuries showed better fruit than the past. The contrary is admitted on all hands: sometimes, perhaps, even in exaggerated terms. Lingard, who stands with Lord Acton far above any other English-speaking Roman Catholic historian in combined industry, learning and candour, made no attempt to plead any general improvement: the generality of Tudor Religious, he admitted, "were men of little reputation", who "had entirely degenerated from their original institution".

We must come now to the third count, that of immorality, open or secret. This is by far the most difficult problem for the modern historian, and not the least important for our estimate of the Reformation as a whole. But its difficulty is in one sense a measure of its necessity. In the words of the latest ecclesiastical historian of Geneva, this is "a subject which it is right to examine without partiality and without reticence. Frankness is demanded by a problem so grave that, in many countries, it contributed strongly to the revolt from Catholicism, and was often the determining factor".(1)

In my previous volumes, I have rather prepared the way for this question than formally grappled with it. In my second volume I dealt at length with Visitors' methods and evidential values (chaps. XVI–XIX) and with general verdicts passed by medieval writers upon the monks of their own day (chaps. XXVI–XXVIII). But here at last is the place to call much fuller attention to the details, as revealed in the records of orthodox visitations. We shall then be better able to judge those reports from Henry VIII's commissioner which, if we are to believe Bishop Latimer, were decisive: "When their enormities were first read in the Parliament House, they were so great and abominable that there was nothing but 'Down with them!'."(2) Let me therefore begin by repeating here what I have often printed elsewhere, that I lay only the lightest stress upon the evidence of Henry VIII's commissioners themselves. Thus, in the case of St Andrew's at Northampton, I have quoted only what they said about finance—facts easily verified—and ignored the so-called "confession" which is made in the deed of surrender forced upon the monks by the King's agents. Those men were sent to make out a case, and their own letters show them far from scrupulous in their methods. Yet the general acceptance of this case by Parliament—and that is indisputable—shows that it must have had some probable foundation. Even satire must have a grain or two of truth to be really effective. And, in this case, we have a wealth of indications, from many different angles, which enable us to ignore for a while everything reported by those suspected commissioners, and to judge independently. Even at the end of the nineteenth century, when first pretence was made of studying the Dissolution with any semblance of full documentary evidence, the abundance of material awaiting our judgment far exceeded men's good will to exploit that material by straightforward historical methods. During the forty years which have since elapsed, a great mass of precious records has been published by the Canterbury and York Society and, still more important, by the Lincoln Record Society with notes by Professor A. Hamilton Thompson which come up to the best standards of Continental scholarship. Some day, perhaps, a student will devote himself for many years to producing, for the help of his brother-historians, such an exhaustive synthesis from Dissolution sources in general as Mr Geoffrey Baskerville has lately produced in the single field of pensions for the dispossessed monks and nuns. But that would involve a collection of details, and especially a labour of sorting and comparison, for which I can never hope to find leisure. One thing, however, I can attempt, in this present chapter, by way of orientation of future research.

First, as to the method of our enquiry. Dom Berlière once suggested that, in view of what may be called Benedictine individualism, we cannot safely argue from one abbey to another; two neighbouring houses, under the same bishop, might differ by a whole horizon from each other. This is doubtless true; we shall certainly never arrive at anything like mathematical certainty; but history must be content with less than that. To collect all the surviving indications concerning all medieval monasteries would be a herculean task; but that would be only a beginning. We should then have to sort them all, assigning to each its true significance, and thus arriving at a clear and comprehensible generalization, correct in all its proportions; a patently hopeless task. No doubt, we of the twentieth century are at great disadvantages for seeing Tudor life in its true relations; but the modern monk is scarcely better off than the layman, unless from first to last he proceeds with something like Socratic awareness of his own ignorance.(3) All, therefore, must be grateful for general verdicts upon monasticism as a whole, expressed either directly or indirectly, by educated and orthodox contemporaries who could judge by their own eyes and ears concerning those men who are divided from us by a gulf of 400 years. A catena of such direct judgments is printed in my second volume (pp. 379–419 and pp. 504–660). The witnesses number 124, including six popes, five cardinals, twenty-three other prelates, ten canonized Saints, and five General Chapters. Of these, only twenty-three are favourable; and even these express themselves far less explicitly or emphatically than the 101 unfavourable. Equally remarkable is the total or comparative silence, on this point, of professed apologists like Netter of Walden in face of the plainest Lollard accusations. Therefore nothing but ignorance can excuse the modern claim that "the evil repute of the monks and friars dates from this period" when Bishop Burnet wrote his *History of the Reformation* (1681).(4) It is far truer to say, with the Roman Catholic Professor Mollat, that "medieval literature, whether rightly or wrongly, blames monastic morality crudely or indiscriminately".(5) Let us therefore, while seeking to avoid indiscriminate crudity, look minutely here into the official documents and see whether they bear out the confessedly unfavourable evidence of the literary sources.

But the study of this official evidence for or against immoralities presents a far more difficult problem than monastic mismanagement, waste, and debt. Dr G. Oliver, a patient Roman Catholic student who was the first to make any statistical attempt in this field, fell into the fatal mistake of assuming that the accusations found in Episcopal Registers constitute an exhaustive record of lapses discovered by the bishops.(6) Cardinal Gasquet adopted this without acknowledgment, and extended it from the single diocese of Exeter to the whole of England, though he had pretty evidently studied none of those other Registers, to which he vaguely and magisterially appealed, with any real care, and though Creighton, reviewing him, had pointed out the weakness of thus relying upon Oliver. Now that the study of the full records is beginning in earnest, some scholar may soon produce a full and trustworthy synthesis. Meanwhile it would be almost impossible, by the discussion of one individual case after another, to arrive at any estimate which would secure even proximate agreement. For there will always be maximizers, who argue that where we have one case proved, or probable, there must be much more behind, and minimizers, who suspect that even plain recorded accusations may be due to personal enmity. Yet here, as often elsewhere, the scientist can help the historian. Adams and Leverrier, independently, discovered Neptune not by straightforward telescopic search among the millions of stars, but by studying the behaviour of Uranus. We may turn away for a while from seeking direct light amid the multitude of individual cases, and study the behaviour of judges, and of the general public, towards those offenders of whom we can be certain. Roman and Canon Law point the same direction to us. *Consuetudo est optima legum interpres*: Custom will show us how the Law works. What does medieval custom tell us here? We may sum up its main significance in a single word, *Impunity*, relative or even absolute. This is the second thread which runs as clear as Exemption through the whole tangle of evidence in Chapters XLIX, L, and our method must be to follow this thread throughout the Dissolution story.

Here, as with Exemption, we naturally begin with St Bernard and his fatherly warnings to Eugenius III. If (he said) the Church was to be saved, then this swelling tide of appeals to Rome must somehow be stemmed. Anyone was heard at that Court who could afford to pay; and, just as money opened the door, so also it might too often influence the judge, since the press of business was too overwhelming for the immediate attention even of a good and able Pope like Eugenius. Thus, while local justice was lamed by the appeal system, justice at headquarters was constantly paralysed by money or powerful friends, and the greatest sinner might have best chances of success. Hence (complained St Bernard) we have something like a Reign of Licence, under "Impunity, offspring of carelessness, mother of indiscipline, root of shamelessness, nurse of transgressions."(7)

The matter will be best understood if we begin with a concrete case, at the Augustinian house of St Peter's, Ipswich, somewhere between 1327 and 1336. It is interesting, first, because it comes not long before the Black Death, and, again, within a few years—perhaps a few weeks—of 1336–7, when Benedict XII made the last general attempt of the Middle Ages to arrest decay by drawing up elaborate and detailed statutes for the principal Religious Orders. Those statutes, in each case, constituted a definite compromise. A century earlier, the papal statutes were far stricter: Gregory IX, the friend of St Francis, had published a series for the Benedictines; and Innocent IV, in 1253 had gone further. He aroused the indignation of English Benedictines, though these were almost alone in carrying out, with some real regularity, the system of General Chapters and regular Visitations decreed by Innocent III in 1215. Matthew Paris writes how

> at this time the Pope, with too censorious intention [*nimis argumentose intendens*], enjoined upon the Bishops that each should visit the Abbots and convents of his diocese. He enjoined them to compel these, under pain of excommunication, to observe certain unimportant [*impertinentes*] articles of the Benedictine Rule, which are not of the substance thereof, and which the said monks had never been wont to keep. But the Black Monks of France, seeing them-

selves wholly destitute of protection from the King, lest they should be exposed to the will [*arbitrio*] of the Bishops, to whom the privileged are especially odious, thought to buy peace for themselves. Therefore they gave unto the Pope 4,000 *livres tournois*, and thus they restrained this tyrannous onslaught. So the Abbot and convent of St Albans appealed to the Pope in person, lest they should be visited by the Bishop of Lincoln; for thus their privileges would be quashed.(8)

A MS. of Worcester cathedral priory contains "the unpopular Statutes of Gregory IX for the Benedictines, as enforced by Innocent IV in 1253, to which the writer has appended, in liturgical parody, *Tu autem Domine auctorem confunde*—'But thou, O Lord, confound the author!'".(9) Since a monastic generation lasted about twenty-five years, three generations would have elapsed between that curse and the episcopal visitation which we are now to study. That is the significance of its date.

Still more significant is its method. It is far more detailed in form than usual, giving us, at least in brief, both the accusations and the defence and the judgment. One other has survived in still fuller form than this, and at far greater length; it is a visitation of the exempt house of Malmesbury by the General Chapter commissary in 1527.(10) This is far too lengthy even for full analysis here; but its evidence for our question of impunity is very similar.

At Ipswich, then, the Bishop of Norwich, Ayermin, summed up the accusations against four of the chief officials.

(1) We object, and in objection we specify, that thou ......* who [*feminine*] hath brought forth unto thee, and Isabella Plais. Item, Mabel. (He confesseth the carnal knowledge, yet saith...he confessed to his Prior and submitted to penance.) Thou hast rashly laid violent hands upon Thomas Makel, subdeacon, in the Cellarer's chamber, even to the shedding of blood; also upon the acolyte John Wylde (he denies...) thou ..... with the brethren during divine service (confesseth, yet he saith that he attendeth in choir in so far as his office [of cellarer] permitteth), that thou makest private breakfasts and suppers in thy chambers with outsiders, consuming the goods of

* Here, and in a few other places, a word or words are illegible. I omit the word *item*, and other pure formalities.

the house (denied). For the three years that thou hast been Cellarer, thou hast rendered no account. (Denied, but he saith that for the last two years he hath rendered none.) Thou wearest padded tunics, one for week-days and the other for holy days. Thou wearest a silver seal with silver chain and bearest... a knife both walking in town and elsewhere and a silken purse and girdle and costly paternosters, contrary to the decency of thine Order and estate (padded tunic denied; knife confessed, yet he saith that this is for fear of Thomas Leu; girdle and purse denied). Thou wanderest commonly and frequently in the town eating and drinking with suspect layfolk in common taverns against the decency of the Order and Religion, wasting the goods of the House (denied). Thou art proprietary for thou hast money and lendest it to suspect women and others to the great scandal of the House (denied). Thou keepest not silence in due places and hast frequent confabulations with women and others in the church doors, against the friars' prohibition (denied). Thou hast a certain suspect enclosure around thy bed in the dormitory (denied; saith that he hath none other than the rest of the brethren). Thou invitest women and other outsiders to the Chapter House where thou eatest and drinkest indiscriminately with them, contrary to the decency of the Order (denied). A lamp which was wont to burn in the church day and night hath been withdrawn by thy counsel (denied). Thou hast removed a certain golden ring of great price offered to the Holy Cross and hast placed there another silver ring of little worth (*denied* cancelled and altered to *confessed*). Thou hast cups and stoops of silver and jewels which belonged to the Lady Nichole de Boville which thou possessest as thine own (denied this Brother Thomas hath a day to purge himself of the matters denied by himself, with his Prior and three canons of the Convent of Holy Trinity at Ipswich on the Tuesday next after St James's day in his own Chapter House, for he hath all his brethren in suspicion. He is dismissed by the Bishop because he purged himself by his single hand). Item, thou hast rashly laid violent hands upon Peter Bellward, even to efusion of blood in church at the High Altar (confessed and the church is under interdict until it hath been formally reconciled). The brethren have commonly sold their mazer-cups which were in the refectory without the Prior's leave.

(2) To thee Brother Clement of Ipswich, Precentor and Sacrist we object and objecting specify that thou possessest money as a proprietary and lendest it to women and others (*denied* cancelled: confesseth that he hath up to the sum of 40*s*. but by the Prior's leave). Thou commonly wanderest in the town eating and drinking with layfolk and other suspect persons contrary to the Rule and estate of thine Order, and thou keepest not silence in due places (denied).

Thou holdest frequent confabulation with women and other suspect folk in the doors of the church and thou invitest women and other outsiders in Chapter House where thou eatest and drinkest with them (confessed). Whensoever thou eatest in the refectory thou sendest the alms of thy food into the town and elsewhere at thine own will, so that there is no almsgiving (denied). Thou with the Subprior and four other of thy brethren hast conspired and sworn to a confederation against Brother T. Verdoun, Cellarer as above (denied). This same Clement purged himself on the aforesaid day of all the articles which he had denied.

(3) We object to thee Brother Richard Hadeleye Almoner that thou hast money of thine own and lendest it to suspect women (denied). That thou commonly wanderest in the town eating and drinking etc. (denied). Thou holdest frequent confabulations, etc. (confessed). Whensoever thou eatest in refectory etc. (he saith that there is no almsgiving). That thou with the Subprior and four other brethren etc. (denied). That thou didst carnally know Idanea or Dionysia Thurstan of Ipswich, and when thou wast Cellarer thou kepst her in thy chamber within the Priory, where she was caught by Sir John, Rector of St Matthew's Church at Ipswich, William Rector of Holbrook and Geoffrey Hemmynge, and that thou didst draw a ... and wouldest have smitten them if they had not fled (denieth the whole article). That thou didst carnally know Jane of Clare and Alice Scrivener (denieth for all time). That thou didst rashly lay violent hands upon Sir Adam of Kersey, Chaplain, in the refectory, even unto shedding of blood (confessed; saith that he did it in jesting spirit and not with violence). Thou art glutonous and drunken so that thou dost frequently vomit, sometimes in choir, sometimes in bed; and thou art contentious quarrelsome and inobedient and hast never rendered thy service according to the manner of the Rule (denieth the whole article yet saith that he hath not yet rendered his service, this Brother Richard purged himself and is dismissed). Item thou hast rashly laid violent hands upon John Scriveyn, Clerk, in the church even to efusion of blood (confessed and was absolved by the Bishop reserving the power of enjoining penance upon him).

(4) We object to thee John of Lyndeseye that thou art proprietary and hast money of thine own etc. (denied). Thou wanderest etc. (denied). Thou holdest frequent confabulations etc. (confessed). Whensoever thou eatest in the refectory etc. (confessed). Thou with the Subprior and others of thy brethren etc. (denied). Thou art quarrelsome, contentious and disobedient and thou hast never rendered thy service according to thy rule (disobedience he denieth: he confesseth that he hath not rendered service). Thou hast been a

monk at Louth Park, and it is believed that thou wast professed (confesseth that he was a monk though not professed). And the handmaid of Amabille the Anchoress who hath twice been with child by thee (denied for all time). Thou didst rashly lay violent hands upon Brother Richard of Hecham, late Prior of Leveringham, even to efusion of blood (denieth and purged himself as above).

It must be noted that the Visitor here is the bishop himself, not a mere commissary. Again, Bishop Ayermin was, like many others, a lawyer. He has not a good record for work in his diocese: he was mostly absent; but so also were many other bishops. His lenience can be paralleled in other visitation records, as will be seen; this case is exceptional mainly for the fullness with which it is reported. The accusations resemble those at St Albans a century and a half later, and at many other monasteries in those intervening years—waste and embezzlement, neglect of almsgiving, sensuality with sexual immorality, and finally *proprietas*, bound up here, as at St Albans, with usury. Yet this lawyer-bishop calls for no evidence whatever from the populous town, where there must have been scores who could have supported or denied (for instance) Verdoun's silk purse and gaudy beads, and tavern-haunting, and the public scandal caused by his usurious practices. The bishop, again, might have used his own eyes as to the "suspect enclosure". Yet on these and other points the accused was allowed to purge himself "with his single hand": that is, by swearing innocence with his hand on the Gospels. Not even compurgation is insisted upon, in which process the accused would have had to produce a few others to swear similar belief in his innocence. The bishop records explicitly here, what may be inferred from many other records, that as Visitor he was content with the single oath, and "dismissed" the man; so also with the other three.

Take again the facts confessed. There is no hint of serious punishment all through, apart from what Verdoun asserts himself to have suffered for his triple incontinences. This is no unusual phenomenon; it may even, I think, be said that it is rather normal than exceptional. I have given many examples in my second volume (chaps. XXII and XXIII and App. 32). Not only do we find very few concrete evidences of full statutory punishment actually carried out, but it is the most respectable churchmen who are most emphatic in exposing the breakdown of discipline. Imprisonment of a bad offender, sometimes nominally for life, involved too many difficulties. A line of less resistance was banishment to some dependent cell: and this was fairly frequent. But it had a double disadvantage; it pleased neither host nor guest, so long as the cell itself kept any decency. Only when these black sheep were numerous enough to turn the whole cell to their complexion, was there a possibility of peace. A line of still less resistance was to attack the offender not through his conscience but through his purse. As a Dominican cardinal wrote in mid-thirteenth century: "When a man is smitten with excommunication, he grieveth not: but if he be smitten with a fine, then is he smitten in the hinder parts, and feeleth the pain."(11) Mr A. F. Leach, in his Camden Society volume on visitations of *Southwell Minster*, judges even more emphatically than I have done (chap. LXXXVII ff.). He writes: "We can only conclude that neglect of duty and sexual immorality were so common that they were never punished, except when some public scandal was created by them"; and he points out the close resemblance between these collegiate clergy and the monastic records. Yet, just as Cardinal Gasquet, whose book has enjoyed the widest currency on Tudor monasticism, blandly assured the public that the monks had no evil repute until Burnet's day, so he flies in face of the most notorious evidence in this matter of Impunity. In 1906 he brought out a new and popular edition, with a preface professedly meeting the recent exposure of his vague and inaccurate appeal to the testimony of the Episcopal Registers. He writes:

> It has of late been pointed out that other "Visitation Records" contain instances of abuses and scandals, and that this is a strong corroboration of the correctness of the scandalous reports of Henry's visitors. The Church, so far from tolerating any abuses of this kind, sternly repressed them by legislation and punishment....On the face of the documents recorded in the Episcopal Registers and elsewhere, it is impossible even for the most prejudiced mind not to admit that wrong-doing was never tolerated by the authorities, and that the punishments meted out were sufficiently drastic to prove their honesty of purpose.

In the face of such a gross perversion of fact, which has been too long supinely allowed currency by historians, it is necessary to clinch here, with evidence drawn from Tudor England alone, the general survey in my second volume. I am here indebted to Mr Warren Sandell, who at my suggestion has worked through the voluminous records with great care, and who allows me to use his results. They must be given in some considerable detail, in proportion to those unconscientious misstatements.

CHAPTER LIII

EXEMPTIONS BY RETAIL

THIS facility of purchasing exemptions from Rome favoured not only selfish patriotism, and selfish parochialism, but selfish individualism also. This made terrible advances, first during the Avignon papacy, when it became necessary to invent new sources of income in compensation for moneys lost by migration from the Everlasting City, and, secondly, when the Great Schism (1378–1417) compelled two rivals, or at one time three, to divide even those resources as best they could. One of these was the creation of Honorary Chaplaincies to the Pope: the title familiar to our day as *Monsignore*.

Let us hear first Father Mortier, who will not be suspected of bias against a system by which so many Dominicans benefited, together with Religious of other Orders. He is dealing with the protests which Hugues de Vaucemain, General of the Dominicans, constantly put up against the efforts of Benedict XII to bring that Order back to the earliest Observance, with its almost complete renunciation of personal possessions. He thinks Hugues was justified in his resistance by the fact that after all, many Dominicans were doing valuable missionary work even under the then relaxed conditions. He concludes:

Master Hugh might have added that, if the tree which St Dominic had planted, on this special ground of Poverty, sometimes produced fruit of inferior quality,—if among the Friars Preachers there were some lukewarm brethren, anxious to shake off the yoke of every observance, and specially of poverty—the fault often lay (be it said with all respect) at the door of the Apostolic See. The Popes were wont to distribute freely, without reckoning, the diplomas of Chaplain or Penitentiary, often in reward for services rendered, often to invite such services, simply to please influential petitioners. Chaplains and Penitentiaries swarmed among the Dominicans. But those dignities carried their ordinary consequence of exemptions and privileges; they had especially the practical consequence of more or less fat revenues. In the friaries, these dignitaries formed a caste which was not the most amenable to observance. And, since their numbers steadily increased,—we may convince ourselves of this simply by reading the Registers of that age—Regular Observance was thereby all the more deteriorated.(1)

Our next witness is equally unexceptionable, and more specific in his facts and reflexions. It is the St Albans monk and chronicler Walsingham, in his "Doings of the Abbots", where he describes the long and beneficent rule of Thomas de la Mare (1349–96). He writes:

In the time of this Abbot, when the Schism had now lasted long in the Church, and the Anti-Pope [Clement] grew in favour of the King of France, since the true Pope, Urban was as it were destitute of help, he sought out many ways whereby he could gain such moneys as would at least maintain his livelihood. Many folk then, perceiving this, among both the Secular and the Regular Clergy, desiring ardently to escape from the yoke of their Superiors, sent money to Rome, where they knew that all things were for sale, begging to be inscribed on the roll of Papal Chaplains, in order that they might thus be absolved from obedience to their Prelates. So some, through the agency of a certain brother Walter Disse, a Friar Carmelite, Doctor of Divinity and confessor to the Duke of Lancaster (to whom the Supreme Pontiff, among other graces, had granted power by a "gracious" bull, nay rather, a shameful, considering the subject—to create fifty Honorary Chaplains in order to collect money in aid of the Crusade of the said Duke of Lancaster against the schismatic Spaniards*), were marvellously—nay, miserably, promoted [*mirabiliter, immo miserabiliter*]. This matter attracted petitions from monks: both Cistercians and Benedictines and Cluniacs, Canons and Rectors of parishes, and even Mendicant Friars. Certain of the St Albans monks, led by a similar desire and moved by those examples, collected money by begging privily wheresoever they could, and sent on this business to the venal Court, receiving the grace in exchange for proportionate money. In this business one condition was kept, that he who spent most earned most grace and favour. For some, even beyond this grace of Chaplaincy and Exemption, obtained leave to become Rectors of parishes, if some lord were willing to present them to a benefice.

It was contrary to Canon Law that a monk should serve a parish, though in fact a certain number of English brethren

* Who, in this quarrel, were allied with France and opposed to England. The lines of division in this great ecclesiastical dispute followed with remarkable exactness the national prejudices of all countries in Europe. (See Creighton, *Hist. Papacy*, Bk I, chap. I.)

obtained dispensations from Rome, and very many Germans. Three of Abbot de la Mare's monks "young, and moved by lightness of head, as such age exacts", bought Chaplaincies, with one old brother who had been fifty years in Religion. This old man, favoured by Lord de Roos, soon obtained the benefice of Gunneby; as for the three, the Abbot steadily refused to keep them *in professione sua*, and "they sought their livelihood in misery".(2)

The *Calendars of Papal Letters* show clearly, for England, Scotland and Ireland, the growth of this system. Vol. III records only four cases: in 1345, 1346, 1348 and 1352. The whole number from 1345 to the end of 1377 comes only to twenty. Naturally enough, the effect is not immediate even then: the decade 1378–87 produces only nine cases for these islands. But the next decade, 1388–97, records 268 cases, and the decade following, 258. And yet, from an early date, the dangers of such exemptions had begun to show themselves plainly, even at the Roman Court. We find in 1368 an "Ordinance, on petition of Hamo, Abbot of Battle, touching the cell of St John, Brecon, in the diocese of St Davids, whose prior, John, asserts that he is a Papal Chaplain, and therefore exempt from the jurisdiction of the said Abbot, thereby causing the dispersion of the monks, and ruin of the buildings. The Prior is declared to be subject to the said Hamo and his successors." That was an individual case, but presently King and Church in England are roused to a general and official protest. In 1395 comes an

Ordinance (on information of King Richard and the Minister and Friars Minors of the English Province and others, to the effect that an increasing number of members of the Order in that Province, without licence of their Superiors, go or send to the Roman Court, and get themselves received as Papal Chaplains, abuse the immunities, liberties, and privileges thereof, despise the obedience and correction of their Superiors, and run about through the world), that all such shall be subject to their Superiors in all things, and be present at divine offices by night and day as if they were not such Chaplains.(3)

Still more significant is the fortieth of the Articles of reform submitted to Henry V in 1414 by Oxford University. "Seeing that the customary [*consueta*] dispensation to many [*plerisque*]

real, but concealed [*suppressis*], apostates, that they may get the name of Honorary Chaplains, is a notable dissipation of Religious Orders, it seemeth that it would be to the profit and honour of Religion if the Supreme Pontiff were not moved by slight suggestions to assist such Religious in future with such dispensations."(4) But such warnings were unheeded; and presently, by a process familiar to all students of medieval history, the evil which had tainted the fountain head and the main current spread also into the smaller streams. Thomas Gascoigne reckons this among the worst abuses which poisoned Church life on the eve of the Reformation. In the days of either Martin V or Eugenius IV, he says (thus, somewhere between 1417 and 1447) "an English Bishop obtained a papal bull that he might have with him, as Chaplains, whomsoever he might choose among Religious or Rectors or Vicars; and so Vicars became his Chaplains, under which licence they absented themselves from their cures and vicarages for years, spending the time in their own delights and in hunting with hawk and hound". He repeats this later on, adding a case which he himself knew, where the absentee hunter-parson "said that this was permitted to him by papal licence; and great sins follow therefrom".(5) In some cases such licence contradicted the express oath of residence which the cleric had been compelled to take by the very constitution of his benefice; and Gascoigne would gladly see the *Fundator* (i.e. the Founder's representative) empowered to eject a man who was thus not earning, but stealing, his livelihood.

These things may go some way to explain the apparent paradox, that the age of greatest monastic prosperity should have been marked by such frequent resignations of abbots and bishops. To put it from the material and common-sense point of view, these enormous business establishments needed economists and disciplinarians at their head, rather than saints. A great Missionary Age [1090–1210] produced endowments far more rapidly than it could secure earnest vocations; at least, after the first generation had passed away. Jocelin of Brakelond is a frank and most convincing witness here. Abbots and bishops had to command, directly or indirectly, a mass of scattered estates or revenues and a multitude of persons often requiring a long arm to reach and a strong hand to control. St Edmund Rich, who in combined scholarship and saintliness stands perhaps at the head of all our primates after Anselm, proved a tactless and unsuccessful ruler. Experience showed this more and more plainly, and fewer saints were appointed: the prelate of [1300] onwards was normally a statesman and business man, in so far as he was fitted for his post at all. But there was an intermediate period during which the saintly prelate had to learn by his own experience that which the world outside him was gradually realizing with increasing clearness. The bitter teaching of inescapable fact gradually blunted sensitive idealism. Discipline, in anything like the sense understood in any modern Church, was rendered impossible by the fact that, at almost every point, a suitor might reasonably hope to buy exemption if he could afford to sue for it. As one generation succeeded another, and exemptions steadily multiplied, the prelate knew perfectly well, from the beginning, that which he had to face. There was no longer, as in ancient times, the heart-break of hope deferred; he had faced the facts, and never hoped for more than moderate success. The fourteenth century, and still more the fifteenth, was an age of disillusion. The better abbots and bishops—Whethamstede and even Fox—had learned, long before their exaltation to high office, the narrow limits within which it was possible to assert the strict law, and the very wide margin of refuge beyond which it would be hopeless to pursue the slippery or defiant sinner. Subjects, on the other hand, knew equally well how far they might hope to go, if they had courage and could command money. Facing these conditions, as all sober men had to face them in Tudor times, we need not wonder why Wallingford was suffered in office by more than one abbot, and why Fox sketched despairingly to Wolsey the limits of his own hopes for monastic reform, even in his single diocese.(6)

CHAPTER LIV

QUIS CUSTODIET? (1)

THERE are three main sources from which the preliminary story of the Dissolution will be written when some historian makes up his mind to study the whole question, without fear or favour, from all or nearly all the original documents. First, the whole series of Episcopal Registers, which at the present rate will soon be completely printed down to the Reformation: but these contain only scattered reports of visitations. Secondly, the General Chapter Records, which have been published very completely by Mr W. E. Pantin for the Benedictines and by Dr H. E. Salter for the Augustinians, and less completely by Canon J. Fowler for the Cistercians. Thirdly, a few special sets of Visitors' reports, systematically recorded, which have seldom survived in their original complete form, but have sometimes, though too casually, been copied *seriatim* into the Episcopal Registers. The fullest and most valuable series of this kind is for the great diocese of Lincoln, which comprised in pre-Reformation days the counties of Lincoln, Leicester, Northampton, Oxford, Buckingham, Bedford, Huntingdon and Rutland. Here we have reports scattered over sixty-two years in all (1420–49 and 1514–47), from five bishops who were very definitely above the average for uprightness and energy in those days of absentee prelates. It is probably on that account that the evidence is recorded by these men and their clerks in unusual detail. Most of these reports have been edited in three volumes for the Lincoln Record Society, by Professor A. Hamilton Thompson, with accuracy and wealth of illustration which may compare with the best Continental standards. They are equipped with an interleaved translation for the benefit of non-specialists. This adds immensely to their value for a work like this present volume; for any reader who is sufficiently anxious to check the use I make of this evidence can do so with the greatest ease. Since, in each volume, the houses are arranged alphabetically, my allusions in this chapter can readily be verified, in most cases without page references.

This huge diocese of Lincoln naturally contained several great and wealthy monasteries. The greatest, St Albans, was exempt: therefore it stands outside the records. Of the rest, Peterborough, Ramsey, Croyland, Eynsham, Oseney, Dorchester, Leicester, Spalding, Wellow and St Frideswide's at Oxford were all of considerable wealth and importance. The first four of these claim our special attention here. For, at different times in the fifteenth century, their Superiors had been appointed by the General Chapter as official Visitors to enquire, and, if necessary, correct at St Albans. Peterborough was thus chosen at least twice, in 1426 and 1465, Bardney in 1429, Eynsham in 1468 and Ramsey in 1492.

Peterborough was one of the greatest houses in England, and we get one important searchlight upon it from those Papal Letters already dealt with in chap. LI. In 1402, the abbot complained that "a number of his monks, asserting themselves to be Papal Chaplains, with the enjoyment of all immunities, etc. granted by John XXII, Clement VI and Boniface VIII [*sic*], refuse to obey their superiors, put off their religious and assume a secular habit, and wander about throughout the world". He besought papal powers to deal with such and bring them forcibly back; his petition was granted. Not long after this, a series of Episcopal Visitations give us far more light. Not only was this great house conspicuous for itself, but it was also within easy reach of Lincoln. Here, then, was an admirable test for the power of those five energetic bishops. It seems evident that the Visitations were not carried out triennially, in strict accordance with Innocent III's decree, yet they seem to have been more regular than the English average, and incomparably more so than on the Continent. In only twenty-four cases have we records of more than one Visitation, and in only five cases, of more than two. This want of continuity renders it difficult to trace the extent to which nominal punishments were in fact carried out. On the other hand, the evidence in these reports is more detailed, in general, than in the average of other Episcopal Registers. When Bishop Gray visited Peterborough in 1432 John Depyng had been abbot for twenty-three years.

The Injunctions, in the light of the fuller disclosures of later reports, clearly indicate the presence already then of the enormous moral and financial disorders discovered later by Bishop Alnwick. There was conspicuous access of women, neglect of hospitality and almsgiving, *proprietas*, accounts not audited, shirking of night-services in choir, and no grammar-teacher for the younger monks. Although the government of spirituals and temporals was then deputed to four monks, it would seem that this arrangement had lapsed before the first Alnwick Visitation of 1437. At that Visitation, besides a mass of testimony concerning waste of revenue, neglect of monastic property, and general financial chaos, there was evidence also of general moral decay, of keeping company and dancing with women in the monastery, and of the neglect of Masses caused by over-night drunkenness. In the end Abbot Depyng resigned the government into the hands of the prior, though apparently keeping the abbacy till 1438, when Richard Assheton was elected in his place. In 1442, there were no serious *detecta*, and thirty-six of the forty reported simply *omnia bene*. That there was a deliberate conspiracy of silence seems certain, not merely because the grossest abuses came to light four years later, but because the nature of these abuses was often such as to make it evident that they had existed longer than four years. It is impossible here to do more than summarize the disclosures made in 1446: they may be read in Professor Hamilton Thompson's translation, detail by detail: they fill twelve pages. Alms are neglected, "by reason of which withdrawal the witness believes that many evils will betide the monastery". Choir-service is neglected.* The abbot has embezzled mass-money for certain departed souls, so that the Masses are no longer said. After compline, instead of going to bed, the young monks "set to drinking, sometimes with the abbot, as freely as if this were allowed them† and are rendered altogether unfit for being present at matins or celebrating [Mass] on the day following". Three (named) drink

* In 1437 the report had run "they are 44 in number, and out of all these there are not more than 10 or 12 in choir in time of divine service". Making full allowance for legitimate absentees, there should always have been about 36.

† It is, on the contrary frequently forbidden, most explicitly, by the Statutes and the Visitors.

so regularly that "they come to Matins or celebrate Masses hardly once in the week". The juniors threaten their seniors when warned, one monk has "withstood the Abbot to his face, with a knife drawn in his hand". The Bishop notes: "The monks keep weapons of attack and defence in places apart in their cells." One has publicly boasted that he will take vengeance on anyone who deposes against him at the Visitation. Again, he "made conspiracies, among the brethren, saying to them 'with whom will you be, on my side or the Abbot's? If on the Abbot's side, you will be accused first'". Another monk has embezzled plate and jewels, including a pyx: he has lent £20 to a citizen (named) at 20*s*. £ per quarter: i.e. 20 per cent. "Light women and suspect have overmuch access to the monastery." Two (named) "do use to drink at eventide in the treasury, where suspect women come in their company to the scandal of the house". One of these "uses to walk up and down of an evening between the monastery and Oxney, drinking in the thorpes that lie between, to the scandal of the monastery". Accounts are irregular. In short, "Except the monastery be put under better government, it will be destroyed."

Grave as were the offences of certain monks there is no record of their punishment; but the abbot's were far graver and supported by numerous and credible witnesses. The interest here is in the bishop's proceedings against him. Briefly, he was charged with adultery with three women, Mrs Parker, Mrs Clerk and Mrs Est, and with enriching them and their husbands with monastic goods and revenue. On September 10 the bishop charged him with these adulteries (which he denied), and ordered him to remove the first two from their dwellings, and to hold no suspect intercourse with any. The next day the bishop, *ex gratia sua*, allowed him to purge with respect to Mrs Est. The Visitation was adjourned till February 8, 1447, but on September 17 a commission was issued to receive the abbot's purgation as regards the other women on the 25th in St John's, Peterborough. On December 3 Mrs Clerk and Mrs Parker appeared before the bishop, and denied adultery. Their husbands were ordered to remove from the monastery property where they lived, and Parker was bound in £40 to do so. On February 8 the bishop treated all day with the abbot and monks about the government of the temporals, and it was not till nightfall that the abbot at last consented to four monastic officers governing temporals for two years. The next day, however, the abbot came and pleaded that to do this would be to the everlasting scandal of his name. He asked to keep the government with the four monks as assessors. The bishop consented, but swore him to submit to his ordinance, and made the condition that for the next two years he should live at Oxney with a small and honest household. We know of no further trouble, and Assheton remained abbot till 1471.

The next recorded Visitation was by the bishop personally in 1518 (*Reg. Atwater*, folios 133ff.). The evidence, here again, is very unfavourable. Some of the conventual buildings are in great decay, by fault of the abbot, who keeps in his hands six of the offices. Thus, while his own lands and buildings are well kept, those of the convent are neglected. He sells timber without the brethren's consent, sometimes to the yearly value of 100 marks or more, and embezzles to his own use. He has a hoard which he increases also by smaller embezzlements. His brother is enriching himself at the expense of the abbey. The abbot "loveth not the studious brethren, but desires the negligent"—*desiderat negligentes*. "Let an injunction be made that the Lord Abbot should use patience towards all; for his impatience impedeth a hundred Masses in the year, and friendship among the brethren." "The same Lord Abbot oppresseth the whole community of the town of Peterborough with his cattle in their commons." He gives no yearly account of his administration: he has founded a grammar school at Kirkton with endowment of £10 a year, and made the Abbot of Swinestead its governor. "Let scholars be sent to continue their studies at the University: for sometimes they are there and sometimes not." "Nowadays, he accepts monks who are too young and untaught, namely boys, by reason whereof there are not so many priests in the abbey as there should be." He has illegally enclosed some of the convent land for his own park. The novices are ill instructed in their religious exercises. "The Abbot sometimes denieth the Sacrament of the Eucharist to brethren who are sick unto death"—*infirmis in extremis languentibus*. He has suggested that he would resign, but will not do this: meanwhile, "he hath left the more grievous delinquents unpunished". "The confessors are ignorant [*ideotae*], and fit brethren are not appointed." Buildings and lands are going to ruin through neglect: young men are put into the offices, while their elders must sit in the cloister. The poor are defrauded of their due alms, and there should be better provision for guests. "Many of the elder monks are wanton and undisciplined [*lascivi et dissoluti*] in choir during divine service, setting an evil example." The abbot is more familiar with layfolk than with his own brethren. Let him be compelled to show his accounts quarterly for audits and to display his hoard. One witness deposes: "The Sacristan is extremely ill-famed [*nimium notatur*] for incontinence. The Prior is ill-famed for having taken certain jewels from St Oswald['s shrine] within the abbey; and the Precentor for going out into the town and excessive levity in his office. The said Prior was not elected by the community, as he should have been." This prior also completely neglects, nowadays, those Masses for the souls of the dead which he is bound to say in the chapel over the Charnel-House. "The Sacristan had in his chamber a certain young girl named Joan Turnour in secret fashion, and hath often times known her carnally, and liveth in incontinence not only with her but with many others." Another witness deposes: "If the [abbey] inn [*pandoxatio*] is deserted for two or three days, at times, then the brethren who are then at Oxney* have no drink but from their own purses." The bishop's comment is: "and within the abbey is a certain tavern wherein the brethren drink at improper times, sometimes too early and sometimes too late. Let it be so ordered that the sub-cellarer permit none of his brethren to procure wine therefrom beyond the seventh hour after noon in summer time. There is too frequent access of brethren to the town of Peterborough, even without licence." He adds, "Let this be reformed."

Even wealthier than Peterborough and almost as important was Ramsey. Here, in 1432, the bishop found that the services were shirked.(1) There were many monks (forty-four at the next visitation, 1439); and there should have been more than thirty

* A dependent cell not far from the abbey, to which the monks resorted for their "recreationes".

in choir. Yet the bishop is content if sixteen are always present in choir, during the Services and High Mass, in addition to those who minister at the altar. More significant still is this scandalous omission of the *Opus Dei*, which all disciplinarians, ancient or modern, characterize as the main object of monastic existence, more important even than almsgiving. This is to be punished with fines in money, a thing which no monk could possess except under those later casuistic interpretations of the Rule which distressed all orthodox reformers. Similar fines were to be imposed for sitting up to drink after Compline, a thing explicitly forbidden by statute and which we might expect to be enforced by spiritual penalties, under pain of 6*d*. fine for an ordinary monk and 1*s*. for the official who was responsible for allowing this offence.* These fines were to be added to the fund for new pavement of cloister, chapter-house and refectory. Similarly, 1*d*. for each unexcused absence from Matins, 1*d*. for absence from other Services or High Mass, and 2*d*. for the Sacristan every time he fails to shut the church door directly after Vespers. We have here a speaking commentary upon that phrase of Cardinal Hughes de St-Cher: a money fine can be relied upon to smite the offender in the hinder parts, and he feeleth the pain. Women, again, are not to be allowed "in the cloister, refectory, dormitory, infirmary or other private places of the abbey", under pain of a month's imprisonment for the introducer. The same penalty for eating and drinking in taverns, especially in talk with women. All must show their private moneys [*peculium*] once or twice a year to the abbot, under pain of suspension from the services; the abbot who fails to maintain this must be fined £10. There was neglect of almsgiving, and too much wandering abroad. The bishop, in conclusion, rehearses how he gives these injunctions to abbot and brethren "for the reform of your manners and the correction of your defects, excesses, and transgressions disclosed unto us at this visitation, which we here pass in silence in order that we may spare your good fame and honour". If they contemn these injunctions, then he will add to the aforesaid fines his Greater Excommunication.

* In 1444, the statutory wage of a freemason or master carpenter was 6*d*. a day: the "rough-mason" had 5*d*. (See my *Art and the Reformation*, pp. 181 ff.)

The next recorded Visitation was in 1439. An old monk could remember "when there were only three households, in the monastery Abbot's hall, refectory, and blood-letting hall; and now there are very many [eating-places], whereby Religion* perisheth and the goods are consumed". The bishop himself puts even more emphatically: "Religion perisheth almost altogether, and the fragments from their tables are not given in alms, but are consumed in [*illegible*] manner." This neglect of almsgiving is emphasized by other evidence. The bishop sums this up in his injunction "That the Almoner shall distribute the alms of the monastery to the poor who are most in need, and in no wise, as he is wont, to his friends or serving-folk." And again:

That the Almoner shall not invite any monks to come to him at Bury† or the Spital for repasts or drinkings; for, at such invitations he receives for every monk so invited a pot of ale containing a gallon and a quarter, a monk's loaf and an entire dish from the kitchen, and, whereas a single monk's vituals should be enough for the repast of all those monks then present, the same almoner applies the whole of the remainder to his own uses, which tends to the great damage of the refectory and the alms; and thus [it happens] that by such repasts, drinkings or noontide surfeitings he keeps the monks away from vespers [and] sometimes from the monastery until 10 o'clock at night.(2)

For at this Visitation again, the choir services are found to be scandalously neglected. "At the canonical day-hours very few attend choir regularly, insomuch as sometimes there are in choir not more than 4, 5, or 6....After Compline also many go out of cloister, neglecting the dormitory, and spend time in drinkings and other irregular doings." There is deliberate malingering. One monk reports this in plain terms, and the bishop meets it in his injunctions, writing:

Each monk, who at any rate is able, shall attend quire and, immediately after compline has been said, shall go to the dorter, nor go out therefrom before 7 o'clock in the following day; whereas many, feigning themselves to be sick, though they be strong enough to eat and drink and roam out of doors, withdraw themselves from

* I.e. the monastic ideal.
† A grange not far from the abbey.

attendance in quire, and many go out of cloister after compline and spend the time in drinkings and other irregularities until ten o'clock at night.

Again, the bishop finds himself compelled to decree "that the monks shall be restrained from the town of Ramsey; for they have public recourse thereunto, and there do they pass the time in taverns, in public drinkings, and other breaches of the Rule". This as usual, is accompanied by familiarities with women, who are "often admitted to too great familiarity within the abbey". This, moreover, may be almost said to occur under the abbot's patronage. For the bishop finally decrees not only that no women be admitted or fed in the abbey "however honest they be except such as the laws suspect of no heinous crime". And, again, he comes to particulars:

> That the monks who stay with the abbot at Byggynd at the noon-day meal shall immediately after that repast return straight to the monastery, and in no wise go, as is their wont, to Bury, where, without asking or obtaining leave, they spend their time in drinkings and other irregular doings with secular persons, even with suspect women for whom they send; and, if they dare not send for them, they go to them in their cottages, where they stay, tarrying there and outside the monastery until ten or eleven o'clock at night.

They transgressed the limitations of Pope Benedict XII upon flesh-eating; and even the bishop is willing to allow something of this excess (pp. 305, 307). There is gross *proprietas*; two monks at the cell of St Ives "hire crofts and lands from lay-folk and sow them with woad and other seeds to their own profit, and not to that of the monastery or of the cell of St Ives; for this Burtone did for this purpose destroy the saffron growing at St Ives, and by reason hereof they are defamed of bargaining and private gain in the neighbourhood". Others make private gain from the gardens which the hostillar allows them. "Several [obedientiaries] behave themselves so indiscreetly and live so delicately that they leave the monastery grievously in debt." For many years past no accounts have been made up and audited. There is much waste and dilapidation. Their conventual church at St Ives "suffers very serious defaults, that threaten ruin".

Yet it is noteworthy here, as in many other cases, that many brethren complacently report with a simple "all is well". No less than twelve testify *omnia bene*, even though the bishop's injunctions show his conviction of the accusations; and indeed nearly all of them must have been either manifest truths or blatant lies. Therefore, warning the abbot and prior of these things [*monemus*], he ends in much the same words as Morton used for St Albans: they and their brethren must reform all these defects, or he will come down upon them again in his yearly Visitations, "sparing no one, according to the degree of their misdoing, so that their penalty, and not their impunity, may be for an example for them that come after" (p. 318). But even Alnwick does not appear to have pursued this urgent matter with special attention, just as he does not seem to have kept up strictly with the statute for triennial visitations. However, the fact that there is no further record in his Register must give the monks of Ramsey a benefit of doubt.

Here comes a gap of more than half a century in the Lincoln Visitation records. Then the Registers of Bishops Atwater and Longland (1514–47) contain a considerable number. Atwater visited Ramsey personally in 1518 (*Reg.* f. 138, *v*°). It is reported that there is insufficient locking of doors, even at night: a chalice has thus been stolen from the church. The prior was not properly elected, but practically forced upon the convent by the abbot, to whom he is slavishly deferential, since the abbot treats him as a dismissible subordinate. One monk holds three obediences, contrary to law. The monks "stipendia" are in arrears; the cellarer will not pay them punctually. There should be fifty monks, but there are only forty. Dom Stowe is a common blasphemer and swearer: the bishop has to take special measures against this sin. The obedientiaries waste the lands and buildings of their offices, and render no account of the moneys which come into their possession: thus "they enrich themselves". Attendance at the services is disgraceful: "for, commonly, there are not more than two monks in the church at time of High Mass, and sometimes none but the Prior alone. The officials come not to choir". "The Prior...is sometimes and often drunken, and then he will reveal the secrets of the abbey and the confessions of the brethren, so that the brethren fear to confess unto him." The bishop adds: "We enjoined as below"; but there is no record of such injunction in the MS. "Dom John Stowe is a blasphemer and a great swearer....The Lord Bishop reserved the absolution of all such blasphemies to himself and his deputies, and decreed sentence of excommunication upon all who shall absolve such blasphemers, either of their own authority or through their brethren." "Many [*plures*] of the monks give themselves up more than is decent to hunting and other games, and sometimes some of them shoot their arrows in the fields without decorous garments, to the scandal of the abbey." Layfolk are admitted to the private dormitory, where "they see and know what is done by the young monks who study there". The accounts are not properly audited. The sub-prior sometimes punishes hastily and harshly, but is "too favourable to delinquents". "It was strictly enjoined upon the Abbot [by the Bishop in person] that he should provide an instructor in the elements of knowledge [*in scientiis primitivis*] for the novices. This hath oftentimes already been similarly enjoined, and he careth not to fulfil it. This was again repeated in this visitation." Dormitory and church are in such bad repair that it rains upon the beds and the high altar and the organ. Choir service is so neglected that, out of thirty monks in the abbey, sometimes scarce eight rise for matins. Other monks besides the abbot are appropriating moneys that pass through their hands.

> The brethren of the abbey, and especially the seniors, frequent and play at dice and games of hazard, and other similar games, at night-time, even for money; and there they swear mighty oaths, by the Lord's Body and His other members. They come not to matins, but play at that time, and this commonly. The seniors, even when they are in choir, sing not but talk together, and the juniors support all the burdens of the choir.

The monks run up debts with the tradesfolk, "to the scandal of the abbey". "There is an outcry against the behaviour of the monks [*illegible*] in the [dependent] convent of St Ives."

Again, in 1530, Ramsey was visited by the Bishop's Commissary (*Reg. Longland*, f. 98*v*). The sub-prior complains "that he is sometimes impeded by the prior from making the necessary reformations of delinquent brethren". On the other hand, the sub-prior himself is accused by two brethren of being "drunken and quarrelsome". The almoner's revenues are managed by the cellarer, to their detriment. The choir-books need repair, and "the pedagogue hath not taught the brethren since last Lent....They lack an instructor in grammar". The sacristan does not render due accounts. "The monks at St Ives come not by night to matins, and the second Mass is neglected, and sometimes there are no more than three [*illegible*]." There is multiple testimony to serious disrepair in the buildings: yet the abbot, the prior, and eleven of the brethren report briefly and complacently *omnia bene*. The Visitor's final injunction, that the reported evils must be reformed, testify to his conviction of their serious character.

Bardney abbey is perhaps even more notable than those two great houses, for transgressions and impunity. We have records of seven Visitations at that abbey; in [1432]; from times between 1437 and 1444; 1519 and 1525. In [1432] Bishop Gray's preamble to Bardney runs "we found that certain things contrary to holy Religion, leading to the destruction of the souls of those set under us and the undoing of Religion, as we relate with sorrow, are daily committed fearlessly therein".(3) He warns them to read their Rule regularly in Chapter, and so to deal with delinquents "that their punishment, and not their exemption, may be an abiding example to the others": this is thrice repeated in the Injunctions. They must "in no wise henceforward gad about or wander, as has been their custom, contrary to the regular observances". There are serious quarrels in the abbey; accounts are not regularly kept, and the abbot has mismanaged financially. Most significant of all, he enjoined "that women, and especially Jane Martyn or her daughter, in no wise enter the cloister or any of the inner precincts, such as the frater, the dorter, or the infirmary or its hall in any manner whatsoever, unless they be mothers or sisters of the monks; and not even these unless they come in honest company to visit their sons and brothers, without suspicion of evil attaching to their companions, and not often". Bishop Alnwick carried out a series of far more thorough Visitations, and recorded many depositions of witnesses.(4) The story is far too long for full reproduction here: it fills twenty-four octavo pages. Much scandal about women, sometimes by name, was bandied about from mouth to mouth. The bishop allowed the accused to "purge" themselves on ridiculously easy terms: but his Injunctions contained one most significant sentence:

He ordained moreover that none of the monks should go out of the monastery without having first asked and obtained leave for a reasonable and lawful cause, nor in any wise drink or eat in the town of Bardney, nor bring any woman howsoever honest into the cloister precincts, nor, if a woman be brought in by anyone, receive her into any familiar converse, such women alone excepted as concerning whom the laws presume that no evil can be suspected.

The choir-service is grossly neglected; hospitality is neglected and the poor are defrauded of alms; the limits of moderation in food and drink are overstepped; the church and other buildings are ruinous; the choir is "almost ready to fall"; they do not keep their statutory scholar at the University; accounts are irregular; Masses for benefactors' souls are sometimes neglected; timber has been cut down and sold in defiance of the bishop's express prohibition. The Visitation injunctions of previous bishops to Bardney have been hidden away, so "unless the lord lay his hand thereunto, the monastery in a little while will be in danger of final extinction".* As to certain abbey muniments, nothing is known of them, "and so the good governance of the whole monastery is going to naught". Its income was 600 marks, and it was 400 in debt. The monks used the grange of Southery for their "recreationes" (as St Albans did Redbourne, Peterborough Oxney, Ramsey Bury, etc.), and their conduct there "is the main cause of scandal to the abbey and destruction to its common possessions". One monk had challenged a serving-man of the abbot to fight. There was dicing among the brethren. A party of four conspirators got possession of the common seal and secretly sealed a blank charter. The prime mover in this affair, who was also mainly responsible for the embarrassed finances of the abbey, "said openly: 'The Bishop has no such jurisdiction in the monastery that he can dispose of the moneys of the monastery: rather will we lay out all that we have in the monastery to defend ourselves against him'".(5) In 1519 Bishop Atwater complains that the monks

* *Exterminium.* Whether *Dominus* refers to God or the bishop must remain doubtful.

hunt and hawk: their dogs and birds defile church, cloister, refectory and chapterhouse. At the Mass of the Blessed Virgin there are generally only two or three monks: the books in the Lady Chapel are "torn, broken, and soiled". Two monks habitually shirk matins and go abroad without leave.

> The Bishop enjoined upon all the brethren that thenceforward all should abstain from familiarity with layfolk, and that they should keep within their inner precincts,* not quitting these on any account without permission: also that no woman should be admitted on any account to the said buildings, but the brethren should set themselves with all diligence to divine service.

In 1525 the abbot had only eleven monks under him, and the bishop found little to note.(6)

* *Loca claustralia.* This term is clearly explained in another visitation record, which adds "namely, church, cloister, dormitory and refectory". (H. E. Salter, *Eynsham Cartulary*, I, 436.)

CHAPTER LV

QUIS CUSTODIET? (2)

EYNSHAM had scarcely a better record than the other three during the 150 years preceding the Suppression.(1) In 1380 the bishop found too few brethren: they were told to raise their numbers to thirty, "as soon as suitable persons can be found". In 1425, they were twenty-two at least; probably twenty-six. In 1417, the bishop forbade their selling further corrodies without his consent. In 1433 the bishop complained that they were reported to have "cast Religion aside", and they were violating the injunctions which he had given at his Visitation. In 1434 mismanagement again: a secular person is appointed to manage and so pay off the debts. Five months later,

the Bishop issues another commission to enquire about the laxity of rule at Eynsham, where it is said the monks have returned to their former indulgence [*luxus*], and disregarded the injunctions which the Bishop with their own consent had made for them. The result of this enquiry was that shortly afterwards, the Bishop, hearing that Thomas, Abbot of Eynsham, had been guilty of gross immorality, publicly and before the eyes of all, since the Bishop's last visitation, orders that certain commissaries should summon the Abbot and ask if he can show cause why he should not incur the penalties of the crimes which he had confessed at the last visitation:* Henry Norwich, Vicar of Eynsham, was implicated with the Abbot. Evidently the penalties had been held over the Abbot since the visitation two years before, in the hope that he would amend; but these repeated commissions had shown that he continued as before. Whether he was deposed or not we do not know.

But this case, among many others, illustrates the difficulties of a capable bishop in dealing with even notorious offenders. The next visitation is undated, but was certainly somewhere about 1440. The bishop found himself compelled to deal with laxity as to wandering brethren and frequentation of the pre-

* Dr Salter here quotes in a footnote from the record: "Adulteries, fornications, incest and rape." *Incest*, in such documents means a monk's sin with a nun, or a priest's with a parishioner.

cincts by women, the statute of flesh-food, and *proprietas*. There was nobody to teach the younger monks; forbidden drinkings were held after Compline; valuables had been pawned, yet the house was still in debt, owing partly to breach of business rules, if not to actual dishonesty: one of the monks had apostatized. At the bishop's Visitation of 1445 the fourteen brethren reported "omnia bene", except that this apostate, or another, had broken prison and run off with a nun of Godstow, but was now in prison again. The next Visitation recorded was in 1517. There was another apostate, and the bishop's chancellor notes nearly all the usual defects of a disorderly monastery. They broke the flesh-rule, haunted the town, frequented taverns with "dice and other indecent games"; let these things, henceforward, be punished by loss of the monk's pocket-money for half a year.

> Let no women, at least of suspicious character, be admitted to consort with any monks within the precincts, and let women who might give rise to any suspicion have by no means any access to the abbey.... The porter hath two daughters, very dissolute and suspect, who oftentimes frequent the abbey, by occasion whereof great scandal ariseth.

"The Prior will oftentimes be drunken, and then will he blab and scandalize and defame his brethren." He, with the subprior and the third prior, are often absent from matins: twice the whole community has shirked this service because these superiors were absent. There was no grammar-master; yet the young monk who makes this complaint joins with five others in reporting "omnia bene". The last Visitation was in 1520, when there was another apostate to report, apart from a senior monk who had apostatized but is now formally pardoned. Again there were only fifteen monks. "The Lord Abbot's sister, who dwelleth within the precincts, is very burdensome to the abbey, and it is believed that the said Abbot's sister is maintained, with many of her kinsfolk, at the abbey's expense, and as is said to the sum of £140 a year,* to the detriment of the abbey." The finances are in confusion: and "the Abbot rendereth no account of his administration": he has been selling timber unlawfully. The third prior shirks matins, and

* The total revenues are reported to the visitor at £469.

the grammar-master "is so negligent that the novices profit not from teaching".

So far the Lincoln Visitations permit us to evaluate four out of the five houses upon which fell the responsibility of visiting and correcting St Albans. From Westminster, the fifth, we have little definite evidence; it was exempt, so we have no bishop's reports. But, though we must give it the benefit of all doubts, the scanty notices show pretty clearly that its fifteenth-century record would not have done credit to the thirteenth century, and still less to any great abbey in any country of modern Europe. Abbot George Norwych, in 1467, was superseded for serious and long-standing financial maladministration. Again, in 1518, Wolsey visited the abbey very strictly and, according to Polydore Vergil, with unjust severity.(2) Like St Denis in France, the abbey was too closely connected with the King's Court to furnish, in general, a model of monastic discipline.

In a question of this importance, involving the whole reality of the Visitation system, we must face the full evidence even at the risk of tedious prolixity. The foregoing instances concern some of the most famous Benedictine houses, in this England where the safeguards prescribed by Innocent III were certainly better observed than the average, and probably better than in any other country of Europe. Let us now turn to one of the most famous among our houses of Austin Canons, that of Merton in Surrey. Here, again, is one of those rare cases where the converging evidence from many different sources has survived with a completeness which enables us to see all round our object.

In 1389, the prior was one of the five heads of houses appointed by the Augustinian Chapter to visit and reform at Cirencester, where some of the brethren were reported to have "committed certain grievous faults and irregularities", with "manifest scandal" and "pernicious example". Yet in 1387 William of Wykeham had found Merton itself in full decay; the brethren protested against his perfectly correct Injunctions as a violation of the "rules, constitutions, privileges and laudable constitutions hitherto observed by the house". Among the Injunctions which they name especially as intolerable are those in which Wykeham specifies fasting for increased neglect of duty or violation of discipline. The offender (he decrees) shall be punished first by a four days' fast on bread, beer and pot-herbs; on a second conviction, by six days; for a third, as many days as the prior may think fit. The faults to be thus punished were (1) shirking Divine Service; (2) breach of silence at due times or places; (3) neglect of the statutory Masses for benefactors' souls, which are "often" omitted; (4) persons "of either sex" haunting the monastery; (5) brethren sometimes "wander beyond the bounds of the priory without honest society and without having obtained licence"; (6) sleeping in other than the statutory night-clothes; and (7) "we have found some of the brethren to be huntsmen", keeping hounds and flying in the face of Canon Law. The prior and brethren complained no less strongly of the bishop's decree that persistent offenders should finally be suspended or removed from their offices. The offences for which the bishop decreed this were the admission of strangers of either sex; the sufferance of those "suspected and other dishonest persons who frequently walk about the church and monastery in dark and shady places, and at times whence loss and various scandals are come"; the wandering abroad without permission; the breach of prescriptions about their bed-clothes, and the fact that "some of the brethren are huntsmen, keeping hunting-dogs" not only at great expense, but in defiance of their Rule and even of Canon Law. Such were the "customs" and "liberties" in defence of which a monastery could openly defend itself against its bishop (who was also one of the most powerful ministers the Crown ever had), and who could yet be chosen by the General Chapter as guardian of virtue for an indisciplined house!(3) Again, in 1506, the General Chapter chose the Prior of Merton "as official Visitor for houses of the Order in the dioceses of Winchester and Salisbury. Yet this man's record in his own house was far from spotless. Bishop Fox, visiting there two years earlier, had been compelled to warn him "under pain of depuration, to reside personally within the house and not to be absent more than a month without lawful and reasonable cause", to join in the convent's choir-services at least once or twice a month, to keep regular accounts for audit, not to alienate jewels or other possessions, "and that thou neither permit nor cause any suspected women to have access to thee within the interior of thy house".(4) Fox carried out a second Visitation of Merton in 1509. He censured the prior for absenteeism: "since the holy Religion of thy priory hath miserably turned aside to that broad way which leadeth to death, by reason of thine absence under pretext of thy priorate of students at Oxford", he must now give up that priorate, quit Oxford, and never leave Merton without episcopal permission for more than a fortnight. The prior is also "defamed with divers women, as specified and declared to [the Bishop] by name, between whom and him is sprung up no little suspicion"; he must therefore give up all intercourse with them. He must also separate entirely from a certain brother of Bishopsgate Hospital, "by access of whom" he is "variously defamed". He is no longer to shirk Matins, Mass, or other services and conventual duties. In many other ways Merton needed serious reform.(5) The Augustinian General Chapters of that year 1509 had to fine twenty-eight heads of houses for non-attendance; in 1506 there had been only forty-four attendances in person, and those of 1512 and 1515 were never held, probably for want of attendants. That of 1518, at which date our William Salyng was still prior, has left a longer record than any other. It is also the most pitiful; though as early as 1434 the assembled fathers had confessed the necessity for radical reform, "since we are beset with the clamorous protests, from both clergy and layfolk, that almost all the conduct of many houses in our Order hath come to such ill-fame and dissolution that this is become a reproach to the whole Order and its condition is thereby dishonoured in many ways".(6) Things had gone so much farther in those eighty years that Wolsey and the prelates spoke independently, almost in the same words, of "your Order which is in peril, threatened with imminent ruin"; "the lamentable ruin overhanging almost our whole Order, and needing reform from top to bottom".(7) Hence came a scene of startling significance. On one of the last days of the Chapter,

the Prior of Overeys,* with hands and fingers clasped, knelt weeping miserably and expatiated humbly upon the literal observance of our

* Of St Mary Overy, commonly called now St Saviour, Southwark, where John Gower's tomb still remains.

Rule, and, as many thought, he obscurely pleaded for his own new mode of life, with much whispering on the part of almost all. The Presidents and many of the other Fathers, and especially the Lord Prior of Merton, alleging our holy Father Augustine's own words and writings, with other laws and sayings and writings of learned men, answered that all the rest, and he himself, had satisfied the said Rule in its strictest sense—*ad verbum*. When these disputations had filled almost the whole morning, we hastened to the Requiem Mass.

Next day, the question was raised again by

a certain canon of Brynmawr, with a declamation like unto that of the day before; a man of extreme ignorance and certainly one who would fain have aroused quarrels: but almost all the rest cried with one voice and answered him. At the next Chapter, to be held at Oxford, we hope, answer shall be given to any who shall propose such things; there shall be public discussion and, with God's favour, they shall be decided.(8)

If there had been a few determined reformers in this great and influential Order, there might have been such a revival, and such a group of Observants formed, as there was in contemporary France and as there had been earlier in Germany. But the General Chapters seem to have represented always, in spite of the reforms they were willing to vote in word, timidity or even retrogression in deed. Dr Salter notes the sense of unreality which seems to have hung about them.

It is remarkable how rarely the triennial Chapters of the Augustinians and also of the Benedictines are mentioned in medieval records. Episcopal registers are almost silent about them, and even monastic chronicles such as the chronicle of Oseney, the register of Barnwell, or the Annals of Dunstable, all of which proceeded from Augustinian houses, show but little interest in the Chapters of the Order.(9)

CHAPTER LVI

FURTHER EVIDENCE FROM LINCOLN

LET us return now to the Lincoln houses, upon which the Visitors' records show so much light. The other greater houses differed not greatly from those four. Something of the same tale is told by Dorchester, Leicester and Spalding. Among these lesser houses, by Daventry, Humberstone, Huntingdon, Newenham, Nutley, St Neots, Torksey, and Ulverstone. The difficulty is rather one of choice among such a mass of evidence for evils so chronic and widespread. But perhaps no single paragraph is more significant than this from the Spalding Visitation of 1438, which displays the reaction of a strong Bishop like Alnwick to an incident of the kind that modern apologists have repudiated as incredible for very grossness:(1)

Brother Roger Seyvelle, when he is in the company of women, behaves himself very wantonly with them, kissing them and otherwise handling and touching them lasciviously, to the foul scandal of the rest and to the bad example of those that are present. He appeared and makes denial, wherefore he has a term half an hour hence to make his purgation with three of his brethren. He produces William Bostone, Robert Sybsey, Nicholas Suttone; and, having brought them forward, confesses to kissing and abjured such kisses, except in case of pilgrimage, and concerning the remainder he made his purgation. And as a penance for his confessions he has that he shall not drink before Easter in a place where a woman is present, except his brother's wife.(2)

Again, it is most necessary to note the commonly farcical character of "purgation" for which I have already given evidence in my second volume (pp. 285 ff., 490 ff.), but which seems to come out with increasing force in proportion as the whole ecclesiastical machinery works with greater friction and inefficacy. Even the Peterborough abbot's case is scarcely so significant here as the record of Huntingdon, a far smaller house. There, in 1439, the prior is defamed with Maud Clerk and both of her daughters, also with five other women specified by name. Dom Overton also is defamed with Maud Clerk. The prior is accused of constant absence from church services, of neglecting to make his statutory confessions to any confessor, and even of leaving out the words of consecration when he says Mass; a device which, as we know from authors of the period, was sometimes adopted by adulterous priests in the hope that they thus escaped the mortal sin of consecrating with impure hands. The other accusations concern cutting down woods, usurious trading, alienation of jewels and other conventual goods. The accusers specify these things in such exact detail that the Visitor could have had no difficulty in verifying at least so many of them as would warrant a judgment upon the rest. Yet the prior was allowed simply to deny or keep silence as to the greater part of them, and to plead flimsy excuses for almost all the rest (II, 153). One of the most damning, however, he was compelled to admit (p. 154):

As for his apostasy by night in a secular garb and the laying of hands with violence upon divers men, where and when his arm was broken in the struggle, about the feast of St Bartholomew, in the year of our Lord 1436, he confesses that he went out at such a time by night, dressed in his riding cloak and a secular hood of a black hue: he confesses also the struggle and [the use of] violence on both sides.

As for the celebration of Masses during such apostasy with no previous absolution, he confesses that he has celebrated Mass a hundred times since such struggle without obtaining any absolution, for he says that he did not incur irregularity for that reason.

As for Overton, he denied and was ordered to clear himself with three of his brethren. He succeeded in bringing two compurgators only: the ruffianly prior, and the sub-prior, Peter Oclee, who had earlier deposed (p. 50) to the prior's defamation with Maud and one of her daughters, and had added to the account of Overton a defamation with Maud alone (p. 150). Yet the bishop accepted these, for the time at least, and his record stands as follows:

He denies the article and was ordered to clear himself with three of his brethren. Thereafter he cleared himself with Peter Oclee, John Madyngley the prior, and then he abjured the said woman and all familiar intercourse with any person from that house, and was admonished under pain of excommunication to observe his oath, etc. [*sic*].

He likewise went forth in apostasy in a secular garb with the prior at the feast of St Bartholomew. He confesses that he so went forth clad in a secular gown of russet hue, which he put on under the constraint of fear after he went out, for he says that he went out in his surplice only with the other under-clothes of his rule. And, having heard these answers, my lord says that he will take counsel against another time concerning the further process against this Overtone by reason of his confessions.

A further interest attaches to this Huntingdon case, as one of the many in which, where other independent records have survived, we get definite evidence for the incompleteness of what the bishop's clerk has noted in his report.* It is even probable that the omitted cases are sometimes the most startling of all, since the secretive spirit—the merciful omission of *tacenda*—comes out as often in Alnwick's *Register* as in others. Here are two side-lights on Dunstable and Huntingdon which we catch only through chance survival from the fragmentary Augustinian Chapter records.(3) In 1446 it is reported to the Chapter

that at the priory of Dunstable there is a canon, a priest and professed, named Thomas Bledlowe, of great age—about 80 years, a notorious murderer and adulterer who had gone into apostasy three times first for 20 years, then for 6 months, and lastly for a year or more. He had recently returned on account of poverty, and remained cut off from the society of his brethren, wilfully dumb and incorrigible. Because of the horrible enormity of his crimes he is feared, yet he is not imprisoned out of regard for his age.

The Chapter directed that he should be kept in custody at St Osyth's, whose abbot accepted the charge. There is no mention of this in the two reports of the Lincoln Episcopal Visitations, and but for the chance survival elsewhere we should know nothing of this aged and savage criminal returning once and again to his monastery, and filling his brethren with a not unnatural fear. Again, this Chapter record of 1446 tells us how "the Visitors have discovered, by the *detecta* at Huntingdon, that three brethren of that house are vagabonds, and have been so for five years, and the prior is negligent in recalling them:

* I have dealt more fully with this in my second volume (pp. 268–72).

wherefore it is decreed that the prior of St Oswald's, one of the presidents, should go unto that house and enquire and reform and should certify fully to the next Chapter". At this next Chapter, 1446, the notice runs: "It is discovered that from the priory of Huntingdon many brethren have gone forth in apostasy and are wandering over the world [*per orbem terrarum*]"; yet even so nothing is specifically decreed by the Chapter. Here, practically without doubt, we have a most significant explanation of the apparently aimless words which Peter Odee had added at the 1339 Visitation: "Seynt Yves, one of our brethren, is at Hull, and Castre, another, in the county of Devon" (p. 150).

The nunneries of Lincoln diocese present no more favourable picture of discipline than the men's houses. We see more distinctly here, what we find scattered hints of elsewhere, private households within the convents, not, indeed, quite on the Continental scale, but sufficiently marked to show a painful contrast with the theoretically strict community life of a Benedictine sisterhood.(4) There are many clearly marked cases of this kind. Three of these may be summarized here. At Bishop Alnwick's Visitation of Catesby, in 1442, the prioress deposes

that sister Agnes Allesley has six or seven young folk of both sexes that do lie in the dorter; that secular folk have often recourse to the nuns' chambers within the cloister, and talkings and junketings take place there without the knowledge of the prioress; that she herself has four nuns in her household, and there are three other households of nuns within the cloister.

The rest of this record shows how fatal the system was to Benedictine discipline. The Visitation resulted in the suspension of the prioress from the administration of the revenues, but not from her office or authority to rule in all other respects. She was convicted of incontinence with a priest, Sir Taylor, with whom she had been caught in the act by a nun, Agnes Halewa. The peculiar scandal of this appears from other depositions which reveal that Agnes was one of the young nuns whom the prioress sent to make the guests' beds. Agnes complained at having to do such work, because she was young and wished to learn religious discipline. Proceedings were begun against Taylor, but the result is not known. The prioress was further charged with having bribed one of Bishop Gray's clerks to reveal the nuns' depositions at a former Visitation, and had beaten the nuns concerned. She also was accustomed to pull the nuns' veils off and call them beggars and whores, sometimes even in choir. Other charges related to gross dilapidation, and the alienation of property. A nun, Isabel Benet, was charged with having had a child by William Smyth, a former chaplain. She admitted the crime, but denied Smyth's paternity, and was admitted to purgation on that score. It was further revealed that, a few days before the Visitation, she had spent the night at the Austin Friars in Northampton, with whom she had danced and played the lute till midnight, and that she did the same the next night with the Dominicans. It is surprising after this to find that Isabel Benet was one of the two nuns appointed by the bishop to take over the administration of the temporal and spiritual goods of the convent, a function they were still performing in 1445, the other administrator being Agnes Allesley, who had danced with her in the friars' convents.

Elstow was a nunnery in which there were five households. It was visited in 1422, 1432 and 1443; the records of these indirectly reveal the kinds of disorders which were discovered. In 1442 it was ordered that no nun who was convicted, defamed, or suspect of incontinence should hold any office, especially that of gate-keeper, until she had been admitted to purgation. Also, the senior nuns were to supervise the dormitory, to see that the nuns went to bed at the proper times before and after midnight, and rose for divine service. No nun was to bring any secular or religious man secretly to her chamber, nor keep them long, if they did come. It was also stated that married boarders had harmed the morals of the house, and that no boarders over twelve years old were to be received without special licence. In 1432 one injunction stated that "since the mutual cohabitation of secular persons, especially of the married, and from the performance of conjugal rites between the same, carnal concupiscence may easily be fomented even in religious women" all secular boarders were to be removed except males up to ten years old, and females up to fourteen. It was noted also that "Dame Petronilla" had often been guilty of fleshly lapse, and was then in apostasy; she was to be brought back and punished.

She may be the Petronilla Gauthorpe present in 1443, when ten of the thirteen nuns reported "omnia bene", and there were no grave detecta. The abbesses at each Visitation retained office till their deaths. A third nunnery of Lincoln diocese was Godstow, with four households; of this house there survive the injunctions of 1432, the appointment of a Commission to visit in 1434, and a Visitation report of 1445. The injunctions are much concerned with the access of Oxford students, which is wholly forbidden. No nun is to receive any secular person in her chamber for recreation [*solacia*], for the Oxford students say that they can have every kind of *solacium* that they desire with the nuns. Prison for a year is decreed for any nun who conveys any token, gift or letter to or from any secular. All doors giving access to the outer precincts when the cloister is locked, are to be blocked up. All beds in the nuns' lodging are to be removed from their chambers except those needed for children.

There remains an important question for our consideration. Even for Lincoln diocese, the Visitation records which have come down to us are very fragmentary. How far are we to take these as a sample of the whole? Is the picture they give us darker, or more favourable, than the actual facts? Or may we take it as fairly accurate, not very different from what we should form from the whole mass of such documents if they had come down to us? My own belief is that Lincoln diocese was in this century, as in earlier ages, rather above the average in discipline, even if we consider England alone. Of its superior regularity to any but a few dioceses on the Continent I feel no doubt whatever. I have indicated in my second volume (pp. 255–8, 478–9) how little regard was paid, in most quarters, to the disciplinary commands of Innocent III. England stands high above the Continent in visitatorial care, as in general social orderliness. Yet, quite apart from literary evidence, we may prove the weakness of the system even in England by comparing carefully one set of official records with another.

The setting up of one Provincial Chapter for the whole of England, according to the provisions of Benedict XII published in 1336, was essentially a measure intended to effect reform. It first provided for reform from outside the monastery, if it would not reform itself from within. But because in actual effect it required the Order to reform itself by using this administrative machinery, it was necessary that there should be a will to reform, sufficiently general and influential, to direct the machinery towards this end. It is here that the extant records of the Provincial Chapters, scanty as they are, seem to show that this will to reform, with any general desire to work the new machinery, was very largely absent. The attendance of heads of houses at the four Chapters of which complete records survive provides evidence of this. Mr Pantin has brought this out in his paper on the *Chapters of the English Black Monks*.(5) He writes:

> Even when the Chapters were duly held, attendance was painfully perfunctory. Strictly speaking, all heads of houses, abbots or priors, were bound to attend the Chapter, unless they had a lawful excuse, such as illness; but from the first the personal attendance was poor. In 1225, only fifteen abbots were present,* and in a list which belongs either to 1253 or 1255 fifteen abbots were personally present, twenty-five sent excuses by a proctor, and eleven were altogether absent. The important Chapter of 1277 did, indeed, draw an attendance of forty-five abbots, but in the beginning of the next century, the attendance was worse than ever. It was particularly unfair, when the greater prelates neglected to come, and the lesser, but more enthusiastic, prelates were put to the trouble of attending, in vain. The true remedy for the absence of the prelates was the sending of proctors; this was soon understood, but at first the proctor's chief business was, apparently, simply to explain his master's excuse for absence (p. 220).

And, again,

> most of the abbots were apparently either inferior old men, or busy feudal lords, who could ill spare the time or expense of a journey, say, from Chester or Tavistock to Oxford or London. Therefore Chapters were constantly breaking down, owing to bad attendance, and had to be prorogued, with a waste of time and patience which penalised the faithful few who came at the first calling. This was a vicious circle; few would care to risk attending an abortive Chapter.

In the early fourteenth century, the meetings seem to have ceased altogether for some years. With Benedict XII's reforms of 1336 onwards, the system revived again. But in 1340 only nine abbots and three priors were present in person, while fourteen abbots and ten priors were not even represented by proctors, and were therefore declared contumacious.

* Out of about sixty (G.G.C.).

In 1343, eleven abbots and two priors were present in person, while one abbot and two priors were absent without sufficient excuse. In 1423 seven abbots and eight priors were present in person; thirty-one were represented by proctors; eight priors were absent, and four were declared contumacious. In 1426 only five abbots and three priors were present in person, while thirty abbots and fourteen priors were represented by proctors.(6)

As regards the Visitations carried out by Visitors appointed at each triennial Chapter, there is little in the extant reports to suggest that they effected any substantial reform. Indeed, except in regard to about four houses, the Visitors purported to find that no reform was required.(7) In 1343 it transpired that only three out of the ten Visitors appointed by the Chapter of 1340 had carried out their visitations, though it is true that two had been prevented by death. It is in the Visitors' reports to the Chapters of 1423 and 1426 that we are able to make something like a direct comparison with the Lincoln Visitations.(8) In 1423 the proctor of the Abbot of Ramsey said he had visited all the monasteries in the Lincoln diocese, he "affirmed without doubt that therein flourished a discipline conformable to Holy Religion, so that he found greater cause for worthily extolling the monasteries, all and several, with the panegyric of praise, than for reforming anything in them with the file of rough correction". And the Prior of Ely reported of Ramsey in terms even more laudatory.(9) In 1426 the proctor of the Abbot of Peterborough reported that he had found all things ordered well and honestly, except for a few unimportant matters which he had left for amendment to the fathers of the monasteries in question. The proctor of the Prior of Ely found that at Peterborough Religion was commendably observed, and everything else governed "under happy rule". Unless we suppose that during the next six years a rapid deterioration took place, which grew worse by the time of Bishop Alnwick, it is impossible to attach any value to these formal reports, either of the Benedictine houses generally, or of Ramsey and Peterborough in particular.

In view of these reports of the houses in the Lincoln diocese, one wonders how grave were the disorders that Visitors elsewhere thought worthy of notice, but by no means suitable to disclose before the whole Chapter. Such were certain findings at Malmesbury and Abbotsbury reported in 1423, and at Abingdon, as reported in 1426. But at the same time it should be remembered that we must take into account differences in zeal, perspicacity, and candour among the different Visitors, as well as circumstances which in one place might promote concealment or connivance, and in another the opposite.

The untrustworthiness of the generally laudatory reports of the monastic Visitors is further supported by the records of Henry V's attempt to reform the monasteries. The abuses aimed at by the Articles of reform proposed by the King in 1421 are all among the irregularities disclosed during the next twenty-five years or so at the Lincoln Visitations. So, again, with the letter attributed to Henry VI in [1450], in which, speaking of the "grete abusions" which he himself has observed during his progresses throughout the realm, he orders the heads of monasteries to attend *in person* at the next General Chapter, and to take in hand the required reforms. Here we have a direct reference to that apathy which caused most of the abbots and priors to attend the Chapters only by proxy, as a plain hindrance to reform.

One among the miscellaneous documents provides a basis for direct comparison with the Lincoln Visitations, if the attributed date is correct, as seems probable, i.e. 1441–4. This is a letter from the Bishop of Lincoln to the Abbot of Chertsey, asking him to release the Abbot of Bardney from the payment of £20, due for certain contributions, apparently in connection with the General Chapter. He gives as a reason the extreme impoverishment of Bardney Abbey. This is strictly in accordance with the state of affairs disclosed at the Visitations of January and March, 1438, and of March and October 1440. Actually the visitations reveal a condition of extreme disorder, and the bishop expressly stated that one of the reasons for his Visitation of March 1440 was the report that "the Abbot, by his sore infirmities had become so powerless that he is insufficient for the rule of himself and of the monastery in things spiritual and temporal". If this letter was indeed written shortly after this visitation, his description of the abbot as "vir satis prudens et circumspectus" seems unduly complimentary; for there was one serious charge against him, which seems to have been substantiated, and that was of causing blank parchments to be sealed with the convent seal without the knowledge of the community. However, in view of the object of the bishop's letter, it is comprehensible that he should represent the abbot as a man worthy of consideration. And in fact it seems to have been his infirmities that were responsible for the extreme disorders of his abbey, rather than any wilful laxity and misgovernment.

It may be added here that the General Chapter Statutes of 1444 give considerable corroboration to the general picture of laxity and disorder presented by the Lincoln Visitations.(10)

All this official evidence supplies, by itself, a sufficient answer to the contention that nothing could have been seriously wrong at St Albans between 1465 and 1476, because we have record that the Chapter visited it in the ordinary routine—or at least proposed to visit it—four times during those years.(11)

CHAPTER LVII

NORWICH AND PRÉMONTRÉ

NEXT to the Lincoln records, for fulness of detailed evidence, come the *Visitations of the Diocese of Norwich*, published by the Camden Society in 1888. These consist of one Visitation by Bishop Goldwell in 1492, and a later series by Bishop Nikke or Nix, at intervals of six years from 1514 to 1532. They were edited by Dr Jessopp, an enthusiastic antiquary whose long and rhetorical preface is full of blunders, and can only mislead readers as to the true historical significance of his text.(1) The evidence of the witnesses, though less detailed, has the advantage over Alnwick's of stretching over a somewhat longer period, and with fewer gaps. On the other hand, Nikke cannot be compared with Alnwick for eminence and episcopal efficiency. He was indeed a zealous persecutor of the Lollards, and repaired part of the cathedral roof. But Godwin, in his Catalogue of the Bishops, records briefly "he hath the report of a vicious and dissolute liver"; and on one page of his *Visitations* we find the disreputable Prior of Wymondham, threatened with the bishop's displeasure, retorting: "Tell both my Lord and my ladie, for I care nott" (p. 99).(2)

The wealthiest and most powerful house in the diocese of Norwich was Bury St Edmunds, with twice the income of the cathedral monastery. But this, as we have seen, had bought exemption and fought Visitation literally to the death—but to the death of the bishop—in the mid-fourteenth century. In 1381 the discipline could not have been very efficient. In 1433, Bishop Alnwick, the future Bishop of Lincoln, attempted to assert visitatorial rights, but (as Abbot Curteys was able to boast afterwards) "the blessed God, who deserteth not them that hope in Him, fulfilled His mercy upon us, graciously restraining the Bishop's malice".(3)

Castleacre also, a considerable house, was exempt because it was of the Cluniac Order. Next to Bury, naturally, came Norwich. Here, as in many other English cathedrals, the bishop was nominally abbot, and the prior was actually working head. We have one Visitation here by Bishop Goldwell in 1492, and four by Bishop Nikke from 1514 to 1532.

Bishop Goldwell reported the following faults, among others:

Women sleep within the priory precincts, contrary to its statutes and the Rule of Religion. The monastery jewels are sold....The Subsacristan lavishly wastes his moneys, and goes out of the priory at night, and sits with the tailor and his wife beyond due hours: and the aforesaid tailor and his wife dwell within the priory precincts, to its great scandal. Certain jewels, offered by the Lady de Blakeney to the Blessed Virgin on the High Altar, have been alienated by the Sacristan. The service in the infirmary is bad, and the sick are most evilly treated there. The pensions of the Harpingham, Wackering, and Tye chantries are not paid. Layfolk sit at table with the monks and brethren. The choir-service is not attended decently by the monks. The monks sit and walk within the Cathedral and its precincts, and talk too much [there] with unhonest and ill famed women. ...The priory doors and gates are not closed at night. No monks are kept to study at the University of Oxford, and this to the great scandal and expense of the priory.

The bishop suspected that benefactors' souls were being defrauded by the monks' negligence, of those Masses for which their endowments had been paid.(4) The next recorded Visitation, by Bishop Nikke's commissary in 1514, shows how little a bishop could keep his monks in check (pp. 72 ff.). Goldwell in 1492 had insisted upon the prohibition proclaimed by his predecessor Bateman, and no doubt by a series of bishops from the thirteenth century downwards, against the presence of women within the priory buildings. But we find one of the first witnesses in 1514 complaining that "it disgusts him to see how young women of suspicious character have access to the cloister, the hostelry, and the infirmary". In this he is supported by two brethren, while others reveal more specific faults of the same kind. The sub-prior and two others "are suspected with the wives of the sub-prior's servants". One monk had recently fathered a child by a servant-girl in the city. "In the hostelry, the brethren are wont to dance, by the Hostillar's favour, at night even to noon." The bishop's commissary reports: "Religion and chastity are not kept here, by the sub-prior's fault, who sets an evil example." There was plenty of unsatisfactory evidence on other points. This cathedral priory, with its huge revenues and its thirty-eight monks, had no schoolmaster. Some of the buildings both in Norwich and in the dependent houses were ruinous: the priory was in debt to the extent of about £2000 modern money. One of the monks, who was also Prior of St Leonard's hospital, had failed to produce his accounts: so also had the prior of one of the cells. Even at the cathedral itself, "the officials have given no account of their office for two years, and no man knoweth how the monastery stands". The chantry Masses were neglected, especially those of Bishop Walter's chantry. "Divine service by day and night is insufficiently performed by the brethren, and especially by the Sub-prior and the Third Prior. A spurious document has been furtively signed with the Priory seal." The only man punished for all these irregularities was the peculating Prior of St Leonard's, who was deposed and forbidden to occupy any office in future. Six years later, in 1520, the monastery was out of debt and the prior was making, but had not yet completed, an inventory of its property and jewels. Only eight boys were kept at the monks' free-school, instead of the statutory thirteen. One of the young monks, aged nineteen, was examined, but "he understood nothing of what he then read at our bidding"; or, as the scribe puts it in a marginal note, "he has not been instructed in any rule of grammar". Another was living alone by himself as parson of Martham, a dangerous relaxation, strictly forbidden by repeated statutes. On the whole, however, this Visitation of 1520 finds comparatively little fault with the cathedral monks.

For 1526, the record breaks off at two important points, where the context seems to indicate serious accusations (pp. 199, 204). There are ugly stories which Dr Jessopp puffs away as evident slanders. Yet that theory would be scarcely more creditable to the priory than to suppose that the witnesses were reporting honestly to the Visitor. "The senior brethren come not to Matins"; the Precentor "hath attended scarce once in two years". The Prior of the Yarmouth cell complains that a monk lately with him frequented dice and other unhonest games, and murmured against his corrections. At Lynn also they play at dice and cards. For "the Prior [of Norwich] is wont to send incorrigible and rebellious monks to the dependent cells". Accounts are not duly rendered by the Obedientiaries. The ex-Chamberlain "took the income of his office for half a year after his expulsion". The cloister is not rain-proof, and ruin is feared there. The fourth prior (who became, later on, prior) "seeth that Religion beginneth to perish by reason of the non-observance of ceremonies; for the younger monks contemn such observation". Of Shelton, the chamberlain, it is reported that he had not been punished for his "grievous crimes and abominable sins"—*nephanda peccata*. He was sent to do penance at Yarmouth where he "lived far more licentiously than at Norwich, haunting the town daily at dice and cards". The cellarer deposes that

> the Sub-prior is easy and remiss in relaxation of the penances enjoined by the Third, Fourth and Fifth Priors, a facility which gives boldness to the juniors in not observing the penalties enjoined upon them. He saith also that the younger monks, after their promotion to the priesthood, obtain the Prior's leave to go on pilgrimage or to visit their friends; by occasion thereof they squander evilly that which hath either been given unto them by their friends or offered at the celebration of their fast Mass; and thus they come back destitute.

Brethren are not adequately instructed for choir-service. "The fragments from the refectory table are not distributed among the poor, but among others who have no need, by fault of the Almoner." There is a violent suspicion that money has been stolen from Doctor Reppis and Flowerdew. "The cloister and dormitory doors are never closed; and boys and layfolk frequent the dormitory."(5) The third prior, one of those who are nominally responsible for the conventual discipline, is reported to have gone out at night disguised as a layman: "he was caught by the cellarer, whom he besought and induced to conceal this fact". His brother, the choir-shirking Precentor, "hath a chamber and a bed therein, contrary to ancient custom, by occasion whereof women resort unto his bedchamber". Another is reported to have been his associate in such matters.

The Visitation of 1532 "is evidently no more than a fragment, and defective at the beginning and the end" (p. 262). It records use of forbidden linen sheets, "an excessive number of hounds in the priory, to the detriment of almsgiving", and the Church with other buildings in sore need of repair—"patiuntur ruinam". Accounts are not regularly rendered: serfs are freed without due registration, which means that their ransom money is being embezzled somewhere. Two in the Yarmouth cell are insubordinate, because their prior "would fain have reformed them in the matter of dice and hazard and other unhonest games". "The juniors apply themselves not to study, but are bent rather upon pleasure and sitting up at night. Dom John Kirby is suspect; he hath converse with many folk by reason of which [*cujus praetexta*] ill-fame ariseth, to the scandal of the monastery."(6) The fifth prior, one of those specially entrusted with discipline, "is light and remiss among the juniors, with whom he is too familiar and holdeth idle vigils and communications,* by occasion whereof the juniors come late to divine service; and at times jewels and precious stones are subtracted from the vestiary": for the fifth prior is also sub-sacristan. The precentor himself causes scandal by his behaviour in his private lodgings. "He is justly deprived of his chamber; for there the juniors congregate and waste time and talk together: he seldom cometh to divine service [of which he is the nominal conductor]; nor doth he ever frequent the refectory." Scholars are not kept at Oxford (as they should be by statute, reinforced by a recent decree of the prior himself). One of the monks at the Lynn cell "is much burdened with debt". One of the Yarmouth brethren "is in debt to many folk and is altogether unlearned"—*omnino indoctus*. All this does not prevent six of the younger monks from reporting "that all is done laudably, in spiritual and in temporal things". The bishop, "for certain reasons of his own", prorogued the Visitation.

There we have, in broad outlines, the difficulties and the lapses of the Norwich community on the eve of the Reformation. It shows the difficulty of exercising real pressure from within and without. And this will come out still more plainly if we regard this record from another angle, by tracing in greater detail the careers of two of the most prominent Obedientiaries, Thomas and John Sall. In 1514, Thomas Sall is precentor, and comes fourteenth on the list. He testifies to

* Vigiliis et aliis rebus non decentibus.

financial irregularities, and to the suspicion of incontinence against three brethren. On the other hand, he himself is accused of withholding moneys which he ought to pay. In 1520, he is among the fourteen who report *omnia bene*, though in fact one brother violates the statutes by living alone at Martham. In 1526,

Dom Richard Lopham says that he heard Dom Robert Frammyngham saying that Dom Thomas Sall, Third Prior, left his monk's habit and went into the city by night in lay clothing; but he knoweth not what he did there. Dom Robert Frammyngham, examined upon the deposition of Dom Richard Lopham, says that he heard from Dom John Martin that Dom Thomas Sall stayed so long in the city; and that, changing his habit, he returned in the night to the priory. He was caught by the Cellarer, who, at his request, granted that he would conceal his deed.

"He is disobedient to the sub-prior." He "quarrelled with Doctor Reppis, saying *that he wolde take him on the face*; and on slight occasion (or rather on none) he calleth him *wastour*".* Later comes the direct testimony of the above-mentioned Martin, who, after dealing with John on a few other points, begins (p. 201): "And also Dom Thomas Sall, Third Prior"—[at this point there is a vacant space in the MS., suggestive of the hesitation and reticence which such records often show at awkward points, after which the scribe proceeds]. "He saith also that it would be expedient to remove the tailor's wife from the monastery, for the avoidance of scandal." Next, Thomas Sall himself is called upon for evidence. "He saith that the tailor's wife (that is, *the wardroper's wiff*) hath suspicious access to Dr Reppis, and embraceth him in the presence of others, to the evil example and manifest scandal of the monastery and of other folk." A later witness (p. 201) agrees with the need for her removal, "yet he believeth not that any thing hath been committed between the Doctor and her". One later witness deposes to a scene between Sall and Lopham which Dr Jessopp tries to rule out on the sole plea that it is a "filthy story...upon the face of it incredible".

* This Doctor of Divinity, in 1520, was Prior of the cell at Yarmouth. In 1514 he had preached the Visitation sermon for the Bishop's Commentary, on the text: "Purge out the old leaven" (p. 71). He finally became Bishop of Norwich (chap. XIX).

In 1532, Sall was one of three who were reported for un-Benedictine dress, though in this case the irregularity seems to have been only in his shoes (p. 263). He was no longer third prior, but infirmarer and one of the penitentiaries, responsible for his brethren's consciences in the confessional. He suspects one brother of incontinence. He complains that the juniors are quarrelsome, and "too wordy, meddling with all cases and matters as captains, aiming at reforming and ruling all except their own selves". The bishop notes that he, "having valuables [*jocalia*] which pertain to that office, setteth many to pawn without the consent of his fellow-monks" (p. 269). He still "absents himself from Church services"; moreover, "he hath places and buildings which he frequents for practising his own arts, by pretext whereof ariseth ill-fame and scandal through those who resort to such places" (p. 267; cf. chap. xx). The editor seems to interpret this as alchemy or sorcery: but we must note the "scandal through those who resort", together with the complaints that "he hath a silken cushion that pertaineth to the High Altar", and that "there are more boarders than usual dwelling within the Precincts and in the chambers belonging to the Obedientiaries" (p. 266): also that this exact phrase, "cujus praetextu oritur infamia", has occurred a few lines earlier in connection with the "suspect" Kirby's "converse with many folk". Moreover, he is explicitly charged later with encouraging waste of time and idle talk in his chamber (p. 267). This seems to point rather to the suggestion that Thomas, like John, had his own rooms in which he entertained unmonastic company (pp. 75ff.). John Sall seems to be the brother of Thomas. In 1514 he complains of financial irregularities, but he himself is withholding moneys which he ought to pay. He is singled out by the bishop as one of the chief offenders in the matter of costume, "wearing linen shirts and long hosen closed-in": in other words the costume which was regarded by moralists as of doubtful decency even for lay-folk. In 1520 he does not appear. In 1526, though as precentor he is nominally in charge of all the services, he is the worst shirker of Matins; "he hath scarce come to them once in two years". Again, "He absenteth himself not only from Matins but also Masses and the Canonical Hours." "Moreover he beareth a silken purse gauded with gold....On holy-days he weareth a bonnet of satin" (p. 198). He is responsible for the ruinous state of the cloister roof, which is no longer watertight. "He hath a chamber deputed unto himself, contrary to the ancient custom, to the scandal of the monastery. Therein he oftentimes passeth the night, therefore evil suspicion is begotten against him; and in his absence he left the keys with Dom Robert Nottell, unto whom (as is believed) women have resorted." Such private chambers with beds were forbidden by the bishop; others have obediently removed their beds, but "J. Sall still keepeth his own."

He weareth sometimes shoes fastened with red silk points, at other times dancing-shoes, and, meanwhiles, long tight hosen with doublet made in inordinate fashion like unto laymen, a pernicious example to the young brethren, especially since this John, even in the Prior's presence, doth not blush to lift up his garments and show to all men his fashion of walking.(7)...He payeth ill the pensions due to his brethren, and [the witness] believeth that he is deep in debt both to the brethren and to strangers, and that it would make much for the profit of the monastery if J. Sall would make up and display the bill of his debts.

"There is a report and a violent suspicion that he stole the money of the Doctor and Flowerdew." It was complained that "the Prior was too remiss in punishment of Dom J. Shelton and Dom J. Sall for their grievous and manifest offences: for he favoureth them too much" (p. 201). Yet the only punishment inflicted by the bishop was that Sall was deposed from his office of *Communiarius*, or steward of the household.

In 1532 (p. 265) he is precentor, yet he is also one of the four who are found to "wear shoes contrary to the Rule". He excuses his brethren who sleep in linen sheets (which are constantly prohibited by statute) "because they cannot provide themselves with blankets", here, in the centre of the woollen industry! He "cometh rarely to choir, to the evil example of the rest". He "hath a cushion of silk that pertaineth to the High Altar".

Next in importance to Norwich—if not even more important—was Walsingham, second only to Canterbury as a pilgrimage church in Britain. Erasmus describes this from outside in a famous chapter of his *Colloquies*: the Visitations show it from inside. The comperta of 1494 reveal disorder and general laxity, but it was in 1514 that the grossest abuses came to light. The chief offender was the prior, William Lowthe, who was abetted by some half-dozen canons. He had been elected in 1503 while a canon of the house, so that his misdeeds were probably of no merely recent origin. He kept the wife of John Smith as his concubine, and enriched both her and her husband not merely with the revenues of the house, but with the money and jewels offered at the famous shrine of Our Lady. These he stole at night himself. Mrs Smith was known as "the Prior's Lady", and kept the keys of malt-house and granary; she went on pilgrimage to Canterbury on one of the prior's horses, and because William Rase called her a whore he had to apologize publicly for it in Chapter. The prior had also committed manslaughter by striking a serf so that he died of it. He had threatened to build a prison for the canons who opposed him, and before the Visitation had several times threatened the canons about their depositions, warning them that he would still rule after the bishop had gone. The upshot was that Lowthe was forced to resign. He was provided with a pension and suitable maintenance. In 1520 he was Prior of Westacre, where complaints were made of his "sensuality". There is no note of any penance for his six chief associates. Lowthe was succeeded by Richard Vowell, Prior of Leighs Parva, Essex.* In 1520 some seven or nine canons were rebellious, refusing to consent to the sealing of a proxy to excuse the prior's absence from the General Chapter summoned by Wolsey, and also refusing to admit new statutes promulgated therein. Their penance was for seven days to take the lowest places in choir, and on the following Friday to fast on bread and beer, and, all kneeling before the high altar, to say five "Our Fathers", and humbly ask pardon. In 1526 and 1532 the complaints are few and not grave.

Westacre. The comperta of 1494 reveal a certain measure of internal strife. The gravest offender seems to have been the sub-prior, Edmund Lichfield, whose mode of life was rather that of a country squire than of a Religious. He neither kept the Rule nor celebrated the obligatory Masses, the Chapter Mass and that of the B.V.M. He kept a rabbit farm, had swans on the

* L. and P. xii (i), 1330 (54).

lake from which he made presents to the local gentry, and was, in short, wholly occupied in temporal affairs. He used abusive language to the prior, and his violence had caused several canons to leave the house. He makes no further appearance. In 1514 a number of charges are made against the prior in regard to financial mismanagement and the misappropriation of funds. He was also suspect with a Mrs Smith. The bishop ordered him to remove the woman and her husband, and to pay certain moneys owing to the brethren. In spite of the considerable evidence of his misrule thus gleaned on June 5, he was put in charge of Walsingham a few weeks later when the prior there was suspended on account of his misdeeds. As we have seen, the latter had succeeded to Westacre by 1520, when the Visitation showed that things had grown worse under his rule. In 1526 William Wingfield was prior; he survived not only to be the last prior, but also to be deprived of his secular benefice under Queen Mary for having married. No charges are made against him. John Barber is noted of having been caught by seculars committing sodomy, of which crime he had been often charged before.(8) He had been a canon since at least 1514, was noted for adultery at the Royal Visitation, and signed the surrender. In 1526 it was deposed that Richard Anger, sub-prior, gave food, which should have gone to the poor, to two women whom the prior had recently excluded from the monastery. He does not appear again. In 1532 there were no grave charges. Two canons deposed that no light burned before the Blessed Sacrament—a seemingly small matter, yet really very significant of the irreligious laxity of the community.

Next in importance was St Benet Hulme, whose abbot was mitred, and therefore of the House of Lords, and whose revenues were so considerable that, with those of Hickling Priory, they formed sufficient endowment for the Bishopric of Norwich from 1536 onwards. Here the comperta of 1494 reveal general laxity, alienation of property, and neglect of Masses for Sir John Fastolf, a great benefactor of the abbey. In 1514 the abbot was John Redyng, who had been chaplain to the former abbot. He was accused of rendering no accounts, and of being responsible for the loss of certain valuables while the abbacy was vacant. He was also involved in a conspiracy to reveal nothing at the

Visitation. From another source we know that he was deprived by Wolsey in 1517, in spite of an appeal from the Duke of Suffolk, who said he was innocent of the charges brought against him.(9) The prior, John Tacolston, had told the brethren to reveal nothing. He was suspect with several women, especially two married women (named). They resorted to his chamber, and he to certain of them at Aldeby. He was still prior in 1520, but makes no further appearance. One monk deposed that often there was no one fit to say Mass. In 1520 and 1526 John Salcot (or Capon) was abbot, and though certain abuses were disclosed, there were no grave personal charges. It is curious that during this period there should be the only record of a definite attempt by the bishop to correct by punishment.(10) It appeared that William Bynham rarely rose for matins, pretending to be sick, though he ate and drank as if he were well. The bishop ordered him to prison in his palace, but relented at the abbot's intercession so long as Bynham should reform himself. In 1532 William Reppes (the Dr Reppes of Norwich) had been abbot for two years. So far as the records go, there would appear to have been considerable deterioration since Salcot's rule. There was a gross neglect of Masses, and of things pertaining to the decencies of divine service, e.g. the wine provided for Mass was sour and not fitting (which may mean that it had ceased to be "valid matter"). A multitude of dogs consumed what should have served as alms for the poor; this had been disclosed in 1526, and an injunction issued. Four monks were said to know no grammar, and to be scarcely able to read. Three had been in the monastery at least since 1526, and one at least twelve years. The sick were neglected, and one monk had died in consequence. Boys slept in the dormitory with the monks. Such are some of the depositions. The abbot acknowledged a debt of over £600, equivalent to about £12,000 to-day. Many of the community are named as responsible for the various abuses, but there is no mention of any punishment.

The abbey of Wymondham is next in importance; and here, in 1514, the bishop found perhaps the worst condition of all. I have summarized this and the subsequent Visitations elsewhere; here I need only add that this brief summary omits two important facts. One, that some improvement took place under a distinguished abbot, Bishop Suffragan and master of St Thomas More. The other that we have here an incident far less infrequent in the Middle Ages than is popularly imagined. Dom Ixworth deposed, "that Dom John Richers revealed the confession of this deponent"; and the bishop issues no injunction on that point (p. 100).

Many other houses supply evidence of relaxed discipline, immorality, and comparative or complete impunity.(11) But perhaps the most significant instance is that of Butley. There is no grave moral offence, but a forgery of priests' Orders, in which two monks were concerned, yet with no punishment recorded. But other details there show the powerlessness or slackness of the bishop to reform even the most obvious defects, where one would think amendment could most easily have been insisted on. There was no teacher of grammar in 1494, 1514, and 1532, and no student at the university in 1520, 1526, and 1532. In 1514 the prior admitted that the monastery buildings and manors were ruinous; in 1520 the church was ruinous and rain fell in the refectory; in 1526 the lead of the church roof let in rain, and the roof-beams were rotten; in 1532 the dilapidation of the chapter-house is expressly mentioned in addition to that of the church. In 1514 the dilapidation of choir-books was said to hinder the celebration of divine service; at the next three Visitations they still remained unrepaired. In 1520 six canons reported that there was no infirmary; in 1526 the sick were given no proper food; in 1532 they had neither food nor beds nor doctor (except at their own expense), and the sub-prior had made away with the pewter mugs given by Sir William Pakenham for the use of the sick.

Redman's Premonstratensian Visitations give us far less detailed evidence from the witnesses than either Lincoln or Norwich; but they have three great advantages. In the first place, they give us evidence for an Exempt Order, and enable us to compare a vicar general's discipline with that of a bishop. Secondly, they give us greater unity of action; and, thirdly, longer continuity.(12) For they record the work of a single Visitor over a period of twenty-seven years, and thus surpass in length of time even the magnificent Register of Odo Rigaldi at Rouen. Moreover, Redman was a prelate distinguished for pastoral activity in an age of notoriously non-resident bishops. He held successively the sees of St Asaph, Exeter and Ely, in conjunction with the abbacy of Shap and the post of vicar for the Abbot General of Prémontré. Thus Redman visited not as bishop but as abbot and vicar from headquarters: yet he had episcopal experience to guide him, and, to some indirect extent, episcopal authority. Though this simultaneous tenure of the well-endowed Shap with his bishoprics rendered him an abbot commendatory, and thus an example of that "leprosy" which began to take real root in England only a few years before the Dissolution, we cannot compare this with the scandals of that system on the Continent. We have here a hard-working prelate, even exceptionally conscientious for his age; so that, if we find him granting points to manifest sin, it was his impotence, and not his will, that consented. But those concessions are in fact very startling, for the continuity of this long series (together with the few Chapter records which are printed in the same collection) enables the student to pursue the sinner's career in many cases from year to year, though in many other cases the clue breaks off disappointingly. The most frequent punishment is banishment for a stated period to another house. An examination of the houses to which culprits are to be sent reveals no clear plan; certainly there was no intention of choosing what seem to be the better regulated houses as being more suitable for the reform of offenders. The only discernible rule seems to have been that not more than one offender from each house should be sent to the same house for correction, and there are only three exceptions to this. Altogether about fifty-nine sentences of banishment were given. About twenty-one of these were actually carried into effect. In two instances it is uncertain whether they were or not. But thirty-six of the sentences were certainly not effectual. In most instances the Visitation report contains the evidence of what happened. Sometimes a sentence is immediately revoked at the intercession of abbot and convent, or in hope of the culprit's amendment. Often it is given expressly as subject to being determined otherwise by the General Chapter. Sometimes the actual sentence is recorded only in the reports of the Chapters, and in some instances where sentence is given for five or ten years in some other house, a scrutiny of the lists of inmates of both houses at relevant times will show whether the sentence was or was not carried into effect.

About fifty offenders either retained their offices or benefices with cure,* or were subsequently promoted to them. Among the latter are five who became abbots, and five who became priors.

In addition to the large measure of impunity enjoyed by individuals guilty of grave offences, there is evidence of that more general impunity which is illustrated by the Visitor's failure to enforce his injunctions. The brevity of the reports, and their demonstrable incompleteness in other respects, make it evident that the occurrence of such positive evidence is largely fortuitous and incomplete. To take a single instance: at St Radegund's, in 1482, "we saw with our own eyes that the monastery would be in ruin unless this be immediately remedied by repair". Yet, in spite of orders repeated at three subsequent Visitations, in 1500 "the whole monastery, as we saw with our own eyes, was very ruinous, beyond all others".† Similar examples could be given which relate to excessive drinking, wandering abroad, wearing knives, the failure to present accounts, and so forth.

There are some ninety to a hundred offenders of various sorts named in the records (besides those involved where general immorality and other abuses are found to flourish); and it is possible here only to deal with a representative selection. At Cockersand in December 1489 John Skypton was convicted of incontinence with Elena Wilson, and given forty days' penance and seven years at Sulby. In April 1491 he was still at Cockersand and had been promoted to cellarer. In 1502 he became abbot. John Bebe was a novice at Dale in 1491. In 1494 he was deacon and sub-sacrist and was convicted of incontinence with a named woman by whom he had a child. He was given forty days' penance and seven years at Halesowen. This was suspended till the General Chapter, which in 1495 sent him to Sulby, where he appeared in 1497. He was back at Dale as cantor in 1500,

* The Premonstratensians, by special privilege, were allowed to serve their own appropriated parish churches, so that a brother might be either cloistered in the monastery or resident outside as parish priest.

† Since the houses are arranged alphabetically throughout vols. II and III of *Collectanea Anglo-Premonstratensia,* all my facts can be easily verified thus or through the index.

and was abbot at the Surrender. William Kyrlew was cellarer of Lavendon when in 1482 he was gravely defamed of incontinence with a named woman, and of alienating goods by gifts to his relatives. He was allowed to purge himself of the former, but was ordered to make full restitution in respect of the latter. By 1491 he had become abbot, and in 1503 was elected Abbot of Langley, on which occasion he is commended as "a man certainly prudent and discreet, of praiseworthy circumspection both in spiritual and in temporal things, very commendable in his life, learning and manners". In 1514 he was summoned to appear before the Chapter in the matter of "certain articles concerning the reformation and health of his soul", i.e. questions of morality or faith. At St Radegund's John Newington was in 1488 excommunicated as apostate and a sower of discord, and said to have been often excommunicated before. In 1492 he was abbot. In 1497 the whole community charged him with the gravest enormities, but the Visitor suspended the investigation of them in the hope that there would be reform. In 1500 he was accused of incontinence with prostitutes and suspect women whom he brought into his lodging and on whom he bestowed monastic goods; also of frequenting taverns on Sundays and feasts, where he indulged in scurrilous and filthy talk. There is no hint of any punishment. At Welbeck Richard Rolston was in May 1488 convicted of incontinence with a named woman, and given forty days' penance and three years at another house not specified. In August 1491 he was at Welbeck, but may have spent three years elsewhere. He is not in the 1494 list, and in 1497 is marked "licentiatus", i.e. he has leave of absence, probably as priest in one of the appropriated parishes. He is not in the 1500 list, but in 1504 he appears as Abbot of Wendling.

Other examples of promoted culprits may be noted. At Blanchland in 1485 (or 1486) John Forest was convicted of incontinence and of having children thereby. He may be the same as John Durham, canon of Shap, who, for reasons not stated, was transferred here in 1475. He was ordered to go to Shap within seven days, but he appears in all the later Blanchland lists, and in 1497 was Vicar of Kyrkharle. At Cockersand in December 1489 Wm Bentham was *multipliciter diffamatus* of incontinence with a named woman, and was given forty days' penance and three years at Croxton. In April 1491 he was sub-prior at Cockersand. In the same house Thomas Pulton was in 1494 convicted of incontinence with two named women, by each of whom he had had a child. On one charge he was sentenced to Barlings for three years, but this was remitted at the usual intercession; on the other the sentence was postponed. In 1497 he was sub-prior and in 1500 Vicar of Mitton, but he cannot certainly be identified with the Robert Pulton who was abbot in 1537. At Halesowen in 1478 John Saunders, circator, was convicted of incontinence and apostasy, but a sentence of three years imprisonment at Cockersand was, at the usual intercession, reduced to eighty days at Dale. He went there, probably at once with the Visitor. He had returned by 1482; in 1488 he was sub-prior; prior from 1491 to 1494; vicar of Halesowen in 1497. At the same house Roger Walsall was in 1488 absolved after doing penance for apostasy. In August 1497 he was convicted of apostasy, procuring an abortion, and organizing with junior brethren a conspiracy against the abbot. He was sentenced to ten years at Croxton with imprisonment, but does not appear there in the list of September 18 following. In 1500 he was at Halesowen, and in 1505 was vicar of the parish.

At Langley in 1478 Thomas Russell was convicted of notorious crimes and unhonest life, and sentenced to forty days' penance and three years at Titchfield—unless he should be dispensed. He may have gone, but in 1482 he is in the Langley list and vicar of Kirby Bedon. The abbot, John Myntlyng, was in 1482 convicted of incontinence and dilapidation. He was ordered to remove women of ill-fame from the precincts within forty days. He was not deposed, but the government was placed in the hands of two canons, who were to pay the abbot a pension and supply him with food. One of these, Walter Alpe the novice master, succeeded to the abbacy before 1488. In 1494 he was greatly defamed for incontinence and wasting the abbey goods. After an enquiry the Visitor failed to find that the *infamia* was founded on truth. But to allay the scandal he ordered the abbot to avoid the society of the woman concerned, to restore the valuables of the house within a year, and to rebuild the refectory within two years. Two accusers, one of whom was Thomas Walsoken who became Abbot of Wendling in 1503, were charged with maliciously defaming the abbot, but penances were suspended till the next Chapter. In 1500 the abbot was charged under pain of excommunication to hold no communication with the same woman, but the Visitor postponed dealing with the charges of apostasy and incontinence till the next Visitation. The abbot resigned in 1502, and (as we have seen) was succeeded by Wm Kyrlew, Abbot of Lavendon.

At Newhouse in 1478 John Hull, with five others—of whom three were also guilty of attempted murder—was convicted of incontinence. He appears here in the 1482 list, but by 1488 had been transferred to Lavendon, though there is no record of his being sent there. There in 1491 he was sub-prior, and in spite of denials was convicted of bringing women into the dormitory to satisfy his lust. At the usual intercession punishment was deferred. In 1494 he was still sub-prior and was convicted of further incontinence, and of trying to poison the abbot. He was removed from his office, and sentenced to forty days' penance and ten years at West Dereham, on the first charge; the second was held to be so grave that its consideration was relegated to the General Chapter. He appears in no further lists, either here or elsewhere.

Robert Bredon was sub-prior of Sulby in 1475, prior in 1478 and sub-prior again from 1482 to 1491. In 1491 he was convicted of bringing women into the dormitory to satisfy his lust, and of apostasy. For the first he was given forty days' penance and seven years at Alnwick; for the second three years at Shap; yet in 1494 he was still sub-prior of Sulby, and was again convicted of repeating the same crimes. He was sentenced by the Visitor to forty days' fast and ten years at St Agatha's, but in 1495 the General Chapter sent him to Dale where he was in 1497. In this year the Visitor, while at West Dereham, licensed him to hold an outside cure for three years. Fourteen similar cases, only a few degrees less gross, may be found in appendix: they can be easily traced through the index.(13)

On the other hand, in rare cases, Redman took really strong action. Here are three of the most conspicuous cases. At Langley, in 1491, he found "that a very great misadventure—*maximum infortunium*—had befallen brother Thomas Ludham". He had quarrelled with a Carmelite friar; "each had laid violent hands on the other, and Ludham unfortunately—*infortune*—cut off the said friar's right hand; to the great scandal and loss of our Order. Wherefore we enjoined upon him forty days of strictest penance—*gravioris culpe*—and that he should be sent within a fortnight to the abbey of Sulby there to be kept in perpetual prison." And indeed, the list of brethren drawn up for Langley at that same time ends with "Thomas Ludham, in prison". But the Visitation of Sulby itself, in that year 1491, reveals grave scandals. In the next Visitation of Sulby (1494) Ludham is indeed there, but without any mention of prison, while Redman's Visitation of Langley (1494) finds Ludham back there, and now sub-prior!

Twice again, we find Redman doing his best to get rid of peccant abbots. He decreed the deposition of John Downham, Abbot of Beauchief, in February 1462. The appalling state of the monastery during a long period is graphically described in an extant letter from John Swyft, who ultimately succeeded Downham. At his prompting a Visitation was held, and Downham was convicted of solemn perjury, dilapidation, incontinence, rebellion, and many other notorious crimes. He had fled into apostasy with seven other canons, and with them had taken arms. The others were involved in the same offences, and all were excommunicated. In the following May six of these accomplices renounce their "opinions", but of the abbot, John Corbridge and John Pownffret there is no further record. Of the others, John Aston and Robert Skipton were summoned as apostates to appear before the Visitor at Titchfield in July 1478, and again at Doncaster on September 5. There is no record of their obeying, and in 1491 Aston was outside the monastery, with licence; in 1494 he was Chaplain of Afferton; and in 1500 Sacrist. Skipton became sub-prior, circator, finally prior. Robert Baxby went apparently into permanent apostasy before 1478. Robert Boland was apostate till 1488, when he was outside "cum licentia". He does not reappear in the monastery till 1500. John Norton, who was apostate also, had come back by 1491, and by 1494 had been elected abbot. William Brotherton was in 1478 Vicar of Afferton, and remained so till 1494.

Similarly in 1482 William Burton, Abbot of Welbeck, was

deposed. He was found to have lived incontinently with diverse women, by whom he had begotten several children who had been maintained with the monastery's goods; he had wasted the goods also upon, and spent whole days and nights with buffoons and such like persons; he had mortgaged property, and alienated valuables, destroyed the woods, and done no repairs; he had sold all the cattle and neglected to pay the canons their stipends. He had been abbot since 1463, yet in the Visitation report of 1478 there is no mention of such things, although it is obvious that at least some of the abuses must have dated back before then. There is no further record of him.

Yet how far did such depositions imply real condign punishment? We have seen that John Mintlyng, Abbot of Langley, was deposed for incontinence and dilapidation in 1482; but pensioned. The convent was specially commanded to give him *in victualibus*, i.e. in food, drink, clothes, etc., "all that hath been administered unto him by ancient custom, without fraud or murmurs, paying also to the said Abbot yearly, without any deception, at the four quarter-days, 50 shillings of legal English money in equal portions". This was when £10 was quite decent for the whole yearly income of a parish priest; and it is perhaps the most moderate pension I have ever met. Yet even in this comparatively decent form it was in flat contradiction to the reforming Statutes of Innocent IV for the Benedictine Order in 1253. These prescribed that "if, perchance, an Abbot's offences require that he be removed from his office, let no provision be made for him of any revenues, but rather let his soul be so provided for that he may do wholesome penance for that which he hath committed".(14) That Statute became a dead letter. Nothing is more notable in these records than the liberal, and sometimes even enormous, pensions of deposed abbots. John de Courtenay, at Tavistock Abbey, had made himself impossible morally and financially. Grandisson of Exeter, a very strong bishop, and one whose noble birth ought to have given him a favourable control over this noble-born abbot, could not get rid of him altogether; he could only seek to put him under control. The conditions provided that the abbot, with his chaplain, should enjoy £80 a year, while only £100 was left to maintain the rest of the brethren, and to pay those corrodies and pensions with which the abbot's maladministration had burdened the house. We have seen how Roger of Evesham, one of the worst monastic ruffians on record, was pensioned off with "the priorate of Penwortham, where he embezzled all that he could of the revenues assigned to the Community".(15) That was in 1213, before Innocent V's Statute; but it would be easy to fill a chapter with concrete cases of pensions to peccant abbots, in complete neglect of that Statute, down to the Dissolution in England, and the Revolution in France. Quite as bad as the Evesham case are those of Bardney in 1318, and Westminster in 1462 and again in 1467, where the pensions were higher than the figure taken by the Statute of Distraint of Knighthood as compatible with knightly rank.(16) There was perhaps no other custom which contributed so directly to the common impunity of crime. For the sinner might hope for rich provision not only in worldly goods, but even in moral whitewash, so long as he could be induced to resign. Halton of Carlisle was a bishop rather above the average, but his transactions with the prior of his own cathedral church are thus summarized by Professor T. F. Tout, as revealed in his *Register*.(17) In 1300 the bishop discovered, and registered, that

his household was a burden to the neighbourhood, and the exactions of his steward and kinsman, Robert of Warwick, excited the indignation of the countryside. He made dishonest profit by trafficking with the convent's goods. He embezzled the funds of the convent and built a "superfluous ship", the profits of whose trade he kept for himself. The prior neglected to visit the sick canons, and told the secrets of the deliberations of the chapter to laymen. Adam was severely admonished for these irregularities, but retained his position for nearly five years longer, when he was induced by very favourable terms to tender his resignation, in September 1304. The elaborate provision made by the bishop for his support in his retirement shows that it was easier to get rid of a negligent dignitary by leniency than by severity. Adam was not only well provided for, but declared to have lived an unblemished life during his whole period of office. His favourable treatment may perhaps be accounted for by the fact that he was sprung from an influential family in the neighbourhood of Carlisle.

In the face of these facts, it seems incredible that Cardinal

Gasquet should have found it in his conscience to write, and the Royal Historical Society should have printed for him without protest, the following summary of the evidence given by these Visitations (preface to vol. I, p. xxxv):

It must in truth be confessed that there was a good deal to correct; but one thing certainly appears, and that is that the Visitor never shirked his duty in any way, and never condoned offences without satisfactory, and indeed frequently severe, punishment of the guilty party.

This makes a curious pendant to what Mr A. F. Leach, not long before his death, told me concerning the difficulties which he had found in persuading the editorial board of that Society to pass his plain strictures upon fifteenth-century Church discipline in the preface to his *Southwell Visitations*. Partly through mere indolence and ignorance, partly through a generous prejudice in favour of fallen adversaries, a monastic legend has grown up in orthodox religious history which is comparable to the old Napoleonic legend of French patriotism. In this case, as in that, the elements of real greatness have been illegitimately emphasized to dazzle the public eye, and our difficulty is to redress this balance with just sufficient, and no more, of the plain ugly facts of Tudor monasticism which impressed outsiders at the time, but have since been partly forgotten, partly discredited by exaggerated Protestant emphasis.

CHAPTER LVIII

FISH OUT OF WATER

THE medieval monastery, if not quite so near to immortality as the Abbot of Evesham reckoned, was certainly far longer lived than any individual. This is the main truth which makes it so necessary to bring in the whole Continental story in illustration of English monastic conditions. That wider synthesis shows how seldom any reformer from outside, however strong his apparent position—Pope or Prince, prelate or city magistrate—was able to enforce any real cure from without. The nearest exception was in Spain, where Cardinal Ximenes was backed up by a despotic queen who took her own way more than once with the Pope. Otherwise, no true successes came except from within; and even those seldom lasted long beyond the first impulse, whether from a man or from a group. Henry VII and his archbishop were exceptionally strong men, but in the end they were beaten by St Albans. They conformed exactly to the common Continental pattern; they gradually experienced the almost impregnable strength of obstinate conservatism, backed by the composite forces of real religion encrusted with superstition, narrow parochialism convinced of its own superior breadth of thought, and wealth such as very few lay-folk could command. King and papal legate struggled no more; and in time they were gathered to their fathers. Meanwhile St Albans and the Northampton Cluniacs went on, tottering more and more to financial bankruptcy unrelieved by any sign of true moral reform. And, all around, there was such a lull on the surface that one of the most widely-read specialists in the period can write:

Who could have supposed, in the latter days of Henry VII, that an extreme time of trial was near? How could such a thing have been credited even in the early days of Henry VIII, who, if tradition be not misleading, had himself been intended for the Church before his brother Arthur's death, and had expected one day to be Archbishop of Canterbury? Indeed, putting tradition aside, we know quite well that Henry VIII had all his days a taste for theological subtleties.(1)

But this it was which gave Henry much of his strength against the conservative theologians. He was not like Busch's Duke of Brunswick, a man physically brave but unnerved by childish superstitions. He would not have shrunk, even for a moment, in face of sheer superstition—rebellious nuns flat upon their bellies, extending their arms crosswise and chanting a sort of Black Mass, words taken from the Roman Liturgy and perverted in defence of sin. He was far nearer to Philippe le Bel, whose obedience to Church ceremonies had always been conspicuous, yet who had employed his lawyers to humble Popes and to plunder a monastic Order. His reign marked the culmination of that lay spirit which had produced Philippe with his clerical pamphleteers, and Marsilius with his use of the most polished ecclesiastical weapons against ecclesiastical despotism. Henry did, in fact, set a scholar to translate Marsilius into English, only omitting those passages which undermine the Emperor's powers almost as much as the Pope's.

Wolsey had taught Henry to exercise many quasi-papal powers. In the matter of jurisdiction over criminous clergy (1515) the King showed himself "no less a theologian than a statesman". He maintained the lay cause with a boldness and persistence which had been impossible for Henry II:

> We are, by the sufferance of God, King of England, and the Kings of England in times past never had any superior but God. Know, therefore, that we will maintain the rights of the Crown in this matter like our progenitors; and as to your decrees,* we are satisfied that you of the spirituality act expressly against the words of several of them, as has been well shown you by some of our spiritual Council. You interpret your decrees at your pleasure; but as for me, I will never consent to your desire, any more than my progenitors have done.(2)

Wolsey, who had done so much to help Henry in acting within his kingdom as Popes would have acted in their great days, was finally succeeded in 1529 by a protégé of his own, Thomas Cromwell, a layman with as few ecclesiastical scruples as the lawyers who had worked for Philippe le Bel. Cromwell may well have suggested to Henry (as Cardinal Pole afterwards asserted) the idea of breaking with the papacy, yet the breach would have been natural enough without any such suggestion.

* I.e. the Papal Decretals in Canon Law.

No modern special pleading has ever succeeded in removing the common-sense objections to having two governments in one country. The academic theory that Church and State are only two sides of the same body has never been realized in actual practice; except, perhaps, in the narrow Italian State of Popes like Pius IX, where the moral and political results were far from encouraging. Henry, to be master in his own house, must definitely reverse the teaching of many centuries past, which had put Canon Law not only beside, but even above, State Law. And the circumstances of the time not only invited him to the fight, but encouraged him to victory. The Popes, while they abated nothing of their theoretical totalitarian pretensions, were steadily losing ground both in religious consideration and in the worldly politics in which their sovereign claims entangled them. Burckhardt suggests with much plausibility that it was only Luther's revolt which, by giving the papacy a really religious issue to fight for, and thus shocking the western Church out of its growing torpor, saved it from becoming a petty secular princedom, hereditary in one or other of the rival Italian or Spanish families. In the England of 1529, the Commons presented the King with a list of grievances against the clergy which, however exaggerated rhetorically, reposed upon facts fully justified by modern research in the original records. Again, there was no more than epigrammatic exaggeration when the Spanish ambassador wrote home to his master from London: "All the people here hate the priests." Bishop Fisher, in natural concern for his own Order, complained at the 1529 Parliament: "Now with the Commons is nothing but *Down with the Church*; and all this, meseemeth, is for lack of faith only."(3) But the Speaker protested hotly against this fashion of treating the nation's representatives as if they had been Turks or Infidels; and we must remember that Fisher himself, in earlier days, had complained in a religious tract dedicated to the mother of Henry VII:

> An we take heed and call to mind how many vices reign nowadays in Christ's Church, as well in the clergy as in the common people; how many also be unlike in their living unto such in times past, perchance we shall think that Almighty God slumbereth not only, but also that He hath slept soundly a great season.(4)

From this time forward the friction between Church and State became so acute that, though half-hearted concessions and truces might have postponed an open conflict, it is difficult to see how that could have been altogether averted except by such unusually far-sighted and generous statesmanship on both sides as no generation has a right to expect. In 1530, under royal stimulus, the Commons passed a series of Acts which have earned for this and succeeding sessions the title of Reformation Parliament. Its most conspicuous work was to support the King in his assertion of Royal Supremacy. Henry, under pretext that the clergy had violated the Statute of Premunire, fined them the enormous sum of £118,000, and pardoned them even thus only on condition that they should formally acknowledge him as "chief Protector, the only and supreme Lord, and, as far as the law of Christ will allow, the supreme Head of the Church and Clergy of England".(5) Soon afterwards, Parliament presented the King with a petition, drafted by Cromwell, against the clerical practice of passing, in Convocation, decrees which conflicted with the Statutes of the Realm. Henry sent word that this practice must cease; and Convocation, resisting at first, were finally compelled to accept this prohibition by large majorities in both Houses. The clergy salved their consciences for abandoning this (for them) fundamental principle, by pleading their confidence in Henry's "excellent wisdom, princely goodness, and fervent zeal to the promotion of God's honour and Christian religion, and also in your learning, far exceeding in our judgment the learning of all other kings and princes that we read of". Gairdner's surmise may well be true: "Though it was a forced surrender of their old acknowledged rights, they threw the responsibility on a really wise and learned king, and further, as is more distinctly shown by the wording of another draft, cherished the vain hope that in future reigns they would recover their lost position."(6) The next steps were that the Pope excommunicated Henry for the matter of Anne Boleyn (July 1533), that in November Henry appealed against him to a General Council, and that, in 1534, payments to Rome and obedience to Rome were formally repudiated. "By these enactments, in the course of one short session was swept away what yet remained of the Papal power in England."(7) The next

Act pronounced the marriage with Katharine null and that with Anne as lawful; all English subjects were commanded to swear allegiance to the Queen. This oath was taken at once by members of both Houses: therefore by bishops and abbots as well as by commoners.

This forms a sordid chapter in English history, from whichever side we regard it. The King showed, at that particular point, a tyranny even comparable to that of the military adventurers who ruled in most of the States of Italy. For it was under this Statute that some good men suffered who were among the truest and most heroic martyrs in history: More and Fisher and the six Carthusians head the list, with Peto the Observantine. Yet, on the other hand, these great figures are almost lost, in full perspective, among the multitude who bowed completely to Henry's will. Lingard, the most distinguished among British Roman Catholic historians who have dealt with this subject for learning and fairness combined, confessed this very frankly to a private correspondent who asked him why he did not, in his history,

> explain why all submitted to the king's supremacy, when there must have been some in every community ready to brave persecution. Unfortunately the fact is that there were not any in most communities ready to brave persecution; and, if I must disclose the reason (he will perhaps approve of my silence in the history) I will answer with Card. Pole, that the monks of that period were men of little reputation, and had entirely [*prorsus*] degenerated from the spirit of their original institute. The only exceptions which he allows are in favour of the Brigittines, a single house, and the Carthusians and Observantines, the least numerous of all the Orders. The rest were a degenerate, time-serving class of men. This I have hinted in gentle terms in note of p. 216, and of it have given a convincing proof in note of p. 194, where, out of 66 theologians who in the convocation voted in favour of their royal master, two thirds, 42, were abbots and priors of monasteries.(8)

Thus, for good or for evil, the King is now his own Pope and in that capacity he will undertake a disciplinary struggle in which the papal record has been, on the whole, one of neglect or of failure. Gregory IX and Innocent IV had indeed published codes of monastic by-laws. Benedict XII, a century later, had published another still more voluminous, yet tacitly confessing failure not only by its repetition of the old well-worn prescriptions, but by its sorry compromise on one of St Benedict's most emphatic prohibitions, that of flesh-eating; a clause in which orthodox disciplinarians had seen an almost indispensable safeguard for monastic morality. That compromise had failed, as a compromise always does when it is based not upon principle, but on concessions to weakness. On the Continent, papal shortcomings had to some extent been made good by the laity: Princes and Town Councils had occasionally fought for reform in the Pope's name. Now at last an English sovereign will undertake this as an obvious State duty of his own. Whatever selfish motives Henry had—and we shall come to that question afterwards—his interference was an action not premature, but rather overdue. Here, at last, was a Prince strong enough and sufficiently confident in the general support of his people to cut the knot boldly: England will do the job herself. The theoretical Internationalism of the papacy had plainly broken down. Popes were now not only like lay princes, but among the pettiest and most quarrelsome of princes in their political outlook. It seemed that nothing short of politico-religious revolution could cure this. Whether Henry had any right to seize the Pope's power will probably remain a debatable question to the end of time. Some will regard it as a barefaced usurpation, while others will justify it on the same grounds upon which we justify papal power itself. The bishops of Rome had been faced with those political and social problems, under the barbarian invasions, which should naturally have fallen upon the imperial authorities. They in their own city, and other bishops in other cities, took the burden, and the powers, and the privileges, of civil magistrates. The Popes gradually supplanted the Emperors even in the political field. Yet in that field they were now as decadent as the later Roman Emperors had been. Local Princes, aided by feelings of nationalism which had been growing steadily for many generations—that nationalism which is a necessary step towards the true internationalism we all long for—could now do what the later Emperors had failed to do, and what the Popes of 1500 seldom even set themselves seriously to do. The political power of the papacy had arisen by the survival of the fittest; and by that law it was dethroned in England. Such is the explanation which would be put forward by many in this country: not only the majority but, if we may judge by the more frequent concessions of the other side, even a growing majority. On one point, however, the main point, both sides may agree. We may look aside, for the moment, from this disputed question of usurpation or rightful inheritance, and regard the question from the point of view of the *fait accompli*. Caesaropapism has succeeded; Henry is *de facto* King-Pope. He is to deal with the monasteries in his papal capacity. How does he justify that capacity in this, the first act of the great drama? Are the acts of Pope Henry I in this monastic field better, or worse, than those of the Popes of the preceding two centuries? Looking thus at that question by itself, must we not recognize that his initial move would have put him high among Popes, if not in the first place? Martin V, the Pope chosen by the Council of Constance for the special task of reform, did indeed draw up an elaborate code for the Franciscan Order, the so-called Martinian Reforms; yet some of its most important clauses were minimized or revoked before his death. No other Pope had trodden even remotely in the footsteps of Benedict XII. Henry, on his side, set his minister Thomas Cromwell to draw up an elaborate series of Articles of Enquiry, and a fairly complete list of Injunctions for general reform of all English houses, exempt or non-exempt. These, so far as I know, have never been fully and fairly discussed in detail, though they have been easily accessible for more than two centuries in the Appendix to Burnet's *History of the Reformation*.(9)

The Articles of Enquiry are eighty-six in number, modelled upon the questions set by orthodox Visitors for centuries past, and differing only in that they are more numerous than in any other single recorded list. They may be said to summarize exhaustively the questions which we find scattered piecemeal in earlier Visitation records. They cover both the spiritual and the temporal management of the house. Concerning these Articles Lingard writes very truly (p. 54):

The instructions which they received breathed a spirit of piety and reformation, and were formed on the model of those formerly used in episcopal and legatine visitations; so that to men not intrusted with the secret, the object of Henry appeared, not the abolition, but the support and improvement of the monastic institute. But the visitors themselves were not men of high standing or reputation in the church.

The Injunctions are less numerous; only twenty-five. The first two are quite unprecedented, since they are adapted to existing and unprecedented conditions. They prescribe that, from henceforward, the abbots, priors and monks must hold and teach "that the King's power is by the Laws of God most excellent of all under God in Earth; and that we ought to obey him afore all other Powers, by God's Prescript; and that the Bishop of Rome's Jurisdiction or Authority heretofore usurped, by no means is founded or established by Holy Scripture". The whole monastic body is henceforth absolved from every oath of obedience which it may have made to the bishop of Rome, or to any other foreign potentate. But the two revolutionary clauses as we have seen did no more than record a *chose jugée*. The great monastic prelates had sat with the bishops in the "Reformation Parliament", and, though Lingard's note on their servile acceptance of Henry's claims was omitted from his fifth edition, yet this was apparently due to a momentary fit of timid reserve; for he strongly emphasized their responsibility, with convincing evidence, in the private letter which will be found in my second volume (p. 458).

The twenty-fourth Article is somewhat of the same nature: it commits the monasteries to an acknowledgment of Anne Boleyn as Queen. Every priest-monk "shall every day in his Mass pray for the most happy and most prosperous estate of our Sovereign Lord the King, and his most noble and lawful wife Queen Anne". But monks had been bound for centuries to pray for King and Queen. The Chapter of Bermondsey, in 1249, decreed at the request of Henry III that the first day of every General Chapter should begin with "a Mass of the Holy Ghost, for the Roman Pontiff and the Roman Court, for the King and Queen of England and their heirs"; again, all houses were to pray daily for King and Queen in their Mass of the Blessed Virgin.(10) As to Anne's queenly rank, that again had been accepted by the monastic prelates.

The twenty-fifth clause, again, has probably no exact precedent among earlier General Chapter decrees. It prescribes

"Also, that if either the Master, or any Brother of this House, do infringe any of the said Injunctions, any of them shall denounce the same, or procure to be denounced, as soon as may be, to the King's Majesty, or to his Visitor-General, or his Deputy. And the Abbot, or Master, shall minister spending Money, and other Necessaries, for the way to him that shall so denounce." But in essence this is no more than Visitors had sometimes found it necessary to prescribe, and what Popes had frequently allowed. The difficulty of enforcing nominal discipline by getting at the actual facts, in the face of conspiracies or intimidation by superiors or undisciplined majorities, was so great that resolute reformers were constantly compelled to encourage, and even to compel, denunciation of the offenders. After all, delation meets us everywhere as a more prominent factor in medieval than in modern discipline. Boys were bound to tell tales to their masters: so also with university students, some of whom even held their scholarships explicitly upon that invidious tenure; and, where there was suspicion of heresy, the very child was bound to report against its parents. This final clause of the injunctions, in proper hands, would make not for the relaxation of discipline, by encouraging unruly brethren against the authority of their superiors, but rather for the importation of reality into nominal sanctions which were too often ineffective. For centuries past, one of the main solvents of discipline had been this facility of appeal to the Pope against the abbot or prior. St Bernard and other holy men deplored this effect from the appeals to Rome; others deplored worse effects still from appeals to secular courts or to powerful friends inside the cloister; as we have here seen Wallingford, a few pages above, maintaining his abusive power at St Albans by appealing against his abbot to local magnates. Jean Raulin, the reforming Cluniac monk who had some experience as Visitor in England, said in one of his sermons: "It is marvellous nowadays how, in matters of monastic discipline, men appeal straight from their Abbot to secular courts; so that there is now no discipline whatever, nor any subjection or observance of the Rule. The devil has long been in possession of such monks, and will still possess them, by reason of this sort of appeal."(11) Those words were spoken somewhere about 1510. Every generation of truly zealous and honest Churchmen was becoming more and more convinced that one essential factor for reform was some Pope or some Council strong enough, and determined enough, to apply inflexibly those sanctions which were to be found everywhere in the Statutes, but which the most hardened offenders were able most impudently to set at naught.

Let us therefore, suspending yet for a while all speculations as to the King's and Cromwell's hidden motives, consider their public actions in the light of their own time. Let us follow this thread through the documentary history of those two centuries and more, to which Henry VIII appealed in the Preamble to his Act of Suppression, in proof of the failure of monks to reform themselves, apart from outside compulsion. Only fragments of that documentary mass have drifted down to us; the greater part has perished not so much through havoc in monastic libraries at the Reformation as through the neglect and destruction before that time.(12) But the surviving records are sufficient to prove on the one hand how seriously great Churchmen deplored certain breaches of discipline and, on the other, how little it availed to legislate against these evils without supporting the Statutes by effective sanctions.

Apart from 1, 2, and 24, which smell of Tudor politics, let us see what may be said for or against the remaining twenty-two Articles.

The first runs: "That no monk, or Brother of this monastery, by any means go forth of the precinct of the same." Here we have simply a plain and brief reminder of the sixty-sixth Chapter of that Rule to which every Benedictine must swear lifelong obedience at his profession. St Benedict writes:

> The monastery, if it may be so managed, should be so constructed that all necessary things, as water, mill, garden, bakehouse, or different occupation may be exercised within the monastery, so that the monks may have no need to wander outside, for this is by no means expedient for their souls. We will that this rule be often read in the Community, lest any of the brethren excuse himself on the plea of ignorance.

This Chapter of the Rule is our natural point of departure. I have frequently dealt with it in earlier volumes: but the evidence needs summarizing and completing here.(13)

The Benedictines, with their reformed branches (Cluniacs, Cistercians, and to some extent Carthusians), constituted the overwhelming majority of English monasticism, supreme in antiquity, in wealth, and in numbers of brethren. They possessed six of our cathedral churches, whereas the Augustinians had only one (Carlisle), and the remaining cathedrals were ruled by secular canons. By far the greatest amount of monastic legislation which has survived in England concerns the Benedictines.

Innocent III commanded them to hold General Chapters and to legislate for their own Provinces, as discipline might require. We may here ignore the division between Canterbury and York, since the Northern Province, when it came to legislate, fell in almost exactly with the Southern. This legislation may now be followed exhaustively through the three volumes of Mr W. A. Pantin's *Chapters of the English Black Monks*.

The first recorded statutes are from 1218 or 1219 at an Oxford Chapter whose decrees were often quoted in later years as classical. Section 17 deals with the subject of claustration and runs: "Let the wanderings abroad [*evagationes*] of monks be altogether prohibited, unless they be sent by the Superior's leave on business or for some very great necessity, to return on the day fixed by the Superior." Clause 25 prescribes the sanction for this rule:

> Again, in order to repress the temerity of those who go forth [the Fathers] have prudently decreed that, when they return after their egress they shall be received into the lowest place, and shall remain perpetually in the grade and rank wherein they are then received, and shall be deprived of all voice in Chapter, until the Superior shall have seen their condign satisfaction and shall think fit to grant them dispensation.(14)

This prohibition was repeated in the Chapters of 1225 and 1277, and at the York Chapters of 1221, 1273, and 1310.(15) Such repetitions are always significant; and the President's foreword to the Chapter of 1363 shows increasing disappointment and impatience. He points out, under the heading of *Concerning the negligence of Superiors*, that this is a prudent statute in Benedictine legislation, and continues:

> We, therefore, considering that this prescription is not only reasonable [in itself] but necessary for [these] modern times, and imputing

culpable negligence of their subjects to those Superiors who do the contrary, or who knowingly permit it to be done, do very strictly command all Superiors of our Order, and all others who are competent, by custom or in other ways, to grant others leave of absence, that they keep this statute in so far as it concerns themselves, and in so far as it concerns their subjects cause it to be inviolately kept.(16)

A similar testimonial to the importance of this clause may be found in the Chapter Statutes of 1277, which base the punishment of the convicted incontinent upon that for going out without leave, with the only addition that he shall never be deputed to sing High Mass until his fault shall be old enough to be ignored.(17)

Vital as this question was felt to be in monastic circles, it aroused perhaps even more concern outside. From almost the earliest days, the monk outside his cloister had been liable to degenerate into the most familiar of social pests. St Athanasius and St Jerome stigmatized him in a pregnant phrase, "fish out of water", which was immortalized in literature by Chaucer, and in jurisprudence by its inclusion in Canon Law.(18) The Emperor Theodosius I, despite his personal reverence for St Ambrose, complained to him in a letter, "monachi multa mala faciunt".(19) The irrevocability of the monastic vow was due far less to any crystallization from within than to compulsion from outside. Turbulent crowds of monks overawed Church Councils; and the order-loving Justinian enacted that the monk must make his lifelong choice, either for the cloister or for the world. Therefore, when Popes drew up codes of monastic discipline, this nuisance of the cloisterless monk was one which most definitely engaged their attention. Gregory IX, who was specially learned in Canon Law, proclaimed in his code of 1236:

We prohibit also very strictly the giving to monks of free power to wander forth [*evagandi*]; nor let the ordinary monks be granted leave to revisit worldly things, except perchance for some reasonable cause and for a brief time; and [on such occasions] let some mature companion be set to guard them; and let them say their hours by the way, and let a book be provided for them; and let no monk be permitted to speak to a woman without two or three honest witnesses. If any monk, whether in abbey or priory, presume to go beyond the precincts of the monastery without licence from his Superior, let him be subjected to the regular penalty.

The next great monastic legislator, Innocent IV, another of the greatest Canonists on the papal throne, repeated this clause verbatim in his own code of 1249.(20)

As Popes were concerned with the vagrant monk, so also were Church Synods. He was a social evil, whether loitering aimlessly as a gossip in the town or village, or wandering about the countryside, or in the more serious forms of sleeper-out for days and days at an outlying grange, or frankly apostate in lay dress. The Council of York (1195) forbade the wandering abroad (*evagatio*) of monks or nuns: "let them not go on pilgrimages, nor go beyond the precincts without certain and reasonable cause, nor without companions whose honesty is sure and undoubted".(21) The Council of Oxford (1222):

> Let not Religious men or women be allowed to quit the monastic precincts without licence from their Superior, nor let them have leave to go forth without definite and honest cause, so that none be free to leave the convent for the sake of recreation or of visiting their kinsfolk, unless he be of such character that no sinister suspicion could or should arise; moreover, let him always have a companion. And, whensoever any shall receive an indulgence to go abroad, let a certain day be fixed for his return.

A Council of 1237 (diocese uncertain) repeats the prohibition: not even "for the sake of prayer, or of visiting his kinsfolk, unless he who begs leave be such as no man should entertain sinister suspicions of him". St Richard Wych, in his Synod at Chichester, decreed severe penalties against Superiors who allowed their monks to "go alone and indecently through villages and towns". Legate Othobon, in his great Council of 1268, whose emphatic decrees were often treated as one of the two main foundations of English Local Canon Law, condemned *evagatio* as "dangerous for the monk's soul"; so also Archbishop Winchelsey in his Constitutions of 1298. One of the most perilous positions was that of a monk alone in an outlying cell. As early as mid-thirteenth century, there were in Europe hundreds of such cells so small that the mother abbey, with its dwindling revenues or through sheer mismanagement, allowed the population to dwindle to two, a prior and his companion. From thence, the step was easy down to a single monk: but at that point Popes had intervened with emphatic prohibitions of any such moral risk. Yet, despite the efforts of Gregory IX and Innocent IV, the abuse spread. Archbishop Odo Rigaldi of Rouen, from 1248 onwards, notes and condemns numbers of solitary cells in his province, though it was certainly above the average in religious regularity. We find reminders of the papal prohibition in the decrees of Durham Synod (1220); Grosseteste bade his archdeacons guard against the abuse in 1230; and, as late as 1518, Wolsey took up arms against it, in repetition from his predecessor Neville in the Province of York.

Meanwhile the cloisterless monk had engaged royal attention, and that very seriously indeed. We must here go back to Henry V, and that solemn convocation of 300 Black Monks which has already been described in chapter XLVIII. The King was earnestly religious: it had comforted him at Agincourt to think of the prayers his monasteries were putting up for him and his army: but his recent pilgrimage from shrine to shrine in England had shown him that all was not well with the monasteries.(22) This concourse which now assembled at his bidding (1422) was greater than that of any recorded General Chapter; and the royal Articles were drawn up with the counsel of six among the most distinguished living monastic prelates, including Whethamstede of St Albans. The King's opening speech expressed his plain intention of recalling monks to their original rule—*de pristina Religione monachorum*. The preamble is equally plain-spoken: Henry and his ecclesiastical counsellors have taken this unusual step "because there are many serious breaches of discipline [*plura exorbitantia et enormia*] among those who profess the Rule of St Benedict in England". In the ninth of these thirteen articles, one sentence deals cursorily and obliquely with this sixty-sixth chapter of the Rule. "If it befall that these cloisterers visit their parents [or kinsfolk] and friends by permission of their Superior, let this be done once at most in every year, and then let them have honest secular folk to escort them thither and homewards." But the eleventh deals with the question directly and drastically. It begins with a patristic quotation which (as will presently be seen) had become classical in this connection, side by side with the concrete case of gadding Dinah's fate in Genesis xxxiv.

Since, as St Augustine saith, among all contests of Christians the battles of chastity are hardest where fight is daily and victory is rare; and since the same Father saith that he who will not avoid the society of women falleth quickly to ruin; and as the Apostle [Paul] saith that there is no remedy but in flight, let it be strictly commanded that no Religious have licence of exit or ingress in the townships or cities where their monasteries are situated; but that their Superiors shall be utterly deprived of the power of licensing them to eat, drink, or talk in those places, except with noble men, since therefrom grievous scandals may arise, and incentives to vice.

The Articles of this Royal Committee were then submitted to the judgment of thirty chosen monastic representatives. Their criticisms have come down to us in two different drafts.(23) Both agree almost *verbatim* in demanding modification of this "olde somdele streit" rule.

As to the 11th Article, seeing that it seemeth to take away the Superior's power of licensing and granting dispensation to his subjects for exit or ingress of the cities and townships where their monasteries are situated, for the sake of eating drinking or talking, we accept not its admission under this form wherein it is proposed; but we agree that it be strictly commanded that no Religious of the said Order [of Black Monks] shall go forth from his monastery into the aforesaid townships or cities, nor eat or drink in the said townships or cities, unless some arduous and reasonable cause demand it, and he shall have obtained special licence in this matter.

This compromise was still further weakened in the statutes as finally drawn up and signed by the monks, as will be seen when we come to the end of the evidence for Cromwell's second article. It is not without significance, perhaps, that the President at this final meeting was Whethamstede of St Albans.

Yet, in those days when the monasteries might still have saved themselves if they had known the time of their Visitation, this chapter of the Rule was always present to earnest disciplinarians and legislators. This is one of the many cases where historians of monasticism have unscientifically narrowed their view down to a single country and one or two generations. The further we look abroad, and the further back we trace the ascertainable facts, the more clearly must we recognize the fatal lethargy of later monasticism in England.

The Cluniacs were always counted among the "Black Monks

of St Benedict". They had only one representative among the six members of Henry V's committee, but this was in rough proportion to their actual numbers and influence. They were subject, not to the English General Chapter, but to the Mother House at Cluny, which issued its Statutes from time to time. Abbot Hugh V, in 1200, complained in his preamble that monasticism was decaying everywhere, but especially in his own Order.(24) He legislated against wandering brethren, and against "consorting with suspect persons".(25) A century later, Abbot Henry compiled another code; here, again, unlicensed vagrancy is forbidden, with added strictness and threats of punishment.(26) About 1480, a far more resolute attempt for reform was made by Jean de Bourbon, one of the few commendatory abbots who were no disgrace to their immense wealth and opportunities. His Statutes of Reform enact that no monk is to eat or drink outside in the town or village; that gates shall be shut after Compline; that none shall perform at plays in women's costume, or haunt funeral-wakes, wedding-feasts, dances and *joculatores*.

Next to the Black Monks, by far the most important sons of St Benedict were the Grey Cistercians. These never lost altogether the spirit which had inspired their founders; even in the sixteenth century, this Order was more alive than the great mass from which it had broken off. Thus we find the Cistercian General Chapter of 1511 fulminating vigorously against "the scandalous wanderings [*discursus*] of certain Fathers of our Order". It prohibited all frequenting of "villages and towns, under pretext of attending funerals or anniversaries, or celebrating Masses for public meetings; unless perchance they be such grave and solemn persons that the Abbots cannot rightly deny this to them".(27)

The next greatest Rule, the Augustinians, supplies less definite evidence, yet sufficient to illustrate Cromwell's injunctions. The nearest document in date is a questionnaire for Visitors of about A.D. 1400.(28) This Rule, in itself, is far less strict than St Benedict's on the question of claustration; yet even here the Visitors are required to enquire repeatedly into this question. Is any brother vagabond or entangled in secular business? Are the cloister doors well kept? Does any wander out of the cloister without reasonable cause? Are any of the brethren hunters or hawkers? Do any practise archery in public with secular folk? Though no such evidence in detail has survived for Tudor times, yet we cannot suppose that there was less need then; very much the contrary. For, at the last recorded General Chapter, in 1518,

the Presidents and the other Prelates treated in general concerning the reform of the lamentable ruin of Religion which hung over their heads, since the monasteries were decaying miserably both in regular observances and in temporal possessions; a decay which seemed to them to arise from God's vengeance, seeing that many, and almost all, despised these ecclesiastical censures arising from the various multitude of Statutes which had been decreed under pain of such censures, and were in no point observed, so that the brethren were compelled to incur them uselessly and almost unwillingly.

Of reformed Augustinian Canons, the most important were the Premonstratensians. Like the Cluniacs and Cistercians, they were governed by General Chapters held at the mother-house in Franck, which legislated for some 1800 dependent houses in Europe. Their Rule prescribed less strict claustration than that of St Benedict; and in fact their brethren frequently served appropriated parishes outside the monastery. Here the prohibition of solitary habitation seems to have been ignored, at least in the later centuries. Bishop Redman's many visitations betray, I believe, no sense of the necessity for Premonstratensians to live, or go about, by twos. On the other hand, we have specific complaint in Chapter that brethren make themselves comfortable outside, enjoying the parson's freehold and rebelling against all orders to return to the cloister. Moreover, the problem of vagrancy was acute here. The Statutes of the Order decree: "We deny absolutely to our Religious the faculty of wandering about [*discurrendi*] through villages or towns; of frequenting fairs, feasts, weddings, or public banquets, and standing as godfathers to infants."(29) King Louis XII, in 1498, "desiring nothing more, next to the salvation of his own soul, than the peace and prosperity of his realm, which could in no wise be attained without the devout prayers of Contemplatives...forthwith [after his accession] yearned greatly for the reformation of the Premonstratensian Order and of all

Religious". He sent his requirements, couched in four Articles, to the General Chapter, which obediently accepted them. The first Article ran as follows:

> The King is minded that the Religious of the Premonstratensian Order, in accordance with the Statutes of their Rule, should religiously lead a most devout life, more obediently and in closer and stricter custody of the cloister than in years past. Let apostates be sent to prison in punishment, without appeal, and His King's Majesty will without fail lend his hand to help.(30)

A century later (1599) Clement VIII undertook a general reform of this Order, in which at last the two-and-two principle is laid down. He decreed (§ 18) "In order to remove all occasion for scandals and wandering abroad, let the monastery be always closed and kept diligently....Let the porter open the gate to none of the brethren unless he be with a companion, and have obtained licence to go forth." Such licence must be given with great formality and very seldom: "let no brother whatever have a general leave to go forth". Violation of this statute entails "severe punishment, even unto prison; let the porter also suffer the same, if he have knowingly assisted the going forth".(31)

The Dominican Rule, again, was founded upon the Augustinian; and, so far from mewing the brethren up in their cloister for life, it assumed that the greater part of their work would be done in "the world", as university students or missionary preachers. Yet it also, in practice, had soon to contend with abuse of that liberty which was assigned to the friars' use. The Chapter Records of this Order have survived in very unusual fulness; and, round about the turn of the fifteenth century, they show anxious preoccupation with this problem. The Chapter of 1505 had to deal with the wanderings of brethren; so again those of 1518–25; that of 1530 repeats the old complaint with still greater emphasis. In 1536 the General rendered account to the chapter of his recent perambulation of the whole Order as Visitor: "We have very often found our Religion fallen from the institution of our fathers....Where can due enclosure be found, and the abolition of useless wanderings abroad?" Therefore, unless the Visitors "apply reformation inexorably" to this and other abuses, and enforce the statutory penalties, "let them, as no true Visitors but rather wolves and destructors of the Order, be removed and deposed promptly, even within the year, from their offices". The matter gains still further emphasis from the General's concluding words. He beseeches the assembled Fathers, "in the bowels of Jesus Christ" for their prayers, that he may be strengthened against "these ingrained evil customs, which for many years past have grown throughout the whole Order, by reason of the wickedness of the times, and have been winked at".(32)

The Franciscan, living under far the most libertarian Rule of all, was most tempted to abuse that liberty. It is he of whom Chaucer writes:

> ...Goddès armès two!
> A frere wol entrerne him evremo,
> Lo goodè men, a flye & eek a frere
> Wol falle in every dyssh & eek mateere.(33)

His Chapter records, though far more fragmentary than the Dominican, bear constant testimony to the disciplinary difficulties thus occasioned. A Provincial Chapter held at Treviso in the later thirteenth century decreed: "The Minister, with the whole Chapter, ordains that whosoever shall go forth from the friary without leave from his Superiors or their Vicars, shall be punished as apostates." "Idle wanderings" [*discursus inutiles*] are to be punished by sitting on the ground in refectory.(34) The Province of France commanded in 1452 "to all Wardens and their Vicars, present and future, in the name of the Holy Ghost, that they licence no brother to go forth from the convent except only once a week. On feast-days or in summer let them grant licence to none whatever, under pain of deposition from their office, unless perchance they be compelled by express and plain necessity." As for exit without leave "for the first time let him eat bread and water on the floor; for the second, let him be flogged in public; for the third, let him be expelled from the convent in confusion".(35) It is plain that there was increasing temptation to violate the two-and-two rule, originally so universal, and so familiar to Dante.(36) It was in his lifetime that the Treviso Chapter legislated strictly on this point. The companion must be chosen and assigned by the warden or vicar, who, "if it seem expedient to them, shall enquire both publicly and privately from the brethren assigned as companions to those who thus go forth, what they have done and whither they have directed their steps; and the brethren shall answer such questions in simple truth".(37) The Tuscan Chapter of 1457 enacted: "Let not the friar ever separate from his companion as they go by the way or beg for alms, or when they sleep in the houses of secular folk, whenever he can thus act in good manners." The first violation is to be punished with stripes, the second with bread and water on the floor. This was repeated in three following Chapters, 1474, 1507 and 1523.(38)

To all this we must add the evidence of the Episcopal Visitation records, which are at last emerging from centuries of neglect, and beginning to attract a few serious students. The complaints of those orthodox Visitors, if no other evidence existed, would be conclusive as to almost universal neglect of the ancient rule of claustration.

Nor were these Visitors pedantically insistent upon the letter of the Rule, or even upon its spirit. They give the superior far more liberty in his interpretation of this sixty-sixth chapter than we have the least reason to suppose that St Benedict himself would ever have allowed. They take no exception to the custom which had established itself at so many great abbeys, where the monks went periodically and frequently either *en masse* or in large parties to some neighbouring cell or grange for "recreation", especially after their periodical bleedings. It is only the excessive frequency of such indulgences that they reprobate, or the irregularities which often accompanied them. It is improbable that any bishop would have forbidden, though he might have regretted, the standing arrangement made by Abbot de la Moot of St Albans (1396–1401).

He granted that on Mondays, Tuesdays, Wednesdays, Thursdays and Saturdays in Lent, not being a red-letter day, they might procure leave after morning Mass to go forth and walk after their wonted manner at other times of year, returning for dinner.

Then, after dinner, on all those days aforesaid, let them go to St German's,* to walk as far as they have been wont in Lententide. He granted further that the licence given unto brethren for walk in

* A cell of the Abbey, about half a mile from the gate; or, by a more circuitous route, a mile.

the morning should hold good for the whole day; but on Saturdays in Lent he decreed that these holiday-makers [*ludentes*] should be present at Vespers and at the Maundy.

The same rules were to apply to dependent cells.(39) No doubt Cromwell's Injunctions would have abolished these concessions; but the question must be viewed in the light of the general evidence which, so far as I know, nobody has yet taken the trouble to collect. Yet nothing short of such evidence—only a fragment of what could be produced in an exhaustive monograph—will suffice to recall the modern reader to the actual atmosphere of Tudor times.

CHAPTER LIX

THE ETERNAL FEMININE

CROMWELL'S next Article, when we look into the sources, will appear even more natural—or, shall we say, inevitable. It runs as follows:

> That women, of what state or degree soever they be, be utterly excluded from entering into the limits or circuits of this monastery, or place, unless they first obtain licence of the king's highness, or his visitor. Also, that there be no entering into this monastery but one, and that by the great fore-gate of the same, which diligently shall be watched and kept by some porter specially appointed for that purpose, and shall be shut and opened by the same both day and night, at convenient and accustomed hours; which porter shall repel all manner of women from entrance into the said monastery.

Here, again, this subject has already been treated in many places of my first two volumes; but it is necessary to summarize and complete the evidence here.(1)

From the very first, monastic legislators had given this subject all the attention which its importance deserved. An enormous proportion of the pre-Benedictine *Lives of the Fathers* turns upon this question. If it is not treated explicitly and in detail by St Benedict in his Rule that is only because it was too axiomatic for the eminently practical saint to waste words over it. It was implicit in the original monk's vow that it should cut him off, with almost negligible exceptions, from all sight or speech of women.

The great Benedictine scholar Martene, in his *Commentary on the Rule*, gives a mass of quotations which readers may trace in his index under the words *mulier* and *femina*.(2) He devotes fourteen quarto pages in illustration of the single passage, of two words only, in which Benedict refers directly to this subject. Chapter IV of the Rule gives a list of brief precepts for the perfect life for each of which a definite Bible precedent may be quoted; these amount in all to the hallowed number of Christ's immediate disciples: seventy-two. For working at these precepts (he says), "our workshop is the enclosure of the monastery, and our stability in the congregation". The sixty-third of these precepts is "to love Chastity" (*Castitatem amare*). Martene enumerates nine props for the maintenance of this duty: fasting, avoidance of idleness, meditation on hell, frequent Communion, prayer, humility, realization of God's omnipresence, patience, and (last and most efficacious of all) solitude with flight from women. In support of this he quotes from that sermon which we have seen Henry V's committee quoting as St Augustine's: St Paul writes: "Flee fornication" (I Cor. vi. 18), as the most effective method of fighting against it. Thence Martene goes on to quote a host of early authorities. Even the bravest souls need to remember St Bernard's words: "to be always with a woman, and not to know a woman, is not this more than to raise a man up from the dead?" St Pachomius, one of the earliest of all monks, "when a man besought him to exorcise his daughter from demoniacal possession, is said to have answered, 'It is not our custom to speak with women'" (p. 164). Originally, therefore, monks kept women away not only from their cloister but from their church. The civil powers helped here; a law of Justinian forbade the burial of women within a male monastery, or of males within a nunnery. Rule after Rule forbade contact with women in unmistakable language. One of the pre-Benedictine codes prescribes the punishment for any abbot who permits women to enter the inner court of his monastery: he must be deposed from his office, and take place as lowest of all the priests. Those reformed Orders, which marked Europe's advance from the Dark Ages to the Middle Ages proper, held emphatically to the same principle. Martene says nothing here of those double monasteries, men and women on the same foundation, which were common in the Early Celtic Church, and repeated later in the experiments of the Gilbertines and the Brigittines, but those were not permanently successful experiments. The general principle "could be proved", says Martene on p. 155, "by almost innumerable examples"; and he goes on to quote an instance from Greece, where "some went so far as to suffer no female animals, as cows and she-goats, and so forth, to be kept in their monasteries". A later Benedictine abbot, St John of Gorze, refused once to rest his weary limbs upon a seat which he had seen a woman vacate (p. 165).

Thus he takes Order after Order, county after county, age after age, often subordinating the chronological to the logical sequence, but always giving the reader means to check his dates and his topography. If he "heaps example upon example, this is to show how our fathers shrank from even the slightest conversation with women, and how much we ourselves ought to fear (and would that we equally shrank!) from talk with them, which in truth can in no way profit and may be most harmful... but enough of this, if indeed we can ever say enough of this matter" (p. 165).

Elsewhere, our Benedictine scholar implicitly apologizes for spending a dozen consecutive pages of commentary upon the bare two Latin words of his text. He pleads, in effect, the common-sense rule of historical method, that one necessary road to accurate generalization is that of marshalling the greatest manageable number of testimonies, from the most various points of view. Dealing with the exclusion of women from abbey churches, he writes (p. 158):

> This was the common Benedictine use, and the general custom of almost all our monasteries. Lest any man should think that I have invented this out of my own head, and tried to distort the practice of a few houses into a general custom, it will perchance be not wearisome, and I hope it may be sometimes profitable, to prove my point if not from all our monasteries, at least by most certain testimonies from the principal and most eminent among them.

And again (p. 163):

> From what I have said, I deem it sufficiently proved that the custom of keeping women out of our churches was not singular, but general to almost all monasteries. The Carthusians and Cistercians seized upon the custom at the very origin of their Orders; and the Carthusians are most highly praised for retaining it everywhere even now. The Cistercians keep it at the Mother-house of Cîteaux and perhaps in some others. But now their churches are indiscriminately [*passim*] open to women; though, as Matthew Paris tells us under the year 1250, at Pontigny no women were admitted but the English, out of reverence for St Edmund.*

* St Edmund Rich, perhaps the greatest of our medieval Archbishops, died in exile at the Cistercian house of Pontigny, where innumerable miracles were wrought at his tomb.

Martene, with all his learning and customary frankness, stops short in mid-thirteenth century. The reason is easy to read between the times of his apology here above. He wrote as one of the reformed Benedictine Congregation of St Maur, at its headquarters of St Germain des Prés, where the visitor to Paris may still linger in the solemn old church, and amid a few fragments of those buildings which, in Gibbon's time, were producing more works of scholarship than either of our English universities. But he knew only too well that the monasticism of his own day was making little pretence of that flight from women which he himself extolled as most efficacious among the nine props for chastity. His master, Mabillon, greatest of all Benedictine scholars, had voiced that complaint in a passage describing the original avoidance of women: "Alas! this is rather turned to the contrary in these days of ours!"(3) Martene, therefore, beyond those two discreet allusions here above, ventured upon no details later than about 1250. That gap of silence must be filled in here.

The earliest set of papal statutes for monasticism, as we have seen, are those of Gregory IX in 1236. These prohibit the entrance of women, with rare and special exceptions. "If any man presume to transgress this rule, the official through whose door the woman hath come in, and also the Abbot or Prior, if he have commanded this, shall fast for one day, upon each occasion, upon bread and water." The Code of Innocent IV (1249) repeats this section almost *verbatim*. Benedict XII's *Constitutions* command to the same effect.(4)

The English Benedictine Statutes, like those of all other nations, recur frequently to this subject. That of York Province in 1221 is brief, and significant of the liberties which the assembled fathers felt bound to guard against: "Let not nuns, or women concerning whom sinister suspicion might arise, spend the night within the monastic precincts." That of 1276 repeated the clause almost *verbatim*.(5) In the Canterbury Province, a chapter met in 1249. It is significant for the story of monastic discipline that the decree should be so markedly indulgent and compromising beyond what was published by Gregory IX twenty years earlier, and Innocent IV in this same year 1249 for the whole Church. They decreed:

Let women be altogether prohibited from ingress to the cloister after dinner [i.e. after noon]. Moreover, let them by no means be admitted within the doors of the monastery to dinner, except by licence of the Abbot and in his presence, except for such consideration as we must have for noble ladies, according to place and time, and according as the Superiors may think expedient.(6)

The next Statute is from the Chapter of 1277, which announced itself as "impelled by the pricks of a zealous conscience to restore, in so far as we can, the state of the Monastic Order to its primitive excellence", as against the new practices which had crept into "almost all monasteries of our Order". Then comes a revised version of 1278, which decrees: "Let none, of what rank or office soever, without asking and obtaining leave from the Superior of his house for the time being, have speech [*colloquium*] with a woman or eat flesh or go forth in any way from the monastic precincts." In 1343 the chapter published a far completer code, which prescribes in chap. VIII:

We will that women be utterly forbidden access to the cloister while the brethren sit there, nor shall they also, in any wise, be admitted to sleep the night or to dine within the gates of the monastery, or outside in the manors, by the brethren who guard [the gates].* Exception may be made in consideration for kinsfolk [*parentes*] of the brethren, and noble women, and others honest and unsuspect, to be granted in view of the place and the time, as may seem expedient to the monastic Superiors.

This was repeated almost *verbatim*, with the added emphasis of "we do more strictly prohibit", in that revised Statute of 1444 which formed the last and standard code for English Benedictinism.(7).

A similar story is found in the model questionnaires. One of 1259 enquires: "Does any monk talk alone with women, except with two or three witnesses who hear everything? Are any women dwelling within the precincts of the monastery?"(8) Another, in 1363, "Are women kept away, especially from entering the cloister while the brethren sit there, and from other private places? as is commanded by the Chapter of Northampton and Benedict XII in the section headed *Let no women dwell within monks' monasteries*."(9)

* Reading *custodibus* for *custoditis*, which seems to make no sense.

In the archiepiscopal councils and episcopal synods we find the same preoccupation: the relation of monks and women was felt to be a major question for the Church at large. The University of Oxford, in 1414, exposed this solemnly to Henry V as an open and intolerable sore.(10) In this matter again, as in my last chapter, we have conclusive testimony of the Episcopal Visitations. This, like that of monks abroad, forms a frequent topic of witnesses' evidence and of visitatorial blame. Moreover, we have plain proof that these are far from exhaustive. It had been frequently decreed in monastic statutes that women must not be employed as servants, sometimes in bare prohibition, and other times with the softening clause that they must be old enough to avert all suspicion. Yet in addition to the instances found in the Visitations, we have multiple evidence, in the monks' own private account rolls, of women employed as a matter of ordinary routine. The scores of examples which I have given on pp. 647–54 of my second volume could easily be doubled if it were necessary to labour the point.

The Oxford petition of 1414 laid special stress upon the exempt houses, as worse sinners in this respect than the mass of Benedictines. We have, in fact, independent testimony to this effect. The Carthusians, as we have seen, were honourably exceptional. But the official Cluniac evidence is in painful harmony with that concrete Northampton instance which stirred King, Legate and Pope. In the reforming Statutes of Abbot Henry [1320] we find:

Item, because a Statute of Pope Nicholas IV of happy memory [1288–92] doth utterly forbid all entrance of women into our cloisters and choirs, We command that, in all abbeys and conventual priories of our Order, the said women be absolutely denied all entrance to the cloister and other places and the common buildings; except such to whom we should defer through reverence to their rank and nobility, and to whom we cannot conveniently refuse entrance.(11)

The Cistercians were, perhaps, the best disciplined of great exempt Orders. Yet a MS. among the archives at Dijon shows that at Wardon, one of the greater English houses, in 1492 "women of evil fame often enter the monastery, whence a very great decay reigns in Religion". It was at that great Council of

Tours, in the presence of Charles VIII, that the Abbot of Cîteaux complained: "women enter everywhere, and the monks go out as they please, whereby chastity and obedience are utterly brought to naught".(12) And, in 1516, the General Chapter fulminated against

the intolerable abuse of certain Abbots who, utterly casting aside the reverence of the monastic state, are not ashamed to keep women under colour of their daily domestic necessities, and sometimes to cause their monks to be served with food by the aforesaid women, who therefore frequent the monastic precincts and the chambers of the abbots and monks, to the greatest peril and perdition of their souls.

In 1518, the Statutes are briefer but equally significant: let there be a special effort now to restoring the three essentials of Poverty, Obedience and Chastity; "for avoiding wanderings abroad, for permitting no entrance of women whatsoever".(13) Things seem to have gone not better, but worse, after the Reformation. The Papal Nuncio Ninguarda, Visitor for Austria and South Germany, reported in 1577: "Certain abbots of the Cistercian Order, whose General is ordinarily a Frenchman, live so licentiously in every respect, especially in the dominions of the most serene Archduke Charles [of Austria], that they are not even ashamed to keep concubines publicly and to maintain them like wives of noble birth. We ought to consult [seriously] on this point."(14)

The Premonstratensians, often scattered about in parish cures, and not seldom under the oft-forbidden perils of solitude, supply very definite evidence on this head. Their early Statutes forbid the presence of women, but with that fatal room for exceptions which crept in everywhere after the first fervour of reform. "We decree that no woman presume to eat in our abbeys with the brethren, nor let them be permitted to spend the night there....Again, within the abbeys or granges of our Order let women by no means be admitted to work, unless they be such that no sinister suspicion can be had of them." Exceptions allowed are very rare, as for the founder's wife, etc. Abbots or priors who give unnecessary permission are to be punished with three Fridays' fast on bread and water.(15) When Louis XII, in 1498, sent to Prémontré that urgent call for reform which we have seen in the last chapter, one fourth of the document was concerned with this matter. The King began:

Herein lieth great deformity. Let your Religious live decently and chastely, in no wise busying themselves with enticements [*illecebris*]; and thus let no suspect women enter their offices or have any the least communication with them; and let the brethren sleep in open chambers. Let them not sell wine within their monasteries, nor let those of them who hold parochial benefices, under pain of deprivation, keep suspect women; let them avoid public feasts, and not wander abroad out of their parishes, but stay at home and busy themselves with contemplation.

Yet the four generations which followed upon the King's well-meant efforts seem to have seen no more betterment than the generations preceding. For in 1614 there was a reforming abbot at Prémontré, Pierre Gosset. He chose the prior, Leau le Paige, as his vicar and coadjutor for a series of Visitations. Le Paige, who afterwards wrote a monumental history of the Order, records on pp. 994–1066 of that volume a full series of the injunctions which he gave in each case, founded on what he had seen or inferred at his Visitation. His first visit was to "the famous abbey of St-Yved-de-Braine". Here he prints the complete text of his "Charter of Reform", running to three folio pages. He warns the brethren against shirking choir-service, "lest our Founders and Benefactors be defrauded of the prayers and suffrages that are due unto them, and we should seem to lead a life of idleness among their labours". As to gaddings abroad and dealings with women, he is more emphatic:

Let the brethren beware of quitting the monastic precincts without express permission from their Superior. We altogether prohibit to the brethren all facilities for wandering about the villages, and public junketings on market or feast days; so also, the standing as godfathers to children; and this We say lest the objects thus set before them should prepare an ambush for chastity, that most delicate of all monastic virtues; or lest any handle be given for offence to layfolk, whose mouths are almost always open to carp at ecclesiastics. If, however, it seems good to walk for refreshment of mind, let them go about the neighbouring fields, meadows, streams or woods under the leadership of the Father Prior. He who doth otherwise, let him pay the penalty due to more grievous offences, for three days....Let women on no account be admitted to the ordinary monastic premises [*regularia loca*], nor let them be suffered to sit at the conventual table. [For privation or suspension has been repeatedly decreed by Popes for those who] presume either to introduce any women to the monasteries (except by chance at times of procession), or to admit them.

This is the type of injunction which Le Paige found himself compelled to follow throughout all but one of the twenty houses he visited, in six provinces of France, which probably afforded as good examples of monastic life, at that time, as any other parts of Europe. At the next place, Belosanna in Normandy, the injunction ran: "Let any be imperilled in it [his chastity], let all shut the doors of the claustral buildings so that no women (even though mothers or sisters) be seen to pass through those places." He habitually begins this particular clause with one or more patristic citations as to the fragile nature of Chastity, often employing that same passage from St Augustine which Henry V used to reinforce his warnings to the English Benedictines. At one of his latest visits (Cambrai), after forbidding mothers and sisters, he adds: "And let no serving-woman, even of honest conversation, be allowed to work at the bakery or wash-house or bath:(16) but let there be a manservant to do all the coarse work, lest [the Superior] incur that pain of suspension which hath been decreed by Pius V, Gregory XIII, and other Popes."(17)

The Friars were, by their very constitution, thrown much more into the world than even the Premonstratensians. True, the cloister was in theory their fortress, which must be kept impregnably against outsiders: "that is no Religion", wrote an early Franciscan, "where all things are open to all men", and therefore "let them never invite strangers, even their familiar friends, to visit the Offices of the Convent".(18) But from that guarded fortress the Friar sallied forth for a great deal of his world's work; and here the problem was to keep his religion free from contact of women. St Francis himself had kept the golden mean; but his Rule forbade "all suspicious intercourse or counsels with women" (chap. XI), and within a generation after his death it had become a source of frequent anxiety, with added warning against "beardless youths".(19) The thirteenth-century statutes for the Provinces of France and Treviso forbid friars to confess women except during the daylight hours.(20) A Chapter of 1452 for the same Provinces had to go much further: it "commanded unto all, in the name of salutary obedience and of the Holy Stigmata of St Francis, and also under pain of excommunication and prison *ipso facto*, that no friar at all, of whatever rank, preeminence or dignity he may be, dare to admit women within the convent precincts or the dormitory or the brethren's chambers, or permit them to enter" (§ 32). The next paragraph forbids no less strictly their introduction into the Offices: in both cases, the superior who permits this is to be deposed.(21) The Tuscan Province decreed in 1457, and repeated in at least six similar documents down to 1507, "*Item*, let no children and adolescents be confessed in the cells, nor be admitted to suspicious places, under pain of public chastisement."(22) All this is supplementary to the evidence quoted in chapter XLIII of this volume. Here, as with the Cistercians and Premonstratensians, the same story goes on after the Reformation. The Nuncio Ninguarda reported in 1577 concerning his Visitations in Austria: "There are some friaries into which a single brother is put, and called Prior, without other companions; and he keeps a woman under the name of 'cook', and God knows how things go. And under this plea the other monasteries, in which there are more brethren, do the like."(23)

The Dominican Chapter Acts in their comparative completeness, enable us to follow this question, like others of great importance, minutely during the years which here concern us most. In 1501, the newly elected general called upon the chapter to help him in "upraising and reforming our Order, which is fallen and utterly deformed". He decreed, under pain of deposition, that no prior or other official

should permit in any wise, or under any colourable excuse whatsoever, that women should enter the dormitories or other offices, or the enclosure, of our convents, unless perchance by reason of some ancient devotion in the cloister or in some part of the convent there should be a concourse of people; or some noble ladies and matrons, with decent company, should wish to visit the convent; and this seldom, by advice of the Fathers of the convent.

In 1530 the decree is still more emphatic: "We command all Superiors of provinces, Congregations, and convents, under pain of deposition from all their offices which will at once be incurred by those who disobey, that they by no means suffer women to serve in the convents, or to haunt [*morarifin*] the kitchen or other offices." In 1553, the General Chapter is still threatening deposition against superiors who fail to "punish severely, by the penalties fixed in our Constitutions, those brethren whom they have caught violating their vow of chastity".(24)

Dom Martene's apology may well be recalled here in application to this and the preceding chapter. In the face of so many other writers who ignore this plain documentary evidence—in some cases, even deliberately—the historian who has taken the trouble to study it is compelled to publish what he finds with a fullness and emphasis which elsewhere might be justly taxed with exaggeration. He can only ask: "Why was it left to me to bring overwhelming evidence for facts which should, long ago, have become commonplaces among all who profess knowledge of this particular subject?" For, apart from the political touches which I have pointed out, these Cromwellian injunctions follow lines which are in harmony both with orthodoxy and with common sense. When (for instance) this royal minister prohibits monks from "demanding to them[selves] any certain, usual, or accustomed duty or portion of meat as they were wont to do", he is there in accord with the best visitatorial traditions. The Premonstratensian General Legislator had found himself compelled to deal with clerical strikes: with brethren who, "because they are not served to their desire in food and drink or raiment. ...Therefore, to the contumely of their superiors and the harm of their own souls, cease of their own accord, and invite others to cease, from divine service".(25) It was found necessary to repeat this prohibition in the revised code of 1505. Again, if Cromwell insists that the monks' leavings should be honestly given to the true poor, and not to friends or dependents, so had all previous Visitors done, with an emphasis and iteration which testified to the frequency of the abuse. His refectory and dormitory rules are irreproachably orthodox. So, again, in his next Injunction, he repeats a prohibition common to other places and ages: "That no brother or monk of this House have any child or boy lying or privily accompanying with him, or otherwise haunting unto him, other than to help him to Mass." His insistence for care of the sick, and for sending students to the universities, had been anticipated with tell-tale frequency during the last two centuries and more. He may indeed innovate in the letter, but not in the spirit, when he goes on to stress the importance of studying and teaching the Word of God, and insists upon the daily reading of a portion of Scripture. Popes and bishops had forestalled him by prescribing that the Rule should be sufficiently read and explained in the vulgar tongue to eliminate all excuse of ignorance; nor could they reasonably have quarrelled with his addition that such explanations should include proof "that the said Rule, and other their principles of Religion (so far as they are laudable) be taken out of the Holy Scripture": or, again, that "true religion is not contained in apparel...and such other kind of ceremonies, but in cleanness of mind, pureness of living". In commanding that accounts should be regularly kept and audited, he lays his finger on perhaps the most frequently enacted and most frequently violated of all orthodox Statutes. So, again, with his prohibition of wasteful felling of timber, and other expedients to raise money by deeds not duly sealed by the convent, and with his command that the monks must take the ordinary business precaution of registering such deeds in a book. He next forbids the reception of professed monks earlier than twenty-four years of age, "and also that they entice nor allure no man with suasions and blandishments to take Religion upon him". This, again, is in harmony with the orthodox spirit; and the next might claim excellent spiritual ancestry: "*Item*, that they show no relics or feigned miracles for increase of lucre, but that they exhort pilgrims and strangers to give that to the poor that they thought to offer to their images or relics." Next comes an abuse never defended but frequently practised under the ever-present temptation of gain: "Also, that they suffer no Fairs or Markets to be kept or used within the limits of this House." Finally come the two semi-political articles which I have dealt with in the preceding chapter. Nor is it true that this claustration, though theoretically just, was in practice enforced by Cromwell with irrational severity. There was divergence upon this point among his agents, and Cromwell took the more lenient side. To what extent, the records do not clearly show, but they distinctly imply that he was willing to listen to reasonable pleas.(26) One such came from Malmesbury, where one of the Visitors took the abbot's part, representing that the head of a monastery

is chosen for his expertness in temporal matters, that he may be a proctor for all the rest, and that they, being provided for by his means, may be released from all outward cares, and serve God the quieter. By the law he ought to be mortified to the world, so as not to be corrupted by outward business; and though divers of them be found otherwise, this can always be remedied by their removal from office. The monks of Charterhouse devised all the ways they could to keep themselves from outward business, and yet they were compelled to have a proctor as their Martha, and their prior to go forth for greater business. Pray consider whether it will be acceptable or convenient that no noble women, or men or councillors, etc., should come to the abbot's table. It will be for you either to qualify your injunctions or determine the exemptions.(27)

For in fact the monks, for centuries now past, were in a position that was no less false for being naturally and gradually formed, and almost inevitable. As monks themselves sometimes confessed, Religion had begotten wealth, and the child was strangling the parent. In most cases, the monks were absentee landlords over widely scattered estates. In so far as they managed personally and directly, this was in more or less contradiction with the Apostolic precept: "It is not reason that we should leave the word of God and serve tables....We will give ourselves continually to prayer, and to the ministry of the word." Monastic practice no longer conformed to what had made its original greatness, that prayer should come first of all, the Opus Dei *par excellence*. Even strict Visitors, while they blame the absence of so many from choir may be found making excuses for the Obedientiaries, who are going about on business or working in their counting-rooms. Thus the institution rendered itself fatally vulnerable: and, the more we emphasize Cromwell's evil qualities and base intentions, the stranger is the paradox that it should have been left to such a man to recall these men of God to the Rule to which they had sworn lifelong devotion. He certainly took bribes greedily; but so did most men in similar positions: "it is impossible to measure the standard of public service which prevailed in those days with that which obtains today".(28)

No less unfair is the criticism sometimes directed against the distinction made by Henry VIII between greater and lesser monasteries. His original dividing line rested upon age-long monastic traditions which Anglican apologists may be excused for not knowing, but which Cardinal Gasquet, Abbot-General of the English Benedictines, had no excuse for ignoring. St Benedict himself had chosen twelve monks as a standard number for a monastery. From time immemorial, other Orders had imitated this example: a cell of twelve or more was looked upon as *conventual*: it could claim to be a full-fledged community (*conventus*), numerous enough to perform all the choir-duties and other activities prescribed in the Rule. Orthodox disciplinarians frequently acted upon the assumption that smaller houses were tempted to greater laxity. St Bernard's exacting piety described the numerous small cells of his own day as "synagogues of Satan". Odo Rigaldi, in that diary of his which shows us so many illuminating details, frequently warned such cells against taking advantage of their smallness to break the Rule. Nothing, therefore, could have been more natural and orthodox than Henry's original distinction. And its commutation, though not so orthodox, was equally natural. For centuries past, the Church herself had commuted penances for money-fines, which were incomparably easier to fix by tariff and to enforce. The same practical considerations moved Henry's commutation: we should probably find that at least nine-tenths of the houses below £200 in income were also below twelve in number of inmates.

Thus, apart from the question of Royal supremacy, which was a *chose jugée*, it is difficult to find anything in Cromwell's Injunctions which St Louis might not have decreed, and Innocent III approved. "The abuse which has been poured on the royal visitors by naïve sentimentalists is based on ignorance of the fact that in this [personal examination], as in other matters, the visitors were following rules which the bishops had always used."(29) However Cromwell's evil intentions may be stressed—and Matthew xii. 24–32 may warn us against assuming evil motives for an action laudable in itself—the fact is that what gave him power to impose these detested injunctions upon the monasteries was the notorious and apparently irremediable degeneracy of their inmates. It is no heretic, but St Peter himself, who warns Religion against this heel of Achilles. "Who is he that will harm you, if ye be followers of that which is good?"(30)

CHAPTER LX

AN ABBOT *IN COMMENDAM*

THE St Albans chronicler, Walsingham, speaks very plainly here.(1) He is describing the reign of one of the greatest among St Albans abbots, Thomas de la Mare (1349–96). He writes:

in the last days of this Abbot, the Church of the Exempt was reduced to such servitude in the Kingdom, that the Pope presumed to quash elections duly made, and set up other [Abbots] at his own pleasure, until the King and his Council assumed a more lively spirit and decreed to resist such great evils.... So the most experienced men feared lest, if the Pope had free power to dispose of the churches of this realm, as in those of Hungary and Spain, he would confer the wealthiest abbeys upon his own Cardinals or familiar servants, who would strive not to increase Religion or augment the numbers of monks, but rather to destroy; for these men coveted naught else than the possessions of such abbeys, as may be proved by such deserted and fallen monasteries in Provence and in the aforesaid realms. For, where of old there were eighty monks, now scarce six or four are maintained: nor are these in the buildings where Religion was wont to flourish, but they are permitted to wander indiscriminately abroad, upon a yearly or daily stipend.* Wherever one or two have died, no new member is taken in, but the numbers are fraudulently permitted to fail, until all are dead and the possessions of such monasteries come wholly into the hands of the [commendatory] Cardinals, and ample monasteries become granges or stalls for beasts. Therefore Abbot Thomas, dismayed by such wicked footsteps, and seeing that no abbey in this realm had escaped the papal traps† (for, when [the Pope] found occasion, he had "provided" candidates to all, and in some—which seemed abominable—he had set not even monks or Religious of the same Order, but into one house of Black Monks he had set a Friar Minor to rule it over the monks in place of a Prior) meditated how he might forestall the time of such wrongdoing, lest the Pope should do to his own house even as he had done with other abbeys around.

* The so-called *portio congrua*: the "living wage" given to the members of a "commended" abbey, while the commendator himself took all the rest of the house's revenues. Wolsey introduced this system at St Albans, and suppressed two of her cells. (Rushbrook Williams, pp. 228–31.)

† The allusion is evidently to the fable of the Fox and the Lion's Den.

He therefore negotiated at Rome, and finally bought, in favour of this one exempt house, for a yearly tribute of twenty marks, freedom from papal interference with the confirmation and benediction of all duly elected abbots.

This pestilence, which Abbot de la Mare had diagnosed so clearly in its earlier stages, had raged with increasing fury from generation to generation on the Continent. In France, especially, where royalty regularly divided the spoils with the papacy, the greatest Churchmen had told the King publicly that these things spelt the ruin of true monastic life. In England, on the other hand, the kings had fulfilled de la Mare's hopes; they had resisted papal pressure; and this "leprosy of monasticism" was almost unknown when the sixteenth century dawned. But in 1519 Henry VIII gave St Albans *in commendam* to Wolsey; and, but for the quarrel with the papacy, the next twenty years would probably have seen him learning to rob the Church in that way as freely and systematically as his brother Francis was doing across the Channel. Of the practical working of *commendam* at this time we have a specimen in our own annals. Redman, Abbot of Shap and Bishop successively of St Asaph, Exeter and Ely, was one of the best prelates of that lukewarm age; he visited steadily, and it does not appear that his abbey suffered from this pluralism. But his younger contemporary, John Smarte, Bishop of Pavada *in partibus infidelium*, was of the pattern which *Piers Plowman* describes contemptuously as "Bishops of Nazareth, of Nineveh, of Naphthali and Damascus...that hop about England to hallow men's altars, and creep among curates and confess against the law" (B. xv. 486, 555). We find him acting as suffragan first in the diocese of Hereford and then in that of Ely. His story has been told once by Froude, who had not searched in the Hereford Registers, and again by Gasquet, who had, but who read them with strangely distorted vision. Yet the full facts are of primary importance for understanding the Dissolution.(2)

In 1518 Smarte was Bachelor of Divinity, and Wolsey, to whom the election was entrusted, chose him for Abbot of Wigmore, an important house of Austin Canons in Herefordshire. In 1519 the diocesan being absent at a Church Council, committed the Visitation of thirteen rural deaneries to his vicar-general and to

Smarte four priories with a hospital. In 1522 the bishop sent notice that he would visit Wigmore itself. In 1523 the bishop petitioned the Pope for a bull appointing Smarte to be his suffragan. In 1526 Smarte was coadjutor to the Bishop of Hereford, and we find him ordaining in the cathedral a batch of sixty-three candidates to different Orders. His episcopal activities, however, were not profitable to his abbey; for in 1529 (August 31) there is a letter from Rowland Phillips, Rector of Croydon, to Wolsey, who had been responsible for Smarte's appointment. It runs:

> I have been with the Abbot of Wigmore, and shown him your gracious mind towards him, and that he should have 40 marks pension: which of late he would have taken gladly; but now, as he trusts to a great change, and specially the extinction of your authority, he refuses the offer. Either, then, he will grow to full authority, and destroy the abbey, or he must be deprived by law.(3)

Less than two months later, Wolsey "fell like Lucifer, never to hope again"; and our bishop-abbot had a brief respite. Yet very soon (January 17, 1530) the diocesan himself was compelled to interfere. For here was the usual trouble, inherent in the *commendam* system, of financial ruin. Bishop Bothe's *Register* tells us how at Wigmore, "by reason of the ruinous state of the church, the chambers and the buildings, and of the chancels of the appropriated churches, and the debts with which the abbey is heavily burdened", the bishop empowers two commissioners to sequestrate and administer the revenues, paying *portions congrues* to the inmates "in order that divine service may be kept up in the monastery". One commissioner is a prebendary of the cathedral, the other is one of the brethren at Wigmore, John Lee, whom we shall meet again. In 1532 there is trouble again at Wigmore arising from that *portion congrue* which was an almost inseparable feature of the *commendam*. Richard Cubley, one of the brethren, petitions the bishop for absolution from this "irregularity" into which he has had the misfortune to fall through manslaughter. His plea is that, when he returned from London to Wigmore,

> he found it and its fruits occupied by certain layfolk with a priest. He petitioned them for maintenance, at least, with his own portion,

as other canons of the said abbey were wont to have; and the said priest and five armed layfolk, after certain threatening words exchanged between them and the present deponent, fell upon the said deponent and inflicted divers wounds upon him: but he, repelling force by force, and necessarily defending himself, with a sword wherewith he chanced to be armed as a wayfarer, slew one John Tykkyl, one of the said layfolk and aggressors.

Thus, however innocent of intention to murder, he finds himself irregular, and applies to his bishop. Bothe, armed with the usual papal licence to absolve penitents in "reserved" cases, absolves him from this and from his sin of having "perchance celebrated Masses and other divine service, yet not in contempt of the Keys" [of St Peter] meanwhile. He is thereby cleansed from all taint of "infamia", and free to accept, if offered, "any dignities, administrations, offices and benefices of the said Order, so long as they be compatible with each other". This canon, also, we shall presently meet again. Meanwhile, next year (August 6, 1533) we have a letter to Cromwell from Thomas Crofte, lessee of the manor of Wigmore. "My neighbour th'Abbot of Wigmore were bound to pray for you, if ye would write unto him to reform himself and his brothers; for in very conscience there is no worse rule kept within England nor Wales than is kept there of all hands." Our next glimpse, however, gives a puzzling cross-light of the kind so frequent in medieval history. The Bishop of Hereford is ill, and cannot carry out his visitation of diocese: therefore he commits this task to his suffragan, together with an archdeacon and a prebendary of the cathedral. This he does, "trusting in their fidelity, moral probity, and industry of circumspection". But we must reflect that he could scarcely exclude his suffragan from such a commission, nor, on the other hand, omit the usual complimentary formulas. In 1534 (July 20) Smarte himself wrote to Cromwell: "The Bishop of St Asaph is lately deceased; and, if I were a man of sufficient qualities, I trust you would help me to succeed him." Whether by Gairdner's mistake or not, exactly the same words are attributed to Smarte again on July 20, 1535.

Then come two documents which cast far fuller light upon Wigmore. One is undated, but there seems little doubt that this came first, if only by a few weeks or days, and that the other followed as a natural consequence. The question of priority, however, is not of primary importance, since the interconnection is obvious.

John Lee, one of the Wigmore canons, sent Cromwell a long letter of accusation against his abbot. Gairdner, who tries to put the matter objectively, knew nothing about this person: but Gasquet, who consulted the MS. *Register* at Hereford (one of the very few cases on which he can be shown to have gone thus to the original in any *Register*), might have discovered that he is the same John Lee whom Bishop Bothe had singled out from the community to work in partnership with that cathedral prebendary for the rescue of Wigmore from bankruptcy. It must therefore be taken very seriously, with only the usual allowance for the exaggerated language of those days whether in praise or in blame. Since Gasquet wrote, the Hereford Registers have been printed. The last volume of the series contains at p. 372 a series of injunctions dated March 26, 1537, and compiled by Bishop Fox from the findings of his vicar general at a Visitation made on September 19 preceding. For the sake of clear comparison, these injunctions may be printed side by side with Lee's accusations.

FOX

(*a*) First, considering that the Superior's life should afford the one model for his subjects, since he cannot with free forehead revile in others, that which he approveth in himself, therefore to thee, beloved brother [Bishop] and Commendatory [of Wigmore], in order that thou shouldst be an example of good, religious and laudable life and conversation, We strictly enjoin and command in the name of holy obedience, that thou shouldst study to avoid the company [*consortium*] of suspected women, and especially of those (if such there be) with whom thou art already noted of incontinence by thine access, under the penalties pronounced by Canon Law against incontinent persons; penalties which, rest assured, thou wilt incur without further *monitio* if thou dost disobey Our injunctions in this matter.

(*b*) *Item*, since Superiors should possess both right-minded mercy and purely-raging discipline with their subjects, lest

LEE, §§ 8, 9, 10, 26

Item, that he the said abbot hath lived viciously, and kept to concubines divers and many women that is openly known. Item, that the said abbot doth yet continue his vicious living, as it is known, openly. Item, that the said abbot hath spent and wasted much of the goods of the said monastery upon the foresaid women.

Item, the said abbot, in times past, hath had a great devotion to ride to Llangarvan, in Wales, upon Lammas-day, to receive pardon there; and on the even he would visit one Mary Hawle, an old acquaintance of his, at the Welsh Poole; and on the morrow ride to the foresaid Llangarvan, to be confessed and absolved, and the same night return to company with the said Mary Hawle, at the Welsh Poole aforesaid, and Kateryn, the said Mary Hawle her sister['s] daughter, whom the said abbot long hath kept to concubine, and had children by her, that he lately married at Ludlow. And these subjects should either be ulcerated by excessive severity or should rush into unlawful deeds through excessive wildness, We bid, enjoin and command thee to treat and address thy brethren and fellow-canons kindly, without contumely or approbrium in speech, and to correct, amend, and punish them for their excesses and faults even as regular discipline and the quality of such a fault do demand, and not more severely. And for such corrections and other capitular business, when thou goest to the chapter-house, thou shalt not bring thy Servants with thee, nor suffer them to be or remain where they may hear what is done there, nor reveal unto them capitular secrets, under penalty of contempt [of Ourselves] and of other sanctions in Canon Law for such offences.*

(c) *Item*, thou shalt not dissipate, waste or consume the lands, effects, possessions or other goods of the said abbey, whatsoever they be, but expend them for the uses of the abbey; nor shalt thou let them out to farm without the consent of the Chapter, whereby the ancient custom of thy monastery such consent was required; nor shalt thou alienate them, nor change, scrape, or increase the dates of indentures or other muniments of the said abbey, or the terms of years, under pain of suspension from the administration of the goods of the said abbey.

(d) *Item*, thou shalt inform thy brethren whether thou hast redeemed the jewels which thou hast pawned in times past; otherwise thou shalt redeem them and restore them to thy monastery, under the penalties ordained for dilapidators.

[there be] others that have been taken out of his chamber and put in the stocks within the said abbey, and others that have complained upon him to the king's council of the Marches of Wales; and the woman that dashed out his teeth, that he would have had by violence, I will not name now, nor other men's wives, lest it would offend your good lordship to read or hear the same.

* Compare Injunction (*j*).

§§ 4, 5, 21, 22

Item, the said abbot hath hurt and dismayed his tenants by putting them from their leases, and by enclosing their common from them, and selling and utter wasting of the woods that were wont to relieve and succour them. Item, the said abbot hath sold corradyes, to the damage of the said monastery.

Item, that the said abbot hath granted leases of farms and advocations first to one man, and took his fine, and also hath granted the same lease to another man for more money; and then would make to the last taker a lease or writing, with an antedate of the first lease, which hath bred great dissension among gentlemen—as Master Blunt and Master Moysey, and other takers of such leases—and that often. Item, the said abbot having the contrepaynes of leases in his keeping, hath, for money, rased out the number of years mentioned in the said leases, and writ a fresh number in the former taker's lease, and in the contrepayne thereof to the intent to defraud the taker or buyer of the residue of such leases, of whom he hath received the money.

§ 6

Item, the said abbot hath alienated and sold the jewels and plate of the monastery to the value of five hundred marks, to purchase of the Bishop of Rome his bulls to be a bishop, and to annex the said abbey to his bishopric, to that intent that he should not for his misdeeds be punished, or deprived from his said abbey.

(*e*) *Item*, in every year now to come, thou shalt render balance account or reason of thine administration during thine incumbency, once yearly in the presence of the convent or at least of four seniors; and thou shalt draw up an inventory of its possessions, under pain of sequestration; and every year, in proportion as those possessions are changed, diminished or increased, thou shalt change, reform and amend the inventory.

§§ 16, 27

Item, that the said abbot hath been perjured oft, as is to be proved, and is proved; and as it is supposed, did not make a true inventory of the goods, chattels, and jewels of his monastery to the King's Majesty and his council.

Item, the said abbot doth daily embezzle, sell, and convey the goods, and chattels, and jewels of the said monastery, having no need so to do; for it is thought that he hath a thousand marks or two thousand lying by him that he hath gotten by selling of orders, and the jewels and plate of the monastery and corradyes; and it is to be feared that he will alienate all the rest, unless your good lordship speedily make redress and provision to let the same.

(*f*) *Item*, there shall be provided a common chest, fitted with at least two keys, whereof one shall be in keeping of one of the senior canons, for storing and preserving the indentures and other muniments of the said abbey: nor shalt thou, or any of thy successors, open it except in presence of two of the seniors, under pain of sequestration from the administration pertaining to the Abbot alone.

(*g*) *Item*, seeing that, where the rudder of discipline is despised, the upshot will be shipwreck for Religion, we enjoin upon you, the canons of the said abbey, all and sundry, in virtue of holy obedience, and command that, as ye are bound, ye bow and obey to our Brother John, the said Commendator, in all things and through all, under pain of regular discipline.

Compare Lee's article 29.

(*h*) *Item*, because it is highly indecent for a man polluted with the stains of lechery to offer [the consecrated] Hosts in the Lord's house, therefore We, desirous that chastity may shine as a gem of all virtues in the Religious dwelling under Our care, do enjoin, direct and command all and sundry of you, the aforesaid canons, that ye keep chastity in all ways, and that each of you keep it, utterly avoiding the company [*consortium*] of all women so ever except in cases permitted by your Rule, under the penalty aforesaid.*

* I.e. that which the Bishop had pronounced in the Abbot's case.

(*i*) *Item*, because, [as Canon Law hath it] "that part is unseemly which agreeth not with the whole", We command in decree

§ 15

Item, that the said abbot consented to the death and murdering of one John Tichhill, that was slain at his procuring, at the said and decree in command that Richard Cubley bear himself religiously in manners, religion, dress, conversation and honesty: that he frequent choir service at both night and day hours together with the rest of the brethren, and abstain from hawking, hunting, quarrels, fights, [*rixis, pugnis*] and all such unlawful exercises, under pain of regular discipline which by Our command shall be inflicted upon him when he shall have trespassed in the aforesaid matters.

(*j*) *Item*, that the things said, discovered, and revealed in Our ordinary Visitation actually exercised through the venerable Master Hugh Coren, LL.D., Our Vicar General in spiritual matters, on the 19th day of September 1536, or any other matters concerning the reformation of the said abbey of Wigmore, be disclosed by none of you, nor let any question be discussed or any discourse be had among you in the presence of any who are not of your body,* under pain of excommunication to be pronounced against those who contravene.

monastery, by Sir Richard Cubley, cano and chaplain to the said abbot; which cano is and ever hath been since that time chie of the said abbot's council; and is supporte to carry crossbowes, and to go whither h lusteth at any time, to fishing and huntin in the king's forests, parks, and chases; bu little or nothing serving the quire, as othe brethren do, neither corrected of the abbo for any trespass he doth commit.

* Compare Injunction (*b*).

It will thus be seen how clearly Bishop Fox had here in mind the very accusations voiced by Lee, and how closely his Injunctions follow them, though, naturally in milder form and more circumspect language. The cautions "if such there be" is a regular formality in medieval, as often in modern, legal documents; it is as often used by the judge who believes as by him who disbelieves; it is a non-committal cliché. Again, there may well have been two sides to these quarrels which the bishop deplores; for Lutheranism was now nearly twenty years old, and "the New Learning" was responsible for much theological friction. Fox also ignores three paragraphs in which Lee accuses Smarte of simony, and selling Holy Orders wholesale to unworthy candidates. This part of the story, apart from Lee's exaggerated figures, could easily be paralleled from Erasmus and other contemporaries.* But it would have needed a bold bishop to take the bull by the horns there. Over John Smarte, Abbot of Wigmore, he had the most definite legal right of judgment, *sedens in tribunali*. But any direct attack upon his

* Compare, for instance, the case of an ex-monk quoted by Baskerville on p. 270 of his *English Monks, etc.* In 1576 at the age of 64, he was found to have been "ordained at Luddington by a suffragan in the time of John Longland, Bishop of Lincoln, having no letters to show, because he was a religious man, ignorant in the Latin tongue and the Scriptures".

fellow-bishop of Pavada would have been a very different venture. There is no allusion, either, to Lee's story of a corrodian inhumanly treated upon his sick-bed for the sake of his little hoard of money. However true the story may have been, it was now ancient history. So also with Cubley's case. Fox makes no allusion to that homicide, now legally whitewashed, but only insists that the chaplain should abstain in future from hunting and hawking, quarrels and fights. The main principle of an Episcopal Register was not to record past offences, but to guard against their repetition. To put it into modern terms, the book is not so much a retrospect, as a record of finger-prints by way of precaution for the future.

Cardinal Gasquet dealt with this story at such length as to make it, practically, a test case between Froude and himself; and his reputation as a specialist is still so widespread, in spite of the growing tide of exposures, that nobody can fully treat the subject without facing that challenge.(4) This is one of the very few occasions on which he shows himself to have actually consulted those episcopal records to which he has confidently appealed as "clearly proving" that "anything like general immorality was altogether unknown among the Religious of England".(5) We might therefore expect to find him here at his strongest; but the actual contrast is instructive. Froude makes no pretence of having studied those Registers which, in his day, were still unprinted and un-indexed. But he does at least print his document from the Public Record Office in full, giving that hostage to fortune. Gasquet, claiming to correct him from the MS. Register, rectifies one serious error of interpretation, into which Froude had fallen through ignorance of the very unusual fact, nowhere accessible in print at that day, that John Smarte was not only abbot but bishop also. Yet he himself, under cover of brief summaries with mere scraps of the original text, goes far worse astray. For he ignores crucial points which come out plainly from that Hereford Register. He ignores the two documents dealing with Cubley's homicide and with the financial chaos which led to the violent remedy of a commission to supersede Abbot Smarte. By ignoring the fact that John Lee was one of those two commissioners, he is able to scoff at Lee's Memorial as "this strange document", a negligible and irresponsible explosion. By misreading the MS. and printing *me* where Lee has quite plainly written *men*, Gasquet finds himself able to impute to him the dishonest suggestion that he, the accuser, should be chosen as an "indifferent and not corrupt" commissioner to sit upon the case. Thus (by manipulating Lee's letter on the one side, and the Injunctions on the other, with suppressions here and quiet distortions there, until he feels able to extract from this confusion, without too patent absurdity, a verdict of "not guilty"), he concludes:

> Thus, after a careful examination, little appears against the character of Wigmore and its abbot, John Smarte. The visitation really discredits the charges and base insinuations of John Lee. If this examination followed upon his complaints to Crumwell, as we have every reason to suppose, then the injunctions must fairly be considered as a verdict in favour of the abbot. In any case, we have in this record a picture of the state of the monastery and a judgment on the character of its superior altogether at variance with that presented in the letter of the discontented canon.

Therefore we may indeed take this as a test case. For it does pretty truly represent the position on both sides of a serious question which is still *sub judice*. Froude's attitude here is that of a man whose wide and discursive reading, with his strong reaction against his early Tractarianism, betrays him sometimes into too easy suspicions. The Cardinal, on the other hand, is so hypnotized by a natural loathing of the Reformation, and has (despite his specialist pretensions, and the masses of quotations which he produces from the *Letters and Papers of Henry VIII*) so little knowledge of the episcopal records and similar sources, that he can take his stand upon so barefaced a *petitio principii* as "much of [Lee's] long document, and notably the accusation of murder, is absurd on the face of it, and may be dismissed". When he wrote this, he had twice appealed to the evidence of the Norwich Visitations, then unprinted, in support of his own contentions. Yet those Visitations show us two cases, at this very time, which flatly contradict any such plea. For they show, at the head of the great monastery of Walsingham, one of the most famous in England, a prior not only homicidal but also adulterous and thieving. At Wymondham, again, the prior had tried to kill two fellow-monks with a sword, and thrown a stone at another in the abbot's presence, and broken open a chest to steal some documents. The Walsingham offender was persuaded to resign by the offer of "a competent annual pension". At Wymondham the bishop decreed no punishment, but commanded that all the lay servants should swear "to keep faithfully the secrets of the abbey"; an injunction strongly reminiscent of Wigmore. Here, again, is another contemporary case, flatly contradictory of Gasquet's pious optimism, though not, this time, in any document which he professed to have studied. There is in the Public Record Office a report upon the character of one Whitehede, Master of the College of Priests at Stoke. The summary in *Letters and Papers of Henry VIII* emasculates this document, as to some extent the Lee articles are emasculated; but Mr Warren Sandell has supplied me with the actual text. It runs:

> Also he is a scandalous person, and by him all the college is slandered, not only by the pitiful death of a poor alms man which he cruelly slew with the poor man's own staff, having a hoop of iron and a pike in the end, 12 men indicting him for the poor man's death of wilful murder as they yet testify, of the which death the college is greatly slandered by the country, and yet as we can perceive he is nothing ashamed....(6)

Disciplinarians and Visitors are frequently concerned with the bearing of lethal weapons by English monks; on the Continent this is even more common.(7) No less absurd, in the light of facts which stare us in the face from Monastic Chronicles and Episcopal Registers, is the cardinal's plea in this same context, that, if the Abbot of Langdon had really been as great a sinner as Henry VIII's Visitors represented, he "could have been got rid of without expense" (II, 363).

CHAPTER LXI

THE FATAL WEDGE

HERE, then, we have the undoubted beginnings in England of Montalembert's "commendam, the leprosy of monasticism". In England, as yet it is only as in the thirteenth chapter of Leviticus; just here a scab and there a patch of open sore; but those are outward visible signs of inward corruption: "the priest shall see the new flesh, and pronounce him to be unclean; it is a leprosy". Such was in fact the verdict of all true priests among us; of all who had the best interests of their Church at heart. Wolsey was in many ways a scheming politician; but he was clear-sighted and far-sighted enough to be reckoned upon that list. He saw the necessity of reform as clearly, perhaps, as anyone else, even where the flesh tempted him to profit personally from the abuses which he professionally condemned. But we have already seen how, when he proposed to the Benedictine General Chapter a series of statutes which, after all, constituted only a recall to the healthy days of two centuries earlier, the assembled fathers told him plainly that they could never keep up their numbers under such conditions, "since in these times of vices, when the world is already declining to its end, very few and very rare are those who desire austerity of life and observance of the Rule".(1) At that very time, Erasmus was writing to Sir Henry Guildford:

O wondrous vicissitude in human affairs! Formerly, it was among the professors of Religion that love of letters flourished; nowadays these, in great part give themselves to belly-cheer and lechery and money, while the love of learning passes to worldly Princes and great men of the Court. For what school or what monastery is there which hath so many men endowed with eminent probity and learning, as your Court? Have we not every reason to blush for ourselves? The banquets of priests and theologians reek of wine and are filled with scurrilous jests; they resound with intemperate tumult and bristle with poisonous slanders, while at the tables of Princes there is modest disputation concerning those things that make for erudition and piety.(2)

Whatever allowance we may make for Erasmus's flattery on one side and love of satire on the other, we cannot dismiss those words as those of an ignorant backbiter. For we have similar evidence from men whose bitter complaints were a measure not of their heretical ill-will, but of their tender devotion to the Spouse of Christ. St John Fisher, as already noted, wrote in a religious tract dedicated to the mother of Henry VII: "An we take heed and call to mind how many vices reign nowadays in Christ's Church...perchance we shall think that Almighty God slumbereth not only, but also that He hath slept soundly a great season."(3) Bishop Fox of Winchester, founder of Corpus Christi College at Oxford, in an enthusiastic welcome of Wolsey's plans for reform, was driven to confess that he was almost tempted to despair of monasticism as he saw it from his episcopal throne, "so depraved by licences and corruptions".(4) Cardinal Pole, in that book in which he tried to dissuade Henry VIII from breaking with the Pope, confessed frankly that, apart from Carthusians, Brigittines and Observantines—the merest handful among our monastic population—the rest "had utterly degenerated from the Founders of their Order".(5) Moreover, that same Reginald Pole, with three other cardinals and four very eminent prelates, sat upon the Papal Commission of 1535 which presented a confidential report upon reform to Paul III. Two clauses of this (11 and 13) concern us very directly here.(6)

Another abuse to be corrected is in the Religious Orders. For many are so deformed that they are a great scandal to the lay folk, and do much harm by their example. We consider that all the Conventual* Orders should be abolished; not so as to do injustice to any, but by forbidding the admission of fresh brethren. For thus they would quickly be suppressed without injustice to any, and good Religious might be substituted for them. But nowadays we hold that it would be best if all boys who have not yet taken the vows should be repelled from their convents. Another abuse troubleth the Christian multitude in the matter of the nuns who are under care of the Conventual friars, where in many [*plerisque*] convents public sacrileges are committed, with very great scandal to all folk. Therefore, let your Holiness take all such cure away from the Conventuals, and give it to the Ordinaries† or to others, as may be judged best.

* I.e. all four Orders of Friars except the reformed minority, the "Observants".

† The *Judex Ordinarius*, normally, is the bishop of the diocese.

The whole of this document casts not only upon the Dissolution, but also upon our Reformation in general, a light which has been strangely ignored.(7) Its preamble to the Memorial proclaims the commissioners' intention of putting before the Pope, without fear or favour, "the most grievous of those sicknesses with which God's whole Church, and the Roman Court in especial, have long been smitten, with the effect that these persistent diseases, growing by gradual degrees, have brought about the mighty ruin which we see". In the forefront of all, they put an article which touches our John Smarte very nearly. For it comes first of all among John Lee's accusations. This bishop-abbot, writes the latter, had abused his position for shameless simony,

giving of Orders, or more truly selling them, and to persons which have been rejected elsewhere, and of little learning and light consideration....So that there be many unlearned and light priests made by the said Abbot, not only in his own but also in Llandaff diocese...a thousand, as it is esteemed, by the space of seven years he hath made priests, and received not so little money of them as £1,000 for their Orders.

With the necessary allowance for medieval figures, here is exactly what the cardinals single out as the first scandal to be removed from Holy Church. They write:

The first abuse in this matter is the ordination of clerics, and especially of priests, wherein no care is taken, no diligence is applied. For everywhere those who are most unskilled, sprung from the basest origin, distinguished by evil manners, mere youths, are admitted to Holy Orders, and above all to the priesthood; that is, to the character which doth most express Christ. Hence spring countless scandals, contempt for Church Orders, and not only a lessening veneration for divine service, but even its almost extinction nowadays.

Here, after all, is what the University of Oxford had complained of more than a century earlier, in their passionate plea to Henry V for the reform of flagrant abuses for which they made the Roman Court in great measure responsible.(8) The other Articles of the 1535 Commission are equally frank about unworthy promotions to parish cures, and especially to bishoprics; the unabashed bargaining which thus defiled the Temple, in evasion of the plainest laws; the system of *commendam*. As a natural result, equally brazen absenteeism: "Almost all the pastors have withdrawn themselves from their flocks: almost all are committed to hirelings."

Another abuse, great and intolerable, whereby the whole Christian folk is scandalized is from the impediments put in the way of bishops in the governance of their flocks, especially as concerns punishment and correction of criminals [*scelestis*]. For, to begin with, evil men, especially clerics, get exemption in many ways from the jurisdiction of their Ordinary. Next, if they be not exempt, they flee forthwith to the [Papal] Penitentiary or Datary, where they speedily find some way to impunity, and (what is worse) for ready money. This scandal, most blessed Father, doth so trouble Christian folk that it cannot be described in words. Let these foul blots be removed, we beseech thy Holiness through the blood of Christ, who redeemed His Church unto Himself and washed her in that same blood.

Apostate friars or monks buy themselves licence to cast off the habit of their Order, and go about with "no vestige of that habit; nay, not even decent clerical dress". Relic-mongers "deceive rustics and simple folk, and entangle them in countless superstitions". Priests

buy licences for marriage, to the unholy joy of the Lutherans. The marriage laws are juggled for money. As for simony, alas! how doth that pestilent vice reign in the Church! so that some shrink not from committing simony, and then hastily begging for absolution from the penalty: nay, buying it, and thus keeping the benefice which they had bought.

Pious legacies are sometimes embezzled. At Rome itself, "all strangers who enter the temple of St Peter are scandalized; for there Masses are celebrated by certain dirty [*sordidi*], ignorant priests, clad in such garments and vestments as they could not decently wear even in dirty houses".

Moreover, in this Rome, harlots go about in the city like married women, or ride on their mules, followed from the heart of the city by nobles and clerics of the Cardinal's households. In no city have we seen this corruption, except in this [which should be] an example to all; for the women dwell even in stately houses.

This outspoken exposure of pestilent sores, this "aureum consilium" from nine prelates whom the Pope had carefully selected for study and confidential report to himself, bore but little fruit in action. On the contrary, when its contents leaked out and the whole was printed in Rome, the papal governor forbade its circulation. Influential courtiers were able to cripple its suggestion that the exaction of enormous fees for any sort of privilege was indistinguishable from the mortal sin of simony. They pointed out, only too probably, that the heretics would take this reform as a vote of censure on former Popes, nearly half of whose income of latter years had come from this tainted source. Contarini and his friends argued vainly that nothing could better blunt heretical weapons than a real reform of the Curia.(9) Next year, Contarini pressed Sadoleto, one of the best of the older cardinals, to attend the Reforming Committee of the Council of Trent. Sadoleto's answer was a mere cry of despair:

> I, if there were any hope whatsoever to establish some good and salutary reform, would offer to devote myself to the work...even unto the cross and death....The body of Christendom is sick too of a malady for which momentary help is of no avail; it would be better by wide and circuitous methods to bring in a partial remedy, just as in the gradual course of time this disease itself was brought in little by little.(10)

As Pastor confesses,

> in consequence of the development of the absolving, dispensing and reserving authority of the Church, such a formidable apparatus of government had been formed within the Curia, with multiplex offices and a vast horde of higher and lower officials, that it had become in and by itself almost unassailable.(11)

And in fact, if we read him carefully, we can find scarcely anything done beyond the solemn republication of regulations ancient in their origin and ancient in non-observance.

Here then, we see that yawning chasm between Established Church and Christianity which had been due so greatly to the *commendam* wedge. In England we never got beyond the thin end: the Dissolution put an end to the rest. Wolsey was our only commendator on anything like the Continental scale: yet even he cuts but a poor figure in comparison with others who dwelt nearer to the fountain head. This contrast has recently been brought out by Mr Egerton Beck in *The Dublin Review*:

One of the charges, however, preferred against Wolsey is that he was a pluralist, but in this regard assuredly no blame can be attached to him. He was not only following the custom of the age, but each of his appointments was made by the Holy See. He was Archbishop of York, administrator in turn of Bath and Wells, Durham, and Winchester, and Abbot of St Albans *in commendam*. Doubtless these were all valuable preferments, but in so far as number goes Wolsey was certainly a very moderate man. The classical instance must surely be that of a Portuguese prelate, who died some twenty years before Wolsey, Cardinal George da Costa. This man was Dean of the Sacred College and so Bishop of Ostia and Velletri, holding also another Italian see, Albano. In Portugal he held the archiepiscopal sees of Braga and Lisbon, together with the suffragan sees of Oporto, Vizeu, and Ceuta. Not content with seven bishoprics, he was also Dean of eight chapters, those of Braga, Lisbon, Oporto, Lamego, Guarda, Vizeu, and Silves in Portugal and Burgos in Spain, and of the last-named he was also precentor. Even this was not enough; he was also commendatory Abbot of eight Benedictine, six Cistercian, and two Augustinian abbeys, in addition to two others, one in Navarre and one in Venetia.(12)

CHAPTER LXII

THE BLACK BOOK

According to an anonymous writer of Elizabeth's reign, Cromwell compiled for Henry's use a "Black Book" of the English monasteries: "this was shewed in Parliament, and the villainies made known and abhorred".(1) The writer is demonstrably vague or incorrect in other particulars; and we cannot place the book higher than as a piece of gossip from an earlier generation. We are on safer ground with Latimer's sermon before Edward VI: "When their enormities were first read in the Parliament House, they were so great and abominable that there was nothing but: '*Down with them!*' but within a while after the same abbots were made bishops, (as there be some of them yet alive), to save and redeem their pensions."(2) It is just possible that Latimer himself was in the House of Lords then; and in any case his is contemporary evidence for facts which must have been well known to all the higher ecclesiastics; so we cannot suspect more than ex-partisan exaggeration here. But he makes no mention of the Black Book; his words might apply to far less systematic summaries of *comperta*, to which we must come presently. There are good reasons for doubting whether the Black Book ever existed. Nobody has ever claimed to have seen it. True, Mary appointed a commission to examine into "sundry and divers infamous scrutinies taken in abbeys and other religious houses tending rather to subvert and overthrow all good religion and religious houses than for any truth contained therein", and it would be natural enough that she should destroy such a volume if it came into her hands; but we can build little upon such a supposition. And, after all, the evidence which lies scattered in many other records, when all its convergent beams shall have been focused, will supply far more certitude than we could have gathered from such a Black Book alone as might have been compiled by an unscrupulous statesman to justify violent action. We must never forget that political side of the question: only we must avoid concentrating upon that side only. We can no more whitewash Cromwell by blackening the monks, than whitewash the monks by the blackening of Cromwell. To his own master each must stand or fall. Cromwell's own correspondence gives the surest evidence of his character; and the monks are most clearly revealed in their own chronicles and business documents, studied in relation to the visitatorial records of bishops and General Chapters. In this present chapter, then, let us focus that evidence, and judge what sort of a Black Book, compiled from irrefragable evidence, might have been laid before Parliament. Much has been anticipated here in my previous chapters; but the question is so important that it calls for detailed and unsparing study here, at the end of this work. Serious writers have too often been deterred hitherto by the sordid nature of the subject. Some have been too generous to associate themselves, even at a distance, with critics whose violence they deplore. Others, to the credit rather of their heart than of their head, repudiate off-hand, without studying the actual documents, such accusations against the Tudor monks as no decent person would make against the monks of our own day in really civilized districts. Yet all depends here upon our realizing the actual Tudor atmosphere; and that can be understood only by patient and penetrating study in the actual records, not only of Henry VIII's time but also of preceding generations.

The testimony of monastic records, with that from other orthodox sources, converges in one direction, and agrees with the popular voice. I have already quoted from Professor Mollat, a Roman Catholic specialist of well-earned reputation: "Medieval literature, rightly or wrongly, blames crudely and indiscriminately the morals of the monks."(3) This includes even the most solemn theologians and disciplinarians; prelates and saints: they judged in terms which might almost be called crude and indiscriminate. Nobody has yet attempted to meet fairly the generalizations of orthodox contemporaries on this subject collected in the Appendix to my second volume. Of these, more than 80 per cent. are strongly condemnatory, often so strongly that, by printing in heavy type the most historically important words of each extract, whether favourable or unfavourable, I have committed the psychological error of seeming to load the dice against the monks. Again, I have shown in that volume that not a single contemporary apologist has yet been found to give the monks of his time such warm and consistent praise as is commonly lavished upon them nowadays by sentimentalists who avoid the documentary sources. St Thomas More himself, in the heat of his violent polemics against anti-clerical critics, goes out of his way to tell two stories, against a nun and an anchoress, which are scarcely outdone by the most bitter Protestant satirists.(4)

The monastic problem cannot be separated from the general question of clerical celibacy. Here, the learned work of H. C. Lea can be had now in a cheap reprint.(5) Some critics have attacked Lea's other books, dealing with more complicated and specialized questions, and have shown that he is vulnerable sometimes on important details, even while his main positions stand firm. None, however, during all these seventy years, has dared to meet him fully on the general question of clerical celibacy. Moreover, two learned Roman Catholics of an earlier generation had already published, apparently without Lea's knowledge, an equally elaborate and, if possible, still more damaging attack upon that question of Roman discipline.(6) These two priestly brothers, one of whom was prefect of the Vatican Archives, were even more unfavourable to the rule of celibacy than the Quaker-bred Lea. The younger brother, in the re-issue of 1845, contends that the prohibition was a mistake from the very first. Therefore he has now undertaken to expose "the terrible immoralities which accompanied it, on the evidence of testimonies persisting through all the centuries, and which it still brings in its train". He has, in these intervening years, collected still more evidence, which he will print as an appendix when his publisher can afford to undertake it [which he never could]. He is confident that "the time is coming when the clergy will no longer be subjected to this law of Compulsory Celibacy, which undermines and ruins their moral health [*sein Heil*] and the efficiency of their pastoral work". It must be remembered, of course, that the brothers Theiner knew little by experience of the far more regular conduct of their clergy in countries like England, Holland, and Switzerland, where they live under the constant observation of a naturally critical society. The Rome in which the Theiners lived and worked so long was still the Rome of the Pope-King, where every office worth having was held by a cleric or a papal functionary, and the greatest of ecclesiastics next to the Pope, Cardinal Antonelli, was notorious for his amours. But it is the mass of documentary evidence produced in this Theiner book which, as in Lea's case, has discouraged all apologists, however bold and bitter elsewhere, from meeting any of the three authors on that particular ground. No student of the Middle Ages can be excused for ignoring Lea or the Theiners: the question they treat is of primary importance for every country and every generation. It is evident that compulsory celibacy has added enormously to the strength of the Roman Church as a working machine; and no fair-minded person can fail to admire the sanctity of many lives lived under that system. But we may find quite orthodox writers in the Middle Ages, increasing towards the end and far more numerous nowadays than their public utterances might lead us to believe, who fear in their inmost mind that the system has been penny-wise and pound-foolish. The question even came openly into the forefront of ecclesiastical politics from 1311 onwards, when Bishop Guillaume Durand suggested it in his memorial to Clement V for the Council of Vienne. Cardinal Zabarella raised it at the Council of Constance; several orthodox princes pressed it upon Pius IV, including the Archbishop of Salzburg: and on each of those occasions the great men had a very considerable backing.(7) Erasmus pressed it very strongly upon his friend the Bishop of Basel.

Erasmus makes no more distinction here between the Regulars and Seculars than public opinion did in general. He writes: "What swarms of priests are nourished in the monasteries! and, beyond these, the multitude of priests is innumerable; yet, among all these, how rare are those who live chastely!"(8) And indeed, though we shall see certain necessary distinctions later on, the two classes are, in essence, inseparable in this particular matter: each casts light upon the other.

Let us begin, therefore, with the Seculars, as far more numerous and lending themselves better to statistical evidence from the records.

In my *Medieval Panorama* I have devoted a whole chapter

to this subject (chap. XIV). The fullest statistics yet printed are from 1397, when an Episcopal Visitation is recorded covering 281 parishes in the diocese of Hereford. The clerics presented to the Visitor for incontinence by their parishioners, nearly all priests, numbered seventy-two. In other less comprehensive records, we find archidiaconal or similar courts dealing with all immoralities within the district, clerical and lay alike. In every one of those cases, from different dates and districts, the clergy supply an enormous disproportion of the accused. So, again, in the very full Visitations of Lausanne diocese in the early fifteenth century. Beyond those sources, mainly accessible in print, I am indebted now to my former pupil, the Rev. J. S. Purvis, for a far more comprehensive record from the Cathedral Archives of York. This is a book of *comperta* from the Bishop's Court, covering nearly 100 years from 1396 onwards. There, again, the clerical sinners presented are overwhelmingly numerous in proportion. The first eleven folios, covering only two years, give 231 persons presented for sexual offences. Of these, two were in minor Orders (that is, were parish clerks). The beneficed clergy supply 90 accused, and the laity (apart from the female accomplices of these clerics) supply 141. Yet the clergy cannot have formed more than about 4 per cent. of the adult population. Taking the whole century Mr Purvis finds the following statistics from the vicars choral and other clergy of the minster itself. The accused number 166, with an aggregate of 483 charges. Only 43 per cent. of these men were charged once only: twenty-six of them had five charges or more, and seven had ten or more. If it be pleaded that this is partly due to the greater public scandal of a cleric's than of a layman's lapse, that will scarcely diminish the significance of these figures. Mr Purvis writes:

> One of the most striking features of the book is the deterioration which sets in when the Wars of the Roses begin, and after. The disturbances seem to have produced a disastrous effect on ecclesiastical discipline. Not that offences became more numerous, but that the machinery for correcting such as reached the Court was vastly weakened.

But the problem had never been really solved all through the Middle Ages. When Gregory VII decreed that parishioners should refuse the Masses of notoriously concubinary priests, that did not give the world a truly celibate clergy, but a series of empty churches: so much so that the Church had to turn on her steps, and the denial of efficacy to the Mass of an unchaste priest became a flatly heretical doctrine. St Anselm, a generation later, was finally beaten by the obstinacy of the English clergy to keep their wives. Even in the long run, incontinence was not conquered but driven underground. The modern plea that these connections were, in fact, a sort of irregular marriage, reposes upon great ignorance of the actual records. These often show the priest accused with a married woman, or with a number of women: nor is any distinction drawn by the sentences among such cases. On the contrary, we find orthodox and devoted churchmen insisting that priestly marriage (the validity of which was steadily denied by Canon Law) was a worse sin than concubinage or random incontinence.(9) Lea's volumes contain many such instances; but St Thomas More, by himself, may suffice us here.(10) In his second pamphlet against Tyndale he stigmatizes priestly marriages as

> worse than whoredom.... For, sith the marriage is no marriage, it is but whoredom itself. And I am sure also that it defileth the priest more than double and treble whoredom, sith that his marriage being as it is, unlawful, and thereby none other but whoredom, doth openly rebuke and shame two sacraments there at once, that is both priesthood and matrimony, and besides that, not only committeth whoredom, but also saith openly that he will commit whoredom, and as a bold beast and a shameless whoremaster, plainly professeth before the face of God, and all Christian people, that instead and despite of his professed chastity, he cometh there to bind himself to shameless perpetual whoredom.

Sometimes the parishioners even compelled their parson to marry for the security of their own family life. A Spanish Council of 1322 found it necessary to legislate against this presumption on the part of the laity; and Nicolas de Clamanges, a century later, asserts that this was the custom "in many parishes".(11)

Similar evidence comes from the system of "cullagium", or tax for the keeping of concubines by clergy.(12) It began by commutation of personal penance for the sin to a money fine;

thence, through the venality of the clerical courts, into a bribe for escaping the fine. It was common enough to engage the attention of Innocent III at his great Lateran Council. His contemporary Giraldus Cambrensis speaks casually of a priest who "after the fashion of almost all parish priests in England", had a concubine in public.(13) The anti-Lollard Chancellor of Oxford, Thomas Gascoigne, tells a story of the contemporary Bishop of St Davids which, however the figures may be exaggerated, cannot be altogether imaginary. In 1451–2, he says, his clergy rebelled; they would rather give up their concubines than continue to pay the "cullagium" of 6*s.* 8*d.* per head. This "Bishop of abominable memory" replied: "I will not grant that your concubines be separated from you and your houses, nor that they be compelled to this. For then I, your Bishop, should lose the 400 marks which I take yearly from priestly concubines in my diocese."(14) The basic fact is practically admitted by St Thomas More himself. Tyndale had treated the system of fines for incontinence as a formal licence to sin, so long as the money was forthcoming. If he had argued, "a practical licence", he would have been able to appeal to what we know from ecclesiastical records themselves, that the man might pay the fine again and again, and that the real original penalty, deprivation of benefice, is scarcely ever found to have been enforced. He therefore lumped England with Germany, Wales, Ireland, Scotland and Spain. More answers him obliquely, but emphasizes very tellingly this weak spot: "I trust he lieth in other countries, for as for England I am sure he lieth." There is, indeed, this system of fines; "but yet are not the amendments made for licences, but devised for punishments and for means of amendment, though the malice of many men be so much that they never amend thereby". Elsewhere he writes: "As for Wales, ye be wrong informed, for wives they have not. But truth it is that incontinence is there in some place little looked unto, whereof much harm groweth in the country."(15) More's friend Erasmus is far franker. Writing to his friend the Bishop of Basel, he suggests abolition of the celibacy rule, and adds: "if Bishops try to change the law, perchance there will be protests from their officials, who smell more gain from the concubines of the priests than they would get from their wives".(16)

For it was Germany that Erasmus knew best; and it was there that the scandal was worst. In the 70th chapter of the *Complaint of the German Nation*, which the Reichstag at Nürnberg laid in 1523 before the Papal Legate Chieregati, we read:

Item, in many [*plerisque*] places, bishops and their officials not only tolerate priestly concubinage so long as certain sums of money are paid, but even compel continent priests, and those who live without concubines, to pay the concubinate-tax, asserting that the Bishop is in need of money, and that, when this has been paid, the priests are free either to remain in celibacy or to keep concubines. Every man must see how abominable this thing is.(17)

From this period, two frank descriptions of the clergy have survived, from authors of irrefragable authority. Archbishop Bourchier of Canterbury, in 1455, proclaimed a Commission of Reform for his province in 1455.(18) He is moved to this by "the constant and loud clamours of many, and by *fama publica*, and the notoriety of the facts". There are rectors and vicars who

like vagabonds and profligates run about through the kingdom and apply themselves to worldly gain, to revellings moreover to drinking bouts, and to wicked adulteries and fornications, and besides, spend their time on all manner of vices, and waste the property, goods, fruits and revenues of their benefices.... Whence it follows, of course, that very many crimes are daily committed by our people, to the contempt of God and holy religion; the dignity of the clergy is disgraced; the health of souls is dangerously neglected; the hope of the poor fails; whilst the duty of sacred hospitality is abandoned by ecclesiastics, amongst whom especially it ought to flourish; decay and all manner of ruin attack church buildings; church goods are vainly and uselessly spoiled and wasted; priests unlearned, untaught, unknown, and unrecognized, and oftentimes without Orders, or suspended from fulfilling their Orders, do by presumptuously administering sacraments and sacramentals, bring the souls of our subjects to ruin and captivity.

Our next evidence is from Bishop Fox of Winchester in a confidential letter to Wolsey, written in 1527, a year before his death. He is giving account of his stewardship:

And as for the secular clerkis, I have not be rigourouse uppon theym in poneshementis except it were for manyfest fornycation or advowtrey. And yet for theme they never dyd open penance to theyr noys [*harm*] or infamy. And also I never pryved person [*deprived a parson*] in noo dyoces that I have be in. And except it be in Suthwarcke,* whiche is under the jurisdiction of tharchedecon, I trowe there be as little oponly knowen synne or enorme crymes, both in persons spirituall and temporall, as is within any diocese of this realme.(19)

This, then, is the retrospect of one of our best bishops after thirty years of episcopal work in four different dioceses, in which we have good reason to believe that the clergy were above the European average. The only point upon which this disciplinarian has been "rigorous" is incontinence; yet even here he has never, in his long career, inflicted either of the standard statutory punishments: public penance or deprivation. Whatever credit we may give him for power of personal persuasion (and in our earlier letter to Wolsey he had confessed to incomplete success with the monks)(20) it remains obvious that, with his parish clergy, he must have fallen back mainly upon the system which we find in the official records of other dioceses; viz. that of pecuniary amendments. From whatever angle our testimony comes it casts a very unfavourable light upon many among the ordinary parish clergy in theory. These, it is true, had taken no vow of chastity; continence was a rule of discipline imposed upon them from above. In the court of conscience, therefore, the monk had stronger demands upon him; but how far did conscience, in ordinary cases, restrain him from following the transgressions of the "worldly" clergy? We have unexceptionable evidence here from one of the frankest and most experienced of orthodox Visitors, Johann Busch. The cloisterers of Sülte were grown old in sin, and quarrelled violently with the new brethren brought in to reform their convent. Reform thus seemed hopeless; but Busch was advised by wise counsellors to grant the unruly brethren their petition for transference to parish work, each by himself in one of the appropriated churches. "Let them, when they beg for leave of absence, promise that they will live in the world according to priestly rule: if you find the contrary, then you will be able to correct them; for in the world, being solitary, they will comport them-

* Southwark was in Fox's diocese of Winchester; it was notorious for its brothels, "the Stews". which brought rents to the see.

selves better through the fear of man than they do now in the monastery, when they fear no man." Busch adds "from that time forth I did thus, and so the monastery thenceforth began to move towards full reform".(21) The inference would seem plain. A man's actions are even more convincing than his words: and here they both agree in a matter where he was in deadly earnest. A priest (he felt) might be more free to follow his unruly inclinations in a monastery (even though that was situated close to Hildesheim, under the bishop's very nose, and subject to the special visitation of an official with powers *ad hoc* from the higher authorities) than he would have been in a parish cure. We need go no further for the explanation why, when decay had once set in, we sometimes find such startling instances of monastic corruption.

CHAPTER LXIII

THE COMPERTA

THIS, by itself, would supply considerable anterior probability for the very unfavourable character of the *Comperta* collected from the Cromwellian Visitations. But there are other sidelights, almost equally strong, which must be briefly indicated.

In studying the immense mass of orthodox disciplinary writings, we find one class of arguments pressed with almost wearisome frequency. They meet us on the very threshold; and, the farther we read, the more inevitable we find them. To sum them up in brief, they run thus: you cannot separate the *Tria Substantialia* of monasticism from each other; nor in practice, can you even separate them from the more important of the non-substantials. The three points from which this train of reasoning most frequently starts are those of *proprietas*, flesh-eating, and wandering. In each of these three cases, argue the disciplinarians, violation of the Rule leads naturally to breach of the vow of chastity.

As to *proprietas*, I have quoted a few of the many examples in my third volume (pp. 405–9). The proprietary monk (it is argued) becomes a gentleman at large, able to pay for his own pleasures and defy his superiors. We have seen that Whethamstede, describing how Wallingford amassed his own hoard, hints at other things as well which he will not specify in writing.

As for flesh-food, contemporaries regarded it as almost inevitable that high feeding, combined with cessation of manual labour, should produce almost insuperable temptations.

Even more fatal, perhaps, was the emancipation from the cloister. I have emphasized this above (chap. LVIII), but it is worth while to add one further instance here. It begins, readers may note, with that same quotation from St Augustine with which the Premonstratensian Visitor continually prefaced his own injunctions against vagabondage. It is the eleventh of those

Articles of Reform which Henry V's Commission proposed for the Benedictines in 1421:

Item, seeing that (as St Augustine saith) among all conflicts that beset the Christian the hardest are the battles of chastity, where the fight is daily and the victory rare; and, according to the same Father, he who will not avoid familiar converse with women falleth swiftly into ruin; nor (as the Apostle saith) doth any remedy remain but by flight, therefore let it be strictly ordained that no Religious of this Order have licence for outgoing or incoming in the towns or cities where his monasteries are situated, but let their superiors be wholly deprived of all faculty for licensing them to eat or drink or talk in such places, except with noble folk; since therefrom grievous scandals may arise, and incentives to vice.(1)

So seriously do the disciplinarians draw conclusions from those three infractions of the Rule which are constantly recorded as actual facts by orthodox visitatorial records and General Chapter Statutes!

If this line of argument stood alone, it would be obviously unfair to press it too far. That a man is beset with temptations, or even that he courts such temptations, does not authorize us to assume lapses as an actual (apart from logical) consequence. But, on the other hand, we must remember the character and qualifications of those disciplinarians who insist upon a strict nexus between cause and effect. The list includes Alvarus Pelagius (who, as Franciscan friar and papal penitentiary, had heard perhaps as many confessions as any other man of the mid-fourteenth century) with Busch and Nider, two of the most energetic and successful reformers of the mid-fifteenth. Here, then, are three eminent and unprejudiced experts. We may refuse to accept implicitly, even on the word of the greatest expert, an assurance that certain antecedents will inevitably produce certain consequences. But common sense should restrain us from ignoring such warnings without the most careful examination. Yet such examination, so far as I am aware, has never yet been attempted in this matter.

Such was the atmosphere. The practically unanimous conviction of disciplinarians was (to quote, as they themselves often quoted, from Ezekiel viii), that, if ever men set themselves to "dig in the wall", it would be seen "what the ancients of the house of Israel do in the dark". Here, then, at last, the civil powers were undertaking a full enquiry throughout the kingdom. Their temptations to exaggerate were obvious, but must it not have been equally plain that these mere politicians were likely to find what the saints had so often predicted?

The more we study the relevant documents from all sides the more we shall find how many lights converge from widely different sources. The Cistercian abbey of Wardon in Bedfordshire supplies a significant instance. We can get here behind Cromwell and his agents to the orthodox official records.

Somewhere about 1536, soon after the Visitation by Cromwell's commissioners, the abbot wrote his reasons for wishing to resign his office. The brethren (he says) reviled him as the cause of their strict claustration in accordance with the Injunctions. "They be in number 15 brethren; and, except 3 of them, none understand nor know their Rule nor the Statutes of their Religion." Only two could be induced to follow instruction in grammar. The sub-prior had been caught in the vineyard with "a brothel woman, and had bribed his discoverers to silence". The abbot names five others as "common drunkards", and intimates his suspicion of unnatural vice also. The divinity lectures prescribed by the Injunctions had led to discord, whether through fault of the conservatives or of the innovators or of both.(2)

Taken by itself, this letter might be construed in very different senses. Does it bear out the Governmental thesis that reform has been long overdue, and it is high time for the lay power to interfere? Or, on the contrary, does it show the dangers and inconveniences of allowing complaints from inside the monastery to the worldly powers outside? Was the main effect of Cromwell's Injunctions to create and foster discontent, and was that Cromwell's main purpose? To help us here, we have two illustrative documents from the MS. Cistercian records at Dijon. One alone is formally dated, 1492; but they are evidently within a few months or weeks of each other, since both emanate from the same pair of Visitors: the Abbots of Stratford and of St Mary Grace by the Tower. They cast light on an abbey exempt by reason of its Order from correction by any but the General Chapter at Cîteaux; and they are contemporaneous with those revelations from St Albans, exempt in virtue of what it can subtly engineer at the Roman Court.

The first is a long and formal complaint from these Visitors to the Abbot of Cîteaux. They regret to have been able to do so little on the Visitation entrusted to them. In these evil days, the reformer must face "great labours, heavy expenses, and the unbearable tumult of Secular folk", to whom sinners appeal for protection. Thus "it is most difficult to correct the perverse, and cunning subterfuges grow daily within the Order". A specially lamentable instance is that of Wardon. The whole neighbourhood cries out against this abbey: our ears are besieged with these complaints (almost the exact words of Morton, two years earlier, concerning St Albans). The abbot is pawning gold and silver, books, chalices and other Church valuables, to the imminent ruin of the house. The Visitor sent him a *monitio* (as Morton did to St Albans) that he should correct himself and his monks; yet in vain; for the abbot has appealed to a certain knight, his personal friend, by whose influence he himself had been elected to the exclusion of more worthy candidates; and between them, these two have formulated the discipline-destroying doctrine that no house of the filiation of Clairvaux is subject to the ordinary Visitor, or to any but the General Chapter itself. There is peculiar piquancy in this invocation of St Bernard's name in the cause of rebellion against ordinary discipline. The abbey's peace is torn also by a quarrel, with reciprocal accusations of murder, and breach of the seal of confession—an offence far more common in pre-Reformation days than modern writers are often willing to admit.

The next Wardon document is a booklet bound, significantly enough, in parchment covers torn in later times from a medieval missal. It records the *comperta* at this Visitation of 1492 by the Abbots of Stratford and St Mary, and the Injunctions which they gave in consequence. The monks "rise not for their vigils"; they hurry indecently through other Services, and often fail to say the daily Mass for benefactors' souls. They wear the forbidden under-linen. They raise the wind by selling corrodies. They have pledged a long list of valuables (rehearsed in detail) including chalices and "12 great volumes" (at the price of £4. 18*s*. 4*d*.). "Women of bad character [*infames*] often enter the abbey, to the extreme ill-fame thereof and to the destruction of Religion." The abbot, in view of the coming Visitation, called the brethren into Chapter and "promised that he would amend all these things, forbidding all and several of the brethren, under severe threats, from telling the Reformer of the truth of the abbey's defects". One monk "deposed that he would willingly say more, but for so many inhibitions on the part of his friends, who firmly asserted that, if in any way he should report to the Reformers any thing disagreeable or adverse to his Abbot, he would certainly come into peril of death; therefore he did not dare to explain further". All that the Visitors could do in that matter was to leave an injunction that the abbot should not "in future, command or impose anything upon any brother or brethren by reason of anything said or done" at the Visitation.(3)

What, then, did these reports actually say? For, though no Black Book may ever have existed beyond the different *Compendia Compertorum* compiled by Cromwell's Visitors, yet enough of these *Compendia* have survived to afford what all students are agreed to take as a sample of the whole.(4)

Let us see, word for word, that report which is the most detailed on the whole, and conveniently brief. It is from the diocese of Norwich, and has this further advantage, that we have for comparison those far more detailed Norwich episcopal visitations from which I have given so much evidence in chap. LVII.

*Shouldham Nuns** J. P. child before entering Religion; M. B. one child by a priest. *Shouldham Canons** J. H.; J. M.; R. T. confess voluntary pollution. *Blackborough* E. D. (Prioress); I. D.; D. S. suspected of incontinence. *Pentney* R. C. (Prior) incont, as appears from the confession of the Prioress of Marham;† J. D. inc. with spinster and v.p.;‡ S. L. v.p.; J. S. with married woman and v.p.; R. C. v.p. *Marham* B. M. one child, and confessed incon. with Prior of Pentney; E. L. one child, by a married man; E. P. one child, married man; D. L., one child, married man; J. M. two children by single men. *Westacre* R. C. with divers women, both married and single; W. S. v.p.; J. T. v.p.; W. C. v.p.; R. P. v.p.; E. M. v.p.;

* This, as a Gilbertine house, was double, of nuns and of brethren.
† Some two miles distant, across the river.
‡ Voluntary pollution.

R. B. v.p.; W. S. v.p.; J. W. v.p.; W. W. (Prior) confesses v.p.;* J. B. with married woman; T. B. v.p.; R. H. with two women and confesses submission to sodomy. *Castleacre* N. B. with spinster; J. B. with spinster; R. H. v.p.; W. E. v.p.; R. S. v.p.; J. L. v.p.; J. H. married woman and v.p.; E. A. v.p.; E. K. with a boy and v.p. *Coxford* W. H. confesses incont. and v.p. *Walsingham* J. L. confesses v.p.; N. M. ditto; R. G. ditto; R. S. ditto; J. C. married woman; J. W. ditto. Here then appeared much superstition in feigned relics and miracles.† *Binham* T. A. with spinster; E. H. with married woman; J. L. suffered sod. *Wendling* T. A. with married woman; he is a great dilapidator. *Beeston* N. W. with married woman. *Bromholm* W. L. (Prior) with spinster; W. A. confesseth incont. S. M. with married woman; H. S. with married woman. Here appeared much superstition with the cross which they call "The Holie Crosse. of Bromeholme". They say that they have here the girdle of St Mary and her milk and fragments from the cross of St Peter and St Andrew. *St Benet* [*Holme*]. R. B. confesseth incont.; J. S. v.p.; J. H. v.p.; T. H. v.p.; Here the Abbot hath made many innovations and hath granted unusual grants under the common seal for fear of visitation. And here we scented no small suspicion of confederation for not giving evidence.‡ *Hickling* R. W. with married woman; R. L. with married woman; R. B. with married woman; R. A. v.p.; J. M. v.p.; M. W. v.p.; *Ingham* J. S. (Prior) with married woman; C. B. with woman. *Norwich Cathedral* R. S. v.p.; R. T. v.p.; R. N. confesseth incont. with married woman and v.p.;§ W. T. confesseth incont.; N. T. v.p.; *Aldby* B. P. v.p.; F. V. v.p. All in this priory desire dissolution with two exceptions. *St Faith's* J. O. with spinster; T. N. v.p. *Langley*. Here almost all are released from Religion. *Buckenham* J. M. (Prior) with spinster; T. F. with married woman and v.p.;‖ T. R. v.p. *Wymondham* T. L. confesseth v.p.; R. Ca. ditto; R. Co. ditto; J. W. ditto. *St Olaves* W. D. (Prior) v.p.; C. M. ditto; H. M. ditto. Among the relics they have a certain linen cloth called "The Wymple of St Ethelrede", through which they draw knotty laces [*fibulas nodosas*] or silken threads which women think good for

* For this man's history see G. Baskerville, *English Monks, etc.*, pp. 194–5.

† See Erasmus's account in his Colloquies (*Peregrinatio Religionis Ergo*, summarized in Froude's *Erasmus*). For the Episcopal Visitation of Walsingham in 1514 see *Vis. Dioc. Norwich* (C.S. 1888), pp. 113ff.; long extracts translated on pp. 33ff. of my *French Monasticism in* 1503.

‡ The MS. has *delegendo*, which makes no sense in this context; a scribal error seems plain for *detegendo*, the ordinary technical word for giving evidence at a Visitation.

§ At the Episcopal of 1526 he was in possession of keys to a private room; "and to him, as is believed, women have had access" (*Vis. Norwich*, C.S. 199).

‖ In *L. and P.* this count is mistakenly omitted.

sufferers in the throat. They have also "The Wymple of St Audrede"* for sore breasts and chest, and her Comb for headache's, and Aaron's Rod for boys that have worms in the belly, and St Etheldrede's Ring which pregnant women put upon their fingers, thinking that they will be more easily delivered. *Fordham*, or *Biggyn* W. B. v.p.; R. B. v.p.; nor are there any others in the priory. *Bury St Edmunds* J. M.; Abbot, delights in the company of women and in sumptuous banquets; he delights in the games of cards and dice, and haunts his granges greatly and preacheth not. T. R., Prior, is defamed for incontinence by reason of their excessive frequentation of women; so also are T. L., T. D., J. W., J. S., J. C., H. A., T. M., and Roger L.; Robert L. confesses adultery; J. O. and J. C. confess v.p., J. B. and Roger L. have apostatized. Among their relics they have, as they say, St Edmund's Shirt and Christ's Blood and portions of the Holy Cross. They have a stone wherewith St Stephen was stoned, and coals wherewith St Laurence was roasted; also nail-parings and hair-cuttings of St Edmund, enclosed in a pyx. They have some skulls, among which they have one of St Petronilla, which simple folk put upon their heads, hoping thereby to free themselves from fever. They have also the boots [*ocreas*] of St Thomas of Canterbury, and the sword of St Edmund. They have the custom there, whensoever rain is desired, to carry in their public prayers or processions a shrine wherein are laid the bones of St Botulph, hoping that rain will thereby come sooner. [*Here the compiler wanders off as follows*: Old woman's superstition. Yet men of Kent are wont to bear away thence a little† wheat and wax tapers, which they burn at the end of the field while wheat is being sown, and thence (as they hope) neither tares nor other ill weeds will grow that year among the wheat.] In the *Comperta* we smell a strong suspicion that the Abbot and brethren were confederate beforehand that they would report [*detegerent*] nothing against themselves; for, though nowhere else do monks live with more licence and irregularities [*licentiosus aut insolentius*] than there, by *communis fama*, yet nowhere was less confessed than there.(5) *Icklesworth* R. F. confesseth v.p. And there also we scent a vehement suspicion of confederation; for, though they are 18 in number, yet nothing was confessed.‡ *Thetford* T. W. confesseth theft. N. H. confesseth v.p. Here also the suspicion of confederation transpires [*colligitur*], since they are 17 in number. *St Sepulchre*,

* *Audrey* was simply the popular form of *Etheldreda*. The cheap little articles sold in multitudes at Stourbridge Fair, Cambridge, christened "St Audrey's Fair", gave rise to the common epithet of *tawdry*.

† *L. and P.* reads *triticum panxillum*, with a natural query as to the meaning. The writer's *u* and *n* are often indistinguishable, and *pauxillum* gives plain sense.

‡ Except, no doubt, that which is asserted of R. F.

Thetford J. C. confesseth incon., and would desire to be licensed to recur to the remedy granted by God, *viz.*, marriage; J. P. v.p.; A. J. v.p.; W. B. confesseth incon. *Rushworth College* One confesses incon., two v.p. *Thetford Nunnery* M. L. confesseth incon. All beg the release [from vows] except the Prioress. *West Dereham* R. W. with married woman; T. M. with spinster; R. Norwold with divers, both married and spinsters, and confesseth sod; J. J. confesseth v.p.; R. W. ditto; T. D. ditto; P. T. ditto; R. G. ditto; T. D. ditto. *N.B.* R. Norwold, *alias* Marke, saith in virtue of his oath and conscience that, if all would so frankly confess their transgressions to my lord King as to speak [out], he would find not even one of the monks or priests who did not lie either with women or with males, or by v.p. or other unmentionable abuses of that kind. Wherefore he wished from all his heart that all might be licensed, whoever desired, to resort to the remedy of marriage; and he hopeth that for this purpose his Royal Majesty hath been divinely sent to earth. So saith also R. W. So, moreover, the said P. T. and R. G., who had cure of souls in country parishes.* Asked concerning the practice of sodomy, they say that this crime reigneth for the most part among priests, both Secular and Regular, and youths who are not yet married. And they would also wish that the remedy of marriage should be granted to such persons. *Crabhouse* M. S. (Prioress) one child; A. S. one, by an unmarried man; C. B., two, one by priest, one by layman; E. B. two, by unmarried men. Here they have alienated certain farms to a certain Konysbie and Gyben, which my Lord [Cromwell] hath sequestered, from [good] causes.

These *Comperta*, then, deal with thirty-three houses. They show sixty-four persons accused of incontinence; in twenty-three of those cases the partner is a married woman, and in two a priest. There are sixty-two accusations of v.p.; three of sodomy; and one of theft.

The whole list of *comperta*, of which this forms an important section, deals with 153 houses visited. They show 239 accusations of incontinence (thirty-two with married women), 161 v.p.; sod. 105. Relics, of a kind which even modern piety regrets as tending to superstition, were found in sixty cases. Specially frequent were girdles for pregnant women; there were nineteen of these, of which fifteen were in the houses of male Religious.(6)

The two most serious of these moral accusations cannot be avoided in any adequate discussion of this subject. At Bishop

* West Dereham was Premonstratensian; therefore the brethren often acted as country parsons.

Nikke's Visitation of Westacre in 1526 one canon gave the following testimony: "Brother John Barbour committed the crime of sodomy with a boy and was caught in the offence by layfolk and hath often been formally accused [*detectus*] of this crime".(7) Dr Jessopp puts this in a parenthesis, with the heading *Erased*; and he writes: "Reading between the lines, I cannot resist the impression that the horror and surprise of this frightful business staggered and perplexed the Visitors." But the "erasure", when the MS. is consulted, shows merely that, in later ink, a pen has been run through the sentence, without any attempt to make it illegible. Dr Gairdner, who began in incredulity, pointed out later that the accusation is repeated lower down without comment, and with explicit reference to the "erased" passage.(8) The colour of the ink would fit in with Bishop Tanner, who found the MS. and gave it to the Bodleian. There are three similar cases, two told with greater detail, in the *Episcopal Visitations of Lincoln*.(9) So far as I remember, no punishment is recorded in any of those, as none is recorded at Westacre. Punishment was nominally, of course, severe. The Cistercian Statutes repeat it more than once: imprisonment for life. No definite testimony, so far as I know, has been produced for the literal application of that severe sanction.

Yet for centuries it had been one of the most serious problems in monastic, and general clerical, discipline.

Bishop Rather of Verona (d. 974) speaks of the cohabitation of his clergy with women as "so customary, so public...that they not only think it lawful but also that none who avoideth this must needs seem unable to be guiltless of that abominable sin of which St Paul speaketh" (Romans i, 27).(10) But the classical authority on this subject is the *Liber Gomorthianus*, which has not been, and probably never will be, translated. This was written in 1049 by St Peter Damian Cardinal and bosom friend to Gregory VII. The book is dedicated to Pope Leo IX. Its theme, from beginning to end, is that criminals of this description must not be suffered to enter the clerical ranks; or, when within, must be ejected.(11) The language is violent, even for the Middle Ages: but those were the days of hottest fight for the rule of celibacy. This is "deep-rooted"; it is a "cancer of the soul"; one "eightfold criminal" is quoted. Yet it is too often winked at: the prelates must bear the guilt of this. The distress of pious folk can be described only in the words of Jeremiah's *Lamentations*. Chap. VI deals with "the Spiritual Fathers who defile themselves with their [spiritual] children"; with "them who confess their crimes to those [priests] with whom they have fallen [into sin]" in the false belief that they can thus trick God into absolving them. Chaps. X–XII deal with those offenders who pleaded apocryphal canons which greatly attenuated the strict punishments proclaimed by genuine Canon Law. He enters into lurid details. He exhorts the sinners to repentance and conversion (chaps. XXIII and XXIV), and concludes with a protest against the man who may accuse him as

> the revealer of his brother's crime. Let such a one [he says], know that I am seeking with all my mind the favour of my inward Judge and fear not the hatred of the wicked nor the tongues of detractors. I would rather be cast into a pit, by a wicked crime, as innocent as Joseph, who accused his brethren to his father, than like Eli be punished with the vengeance of God's fury for that he saw the wickedness of his sons and held his peace.

He claims with St Paul: "I take you to record this day, that I am pure from the blood of all men: for I have not shunned to declare unto you all the counsel of God." Roger Bacon wrote his *Compendium Studii Philosophiae* in 1271, for and at the bidding of Pope Clement IV. He sets out to expose the weaknesses of Theology, Science and Philosophy in that day, and finds one of the main causes is the lack of sound morality.

> University students [he writes], give themselves over in youth to lechery and gluttony: and, when they are old, they depart not (as Solomon saith) from their evil customs; nay, they are confirmed therein, save only a very few to whom God giveth special grace. They are more and more blinded by lechery, as was proved in this very year; for many theologians at Paris, and men who had lectured in theology, were banished from that city and from the realm of France for vile sins of sodomy.(12)

Bacon's younger contemporary, Dante, finds a multitude of these sinners in hell, especially from the universities, where the rule of celibacy was nearly always enforced.(13) His greatest medieval commentator, Benvenuto da Imola, expatiates at length upon this passage.(14) He also accuses the universities first and foremost.

I myself have known certain old men infected by this disease.... Certainly, when first I saw these words of Dante, I was very indignant; but afterwards I learned by experience that our most wise poet hath here done excellently. For in 1375, when I was at Bologna* and lectured upon this book, I found certain vermin bred of the cinders of Sodom who infected the whole of that University; and, being unable to bear longer with that great stench, the smoke whereof was already dimming the stars, I disclosed the matter, not without grievous peril to myself, to the Cardinal of Bourges, who was the Legate at Bologna. He, as a man of great virtue and learning, who detested such abominable crimes, commanded an enquiry for the principal offenders, some of whom were caught while others fled in terror. And, but for the hindrances wrought by a certain traitorous priest to whom the commission had been entrusted and who was infected with that same disease, many would have been given over to the flames of fire....Thereby I incurred the deadly hatred and enmity of many men: but God's justice hath graciously protected me hitherto from these enemies of nature.

Warnings of the kind are frequent in General Chapter Statutes of the Mendicant Orders.(15) St Bernardino, who was one of the greatest of missionary preachers and confessors under the new Observant revival, is most emphatic on this subject. He regarded it as the worst moral plague of his age. In his open-air sermons to multitudes at Siena, he warned them of fire from heaven, and bewailed the deep-rooted prevalence of the evil: "As thou hast this sin, so also had thy father...your children may say, when they commit it, 'so did my father too'."(16) A few years earlier, about 1410, a grave warning came from Jean Gerson, Chancellor of Paris.(17) It is in this connection that Gerson writes elsewhere: "Believe those [of us] who 'dig through the wall'...for what old men do with their juniors both in monasteries and in universities and elsewhere."(18) And, finally, Erasmus to his friend the Bishop of Basel, in criticism of Regular and Secular clergy: "I touch not upon the mysteries of their secret lusts; I speak only of those things which are notorious to the multitude."(19)

The documentary evidence of these foregoing chapters could be multiplied almost *ad infinitum*; but this much should suffice. Indeed, it might indeed be suggested that this is more than

* The greatest university in Christendom, next to Paris.

sufficient, and that the chapters read less like history than like an accusing barrister's arraignment. This, I should plead, is mainly due to the almost incredible indolence of some among my predecessors, and want of candour in others, while academic critics have too often judged the question from their comfortable arm-chairs, impatient that there should still be so much written about this ancient bone of contention, and deciding for their own selves on the easy principle "six of one, and half-a-dozen of the other". The frailties of Henry and Anne are known to all men; but, by those conventions of clubland which are often strong in academic circles, it is more indecent to expose recorded vice than to ignore or palliate. A similar temptation to one-sided "impartiality" lies in the confessedly unsavoury character of many among Cromwell's agents. They were chosen for unpleasant detective work which, for centuries past, had been reserved for ecclesiastics, but which, by the confession of the most zealous orthodox reformers, had seldom been adequately performed. These new State instruments were, necessarily, the very opposite of their predecessors. The temptation of the Episcopal or General Chapter Visitor had been to ignore inconvenient facts: St Thomas More does not venture to meet directly St Germain's complaint that even the best Churchmen were too often inclined to shield the sinners of their own cloth rather than to grapple sternly with the sin. The Church courts, on which the Visitor had mainly to rely, were notoriously corrupt from top to bottom. We must again remember here that complaint of the Abbot of Cîteaux, at the great Royal Council of Tours in 1493. Monks (he said) who had money enough to press appeal after appeal at Rome or in the Court of Arches were pretty sure of success, since "Many Abbots and Visitors, who cannot maintain such heavy expenses, even those who have a great number of subjects, are oftentimes constrained to dissemble, and, in trust upon divine mercy, to keep patience until some other day when God shall vouchsafe to provide a remedy thereunto".(20) The remedy which God found at last was bitter to swallow: Henry VIII and his agents: brought unscrupulous powers to bear upon privileges which were unconscientiously abused. The tables were now completely turned, and these undisciplined monasteries were faced with men whose temptation was on the side of over-severity. The Church courts were swallowed up, for this purpose, in a State judicature almost, or possibly quite, as corrupt as they had been. Bishops and archdeacons had been tempted to take a privy bribe and remit the punishment; Cromwell and his agents took such bribes unabashedly. Prominent in the modern condemnation of these men is the fact that among those who got the richest pensions are monks whom the Visitors had condemned as greatest sinners; yet, here again, we have simply the same sudden reversal of parts. We have seen in an earlier chapter how, under an unusually competent and careful bishop, five of the worst offenders were promoted to abbacies within a single generation and in a single not very numerous Order. Even among the fragmentary surviving records we could probably find as many such orthodox cases as in the Cromwellian Visitation. In 1467 Abbot Norwych of Westminster was suspended for serious and continuous mismanagement of the abbey's revenues, from which it took long to recover. He was granted a pension of 100 marks, something like £1000 modern. Thus, though we are bound to distrust the Cromwellian blackening, we have similar reasons for discounting the pre-Cromwellian whitewash. Has any of Henry's accusations in 1536 been shaken so thoroughly, by unexceptionable side evidence, as the flattering reports of those Benedictine Visitors have been shaken by the contemporary evidence from those same houses which has happened to survive in the episcopal *Registers* of Lincoln?

CHAPTER LXIV

REVOLT AND PENSIONS

THE Pilgrimage of Grace has been unduly emphasized as evidence in favour of the monasteries. In that, and the Lincolnshire Rebellion which preceded it, the Dissolution was indeed put forward as one of the main grievances against Henry's government; and monastic doles must have been specially missed in the North, with its more scattered and poorer population. But the militia of the South, though far from enthusiastic in defence of the Government, could yet be trusted to march and fight; and in those counties past rebellions had been rather against the monastic landlords than in their favour. Even in Lincolnshire, the few monks who joined the rebels did so only under compulsion; or at least they so pleaded when the day of reckoning came; and that plea is almost equally significant whichever way we take it. Concerning the whole movement, the Misses Dodds sum up:

> It is curious that their most ardent apologists dwell particularly on the small share that the monks took in it, as this does not at first sight appear to be to their credit. The Pilgrims were putting themselves, "lives, wives, children, lands, goods and chattels...to the utter adventure of total destruction", on behalf of the monks. In return they were received with terror, helped grudgingly, and dismissed as soon as possible. Their champions might risk their all, but the monks would risk nothing in return if they could help it. They were ready to share the fruits of victory, but they had no mind to suffer for a possible defeat. The attitude of the Abbot of Furness was only too common—they wanted to be safe with both sides.
>
> In extenuation it may be urged that the arrival of a band of rebels at a monastery was often indistinguishable from the arrival of a gang of marauders. At the beginning of the rebellion, moreover, the commons often compelled the monks to serve in their ranks, which was contrary to the monastic vow; it is not suggested that the religious should have borne arms, but that they might have been more liberal of money, encouragement and prayers.
>
> Then too the monks were landowners, sharing all the interests and terrors of the propertied class. They might on the whole be better

landlords than laymen were, but in individual cases they had aroused hatred, and they feared the consequences. The Abbot of Jervaux's tenants were ready to murder him. Mackerell said that many of the commons were his mortal enemies. The poor were groping towards a policy of their own, that they would defend the monasteries if the landlords would remedy their grievances. The religious were not farsighted enough to understand and adopt this policy. They would not take part with the commons; they were merely afraid of them and thought that somebody ought to keep them in order. They did not see that by their own faith they might convert a disorderly rabble into a body of crusaders. It was not impossible; the miracle had been wrought before and would be again, but the English religious of that age were not the men to perform it. They were in the main worthy creatures enough, but incapable of either a martyr's complete self-abnegation or a rebel's courage and decision...

When the order came for the monks to go, they lamented—and accepted the King's pension. There were among them some martyrs and some rebels, but even out of those who were executed many would have submitted to the King on any terms if he would have accepted their submission.(1)

In Lincolnshire, the insurgents showed neither discipline nor courage: they had no efficient leader and no definite policy.(2) One cause of discontent, even, was the unwillingness of the clergy to face an examination by a Royal Commission into their morals, their education, and their politics: a monk testified that he himself had hoped to "succeed to the room of some of these unlettered parsons". In short,

the Rising was not simply religious or agrarian or political, but a little of each. It was as much against an unpopular tax and an unpopular bishop [of the diocese] as against the King's religious policy and his chief minister. The rebels protested against the Dissolution of the Monasteries; but the vital question of the Royal Supremacy was only once, and then the rebels expressed their willingness to acknowledge the title. The gentlemen hated Cromwell and the Statute of Uses, but they wavered on the question of the abbeys, and were very much afraid of the commons and of civil war.(3)

The Pilgrimage of Grace, again, is similarly summed up by the same two authors after an exhaustive study of the whole documentary evidence. It "failed completely: its only result was to hasten the very events which the Pilgrims dreaded.... It is not a sufficient explanation of this failure to say that the

Pilgrims were contending against the spirit of the age." The main causes were fourfold. First, they entirely mistook the King's character. "They believed him to be a weak, good-tempered sensualist, always the tool of some favourite", while in fact he "took some pains to hide his despotic temper and his iron will under a mask of careless good-humour, and with his northern subjects the deception was completely successful".

Secondly, it had no leader of genius to stand against Henry's undoubted political genius, good or bad.

Thirdly, there was a fatal rift between the gentlefolk and the common people. "Briefly, the gentlemen wanted higher rents and lower wages, while the commons wanted lower rents and higher wages. It seemed impossible that anything could reconcile these discordant aims."

Fourthly, "Though the force of religion accomplished much, the clergy of England as a body gave little countenance to the Pilgrims. The lower clergy, both regular and secular, devoted themselves to the cause; but the higher ecclesiastics were supine.... The Papacy ignored the Pilgrims while they lived and forgot them after their death; they were not sufficiently well born to do her credit."(4)

Mr Baskerville comes to much the same conclusion. He writes: "A great deal of the clerical discontent which found expression in the Pilgrimage of Grace and similar movements was due, as has been pointed out, to the substitution of efficient royal collectors of revenue for inefficient papal ones."(5) And he adds:

The general bewilderment was increased, also, by the fact that the matrimonial and semi-matrimonial affairs of most of the great personages who were involved in the business were tangled to an amazing degree. Two of the King's brothers-in-law had been divorced, while another had married his deceased wife's sister. Pope Clement himself was a bastard; at least nobody has so far discovered the surname, much less the marriage lines, of his mother, Fioretta. Of the two Cardinals who tried the case, the English one had a son who was a clergyman and a daughter who was a nun, while the Italian brought his son with him to England and got him included in the birthday honours; at any rate he was knighted at the next tournament. The forces which respectively opposed and supported the King were of an equally bewildering kind. Against Henry, the Pope, in dread of the Emperor; yet who could offer the King two wives at the same time, an expedient which had already occurred to the patriarchs of the Old Testament, and which was afterwards to be suggested by Latitudinarian bishops to Charles the Second and by Rosicrucian divines to Frederick William the Second of Prussia, as a solution for the very similar difficulties under which those monarchs laboured.(6)

Henry VIII himself saw these things sufficiently clearly in his own generation, though modern writers often ignore them. He had his finger on the pulse of his people far more truly than any despot of his own time. For all his hacking and bullying of Parliament he could not deprive it of a real power which foreign nations envied us even in the Middle Ages. "Indeed, even the monarchy of the Tudors enhanced its power, dignity and authority."(7) He did not "rob England of her religion". Side by side with his people, he felt his way to change from many frozen conventionalisms which, in their dead unreality, had become corrupt and poisonous. This remains true even when we emphasize the worst that can be honestly urged against his methods. When Philippe-le-Bel, Eldest Son of the Church, suppressed the Templars in partnership with the Pope, their main weapon was the rack. In France, where this was mercilessly used, the victims were brought to confess that at their admission they regularly adored a pagan idol, and swore to a treasonable charter of which a copy was kept at every one of their houses. Yet, though everything had been sealed up at the moment they were attacked, no such idols or charters were ever found by the police. Many, when the torture was over, revoked their confessions and were burned for it. One recounted how, in the torture-chamber, he had "deposed upon oath...that all the errors imposed upon the Templars were true", but he added that, in those circumstances, "he would have confessed even to have slain the Lord, if this had been demanded of him".(8) Where, as in England, the law of the land forbade torture in the courts, no such evidence was found. But the Pope insisted that it should be introduced among us also, and even circularized the whole of Europe for its employment against an Order whose condemnation had, by that time, become a matter of papal prestige.(9) Here also, as with our own monasteries, one of the greatest temptations lay in the immense wealth of the victims. Another parallel is in the French Revolution which swept the religious Orders away at a single stroke, with less formalities of justice, greater violence, and more complete confiscations than anything in English history. Even the papal suppression of the Jesuit Order in the eighteenth century had its episodes quite comparable with Henry's Dissolution. Every monk, therefore, could claim compensation from the Crown, unless he was prepared to take the consequences of open rebellion against the Act. And, on reflexion, it need hardly surprise us that scarcely a score, all told, were willing to take those consequences. We must not attribute to these men, as revealed to us in their own records, the mentality of a modern writer in his arm chair. Extremes meet in psychology; and centuries of implicit obedience to a spiritual autocracy had gone far to restrain not only extreme individualism but even independent judgement in the ordinary public. It is one of the most frequent historical phenomena that the most violent reactions follow upon the most ancient and sheep-like loyalties; and the common man will change one master for another with a facility which confounds the speculative politician.(10)

Another point of capital importance must be mentioned, upon which the misrepresentations or exaggerations of sentimentalists have been corrected recently by the simple process of studying all the relevant documents. This is, the fate of the dispossessed Religious. Abbé Constant's book will best serve for our text here, since he sums up the exaggerations of his predecessors, and his footnotes show how he relies upon their evidence. His conclusions run:

> there were some pensions promised, but only for the Superiors. The ordinary Religious were dismissed with a small gratuity. In certain areas the people were roused by these long processions of monks and nuns, from whom they had formerly received alms, work, and pensions, and who now went from door to door begging for food and lodging.

And again:

> the nine or ten thousand monks and nuns who had been driven out received very little, with the exception of the Superiors, and many led a deplorable life of vagrancy and poverty, of the three million

inhabitants, from forty to eighty thousand depended upon the monasteries, because they were sick, or poor, or else employed as servants, and all at once they found themselves deprived of their daily bread.

For this he quotes five authors, not one of whom is an original authority and who vary in date from Burnet (1679) to Gasquet (1888). His footnote on p. 194 does indeed refer to Mr Baskerville's brief essay on this subject (the complete book was not then published), but in words which make it very doubtful whether he had read even that essay with any care.(11)

Mr Baskerville, whose industry has collected and focused all the available evidence, in print and in MS., comes to a very different conclusion. Concerning the three successive Pension Commissions (1552, 1554, 1569) he writes:

> Some, but by no means all, of their reports are extant. If only they had been studied more carefully, we should have been spared a great many of the tears which sentimentalists have shed over the fate of the former Religious.... Former monks who held livings were actually better off than their fellow-parsons who had never been in Religion.(12)

Of this he gives the concrete instance of a Lincolnshire vicar who had his benefice, his vicarage, his own pension of £2 as ex-monk and his wife's of £2. *6s. 8d.* as ex-nun, sums which should be multiplied by about thirty to bring them into terms of A.D. 1900.

The arrangement, briefly, was as follows. The pension, in all cases, was dependent upon the acceptance of the Act of Supremacy and the Queenship of Anne Boleyn. This, however, applied to every man or woman in the land, and the matter had been decided by the monastic superiors long before. In 1531 they had accepted, after feeble resistance, Henry's claim to be Supreme Head; and, in 1534, the Act of Succession declared it high treason to contest Anne's position as Queen. Although the Spanish Ambassador Chapuys may have been substantially right in telling his master that Anne was "hated by everybody", yet

> at her coronation on June 1st, 1533, the monks of Westminster, all in rich copes, and many bishops and abbots in copes and mitres, received her in Westminster Hall; at the banquet which followed, bishops and abbots sat at table in their parliament robes. When the

King and Queen were on progress the Abbot and Convent of Gloucester received them in state at the west door of the abbey church with crosses, copes and cushions. Abbots ended their letters "God save Queen Anne", and when the Abbess of Bruisyard said in her letter to Cromwell that she prays for the Queen and Princess, she was referring to Anne and her daughter Elizabeth, and not to Katharine and her daughter Mary.(13)

The monk, then, had to accept what was imposed upon all other subjects, and what he had already accepted tacitly when his superiors voted for it. We must not blame the multitude for not preferring martyrdom, as a handful did; but it is anachronistic to credit these people with any such violent shock to their conscience as is often supposed. Extremes meet; and the man whose acquiescence in one form of despotism has rendered him insensible will adapt himself with astonishing callousness to another quite different. The papal requirements of implicit, unquestioning obedience, for centuries past, had gone far to send individualism to sleep. It has often been noted how Wolsey's despotism in the Church helped Henry's in the State. The ablest Roman Catholic historian of this period, Lingard, confessed quite frankly to a private correspondent the reasons which restrained him from any attempt to whitewash this episode. "Unfortunately the fact is that there were not any in most communities ready to brave persecution." There were, indeed, such among the few Brigittines, Carthusians, and Observantines; but "the rest were a degenerate, time-serving class of men. This I have hinted in gentle terms in note of p. 216, and of it have given a convincing proof on p. 104, where, out of 66 theologians who in the Convocation voted in favour of their royal master, two thirds, 42, were Abbots and Priors of monasteries."(14)

Again, in June 1530, Henry sent, in the name of the whole realm, a plain letter of remonstrance to the Pope, showing what harm was being done by his inability to make up his mind as to the Divorce. It ran:

It should in any case have been sufficient that the justice of the cause itself has been proved everywhere by the votes of the most famous Universities; by the English and French and Italian....How unhappy it is that a thing which is asserted as true by our own two

Universities and that of Paris, with many others in France, by the most learned and erudite men both at home and abroad, who show themselves ready to defend it both with tongue and with pen, should not be granted as true by the Apostolic See to that Prince through whose word and protection the Apostolic See standeth in authority [in England].

Through these papal hesitations we English are threatened with a bloody War of Succession like that of the Roses.

If our Father will not [pronounce as so many learned men have already done,] but has decreed to leave us as orphans and to cast us off, this will certainly be thus interpreted, that we are left to care for ourselves, and to find our own remedies elsewhere. . . If your Holiness doth not so, or even delayeth so to do, our condition will be all the more wretched that we have laboured so long in vain; but we are not altogether destitute of every remedy. Extreme remedies, indeed, are always harder, but the sick man is concerned to relieve his sickness by any means.

This, no doubt, hints at Henry's threat of appealing to a General Council. The document was signed by two archbishops, two dukes, two marquises, thirteen earls, four bishops, twenty-five barons, twenty-two abbots, and eleven "knights and doctors in Parliament", including Gardiner, the future bishop.(15)

Submission, therefore, was a preliminary condition for the monk; and no instance (I believe) has been produced of any who refused and lost his pension—apart, of course, from the heroic Carthusians with less than a dozen others who faced actual martyrdom. The commissioners of 1536 divided them into three categories. First, in each house, the superior had a life pension suitable to "his degree and quality". This was punctually fulfilled; they were on the scale usual for retired abbots or priors in the past. Secondly, of the brethren; each who chose to remain was sent to another house of the same Order: thus two Dover monks went to the Cathedral priory, and one to St Augustine's, at Canterbury. Thirdly came those who chose to abandon their profession. The choice varied enormously at different houses. From some, all out; and none from others; but the records are too fragmentary to give statistical certainty for the whole. Mr Baskerville, however, judges it probable that more than half went out.(16) This class it was which provided the only real difficulty. To these, the Commission granted dispensation from their vows, as Popes had done, virtually if not formally, in such rare cases as that of Erasmus. With this, the outgoing Religious received a "capacity", such as had long been purchasable at Rome by monks who could afford it, for serving a parish cure. Thus provided, they went out of their own choice to face the world.

They did not, however, leave their houses without being given any provision, as writers of lachrymose disposition would have us believe.... Their wages, long in arrear, were paid, and a "reward", or species of bonus, was given as well. This sum was to go towards the purchase of new clothes suitable for their new careers as secular clergymen and to tide them over generally until they got a new job. Rewards for the Religious were on a generous scale.... Nevertheless the Religious were not generally satisfied with this provision; to their discontent may be attributed one of the causes of the risings in Lincolnshire which began in the autumn of 1536 and of the more serious rising in Yorkshire which followed.(17)

It was natural that the monks should resent this uprooting; and certainly it fell far more hardly upon the nuns. At first, in 1536, they had the same choice as the men: transference to a larger unsuppressed convent, or freedom to go back to the world. Those who chose such dispensation received a lump sum sufficient to buy worldly clothing and to keep them for a short while. The majority of these, probably, fell back upon their home.(18) Within a year, considerable relief came; for from 1537 onwards, whenever a convent "surrendered" to the King, each inmate received a pension, whatever her moral record might have been. Thus handsome pensions are recorded to a lapsed Prioress of Littlemore and a lapsed and truant nun of Basedale.(19) The tales of attempts by Cromwell's Visitors upon the nuns' virtue repose, to begin with, only upon far later hearsay. The earliest is from Fr. Sanders, a papal nuncio who was only nine years old at the Dissolution, and who wrote fifty-five years later without producing any corroborative evidence.

The other similar story comes to us at second hand from Sir William Stanley, through the historian Thomas Fuller (d. 1661) who adds:

All I will say to this story is this, that if this Sir William Stanley was he who, contrary to his solemn oath to the Earl of Leicester and the United States [of Holland], betrayed the strong city of Deventer to the Spaniards, and lived many years after in a neglected, forlorn condition, one so faithless in his deeds may be presumed false in his words, and the whole credit of the relation may justly at least be suspected.

Cardinal Gasquet not only suppresses these last sentences, but goes out of his way to print Fuller as saying the exact opposite: "It was evident that the blood of the old Puritan was stirred within him, and he must have felt that the disgraceful relations made to him were only too true."(20) The whole story of the Dissolution in England needs to be re-written, as Mr Baskerville has done, from the original sources. Here and there he has been able to trace the career of dispossessed monks and nuns, both before and after the Dissolution; and certain pages in particular throw a very unfavourable light on the sentimental pictures by modern historians: see pp. 184, 191–5, 217, 221, 223.

CHAPTER LXV

RICH AND POOR

THIS brings us to a third subject upon which a great deal of bad history has been written: that of pauperism. The worst offender on this point, as often elsewhere, is the generous, eloquent and ignorant farmer William Cobbett. His *History of the Protestant Reformation* has perhaps had, and still has, more readers than any other; for it has recently been reprinted in a very cheap form by the English "Publishers to the Holy See, revised, with notes and preface, by Cardinal Gasquet".(1) Cobbett exposed more than one complacent Protestant exaggeration, but fell instead into blunders always serious and often ludicrous. Having himself an infallible eye for the number of beasts in a stall, he undertook to estimate our medieval population by the number and size of our medieval churches. "If the father of lies himself were to come and endeavour to persuade us that England was not more populous before the 'Reformation' than it is now, he must fail with all but downright idiots."(2) The Cardinal himself can scarcely escape this unsavoury category; for he has always elsewhere accepted the ordinary historian's computation for Reformation times, of five millions at the very most, and probably little over four. In Cobbett's day there was a real census, which gave nearly twelve millions, in 1821. Yet the seven pages in which Cobbett emphasizes our diminished population as one of the cursed results of the religious revolution are reprinted *verbatim* by this present-day editor without the least note of warning.

So, again, with the lengthy passages where Cobbett deals directly with the question of pauperism; the Cardinal not only reprints them in the text, but expatiates at great length in his Preface (pp. v–xii). The Reformation (he writes) "was in reality the rising of the rich against the poor". And the text itself recurs to the point over and over again.(3) The Reformation is one of the causes why Cobbett's England is "covered at last with pauperism, fanaticism, and crime". "There were no poor-rates and no church-rates as long as Waverley Abbey existed and as long as Bishops had no wives." "Usury among Christians was wholly unknown, until the wife-killing tyrant laid his hands on the property of the Church and of the poor." "When the Protestant religion came and along with it a married priesthood, the poorer classes were plundered of their birthright and thrown out to prowl about for what they could beg or steal." "When Elizabeth had put the finishing hand to the plundering of the Church and poor, once happy and free and hospitable England became a den of famishing robbers and slaves." In her reign "we have the great, the prominent, the staring, the horrible and ever during consequences of the 'Reformation'; that is to say, pauperism established by law". "I will now show not only that the people were better off, better fed and clad, before the 'Reformation' than they ever have been since, but that the nation was more populous, wealthy, powerful and free before than it ever has been since that event." These assertions cannot safely be ignored, since they are officially championed by a powerful hierarchy and presented, perhaps, to the actual majority of English-speaking readers. Mr Baskerville dismisses Cobbett's book in a single sentence as "one of the most amazing pieces of rubbish that was ever written", yet this is not enough in itself, so long as the great majority of scholars suffer its continual circulation in contemptuous silence. In history, as elsewhere, there is a Gresham's law; free circulation helps bad coin to drive out the good.

The problem of pauperism, though certainly hastened by the Dissolution, was already acute in the days when orthodox Visitors were still wearying themselves with constant complaints that the monasteries neglected their duty of almsgiving, and sometimes even embezzled the charitable moneys of which they were only trustees. Miss Leonard gives full details in the early pages of her *English Poor Relief*. In 1349, during the Black Death, the Royal Ordinance of Labourers prohibited relief to the able-bodied poor; they must be compelled to work. This led to an exodus from villages where it was strictly enforced. Hence, in 1388, regulations restricted the movements of all beggars and labourers; they must carry letters testimonial with them, or they must be taken and put in the stocks. The impotent poor must be supported by their own neighbourhood. This has some right to be called our first real Poor Law, providing for all cases. City authorities also, as in London, legislated against not only vagabonds, but all who harboured such. Henry VII enacted two statutes against them. All this while, from Richard II onwards, Parliament had been compelled to move for the enforcement of that church law by which, nominally, one-quarter or one-third of the revenues of every benefice was reserved for the poor of the parish. Documentary evidence proves that, even in the cases where it was seriously attempted to enforce these new Parliamentary regulations, the proportion aimed at was far below what the Church had preached in theory and never fulfilled in practice, even approximately.(4) Similarly, even the hospitals and almshouses were coming more and more under lay control. "Thus, before the sixteenth century, state and town had begun to make regulations for the relief of the poor. Some of these regulations were dictated by...a growing tendency for the state to interfere to prevent the maladministration of ecclesiastical revenues."(5) Still the measures were found insufficient. A story of at least as early as 1521 has, for its main point, the great numbers of beggars in our population. Things were the same on the Continent; this provoked a book in Germany as early as 1514. Unemployment was rife, mainly through the break-up of feudal conditions, the cessation of civil war, with the growth of order in the state, and the increase of commerce and industry. "In the first place, the peaceful life of the craftsman was favourable to the growth of the population; and, in the second place, the new occupations were less stable than the old industries had been."(6) The influx of silver from America caused a great rise of prices; and successive debasements of the coinage from 1527 to 1551 increased the evil greatly. But, for England, the most fatal cause of all was the conversion of arable to sheep farms, and consequent destruction of whole villages; a system which, as St Thomas More pointed out, was pursued by abbots as well as by lay landlords. Again, "the charity distributed by the monks...was to a great extent unorganized and indiscriminate, and did nearly as much to increase beggars as to relieve them".(7) The general increase called for two statutes in Henry VIII's reign. The first, in 1531, provided that impotent poor should have written license to beg. The able-bodied beggars were to be whipped in the nearest market town, and thence sent back to work at their place of origin. In short, it very nearly repeated the Act of 1388. Henry's Act of 1536 added to these negative provisions an arrangement for positive relief. "This Statute is the first in which the state not only enacts that the poor shall be provided for in their own neighbourhood, but also makes itself responsible for the administration of relief and the raising of funds." So little can it be considered (as Cobbett and his imitators would have it) in the light of a Machiavellian prelude to the Dissolution, that it is "similar to measures passed at almost exactly the same time in France and Scotland".(8)

The problem of pauperism, therefore, was far older than the Reformation, and was far from being confined to districts which lost their monasteries. The most recent studies of economic historians have dissipated many exaggerations, and even some categorical mis-statements, as to the influence of the Reformation upon the eternal struggle between Riches and Poverty. Professor Savine of Moscow, in that study of the *Valor Ecclesiasticus* which has held its ground for thirty years among the most valuable and accurate treatises on English medieval history, concluded from the documentary evidence that there was no justification for the exaggerated pictures often drawn of a world left desolate by the ruin of the monasteries. More recently, Professor Tawney has published a still more important volume, welcomed still more warmly by the most competent critics, *Religion and the Rise of Capitalism*.* In that volume he is constantly faced by the view which would date most of our present economic difficulties from the Religious Revolution of the sixteenth century; and he brings the most convincing documentary evidence against it. He shows how closely nearly all the Reformers clung to the time-honoured economic theories of the Middle Ages; and how the full divergence, when it came at last in the seventeenth century, was due less to religious changes than to that expansion of material prosperity which had begun long before the Reformation, and for a long time developed

* My references throughout are to the 1st ed. (1926).

most completely in such irreproachably Catholic regions as Southern Germany and Belgium.

When we look from theory to practice, we often find the medieval gilds acting tyrannically, and unfavourably to the struggling man (p. 27). Nationalism, again, had begun to influence trade greatly long before the Reformation (p. 27). The enormous majority of the population were peasants; yet "in reality, as far as the servile tenants, who formed the bulk of medieval agriculturalists, were concerned, the golden age of peasant prosperity is, except here and there, a romantic myth, at which no one would have been more surprised than the peasants themselves. The very essence of feudal property was exploitation in its most naked and shameless form" (p. 57). The official Church not only recognized serfdom but profited heavily by it* (pp. 58–9). Usury, the canker of society, was practised most shamelessly under the eye of, and it may almost be said by command of, the Popes, whose Court could not have been maintained without wholesale and public infringement of Church Law on that subject. To the Reformers, this sin "was the more horrifying because it was in the Capital of the Christian Church that it reached its height" (pp. 29, 44, 110). Modern capitalism began in Italy, centuries before the discovery of America. Columbus was able to remark: "Gold constitutes treasure; and he who possesses it has all he needs in this world, as also the means of rescuing souls from Purgatory, and restoring them to the enjoyment of Paradise" (p. 89). When the English monasteries were dissolved, "Portugal had been master of an Indian Empire for almost a generation" (p. 70). Spain followed Portugal rapidly in this scramble for "parasitic wealth", while her mad tyranny did its best to capture the far more real wealth of her subject populations in Holland and Belgium. Antwerp had been, before this tyranny, the most modern of trading centres in Europe. Before Henry VIII was out of his boyhood, this "microcosm which reflected the soul of commercial Europe" was exploiting the discovery of the New World, and becoming "the capital of the European money-market"—at a time when London could count only in the second rank (p. 75). Thus

* Wyclif seems to have been the only Schoolman who objected to serfdom on principle.

Antwerp was the most natural place for St Thomas More to choose as the scene of his meeting with the much-travelled trader who told him the strange story of Utopia. While the clergy of Antwerp were fiercely intolerant of heresy, her traders were wresting from less orthodox Venice her earlier supremacy in "big business". For she was so situated as to tap not only the new discoveries, but the startling capitalistic advantages of Southern Germany where, already in the fifteenth century, money was rising to a social and political power which has seldom been exceeded. There, from 1476 onwards, "scarcely a decade had passed without a Peasants' Revolt" (p. 81). When the Reformation came, the yearning for the imaginary Golden Age of the past "was the cry for spiritual peace of a society disillusioned with the material triumphs of a too complex civilization" (p. 85). Before the Reformation, the Trust system was growing up in Germany, "defended and attacked by arguments almost identical with those which are familiar to-day" (p. 87). From at least 1440 onwards, far-reaching schemes of social reconstruction were suggested by anti-capitalist writers (p. 88). For commercial corruption took no pains to hide itself: it could afford to be notorious.

The City interest was one of the great Powers of Europe. Publicists might write that the new Messiah was the Prince, and reformers that the Prince was Pope. But behind Prince and Pope alike, financing impartially Henry VIII, Edward VI and Elizabeth, Francis, Charles and Philip, stood in the last resort a little German banker, with branches in every capital in Europe, who played in the world of finance the part of the *condottieri* in war, and represented in the economic sphere the morality typified in that of politics by Machiavelli's Prince. Compared with these financial dynasties, Hapsburgs, Valois and Tudors were puppets dancing on wires held by a money-power to which political struggles were irrelevant except as an opportunity for gain (p. 78).

There were at least six of these multi-millionaires as we call them, considering the value of coin in those days. Most powerful of all were the Fuggers* who, "thanks to judicious loans to

* For Jakob Fugger's boast to a Spanish cardinal's secretary that he had made every bishop in Germany, and had sometimes filled the see twice or more, and this was the most lucrative of all his sources of income, see chap. xx here above.

Maximilian", had acquired enormous concessions of mineral property, farmed a large part of the receipts drawn by the Spanish Crown from its estates, held silver and quicksilver mines in Spain, and controlled banking and commercial businesses in Italy and, above all, at Antwerp. They advanced the money which made Albrecht of Brandenburg Archbishop of Mainz; repaid themselves by sending their agent to accompany Tetzel on his campaign to raise money by indulgences and taking half the proceeds; provided the funds with which Charles V bought the imperial crown, after an election conducted with the publicity of an auction and the morals of a gambling hell; browbeat him, when the debt was not paid, in the tone of a pawnbroker rating a necessitous client; and found the money with which Charles raised troops to fight the Protestants in 1552. The head of the firm built a church and endowed an almshouse for the aged poor in his native town of Augsburg. He died in the odour of sanctity, a good Catholic and a Count of the Empire, having seen his firm pay 54 per cent. for the preceding sixteen years (p. 79). "It was predominantly Catholic cities which were the commercial capitals of Europe, and Catholic bankers who were its leading financiers" (p. 84, cf. p. 319). On the other hand, in the lower stratum of society, lived "a wage-earning proletariate, dependent for their livelihood on capital and credit supplied by their masters, and alternately rising in revolt and sinking into an ever-expanding morass of helpless pauperism" (p. 86).

If in England things were not so bad as this, it was not due to our superior religious orthodoxy, for Lollardy was still a strong leaven in spite of the religious bonfires, and the Bishop of London complained in 1514 that no cleric could get justice in the King's Courts by reason of the leanings of the people towards heretical pravity. The reason was that we were still backward in trade, undisturbed by the enormous economic expansion of the Low Countries and Italy, Spain and Portugal. Yet, long before the Reformation Parliament met, England had suffered from every evil that beset her after the Dissolution of the Monasteries, except depreciation of the currency (p. 137). Enclosures had been going on for nearly a century. Government had tried to grapple with this abuse in 1489, 1515, 1516, 1517 and 1534. Cold business documents prove that "the monks, after all, were business men, and the lay agents whom they often employed to manage their property naturally conformed to the agricultural practice of the world around them....Holy men reclaimed villeins, turned copyholders into tenants at will, and, as More complained, converted arable land into pasture" (p. 139). There can be no doubt that the Dissolution aggravated these evils for the time being: but its effects are sometimes exaggerated beyond all reason.

False as is the legend that capitalism, with attendant pauperism, was an invention of the Reformers, equally false is the contention that they welcomed it.

> To think of the abdication of religion from its theoretical primacy over economic activity and social institutions as synchronizing with the revolt from Rome, is to antedate a movement which was not accomplished for another century and a half, and which owed as much to changes in economic and political organization, as it did to developments in the sphere of religious thought. (p. 84.)

Protestant theologians, like their Catholic predecessors and contemporaries, insisted that the Church had the right not only to dictate social morality, but to punish the disobedient (pp. 9, 81, 152ff., 157–9). They rather interpreted the medieval theories of Usury and Just Price with added strictness, in protest against the lax morals of the Renaissance, and the greed of the Papal court (pp. 85, 91). They sighed for an imaginary age of peasant prosperity, as romantic Catholics do now in the twentieth century (p. 92). They accepted, like the medieval thinkers, that natural stratification of society which rendered it dangerous, if not sinful, to struggle for a rise above one's native rank (pp. 56, 103). Zwingli complained of the great Catholic Councils of Constance and Basel for their indulgence towards mortgage of land on the security of the crops (p. 103). While Luther denounced usury with a vigour which refused to admit the Schoolmen's modifications, it was Eck, Luther's orthodox enemy, who journeyed to the University of Bologna for authoritative confirmation of his daring argument that "interest could lawfully be charged in transactions between merchants"; and the expenses of his journey were paid by the arch-usurers, the Fuggers (p. 81). Nor was the Church alone, after the Reformation, in this social conservatism. The Privy Council, under Elizabeth and beyond, punished offenders, and interfered sometimes to stop the oppressive assertion of a landlord's strict legal rights, and to remind him of his wider duties to society (p. 167). To churchmen and statesmen alike, the State was something more than an institution created by material necessities or political convenience. "It was the temporal expression of spiritual obligations" (p. 170). As to enclosures, "in the 4 years from 1635 to 1638 a list of some 600 offenders was returned to the Council, and about £50,000 was imposed upon them in fines" (p. 173). The Puritan Richard Baxter discusses Usury at great length: "and the first characteristic to strike the modern reader in all this is its conservatism.... He differs from one of the later Doctors, like St Antonino, hardly more than St Antonino himself had differed from Aquinas" (pp. 224–5). For Luther and Calvin, as for the Schoolmen, the landlord "is not a *rentier*, but an officer; and it is for the Church to rebuke him when he sacrifices the duties of his charge to his greed for personal gain" (p. 149). If all this broke down before the seventeenth century was out, that was because it was too conservative, and ignored those world transformations which had inspired the age of Francis Bacon and Descartes.

If the anti-Reformation legend deals thus falsely with Protestantism in general so far as this matter is concerned, still more patently is it unjust to Calvinism. Just as superficial writers of to-day, who have evidently never read either him or the Schoolmen, talk as though he had invented the doctrine of Predestination, so they ignore how nearly his attitude on commercial morality agreed with that of the Middle Ages. Especially absurd is the idea that he taught men to find salvation in riches. Professor Tawney sums up: "Calvinism had little pity for poverty; but it distrusted wealth, as it distrusted all influences that distract the aim or relax the fibres of the soul, and, in the first flush of its youthful austerity, it did its best to make life unbearable for the rich" (p. 132). Calvin's own doctrine on the questions of Usury and Just Price did not essentially differ from that of the Schoolmen. He did indeed make a little more allowance than they had done for just interest upon money lent; but he insisted, as they did, upon the wickedness of taking unfair advantage of a neighbour's necessities. "Against monsters of this kind the [Calvinist] ministers rage without ceasing" (p. 120). "The contents of the programme were thoroughly medieval....Throughout there is a prolonged warfare against the twin evils of extortionate interest and extortionate prices" (p. 119; cf. pp. 113, 118). With Usury, as with Folk-dance, the medieval Church had consistently preached a theory which broke down badly in practice. The usurer and the village dancers, despite all prohibitions, went on their own way with even greater licence of behaviour than was shown in America under the Volstead Act; and the result was a corresponding weakening of morality and respect for the law. Calvin, on the other hand, in his authoritarian State of Geneva, fought the battle more boldly and consistently than the medieval hierarchy had ever attempted. His success was far from complete: but it went a very long way beyond theirs. His followers in England and Scotland fought sometimes with the exaggeration of men whose power is not sufficiently legitimate and enduring to permit a generous gesture. In that sense, as with certain exaggerations of the Predestinarian doctrine, the great reformer might have protested, "I am not a Calvinist" (p. 107).

In England, an Act of 37 Henry VIII (1545) permitted interest up to 10 per cent.; in the days when, by the recent Statute of the Six Articles, men were to be burned for denying Transubstantiation, and condemned as felons for contesting the necessity of auricular confession. It was the Reformers who, by the Act of 1552, prohibited all interest as "a vice most odious and detestable", thus going back to the earlier doctrine of the medieval Church and abolishing the relaxations which had been allowed by Aquinas, Antonino and the Schoolmen in general. Elizabeth's Act of 1571 repealed this. Thenceforward "the exaction of interest ceased to be a criminal offence, provided that the rate did not exceed ten per cent." (p. 180). This was stricter than the French law in the fourteenth century, when kings paid no attention to the Church's legislation on this subject, but simply aimed at restricting the tariff. The rates varied: but from 1312 the practically legalized rate of interest was 20 per cent. in general, and 15 per cent. at the fairs of

Champagne, where credit was good among solid merchants. An edict of 1378 even licensed certain usurers (who of course had to pay for their licences) to take interest up to 50 per cent.(9) Thus there is great exaggeration in Max Weber's theory that English Calvinism was the parent of capitalism. Not only is capitalism a good deal older than the Reformation, but the seventeenth-century revolution in thought owed more to economic than to religious changes, more to fact than to theory (pp. 212, 319).

Thus, deep and far-reaching as were the changes at the Reformation, we cannot set them all on one side of the balance. If the monasteries, at certain times and places, had been the only secure bulwark against pauperism, that had ceased to be true long before 1500. Henry's spoliation, quite apart from the creation of six (or five) bishoprics and cathedral staffs, and of forts for national defence against invasion, was far less truly a "rising of the rich against the poor" than the victory of a lay squirearchy over a Church squirearchy. An enormous share of all the land (in days when land was by far our greatest wealth) was taken from men who had been almost completely protected, even in their worst mismanagements, by the maxim *Touch not mine Anointed.* The men thus expropriated were those to whose holdings the Statute of Mortmain gave an official name: monastic possessions were held under the Dead Hand. The mismanagement of their land in Tudor times, if not general, was indisputably common enough to constitute a public scandal in many places. Yet it was a vested interest, growing more and more irreformable from day to day. The victorious squirearchy, on the other hand, was not protected from the natural consequences of its own mismanagement. Although Spelman's *History and Fate of Sacrilege* is utterly unhistorical in its sentimental exaggeration of isolated instances into a Providential law, yet there is that truth in it which we might find in any equally laborious collection dealing with suddenly acquired wealth of any kind. *Soon come, soon go*, holds true for every age. If not the very man who got or bought monastic spoil for himself, yet at least his son or grandson was not infrequently vicious or thriftless enough to disperse much or all of his lands. These were bought piecemeal by small men; and thus a comparatively new class of yeomen farmers was created, to the lasting benefit of the land.

We may apply, after all, a very simple test. Can it be seriously maintained that the poor, before the French Revolution, were better off where monasteries still abounded—in France, Italy, and Spain—than here in England?

We cannot reconcile recorded facts with the modern legend that monasticism, apart from its ideal Rule, went far in practice to correct the aristocratic spirit of feudalism. Professor Savine thus concludes his scientific study on English monasteries on the eve of the Dissolution:

> However heterogeneous the interests of the professed "religious" might have been, the majority of them could not but sympathize with the upper and middle classes, in a way altogether at variance with anything like a democratic spirit. In a society full of discord between classes so various, the Roman Catholic Church failed to remain thoroughly and sincerely democratic because it was as it still is, the Church of general unity. It undoubtedly expressed sympathy with the masses and the poor, but at the same time it continued to be on good terms with the few and the rich. It enjoined simplicity, poverty, privations, but at the same time it knew how to find excuse for riches and luxury. In the great drama of class warfare it was compelled to shift its fighting-place or to stand between the hostile camps. It was stronger abroad than at home. It became bold and mighty when it girded itself with a sword against the infidels; in the hard struggle for life among its own children it confined its energies to a policy of pious appeals to love and mercy.(10)

CHAPTER LXVI

ORTHODOX ADMISSIONS

It is thoroughly unhistorical to ignore the extent to which pious churchmen of the Middle Ages sadly anticipated, or even approved in principle, the Dissolution of the Monasteries.

Let us begin with those who more or less definitely foretold it. The well-known prophecy in *Piers Plowman* has already been quoted. In 1492, while Morton was struggling vainly in the ecclesiastical lawcourts against St Albans, the great Strassburg minster-preacher Geiler preached before the Emperor Maximilian. The bishop, the chapter and many princes and lords were there.

Geiler had harped on his favourite theme, the necessity of reforming abuses; and he said in conclusion that, since all efforts had hitherto failed, "God would send other reformers; these were already on the way; he himself would not live to see them, but many of his hearers might. They would then regret too late, for there would be no mercy. Let every man think this over carefully; things cannot last; *es muss brechen*." The audience were deeply disturbed, says the chronicler; the Emperor conversed with the Bishop on the subject of the abuses denounced by the preacher, but it ended in nothing.

Later on, the same theme was repeated before the Emperor: "Since neither Pope nor Kaiser, King nor Bishops, are willing to reform our lives, God will send a man to do this and to revive our fallen religion." There were two other conferences in consequence; but "all vanished in smoke".(1) Next year, in 1493, the scene changes to France. Louis XII held a Great Council at Tours; the main theme was Church Reform. To the abbots he said: "The King wills that all the Statutes [of your Order] be kept inviolably by you and your Religious. If ye do thus, ye shall do a thing pleasing to God and most pleasing unto the King. If not, it shall be done by others, of other vocation, even as right shall dictate and reason shall advise."

At this same time, the most distinguished Benedictine in Germany, for learning and piety combined, was Abbot Tritheim.

He died in the year in which More wrote his *Utopia*, while Luther was still an obedient papalist cloisterer. Tritheim, preaching to a solemn assembly of fellow abbots, reminded them of the catastrophic changes in the atmosphere. The laity (he said) who of old endowed our abbeys, are now far more concerned to disendow them.

For they say: "Lo! these sinful priests and monks have grown rich! Lo! they now despise the worship of God and consume their wealth with harlots! they care not for honesty, holiness of life is nothing to them! Why therefore do we hesitate and hold back? Wherefore do we not fall upon their worldly goods, that these men's sinful pride may be brought low?" It is our sins alone which have made us thus contemptible before God and man.*

Again, we may practically reckon it as a forecast of 1536 when, about the turn of the fifteenth century, the Abbot of Combe in Warwickshire appealed to the General Chapter at Cîteaux against the promiscuous admission and entertainment of women, "talking, drinking with the brethren at all hours of the day—and (would I were not compelled to say)—of the night". For this cause, he writes, "not only do many bishops and prelates, but also temporal princes and lords, speak against us, but they are also deservedly indignant".(2) It was upon indignation of this kind, hitherto sporadic, that Henry worked by focusing it. Professor Pollard has brought out most clearly the extent to which he felt the pulse of the nation, and carried his people with him.(3) Thus, when the time came for his political stroke, he knew that he could reckon upon many who had long foreseen the application of force to the abbeys.

Bishops also were feeling that the evil called for drastic, and almost revolutionary, interference. It was not only that the suppression of so many priories for educational foundations was easily carried out with papal approval—for Eton and King's and other colleges at Oxford and Cambridge. But we also find a pious and energetic prelate like Fox of Winchester recording his despair of ever living to see any real reform of the monasteries, even in his own diocese.(4) His younger contemporary at Lincoln, Longland, we have seen using his legal position as

* *Opera Pia et Spiritualia* (1604), p. 859. The words were spoken to the Abbots of his own Order.

"founder" to break down the Cistercian exemptions which sheltered vice at Thame. Holinshed is probably not exaggerating much, and may indeed be literally correct, when he reports:

What, my lord, shall we build houses and provide livelihoods for a company of bussing monks, whose end and fall we ourselves may live to see? No, it is more meet a great deal that we should have care to provide for the increase of learning, and for such as who by their learning shall do good in the church and commonwealth.(5)

St Thomas More, under the temptation of violent controversy with Tyndale and others, and on the very eve of the Dissolution, came nowhere near the warmth of many modern apologists. Perhaps the least ambiguous of all his apologies for the monks is that on pp. 883ff. (of his *English Works*), where he asks which of the critics would care to live as a monk ought to live, or even as the average monk does live. Not many, no doubt; but, on analysis, this amounts only to saying (what all reasonable modern students have long been willing to grant), that the average monk lived a definitely less undisciplined life than the average worldling. To that alone More's argument commits him; and his own friend Fisher's words preclude our pressing it much further than this; for Fisher, in a very interesting passage written in prison during the last weeks of his life, at a moment when he had all More's controversial excuses for upholding monachism, argues at considerable length that the hunter lives a harder life than the monk. Taking all More's later apologetics together, they amount to no more than a plea for sparing the monks still, in the hope of amendment.(6) Even when Dissolution was not only talked of but put into effect, it had qualified approval from some of the most orthodox among Henry's adversaries. The Observantine Peto risked perhaps his life, and certainly the King's violent displeasure, by openly preaching against the Divorce. He took refuge on the Continent, and was afterwards raised to the cardinalate. Yet Hutton wrote to Cromwell on January 20, 1538:

Yesterday came to my hands a letter from Friar Peito, here enclosed....He is very earnestly against the abuses of Religious men, but that the Bp of Rome should not be head of the Church will not stick in his stomach. The suppression of the abbeys he makes light of, but thinks they might be put to better use. Except in these two points he seems consonant to reason.(7)

Bishop Gardiner, again, is best known for his severity towards the Protestants under Mary. Yet, in a sermon at Paul's Cross in 1540, while he attacked the Lutherans for their revolutionary doctrine of Faith and Works, he spoke contemptuously of the now dissolved Orders of Friars. In former days, he says, the Devil tempted the unreal Christian

with a wanne hope to lyve merely [i.e. merrily] and at his pleasure here, and yet have heaven at the last; and for that purpose procured out pardons from Rome, wherein heaven was sold for a litle money, and for to retayle that marchaundise the devyll used freres for his ministers. Nowe they be gone with all their tromperye, but the devyll is not yet gonne. And now he perceyveth it can no lenger be borne to buy and sell heaven (both the marchaundyse is abhorred, and the ministers also—we can not away with freres, ne can abyde the name), the devyll hath excogitate to offre heaven without workes for it, so frelye that men shall not nede for heaven to worke at all, what soever opportunite they have to worke.(8)

Again, when the Statute of 1545 had put all the hospitals and charities into Henry's hands, Gardiner sent to the royal secretary, Paget, a letter which will surprise only those who have not followed in detail the frequent decay, mismanagement or embezzlement of medieval hospitals and other religious foundations.(8) He wrote:

Master Secretary, after my most harty commendacions: I understand it hath pleased the Court of Parliament to geve in to the Kinges Majesties handes the disposition of al hospitalles, chaunteries, and other houses; wherof I am very glad and, thus far, if I might without displeasour, wold be an humble suter, both by myself and my frendes, that it wold please his Majestie to have respecte, as I doubte not but his Highnes wyl, to the Hospitalles of Saincte Crosse besides Winchestre and of Mary Magdalene, wherein poore folkes be releved.(9)

A select commission of prelates was chosen by the Pope to report to the Council of Trent on the reforms most urgently needed in the Church. It consisted of four cardinals (our own Pole and a future Pope among them), two archbishops, one bishop, one abbot, and the master of the papal palace. It was sworn to secrecy; the report, therefore, is a document unwarped by political bias or temptations to rhetoric; it is a naked statement of primary moral necessities and was presented two years after the Dissolution of the smaller monasteries in England.(10) The commission's first complaint is against the promiscuous ordination, ignorance, and moral unworthiness of the clergy in general; their plain words go far to justify St Germain and Tyndale, and to discount More's apologies. Thence they complain of the impunity of clerical offenders in general and finally they come to the monasteries.

Another abuse which must be corrected is that in the Religious Orders; for many are so disordered [*deformati*] that they are a great scandal to secular folk and do much evil by their example. We are of opinion that all the Conventual Orders,* yet not so as to inflict injustice on any man, but by prohibiting their reception of fresh novices; by which means, without injustice to any, they would soon be destroyed and good Religious might be put in their places.... Another abuse troubles Christian folk in the matter of nuns who are under the care of the Conventual Friars, among whom, in many [*plerisque*] nunneries, public sacrilege is committed, to the extreme scandal of all men. Let your Holiness, therefore, deprive the Conventuals altogether of that care, and give it to the Ordinaries or to others, as it may seem best.

At an earlier date, Pole had condemned all the English Religious with the exception of a small minority, viz. the Observants, the Carthusians and the Brigittines. He concludes: "whom will you find to compare with those three? Or rather, when you exclude those three, whom can you find who have not utterly degenerated from the founders of their Orders?"—*qui non prorsus ab instituti sui authoribus degeneraverint?*(11)

Perhaps the most unforgivable count against Henry VIII, to the modern mind, is his wanton destruction of so many splendid buildings and so much of medieval art. But here, again, without for a moment attempting to excuse him, we must take into account the spirit of Henry's own time, and of his predecessors and successors. The medieval artist was pitiless towards other men's work. His strength lay in the impulse to express his own individuality; or, more often still, the fashion of his own genera-

* I.e. all the Mendicants except that small minority which had adopted the Observant reforms. In England, there were only seven Observant houses.

tion.(12) The Renaissance artist was more pitiless still, for he often destroyed the old with missionary zeal. An enormous amount of disrepair is noted by orthodox Visitors even from the thirteenth century onwards, and increasingly as the Middle Ages wear on. If our abbeys had been left alone, and the *commendam* system had grown with us, as it bade fair to grow, almost to Continental standards, then many buildings would have perished in literal ruin, and more still would have been rebuilt from bottom to top, according as funds could be raised for the reconstruction. That wonderful series of drawings which the St Maur Benedictines prepared for their *Monasticon* at the turn of the seventeenth century bears irrecusable testimony to this. Turn where we will, though the church is nearly always old, and often the cloisters also, the rest of the buildings have nearly always been reconstructed in the most approved modern style.(13) Thus, when we are told by an enthusiastic American writer on Gothic art that "through the destruction of the monasteries by Henry's cut-throats...most of the very noblest examples of Gothic in England have utterly perished from the earth", we may return for consolation from this exaggeration to the able and zealous Catholic Montalembert, who knew England very well, and who noted regretfully that "if we wish to form an idea of the majestic grandeur of monastic buildings, we must visit England. The work of devastation has been less complete and irreparable than elsewhere."(14) Yet, even after we have said the most we can in palliation, the story is still one of shame; for the buildings might have served everywhere throughout the country, as they have done in two or three cases with us and more often in Germany, for schools and colleges, and thus for such a national network of education as our medieval ancestors never had, nor we ourselves until the memory of living men. Among the exaggerations which Robert Aske pleaded in justification for the Pilgrimage of Grace, one article remains literally and undeniably true: "Also the abbeys were one of the beauties of this realm to all men and strangers passing through the same."

CHAPTER LXVII

POST-REFORMATION FRANCE

MUCH confusion has been introduced into monastic history by the easy assumption that the Counter-Reformation gained anything like full success. The most it did anywhere, among the monasteries, was to stem further decay: and even there it was often unsuccessful. I have given evidence for this in my second volume, from Germany, Scotland and Austria, between 1562 (when the fathers of Trent had already been seventeen years at work) and 1572.(1) But fuller proof is needed here. For the question: What harm was done by the Dissolution in England? is inseparable from that other: What good was obtained by sparing the monasteries on the Continent until the French Revolution? In answer to this question we have two very valuable books, crammed with first-hand evidence. The first is by a Benedictine monk of to-day, Dom Paul Denis, who has been the first to work exhaustively through the whole mass of material. I shall quote freely from him, as far as possible in his own words, as a safeguard against exaggeration.(2) Dom Denis, in his introductory chapter, has little to say which would encourage us to put French religion higher than English in 1600. It is a dismal picture, and he finds the main causes in *Commendam* and the Wars of Religion. But *commendam* had been steadily resisted by English kings; and even Wolsey under Henry VIII had not been able to introduce anything like the Continental gangrene. Religious wars, again, we had escaped by the simple process of arming ourselves adequately and keeping out the foreign lord, while to religious malcontents at home the Government put what they loathed as "the Bloody Question": namely, *In the case of war between your sovereign and the Pope, which side would you take?* Civil wars had done much to impoverish the French abbeys, but far less than *commendam* had; and, at the worst, the monks might have been expected to accredit their vow of poverty by managing to live upon a scale quite equal, on the average, to that of the middle class. When, again, it is pleaded that the religious revolution had ruined true faith with its Lutheran or Calvinistic poison, must we not ask whether true faith cannot be expected to hold its own except in countries where religious nonconformity is suppressed? Henry IV, as early as 1608, had favoured certain beginnings of reform within the Benedictine Order. That of Cluny went further between 1613 and 1627; but still timidly. When Richelieu became Prime Minister, in 1624, he recognized this as one of the first of his tasks. So, again, did his successor, Cardinal Mazarin. There was a growing movement in France towards unity of faith and discipline in Church and in State. Richelieu was the first to see the immense importance of this from the purely political side. But he knew also how many times the secular arm had failed when it went further than to second the Church; and therefore he began by obtaining powers which would give him papal as well as royal authority. Great realist and opportunist as he was, he utilized the *commendam* system here as a lever against the worst vices that *commendam* had produced. In order to obtain full powers of visitation, he persuaded the Pope to appoint him abbot-general of the three greatest among Possessionate exempt Congregations; Cluny, Cîteaux, and Prémontré. He held also *in commendam* others of the greatest abbeys in France or in Europe, such as Marmoutier and La Chaise-Dieu. The income of these houses formed his salary as Prime Minister; and the ecclesiastical titles enabled him to frustrate many of those appeals to Rome which had maimed the hand of so many other disciplinarians.

He began active reform in 1627, as coadjutor to the Abbot-General of Cluny. In 1621, the abbot had been the Cardinal de Guise, "who, despite his title as Archbishop of Reims, had married a cast-off mistress of Henry IV, Charlotte des Essarts, by whom he had five children; and he had once compelled the King to shut him up in the Castle of Vincennes to prevent his fighting a duel with the Comte de Nevers". This abbot, shortly before his death, had signed a series of Articles of Reform drawn up by the grand prior, D'Arbouze, who desired reformation, but had not the force of character to bring it to effect. He therefore chose as his coadjutor the man who for five years had been cardinal, and for three years past had governed the whole of France. Richelieu strove vainly for a union between Cluny and the one really reformed Benedictine Congregation in France, St Maur. But the large majority of Cluniacs were opposed to reform; and Richelieu never succeeded even after he had become abbot-general by the resignation of d'Arbouze (1629). For in 1638 the situation was becoming desperate; the chapter confessed how "all that remains of the Order of Cluny is composed of benefices or priories in which already there are no monks left, or so many that they cannot form [real] communities". "Nothing but this union" with St Maur, it was pleaded, "could remedy all those evils and prevent the fall of the Order and of its benefices and conventual priories." "Divine service was being abandoned, and the buildings ruined." Here is the state of things in 1638, as reported by the Mauristes in support of their efforts to reform Cluny by union with their own reformed Congregation:

Complaints against the commendatory Priors of Cluny, proving the desolation of their priories; suppression of divine service, ruin of conventuality,* lamentable state of the buildings, moral lapses, and so forth. Such was the situation of almost all the Cluniac houses! A few official visitations have been held in these disorderly places: hitherto they had been made only as a mere matter of form, since the monks had taken care to offer the Visitors bribes to shut their eyes. The discoveries [at these recent visits] have been frightful. We must procure the union at all costs.

The 1341 reformed Cluniacs, spread over thirty-eight houses, would thus have reinforced the 8760 reformed monks of the St Maur Congregation, and would have had great opportunities for making converts among the unreformed majority of Cluniacs and Benedictines: the more so, because Richelieu had forbidden the unreformed, the "anciens", to receive fresh novices. That was Richelieu's dream. But among the parties which did most to frustrate this was the Roman court itself, which succeeded in mollifying even papal and royal favour to this scheme. It insisted, obstinately and repeatedly, upon one concession to the "anciens" which "went directly against obedience and good

* The number of twelve brethren was fixed by custom as necessary for a full *conventus*: with any smaller number there were difficulties in fulfilling the full task of services, household management, etc.

order, and would weaken regular discipline", and upon another which "went directly against the vow of poverty". At last, after seven years of quibbling litigation at Rome, true reform was farther off than ever. Then "at the beginning of 1642 came the brutal revelation of the secret motive, long unavowed, which had caused these indefinite procrastinations, it was the fear lest the reform of the Order of Cluny should diminish the revenues of the Papal Datary". It was vainly pleaded that, if this Roman opposition ceased, Richelieu "can farther advance the reformation of the Order [of Cluny, Cîteaux and Prémontré] in a single day, as he is doing, because of the post which he holds, than others could do in whole years". It was equally vain to represent that, under the conditions upon which Rome now insisted, "no reform can be hoped for, but only the continuation of the disorders and public scandals on the part of the ancient monks, which are beheld only with horror".

Thus, even at the end of Richelieu's life, he was obliged to procure a decree of the Parlement of Paris against the "ancient monks" of the Benedictine, Cluniac, Cistercian and Premonstratensian Orders, who broke even the wide bounds allowed to them by the concord between reformed and non-reformed brethren.

> After painful and scandalous incidents, which however did not go beyond the limits of the cloister, they had gone forth one fine day without leave, and thenceforward they scoured the streets of Paris and other towns which had a Parlement, under pretext of lawsuits and personal business....At this rate, several had soon discarded the frock, and there were public scandals.

Richelieu died without realizing his dream of union, "and Cluny collapsed, while Cîteaux and Prémontré did no more than linger on in gloomy and mutilated life until the Reformation". Yet wherever his strong hand was able to act freely and leave its imprint—we see this at Marmoutier, and throughout the story of the St Maur Congregation—he was able to build, and secure for a long future, that tranquillity in the Order which is so happily expressed in a single word by the Benedictine motto of "PAX". His successor as Abbot of Cluny was elected by the "Anciens", who by the Concordat had renounced all share in future elections. They chose a deformed boy of thirteen, son to the Prince de Condé, who moved heaven and earth to secure papal confirmation. The King dared not offend the most powerful Prince of the Blood, and the Pope confirmed the election, absolving all its irregularities of procedure. "That was the death of Cluny." When Cardinal Mazarin, in 1655, was himself Abbot of Cluny, Colbert wrote him a letter urging the necessity, among his first tasks, that of Cluny,

the reform whereof was undertaken with great care and great labour by his Eminence the late Cardinal de Richelieu, and even executed, but upon such feeble foundations, (not being supported by the authority of the Holy See), that immediately upon his death, being abandoned by his powerful protection, it has received such rude shocks that, within a short time, it has been reduced of itself to a worse state than when his Lordship the Cardinal was invited to set thereunto his strong hand.... In all the houses occupied by the *Anciens*, there is nothing to be seen but the consequences of bickering [*chicane*], evil living, the waste of monastic property and the lack of obedience and of command; to the great scandal of all the towns where the monasteries are situated, and of all the country around. As to the Observants,* there are now only 14 houses left; and in these not all the monks believe themselves bound to observe their vows, because the establishment of their Observance has not been confirmed by the Pope; and your Eminence may judge from thence the disorder which may creep into the mind of a monk who lacks that foundation. Thus we see that, apart from a few details of community-life which they still observe, the same disorders which reign among the *Anciens* are also among the Observants; the more so, that they quit and go forth from their monasteries without scruple and with impunity, and that the possessions of the principal houses are in such a state, by reason of their evil husbandry, that this reason alone would oblige them to quit.

Thus (adds Dom Denis)

the two Observances went on side by side. The *Anciens*, in spite of Richelieu's prohibition to receive novices, went on receiving them after his death; or, to speak more properly, continue as of old to transmit their prebends to younger sons of good families, and, under the title of "Monks of the Ancient Observance", to live the daily more luxurious life of idle canons, without succeeding in distinguishing themselves by a single man or a single work; until at last, on the eve of the Revolution a decree of Louis XVI's State Council (1788, March 27), and a brief of Pius VI (July 4) sup-

* Those who had definitely joined the reform of St Maur.

pressed them definitely, and thus spared the Assemblée Nationale the supreme injustice of confounding this useless dead branch with the trees, still green and sappy, which it was about to cut down pell-mell by its great scythe-stroke of February 13, 1790.

The decay of Cluny transpires in wide general terms from these documents; and so also with the Orders of Cîteaux and Prémontré. But we get vivid details from the other great abbeys of which Richelieu had procured the *commendam* in order to reform them.

The abbey and Congregation of Chezal-Benoît, as we have seen already in chap. XXXIX, had been in the vanguard of monastic reform a century earlier. But it was now as decayed as the rest. In 1632, the Visitor General, Dom Mercier, inspected two of the greatest houses: "he found deplorable abuses there, but was powerless to reform them". In his own abbey, Mercier "tried to suppress private property, promenades about the town, good feasts, luxurious dress, and gaming: but his monks had been so long accustomed to these that they considered them as acquired rights; they fought to preserve them with that ferocious energy which luxury can display when it comes to self-defence; they even denounced their Abbot to the Parlement at Paris". But Richelieu put all his energy and influence into the matter. In 1635, he procured bulls from Rome naming him Abbot-General of Chezal-Benoît. The reformers now sent him a memorial. A few heads of houses had promised reform, but "so far are they from having since fulfilled their promises, that, on the contrary, they have so increased disorder in their houses that we may speak of Observance as utterly extinguished therein". The superiors "are almost all young men, foisted in by intrigues and monopolies"; their houses are so deep in debt that credit is dead: even when they have spent a few days in their monasteries, it has been to make good cheer, with profusion of viands, and to employ vengeance and indignities against the other Religious whom they knew to be persistent for the cause of reform. The memorial then beseeches Richelieu's intervention, "seeing that it is impossible for the Congregation to subsist of its own strength, or to be reestablished in good reform by the said Superiors, considering their libertine and licentious life and the disorders which they create in the monasteries". Richelieu obtained royal and papal help. Thus he was able

without any violence, almost without once interfering directly, to bring a whole congregation to the cause of order, edification and regularity. Before his time Chezal-Benoît was in full decay and all its monks knew this. But they loved this loose life and wished to defend it towards and against everyone. The prescriptions of the Council of Trent were evaded, they used ancient privileges to keep off all attempts of reform, they escaped from the supervision and visitation of Bishops who were their neighbours and they hoped to continue indefinitely leading this luxurious and pleasant life which excluded neither hunting nor dancing. We may see on the contrary in consequence of the patient and persevering efforts of Richelieu how all these monasteries flourished again and became centres of austere, dignified and fruitful life.

St Médard-de-Soissons was one of the great abbeys of France. About 1635 it was reduced to a deplorable state. There were only eight monks left. These had indeed taken the Benedictine vows; but in fact they followed no Rule. All the conventual buildings were uninhabitable. The beautiful cloisters were full of rubbish; the refectory vault had fallen in; the chapter house was in a very bad state, and grass grew in the dormitory. The only habitable corner was the building which, in old time, had served as a prison for Louis the Pious (840). The ancient and magnificent church was ruined from top to bottom; the commendatory abbot had built another through a heretical architect, whose one idea had been to shape it like a Protestant meeting-house. The sacristy contained but one alb and a pewter chalice. Richelieu took advantage of the vacancy of the abbey to interfere, and introduced the reform of St Maur.

St Savin is famous for the completest series of eleventh-century paintings in France.

From 1611 onwards it was held as a benefice by the Baron de Francs, Lord of Neuchêze, who installed himself there with his wife and children, his numerous concubines and bastards and a band of cut-throats with whom he abandoned himself to acts of violence and pillage which seem improbable at the beginning of the seventeenth century. The monks had soon been obliged to take to flight...in consequence of a series of complaints and judgements which had not been able to put an end to this scandalous situation. A decree of the Grand Council of Poitiers (1634) ordered that the said Abbey of

Saint Savin should be reformed by the Bishop of Poitiers or his Grand Vicar, assisted by two monks of the Order and monastic discipline and observance re-established according to their original institution. The violence of Lord de Francs paralysed this attempt, nothing could be done until this ruffian was put into prison.

Richelieu undertook this and arrested the baron by a sudden stroke; he died soon afterwards in the Bastille.

The state of the abbey was lamentable. Part of the vault of the church had fallen in, the pillars were damaged, the chapels and choir screen ruined, the roof timbers rotten, the windows unglazed and half walled up, the choir without screens or stalls. There were only two bells, one cracked and the other worn out. The only ornaments were an alb, a chasuble, a challice and ciborium of pewter, a wooden crucifix with a broken copper Christ was tied up with string. Divine service had ceased, the monks were dispersed, all the buildings which had formerly been cloister, dormitory and other monastic dwellings were entirely ruined and overturned, with only a few pieces of wall remaining.

After two years' work at repair the Maurist monks were able to come into the abbey. That year, however, Abbot Beni, with the help of his relative the Bishop of Chalon, "obtained a revocation of the prohibition to reappear at Saint Savin and soon renewed his father's violence".

Marmoutier was one of the greatest abbeys in Europe, and the head of a Congregation. "In 1603 six monks of this Abbey, no longer able to support the scandals which they witnessed daily, left the community to practise among themselves regular exercises and a more worthy life...the mother Abbey, although it had given birth to these two religious institutions, was itself in great need of reform." Of its three abbots from 1604 to 1629 two were royal bastards.*

Disorders steadily increased. The monks would no longer hear of discipline and regular Observance. That was a foreign speech to them. Louis XIII attending High Mass one day of 1619 in the Abbey church had been much shocked by the ill behaviour of the monks. Their licence had reached such a pitch that the regulations and observances of the Superiors were obliged to forbid them from absenting themselves from Divine Service, from leaving the Abbey and sleeping outside without permission, from wearing garments unsuitable to

* The last, Grand Prior of Vendôme, is immortalized by Dumas.

their profession, from swearing by God, from frequenting masked balls and so forth. These monks had dancing masters and fencing masters in the house. Their most innocent pastimes were riding and hunting and nothing but prison was capable of bridling their excesses.

In 1629, the Cardinal de Bèrulle was put in by the King as reformer; on his death a few months later, Richelieu was chosen. He at once issued some statutes of reform, very mild. Then he proposed to introduce reformed monks from Cluny. The monks, anxious to avoid this at all costs, offered to accept reform from St Maur. Richelieu negotiated a concordat between the two abbeys. Negotiations dragged on; and meanwhile the unreformed at Marmoutier broke out into rebellion. The grand prior, who was responsible for the discipline, tried to enforce it to some extent.

But all his efforts came to nothing in face of the ill will of the rebellious monks. A young novice once put a pistol to his head threatening to kill him if he was still bold enough to go on with his remonstrances and correction. The *Anciens* themselves, though very undisciplined, were indignant at the attitude of the young monks: as for the poor Prior recognizing too late the fault that he had committed all he thought of now was to make his life safe by letting reform establish itself in his Abbey as soon as possible.

Richelieu procured royal letters, and arranged with the General of the Mauristes to send twenty-four of his reformed monks to Marmoutier. The royal envoy escorted these missionaries round the buildings; they and their hosts attended High Mass and chanted in choir together.

When Mass was over the Royal Commissioner led the reformed monks into the cloister, chapter-house, dormitory and refectory, gave them the keys of the sacristy and put them in possession of all the monastic buildings. When evening came he returned to Tours where the monks went to their cells for a sleep which was rendered necessary by the fatigues of the day and the long ride on horse back which most had had to reach Marmoutier. But lo! at nine o'clock at night a strange concert broke out under the cloisters and in the dormitory. The young monks had hidden there and until one in the morning they did nothing but howl, imitate cries of animals, blow their hunting horns, discharge firearms and belch out a thousand insults against the newcomers. At 2 in the morning all the monks of Saint Maur were in the church to sing matins, they would employ no other arms but prayer and patience. The young monks repeated their insults of the night before; but all the decent folk among the *Anciens*, scandalized by such conduct and already full of admiration for the virtue of their new hosts, sent some of them to Tours begging the Royal Commissioner not to depart until the young monks, who by the concordat were bound to go and study or to be sent to priories, had left the Abbey....There were a few relapses still. The young monks who had been sent to study and to the priories came back from time to time to the Abbey: they came to choir in riding boots and amused themselves with disturbing the service by singing false. The third Prior's lodging remained their headquarters; they learned dancing and fencing there with hired masters; days and nights were spent in eating and drinking; nothing was heard but oaths, blasphemies and obscenities, the echo of hunting horns and musket shots. Moreover, as nothing is more insupportable to the wicked than the virtue of the good, these rascals went once so far as to overwhelm the Proctor of the reformed monks with fisticuffs and kicks. The Prior, weary with all these disorders, died of grief (1638). The young monks counted greatly on the General Chapter which was about to meet in order to shake off the yoke of reform; but Richelieu, warned of this, forbade the Chapter meeting and cut down the monks' pensions; this calmed the excitement.

At Richelieu's death the troubles began again. "The Prince de Condé acted as a troublesome meddler to compromise and sometimes ruin the Cardinal's work"; only "the firm conduct of the pious Queen and of Austria saved what could be saved of this work".

All these facts form a living commentary on Richelieu's own words in his *Testament Politique*. He is addressing Louis XIII:

When I remember that in my youth I saw nobles and other layfolk possessing in *commendam* the majority not only of priories and abbeys but also of parishes and bishoprics, and when I consider that in my earlier years so great was the licence in monasteries of men and women that in those days nothing but scandals and bad examples were found in the greater part of those places where we ought to seek edification, I confess that I receive no little consolation to see that these disorders have been so absolutely banished in your reign that nowadays *commendam* and disorder in the monasteries are more rare than legitimate possessions and truly living religious houses were in those days.

The researches of Dom Denis do indeed compel us to discount somewhat from this complacent conclusion; he shows how much of Richelieu's work fell to pieces after his death, leaving Mazarin to face the same problems as his master. But the documents prove also how much the great cardinal had done, which no other man could or would have accomplished, in face of the frequent lack of support at Rome. While so many ecclesiastics were indifferent or hostile, these two cardinals did the work rather as statesmen than as priests. They saw that decency and discipline in the vast and immensely influential monastic world were essential for sound life in the State: some sort of regularity was necessary if the King's Peace was to run in France. In so far as the Catholic Reformation became a reality in France, this owed perhaps more to the aid of the Secular Arm than to any fighting tenacity of the Popes.

CHAPTER LXVIII

POST-REFORMATION ITALY

SCIPIONE DE' RICCI was descended from one of the most ancient families in Tuscany.(1) Born in Florence (1741), he was sent at the age of fifteen to study under the Jesuits in Rome. He was cured of a tuberculous swelling in his knee by the application of a printed portrait of the Venerable Ippolito Galantini to the part affected; and he always remembered gratefully the three professors who had taught him in history and the exact sciences. The famous "promise" to St Francis Borgia, that all true Jesuits are sure of heaven, tempted him to think of entering the Order; but his parents, hearing of this, at once recalled him to Florence (1758). At the University of Pisa, and then under the Benedictines at Florence, he came under the influence of St Augustine. He was ordained priest in 1766. His advancement was so rapid that in 1775, at the accession of Pius VI, he was offered a prelacy at the Roman court which would have assured his future fortune. He steadily refused, having convinced himself by observation "that there is no place in the world where the project of making one's fortune (as the phrase goes) and reaching exalted posts is so incompatible as this with the possibility of remaining an honest man".* He went back to Florence, and was soon made vicar-general to the archbishop. In 1780 he was promoted to the double bishopric of Pistoia and Prato. By that time he had the confidence of the Grand Duke, Leopold, who was one of the most enlightened princes in Europe. Leopold's civil reforms were remarkable, and he was equally anxious to remove Church abuses. With his assistance, de' Ricci held a Synod at Pistoia in 1786 which unanimously passed a number of decrees for radical reform, showing itself in other matters definitely "Gallican", and impatient of papal absolution. The next step was to convoke all the bishops of Tuscany to ratify these. Here the bishops

* De Potter, I, p. 21. Wherever in this section I quote verbally, without further warning, it will be from de' Ricci's own words.

allowed no voice in discussion but to their own Order; and only three voted for the reforms, which were finally condemned in 1794 by a papal bull, *Auctorem Fidei*. The grand duke, succeeding to the Empire as Leopold I, lost his special interest in Tuscany; de' Ricci was threatened with mob violence, and he retired into private life. From this he was drawn by the reactionary government of the Kings of Etruria (1801–7), which re-established the Inquisition in Tuscany. In 1805, Pope Pius VII passed through Florence, summoned de' Ricci to his presence, and demanded an unqualified public retractation of his errors and signature of adhesion to *Auctorem Fidei*. De' Ricci signed on the impulse of the moment, as he pleaded privately; yet he repeated his retractation in later years and died in 1810.

He had lost heart, as thousands have lost heart before and after him, in the face of evils which he felt himself unable to conquer. Thus the Synod of Pistoia was utterly abortive; yet Scipione's own memoirs and family papers are of the utmost evidential value: for it is precisely the most staggering details which are supported by the confessions of the culprits, signed by their own hand with due notarial attestation. They show the frequency, and above all the impunity, of vice in a society where the clergy were notoriously disproportionate in number, deficient in education, and protected from exterior discipline by so many generations of privilege that the prince himself could touch them only with the greatest caution.

When Scipione took up his work at Pistoia, the first business he found to his hand was that of persuading the grand duke to hush up a public scandal by quietly imprisoning a thieving canon in a monastery under ecclesiastical penance. His next task was far more difficult and important. He suspected the Dominican nuns of Sta Lucia at Pistoia of the same relaxation which he had already found at Florence. And presently, among those of Sta Prato, his worst suspicions were confirmed. Here he made no direct attack upon the privilege which reserved confessions to the friars themselves, who could make sure that the convents consumed their own smoke. But he appointed for himself a Dominican whom he could trust; and this confessor found himself compelled to refuse sacramental absolution to two of the senior nuns. They believed "neither in eternity nor in the Sacraments nor in sin, especially sins of the flesh" (p. 70). Ricci approached the Dominican authorities, in order to settle the affair as secretly as possible; but he was rendered powerless by the obstinacy of the general, who answered that he had punished the culprits sufficiently, and fell back upon his privileges to prevent any further enquiry. This, said Ricci afterwards, was providential; for he himself was so willing to avoid scandal that this "pestilent gangrene" might never have been probed fully to the root. The Grand Duke, appealed to, gave strict orders for cutting off all communication between the nuns and the friars. As early as 1642 the city magistrates had exposed to the Pope "the indecent conduct of the friars in the convents of S. Caterina and S. Lucia", "things which, for respect and decency, should not be named" (pp. 77, 337); but the then Grand Duke had not ventured to interfere. Leopold was of very different temper; and he was already sure of his ground, for he had procured papal permission in 1776 for transferring the nuns from Dominican to episcopal supervision. The friars managed to nullify this to a great extent by their intrigues; yet it rendered possible much of that "digging of the wall" which was so sorely needed. In 1774 a petition was sent to Leopold by six nuns of Sta Caterina at Pistoia who desired to live a decent and regular life. Each signed her name with her own hand; three were seniors, of the Conventual Council (I, 339 ff.). It began:

Declaration of the conduct of the fathers of St Dominic, in their direction of us, nuns of S. Caterina at Pistoia. Instead of leaving us in our innocence, they corrupt us by word and deed, and often come from the Sacristy, whereof they have almost all the keys; and, the grating being of sufficient size [of apertures], they act a thousand improprieties there.*...They put their hands into the bosom of their "friends", etc. [*sic*]. If again they get an occasion of entering the convent by some false pretext, they go to the rooms of their favourite [*parziali*], even alone. They are nearly all smeared with the same pitch, even to the Provincial Ministers; and these are the things for which they take advantage of their visits. They drop bestial sentiments from their mouths, saying that they are considering our own happiness; that we may satisfy ourselves without the pains of child-

* Here follows a detailed description, which would scarcely be credible but that it is repeated, under the most formal notarial attestation, in the confession of the nuns of Prato.

birth; that, when this world is finished, all is finished; that St Paul also teaches us how he "laboured with his own hands" (I Cor. iv. 12), and therefore let us help ourselves to take our pleasures. They suffer all sorts of improprieties to go on in the parlour. Though we have often warned them, they do not remove or cut off perilous friendships; and hence it has befallen that folk have many times entered by night-time to enjoy themselves and sleep with the nuns, having by subtlety caused keys to be made. They suffer likewise that a nun of this sort abstains from the Sacraments, nor do they care to introduce mental prayer; nay, they preach nothing but the peace of this world. Those who live after their ideas are exalted by these men and contented even in the most extravagant matters, while the rest must betray their own conscience by adapting themselves, or must suffer perpetual war, as indeed is the case at this moment.

This is the pure truth, without passion, and formally attested in conscience by us the undersigned. [Six names in full.]

Ricci kept other autograph letters from this group, complaining to Alamanni that the unreformed sisters daily threatened them, even with poison (I, 350). He received corroborative evidence in later years from a page-boy who confessed to have been a frequent intermediary between the friars and nuns; and the Grand Duke obtained a signed report from three of the workmen employed upon the convent buildings. One Easter Day, the Dominican prior and confessor, with two other friars, were surprised "passing the time at table, each with his respective nun" (I, 345). But this (1774) was six years before Scipione's appointment. The then bishop, Alamanni, an octogenarian who lived at Florence, was commanded by the Grand Duke to appoint at once a director for the nuns; the Dominicans were warned off from approaching the convent, under pain of prison. About the same time (1777) four nunneries were removed by Rome from the care of the friars: three Franciscan and one Dominican. "The abuses alleged by the Bishops of the dioceses concerned are grave: they make one suspect that there has been sollicitation to crime and seduction by means of auricular confession" (I, 356). The nuns protested: subjection to the friars was regarded as essential to their vow. When Ricci came into power, he found that "these unhappy victims of the friars' evil teaching [*della fratina seduzione*] were obstinate against recognizing the Bishop's authority: some of them would rather remain deprived of the Sacraments, than receive them from the hands of those priests, Secular or Regular, whom the Bishop had assigned to them". He appealed to the Pope, whose decision justified him: but he adds: "I knew I must now be always on my guard against the crooked machinations of the Dominicans" (I, 54). In fact, though the nuns of Sta Lucia and Sta Caterina at Pistoia finally gave way, the Prato affair caused him far more difficulty. For he was determined to probe it to the bottom, while the friars and nuns defended themselves desperately. He was met by "menaces of riot, intrigues to spirit away the two victims of seduction, machinations between friars and nuns to suppress papers and books and hide the scandals, and dark manœuvres to intimidate the Bishop; such were the methods of those wretches" (I, 95). Meanwhile, he writes: "I was met on every side by new specimens of the misuse which the friars made of their authority over the nuns, and the indecent liberties with which they associated together. The Provincial's wife, the Confessor's mistress, were talked about with a frankness which is sometimes unusual among worldly folk" (I, 97). Two autograph letters, sent in formal testimony from the Prioress of Sta Caterina at Pistoia to the Rector of the Episcopal Seminary in 1775, run to eight pages of print (I, 557 ff.). She records her experience of twenty-four years; she will not recall the dead, but she brands sixteen of the living friars by name including a Provincial.

But why name more? Apart from two or three friars, among so many living or dead, whom I have known, there was not one who was not of the same stuff. All profess the same maxims, and behave alike. They live with the nuns more familiarly than if they were married folk. It is customary that, when they attend a sick nun* they sup with the nuns, sing and dance and play, and sleep within the walls. Their maxim is that God has forbidden hate, and not love, and that man is made for woman and woman for man....One of those I have named was found in a chamber with a nun, and then he fled; but they appointed him afterwards Confessor Extraordinary....How many Bishops are there in the Papal States who have similarly discovered disorders in the convents of their dioceses, and made examinations and visits! Yet they have never been able to extirpate the evil they

* One of the few occasions upon which the Statutes permitted entry into a convent.

knew of; because the friars instil the belief that all are excommunicated who reveal that which passes within the Order. I said one day to a Provincial, an Englishman whose abode I have forgotten: "Poor creatures! they believe that they are quitting the world to avoid dangers, yet they find worse: our fathers and mothers gave us a good education, and here we find the *Ave Maria* spelt backwards!" He knew not how to answer me....Poor wretches, God knows whether they are not in hell! How ill they are assisted [on their deathbed]! That is a carnival-time [in the Convent]....And tell me not that ours is the only convent where this is done. It is the same at Sta Lucia, at Prato, at Pisa, at Perugia, and I have heard tales which take your breath away. Everywhere the same fashion; the same disorders and abuses. One friar said to me that, if a nun's veil were hung at one Pole, and a friar's frock at the other, such is the force of sympathy that they would come together. I say, and say it again, that however much our Superiors may suspect, they know not the least fraction of the great evils that pass between friars and nuns.

She adds "at San Vincenzo, which passes for a sanctuary, the nuns have also their lovers". She emphasizes the impunity, or even popularity, of some of the worst friars named. The papal nuncio defended and protected the Dominicans. In 1782 he scandalized right-thinking folk in Florence by patronizing the comedies and masked balls which the friars gave there (I, 370).

This is the most explicit arraignment, apart from the signed confessions of the two main sinners at Sta Caterina. But the book contains overwhelming evidence for the prevalence, down into modern times, of those abuses which the most saintly reformers had never been able to eradicate in the fifteenth century. Given the system of dumping younger daughters into nunneries, and the social licence of most Continental countries among the laity, there is nothing here that need surprise us. But those are precisely the two crucial points which are ignored by modern apologists, who imagine past monasticism after the pattern of our own day, where the votaries of both sexes form, in comparison, an infinitesimal proportion of the whole population, and live under free criticism, and cannot altogether subtract themselves from the discipline of ordinary State law. Another point which needs some imagination nowadays, but which is brought out very strongly in these nuns' evidence, is the immoral use which follows quite naturally from any exaggerated belief in the peculiar sanctity of the priesthood. It is not only that the nuns repeatedly name priests as seducers and as teachers of abortion, but they also explicitly accuse them of using the confessional for the very purpose of seduction.(2) Moreover, they preached the moral innocence of that which would be sinful with any other than a priest.(3) The consecrated Host played its part here, as in the similar scandals at Louviers about the same time, and as Caesarius of Heisterbach tells us in the thirteenth century.(4)

It would be unjust to emphasize too much, in itself, the hideous nature of these revelations which confronted Ricci as soon as he set himself to unsparing enquiry. But it is more important that several witnesses testified to these abuses as general; for there were 3000 priests among the 80,000 inhabitants of Florence, and Ricci stigmatized the secular clergy of his own diocese as "for the most part ignorant and ill-educated"; "many knew not Latin and could not read it" (I, 55; III, 318). The Senator Rucellai, in his memorial to Leopold for reform throughout Tuscany, insisted upon the diminution in numbers of priests, who formed 3 per cent. of the total population and of whom (as he said) the majority had taken Orders only for the sake of immunity from the ordinary lawcourts (III, 174). Moreover, we may perhaps find the most damning evidence of all in the almost universal impunity of offenders, even when they did not actually go on from promotion to promotion.(5) Ricci himself, after years of struggle, had still to interfere severely for the punishment of nuns who acted comedies and gave dances in their convents, as their predecessors had done in Traversari's time (II, 29, 293). The two worst nuns when Ricci came upon the scene were put under strict detention, separately, in other religious houses, where they lived many years afterwards. But, at the time of their first discovery, when the matter was left to the Dominicans, their legal directors, the discipline was such as St Thomas More allows himself to describe with what might almost be called heretical relish. One of their signed confessions runs: "*Q.* What penance did [the Franciscan Dr Ulivi], give you? *A.* Five *Paters* and five *Aves* to the [five] Holy Wounds, which I must recite daily till further notice; but I did nothing of that, and this was about 7 or 8 months ago." Two Dominicans, at different times, had imposed the penances of reciting the daily Office (to which in any case she was morally bound) "without intention and without attention", so long as she said the words. Afterwards, she long maintained that her infidel beliefs could not be wrong, "because she had twice revealed them fully in confession to Dr Ulivi, and that friar had prescribed no penance". So again with the other, the sub-mistress.

> *Q.* What penance was imposed upon you when you abjured? *A.* None at all. *Q.* Did neither your first Confessor nor your second give you any penance at these abjurations? *A.* I think not; I do not remember. *Q.* When the Confessors gave you absolution, did they impose a penance? *A.* Yes. *Q.* What did they give you? *A.* I have no recollection; they will have given me prayers; the seven [penitential] psalms, and rosaries; and I think one of them gave me a little fasting (*rata di digiuno*).(6)

They were admitted frequently to the Holy Communion, which they insisted upon approaching in token of innocence.(7)

Most serious of all, however, was the Pope's direct responsibility for this impunity. In 1781 Ricci sent a long and formal letter to Pius VI, describing the errors of the two nuns at Pistoia in general terms, and adding that, at one time, there were six such; he had not been able to prove it documentarily because the friars had burnt or subtracted them. He wrote at the same date a more intimate letter to Cardinal Corsini, appealing to the formal depositions of nuns "which I cannot put into my letter to the Pope: for they would fill you with horror. Yet of what are these miserable Dominicans capable! The Provincials and Priors, instead of remedying all these disorders of the Confessors, have suffered them, or even have committed themselves the same iniquities." Ten days later he wrote to the cardinal, emphasizing their confession of "the horrible abuse made of the Sacrament of the Eucharist". A little later, he wrote again to the Pope direct, enclosing an abstract of their judicial confessions, including their tenet that their "union with God" is lawful with a priest, though not with other folk. The cardinal backed Ricci up; so did the archbishop-elect of Florence, "fearing his diocese also contained nuns perverted by the friars". But their support was timid, and the Pope allowed a Jesuit and a Dominican to draw up an answer in praise of the friars and in rebuke of the calumniator and seditious busybody who attacked them. Ricci, in a letter approved by Leopold and by the Archbishop of Florence, wrote a letter with details of the friars' immoralities, and the general scandal caused by their public and notorious improprieties. The Grand Duke accompanied this with a letter of plain-spoken rebuke to the Pope for this treatment of a prelate whom he himself was resolved to support with all his power. He added that he would himself take these disorderly nunneries in hand, with all others in Tuscany, if Rome did not hasten to submit them to the spiritual authority of their Ordinary. The Pope gave way at once, sent Ricci a brief essentially contradictory of the first, and the reforming bishop had nominally a free hand. But, as he knew well enough, the friars were too powerful to yield; and Rome began from thenceforth to work secretly against the reforming zeal of the House of Austria: Leopold and his brother the Emperor Joseph II.(8)

The Jesuit historian Tacchi-Venturi speaks very frankly of the state of things in the mid-sixteenth century and beyond. The saintly Giulio Mancinelli, who joined the Company of Jesus in 1558, had long been held back by his unfavourable experience of other religious Orders. He was of noble birth; and all round him he saw the convents filled with coarse rustics. In his own words:

> In [my city of Macerata] I had never seen a man enter into Religion but such as were of senseless and eccentric [*humoristi*] nature, mis-shapen of body and very deformed, of vilest parentage or of bastard birth....As to their manners, there had befallen at that time, among the Religious, very scandalous cases, wherefore they were commonly in evil and vile reputation; and I believed not that any lived in holiness, without mortal sin, as I desired in Religious life.

Tacchi-Venturi cites another witness, the priest Lorenzo Davidico (d. 1574), who dedicated his *Anatomy of Vices* to Julius III. "The 88th chapter of part I, destined to pass through the hands of all men indiscriminately, runs from beginning to end in the most ardent exhortations or the bitterest philippics addressed to the priests of the day." Repeating in substance, though with changes of form, the oration of Antonio Pucci at the Lateran Council of 1514, "he gives to his own work a highly individual colour, well adapted to portray the miserable state of debasement in which so large a part of our clergy lay buried".(9)

Thus post-Reformation monastic history is simply a natural continuation of pre-Reformation conditions. It was impossible to bring the monks, without violent revolution, into line with ordinary citizenship. Their privileges, though originally of mere mushroom growth, when we take the long perspective of history, had acquired what to their contemporaries seemed immemorial antiquity. Behind these they resisted ferociously and unanimously; and even Popes dared not to drag them from their holes. The good and the moderate were outnumbered and terrorized by the degenerate. Thus, at last, monasticism not only cumbered the ground but infected it; and every Government was compelled to lay its axe to the root of this tree of privilege and exemption. That tree is now compelled to show its fruits, and is immensely improved by the drastic surgery of 1792 and following years. The institution has outgrown recognition and perhaps the historian's greatest difficulty lies in his temptation to judge the monk of 1500 by the monk of to-day.

CHAPTER LXIX

THE TUDOR BACKGROUND

THERE cannot be even an approximate opinion on this great revolution until disputants on both sides have accustomed themselves to bear constantly in mind the great differences which divide Tudor mentality and Tudor customs from those of our own day. At present, even the most glaring anachronisms pass muster. Professor Tawney points out that nobody would be more surprised than the Tudor peasant to be told that his lot had corresponded to the glowing picture painted by many modern writers from Cobbett onwards. Another very strong example is the treatment meted to Cromwell's choice of twelve as the rough line of division between efficient and inefficient monasteries. Sheldon Amos treated this as an *ad captandum* figure. That was natural enough in a modern lawyer who made no pretence of specialization in monastic history. But our ecclesiastic historians have sometimes passed a similar condemnation, in evident ignorance of the elementary fact that twelve was always a sacred number in Benedictine history. The saint's own original foundations were of twelve each; and this became so definitely the accepted standard that it was constantly erected into a test: houses of twelve or more were dignified with the adjective "Conventual"; below that number, the congregation did not form a *conventus* in the strictest sense. When, for instance, Bishop Scipione de' Ricci and others set themselves to reform the eighteenth-century monasteries in Tuscany, *twelve* was their rough distinction between competence and incompetence; and they, also just like Henry VIII and Cromwell, proposed an age-limit to the life-long vow: in some cases twenty-one, in others twenty-four.(1) Yet Cardinal Gasquet, who claimed special authority on Benedictine constitutional history, allowed himself to echo Amos's condemnation: "Such a limit [as the number of twelve], however, is made ridiculous when it is set as the line of demarcation between virtue and vice." We have here only an outstanding instance of the ignorance or want of candour which, even today, often distorts Reformation history.

Men brought up in modern English-speaking countries, with their traditions of political and religious liberty, need a great and continual effort to realize the state of things which confronted Tudor statesmen and the Tudor public: every man or woman who was honestly concerned for pure religion and good morals. Those who ignore these things, and even those who minimize them, run blindly into that very fault which they lightheartedly impute to others, of failing to visualize the actors on that stage in the true light of their own day. No man can understand either Henry VIII on one side, or More and Fisher on the other, who allows himself for one moment to forget the first postulates of those men's thought. Serious minds were soaked through and through with beliefs which are in great part abandoned even by the most conservative minds of today: and the thoughtless mind was often still more swayed in its blind actions by the subconscious influence of those traditional beliefs. Apart from the growing scepticism of a small minority, religion was a picture of glaring—it may almost be said, of blinding—contrasts. Every baptized creature was destined for an eternity either of unimaginable bliss or of indescribable physical and mental agony: for of course purgatory did no more than postpone the execution of that irrevocable separation between sheep and goats. The final decision between this Heaven and that Hell depended, above all, upon the soul's last state as it quitted the mortal body. Moreover, the most definitely saving or damning question here was that of the dying man's attitude towards God: and this, again, was practically narrowed down, in men's belief, to their attitude towards the Church: which, again, too often meant simply, towards the priest and his rite of Extreme Unction. For, in spite of hair-splitting academic logic, it was almost impossible in practice to separate that Church from its clergy: indeed, it was sometimes academic orthodoxy itself which obliterated in practice its own wire-drawn distinctions. For orthodoxy insisted upon the doctrine of *opus operatum*; the priestly ceremonies possessed great value not only as sacraments but even as spells and incantations. The most sinful priest conceivable could "make" Christ's own Body (to quote the crude phrase sometimes used by sacerdotal extremists) as efficaciously as any Pope; and the most polluted fingers, handling this, could pass on certain miraculous graces to the most unthinking soul. The person of the ministrant was thus swallowed up in the supernatural glory of the altar; and, as a bad priest could, to some extent, efficaciously bless a bad man, so also was the sacerdotal curse hated and to be feared even by the man whose conscience did not otherwise reproach him. *Touch not mine anointed*, and *To obey is better than sacrifice* were principles with which all men were necessarily familiar in practice, whether they knew the Biblical texts or not. Thus even the stoutest anticlericals were sometimes subconsciously influenced by what may be called the talismanic side of official religion. This same natural tendency has survived to our own day in Spain, Mexico and Southern Italy.

Nothing short of this could explain the grovelling subjection with which Leopold and Ricci had to contend, and which, in the end, went so far to thwart their efforts and those of other enlightened rulers on the Continent. To this we must add a second consideration of great force: that passion for unity which, fanned to fever-heat by the centuries of anarchy following upon the break-up of the Roman Empire, often mistook shadow for substance, and led to a worship rather of the name than of the reality. It has needed the experience of twelve later generations, with all their quarrels, their wars, and their sincere or patched-up reconciliations, to convince the world—if indeed it is yet convinced—that men are born different; that their natural instincts and thoughts must always vary; and that, though a minority must always live at a disadvantage, the majority can never gain by suppressing minorities altogether. Therefore in Tudor England, so crude still in its religious and political conceptions, what baulked the social reformer was the ineradicable and often unconscious confusion between Christian principle and pagan traditions or practices. The Church, strong in immemorial possession, fiercely resented all attempts to eliminate ulcers which had grown into the flesh, and were confessedly more pestilent now than two hundred years earlier. St Thomas More himself, in his answer to St Germain's complaints, could not deny that the good clergy themselves were often more concerned to shield their erring brethren from legal and public punishment than to expel them resolutely as scabby sheep. Perfectly legitimate criticism, though coming from men untainted by heresy, was too often blamed as a fouling of the untouchable nest of Unity. To wash the soiled ecclesiastical linen was treated as an encouragement to those who would fain rend the Seamless Robe of Christ. Evil vested interests, under the respectable quasi-legal title of Custom, constantly superseded good reflective Law. We have already seen how, under Paul III, one of the strongest arguments against reform at the Roman court was the certainty that Lutheranism would rejoice in so manifest a retractation, with its implied confession of sinful and filthy gain for ages past. St Thomas More, again, could deny the truth of St Germain's quotations from Gerson; but only pleaded that those scandals, which the great Paris chancellor had branded for his fellow-clerics in a Latin as scathing as Juvenal's, ought not to be translated into plain English for the multitude to read.

Tolerance, therefore, difficult enough in any day, was practically impossible then. Theoretically, if only we could be sufficiently convinced of the rightness of our own belief and the wrongness of another man's, it would be our duty as citizens to prevent the spread of the wrong. Yet even philosophers have often been slow to realize how rare such certainties must be, so that truth can very rarely gain so much by Protection as by Free Trade. It has needed many generations of bitter experience to bring even theoretical tolerance so far as that. In 1500 there were myriads among the best in Europe who had not yet come within distant sight of any such conclusion; they would not have been tolerant if they could, and could not if they would. Therefore the step from a war of ideas to a war of bloodshed or terrorism was as nearly inevitable as we can call anything inevitable in history. Paul III, in his bull of 1538, called upon the orthodox princes of Europe to invade England and treat as slaves all Englishmen who might be captured in defence of their King. In 1545, again, he bound himself by contract to supply 12,500 men and 100,000 crowns for the war against the Protestants of the Continent.

Those were the forces against which Henry had to work, just

as the Popes had to reckon with an increasingly despotic King in an age when the general trend was towards despotism. We must judge both, therefore, in their relation to that background. The Pope relied upon conceptions of the Vicariate of Christ which were rapidly breaking down; Henry was of a generation which grew increasingly heedless of papal thunders, and he was bold enough to fight for the mastery in his own kingdom. That, after all, is what Philip IV of France had said two centuries earlier: "The King means to be master in his own house." Henry's plundering was not more barefaced than Philip's; and his methods were far less brutal. His worst deeds cannot be compared with the systematic foul play in court, and the cruel punishment of burning, inflicted upon the Templars by King and Pope in collusion.(2) But he had to break down a series of papal fortresses; he was the despotic and cruel ruler of a nation which, like the rest of Europe, consisted of men far more blunted to cruelty and blood than the average person of to-day. Again, he had equally cruel adversaries abroad. Yet, with all this, it was not until the reign of his daughter Mary that judicial torture became almost as familiar to England as to France and Italy and Spain and Germany. Among all those who blame the rupture of the sixteenth century, and who harp upon the well-worn theme that much bloodshed would have been avoided, and far better religious results obtained, by such a gradual reformation as Erasmus might have sketched, how many are there who show that they have thought out that attractive speculation in detail? Let us suppose the enormous good fortune of a Pope like Eugenius III at Rome, with a saintly master like St Bernard to advise him, and a sovereign like St Louis to deal with. If such a pontiff had begun as Contarini and Pole advised, by cutting off at one stroke, as shameful and simoniacal, the greater part of the income of the Roman court, how long would he have lived? Or, again, if the saintly King had assumed Charlemagne's role of Episcopus Episcoporum, and proclaimed resolutely that religious foundations richly endowed by lay-folk for prayers and masses and almsgiving were answerable to the lay powers, in the last resort, for something like loyal fulfilment of their share in the contract? If, in short, he had applied that writ *cessavit* which the Second Statute of Winchester put into his hands, would even St Bernard's zeal for righteousness have brought him to admit that a layman might withdraw anything which had once been consecrated to Church uses, thus snatching the sacrifice from the altar?(3) Does not the intensive study of medieval history show more and more plainly that abuses, often natural and even harmless in their origin, had so woven themselves into warp and woof of a Church which could defend herself against almost any change by raising the alarm-cry of *sacrilege*, that no single ruler, nor even any two in concert, could attack the canker at its root? His tyranny, at the worst, pales beside that of the Italian princes of his time. Therefore, there is no need to attempt retracing here that story of Henry VIII and of Wolsey which has been told by Professor A. F. Pollard with such mastery of the sources and balance of judgment: a story which agrees in all essentials with that of the learned and honest Roman Catholic Lingard. To his own master Henry stands or falls; the Master by whose law all historians must, independently, estimate the privileges and the services of the monasteries. But, for completeness even in that field, we must face certain points upon which the correct authorities have too often falsified the actual relations between Monasticism and Royalty under Henry VIII.

The matter of Cromwell's Injunctions has been dealt with already.

The acceptance of Royal Supremacy by Convocation and the inertness of the Religious in face of the Suppression, were very human; and, in face of what has happened throughout Europe in our own day, few would venture to cast the first stone. But, here again, we must visualize them in the light of their own time, and bear in mind how superhuman their claims were. *Nolite tangere christos meos.* Unless these men's righteousness could be said to exceed clearly that of the multitude, there was no reason for their existence as a caste apart from the laity.

On the other side, again, even those who are most anxious to avoid extremes are sometimes most ready to forget the difficulties under which Henry laboured, like all who have the courage to risk a radical change.

Thus any reforming prince, whether his intentions were good

or bad, had to reckon with a spiritual sovereign who was fiery in defence of his own privileges and claims, yet tepid in the face of organized monastic resistance.

Moreover, the Councils had been far from completely successful, even in the years when they asserted, and to some extent exercised, a more than papal power. The Council of Basel made certain concrete experiments which Henry probably did not know in detail, but which in their totality were notorious. The statesman who drew up the Preamble to the Dissolution Statute if he had been challenged for that clause "by the space of 200 years and more...little or none amendment is hitherto had", need have gone no further than to Abbot Martin v. Senging. This man, one of the most zealous among the fathers of that council, reminded his assembled brethren that their most necessary motto must be taken from the Gospel text: *Physician, heal thyself*. For

the Abbots of certain monasteries have rejected the Visitors appointed for them by the Holy Council in the dioceses of Augsburg and Constance. They have treated these men with contempt, being well armed with the help of lawyers who get the fattest of fees from them....This, most Reverend Fathers, was the cause of their resistance and of the irreverence which they showed; their contumely and derision and disparagement, not only against the Visitors but even against the Council. For at length they were brought to such a pitch of madness by the evil persuasions of these members (as I cannot doubt) of the devil, that, when the Visitors would have executed the [Council's] mandate against their will, and when, under their pertinacious and obstinate persistence, those Visitors had proceeded to excommunication and interdict, then, the Abbots being unable to go further, closed all the abbey gates to prevent their entrance. Thus they did in two monasteries. Note, I pray, most reverend Fathers, this ignominy and contempt shown to the Sacred Council even more than to the Visitors by these men who, in a manner, are under the wings of this Assembly—nay, in its very face! For, when cited by the Papal Legate, they departed unpunished. What, think ye, do those who are far away from the Council? I fear they have been encouraged. Listen, most reverend Fathers: these rebels not only departed unpunished, but went away in glee, well rewarded; for they obtained what they coveted, Visitors whose lives resembled in all respects those of the brethren who were to be visited, men after their own heart!(4)

Here, written large, we have pretty exactly the experience of Henry VII and Cardinal-Legate Morton at St Albans.

I have sometimes been inclined to believe that the Tudor monasteries were beginning seriously to march with the times; and that here, as often elsewhere, the crash came not when things were at their worst, but when they were already mending. This may indeed be so; but it can scarcely be argued that the records point clearly in that direction. Moreover, we cannot read this theory into St Thomas More's lengthy and forcible polemical writings. More, with the faith of a martyr and the acumen of a trained lawyer, seems to avoid what would have been far the most telling plea: "You yourselves can see how things are mending; give them at least a further chance to show what can be done." He never gets beyond the somewhat half-hearted plea that good monks are people of true self-denial, and that it is unjust to condemn all for the shortcomings of some. Nowhere, I believe, does he venture upon the vaguest suggestion of the proportion which the good may bear to the bad or indifferent. The best that he says amounts to no more than can be pleaded in all ages for any institution which has once been honourable, and is still useful though it may now be decadent. Nowhere does he raise the question definitely above mere morbid anatomy; and modern historians who wish to go farther than More must definitely show their vouchers. Above all, they must not ignore, with however generous intentions, facts which, once faced, cannot be set aside as irrelevant. The cancer was there in later monasticism: orthodox contemporaries often branded it in terms of what might seem bigoted Protestantism. That cancer history must probe to the roots, yet without losing sight of the living tissue behind. It is, in fact, the comparative soundness of modern monasticism which constantly tempts to the anachronism of judging William Walingford and his brethren by the standard of (let us say) Dom Berlière and his brethren of Maredsous. That is the contrast which displays a lofty ideal even to those of us who cannot bring ourselves to regard it as the loftiest of all.

APPENDIX I

THIS Appendix and Appendix II, I owe to Mr Warren Sandell, who has made an exhaustive study of the original documents.

Authors responsible for the so-called "rehabilitation" of the monasteries condemn, often in hysterical terms, the "filthiness" of the Visitors' reports and letters, and—by inference—of their minds. "Foul as it is, with a most unspeakable foulness" is a phrase used by Gairdner of the *Compendium Compertorum.* (1) Gasquet at one point seems to endow the dust of ages with an ethical import. Layton's letters, he says, "abound in the most filthy accusations.... They manifest the prurient imagination of one who was familiar with vice in its worst forms. His letters...are the outpourings of a thoroughly brutal and depraved nature; even still they actually soil the hand that touches them" (*sic*). (2) Dr Jessopp reaches the apex of hysteria. He says, among much else, that the comperta "could only have been penned by a man of blasted character and of so filthy an imagination that no judge or jury would have believed him on his oath". He cannot believe such charges against "some eighty gentlemen and ten ladies" in East Anglia. (3) These are fair examples of the rhetoric which such writers substitute for a calm examination of evidence. To judge the validity of such advocacy it seems necessary first to distinguish between the *Compendium Compertorum* and the Visitors' correspondence. The former simply states the names of religious persons and the offences charged against them. Adultery, fornication and unnatural vice are indeed "foul". But if "foulness" is thence to be attributed to any persons, it depends entirely upon whether the charges are true or not who is to be regarded as foul, the accused or the accusers. The objective "foulness" of the record cannot in itself discredit the Visitors. If it could, then what is to be said of ecclesiastical Visitors whose records contain accounts of depravity more detailed and graphic than anything in the comperts of the royal Visitors? (4)

Some of the letters written to Cromwell contain racy accounts of delinquencies and abuses, recorded with an obvious appreciation of their humorous aspects. But there is nothing in them approaching the, to our minds, ribald obscenity of St Thomas More's story of the shrine of St Walery in Picardy. (5) Yet the Visitors' letters were secret and highly confidential, whereas St Thomas More's story was published for all to read. The truth is that it is a gross anachronism to import into the sixteenth century the decencies and pruderies of a later age. Yet it should be stated that, in his reply to More, Tyndale administered a grave and restrained rebuke.

Another charge against Cromwell and the Visitors is that their sole object in the Visitation was to provide, and if necessary concoct, evidence which could make a plausible pretext for suppressing the monasteries. Gasquet tried to prove that from the very beginning of the Visitation Cromwell told Dr Layton that "he had not been sent on his round for the purpose of approving". To do this he quotes a letter dated September 16 in which Layton abjectly asked pardon for greatly praising the abbot of Glastonbury at the time of the visitation (i.e. August 1535). The letter was in fact written four years later, after the commission which preceded the abbot's execution. (6)

Apart from other internal evidence of its date, Cromwell is addressed as "your Lordship", which he was not till July 1536, a fact which Gasquet states on another page.(7) Although the letter was printed in a collection from which Gasquet elsewhere quotes, (8) he here gives a not easily verifiable reference to the P.R.O. MSS. The letter proves the exact opposite of Gasquet's contention. Moreover, the various Visitors frequently gave favourable reports, besides exempting a third of the northern houses from any immorality.(9) If the Visitors invented what they could not discover, or took baseless rumours as fact, why so many "clean bills", why distinguish, as at Blackborough and Coverham, when there was only a "suspicion"(10) of immorality, and why admit their inability to get comperta in some places?

In all this secret correspondence there is no evidence that Cromwell ordered or connived at fictitious comperta, but there is good reason to think that the Visitors would not dare to send him false reports. The obvious desire to suppress the monasteries does not in itself prove that the alleged abuses were fabricated and not discovered. It does not follow that we must blindly accept every charge as judicially proved; but the reliability of the comperta must be assessed by their probability in the light of previous Visitations, and other records.

The comperta are distinguished from ecclesiastical Visitation reports by the charges of solitary vice. Canonically such purely private sins would be outside the scope of ecclesiastical Visitations. But from the evidence we have of the Visitors' "direct method", it is unnecessary to assume with Gairdner that such faults could only be known by sacramental confession. (10)

Finally, the judicial procedure of orthodox ecclesiastical Visitations, though designed to safeguard individual and corporate rights and privileges, was not necessarily the most effective way of discovering existing abuses. Modern experience tends to show that less formal questioning may be more effective in disclosing offences and convicting offenders. Both methods may be abused. One may give immunity to the guilty, the other may endanger the innocent. But at any rate the methods described by Layton would have been superfluous if, as is suggested, the Visitors could furnish the required crimes from the fecundity of their filthy imaginations.

Cromwell is charged with pursuing, through the Visitors, a deliberate policy of harshness, especially by enforcing rigorously the Injunctions forbidding them to leave their precincts, and ejecting those professed under a certain age. On August 20, 1535, Legh wrote urging that Layton should keep the heads of houses as well as the brethren from going abroad, as he himself did, or else that he should be allowed to give licence to the heads so that the Visitors' procedure should be uniform. He was against giving this licence because it would cause discontent among the brethren (11)—a view supported by a later letter of the Abbot of Warden. (12) On the 24th he visited Bruton, four days after Layton, and wrote again in similar terms. (13) His companion ap Rice had, however, written on the 20th complaining of Legh's severity, and urging that some of the Religious should be allowed to go abroad on necessary business. He instanced the Carthusian proctors to show that this need not impair religious discipline. (14) A letter from Legh on September 3 proves that Cromwell followed ap Rice's advice, so far as to give Legh discretion to license heads to go abroad on necessary business. (15) Yet Gasquet says of Legh's first letter that its opinion was "no doubt conclusive from Cromwell's point of view". (16)

Legh still advocated his own policy as causing the heads to depend more on the authority of the King and Cromwell, and he said he would not give the heads leave until he had spoken with Cromwell, or had his express command to give it. Layton, meanwhile, continued his more lenient policy without rebuke. Legh met Cromwell in the middle of September at Winchester, and had been severely rebuked by him in a letter before October 16, when he wrote to excuse himself. (17) On the same day ap Rice wrote a graphic account of Legh's conduct to Cromwell, who had evidently blamed him for not reporting it before. (18) The next day he wrote again about his fears if Legh should know of his report, and giving reasons why Cromwell should not use "any extremity against Dr Legh". (19) It is significant that he should suppose that this would be the natural effect of his report.

Legh wrote again on the 19th more humbly, (20) but Cromwell sent a further rebuke on the 17th, to which Legh replied on the 21st. (21) No further evidence of this conflict survives. The natural inference is that Legh was brought to heel, and it is clear that the facts do not justify Gasquet's assertion that Cromwell approved of Legh's "excesses and unscrupulous violence". (22)

The facts about the dismissal of religious are similar. On September 24 ap Rice suggested to Cromwell that because of women's earlier maturity, and the greater risk of scandal from their leaving their convents, the age up to which they might be released should be twenty-two not twenty-four. He says that Legh had refused this modification. (23) Before October 20 Cromwell ordered that none were to be expelled over the age of twenty. (24) This followed ap Rice's denunciation of Legh on October 16, in which he said: "He does not follow your instructions, for whereas you ordered that all of both sexes between 22 and 24 should choose whether they tarry or go abroad, he sets religious men only at liberty. He has inserted a clause in his injunctions that all of any age may go abroad". (25) It is soon after this that Legh begins to paint pathetic pictures of Religious begging to be released, and asking what he shall do. (26) No reply is recorded, but the subsequent comperta of East Anglia show that Legh did not venture to release any, but merely recorded the names of those who wished release. Thus it seems that at this time Cromwell did not countenance Legh's plan to depopulate the monasteries. There seems to be no grounds for Gasquet's assertion that, as distinct from ap Rice, who was "not so deeply in Crumwell's counsels", it is Legh who "discloses the truth as to the secret policy pursued by Crumwell". (27)

APPENDIX II

THE ITINERARY OF THE ROYAL VISITORS

THE great speed of the Royal Visitors in 1535–6 is repeatedly cited to prove that their reports are incredible and worthless. "The rapidity of their tour", says Gasquet, "rendering investigation impossible, makes their comperts or reports utterly valueless."(1) Gairdner writes: "Considering the rapidity with which the work was done, the investigation could hardly have been very judicially conducted."(2) While in other parts of England it can easily be shown that their progress was not extraordinarily rapid, the criticism does at first sight seem substantial when applied to the visitation of the North.

The visitation began at Lichfield on December 29, 1535, and ended on February 28, 1536, when the Visitors left Ludlow for London,(3) thus occupying 62 days, i.e. one day short of 9 weeks. The territory falls naturally into two parts. On the east it extended northwards to Bamburgh, some 50 miles north of Newcastle. On the west it stretched southward from Carlisle to Cumbermere (probably the last house visited), about 26 miles south-east of Chester, and 53 miles north of Ludlow. The houses visited numbered 121. The comperta of forty houses contain no charges of any offences.

The Visitors were Dr Legh and Dr Layton. Layton, after visiting southern England, had been busy at Sion till at least December 17.(4) He next appears at Leicester, having visited on his way Chicksand, Harrold, and St Andrew's, Northampton. Since the end of October, when he visited Cambridge, Legh had conducted a Visitation of East Anglia. In Layton's letter from Leicester he says he has arranged to meet Legh at Lichfield, and announces: "This morning we depart towards Lichfield church, and from thence to certain abbeys upon Trent side, and so to pass on to Southwell, and to be at York on the day after 12th day we intend."(5)

This letter is dated "*crastino divi Thome*", and hence has arisen a strange error about the date when this visitation began, for all writers who refer to the fact at all assume that this refers to the feast of St Thomas the Apostle, on December 21. Two documents prove that this is not so. An undated letter from Hugh Wytwyck, Prior of Huntingdon, states that Legh visited Hinchinbrook, near Huntingdon, on December 23.(6) On January 15, 1536, Thomas Bedyll, then visiting Ramsey, wrote that "doctor Legh now at Christmas gave liberty to half the house at Sawtrey to depart".(7) Sawtrey is about

10 miles from Hinchinbrook, and near the route which Legh would naturally take towards Lichfield. There is no doubt, therefore, that the St Thomas in question is St Thomas of Canterbury, commemorated on December 29. It should be remembered that he had not yet been "unsainted", and there was no reason why such a letter should not be dated from his feast. One from Cranmer to the King on January 18, 1536, refers to "St Thomas' day in Christmas" (i.e. in the octave of Christmas).(8)

Another similar error (I think universal) is to date the Visitors' arrival at York as January 11. This seems to arise from Legh's letter dated from York on the 13th, in which he says "master doctor Layton and I the 11th day of January were with the archbp of York".(9) But the Archbishop on the 13th was certainly at Cawood, 10 miles south of York.(10) Also Layton's letter of that date shows that the visitation of the York houses did not begin until the 13th.(11) Roughly between Cawood and York lay four or five of the visited houses. It seems certain, therefore, that the Visitors examined the Archbishop at Cawood on January 11, and arrived at York on the 13th, after visiting some intervening houses.

Thus this first stage of the Visitation occupied 15 days and, from their geographical situation, could not have included more than thirty-nine houses. According to the dates accepted by Gasquet and others hitherto, this stage would have taken exactly 21 days, yet Gasquet writes: "Some eighty-eight monasteries are reported on within the fortnight."(12) This statement illustrates not merely Gasquet's unscrupulous inaccuracy, but even more his gross incompetence. How did he get the number eighty-eight? By counting the houses in the *Compendium Compertorum* until he came to the first York house mentioned, and that number is, in fact, eighty-eight. Not only did he fail to observe that his calculation left 6½ weeks for visiting thirty-three houses (thus destroying for nearly three-quarters of the visitation his argument from speed), but he neglected the five minutes' scrutiny which would have revealed that among his eighty-eight houses were places as far apart as Derby, Middlesbrough, Chester, Carlisle, and Brinkburn in Northumberland. The habits of Roman Catholic "historians" are further illustrated by the Abbé G. Constant who, in his recent substantial history of the English Reformation, roundly states that "ninety, for instance, (were visited) in a fortnight in the diocese of York".(13)

Any attempt to construct a detailed itinerary would be mainly conjecture, though firmly based on (1) the geographical situation of the houses, (2) eleven documents which give the whereabouts of the Visitors at certain dates, and (3) the fact that sometimes the two

Visitors worked separately, which the documents witness, and the geographical situation of the houses shows to have been inevitable over the greater part of the visitation. From the Visitors' arrival in York there remained eighty-two houses to visit in 47 days, but in mitigation of the speed which at first sight would seem to be necessary, these two factors must be taken into account, viz. (1) that the two Visitors were dividing the houses roughly between them; and (2) that of these houses, five were in York, three in Chester, and two in Richmond, i.e. ten *houses* in only three *places*, so that the number of *places* to be visited in the 47 days was seventy-five.

I have plotted the visitation itinerary on the ¼ inch to the mile Ordnance Survey maps. Having regard to the factors mentioned above, I calculate that each of the Visitors during 61 days (i.e. to the probable date of visiting Cumbermere) covered about 1015 miles, giving an average of less than 17 miles a day. The significance of these figures can better be gauged if they are compared with others derived from the itineraries of ecclesiastical Visitors. The most convenient, chiefly because they cover a very large area of the country, and are available in detail, are those of the two Premonstratensian Visitors, Bishop Redman (1478–97) and Abbot Wilkinson (1506). Of the latter Gasquet says: "It is impossible not to be struck with the rapidity with which he frequently moved from one point to another." Four things must be borne in mind about ecclesiastical investigations, viz. (1) that the visitors had no need to inconvenience themselves by haste, whereas we know that the Royal Visitors were directed to use "all speed with diligence" under a ruthless superior, Cromwell; (2) that ecclesiastical Visitations were conducted with prolonged ceremonies, usually including a sermon, and a canonical procedure to which might be added the purgation of offenders and the deposition of superiors, whereas the Royal Visitors certainly cut out most of the ceremony, and used a "direct method" which Layton described in his letter from Leicester; (3) that, on the other hand, the Premonstratensian Visitors had one reason for not dawdling unnecessarily on the road, in that they had to provide for their own expenses when more than one day's journey from one of their houses, and (4) that Royal Visitors could command facilities on the road superior to those available to ecclesiastics. Here are the calculations:

(A) *Bishop Redman*

May 21–Aug. 1, 1478. 71 days. 976 miles. Average: 13·7 m.p.d. 20 visits.

May 20–July 25, 1488. 67 days. 838 miles. Average: 12½ m.p.d. 20 visits.

Aug. 8–Oct. 16, 1491. 70 days. 912 miles. Average: 13 m.p.d. 25 visits.
(Oct. 3–16, 1491. 14 days. 256 miles. Average: 18·2 m.p.d. 5 visits.)
Aug. 21–Oct. 24, 1497. 65 days. 942 miles. Average: 14½ m.p.d. 24 visits.

(B) *Abbot Wilkinson*

April 25–May 23, 1506. 29 days (21 travelling). 551 miles. Average: 19 (or 26) m.p.d. 9 visits.
(May 9–23, 1506. 15 days. 351 miles. Average: 23·47 m.p.d.)
Sept. 9–Nov. 7, 1506. 60 days (38 travelling). 800 miles. Average: 13·37 (21) m.p.d. 17 visits.

During these periods of his Visitations, Wilkinson covered from 20 to 30 miles on 20 days, and from 30 to 40 miles on 15 days, while from May 9 to May 20 his daily mileage was 40, 18, 30, 0, 41, 0, 30, 23, 0, 51, 38, 26.

Finally, it seems certain that to impugn the credibility of the charges which are made against the religious in the comperta of the Northern Visitation on the ground of the speed with which the Visitation was conducted, is an argument which has no substance or foundation in fact.

NOTES

Fuller descriptions of many of the authorities quoted here will be found in the lists of *Abbreviations and Authorities* included in Vols. I, II, III of this work.

INTRODUCTION

(1) Joinville, § 445.
(2) Douais, *Doc. pour servir à l'histoire de l'Inquisition* (1900), II, 100.

CHAPTER I

Colet, More and Charterhouse

(1) See p. 660 of my second volume.
(2) *Epistolae*, ed. P. S. Allen, IV, 521; *Opera* (Leyden), III, ii, 459. For the severity of Carthusian life in its full strictness see J. H. Lupton's *Colet* (1887), p. 217. "How severe were the rules of the Order may be seen from the contents of a little manuscript volume, that apparently once belonged to the monastery at Shene, entitled, 'Formulare Carthusianorum'. In the form of admission of a novice, after setting forth the 'lenght and prolixitie of the divine office', the prior is directed to say: 'For your body you are to weare a shirte of heare, and a cord aboute your loynes, and a wolen shirte. You are to lye upon strawe or a bed of chaff, with a blanket betweene. For your diet, it is a perpetuall abstinence from flesh, in so much that in the greatest or most daingerous sicknes you can expect no dispensation therein. Also a good parte of the yeare wee abstaine from all whitmeates, as in Advent, Lent, and all the Fridays of the yeare.... For silence and solitude, it ought to be perpetuall, except when our statutes giveth licence, or that you aske leave.' Then follows an enumeration of certain services to train and discipline the novice 'in the purgative way', menial tasks of sweeping, and the like; 'which workes, by howe much they are more vile and contemptible in the eyes of the world, by soe much they are more pretious and meritorious in the sight of Almighty God'."
(3) Compare the words of a very learned and orthodox champion of monasticism, in *The Downside Review* for 1899 (XVIII, 50): "The next three centuries [from the early thirteenth century onwards] show the solid spirit which animated Benedictine monasticism in this land. The history of our monks of this Order stands alone in Europe during this period; it is time that this matter should be made clear, and that they should not be judged or condemned on the score of the contemporary state of things in France or Germany, Italy or Spain. English Benedictinism was not suffered to become *déchu*, and to fall into the desperate state which necessitated the heroic remedies of Bursfeld and Melk, St Justina and Subiaco."

CHAPTER II

Sporadic Reforms

(1) Wherever no other reference is given, this story is taken from the *Chronicon Villarense* (Martène, *Thesaurus*, III, 1267 ff.).

CHAPTER III

The Shackles of Materialism

(1) For all these details I have used D'Achery's *Spicilegium* (1666), VII, 437 ff. The *Chronicle* is also printed in *M.G.H. Scriptt.* X, 272 ff., and in Migne, *P.L.* CLXXIII, 113.

(2) Evelyn's *Diary*, under September 1646.

(3) *The Medieval Stage*, I, 121; cf. II, 119, 136.

(4) See H. Grundmann, *Religiöse Bewegungen im Mittelalter* (1935), pp. 29, 31 ff., 36, 45. I feel that the author exaggerates considerably the extent to which *textor* lost its plain sense of *weaver* and became synonymous with heretic; the present passage does not stand alone in implying that the unpopular *textores* were actual craftsmen. At the same time, the analogy of Freemasonry, when the "operative" craftsmen finally evolved into "speculative" and somewhat free-thinking internationalists, gives some force to Dr Grundmann's contention, when we discount his exaggerations.

CHAPTER IV

The Wider Problem

(1) Albero, III, 72.

(2) *Menses*, p. 42; cf. pp. 46, 73, 95, 120–4.

(3) Bulliot, I, 193.

(4) Mabillon, *Annales* (1739), VI, 190; cf. V, 370–1.

(5) *P.L.* CCIV, 968; cf. Calmet, *Hist. de Lorraine* (Nancy, 1745), II, preuves, col. L ii. Cf. the case of Thurgarton Priory in *Reg. Corbridge* (1304), I, 272 ff.

(6) *Ann. Colmar*, p. 9, note.

(7) St-Martial, p. 77.

(8) Le Paige, pp. 663 ff.

(9) *Decret. Greg.* lib. III, tit. XXXV, c. 6.

(10) B. Pez, *Thes.* III, ii, 528.

(11) Mansi, *Concilia* (1780), XXIV, col. 119, c. 26.

(12) H. E. Salter, *Augustinian Chapters*, p. 16.

CHAPTER VI

The Council of Constance

(1) H. v. d. Hardt, I, v, 91–3.

(2) H. Finke, *Acta Concilii Constanciensis*, IV, 539 ff.; also H. v. d. Hardt, *Magnum Concilium Constantiense*, I, ix, 506 ff.

(3) This is much more accessible to English readers; it is printed in E. Brown's *Fasciculus*, I, 406. See also H. v. d. Hardt, I, viii, 409 ff.

(4) Finke, II, 394.

(5) Printed in E. Brown's *Fasciculus*, II, 560, 562.

(6) Cf. Finke, II, 497 (Matthew, a Cistercian representative): "We are become a byword and a derision to all people...even in the streets and taverns, at feasts and at theatres (I say it with tears) we are lacerated and mocked by the most impious persons, hammering upon our backs. For the vulgar folk, unable to discern between good and bad prelates, shun all and love none", etc. Cf. H. v. d. Hardt, I, x, 635, and I, viii, 428, where the public scandal is taken as a basis for argument; also Finke, II, 439; the orator repeats his accusations here in the Council "though they are known to the whole world".

(7) Finke, IV, 731.

(8) Finke, III, 759. This question of simony is mentioned in almost every speech.

(9) Finke, II, 501.

(10) Ibid. p. 387.

(11) Ibid. p. 425.

(12) Ibid. p. 428.

(13) Ibid. p. 430.

(14) Ibid. p. 436.

(15) Ibid. p. 442.

(16) Ibid. p. 460.

(17) Ibid. p. 465.

(18) Ibid. p. 469.

(19) Ibid. pp. 497–8.

(20) Ibid. p. 524. He continues: "For there are innumerable priests who keep concubines in their houses, begetting carnal sons and daughters, and celebrating daily three or four Masses, handling the flesh of the unblemished Lamb from the Virgin's womb with those hands wherewith a little earlier they had handled the flesh of harlots."

(21) Ibid. pp. 582ff.

(22) Finke, IV, 584ff.; also in H. v. d. Hardt, I, 277ff.

(23) Finke, IV, 671ff.

(24) Ibid. pp. 740ff.

(25) The two sets of decrees are printed in H. v. d. Hardt, I, x and xii (coll. 616–722).

(26) Finke, IV, 726.

(27) The decrees are printed in Trithemius, *Opera Pia et Spiritualia* (Mainz, 1604), pp. 1032ff.

(28) *Annales Hirsaugienses* (1690), II, 349; cf. p. 351.

CHAPTER VII

Italy and Spain

(1) See his *Chronicle* in *M.G.H. Scriptt.* XXXII, 213.

(2) Turin, 1843. The book covers six dioceses; but Italian dioceses were much smaller than ours.

(3) Spondanus (Lyons, 1678), I, 68 (ann. 1212, § 12).

(4) L. Tosti, *Storia della Badia di Monte-Cassino* (1842), II, 289.

(5) Ibid. III, 53.

(6) A. Dantier, *Les monastères bénédictins d'Italie* (1867), II, 171.

(7) *Opere* (Milan, 1802), II, 209 (Nov. x).

(8) *Novellino* (H. Waters, 1895), I, 19.

(9) *Dialogo*, ed. Gigli.

(10) *Lettere*, ed. Gigli, II, 6.

(11) Gigli, p. 215 (127).

(12) *Prediche* (ed. G. Baccini, 1889), 93 (serm. iv). Compare his rough notes for a sermon in P. Villari, *Life and Times of S.* (1899), app. p. 776

(13) *Discorsi*, bk. I, chs. 13 and 55 (translation of E. D[acres], 1636, pp. 68, 216).

(14) *De Planctu Ecclesiae* (Lyons 1517), f. 83*a*. For his sweeping condemnation of the Religious in his time (1335) see my vol. II, pp. 544ff.

(15) *Tractatus*, f. 51*a*.

(16) Ed. Turin (1880), pp. 465ff.

(17) Copies made from the archives by O. Mazzoni Toselli, vol. II, fasc. 4, pp. 161–9, at the Biblioteca dell' Archiginnasio, Bologna. I have procured a full transcript, which will be found among my papers at Chicago. Witnesses deposed that she cursed her parents who had put her into the convent, that she had one haunt in church grounds in which she had given herself at different times to "a good forty men"; and another in a vault by the town

gate. One Dominican friar at least, and one Franciscan were among her regular frequenters. This had gone on for many years, not without occasional punishment, but without any effective check.

(18) E. Rodocanachi, *La Réforme en Italie*, I, 128; compare the concrete cases which he quotes from legal documents. The whole of this section, *Mœurs du Clergé* (pp. 96–134), should be read by all who would follow that side of Italian life in the sixteenth century.

(19) I, 39; cf. pp. 125–6. See further, for the decay of that house, II, 181; for attempted reforms, I, 74, 108ff., 114, 132.

(20) "History and Cartulary of Carbone", in *Orientalia Christiana*, XI, 5ff. and XV, 2ff. (May 1928 and June 1929).

(21) Loc. cit. I, 116, 117, 126.

(22) *De Planctu Ecclesiae* (1517), ff. 27*a*, 122.

(23) *Speculum Humanae Vitae*, lib. II, cc. 26–7. I have printed extensive extracts in my second volume, pp. 607ff.

(24) *The Life of Cardinal Ximenez* (trans. Canon Dalton, 1860), pp. 197ff. The original German is rather stronger; in three places where this has some importance, I have supplied the full sense in square brackets.

(25) Ibid. p. 203.

(26) Ibid. p. 215.

(27) Ibid. p. 217. Hefele adds: "Such, at least, is the account given by Petrus Delphinus, and after him by Raynaldus in his continuation of Baronius."

CHAPTER VIII

From Constance to Basel

(1) H. Rashdall, *Universities of Europe* (1895), I, 529ff. and II, 29, 38. The Popes had, indeed, their "University of the Court", founded about 1244 when seventeen other universities already existed in Europe: but this was peripatetic like the medieval law-courts, following the Pope wherever he went; in 1415 it was at Avignon, if it existed at all. A "University of the City of Rome" had been founded in 1303, but it had collapsed during the Great Schism; and when Eugenius IV revived it in 1431, he counted as its second founder. In neither University was the Theological Faculty of any distinction; Civil and Canon Law overshadowed it, "And the Popes themselves were lawyers rather than theologians....At no period of the Middle Ages was the University [of the City] of much importance from an educational point of view." It was not until Leo X united the two in what was afterwards called the Sapienza that they became a real school of thought (Burckhardt, p. 107).

(2) Rashdall, loc. cit. I, 529ff.

(3) See my second volume, pp. 535–6.

(4) *De Recuperatione*, § 30.

(5) Mansi, *Concilia*, XXIV, 120, 130.

(6) *Revue Bénédictine* (1923), XXXV, 162ff.

(7) Le Paige, *Bibliotheca Praemonstratensis*, p. 665.

(8) Addy, *Beauchief*, p. 76; Taiée, I, 131.

(9) Finke, IV, 606, 608.

(10) *Chronicon Hirsaugiense*, I, 226.

(11) For this evidence see vol. II, 400–1 and 576–88.

(12) Pantin, *Chapters of the English Black Monks*, II, 110ff

(13) See vol. II, pp. 599ff. and 655ff.

(14) For Janssen, see the facts I give in vol. I, pp. 408–9, and consult his index to note how often he appeals to Trithemius, yet how studiously he avoids quoting that specially competent author's exposures of the radical faults in the monasticism of his own time.

Pastor is more frank; yet his omissions are remarkable and serious. I quote from the authorized translation by Antrobus. In vol. I, pp. 148–50, he describes the reforms of Groote and of Windesheim without quoting from the contemporaries who contrasted those reforms with the intolerable abuses which they combated. On p. 335, a contemptuous reference to "the so-called decrees of reform" at Basel falsifies the whole perspective; no reader would realize that Basel did at least make one serious fight for the Windesheim reform. On pp. 355–7, he speaks of Eugenius IV and reform in terms irreconcilable with what we learn from the Pope's own friend Traversari. Again, while quoting from Nider and Schieler, he omits what they both emphasize, the success with which a nunnery managed to resist the whole reforming efforts concentrated upon it by the Fathers of Basel. In his second volume (p. 137), there is a gross *suppressio veri*. He quotes from Trithemius half a page which he uses to imply the final success of Cusa's reforms, ignoring entirely that Abbot's repeated and emphatic contrary evidence to which I shall come in Chapter XVII. In all his first seven volumes (the only relevant ones), Trithemius is never quoted except with deceptive implications; and although this is apparently due to Pastor's own unfamiliarity with the originals, the effect is none the less mischievous. True, the original sinner here is Janssen, whom Pastor gives as his sole authority; but the incident is characteristic of the echoes from apologist to apologist by means of which the reader is lulled into false security. In all the first five volumes, I find only one further reference to Trithemius (v, 292); here, again, it is a quotation designed only to reassure the reader.

(15) *Rev. Bénéd.* (1897), XIV, 370; see also my third volume, p. 465.

(16) *Formicarius*, pp. 33ff., 167ff., 175; H. v. d. Hardt, I, iv, 164.

(17) Leibnitz *Scriptores*, II, 486; cf. Grube, *Johannes Busch*, p. 51.

(18) Chmel (1859), p. 241.

(19) Grube, loc. cit. p. 50.

CHAPTER IX

WINDESHEIM

(1) The best brief account of the Brethren is by Mr H. S. Gem in Hastings, *Encyclopaedia of Religion and Ethics*, II, 839ff. Ullmann's *Reformers before the Reformation* and S. Kettlewell's *Thomas à Kempis and the Brothers of Common Life*, give fuller details, and are still valuable. W. Mulder has published Groot's own letters, *Gerardi Magni Epistolae* (1933).

(2) Busch fully recognizes how much his beloved Windesheim owed to Groot (p. 254). This present chapter, with some of those following, is mainly built upon these invaluable records (J. Busch, *Chronicon Windeshemense* and *Liber de Reformatione*, ed. K. Grube, 1886). Grube himself wrote a separate study which is now unfortunately out of print. It is excellent in its appreciation of Busch, and gives also much valuable collateral information; but here and there the author's ultramontane enthusiasm betrays him not only into untenable inferences but into plain inaccuracies. A translation of both Busch's books, with only slight omissions of redundant portions, is at present in preparation by Mr Francis Darwin of Oxford. A remarkable monograph of Acquoy on Windesheim and its influence (*Het kloosterte W. en zijn Invloed*) is now unprocurable; the Cambridge University Library owes its own copy to a lucky legacy.

(3) Busch (ed. Grube), p. 44 (cf. Acquoy, II, 370, 371).
(4) Ibid. pp. 308, 373.
(5) Ibid. p. xxxiii.
(6) Ibid. p. 654.
(7) Acquoy, II, 369.
(8) Busch, p. 137.
(9) Acquoy, II, 375.
(10) Busch, pp. 149, 153.

CHAPTER X

True Monks

(1) St Gregory's *Dialogues*, bk. IV, c. 38 (*P.L.* LXXVII, 392). The demons congregate round the deathbed of "a very great man in the world", and he expires with those words in his mouth.
(2) Compare the case of St Catharine of Siena about this same time.
(3) Busch is here alluding to a famous utterance of Gregory the Great (Homilies, bk. II, no. 29). The full passage, with other medieval echoes from it down to Dante, is quoted on pp. 28ff. of my *Christ, St Francis and To-day*.

CHAPTER XI

Model Monasteries

(1) The value of the Rhenish florin may be estimated from Busch himself, pp. 350, 704, and 786. A capital sum of 75 florins defrayed the lifelong expense involved in adding one more monk to the population of a monastery: again, a very small monastery could be founded on a capital of 75 florins for the buildings, and a guarantee of 150 florins a year for endowment. We can get sidelights from the almost contemporary account-rolls of the Bishop of Utrecht. A cask of herrings cost just over 3 florins; therefore this sale of fish would come to about the price of from 30 to 60 casks of herrings. Again, the bishop's charge for absolving Sister Dorothy, who wounded her fellow-nun in a nunnery, was 3 florins; and a Scotch priest's expenses in prison come to a florin per month (*Rekeningen van het Bisdom Utrecht*, ed. K. Heeringa, part II, 1932, pp. 68–70).
(2) G. Anton, *Gesch. d. teutschen Landwirthschaft*, III, 487.

CHAPTER XII

Johann Busch

(1) Compare the description of a thoroughly decayed Cistercian monastery, the great abbey of La Trappe, just before Rancé's celebrated reform of 1660 (Gaillardin, *La Trappe*, I, 46ff.). Busch gives two cases even worse on pp. 735–7 but without naming the monasteries. These two, apparently, are not historical but *ben trovati*; yet, such stories have their significance for social history, for Busch himself believed that the reformer in those cases was Duke Albert of Austria.

CHAPTER XIV

Recalcitrant Sisters (1)

(1) Gratian, *Decretum*, pars. II, C. xxvii, q. 1, cc. 14, 21, 24. The nun has entered into a "spiritual marriage", and, if she marries a man, she becomes a "bigamist". Cf. C. L. Richard, *Analysis Conciliorum* (1778), IV, 135.
(2) See my second volume, p. 11.

(3) E.g. Richardinus, pp. 108, 171. One of the main causes of decay in the Augustinian Order is "the frequent wandering forth from the monastery of brethren and superiors".

(4) Cf. Eileen Power, *Medieval English Nunneries*, pp. 344ff.

(5) For this and the other details of Busch's visitations in this chapter, see his *De Reformatione*, pp. 555ff., 562ff., and the figures bracketed in my text.

Dr Grube, in his long summary of this scene (p. 155), omits these interesting traits, apparently because they scarcely fit in with his apologetic scheme. Miss Eckenstein (p. 420) follows Grube here as elsewhere; she evidently knows nothing of Busch's own text.

(6) The Duke, it will be observed, would have thought it perfectly natural if either of those two bishops had sent him a letter of military defiance, a *Fehdebrief*, after Götz v. Berlichingen's pattern, as the result of some quarrel.

(7) Just as the nuns tried to curse Busch with the funeral *Media vita*, so they did their best to imitate the priest's excommunication with bell, book and candle. After that came the prehistoric pagan curse of biting the earth and throwing dust.

(8) Myrc's *Instructions for Parish Priests* (E.E.T.S. 1868), p. 10. Gerson condemned this as a suicidal superstition, since folk must necessarily see frequent cases of its falsity.

CHAPTER XV

Recalcitrant Sisters (2)

(1) E. Vansteenberghe, *Le Cardinal Nicolas de Cues* (1920), p. 118.

(2) Ibid. p. 143.

(3) For all these Austrian nunneries, see ibid. pp. 144ff.

(4) B. Pez, *Bib. Ascet.* VIII, 660ff.

(5) Printed in *Franziskanische Studien*, Beiheft 7, pp. 33–5, 93–120

(6) L. Dacheux, *Jean Geiler de Kaysersberg*, ch. XIV.

(7) *Formicarius* (1602).

CHAPTER XVII

The Windesheim Influence

(1) See my first volume, pp. 88, 317, and App. III.

(2) Ibid. pp. 142, 156, 162, 367–8, 500 and App. XVII.

CHAPTER XVIII

Bursfelde in the Ascendant

(1) For the epoch-making Chapter of Petershausen, see Trithemius, *Annales Hirsaugienses*, II, 346ff. For Bursfelde, see Fleury, *Histoire Ecclésiastique*, an. 1410, §§ 5ff.; and especially Dom Berlière's valuable articles in the *Revue Bénédictine* (1899), XVI, 385ff., 481ff. and 550ff.

(2) Busch, p. 356.

(3) For Constance, see Pastor, *Gesch. d. Päpste*, bk. I, c. 3 ad fin. For Basel, Berlière in *Revue Bénédictine*, XVI, 399.

(4) Berlière, loc. cit. p. 400.

(5) For this and much more, with full references, see my second volume, pp. 612–16.

(6) *De Vera Studiorum Ratione*, quoted by Berlière, loc. cit. p. 502.

(7) Heinrich Bode, in Leibniz, *Scriptores*, II, 349.

CHAPTER XIX

The Background of Reform

(1) The passage here translated is from bk. I, c. 7 (Douai, 1602, p. 52).

(2) *Formicarius*, pp. 22, 26, 66; *De Reformatione*, p. 136.

(3) *Joannis Tritemii ad Monachos Dehortationes* (Romae, typis Vaticanis, 1890), pp. 4, 43ff., 128, 236, 267. On p. 128 Trithemius, describing the state of Spanheim when his predecessor began the reform, appeals to the evidence of a surviving witness among his present hearers, Brother Heinrich. It is inexplicable that Janssen, and even the more candid Pastor with wider opportunities, should so neglect this most conspicuous witness.

(4) For the most that can be truly said in favour of the Bursfelde reform and Cusanus's legation, see Dom U. Berlière's article in *Revue Bénédictine* (1899), XVI, 481ff.

(5) See Dom Berlière's article in *Revue Bénédictine* for 1929, pp. 46ff., and 1930, pp. 55ff.: *Bursfelde und Abstinenzindult von* 1523.

(6) For Legatius see Leibniz, *Script. Rev. Bruns.* (1710), II, 413.

CHAPTER XX

Bursfelde in Decline

(1) The question is very fully discussed by Dom P. Volk in *Revue Bénédictine*, 1938, 1939 and 1940 (vols. XL, XLI and XLII).

(2) Volk, loc. cit. XL, 341–4. He adds: "The general judgment upon this pen-warfare must be that the obstinate refusal of those dietary mitigations of Benedict XII did more harm to the reform of Melk than any profit which resulted from their fleeting and compulsory adhesion to their principles." For Melk, like Bursfelde, gave way in the end. Cf. XLI, 56ff.

(3) Vol. XLI, pp. 56ff.

(4) Vol. XL, p. 360, and vol. XLI, p. 51; cf. p. 53. Compare also L. Pastor, *Die Reise des Kardinals Luigi d'Aragona*, 1517–1518 (Freiburg i. B. 1905), p. 97. The Secretary's words run: "The Fuggers are nowadays among the greatest merchants known to Christendom; for, apart from other resources, they can lay hands on 30,000 ducats in ready money without touching an atom of their real estate, which is of no small worth. This wealth they have gained by expediting bishoprics, abbacies, and rich benefices in Germany; for, as the said Master Jakob boasted, in his own time he has expedited all the bishoprics in that land, many of them twice or thrice; and yet he is not past 70 years of age." They also gained an enormous income from their leases of royal mines.

(5) Leibniz, *Scriptores*, II, 361.

(6) Vol. XLII, p. 70.

CHAPTER XXI

The Great Legation

(1) Creighton, op. cit. III, 46.

(2) F. A. Scharpff, *Nich. v. Cusa* (1843), I, 154.

(3) Ibid. pp. 156–62.

(4) See my *Sectarian History* (Wessex Press, Taunton), pp. 39-45.

(5) E. B. Swalue, *De Kardinaal Nicolaas van Cusa* (Leiden, 1838), pp. 112, 264, 269.

(6) Scharpff, I, 252; *Düx. Nic. v. Cusa*, II, 128.

(7) Creighton, op. cit. III, 236ff., 256ff.; Scharpff, I, 284ff. Creighton seems hypercritical here; only in his last volume (VI, 8, 9) does he render full justice to Cusanus.

(8) Düx (II, 451) prints the original Latin; Scharpff gives it in full translation (I, 284). Summarized in Pastor-Antrobus, III, 270, with a similar project submitted to Pius by Domenichi.

(9) Scharpff, I, 155–6, 163–6.

(10) Vansteenberghe, loc. cit. p. 121.

(11) Ibid. p. 152; cf. pp. 119, 120–1.

(12) Pastor-Antrobus, II, 115.

(13) Trithemius, *Annales Hirsaugienses* (1690), II, 423–50; *Liber Pentichus*, c. xi; *Dehortationes*, p. 267.

(14) Düx, loc. cit. II, 464–5.

(15) Vansteenberghe, loc. cit. p. 159.

CHAPTER XXII

The Congregation of Melk

(1) H. Pez, *Scriptt. Rer. Austriae.* (1725), II, 658.

(2) For these "Scottish" (i.e. Irish) abbeys see M. Heimbucher, *Orden und Kongregationen*, I, 258ff. For the fifteenth-century attempt to reintroduce the Scoto-Irish element into Germany, see my second volume, pp. 313ff.

(3) This memorial was printed by B. Pez, *Bibliotheca Ascetica*, VIII, 508ff.

(4) A much briefer, but very significant, description of the monastic conditions of that time may be found in vol. II of Pez's collection, pp. 83ff. It is a sermon to monks by the Venerable Peter v. Rosenhaim in [1432].

(5) B. Pez, *Bibl. Ascet.* VIII, 574ff.

(6) H. Pez, *Scriptt. Rer. Aust.* II, 637.

CHAPTER XXIII

Sta Giustina at Padua

(1) B. Pez, *Thesaurus*, II, iii, 270ff.

(2) Salimbene in *M.G.H. Scriptt.* XXXII, 39; fully translated in my *From St Francis to Dante*, 2nd ed. pp. 45ff.

(3) A. J. C. Hare and St C. Baddeley, *Walks in Rome*, 1905, p. 616.

(4) Ibid. pp. 616, 619.

(5) B. Pez, *Thesaurus*, II, iii, introd. p. lix.

CHAPTER XXIV

The Holy Grotto and Monte Cassino

(1) *Catholic Encyclopaedia*, article "Subiaco".

(2) Benvenuto da Imola, *Comentum*, V, 302 (on Dante, *Parad.* XXII, 72ff.).

(3) B. Pez, *Bibl. Ascet.* VIII, 497.

CHAPTER XXV

The Italian Scene

(1) M. Creighton, op. cit. (1882), II, 327.

(2) For full translation see my *Life in the Middle Ages*, I, 229.

(3) The best study of the Italian Renaissance is still that of Jakob Burckhardt. An excellent English translation, lavishly illustrated from the best works of art, is published by George Allen and Co. It is from this edition that I quote here.

(4) Traversari, *Epistolae* (Mehus), p. 264.

(5) For Piero de' Pazzi, see Voigt (1893), I, 291, and Symonds, *Renaissance* (1877), p. 41. For S. Raniero, see Ruskin, *Praeterita*, vol. II, § 120.

(6) Muratori, *Rer. Ital. Scriptt.* (1914), XIX, iii, 431. Bruni lived from 1369 to 1443. His classical scholarship finally earned him the Chancellorship of the Florentine Republic (1427–43). It was in 1396 that Chrysoloras became Professor of Greek at the University of Florence.

(7) Symonds, loc. cit. p. 520. Compare Bertrand Russell in *Mysticism and Logic* (1932), p. 61: "Real life is, to most men, a long second-best, a perpetual compromise between the ideal and the possible; but the world of pure reason knows no compromise, no practical limitations, no barrier to the creative activity embodying in splendid edifices the passionate aspiration after the perfect from which all great work springs. Remote from human passions, remote even from the pitiful facts of nature, the generations have gradually created an ordered cosmos, where pure thought can dwell as in its natural home, and where one, at least, of our nobler impulses can escape from the dreary exile of the actual world."

(8) Burckhardt, pp. 57–68.

(9) See (to choose a recent book of great ability) *The Constitutional History of Medieval England*, by J. E. A. Jolliffe (Black, 1937). We there read on p. 157: "There is, therefore, no inevitable antagonism between the crown and the legalized feudalism of the twelfth century, and such expressions as 'feudal anarchy' are peculiarly inapt to describe the normal mind of feudalism, which maintained, on the contrary, an all-pervading respect for law, a respect so strong that it asserted its sanctity above that of any of the authorities which were empowered to carry it out. The rule of law was the most clearly realized political principle of the feudal age, governing the conduct of lord and vassal alike." But the balancing sentences come later on (p. 239): "With the reign of Henry II a new device, the assize, comes into politics. It is something set by agreement—*assisa statuta*, *assisam statuere* are common amplifications—and it marks the first realization that custom can be changed by the will of those who live under it or govern by it." In other words, law to be complete must not simply embody what has been followed from time immemorial, but also the expression of later lawgivers, working in the face of changed conditions, and aiming at a logical synthesis.

(10) Burckhardt, pp. 223, 227, 233.

(11) *Inferno*, XXIX, 3–36.

(12) Full account in Symonds, loc. cit. p. 175. Compare Burckhardt, p. 100; where, however, he gives more credit to monastic copyists than modern research would warrant.

(13) Burckhardt, p. 92.

(14) Ed. 1903, vol. III, pp. 63–5.

(15) In the Basel editions of his works this is letter No. 15; in R. Wolkan's elaborate edition of his letters it is No. 78. He writes: "Certainly thou hast begotten a son neither of stone nor of iron, being thyself a man of flesh. Thou

knowest what a stallion thou hast been [*scis qualis tu gallus fueris*]. This plague is spread far and wide, if plague it be, to employ our natural members; though I see not wherefore copulation should be so condemned, seeing that nature, who worketh nothing in vain, hath implanted this appetite in all living creatures, in order that the human race may be perpetuated." Julius Caesar was no pattern of chastity; and, "who shall blame an insignificant fellow like me if I do as the greatest have not disdained to act?"

(16) See, for instance, *Decret. Greg.* lib. III, tit. I, cc. 3, 13, 15, and Pecham's constitutions in Wilkins's *Concilia*, II, 53b.

(17) Ep. 93 (Basel).

(18) *Hist. of the Papacy* (1903), III, 63. We must, however, qualify this by the case of Gregory of Heimburg. Pius having condemned him as "a child of the devil", Gregory retorted, "Nay, I am born not of any condemned copulation but of lawful wedlock, a thing which the Pope hates, he who favoureth bastards and who made a very long oration, well-nigh for three hours, wherein he sounded the praises of Ferdinand the Bastard at Mantua." In a later sentence he seems to allude to Pius's letter to his father about his own bastard (Brown, *Fasciculus*, II, 127).

(19) Basel, Ep. 395.

(20) Basel, Ep. 50; Wolkan, p. 125.

(21) Wolkan, *Priester*, p. 28.

(22) Basel, Ep. 92.

(23) Basel, Ep. 93.

(24) *Wiederbelebung*, I, 438.

(25) Burckhardt, p. 225. "The Italian of the Renaissance was the first gambler on a large scale in modern times. Pictures of future wealth and enjoyment rose in such life-like colours before his eyes that he was ready to hazard everything to reach them.... That great lottery-bank which was called the Court of Rome accustomed people to a need of excitement, which found its satisfaction in games of hazard during the intervals between one intrigue and another." St Bernardino and Savonarola thundered unceasingly against the gambler's intoxication, and his furious blasphemies when he lost.

(26) Ibid. pp. 31, 39, 46, 49, 50. "Great as was the terror felt for the Turks and the actual danger from them, there was yet scarcely a Government of any consequence which did not conspire against other Italian states with Mohammed II and his successors....From a scoundrel like Sigismondo Malatesta nothing better could be expected than that he should call the Turks into Italy. But the Aragonese monarchs of Naples,...afterward hounded on the Sultan Bajazet II against the Venetians. The same charge was brought against Lodovico il Moro."

(27) Ibid. p. 239. For mission-preacher in Renaissance France see A. Méray, *Libres Prêcheurs*, Introduction.

CHAPTER XXVI

Ambrose of Camaldoli

(1) The main source here is *Ambrosii Traversarii Epistolae et Orationes*, ed. L. Mehus (Florence, 1759). I shall quote this edition, the only complete but unfortunately very rare, under the short title of "Mehus". Numbers refer to columns.

(2) Migne, *P.L.* CXLIV, 966: cf. Mehus, 484 note. The rest of this brief sketch is mainly based on P. Hélyot's *Ordres Monastiques*, with the article on Camaldoli in *The Catholic Encyclopaedia*. A description of its present state may be found in a small book recently published: Stephen Ouseley, *From Camaldoli to Christ* (The Harrison Trust, 1931). The reader will easily make the necessary discount.

(3) Mehus, 783.

(4) S. Baluze, *Vit. Pap. Avenion* (1693), I, 389 (cf. pp. 218, 285, 806 for the Benedictine average of that time).

(5) Mehus, 605.

(6) *M.G.M. Scriptt.* XXXII, 166, etc. Cf. my *From St Francis to Dante*, 2nd ed. p. 195.

(7) For these and many other details, see the full and careful biography by A. Dino-Traversari, *Ambrogio Traversari e i suoi tempi* (Florence), p. 31.

(8) *Hodoeporicon* (ed. A. Dino-Traversari as appendix to his *Ambrogio Traversari e i suoi tempi*), p. 96. Where not otherwise stated, I shall quote this excessively rare book from Dino's edition, which, after many years of fruitless search, I owe to the kind generosity of Fr. D. B. Zema, S.J. It is out of print and very rare: the original Lucca edition of the seventeenth century is rarer still: it is in the British Museum and the Bodleian, but not at Cambridge.

(9) Mehus, 309.

(10) Ibid. 309, 312, 313, 317, 318, 320.

(11) *Hodoeporicon*, p. 93: Dino (p. 36) writes by a slip 96.

(12) Dino, p. 36. Though he asserts on the next page that some of the brethren were copyists, he gives no original evidence, but refers to Müntz, *Hist. de l'art pendant la Renaissance*, pp. 698–9.

(13) Mehus, 561. Dino (p. 38) undertakes to prove monastic activity in this direction by references to Mehus, epp. 44, 260, 281, 305, 439, 441, [485], 503. This which I have bracketed contains nothing about writing. Of the rest, 305 and 441 may possibly refer to monastic copyists, and 439 certainly does; it is addressed to Jerome.

The following pages of Traversari's correspondence supply evidence, of one kind or another, for the writing, keeping, price or accessibility of books at his own most favourable time and place: 6, 13, 20, 50, 82, 88, 211, 232, 303, 306, 316, 318, 339, 362, 367, 369, 371, 375, 377, 383, 395, 407, 415, 417, 420, 421, 487, 491, 492, 494, 504, 506, 517, 535, 561, 566, 619, 983, 984, 1021, 1028, 1050, 1113, 1115, 1116, 1128.

(14) Mehus, 983 note, 984, 1073. Poggio Bracciolini writes of St Gallen: "we found Quintilian still safe and sound, but all mouldy and covered with dust. For the books were in the library not as their dignity demanded, but in a hideous and dark dungeon, at the bottom of a tower, to which not even a criminal condemned to execution would be relegated." Bartholomew of Montepulciano writes "buried by some fate in places of darkness" (984). Gregorio Corraro, Protonotary Apostolic, rejoices to have liberated certain precious volumes on his way back from the Council of Basel, "from German prisons": *de Germanorum ergastulis* (1073). See also J. A. Symonds' *Revival of Learning in Italy* (1877), pp. 129–38.

(15) *Hodoeporicon*, pp. 28, 31; cf. Mehus, 407.

(16) Voigt, *Wiederbelebung*, I, 186.

(17) Symonds, p. 103.

(18) Mehus, XXII.

(19) Ibid. 178 ff.; Voigt, I, 295 ff.

(20) Dino, p. 38.

(21) Mehus, 354, 358, 362, 387, 392, 394, 397.

(22) Dino, p. 78, quoting from Valla, op. cit. lib. I, cc. 22, 46.

(23) Mehus, 565 (but see 566–7, where the suspicion is dissipated) and 1060.

(24) Ibid. 1062. Michael was monk and librarian at Sta Maria degli Angioli.

CHAPTER XXVII

The Visitor's Mind

(1) Mehus, 649. For the next few pages I shall give references to his correspondence sparingly in brackets. In an Appendix, I supply the other very numerous figures which a specialist reader might be glad to have as vouchers.

(2) *Prediche Volgari* (1884), II, 98, 108, 140, 142, 150.

(3) Mehus, 52; cf. Dino, p. 288.

(4) See my *From St Francis to Dante*, 2nd ed. p. 284; cf. pp. 95, 180.

(5) Mehus, 109. St Bernardino himself, in one of his sermons, speaks of the almost insuperable difficulties which the higher clergy found in avoiding nepotism (opp. ed. de la Haye (1745), I, 303).

(6) Burckhardt, pp. 243–53.

CHAPTER XXVIII

The Visitor in Actio

(1) *Hodoeporicon*, p. 12.

(2) Ibid. p. 65.

CHAPTER XXIX

Uphill Work

(1) Mehus, 829.

(2) *Hod.* pp. 57ff. The long struggle is one of the most prominent subjects in his whole correspondence: Mehus, 323, 325, 558, 560, 563, 564(?), 565, 586, 664, 781, 855, 857, 861–2, 866, 867, 870, 871, 874, 877, 878, 888, 893, 900, 920, 1000, 1002.

(3) Pico della Mirandola, one of St Thomas More's heroes, sent an open letter to Leo X in the very year of Luther's revolt (1517). The clergy, he said, behave worse than Eli's sons at the door of the tabernacle: sodomy is systematic among them, and "the ignorant people are deterred by their example from divine worship and from all piety". The theologian Wimpfeling, writing to the Emperor Maximilian in 1511, asserted that sodomy was a means of promotion in the Church, and Wicelius wrote "the whole earth is full of fornication, adultery and sodomy" (Brown, *Fasciculus*, I, 338, 340, 732). St Bernardino speaks of this again and again in his sermons.

(4) Mehus, 888.

(5) *Hod.* p. 115.

(6) Mehus, 562.

(7) Ibid. 836.

CHAPTER XXXI

A Commendatory Abbot

(1) Mehus, 178. The other letters on this affair are (in chronological order) on coll. 45, 180, 219, 714, 47, 220, 183, 186, 187, 50, 190.

CHAPTER XXXII

The Pope's Help

(1) M. Creighton, *Hist. of the Papacy* (1882), II, 510. For St Antonino see his *Chronicle*, pars. III, tit. xxii, c. x. §5 (ed. 1586, vol. III, p. 526*a*).

(2) Creighton, loc. cit. p. 28: *Rev. Bénéd.* (1923), p. 162.

(3) Ibid. p. 327.
(4) Ibid. pp. 246–7.
(5) Ibid. p. 404.
(6) Ibid. p. 483. Compare two other sayings by this "master of proverbs". "He who knows most is most persecuted by doubt." "Serious matters are settled by arms, not by laws."
(7) Pastor-Antrobus, *Hist. of the Popes*, III, 278.
(8) Vatican Archives, *Reg. Secret*, vols. 468, 32; 469, 237; 470, 107; 471, 126; 472, 235; 473, 250; 481, 295; 493, 132; 494, 8; 499, 164; 500, 10.
(9) Dino has collected the evidence (pp. 315–20), quite conclusive as to the suspicion, but far from sufficient to establish the probability of the fact.
(10) Mehus, 1060.
(11) *Dino*, p. 321.
(12) Mehus, 1055–7: cf. Introd. p. ccccxxxii. Ambrose himself, writing six years earlier to Poggio in lament for his own dear brother and yoke-fellow Jerome, had celebrated him as *Virgo purus et monachus integer* (ibid. p. 103).
(13) Ibid. p. ccccxxxiv.

CHAPTER XXXIII

Custom and Tradition

(1) *Reg. Secret.* Pius II, vol. 500, f. 10.
(2) *Hod.* p. 70. "When we came to the monastery of Monte Croce, we found a place admirably fitted for a religious house. For it is a lofty hill, planted with vines and olives and trees, and clad on one side with thicket-wood, bears the monastery on its summit; a place furnished with honourable and necessary buildings, if only anyone were there who would live according to the Rule (*religiose*). At first we were delighted with the pleasantness of this place; then we deplored its miserable condition, to think that such commodity was wasted, without fit occupants to inhabit it. We found the Prior with one monk and a lay-brother. We found that the Prior was a man of honest life, but his companions complained bitterly that he was very avaricious, and did not provide them with necessaries, while he neglected their possessions and the monastery itself" (29 June). At five other places, within those few weeks alone, he found one monastery "desolate and destitute" (pp. 73, 79) at others "the buildings in ruin" (p. 75), "vast ruins" (p. 91); "a nunnery now destroyed" (p. 97); an abbey "desolate, and verging upon ruin" (p. 99). For other badly dilapidated or ruinous houses see pp. 40, 66, 101, 103, 104, 111, 129, 130.
(3) Thorne's *Chronicle* (Twysden *Scriptt.* col. 2054 (p. 463 of A. H. Davis's translation)). For monastic vows and papal dispensations see Dionysius Cartusianus, *Opera*, XXXVI, 581 ff., 645; and cf. p. 539.
(4) E.g. *De Ref. Relig.* (1611), pp. 119, 153–6.
(5) E.g. *Opp. Pia.* pp. 350, 448.
(6) F. A. Scharpff, I. 191.
(7) B. Pez, *Bib. Ascet.* VIII, 660 ff.
(8) Leibniz, *Hist. Bruns. Scriptt.* (1710), II, 351.
(9) E. Brown, *Fasciculus*, II, 104.
(10) Ibid. p. 229.
(11) *Opera*, XXXVIII, 251 (*De Ref. Monialium*, art. XV). Compare Rob. Richardinus, writing from a reformed Augustinian house in France: one of the main difficulties is the offender's reply: "Everybody breaks the Rule on this point: why not I?" (p. 177).
(12) *Fontévrault*, p. 37.

(13) Claude Fleury, *The Historical account of the Manners and Behaviour of the Christians* (London, 1698).

(14) *Le Recrutement des Monastères.*

(15) H. v. d. Hardt, III, 150. Here is a concrete case from the same time (*Cal. Pap. Letters*, VII, 77, 1418 A.D.). "Mandate at the petition of Richard Sywel, priest, of the diocese of Lincoln...who states that when he was only in his thirteenth year he was fraudently induced by certain enemies to enter the Cluniac Priory of St Andrew, Northampton, in which he assumed the monastic habit, but before completing the year of probation refused to make his profession and left the said priory and abandoned the habit. If he find the facts to be so, to declare that he is not bound to the observance of the said or other religious order, but is free to live in the world."

(16) *Environs de Rouen*, p. 12.

(17) Quoted by A. Méray, *La Vie au Temps des Libres Prêcheurs*, II, 185; L. Dacheux, *Jean Geiler*, p. 185 note, where there is a quotation to the same effect from Wimpheling. Compare also J. J. Hottinger, *Helvet. Gesch.* II, 843, 845 and La Tour-Landry (E.E.T.S.), p. 165.

(18) *Oeuvres de Ste Thérèse* (Migne, 1863), I, 160.

(19) *Nouveaux Sermons Inédits*, pp. 39–42; quoted in *Anthologie Brémond*, pp. 311–14. For the present day, see A. Houtin, *Une Vie de Prêtre*, p. 119. Diderot's novel, *La Religieuse*, is corroborated by many unexceptionable documents.

(20) *Mem. St Edmunds* (R.S.), III, 65ff. The privileges of St Albans were even greater: see Trokelowe (R.S.), pp. 439, 440.

(21) See my second volume, p. 586.

(22) *Opp.* II, 527.

(23) *Loci e Libro Veritatum*, p. 203.

(24) H. Pez, *Scriptores*, II, 638. The date is 1464.

(25). The papal Commissary, Ninguarda, in his general report for the year 1577, emphasizes the evils of exemption; many of the exempt Orders are subject (after the Pope) to Ministers General in distant countries. Thus they are rarely visited; and "it befalleth sometimes that the hereditary Visitor is himself a person of ill fame, leading a dissolute life" (*Quellen und Forschungen d. Preuss. Instituts* (1898), I, 183). Even among the Carthusians in the Austrian dominions, "whose General lives in France, Monastic discipline has long ago begun to decay in some places for, though they have their own Visitors in the district, yet these are sometimes such as to need visitation themselves, rather than to visit others. Wherefore many pay little attention to their own institutes; nay, some even eat flesh, under pretext of infirmity" (p. 183). Some Abbots of the Cistercian Order, whose General is ordinarily in France, live in such universal licence, especially in the countries subject to the most serene Duke Charles [of Austria], that they are not ashamed even to keep concubines publicly and nourish them as though they were noble wives" (p. 194).

(26) *Institution au Droit Ecclésiastique*, ch. XXVI (ed. 1688, I, 224).

CHAPTER XXXIV

EGMOND. FIRST PHASE

This and the next chapter repose upon the valuable collection of original documents published by E. S. Dessing for the Historical Society at Utrecht, *Bescheiden angaande de Hervorming der Tucht in de Abdij van Egmond in de 15^e Eeuw* (1930).

CHAPTER XXXVI

Reform in France

(1) *Revue Mabillon* (1931), XXI, 36–7.

(2) Both books, unfortunately, are out of print and almost unprocurable. My debt to both is very heavy. Page references in brackets are to Renaudet.

(3) Rashdall, *Univ. Europe* (1st ed.), II, 536.

(4) *Chron. Wind.* II, 68, p. 205.

(5) Mehus, p. 136, No. 106. I have translated the whole passage in my *Europe's Apprenticeship*. For Cluny see my first volume, chapter XIV.

(6) *Analecta Gallicana* (1911), II, 340.

(7) Ibid. p. 344.

(8) Georges Goyau, in Hanotaux, *Hist. de la Nation Française*, VI, 320.

(9) Ibid. p. 324.

CHAPTER XXXVII

Visitors' Reports

(1) This chapter reposes on reports hitherto unpublished, in the *Archives d'Eure-et-Loir*, Reg. H (1423), ff. 13–16, 25ff., 29–30, 33, 139, 195–6; Reg. H. (1424), ff. 53–4.

(2) Similar cases of churches used as store-houses are not uncommon; see the visitations in Stapledon's *Register* and in *E.H.R.* XXVI, 108ff.: also the visitations of Worms diocese in *Zeitsch. f. Gesch. d. Oberrheins*, vol. XXVII, and for dio. Lausanne, published in the *Doc. Hist. Suisse Romande*.

CHAPTER XXXVIII

Individual Cases

(1) See my *Black Death* Benn's Sixpenny series, p. 51, for full details.

CHAPTER XXXIX

A Benedictine Reform

(1) *Origines de la Réforme*, II, 500ff.

(2) *Revue Bénédictine*, 1900, 1901. He seems scarcely to have grasped, in those earlier days of his work, the historical background of that time: his errors in the later portions of these articles are plainly exposed by Dom Paul Denis in his *Le Cardinal de Richelieu et la Réforme des Monastères Bénédictins* (1913), p. 116. Fernand's tract is in the British Museum: it deals more briefly with the same subjects as Jouenneaux.

(3) Berlière, pp. 348, 353.

(4) Ibid. p. 40.

(5) I have printed a full analysis of this extremely rare book, with full translations of the more important passages, in the eleventh of my *Medieval Studies, French Monasticism in* 1503 (Galloway and Porter, Cambridge, 2*s.* 6*d.* post free).

(6) *Tusis carnibus*, i.e. the "mortrewse" in which Chaucer's Cook showed such professional skill.

(7) Peter the Venerable confesses that his fellow-monks of Cluny, as early as the first half of the twelfth century, were accustomed to violate the Advent fast by eating the fat which, at that season, was avoided even by pious layfolk. (Migne, P.L. clxxxix, 1028.)

(8) It was forbidden for monks to become godfathers, not only because this involved them in a fresh spiritual relationship incompatible with their ideal, but also because it entangled them with worldly folk and worldly affairs. The temptation, however, was very great; cf. the letter of an abbot at Bordeaux in Father Denifle's *Désolation des Eglises, etc.* I, 583 (A.D. 1419). The abbey had been so impoverished by war that the Abbot begged for a papal indult permitting him to stand godfather to forty children of noble or wealthy families; the pope granted only four. The infraction of this rule is commonly noted by medieval visitors, and we have seen it in the case of Ambrogio Traversari.

CHAPTER XL

Windesheim Again

(1) There were only 150 houses of Augustinian Canons in the whole of France, as against 1460 Benedictine, Cluniac and Cistercian abbeys with some 6000 dependent cells, and 400 friaries. (Imbart, II, 199.)

(2) Contemporaries corrupted his surname sometimes to Momburnus, Manburnus, Monboir. For the whole of his life and work, I rely mainly on the excellent volume by Dr P. Debongnie, C. Ss. R., *Jean Mombaer de Bruxelles* (1927).

(3) See P. S. Allen, *Erasmi Epistolae*, I, 199 (No. 73).

(4) The full story is admirably told by Père Debongnie (ch. III).

(5) Renaudet, 459, dealing with the year 1509, and the gradual slackening of reforming energy. "In the tumult of quarrels between Medicants and Secular Clergy, and between rival Congregations, the silent virtues of cloisterers were lost; and the public, which more and more loudly accused the leaders of the Church, even began to suspect the sincerity of the Observants...Gringoire, like Bouchet, blames the reformers, whose work he attributes in most cases to hypocrisy or ambition, and who need reformation themselves."

(6) Migne, *P.L.* LXXXIX, 514*c*. It has sometimes been suggested that this letter was drawn up by his officials; but this, even if true, would not alter the question here.

(7) Debongnie, p. 62.

(8) Debongnie, pp. 73ff.; Imbart, II, 506.

(9) Debongnie, p. 76. Note this evident proof that the then monks did not habitually confer with each other in Latin, and compare p. 75 "ces chanoines étrangers" and p. 83 "un autre sachant le français".

(10) Ibid. p. 90. He shows that even Dr P. S. Allen's care had gone somewhat astray here (*Erasmi Epp.* I, 199), and that this letter refers not to the abbey of Livry but to the Cabrin affair.

(11) The abuses, serious enough, are detailed by Debongnie, p. 101.

(12) P. S. Allen, *Erasmi Epp.* I, 92.

(13) Compare Debongnie, pp. 101 with 110.

(14) Debongnie (pp. 127–8) brings out its supreme importance for reformers. That chapter of his book continues with a picture of Austin Canons' life under the reformed scheme.

(15) Ibid. p. 286.

(16) Ibid. p. 287. "In 1544 Antoine Caracciolo was made abbot of St Victor by the influence of Marguerite de Navarre, with papal ratification. He had published, in the days of his expectancy, an edifying little book, *Le Miroir de religion*. Once firm in the saddle, he said openly before the Chapter-General, in answer to the request that he should take the usual oath of obedience to

the Constitution of the Order; 'know that I care not for those things; for the King of France hath given me this abbey in order that I might be able to dower my sisters with decent marriage-portions'. He then 'left the hall, laughing'" (Bonnard, *Hist. de l'Abbaye de St Victor*, II, 41).

CHAPTER XLI

Robertus Richardinus

(1) This Chapter, like much of the last, is based upon the edition of Richardinus's *Exegesis in Canonem Divi Augustini*, printed at Paris in 1530 by Wechel (Scottish Hist. Soc. 1935). Nearly all my summaries may be easily recognized in the side-notes to that edition, to which also the few page references in my text refer.

(2) Debongnie, p. 101.

(3) Cf. Percy Scholes, *The Puritan and Music in England* (1934).

(4) This should fill a chapter of my fourth volume. It will be noted how exactly this description in Richardinus bears out Chaucer's satire (Prologue, 193 ff.).

CHAPTER XLII

Germany Again

(1) *Opera*, p. 651.

(2) *Opp.* VII, 351; cf. II, 498 and XIV *bis*, 656.

(3) See vol. XXXVII, pp. 41, 48, 143 (whole Article XIX), 151, 316.

(4) *Chron. Cartusiense* (1608), p. 401.

(5) Walch, I, 182.

(6) *Opp.* (1706), IX, 1201; cf. Jortin, II, 19, 23, 33, 37–8, 39, 74.

(7) Pastor-Antrobus, I, 156.

(8) Vol. I, p. 129.

(9) J. Chmel, "Zur Kritik d. Oest. Gesch." (*Denkschriften d. K.K. Akad. d. Wiss. in Wien* (1850), I, 232 ff.).

(10) Paul Lehmann, *Corveyer Studien*, p. 21 (*Abh. d. K. Bayer. Akad. Phil-Hist.* (1919), Bd. XXX); *Studien und Mitteilungen* (1899), XX, 563.

(11) Wolff, *Des Klosters Pforta* (Leipzig, 1843), II, 617 ff. Bertuch, *Chron. Portense*, pp. 104 ff.

(12) *Origines de Réforme à Genève* (Geneva, 1936, vol. I only).

(13) On pp. 226–49 Naef deals with the question of pre-Reformation and post-Reformation morals in Geneva. In the former period a Canon's house was let as "a very den of prostitutes": the artisans revolted against the facilities afforded to brothel-keepers.

CHAPTER XLIII

The Franciscans

(1) *Annals of Ireland* (Irish Archaeol. Soc. 1849), p. 39.

(2) See chapter III of my *Black Death* in Benn's Sixpenny Series.

(3) *Opp. Ined.* ed. Brewer (R.S.), p. 399; Coulton, *From St Francis to Dante*, 2nd ed. p. 57.

(4) *Parad.* XI, 124 ff.; XII, 112 ff.

(5) *De Recuperatione Terrae Sanctae*, pp. 84 ff.

(6) Edition of 1529, vol. IV, ff. 243.

(7) Glassberger (1887), p. 58; Potthast, 10,308, 10,309, 16,077; Sabatier, *vie* (1894), p. 407 (Appendice I).

(8) *Handbuch d. Gesch. d. Franziskanerordens* (1909), p. 83. An excellent book, which needs only the ordinary natural discount for the author's ultramontane convictions.

(9) Heimbucher, *Orden und Kongregationen*, II, 370ff.; Holzapfel, pp. 91ff.

(10) The best biography, by A. G. Ferrers Howell, is unfortunately out of print and very scarce. But there is also a good life by Paul Thureau-Dangin, translated into English.

(11) *Die Martinianische Reformbewegung* (Münster, 1921), pp. 2ff.

(12) *Gesch. d. Kölnischen Franziskaner Ordensprovinz* (1904).

(13) Mehus, II, 39 (col. 109).

(14) Printed in full, *A.F.H.* II, 615ff.

(15) Holzapfel, p. 156.

(16) Vansteenberghe, p. 118.

(17) *Ana. Gallica*, II, 345–6.

(18) *Camb. Mod. Hist.* II, 499ff.

(19) *The Grey Friars in Oxford* (1892), p. 111.

CHAPTER XLIV

The Dominicans (1)

(1) *Histoire des Maîtres Généraux de l'Ordre des Frères Prêcheurs* (1903–11). My figures in brackets refer to vol. and page of this book.

(2) R. F. Bennett, *The Early Dominicans* (1937), ch. III *passim*: he there corrects the too absolute assertions of Mortier.

(3) See my *Black Death* in Benn's Sixpenny Series.

(4) Quoted in full on pp. 66ff. of my *Black Death.*

CHAPTER XLV

The Dominicans (2)

(1) Mortier, IV, 169.

(2) Ibid. p. 170.

(3) Ibid. p. 174.

(4) Ibid. pp. 198–9.

(5) Ibid. p. 502 note.

(6) Women appear very early in the Chapter Acts; see the years 1240, 1242, 1245, 1247, 1249, 1250, 1255, 1256, and so on continuously. See also *Teutonia*, pp. 32, 33, 58, 67ff., 88, 111, 112, 136, 141. For potations, see *Teutonia*, p. 58; wine-shops, ibid. p. 60; flesh, ibid. pp. 61, 67, 99; vagrancy, ibid. pp. 56 (cf. 67), 62, 105; fighting, ibid. p. 61; services, ibid. pp. 54, 55; Visitors' difficulties, ibid. pp. 3, 19, 22, 26, 33, 47, 115, 145; general decay, pp. 23 (note), 47, 49, 90.

(7) *Mon. Ord. Praed.* vol. IX (*Acta Cap. Gen.* IV, 3ff.).

(8) Mortier, V, 116.

(9) *Registrum Turrianum, etc.* ed. B. M. Reichert, pp. 128, 135.

(10) Mortier, III, 664; V, 357–69.

CHAPTER XLVI

Citizens and Cloisterers

(1) H. Pirenne, *Livre de G. de Ryckel*, XLIX, 15, 18.

(2) Löhr, II, 346, 350.

(3) Taiée, I, 134.

CHAPTER XLVII

The Secular Arm

(1) I have produced evidence against such exaggerations in an article printed by *The Cambridge Historical Journal* (1935), v.
(2) *Brit. Soc. Franc. Studies* (1920), v, 63–4; A. F. H. (1934), iv, 163.
(3) See, for instance, Löhr in *Quellen und Forschungen* (1924), Heft 19 p. 24 note.
(4) *P.L.* ccxvi, 405.
(5) *P.L.* cxliii, 851.
(6) *Opera* (1565), p. 790.
(7) *Op. Pia* (1605), p. 862*a*.
(8) *Rev. Bénéd.*
(8*a*) J. Hashagen, *Staat und Kirche vor der Reformation* (Baedeker, Essen, 1931), p. 354. I discovered this learned and valuable book only after this present chapter had been written. Pp. 324–55 are specially valuable, in this connection. He quotes the confession of the Abbot of Tegernsee to Cardinal Cusanus, that the authority of the Ordinary was not sufficient for effectual reform of the monasteries, without the help of the Secular Arm.
(9) Oefelius, *Rer. Boic. Scriptt.* (1763), i, 346*a*.
(10) Chmel, *Regest. Fried.* (1859), iv, 276, No. 2701.
(11) *Ana. Fra.* (1887), ii, 342.
(12) *Quellen und Forschungen* (1924), Heft 19, p. 24. Another list in Heft 3 (1908) gives twenty-three reformed houses on the authority of a Dominican of about 1460: five had been reformed on lay initiative, and nine more with lay help (p. 11).
(13) Naef, i, 249, 251.
(14) A. Störmann, *Die Städtischen Gravamina gegen den Klerus* (1916), p. 249.
(15) Finke in *Röm. Quart.* Suppt. (1896), iv, 5.
(16) Vansteenberghe, p. 148.
(17) H. v. d. Hardt, tom i, pars v, p. 170.
(18) Störmann, p. 275; Löhr, p. 25.
(19) *Martinianische Reformbewegung*, pp. 137–40.
(20) *Conciliorum Omnium Volumina Quinque* (Venice, 1685), v, 205ff.
(21) Calmet, *Münster*, p. 159.
(22) D. Branche, *L'Auvergne au M.A.* (1842), i, 412.

CHAPTER XLVIII

The English Position

(1) M. Paris, *Chron. Mag.* v, 407.
(2) *Lib. Verit.* p. 4; cf. pp. 72, 147, 149, 151. Elsewhere he predicts religious revolution (pp. 12, 14, 40).
(4) Walsingham, *Hist. Ang.* R.S. ii, 337; Gale, *Scriptores* (1684), p. 513.
(3) W. E. Pantin, *Chapters of the English Black Monks*, i, 203.
(5) Pantin, ii, 110ff.
(6) Ibid. pp. 120, 124, 133.
(7) Bekynton, loc. cit. p. lxxxix.
(8) *Lib. Verit.* p. 151; cf. p. 4.
(9) Wilkins, *Concilia*, iii, 619.

CHAPTER XLIX

The St Albans Case (1)

(1) See F. A. Gasquet, *William Wallingford* (Sands and Co., about 1910). Though Dr James Gairdner, an historian of very different quality, told the same story at some length in the *E.H.R.* for 1909 (XXIV, 91 and 319), he was frankly dependent upon what Cardinal Gasquet supplied from the Vatican Archives; fragments falsified by *suppressiones veri* and *suggestiones falsi*. My own vouchers, in transcripts and photostats from the Vatican Archives, are to go with the rest of my library to the University of Chicago. I must here pay special tribute to the kindness and courtesy of the Prefect, Mgr. Angelo Mercati, who put himself to considerable trouble in verifying the Cardinal's references, of which one was incorrect and others superannuated.

(2) *Ana. Gallica*, II, 179.

(3) *Camb. Mod. Hist.* I, 384.

(4) Rushbrooke Williams is hopelessly superficial here.

(5) *Reg. Whethamstede*, R.S. *Reg. Amundesham*, R.S. I.

(6) *Reg. Amundesham*, I, 344.

(7) On this point writers of different schools are agreed: see pp. 310ff. of my third volume. Compare T. F. Tout, *Medieval Forgeries* (1920), p. 15 with the Roman Catholic, Dr W. Barry in his *Papal Monarchy*, p. 133.

(8) Pantin, III, 223, 233, 236, 240, 242, 244.

(9) Walsingham, *Gesta Abbatum*, R.S. II, 95ff.

(10) Ibid. II, 177.

(11) Ibid. II, 511ff.

(12) Ibid. II, 420ff.

(13) Amundesham, I, 101ff.

(14) Ibid. pp. 159, 187.

(15) *Reg. Whethamstede*, II, xxxii; Galbraith, p. 57.

(16) See *Evesham Chronicle*, R.S. p. 142; E. F. Jacob in *Mildred K. Pope Miscellany* (1939), p. 168.

(17) *Amundesham*, I, 344. Rushbrooke Williams (p. 202) points out the gross forgery, but gives no details.

(18) Vatican Archives, Arm. XXXIX, tom. 21, f. 235*b*.

(19) Wilkins, *Concilia*, III, 630. For more details see my second volume, p. 619.

(20) Gasquet (p. 54) applies this to Innocent's later bull of 30 July. The quotation professes to come from St Augustine (Serm. XIII). Yet, in fact, the cause had been determined by two Councils; the Pope had only ratified them. This was pointed out long ago; yet the misquotation is still repeated everywhere, though even Newman's colleague Fr. Ryder had to confess "no doubt it involves a certain rhetorical exaggeration". See R. F. Littledale, *Plain Reasons*, p. 105. and H. I. D. Ryder in his reply (*Cath. Controversy*, p. 189).

(21) This "perchance", inserted with legal caution to cover a *possible* case, is taken by Gasquet as an *assertion* that the abbey's immunity had been "quite recently confirmed by His Holiness himself" (p. 51). In the next sentence he asserts that the abbey had a privilege of exemption even from Legates, unless "the abbey was specifically named" among those which might be visited. There is no authority for these words either in the monks' petition or in the Pope's indult.

(22) *Archiv. Vat.* Inn. VIII, Suppl. vol. 913, f. 66.

(23) Mortier, as quoted in earlier chapter.

(24) Bull quoted by Marc Bloch, in his contribution to the volume in honour of Enrico Besta, p. 7.

(25) Here are the words which Gasquet gives to his readers as a fair equivalent for the whole remainder of Morton's *Monitio* (pp. 43–4): "Then follow a series of the gravest charges against the moral character of one of the nuns of Pray and some of the monks; the name of one of the younger religious, Thomas Sudbury, being mentioned. Sopwell, too, had been put into the care of monks who have dissipated the property and brought it to ruin. The same has been done in regard to the property of the cells dependent on St Albans. As to the Abbey itself, Wallingford is charged, according to report, with getting rid of property and jewels, of cutting down the woods, and especially of selling all the oaks and timber trees to the value of 8000 marks. As to the monks, some are said to be given to every worldly evil; divine service is neglected, and some consort even within the monastery precincts with bad women; others purchase promotion by theft of chalices and church plate and jewels, even from the shrine of St Alban itself. Report also accuses the Abbot of defending the evil doers, and humiliating and keeping in the background those of his Community who are good and desire to live in a religious manner."
(26) Wilkins, *Concilia*, III, 632.
(27) *Reg. Inn.* VIII, vol. 884, f. 127.

CHAPTER L

The St Albans Case (2)

(1) See my second volume, p. 321.
(2) Dugdale-Caley, V, 186; *V.C.H. Northants*, II, 108; *Rolls of Parlt.* VI, 434.
(3) T. Wright, *Letters Supp. Monast.* (1843), p. 92.
(4) *Reg. Whet.* R.S. I, 104.
(5) Ibid. p. 112.
(6) Ibid. p. 115.
(7) Ibid. p. 118.
(8) *Chron. Joc. Brakelond*, C.S. p. 90. For this monastic use of *scandalizare* for "put to shame", see the exactly similar incident at Bury (ibid. p. 23).
(9) Ibid. pp. 128, 130.
(10) Ibid. p. 134.
(11) C. Leber, *Fortune Privée*, p. 66 (royal wages account for 1340).
(12) Pantin, I, 36, 72; III, 51; *Mon. O.P.* IX (Acta Cap. IV, 1901), 34; cf. p. 180, "money-changers". Cf. also Pantin, III, 291–2: one monk is "a notorious *proprietarius*" and "a public merchant in the matter of buying horses and other merchandize". Another is suspected "of possessing a great sum of money, so that is named as a public proprietor". Another "is said to keep in his possession a great sum of gold and silver, so that he can reasonably be called *proprietarius* (p. 295). I have given evidence on this subject on pp. 35, 51, 52, 98, 252, 267, cc. XVI, XVIII, pp. 367, 400, 477, 504, 541, 562–3, 568, 583–4, 616 and 671 of my third volume.
(13) Fifth Edition (1849), V, 37.
(14) *La Réforme en Angleterre*, vol. I. English translation by the Rev. R. E. Scantlebury (1934). Though Professor Constant has certainly read very diligently, yet he has obviously, in some cases, scarcely looked at the book with which he deals, but has picked up his idea of it from a review.
(15) F. A. Gasquet, *Abbot Wallingford, a Monograph*, reprinted in *Monastic Life in the M. Ages* (1922); L. F. Rushbrooke Williams, *Hist. of the Abbey of St Alban* (1914). Far more valuable is the much briefer prize essay by V. H. Galbraith, *The Abbey of St Albans* (1911).
(16) *Reg. Whet.* R.S. I. 479. I here adopt Cardinal Gasquet's translation, except where it is too loose or (as here and there) incorrect.

(17) Dugdale-Caley, II, 243.
(18) *Reg. Whet.* I, 476–7; cf. pp. 423, 472.
(19) *Ibid.* p. 208.
(20) *Reg. Whet.* R.S. I, 476.
(21) Rushbrooke Williams, p. 226.
(22) *Reg. Whet.* R.S. I, 128, 130.
(23) *Reg. Whet.* R.S. II, 155, 158; cf. I xix and II, 154.
(24) *Reg. Whet.* R.S. I, 130.
(25) *Chronica Joc. de Brakelonda*, C.S. p. 23.
(26) See my *Ten Medieval Studies*, p. 164.
(27) *Abbot Wallingford*, pp. 16, 45, 47, 48. Mr Rushmore Williams, following him as uncritically as usual, speaks of the *monitio* as "bluff" (*Hist. Abbey of St Albans*, p. 221).
(28) Gasquet, *Abbot Wallingford*, pp. 46–7. Here, as usual, he is blindly followed by Mr Rushbrooke Williams (p. 222): "That there was any substantial truth in Morton's general charges is tacitly contradicted by the Admonition itself. Not the least remarkable part of the letter is the request that the Abbot, who, if half the charges made against him have any truth, must be a monster of iniquity, will himself correct the faults of which he is accused. ... It certainly looks as though Morton were merely taking advantage of the rumours which had been in circulation about the administration of the House to strengthen his hand for the inevitable appeal to Rome."
(29) Gasquet, p. 59; Williams, pp. 223, 225.

CHAPTER LI

Exemption Wholesale

(1) All this much seems to be implied, and certainly far more is taught, in Professor R. G. Collingwood's *The Historical Imagination* (Inaugural Lecture at Oxford in 1935). Let me quote also from p. 19 of this lecture: "Everything is evidence which the historian can use as evidence. But what can he so use? It must be something here and now perceptible to him: this written page, this spoken utterance, this building, this finger-print. And of all the things perceptible to him there is not one which he might not conceivably use as evidence on some question, if he came to it with the right question in mind. The enlargement of historical knowledge comes about mainly through finding how to use as evidence this or that kind of perceived fact which historians have hitherto thought useless to them."
(2) Rushbrooke Williams, loc. cit. pp. 215, 221, 224; Gasquet, loc. cit. p. 2; for other anachronistic pleas, cf. pp. 20, 78.
(3) Com. I, c. 51; for further evidence see my *Art and the Reformation*, p. 216 and Chapters XVI, XVII.
(4) Pasquale Villari, in *Encyc. Brit.* 11th ed. XXIII, 346. Compare Huizinga, *Waning of M. Ages*, p. 163. "Among the princes and the lords of the fifteenth century, more than one presents the type of an almost inconceivable mixture of devotion and debauchery. Louis of Orleans, an insane lover of luxury and pleasure, addicted even to the sin of necromancy, has his cell in the common dormitory of the Celestines, where he shares the privations and duties of monastic life, rising at midnight and sometimes hearing five or six masses a day." He instances also Philip the Good of Flanders, and Gaston-Phebus, Count of Foix. This (he adds) must not be accounted hypocrisy, but rather "a kind of reconciliation, hardly conceivable to the modern mind, between two moral extremes. Its possibility in the Middle Ages depends on the absolute dualism of the two conceptions, which then dominated all thinking and living."

(5) Camden Soc. (1840), p. 3.
(6) Stephen's own letters are in Migne, *P.L.* CXI, 496 ff.
(7) *Chronicon Abbatiae de Evesham*, R.S. introd. p. xxx.
(8) *De Offic. Episc.* §§ 33, 37; cf. his *De Consideratione*, lib. III, c. iv, § 18, to Eugenius III.
(9) Peter of Blois, *Ep.* 68.
(10) *Opp. Pia* (1605), p. 993.
(11) Mortier, v, 297 ff.
(12) *Act. Cap. Gen.* IV, 214.
(13) Mortier, v, 279.
(14) Ibid. p. 281.
(15) See my *St Francis to Dante*, index s.v. "Last Judgement".
(16) *Summa*, III, col. 920*b*.
(17) Cardinal Gasquet's computation (*Henry VIII and the Eng. Mon.* II, 323) can be accepted as sufficiently accurate. It takes no notice of the few exempt Benedictine houses: we may roughly count the inmates of these at 200, adding this figure to the exempt total, deducting it from the other. This will give the totals in my text.
(8) *Chron. Evesham*, pp. 114, 138.

CHAPTER LII

Impunity

(1) H. Naef, *Origines de la Réforme à Genève* (1936), I, 237.
(2) *Sermons* (Parker Soc.), I, 123.
(3) Compare the instance already given, where Cardinal Gasquet treats as absurd the idea that a disreputable Abbot should be formally called upon to reform his own community; or, again, the passage in his *Henry VIII, etc.* (II, 307) where he is evidently ignorant of the importance attached among Benedictines, from the earliest days, to twelve as the probable requisite for efficiency in a convent. Everywhere, again, he shows ignorance of the important technical difference between *comperta* and *detecta* in visitations. He blunders even over the common term of "Frayter", a corruption of *refectory*, imagining it to mean "the community recreations" (I, 278). In this he is faithfully followed by Fr. Ethelred Taunton (*Black Monks of St Benedict*, I, 86).
(4) Gasquet, *Hen. VIII, etc.* II, 492.
(5) G. Mollat, *Papes d' Avignon* (1912), p. 234.
(6) *Monasticon Dioecesis Exoniensis* (1846), introd. p. vii.
(7) *De Consideratione*, lib. III, c. v, § 20.
(8) *Chron. Maj.* v, 380. The King, of course, was St Louis.
(9) W. E. Pantin, in *R. Hist. Soc. Trans.* (1927), p. 380.
(10) W. E. Pantin, *Chapters of the English Black Monks*, III, 124.
(11) Hugo de S. Caro, *Comment. in Psalm LXXVII.* Here he is speaking primarily of the clergy in general: but we shall see in Chapter LIII how aptly it applies to cloisterers in especial.

CHAPTER LIII

Exemptions by Retail

(1) *Maîtres Généraux*, III, 162.
(2) *Gesta Abbatum*, II, 417.
(3) *C.P.L.* IV, pp. 75, 508.
(4) Wilkins, *Concilia*, III, 365.
(5) *Lib. Verit.* pp. 132, 168.
(6) See my second volume, p. 642.

CHAPTER LIV

Quis Custodiet? (1)

(1) This seems to have been almost endemic at Ramsey. In 1395, the visiting Bishop had found irregular attendance, with its frequent concomitants—hunting-dogs, dilapidated buildings, and embezzlement (*V.C.H. Hunts*, I, 381). It is necessary here to enter a *caveat* against the *Hunts* and *Beds* volumes of this generally valuable, but sometimes strangely unequal work. They are by "Sister Elspeth, of the Oxford School of Medieval History". With references to the Gray and later injunctions, she writes "they are mainly of a formal kind...there seems little doubt that the standard of life [at Ramsey] was fairly high for the fifteenth century".

(2) Quoted fully in vol. v, ch. LIII, p. 36. *Lincoln Visitations*, III, 308.

(3) Lincoln Record Soc. VII, 1 ff.; cf. pp. 79, 103.

(4) Ibid. XIV, 9 ff.

(5) Ibid. p. 29. One deposition, from John Bracy, a senior monk, must be left in its original Latin (p. 17): "Dicit quod quidam monachi tam tempore refectionis quam ante et post non verentur eructare vilissimo modo ventum ab inferiori latere, et si quis eis in hoc dixerit statim prorumpunt in verba contumeliosa."

(6) *Reg. Atwater*, f. 51 *a*.

CHAPTER LV

Quis Custodiet (2)

(1) See H. E. Salter, *Cartulary of Eynsham*, I, xxvii ff., 431 ff. and *Lincoln Visitations*, vols. I and II under Eynsham.

(2) Widmore, *Hist. West. Abbey*, p. 123; *V.C.H. London*, I, 446 ff.

(3) Heales, *Merton*, pp. 265–79. The Editor permits himself the absurd suggestion that, as the like injunctions were sent to others, this "indicated that they were a sort of circular" and therefore not of serious significance. He appeals for this to the Injunctions for Selborne priory, printed in full by White in his *History* of that parish (App. to 1st ed.). But a careful comparison shows that each set was modified with special reference to the particular house to which Wykeham addressed it: and in both cases his preamble claims that the Injunctions rest upon "repeated" irregularities disclosed by his visitation. In each case also, the Injunctions prescribe for *the future* things which, his words clearly imply, had not been kept in the past. Moreover, we have independent evidence in the case of two Injunctions. The diliquidation of buildings at Merton was confessed in lamentable terms by a plea of the monastery to the Bishop in 1393 (Heales, p. 284). The pawning of Church jewels, vestments and relics at Selborne, and their non-redemption even ten years later, is proved by another episcopal Visitation (White, ch. 14, note). The Merton Editor, without even this excuse of finding similar Injunctions addressed to other houses, presumes in the case of the 1504 visitation that "from the general nature of these Injunctions, it might be supposed that they were intended to be addressed to monasteries generally".

(4) Heales, *Merton Priory*, pp. 316–17.

(5) Ibid. pp. 318 ff., from Fox's *Register*, II, f. 139.

(6) H. E. Salter, chapters of *Aug. Canons*, p. 177.

(7) Ibid. pp. 133, 135.

(8) Heales, *Merton Priory*, pp. 138–9.

(9) Ibid. p. xxxviii.

CHAPTER LVI

Further Evidence from Lincoln

(1) For instance, Dr Jessopp as quoted in my next chapter.

(2) *Alnwick Visitations*, III, 334: "Cum fu[er]it in comitiua mulierum, multum lasciue habet se cum eis in osculando eas et aliter per ubera vel alia secreta tractando et tangendo in pessimum scandalum ceterorum et malum exemplum interessencium."

(3) Ed. H. E. Salter, pp. 90, 114.

(4) See Eileen Power, *Med. Eng. Nunneries*, pp. 310ff. The Lincoln cases are: Legburn 1525; Littlemore 1517; S. Egid in Bosco 1530; Ankerwyke 1519; Greenfield 1525.

(5) *Trans. R. Hist. Soc.* (1927), p. 221.

(6) Pantin, *Chapters, etc.* (P. Hist. Soc.), II, 18, 19, 137, 160.

(7) Ibid. II, 21.

(8) Ibid. II, 142–3.

(9) Ibid. II, 165.

(10) Ibid. II, 134ff.

(11) Gasquet, *Abbot Wallingford*, pp. 21–5.

CHAPTER LVII

Norwich and Prémontré

(1) His description of visitatorial procedure is to a great extent evolved from his inner consciousness; it should be corrected by Professor Hamilton Thompson's Introduction in his first volume. He takes the liberty of dismissing the most compromising evidence as on the face of it incredible (p. xx).

(2) Ed. 1615, p. 431. Godwin sometimes reports mere gossip, and this may be an echo from the bitter and often inaccurate Bale but the Prior's words seem plainly to refer to some such suspicion.

(3) Dugdale-Caley, III, 136; see full translation by Professor Hamilton Thompson in his *Lincoln Visitations*, II, xix.

(4) Pp. 3–6. It is characteristic of Dr Jessopp's off-hand inaccuracy that he thus sums up this report (which I have translated literally with only a few omissions). "There are no signs that in the year 1492 there was anything like general laxity of conduct among the Norwich monks" (p. xvii).

(5) P. 266. It is characteristic of Dr Jessopp that he sums up this 1532 visitation "Of any gross vices we hear not one single word." Dom Thos. Sall also was doing things "cujus praetexta oritur infamia et scandalum".

(6) Loc. cit. XX, 204: Dn Nicolanus Fraunsham dicit quod D. Thos. Sall tertius prior in camera osculabatur D. Ricardum Lopham et tetigit pudibunda ipsius et amplexatus est eum. For Lopham's character see p. 265.

(7) This is a far more important matter than might seem at first sight: especially since Jessopp, whose introduction to his visitations is followed by far more readers than those who take the trouble to read the text, has blundered egregiously over it. In three consecutive lines (XXI) he misprints *crepidis* as *trepidis* (a substantive which he naturally cannot find in any dictionary); he misquotes *longis* as *largis*; and he grossly mistranslates both *diploide* and *caligis*, thus reducing it (as he complains) to a "queer passage". *Crepida* was a light shoe or slipper, both in classical and in medieval Latin.

Caliga in classical Latin was a heavy high-low boot, such as the soldiers wore; but from at least 1150 or so we find its meaning very much changed. It has crept up the leg and become *hose*, and it is made no longer of leather but of cloth. Gradually these hosen became longer and longer, until they joined at the top into one garment, which betrayed its dual origin by keeping the plural number—*hosen*, equivalent to the later breeches and trousers. In post-Reformation times this garment, having joined above, now separated below, into knee-breeches (*haut de chausses*) and stockings (*bas de chausses*, or, in brief, *bas*). But in the fifteenth century, while the hosen still fitted more or less tightly to the body this fashion was attacked as definitely indecent even for laymen. The former fashions of long tunic and cloak had passed away; the short *cotte hardie* was followed by the short doublet (*diptois*) and scanty cloak. Yet it was only gradually that the tight hosen joined up completely; and, even then, there was the *cod-piece*, or *braguette*, which gave considerable anatomical emphasis. As early as 1342, Archbishop Stratford in the Council of London fulminated against clerics who dressed like laity, "with red and green chequered *caligae*, and beaked shoes". In [1410], when the fashion had gone still further, the martyr John Hus attacked it as one of the glaring immoralities of his age. In [1450], the Oxford Chancellor Gascoigne wrote even more strongly (*Lib. Verit.* p. 144). It offends him worse than a décolletée woman; it is an unabashed indecency, and a cause of the foulest vices. "Ornatus virorum, jam nuper inductus, citra annum 1429, plura mala causavit, in superbiendo, et in fornicando, et in adulterando, et in Sodomia, ut notum est pluribus. Homines enim femorum formam ostendunt et genitalium per aperturam togae, et braccis jam non utuntur, sed caligis, in quibus forma magnitudinis membrorum turpiter ostenditur." The monastic reformer Johann Busch [1460] describes how a nun eloped with the aid of her lover. He writes: "so, by counsel and assistance of this priest, she clad herself in man's attire, that is, doublet and breech-hosen" *diploidem et caligas bracatas*.

(8) This has been scrawled over for deletion, but roughly in much blacker, newer-looking ink, probably by Bishop Tanner, who gave the MS. to the Bodleian.

(9) *L. and P. Hen. VIII*, IV, 3772.

(10) At Woodbridge he decreed that, if the Prior could not otherwise restore discipline by imprisonment, he should send them to the Bishop for punishment (p. 181). At Norwich two accused were imprisoned until the morrow, when their punishment would be carried out (p. 203).

(11) *L. and P. Hen. VIII*, IV, 5158.

(12) For full details, see my *Ten Medieval Studies*, App. II.

(13) Christopher Hesyll of Welbeck, William Bradford of Sulby, William Hynmers of Alnwick, John Lincoln of Barlings (possibly the same as the "John Barlynges" of 1494), William Gillyng of Coverham, William Hall of Eggleston, John Wakefield of the same, Thomas Sall of Langley, Gilbert Eggleston of Newhouse, Edward Seyton of Sulby, Thomas Pynderwell of Tupholm, Edward Colynsouf Welbeck, Richard Holyngbridge of the same, and William Farley of West Dereham.

(14) Matthew Paris, *Chron. Maj.* VI, 246.

(15) *Five Centuries of Religion*, II, 377; *Chron. Evesh.* R.S. p. 253. This was in 1213.

(16) *Five Centuries of Religion*, II, 341.

(17) *Register of John de Halton* (Cant. York Soc. 1913), introd. p. xxxiii.

CHAPTER LVIII

Fish Out of Water

(1) J. Gairdner, *The English Church in the sixteenth century* (1902), p. 5.
(2) Ibid. pp. 45–7.
(3) Ibid. p. 104.
(4) Fisher's *English Works* (E.E.T.S. 1876), p. 170.
(5) Lingard, IV, 559.
(6) Ibid. p. 566; Gairdner, p. 122.
(7) Lingard, V, 22.
(8) See my second volume, p. 458, for the full quotation.
(9) *Records*, cc. 1 and 2.
(10) Pantin, I, 31, 43, 45.
(11) Raulin, f. 55*f.*
(12) See, for instance *A.F.H.* III, 98, where Fr B. Kruitwagen, O.M., explains why so few of the Franciscan Chapter Records have survived. Quite apart from the Chapter Decree of 1260, under St Bonaventura, for the destruction of earlier statutes as soon as new had been published Fr Kruitwagen points out "one great danger before printing had been invented, viz. that the brethren either in parsimony or through indolence, tried to bring the old editions up to date by scraping or cancelling or adding in the margin and similar foolish devices, whereby they miserably corrupted the text and the words". As to the inaccuracy of Benedictine texts, see Pantin, I, xiv, 5. Jean de Bourbon complained that Cluniac Priors often neglected the Statutes so shamefully that they did not even trouble to bring copies away from Chapter meetings and publish them in their own houses (Marrier, a.c. 1614).
(13) See Index to my vol. I under "Monks and *stabilitas loci*" and to vols. I and II under "Monks wandering".
(14) Pantin, I, 11, 13. The York Chapter of 1310 prescribes a similar sanction for "fugitives", and glosses this word as "those who go forth from the gates of the monastery or cell where they dwell, for the sake of wandering or walking abroad, without special leave of their Superior" (ibid. p. 269).
(15) Ibid. I, 67, 83, 236, 249, 269.
(16) Ibid. II, 70.
(17) Ibid. I, 84.
(18) *Cant. Tales, Prol.* l. 180.
(19) Gratian's *Decretum.*
(20) *Registrum Odonis Rigaldi*, p. 646; M. Paris, *Chron. Major.* add. under year 1249.
(21) D. Wilkins, *Concilia*, I, 502. For the other Councils see ibid. I, 583, 592, 628, 693; II, 16, 248–9, 250; III, 674.
(22) Pantin, II, 98ff.
(23) Ibid. pp. 120, 124.
(24) Marrier, *Bib. Cluniacensis* (1614), c. 1447; properly 1457.
(25) Ibid. 1599, 1604, 1606, 1612.
(26) Ibid. 1564 (should be 1548), 1569 and 1575.
(27) Martene, *Thesaurus*, IV, c. 1636.
(28) H. E. Salter, *Augustinian Chapters*, pp. 204ff.; cf. p. 133.
(29) Le Paige, c. 1060.
(30) Ibid. c. 952.
(31) Ibid. cc. 145, 325.
(32) *Acta. Cap. Gen.* (ed. Reichert, 1901), IV, 33, 167, 200, 222, 256, 259, 260, 268.
(33) Wyf of Bathe, *Prologe*, l. 834.
(34) *A.F.H.* VII, 461, 474; cf. p. 458.
(35) *A.F.H.* XXVII, 89, §§ 27, 35.
(36) *Inferno*, XXIII, 1–3.
(37) *A.F.H.* VII, 458.
(38) *A.F.H.* VIII, 175, § 7.
(39) *Gesta Abbatum*, R.S. III, 471.

CHAPTER LIX

The Eternal Feminine

(1) See vol. I, pp. 398ff. and 424ff.; vol. II, pp. 647ff.

(2) I quote here from the original of 1690; but this invaluable *Commentary* was reprinted by Migne with the text of the Rule itself.

(3) *Ann. Benedict.* (1740), V, 489.

(4) *Registrum Odonis Rigaldi*, p. 646.

(5) Pantin, I, 234, 252.

(6) Ibid. pp. 42, 67, 99. The Fathers of later date similarly whittled down Benedict XII's decree about flesh-eating.

(7) Ibid. II, 45, 208.

(8) *Annales Monastici*, R.S. I, 486.

(9) Pantin, II, 87.

(10) See Wilkins, *Concilia*, II, 245, 246, 249, 250, 298; III, 363.

(11) Marrier, *Bib. Cluniac.* 1551.

(12) *Analecta Gallicana*, II, 345.

(13) *Five Centuries of Religion*, II, 653; Martène, *Thesaurus*, IV, 1636, 1638.

(14) *Five Centuries of Religion*, II, 646.

(15) Le Paige, p. 817 (lib. IV, dist. iv, c. 14).

(16) Ibid. pp. 994ff.

(17) Ibid. p. 1060.

(18) See my *From St Francis to Dante*, 2nd ed. p. 344.

(19) Ibid. pp. 96–7, 146; see also my *Ten Medieval Studies*, pp. 184–6.

(20) *A.F.H.* VIII, 457.

(21) Ibid. XXVII, 90.

(22) Ibid. VIII, 175.

(23) See my second volume, p. 646.

(24) *Acta Cap. Gen.* O.P. (ed. Reichert, 1901), IV, 5, 12, 221, 348.

(25) Le Paige, *Bib. Prem.* pp. 835, 856.

(26) To the cases listed by Gairdner on pp. xxff. Of *L. and P.* IX, we may add Nos. 139, 159, 686. In all alike, the monks complain that business necessities call them much abroad. The grounds on which Gairdner suspects Cromwell of having refused the Prior of Canterbury are unconvincing.

(27) Ibid. IX, 139.

(28) Baskerville, loc. cit. p. 124.

(29) Ibid. p. 77.

(30) I Peter iii, 13.

CHAPTER LX

An Abbot *In Commendam*

(1) *Gesta Abbatum*, II, 417.

(2) Refer for all this story to J. Gairdner in *Letters and Papers of Henry VIII*, IV, iii, No. 5898; VII, 992; VIII, 1073 (cf. 290, § 46); J. A Froude, *Short Studies*, I, 419. "The Dissolution of the Monasteries." "Everyman" edition of his "Essays", pp. 163ff.; F. A. Gasquet, *Henry VIII, etc.* (1888), I, 365; *Registers of Bothe and Fox* (Cantilupe Soc.), VI, 36, 65, 129, 145, 177, 232, 269, 271, 286, 293, 322, 362, 372; G. G. Coulton, *Ten Medieval Studies* (1930), p. 214, Ely.

(3) *L. P.* IV, No. 5898.

(4) *Henry VIII, etc.* (1888), I, 365–70.

(5) Ibid. p. 38.

(6) The summary gives only: "A third (decree) for immoral conduct in slandering the college, frequenting bad company... ." *L. and P.* IV, 2752 (iv).

(7) For instance, the Augustinian Canons in [1400] and [1450]; H. E. Salter, *Chapters, etc.* pp. 196, 201.

CHAPTER LXI

The Fatal Wedge

(1) Pantin, III, 124: "Quoniam in hac nostra tempestate (mundo iam in suum finem declinante) perpauci sint atque rarissimi, qui vite austeritatem et observanciam regularem cupiant." The document is given in abridgement in *Letters and Papers of Henry VIII*, IV, i, No. 953. Dr Brewer, the Editor, has softened it down considerably, according to his frequent custom.

(2) *Opera*, III, i, 438; *Ep.* 417.

(3) Fisher's *English Works* (E.E.T.S. 1876), p. 170.

(4) See my second volume, p. 643.

(5) Ibid. p. 458; cf. Pole's *Pro Ecclesiasticae Unitatis Defensione* (Rome, 1536), f. 103.

(6) B. J. Kidd, *Documents illustrative of the Continental Reformation* (1911), pp. 307 ff.

(7) Lingard did indeed know Pole's condemnatory words in the *Defensio*.

(8) Wilkins, *Concilia*, III, 364. The University complains: "Among both Regulars of all sorts and also among Seculars a great multitude [turba multa] of undisciplined and untaught persons cease not daily to flee [comvolare] to Holy Orders", let all, in future "undergo a strict examination". And again: "Seeing that those whom the Ecclesia Anglicana admitted not to the height of priestly Orders, but hath repelled as unable and unworthy, the Roman Court is oftentimes wont to send back, however untaught and ignorant, as fit and ordained men, let the Supreme Pontiff be approached with a supplication that such illiterate, simple and ignorant folk, from this time forward, be not promoted to Holy Orders, to the scandal of the Court and of the whole Church."

(9) Pastor, *Hist. Popes* (Eng. trans.), XI, 176. Here, then, is a document of capital importance for any history of Henry VIII's monastic policy; yet it has been strangely neglected. Lingard, at his earlier date, might be excused for not having discovered it. Dixon makes no allusion to it. Gasquet, who owed so much to Dixon, is equally silent. Constant, whose book has far more claim to fulness of detail, does indeed quote the title, but has nothing whatever to say concerning the contents of this document. Pastor, with all his immense industry, amid the 1260 pages which he devotes to the years of Paul III's pontificate does make three pages of room for an analysis of the document. His attitude is far more impartial than that of the English-speaking apologists: yet the reader could form from him no adequate idea of its significance. Dr James Gairdner, when he was still an apologist for monasticism, did indeed call definite attention to the document, though he gave no quotations, nor any adequate idea of its great significance. This may, after all, have been one of those discoveries which, at the end of his life, compelled him to disavow publicly his earlier warmth of championship.

This story is told fully in the twentieth of my *Medieval Studies*, pp. 23 ff. As early as 1906 Dr Gairdner, while still disagreeing with me on the whole, allowed me to publish a letter in which he disavowed the unconscientious fashion in which his own *obiter dicta* of seventeen years earlier were being used to prove his hearty agreement with Gasquet. Again, in 1909, he wrote in answer to Mr Royce in *The Nineteenth Century and After* (July, p. 54): "I must confess that my treatment of monasticism is exceedingly defective." In 1911, again, he did what few men ever have the moral courage to do—published a set of cancel-pages in correction of the errors which had been pointed out, with regard to monastic and clerical morality in the first two volumes of *Lollardy and the Reformation*. Yet his original testimonial to Gasquet is still utilized by Roman Catholic apologists, as though no retractation had ever been published.

(10) Ibid. p. 154; cf. pp. 149, 150.
(11) Ibid. pp. 149–50.
(12) *Dublin Review*, April 1927, p. 238.

CHAPTER LXII

The Black Book

(1) Printed in T. Wright, *Letters, etc.* C.S. pp. 112ff. For the whole subject see Gasquet, loc. cit. I, 289, 302ff., 339, 348.
(2) *Works* (Parker Soc.), I, 123.
(3) *Les Papes d'Avignon* (1912), p. 234.
(4) For the passage in full, see my vol. II, p. 498, from More's *English Works*, p. 134 (wrongly printed, p. 154).
(5) Watts and Co. 2*s.* 6*d.* net. This contains the whole text (apart from notes) of Lea's two volumes.
(6) J. A. and A. Theiner, *Die Einführung der Erzwungenen Priester-Ehelosigkeit* (1828; reissued 1845).
(7) H. C. Lea, *Sacerdotal Celibacy* (3rd ed. revised), II, 25ff., 192–7, 200–3.
(8) *Opp.* X, 1201.
(9) Lea, loc. cit. I, 166, 230, 305, 395, 412, 435, 454.
(10) *English Works*, p. 485. Compare Gerson for a similar comparison, as quoted in Lea, loc. cit. I, 440.
(11) Lea, loc. cit. I, 381, 440; II, 1. In this last place, however, he exaggerates the "many" of his text (*plerisque*) into "the majority". Compare More, *English Works*, p. 231.
(12) Lea, loc. cit. I, 309, 346, 406; II, 55, 239; Ordericus Vitalis in *P.L.* 188, c. 382.
(13) *Opp.* R.S. III, 129.
(14) Gascoigne, *Lib. Ver.* p. 35.
(15) *English Works*, pp. 231, 618.
(16) *Opera*, X, 1201.
(17) A. Störmann, *Die Städtischen Gravamina, u.s.w.* (1916), p. 283. In answer to modern whitewash of this evil, Störmann adds in a footnote: "In my opinion it can as little be denied that there were Bishops who did indeed inflict money fines upon concubinaries, but left them otherwise in place. Against this 'unworthy tolerance' Eck expresses himself at one place in his *Memorials* under the year 1523: 'Let Bishops not suffer notorious concubinaries, and let them especially drop the abominable word and deed of tolerance, wherein they take money and leave delinquents unpunished, so that he that is filthy may be filthy still'." It must be borne in mind that Eck was one of Luther's arch-adversaries.
(18) Gee and Hardy, *Documents, etc.* (1896), p. 141.
(19) Fox's *Register* (ed. Howden), p. xlix.
(20) See my second volume, p. 643.
(21) *Lib. Ref.* I, vii, 417.

CHAPTER LXIII

THE COMPERTA

(1) Pantin, loc. cit. II, 110.

(2) T. Wright, *Letters Relating to the Suppression* (C.S.), p. 53.

(3) See the Dijon archives, *Monastères Anglais*, H. 407; bundle *Abbates Conjuncti*. There is also a letter of 1521 from the Abbot of Neath as Visitor, rehearsing that "all the abbeys of our Order in Wales have deviated far from our Rule". In 1501, the Abbot of Mellifont reports similarly "the ruin, desolation and disuse, alas! of our Order in Ireland". An earlier complaint in the same collection, from Ireland to the Abbot of Cîteaux, specifies one of the main causes of this decay, "the pensions and *ad commendam* appointments imposed by the Apostolic See, contrary to privileges granted to our Order". It is somewhere about 1500 that these records show the Abbot of Combe appealing also to Cîteaux for effectual measures against "the entering and frequentation of women in our abbeys; otherwise there will never be honesty of Religion nor will observance be in good repute among the monks; for it hath been, and is, the ruin of many....Not only do many bishops and prelates speak against us, but they are also deservedly indignant; so also are temporal princes and lords".

Such indignation, recorded at many times and places, shows why we must recognize essential probability, at the bottom of partisan exaggeration, in Latimer's story how, when the *Comperta* were read in the House of Lords, the one cry was, "Down with them!"

(4) See Appendix, *Cromwell's Comperta*.

(5) Compare here Wright, *Sup. of Monasteries*, c. 5, 85 for a letter to Cromwell from the Visitor, J. ap. Rice. Gasquet (I, 343 ff.) attempts to convict ap Rice of dishonesty by translating *communis fama* as "nothing but vague reports", and *fatentur* as "are reported". Thus this President of the Papal Commission for editing the Vulgate either confused *fateri* with *fari*, or deliberately mistranslated in order to disguise the fact that ap Rice was asserting actual confessions.

(6) See *L. and P. Henry VIII*, x, No. 364, pp. 137 ff.

(7) *Vis. Dioc. Norwich*, C.S. pp. 250, 309, xxxiii.

(8) *Lollardy and the Reformation*, III, xxix.

(9) *Linc. Rec. Soc.* XIV, 188, 194, 197, 275; MS. *Reg. Longland*, f. 75. At Peterborough the abbot is suspected; at Leicester and Missenden there are multiple cases. In no case is there hint of the theoretical statutory punishment.

(10) Migne, *P.L.* CXXXVI, 619. See ibid. p. 586 for this view of clerical morality in general.

(11) Migne, *P.L.* CXLV, 159 ff.; see especially 161*b*, 162*a*, 166*b*, 177*e*, 179*d*; 183*d*.

(12) *Opp. Ined.* R.S. p. 412.

(13) *Inferno*, XV and XVI.

(14) *Comentum* (ed. Lacaita), I, 505, 523, 529.

(15) *E.G. Acta Cap. Gen. O.P.* (Reichert, 1901), IV, 104; *A.F.H.* VIII, 175, § 5 and quotations given above in my Chapter LIX.

(16) *Prediche Volgari*, II, 135–6; III, 98, 108, 140, 142, 150; *Opera* (ed. Delarne), I, 216*b*. See my second vol. pp. 404, 595, for the Saint's arraignment of monastic morals as a main cause of the growing infidelity; "men believe in nothing higher than their own roof".

(17) *De Confessione Mollitiei* (Opp. ed. 1606), II, 309. This is mainly concerned with v.p. See also *Gesta Abbatum*, R.S. II, 436.
(18) Ibid. p. 629; fully in my second volume, p. 589.
(19) *Opp.* X, 1201.
(20) *Ana. Gall.* (1911), II, 345–6.

CHAPTER LXIV

Revolt and Pensions

(1) M. H. and R. Dodds, *The Pilgrimage of Grace*, II, 156–7; cf. I, 74–6.
(2) Ibid. I, 91.
(3) Ibid. I, 92, 102, 139.
(4) Ibid. II, 329ff.
(5) *English Monks, etc.* p. 121. For exposure of other exaggerations in current modern accounts of the Lincolnshire Rising, see ibid. pp. 153, 159, 162, 165, 168.
(6) Ibid. p. 111.
(7) G. L. Haskins in *History* (1940), XXIV, 297.
(8) *Dossier de l'Affaire des Templiers*, ed. Lizeand, pp. 188ff.
(9) Cf. my *Inquisition and Liberty*, ch. XXII.
(10) Witness the acceptance in Modern Germany of the Soviet alliance.
(11) Eng. Translation, pp. 170, 194.
(12) Loc. cit. p. 257.
(13) *English Monks, etc.*, p. 113.
(14) Letter of 25 November, 1820, in the library of St Cuthbert's College Ushaw, printed in my second volume, p. 458. One of the footnotes to which Lingard refers, however, was removed from later editions of his *History*, apparently for prudential reasons.
(15) Herbert of Cherbury, *Henry VIII* (1649), p. 303. Constant gives an attenuated summary, and blinks entirely the significance of these prelates' signatures.
(16) Ibid. p. 150.
(17) Ibid. p. 153.
(18) Ibid. p. 219.
(19) See my *Ten Medieval Studies*, p. 210, where I expose his even more glaringly false quotation from Thorold Rogers, to which I drew the Cardinal's attention by registered letter, but which he reprinted presently in cold blood. For the value of Sanders as historian, see my *Monastic Schools in the Middle Ages*, p. 18.
(20) Ibid. p. 219.

CHAPTER LXV

Rich and Poor

(1) The second edition is dated 1896. The Cardinal writes in his preface (p. iv):

"For the purpose of this edition I have been at some pains to enquire into the truth of the few assertions made, and to set down the results in the shape of notes, either giving authorities which may be taken to bear out the writer's statements, or pointing out wherein my opinion he was mistaken, or has somewhat mis-stated or exaggerated the bearing of some fact. I confess that I was surprised to find how few were the instances for which some satisfactory authority could not be found to bear out the picture prescribed in Cobbett's pages."

The following are among the other astounding blunders to which the Cardinal tacitly gives his voucher for the benefit of modern Roman Catholics: King Alfred founded Oxford University and invented Trial by Jury, counties, and hundreds, and tithings and courts of justice (§ 185). "The Spanish Inquisition...from its first establishment has not committed so much cruelty as this first Protestant Queen [Elizabeth] committed in any one single year of the 43 years of her reign" (§ 340). We cannot, with Mr Baskerville, dismiss Cobbett's book briefly as "one of the most amazing pieces of rubbish that was ever written", so long as it is published with the assistance and the blessing of a writer who earned his Cardinalate by his reputation as an historian.

(2) Cobbett, p. 453.

(3) *Hist. Prot. Ref.* §§ 145, 184, 206, 329, 331, 332, 374.

(4) Full details in my third volume, pp. 175 ff.

(5) Leonard, loc. cit. p. 9. My fourth volume should show many particulars of this very frequent maladministration.

(6) Ibid. p. 15.

(7) Ibid. p. 18.

(8) Ibid. p. 54.

(9) I owe these details to Mr H. G. Richardson, who has exhaustively studied both printed and MS. sources. In the strictest legal sense, the French royal edicts of 1312 and 1333 did formally condemn usury; but they revoked in the same breath their own general condemnation. From 1378 onwards the Government sold to certain usurers a licence to take up to 50 per cent. The legislation thus created a Black Market.

(10) *Oxford Studies in Social and Legal History* (ed. Vinogradoff), I, 267.

CHAPTER LXVI

Orthodox Admissions

(1) L. Dacheux, *Jean Geiler*, pp. 496–7. Abbé Dacheux casts doubt upon the exact words of Geiler, yet admits that they are *ben trovati*.

(2) Dijon, *Archives Départementales* (*Monastères Anglais*), bundle *Abbates Conjuncti*.

(3) *Hen. VIII* (new ed. 1905), pp. 430 ff.

(4) See my second volume, p. 643.

(5) Holinshed (1808), III, 617.

(6) I have printed More's words in full on pp. 658–60 of my second volume. Fisher's are from his little treatise written for his sister, on the Religious life. He wrote "For Loue maketh euerle worke appeare easie and pleasaunt, though it bee ryghte displeasaunt of it selfe.... This thing may wel appear by the lyfe of hunters, the which out of doubt is more laborious and painfull then is the lyfe of relygious persons, and yet nothing sustayneth them in theyr labour and paynes, but the earnest loue and hartie desire to fynde theyr game." And so on for nearly five octavo pages, embroidering in detail upon the theme that "so many Religious persons so diligently pursue not the wayes of Religion as doe the hunters". (English Works, *E.E.T.S.* 1876, pp. 364 ff.)

(7) *L. and P. Henry VIII*, XIII, i, 115.

(8) Note the plain admission that Indulgence had been bought and sold.

(9) *Letters of Stephen Gardiner* (ed. J. A. Muller), pp. 169, 218. St Cross Hospital still survives, and supplies bread and ale to all wayfarers on request.

(10) Kidd, *Documents of the Continental Reformation*, p. 307; also by

J. Le Plat, *Mon. Hist. Trident.* II, 596; and by E. Brown, *Fasciculus*, II, 231. Le Plat finds it difficult to explain satisfactorily why, while a Protestant edition of this frank document was promptly put upon the Index, it found its way into none of the great collections of Council Acts until Mansi published it nearly two centuries later. In fact, the orthodox disputed its authenticity until this was admitted by Cardinal Pallavicino in 1656.

(11) *Defensio Ecclesiasticae Unitatis* (Rome 1536), f. 103.

(12) See my *Art and the Reformation*, ch. XXII.

(13) *Monasticon Gallicanum*, ed. Peigné-Delacourt (1871), 2 vols, 4to. In the first forty abbeys here dealt with, only four have kept any important portion of their medieval domestic buildings. Compare my *Art and the Reformation*, p. 410 and Chapter XXII and G. Baskerville, loc. cit. p. 278: but this is not just to the actual churches.

(14) R. A. Cram, *The Gothic Quest*, p. 125; *Moines d'Occident*, l. XVIII, ch. V (ed. 1882, vol. VI, p. 247).

CHAPTER LXVII

Post-Reformation France

(1) Pp. 644–6.

(2) "Le Cardinal de Richelieu et la réforme des monastères bénédictins" (1913).

CHAPTER LXVIII

Post-Reformation Italy

(1) See M. De Potter, *Vie de S. de' R.* (Brussels, 1835). The author is strongly anti-papal; but his book has permanent value from the numerous verbal quotations from de' Ricii's own papers, especially his *Autobiography*.

(2) I, 374: "A friar who had been Confessor to us for four years, and who afterwards became Minister Provincial, wrote me letters so abominable that I cleared my conscience by showing them to a priest. He was taken aback, and said with a sigh: 'For many years I have heard confessions, but never have I met with anything so bad as this!'. I told to this same Provincial the great scruples which [his words] had aroused in me. He answered, 'I must tell you plainly, you are just a silly girl. Try, and you will be grateful to me, and your scruples will pass.' Moreover once, on the occasion of a visit, he attempted to compass his design." See also I, 440, 445, 459: "the true union with God, beyond that which is in the Eucharist, consists principally in uniting ourselves with the priests." There were 3000 priests among the 80,000 inhabitants of Florence (III, 219). The same witness accused the friars of revealing the secrets of the confessional (I, 376; cf. II, 452 for its use in politics). For the confessional and seduction see also I, 445, 489, 492–3, 495; III, 154, 163, 218. For unreality and confession, I, 447; for revelation of secrets, II, 452. For abortion see I, 375.

(3) I, 410. One nun told another that a method of union with God "was carnal copulation; and she indicated to her, for this purpose their then Confessor, Father Gamberani, because the thing should be effected with a priest".

(4) I, 404, 416, 434, 455, 461. For the priest and his Host as a love-philtre, see Caesarius, *Dial. Mirac.* (ed. Strange), II, 170.

(5) For the frequency of clerical immorality, see I, 377, 384–6, 388, 391, 431, 442, 450, 460, 465, 473; III, 161, 168–9, 172–4, 207; II, 309, 442, 474–5.

For the side of mysticism, I, 388–98. For homosexualities as in the *Black Book*, I, 360, 388, 391–2, 394, 400, 403, 407, 420, 425, 430, 435, 459; II, 297, 299, 311.

(6) I, 424–5, 448–9, 481.
(7) I, 422, 443–4, 447. But they were sometimes repulsed, 384.
(8) I, 104, 108, 372, 454–64, 470–4.
(9) *Storia della Compagnia di Gesù in Italia* (Rome, 1910), pp. 47–51.

CHAPTER LXIX

The Tudor Background

(1) De Potter, III, 207, 214–15, 217.
(2) See H. C. Lea, *Inq. of the M. Ages*, bk. III, ch. V, and my *Inquisition and Liberty*, ch. XXII.
(3) See my third volume, pp. 76–7 and 576.
(4) B. Pez, *Bib. Ascet.* VIII, 511 ff.

APPENDIX I

Cromwell and his Agents

(1) *Loll. and Ref.* II, p. 84.
(2) *Henry VIII and English Monasteries*, I, 437.
(3) *Norfolk Antiquarian Miscellany*, II, 440–41.
(4) E.g. *Visitations of Religious Houses in Diocese of Lincoln* (Cant. and York Soc.), II, 49, 70, 197 (note); III, 257, 333–4. *Reg. Ralph of Shrewsbury* (Somerset Record Soc.), p. 683.
(5) *Dialogue concerning Tyndale*, bk. II, ch. 10.
(6) *Op. cit.* I, 439.
(7) *Op. cit.* I, 393–4 note.
(8) *Op. cit.* I, 416; Ellis, 3 S; III, 247.
(9) E.g. *L. and P.* IX, 68, 139, 160, 457; X, 364.
(10) *Loll. and Ref.* II, 78; *Norfolk Antiq. Miscellany*, II, 444–49; *L. and P.* X, 364.
(11) *L. and P.* IX, 138 (Wright, p. 56).
(12) Ibid. IX, 1167 (Wright, p. 53).
(13) Ibid. IX, 167.
(14) Ibid. IX, 139.
(15) Ibid. IX, 267 (Wright, p. 65).
(16) *Henry VIII and English Monasteries*, I, 264.
(17) *L. and P.* IX, 621.
(18) Ibid. IX, 622.
(19) Ibid. IX, 630.
(20) Ibid. IX, 640.
(21) Ibid. IX, 651.
(22) *Op. cit.* I, 448.
(23) *L. and P.* IX, 423.
(24) Ibid. IX, 641.
(25) Ibid. IX, 622 (MS.).
(26) Ibid. IX, 651, 694, 708, 735 (Wright, p. 82).
(27) *Op. cit.* I, 256–7.

APPENDIX II

The Itinerary of the Royal Visitors

(1) *Hen. VIII and Eng. Mon.* I, 287.
(2) *L. and P. Hen. VIII*, Pref. p. xlii. *Loll. and Ref.* II, 79.
(3) *L. and P.* X, 363.
(4) Ibid. IX, 986; Wright, Supp. 48.
(5) *L. and P.* IX, 108; Wright, Supp. 91.
(6) *L. and P.* IX, 1009.
(7) *L. and P.* X, 103; Wright, Supp. 98.
(8) *Letters* (Parker Society), p. 319.
(9) *L. and P.* X, 91; cf. Gairdner, *Loll. and Ref.* II, 74.
(10) *L. and P.* X, 93.
(11) Ibid. X, 92; Wright, Supp. 97.
(12) *Loc. cit.* footnote.
(13) *Reformation in England* (1934), p. 142.
(14) *Anglo-Premonstratensia* (Camden Soc.): Redman's Visitations in vols. II and III. Wilkinson's itinerary, I, 193.

INDEX

Note. In the appendices, personal and geographical names are fully indexed, but subjects are entered only under general headings.

33 1/3 %
c8/90c
#70